A World Made for
MONEY

ECONOMY, GEOGRAPHY, *and*
THE WAY WE LIVE TODAY

BRET WALLACH

University of Nebraska Press | Lincoln and London

Library of Congress Cataloging-in-Publication Data

Wallach, Bret, 1943–
A world made for money: economy, geography, and
the way we live today / Bret Wallach.
pages cm
Includes bibliographical references and index.
ISBN 978-0-8032-9891-0 (hardback: alk. paper)—ISBN
978-0-8032-9894-1 (epub)—ISBN 978-0-8032-9895-8
(mobi)—ISBN 978-0-8032-9896-5 (pdf) 1. Economic
geography. 2. Commercial geography. 3. Natural
resources—Management. I. Title.
HF1025.W27 2015
330.9–dc23
2014049412

Set in Arno Pro by Lindsey Auten.

Contents

Introduction

I'm stopped at a traffic light in the college town where I live. It's a recently renovated intersection, an expanse of new and very white concrete about a hundred feet square, six lanes crossing four, plus right- and left-turn lanes. One corner is occupied by a Walgreens. Kitty-corner there's a CVS. They seem evenly matched, but the Walgreens parking lot has two or three times as many cars as the CVS lot. I don't know why. Walgreens is open twenty-four hours a day, but can that explain the difference? It's a puzzle.

A third corner is occupied by a bank built a few years ago on the site of an old gas station and low-rent convenience store. I forget the bank's name, but I have an excuse: this town of 150,000 people has at least fifteen banks, some with several branches. It must not take a lot of money to open a bank, because I saw this bank under construction and, with the exception of the vault, it's a balloon-framed wood building faced with brick and trimmed with synthetic stone. Apart from the tower adorned with a nearly illegible clock, the building might be mistaken from where I'm stopped for a new house.

The fourth corner is more unusual. It's occupied by a freestanding dentist's office built to look like a small-town railway station in the Old West. It has another tower and another clock, but beneath the clock there's a sign stating the elevation to the hundredth of a foot. The owner, it seems, is a serious railway buff. In front of the building there's even a full-sized wooden model of a funnel-stacked, wood-burning locomotive.

There used to be a restaurant on the site. It was part of a chain and had been built about fifteen years earlier. It served Southern-style meals—mostly fried chicken—throughout the day. Eventually it closed, and the building sat vacant for a couple of years. I thought we might get another bank—you can't have too many—but the dentist came along, demolished the restaurant, and built what he calls the Dental Depot. He keeps it open six days a week, but he's never there. Two young dentists, recently joined by a third, run the place while the owner concentrates on building more depots. The chain already stretches from Phoenix to Dallas and Tulsa.

The corner where I'm stopped was first settled by whites during the Oklahoma land run of 1889, and though it's only half a mile from the center of town, it was at the city limits until about 1940. Since then, it has gone from farmland through a complete cycle of construction and demolition. It is now well into the second cycle. This kind of churning bothers me because I retain the childish assumption that the world is permanent. I know better, but habits die hard. Right now, in the minute while I'm waiting for the light to change, I'm struck by something else, something that has never occurred to me. It is that everything I see has been built to make money.

This is like realizing that baseball involves bases and basketball involves baskets. In elementary school I delivered 282 newspapers twice a week. Folded into hatchets and tossed to lie near front doors, the newspapers formed a tiny fragment of my neighborhood landscape. They were my own bit of blight, thrown there because I wanted to make money. I never thought of it, but I knew it as fish know water.

Now, sixty years later, I look for exceptions. Clearly, the city did not pave the streets and install the new traffic lights to make money. On the other hand, these things exist primarily to help the town's residents get to or from the town's businesses. Indirectly, the lights and streets exist largely for money.

I think of the town's residential neighborhoods. Years ago, one of the builders told me that he stayed small because he couldn't build more than a hundred homes annually without sacrificing quality. Now he's up to almost 500 a year. In fact, he's now on the list of the top-hundred builders in the country. More power to him, but he's sacrificed quality. We could be polite and say that quality was trumped by the builder's competitive spirit, but the measure of that spirit is his bank account.

The developers of the town's commercial space are mostly from out of town. I remember the architect for a chain restaurant who came by to check a new location. It was on the edge of a small lake. Somebody suggested that he modify the restaurant's layout so customers could see the water. No way, he said. He had to be at his next site by Thursday.

Someone might object that this is a college town and that the college is by far the town's biggest employer. True, but the sorry response is that under a rhetorical veneer—Oxford and all that—the students are here (and their parents certainly are paying for them to be here) to learn how to make money.

I look at the wider world. The corner I have just described is a bagatelle compared to the superregional centers of America's big cities. It's a good thing card readers don't make as much noise as old cash registers; otherwise, the people near those centers would all be deaf.

It's no better out of town. If I drive 30 miles in any direction I am likely to see old cotton fields ruined by erosion that nobody worried about so long as cotton made money. If I travel a bit farther, I can find oil fields and coal mines that exist only because someone hoped to make money and in many cases makes money still. Occasionally I fly through Dallas–Fort Worth International Airport and notice from the air what appear to be freshly cleared building sites, hundreds of them scattered and isolated on the prairie as though for people redefining large-lot living. The clearings aren't what they seem. In fact, they mark gas wells tapping the newly prodigal Barnett Shale, the first big success for hydraulic fracking. Last I looked, the Barnett had sixteen thousand wells spread over 5,000 square miles, and not one had been drilled for any reason other than to make money.

I hope I am not misunderstood. Sitting at the intersection I've been describing, I like being able to adjust the air-conditioning in my fine American automobile. I can point you to a good cheese shop up the road and to a classic diner down the other way. On a less bouncy note, I know perfectly well that I would be dead if it weren't for the world made for money. Modern medicine has saved my hide at least once and has repaired significant damage more than that, and I know that modern medicine could not exist without the immense undergirding provided by the world made for money.

And so I waffle. I know I am supposed to hate Walmart. The trouble is that I also believe that Walmart is a lifesaver for the poorest people in a thousand towns—and not just for the people who shop at Walmart—because the Beast of Bentonville pushes down prices at all its competitors. It gets worse, I'm afraid, because I also defend Monsanto. How could I do such a thing? The answer is that I believe that if all the farmers in the world suddenly adopted traditional methods of growing heirloom varieties, we would quickly find ourselves in a global famine. In the same way, I know—trust me, I'm well trained— that I'm supposed to hate ExxonMobil, but the world uses about 25 billion barrels of oil annually, and the implications of oil spills, carcinogens, and greenhouse gases are insignificant next to the prospect of our tanks running dry.

I do understand that the Chinese factories churning out cheap clothes and iPads aren't much better than the coal mines of the Industrial Revolution. In a way, they may be worse, because coal miners at least kept their pride. I do understand as well that a world made for money exacts a terrific environmental price. Smog used to be the obvious symbol of it, but climate change may soon be a more engulfing one. There's something else wrong with a world made for money: it's unbelievably, never-endingly, stupefyingly ugly and boring. I can tweak that a bit: nobody ever loved a landscape made for money.

Well, I'm probably wrong. There are people who will insist that they love Dunkin' Donuts. Fine: the *L* word is elastic. I will say instead that the places I have loved have not been made for money. What bothers me most when I consider this fact is that I am so completely immersed in the world made for money that I forget that there is a choice.

Every now and then something comes along and sets me straight. My brother, for example, has the misfortune to live on the fringes of the San Francisco metropolitan area, which I escaped nearly five decades ago. He recently picked me up at the San Francisco airport and we headed east over the Bay Bridge. (How many times I crossed that bridge in years past! How pleased I was in my car with its 413-inch engine, high-lift cams, and high-ratio differential. I miss its sound still.) We drove through the infinity of Oakland, crossed the once-beautiful San Joaquin Valley, then began rising (in more senses than one) into the Sierra.

I hadn't been to Yosemite Valley in over forty years, and though it was very familiar, I reacted to it differently now than I had then. In my twenties I had taken the valley as a challenge and walked lickety-split up to the top of Yosemite Falls, leaned over the safety bars up there for all of five minutes, then jogged back down to the valley floor. Now I stood in the meadows, walked very little, and thought what an incredibly beautiful place this was. Yes, that's the voice of decrepitude for you, but it's also something else. When John Muir railed against the construction of a dam at Hetch Hetchy, he said that we might as well wall up our churches to make water tanks. Forty years ago and more I got the metaphor, but now it was more meaningful. For this, I blame experience. Only after seeing Scotland and Morocco and the Karakoram and Java do I appreciate how remarkable Yosemite is, how with its waterfalls in spate it is as breathtaking as Europe's cathedrals.

Blame the mountain air; I will desist. I want to correct, however, the idea that the only alternative to the world made for money is the natural world. Of course, it's true that the natural world was not made for money, but neither were most of the world's cultural landscapes, certainly not those made more than a few centuries ago. Think of the famous monuments that form a daisy chain across Eurasia. They are draped from the Alhambra to the Parthenon, from Hagia Sophia to Al-Aqsa, from the tomb of Jahangir to the Sun Temple at Konark, from the tortured stones of Angkor's Ta Prohm to the inconceivably perfect carpentry at Nara and Horyuji.

Think of simpler things too: the stepped paddy terraces of the Orient or a homesteader's cabin in Nebraska. The world made for money, I remind myself, is a recent thing, its current near-ubiquity a matter of perhaps a lifetime or two. I won't quibble about a precise date of birth, though for myself I see Sir Francis Bacon as the pivotal figure in the emergence of the new world. With his insistence on practical knowledge for practical ends, he was laying the foundation for Watt's steam engine and Edison's electric light and all the rest.

I think of *Let Us Now Praise Famous Men* and James Agee's agonizingly detailed description of an Alabama sharecropper's cabin. Agee presses himself against the rough planks of the building and tries to understand them through the sense of touch. If memory serves, Tolstoy does something similar in the harvest scene in *Anna Karenina*. So does Mark Twain when, in *Life on the Mississippi*, he writes about Captain Bixby's knowledge of every bend, bar, and ripple along a thousand miles of ever-changing river.

For my part, I remember a house I rented for half a dozen years in far-northern Maine. It lay out of town in a sparsely settled, hilly landscape with valleys so broad that the view from the house stretched northwest over 5 miles of potato fields and fir trees to the St. John River, which marks the Canadian border.

I do not know when the house had been built, but this was and is an Acadian neighborhood, settled after the British in the 1750s drove the Acadians from their homes in what are now the maritime provinces of Canada. I don't think the house was anywhere near that old, but it had been built with methods older still. It measured about twenty feet by thirty, excluding a simple lean-to probably added in the 1950s for a kitchen and bathroom. The original part of the house had two stories, each with four rooms, and there was a full basement stuffed tight each fall with eight cords of firewood.

Snow covers this part of Maine without a break from late November into May. By then the basement was empty, all the wood carried armload by armload up a tight staircase to a simple wood-burning stove on the floor above. The firewood was either sugar maple or American beech, both of which burn very hot, but the house stayed warm also because its walls were solid planks between two and three inches thick. They were laid horizontally, narrow edge on narrow edge and held together not just with dovetailing at the corners but with finger-thick wooden pins inserted in holes drilled every few feet along the narrow edges of the planks. Cedar shingles covered the outside, though by the 1970s they had disappeared under a layer of green asbestos siding.

A few years after I left Maine, the house was demolished by the owner's son, who wanted central heat, maybe even air-conditioning for those six days of August. Perhaps he didn't like the idea of sleeping in the same room used by his father, grandfather, and great-grandfather. The old house in any case didn't go gently. A bulldozer came to knock it down, but instead of collapsing the building just shuddered and moved, intact, off its stone foundation. I miss the house even now, though it's been gone for almost thirty years. I find myself mentally touching its rough planks or patting the always-cool stones of the basement walls.

A decade before moving to Maine, I had managed a small apartment building in Berkeley. It was brand new and I thought it was great, partly because it was new and partly because it was modern, which is to say absolutely functional. It had eight two-bedroom units divided into two blocks each of four identical apartments, two up, two down, a garage below. Between the building and the sidewalk there was a pathetic foundation planting—a few uncared-for shrubs buried in mulch. Nobody ever paid them any attention.

A real-estate company managed the building for the young Hong Kong couple who owned it. I met them only once and briefly, I suppose because they wanted to approve the real-estate company's plan to let me collect the rent and take care of things in exchange for a discount on my own. It worked well because there was really nothing to do except occasionally calm noisy students. The last time I passed by— and it was a decade ago or more—the building was still there. I saw it but didn't look for long. It made me vaguely uncomfortable, perhaps because it had lost the newness that had been its appeal or perhaps because a closer look would lead me to wonder at how I could have considered an investment property to be a home.

Or I think of a shop that opened a few years ago near my office. It sold Indian imports, including food. There was a shelf with those small boxes that contain a foil bag that you dump in boiling water for three minutes. You fish it out, cut the corner, and pour the contents into a bowl. Bon appétit!

I asked the shopkeeper which variety he liked best. He said, "I don't eat any of them. My wife cooks proper food." With honesty like that his shop was bound to fail, and it did, quickly. Still, the question lingers: What's wrong with those little pouches? Why wouldn't the shopkeeper (or me) like them any better if they were prepared according to a master chef's recipe by well-paid workers in a sparkling factory using only organic, fair-trade ingredients? The answer, I think, is that the people chopping eggplant in the factory are making money, not food. In exactly the same way, the house in Maine was built as a place to live, while the apartment building in Berkeley was built to make money. It's a pretty basic distinction. Cue the dying Kane: "Rosebud, Rosebud."

So it's a conundrum: the world made for money is a literally lifesaving triumph while, simultaneously, it is a prison. This is not a conundrum that I will settle in these pages. My much more modest aim is to describe, survey, or take stock of this world we have made for money. I allow myself only the occasional judgment, so that the reader may read a page, think that the things I'm describing are appalling (or amazing), yet remain unsure whether I agree. Often enough, I am myself unsure on which side of the fence I stand. I have a habit of standing simultaneously and uncomfortably on both.

I have begun in that most familiar territory, the shopper's world, where I start with fast food (Ah! The reader's judgment bursts so quickly into reactive flame!), department stores, Walmart (how not), supermarkets, and shopping centers. Then I turn to manufacturing. I begin with something with which we are intimately familiar—soft drinks and beer—then turn to clothes, automobiles, airliners, and some general remarks about the industrial battlefield.

I spend a great deal of time on transportation, without which we would promptly starve or freeze, and then turn to the oil industry, without which the wheels would stop. I consider mining, without which those wheels (and so much more) could not be made, and then I come to industrial agriculture, which amounts to farming for money.

Industrial agriculture is growing at the expense of subsistence agriculture, which is to say farming not for money. Here I consider both the many programs designed to ameliorate rural poverty (how words from Latin make everything so pleasant!) and the much more powerful force of migrants abandoning their villages and ancestral lands.

This brings me to cities. I begin with Asia, where urbanization is occurring at a speed and with an energy greater than any adjective conveys. I scan Europe—London, Moscow, Paris—then come home. Americans are terminally ambivalent about cities, which brings me to my final section, which begins with the American suburb—an expression of anti-urbanism if ever there was one—and goes on to consider some of the other ways in which people express their need to escape a world made for money.

The net is thrown widely, yet there is nothing about banking and other financial services. For this omission I have an excuse, namely, that I'm interested in the visible world, and money can't be seen. An honest explanation would also have to include the admission that I do not understand banking, though in that department I have much company. I recall an author some years ago who, superb in his research into the oil industry, said that nobody would ever penetrate the secrets of the world's banks.

There is nothing here about African or South American cities—or Australian or Canadian ones. There is nothing about the automotive industries of China or India, huge as they are. There's nothing about inland waterways, nothing about the forest industry, nothing about fisheries, nothing about the mining of copper and the quarrying of limestone. Originally I touched on all these things—well, everything except the limestone—but the pages fell to the floor for brevity's sake. So I too have done my best to avoid history, not from disinterest but because if I dwelt more on the past I would have had to say less about the present.

One thing I have kept in abundance. More than newsmagazines, I like newspapers, and the reason is that newspapers often let their sources speak for themselves, without paraphrase. On almost every page that follows I have borrowed a quotation or two caught by a newspaper reporter. The quotations are almost always informal, yet they have an authority that paraphrases and syntheses cannot match. I do try to write clearly—no easy thing—but the gold is in the quotations, which are like the master strokes in a landscape painting, in this case not of a meadow or seascape but of a world that, for better and for worse, we have made for money.

A WORLD MADE FOR MONEY

1 Shopping

John Locke uses the word *consumer*, but there is no fun in it; the word for him is a mathematical expression, standing on one side of an equation and balanced against *producer*. Daniel Defoe uses the word in an equally analytical way. So does our own Ralph Waldo Emerson. Then the clouds break. Richard Sears comes along and, it's no exaggeration to say, changes the world. Calculation is gone, and with the "Consumer's Guide" section of the Sears, Roebuck catalog for 1897, Richard Sears invites the world to dine.

FAST FOOD

Burger Wars

And so, 115 years later, Americans spent $175 billion annually on fast food. The leading provider was headquartered in Oak Brook, a Chicago suburb. There, a nondescript, eight-story office building on McDonald's Drive housed the center of an empire with over 14,000 restaurants in the United States and that many again spread over 120 other countries.

The average McDonald's had annual sales of $2 million. The most popular item for several years had been the Double Cheeseburger, anchor of the Dollar Menu. The average restaurant sold 350 of them daily, but many franchisees in 2008 said they were losing money on the Double Cheeseburger. What could be done? The solution was simple: remove one slice of cheese, call the result a McDouble, and swap it for the Double Cheeseburger on the Dollar Menu. What else? On the assumption that people lusted after fries, the company took them (and Coke) off the Dollar Menu, raised their price above a dollar, and replaced them on the Dollar Menu with ice cream and cookies. Anything else? In 2012 McDonald's rolled out the Extra Value

Menu to compete with Burger King's Value Menu and Wendy's Super Value Menu. None of the items on it were new, but customers might be drawn to what now appeared to be a special.

Three-quarters of the company's restaurants in the United States opened at five in the morning, and many ran twenty-four hours. No wonder: breakfast provided a third of McDonald's revenues in the United States. The chief operating officer for the United States said, "I'm amazed at the people who work for me who take their kids to hockey at 4 a.m. and 5 a.m. I want us to be open when they need us." Most of those customers didn't have time to park and come in. That's why two-thirds of McDonald's business in the United States was at the drive-through. The company introduced double-lane drive-throughs. To save another dollar, they spelled them "drive-thrus."

McDonald's looked hard for another blockbuster on the scale of the Egg McMuffin. That popular breakfast sandwich had been the invention in 1975 of a Santa Barbara franchisee named Herb Peterson. Who could match him? The Arch Deluxe failed in 2005. Over the years subs and pizzas had been tried and abandoned. A spicy chicken sandwich, introduced early in 2006 with "a bold blend of chipotle spices," was axed after six months. In 2013 the Angus burger bit the dust. Hope rose with the Asian salad, with arugula, mandarin oranges, and sesame ginger sauce, but that died too. The chicken snack wrap looked like it might be a hit with consumers who wanted something between lunch and dinner.

One retired McDonald's executive warned of the perils of a long menu. "You try to push people through the drive-thru," he said, "but you give them a menu that takes a half hour to read." McDonald's already had over a hundred items on that menu. The president of McDonald's USA in 2014 lost his job after less than two years, in no small part because a growing menu slowed things down. "In retrospect, I would have taken more time on that," he said. Ironically, a *Consumer Reports* survey of its 32,000 readers rated McDonald's hamburgers as the worst of twenty brands, which hinted why the unfortunate president had been in a hurry to introduce new products.

Tim Hortons, a Canadian chain, set a goal: customers should wait no more than a hundred seconds between placing an order and taking delivery—and they shouldn't stay at the delivery window for more than twenty-five seconds. A British chain, Pret a Manger, put so many clerks at the counter that transaction times never exceeded a minute. McDonald's tried a third approach: dual-point service with ordering at one end of the counter and pickup at the other. Like Burger King and Subway, it also experimented with touch-screen order kiosks. The machines were made by NCR, and those that took cash as well as plastic cost $18,000. Customers took a receipt from the machine and exchanged it for food at the counter.

Still, McDonald's lagged not only Tim Hortons and Pret a Manger but Wendy's. By 2012 Wendy's had drive-through orders down to 130 seconds, while customers took 189 at McDonald's. In 2006 McDonald's tried something radical. Customers in Northern California would talk to somebody not inside the building but at a call center hundreds of miles away. A clerk there, facing a battery of waiting callers instead of a line of cars, had no dead period between orders. Employees had to keep their eyes on their monitors too because every now and then a red box appeared to check up on them. The workers had 1.75 seconds to hit their mouse. The boss of Bronco Communications explained, "You've got to measure everything. When fractions of seconds count, the environment needs to be controlled." Other chains, including Jack in the Box and Wendy's, tried the technology.

To keep his lines moving, Dave Thomas of Wendy's for many years sold milk shakes in only one flavor, a vanilla-chocolate combination. Thomas died in 2002, and new flavors soon made their entrance, starting with vanilla. Wendy's also tried breakfast, which Thomas had resisted. With practice Wendy's might have been able to make breakfast profitable, but its stockholders weren't waiting. In 2007 Triarc forced Thomas's successor out, and a year later it bought the company for $2 billion. By 2011, and measured by revenue, Wendy's was on the verge of overtaking Burger King.

Nagged by bad publicity, the industry began offering salads. Lettuce for fast-food restaurants became big business in California's Salinas Valley, where Taylor Farms sold McDonald's 900,000 pounds of iceberg lettuce every month, plus 800,000 pounds of a specialty mix of sixteen lettuces. McDonald's was also the biggest restaurant buyer of fresh apples.

The problem with salads was that they lost money, partly because few customers bought them. A bumper sticker explained why: "Eat beef. The West wasn't won by eating salad." So a typical Burger King sold 300 Whoppers a day but only three salads. Still, salads stayed on the menu, as Burger King's CEO explained, so health-conscious moms couldn't cast their "veto vote." Hoping to find the holy grail of a healthy French fry, Burger King began offering Satisfries. With reduced fat absorption, they were the company's fourth attempt since the 1990s to increase sales of this critical product. In 2014, after less than two years, Satisfries were pulled from the menu.

Pizza

Americans meanwhile spent $30 billion annually on restaurant pizzas. The biggest chains were Pizza Hut, with 7,500 restaurants in the United States; Domino's, with 5,000; and Papa John's, with 3,000. In 2001 Papa John's became the first to allow online ordering, but by 2014 all three got 40 percent or more of their orders that way. It made a huge difference, allowing the chains to increase their market share from a declining 40 percent in 2000 to a rising 51 percent in 2014. Convenience trumped atmosphere and food, and by 2014, 6 percent of all the independent pizza shops open in 2001 had closed. At the same time, however, Sbarro, a chain with over a thousand restaurants, declared bankruptcy in 2014 and blamed an "unprecedented decline in mall traffic."

Casual Dining

A notch above burgers and pizza, "family-restaurant" chains like Denny's, Big Boy, and IHOP struggled as they lost customers to "fast-casual" restaurants like Panera Bread and Chipotle and to still more expensive "casual-dining" places like Olive Garden, Outback Steakhouse, and Ruby Tuesday—places with table service and beer and wine. Casual dining had problems of its own. The global chief brand officer for McDonald's put his finger on the core issue when he said that millennials had "a wider range of choices than any generation before them" but were "promiscuous in their brand loyalty," which was to say that they had none. The average customer spent more than ten dollars and wanted aspirational fast food. That's how a Red Lobster official explained a dish called "fire-grilled grouper rubbed with fresh basil oil." The Red Lobster officer said that aspirational consumption was "well into food now, and the expectations were high." Bennigan's tested a "seared poppy-seed-crusted ahi tuna," only to give up and call it a failure. The company's "chief concept officer" said, "Our consumer didn't have as sophisticated [a] palate as we may have thought."

Applebee's, with more than 1,900 restaurants, also had menu troubles. The company offered fifteen-dollar steak dinners. One of its cofounders, who long ago had sold her interest in the company, didn't like the steaks. "That kind of stuff is out of their element," she said. She ordered a bruschetta burger but reported, "I didn't like it at all." It didn't help that just down the road there was a line of competitors, including a Chili's, an Olive Garden, and a pneumatic Hooters. Eventually, in 2007, IHOP bought Applebee's for $2.1 billion. The next year, Steak and Ale and all company-owned Bennigan's closed, leaving 200 fewer restaurants for Applebee's to contend with. Meanwhile, the fast-food giants started elbowing into fast-casual territory. Taco Bell offered a new line of salads and burritos at Cantina Bell.

Nobody could rest easy. As the CEO of Panera said, "What was good enough yesterday will not be good enough tomorrow." He himself was opening stores in Manhattan, far from Panera's usual suburban locations. It was a challenge because the usual Panera couldn't handle so many customers walking in the door.

Dunkin' Donuts, founded in 1950, grew by 1963 to 100 stores. By 2006 it had 5,800 and was opening 550 more annually. The target was 15,000 stores by 2020.

Dunkin' sold almost 3 million coffees every day, but it was squeezed. On one side there was fast food and on the other there was the company Dunkin' called Sixbucks, which sold 4 million coffees daily. The two had very different customers. Dunkin' spoke to its customers by offering small, medium, and large drinks. Starbucks had its own language: "tall," "grande," and "venti."

A typical Dunkin' customer said, "If I want to sit on a couch, I stay at home." This was music to the ears of a Dunkin' franchisee who said, "I don't want them hanging around for hours." Dunkin's own research suggested that its customers wanted to be part of a crowd, while the Starbucks customer wanted to be appreciated as an individual. (A similar divide separated Sheraton's customers, who liked to chat with each other, from Westin's, who didn't. The difference didn't bother Starwood, which owned both chains.)

Between 1990 and 2005 Dunkin' had been owned by French investors, but they sold the company to a group of Americans who planned a major expansion. The new boss, distressed that there were only sixty Dunkin' stores west of the Mississippi, said that his predecessors "believed this was a great regional brand, but for them the world ended at the Hudson River." You could hear the optimism in the voice of the Dunkin' spokesman who said, "There's a whole lot of white space for us to cover over the next fifteen years." In 2007 the company announced plans for 125 shops in the Dallas–Fort Worth metro area alone. The market there already had 287 McDonald's and 174 Starbucks—not counting shops in supermarkets. Starbucks fought back by opening a second chain of shops called Seattle's Best Coffee. In 2014 eight of these ten new stores closed; the other two were converted to Starbucks.

Starbucks had grown from eleven stores in 1988 to thirty-one stores in 1991. Then it took off, rocketing to 12,000 stores in thirty-seven countries in 2007. In 2012 the Starbucks boss insisted that his company had "never been more enthused and more aggressive." His company now had 17,000 stores, including 12,000 in the United States. Already with about 550 in China, Starbucks, in a joint venture with Tata, began opening stores in India. A market researcher there observed that the company had bright prospects because "there really are no nice places to meet in our big cities, outside the lobbies of five-star hotels."

Dunkin' was far behind in these countries, although it was strong in South Korea, where it began operating in 1992. By 2009 it had 663 Korean outlets and was planning to double that number. Dunkin's Korean customers got comfortable chairs and wireless Internet, and they were encouraged to sit as long as they liked. In 2012 Dunkin' opened its first store in India. Its Indian partner already operated Domino's Pizza restaurants there.

Back home, Dunkin' didn't want to lose its traditional customer, but it did want to attract the other kind, so it renovated its stores with fake-granite countertops and a fancier menu. But not too fancy! No paninis. Instead, Dunkin' began selling what it called a "stuffed melt." Verdict? Too messy. Presto—the melt was gone, replaced by warm sandwiches on flatbread.

Dunkin' was not alone in hoping to capture Starbucks' customers. "Large," McDonald's said in plain English, "is the new grande." It opened its first McCafé in Australia in 1993. Offering "specialty coffee in a relaxing setting at an affordable price," 300 McCafés operated in Asia and the Middle East, along with a hundred each in Europe and Latin America. There were only a few in the United States, however, where the drive-through was king. Still, in 2008 the company announced that it would install coffee bars in all its American restaurants. Cost: $100,000 per location. Coffee sales had already jumped 30 percent after the company started using thicker cups with the words "fresh brewed custom blend . . . rich, bold and robust." Add in wireless Internet and softer lighting, and McDonald's was brushing against Starbucks territory. Franchisees weren't always happy, however. One said, "We are not even paying for the electricity to run the machine." Perhaps the happiest entrants in the coffee business were the artisanal chains like Blue Bottle Coffee. Providing a cup of coffee that actually tasted good, they seemed to have a bright future, bright enough at least to attract seasoned investors.

Krispy Kreme

Investors in Krispy Kreme watched as the chain shrank from 440 outlets in 2004 to 300 two years later. The first West Coast Krispy Kreme, which opened in La Habra, California, in 1999, closed in 2006. The franchisee for Arizona and New Mexico closed its ten stores. Stores closed in Pennsylvania, Texas, and Oklahoma. The company was still growing overseas, which pushed the store total to 800 by 2013. The new Krispy Kreme store, however, was half the size, or less, of the 4,000-square-foot store of the theater vintage. Good-bye to the doughnut theaters, where customers looked through glass walls at dough rings on parade. One analyst said, "I give it a 10 percent chance that Krispy Kreme will ever regain the luster it once had. . . . They had their moment, but the lines are no longer out the door." Another agreed: "People just won't line up for doughnuts forever and ever." For people who had been part of the fanfare at the openings, the closings were as distressing as piles of money going up in smoke, which in a way they were.

RETAIL

Through most of the twentieth century, department stores were the dominant supplier of dry goods, at least for urban consumers. The leaders were still huge companies—by revenue Sears and Macy's came first, followed by JCPenney and Kohl's, then Nordstrom and Dillard's— but department store revenues peaked at $232 billion in 2000 and by 2012 had declined to $180 billion.

In a brave effort to resist the trend, Federated Department Stores in 2005 consolidated nearly all its stores into a single national brand, Macy's. Federated had already gobbled up Rich's, Lazarus, Goldsmith's, Burdines, and the Bon Marché. Now it bought May Company for $17 billion. It was the end of the line for Marshall Field, Robinsons-May,

Hecht's, Filene's, Famous-Barr, Kaufmann's, L.S. Ayres, Meier & Frank, Strawbridge's, and the Jones Store. The only name that Federated kept, besides Macy's, was Bloomingdale's, with forty stores.

By late 2012 there were slightly over 800 Macy's, with revenues of about $26 billion. But why would Macy's as a national brand do better than a dozen brands with deep regional roots? Buying power helped. So did advertising, because for the first time a department store would have a national ad campaign. Also, with so many stores Macy's would now be able to offer exclusive merchandise, a practice pioneered by Target's line of home furnishings by Martha Stewart.

Macy's aimed for the space between discounters like Target and specialty retailers like Gap. To hold that space, it sought to stock products with a range of qualities on the assumption that shoppers who saw a spectrum of good-better-best items tended to buy near the top. Federated divided its female customers into four groups, nicknamed Erica, Katherine, Julie, and Alex. They represented the brand seeker, the traditionalist, the traditionalist who also wanted to be stylish, and the fashionista.

A skeptical analyst said, "They've put together two companies [Federated and May] in a niche that no one wants to be in anymore." Stubbornly, the company intended to prove him wrong. It focused on maintaining low prices rather than cycling between sales, and it developed branded products by Tommy Hilfiger, Sean Combs, Jessica Simpson, Madonna, and—wonders never cease—Donald Trump. Still, store sales in late 2012 remained flat. Customers demanded discounts, and revenue growth for 2015 was projected at less than 2 percent.

Despite its problems, Macy's disdained JCPenney, which had more stores than Macy's (1,100 versus 800) but lower revenues ($18 billion versus $25 billion). Macy's boss sniffed, "It's kind of like comparing apples and monkeys—not even oranges." JCPenney fought back with its own version of good, better, and best: the fighting price, the core price, and the aspirational price. Sephora was an example of an aspirational product line at JCPenney, and it did very well for the company, even in slow seasons. The store tried its hand at fast fashion too, partnering in 2010 with Italy's Mango, which hurried new styles from design studio to store in a month. What was the appeal for JCPenney? Its CEO answered the question simply: "If you only deliver four times a year, there's only a reason to come to the store four times a year."

A new JCPenney CEO arrived in 2012. He had previously devised the layout of the brilliantly successful Apple stores, and he set out to work his magic on JCPenney. "People won't tolerate big stores," he said. "You have to break it down for them." His plan was to convert the center of each store to a "town square," a social space with entertainment and room to gather, surrounded by a constellation of specialty shops. Would it work? One analyst was skeptical. "The Apple store is a shining example of how to sell a few products well. I don't believe it's possible to have the same approach across a department store." The analyst apparently was right, because Penney's revenues fell that year by 25 percent, and the new CEO was shown the door after only seventeen months. An analyst seemed to hint at the company's demise when she said, "The entire value of this company [JCPenney] is in its real estate."

Another analyst had been watching somebody else. "As I look at the whole equation," he said in 2006, "the big winner over the next 12 to 18 months is going to be Kohl's." That company, which opened its first department store in 1962, by 2012 had almost 1,100 stores with revenues equal to JCPenney. It had exclusive designer merchandise too, in its case from Jennifer Lopez and Marc Anthony. Yet Kohl's too had its troubles, particularly in slow restocking of popular merchandise.

Perhaps the lion's share of merchandise would in the future come not from a store but from the Internet—not from a big box, some people said, but from a cardboard box. A consultant warned, "We will hit a tipping point soon, if we have not already, when online will become so mainstream that retailers will wonder what they need some of these big boxes for, when you have a retail presence in everyone's pocket via your smart phone." By 2012 some online retailers were offering lower prices to customers close to a competitor's physical store. JCPenney and Nordstrom fought back by fulfilling online orders from nearby stores, rather than distant warehouses. Inventories could be managed better this way, and delivery was cheaper and faster. A Macy's executive said, "We've spent the last 153 years building warehouses. We just called them stores."

Early Discounters

For decades the biggest threat to department stores came from discounters. They too had traveled a long and sometimes rough road. In 1929 Frank Woolworth's company (he himself had died ten years earlier) operated 2,000 stores in the United States. A 1993 newspaper story, however, covered the company's terminal decline: "The Woolworth Corporation said yesterday that it planned to eliminate 13,000 jobs and close 970 stores, including half of its remaining five-and-dime variety stores, in what would be the largest, most costly reorganization in the retailer's 114-year history." A skeptical consultant said, "I'd not be surprised if within three years, Woolworth will not have a Woolworth." His aim was good: the last Woolworth in the United States closed in 1997. Blame parking lots. Woolworth's didn't have any.

In 1946 a newcomer, E. J. Korvette, opened a luggage store on East Forty-Sixth Street in Manhattan. Undercutting fair-trade laws, Korvette soon had fifty-eight stores as far west as Chicago and offered bargain prices on a wide range of items. It was too wide a range, it turned out, because its founder, Eugene Ferkauf, either quit or was pushed out in 1968. Six years earlier he had made the cover of *Time* magazine; twelve years later, in 1980, Korvette was liquidated.

Along came another would-be assassin. Kmart had a huge advantage over Woolworth because it offered not only much more floor space but plenty of parking. Then something went wrong. An analyst said, "Some time in the mid to late 1970s they got frozen in time and continued to do things in the same old way, and the world passed them by." Kmart in 2005 still had enough financial power to buy Sears, however. It promptly announced that Sears would no longer help pay the medical expenses of retirees younger than sixty-five; older ones would get reduced support. Pow! But the cuts weren't deep enough. In desperation Sears began allowing other retailers to sell its Craftsman and DieHard products. A consultant explained that this new policy went against "what every retailer in the United States is doing, what every retailer is trying to accomplish, which is to differentiate themselves from their competitors." Sears, he continued, was in a state of "total collapse." Late in 2013 Sears announced that its flagship store in Chicago would close. The next year the company decided to raise cash by selling its shares in Sears Canada.

In 2012 Sears, like Montgomery Ward and Woolworth before it, was dropped from the S&P 500. In 2002 Kenmore appliances, made for Sears by Whirlpool, had been the nation's top seller. A decade later Kenmore was third, after Whirlpool and General Electric. Sears in that decade saw its share of major appliance sales in the United States slip from 40 to 29 percent, while Lowe's rose from 12 to 19 percent and Home Depot rose from 4 to 10 percent.

The Rise of Walmart

Like the first mammal setting foot on dry land, Walmart ventured in 1975 to open a store in Mount Pleasant, Texas, an hour's drive from the Arkansas line. A dozen years later, Walmart opened its first two Supercenters. They were in the Dallas suburbs of Garland and Arlington and were joint ventures with Cullum, the operator of a local supermarket chain called Tom Thumb. Cullum taught Walmart how to do food but soon sold its half of the partnership back to Walmart. Brooks Cullum explained, "They wanted to expand more rapidly than we could. It was a sheer disparity in size."

By 2006 over 62 percent of Americans lived within 5 miles of a Walmart. More than 99 percent of them lived with 25 miles. Ten percent of all retail sales in the United States were made at a Walmart. (Second place, with a measly 2.7 percent, went to CVS pharmacies, while Kroger, Costco, Target, and Home Depot all floated around 2 percent.) The square footage of the stores opened by Walmart in 2006 equaled the total square footage of the approximately 2,000 stores operated by Britain's Tesco, by most measures a huge company. Still, a Walmart official said, "We haven't even scratched the surface of the urban cores. Think about New York, Boston, Detroit, San Francisco, Washington DC. There are thousands of new Supercenter opportunities."

By 2010 Texas had 453 Walmarts, more than twice as many as runner-up Florida. In the Dallas–Fort Worth metro, with 5.2 million people, Walmart by 2008 had 102 stores, including 58 Supercenters, 19 Sam's Clubs, and 20 Neighborhood Markets. Saturated? Not according to a spokesman who said, "The metroplex is still targeted for growth." The original Garland Supercenter had already closed and been replaced by a new store a mile away and tailored to the Latino market. Tom Thumb still operated a hundred stores, but Cullum had sold out, and the chain became the Texas subsidiary of Safeway.

An analyst said that the United States no longer had an economy of supply and demand but one of "supply and command." He was talking about Walmart. For a century Coca-Cola had operated through bottlers that delivered and stacked drinks on store shelves. Walmart in 2007 demanded delivery instead to its warehouses and told Coke that, if the answer was no, Walmart would start selling a house brand of sports drinks, which would marginalize Coke's Powerade. Coke capitulated.

(This was more than the story of Walmart and Coke. At the start of the twentieth century, retailers had dominated their partnerships with manufacturers, who were more or less invisible. The rise of branded products changed the balance of power and reduced retailers to agents. As Walmart demonstrated with Coke, however, power was shifting back to retailers, in part because retailers were now so big and in part because they sold house brands.)

Walmart set out to bypass wholesalers and deal directly with manufacturers and growers. In 2009 the company sourced about 20 percent of its goods directly from producers. It planned to raise that number to 80 percent—and save about $10 billion in the process.

Walmart in 2003 warned its hundred biggest suppliers that it would soon demand radio-frequency tags on all shipments. Consultants estimated that this would cut the cost of checking inventory by 65 percent. It would also help eliminate every retailer's nightmare: too much (or too little) stock. Radio-frequency identification, or RFID, technology was slow in coming, however, and at the start of 2007, it was installed at only five of the company's 120 distribution centers, plus a thousand stores. A few months later, the company dropped the requirement. It did not give up, however. It started the push all over again in 2008, when it demanded that all suppliers shipping to its Sam's Club distribution center in DeSoto, a southern suburb of Dallas, have tags on every pallet—or pay Walmart two dollars per pallet to put one on for them. The company said that within a year it would demand labels on every box and by late 2009 on every item. The company came close to this target: labels actually began appearing on individual items in 2010. Clothing came first, with sensors on removable labels or packaging.

Walmart pressed overseas suppliers too. Jiaxing Yishangmei Fashion had an order in 2005 for 160,000 sweaters from Walmart. The boss said, "The orders are big and the price is cheap and it's hard." With rising costs in China and falling demand in America, Walmart quit sourcing from Jiaxing. The understated owner said, "We are very worried in this business." In 2008 Walmart decided that it wouldn't be buying anything from Shandong's Boshan Linar Garments Company. The head of sales for Boshan said, "It's always hard to make money from Walmart orders, but without them, we are finished."

Resistance

Yet things did not always go Walmart's way. The boss of New York City's United Food and Commercial Workers Union called Walmart "the retailer people love to hate." The speaker of the city council said, "Walmart can say they are a different company, but we are not going to roll the dice in New York City." The president of the Retail, Wholesale, and Department Store Union said, "Walmart is leading us on a race to the bottom." Predictably, there were no Walmarts in New York City. Would-be customers went to New Jersey. Residents of San Francisco, Seattle, and Boston had to head to the suburbs too. Boston's mayor said, "Walmart does not suit the clientele we have in the city of Boston. They don't pay wages that are sufficient. Their benefit structure is poor. I don't need employers like that in our city." The nearest store was in Walpole, several miles beyond the city limits.

Over on the West Coast, Walmart opened its first California Supercenter in 2003 at La Quinta, 20 miles southeast of Palm Springs. In 2004 it won permission to open a Supercenter in Rosemead, east of Pasadena and in a community where 90 percent of the residents were Asian or Latino. About twenty smaller Walmarts were open in Los Angeles proper. Almost all were east of the Harbor Freeway, however, and no Supercenter had yet opened in the city.

Was the company going to give up? Its boss said that critics opposed to its entry "need to bring their lunch, because we're not going to lay down." (What? You want him to respect intransitive verbs? No problem: write to customer service.) In 2012 the company secured a building permit for a small-format Neighborhood Market in LA's Chinatown; miraculously, the permit arrived one day before the city council banned chain stores from that neighborhood. An unhappy resident said, "They're going to take over everything." Another said, "They are going to erase the cultural community." A third said, "If they don't open, I'm happier." A company official, however, predicted, "The day our store opens thousands and thousands of local residents are going to shop." A businessman agreed and said, "This community has not had a mainstream grocery store in 74 years." Another added, "The opposition comes from outside Chinatown." He may have been right because Safeway, Supervalu, Giant Food, and Jewel-Osco had all, over the years, hired Saint Consulting Group to covertly organize community opposition to Walmart.

Walmart was more successful in Chicago, where the mayor vetoed a measure that would have kept the company out. Two stores were open by 2013, along with many more in the suburbs.

Walmart was more successful in Washington DC too. Members of the city council in 2013 pushed for passage of a "super-minimum-wage" or "living-wage" bill that would have paid Walmart workers $12.50 an hour, more than four dollars above the existing minimum wage. Walmart said that it would cancel plans for three Supercenters and study its options for three already under construction. A city council member in favor of the measure said that it was regrettable for the company "to now stick guns to council members' heads." The president of a local civic association came down on the other side. All the stores were in the city's poorer, eastern half, and she said, "We have been working on making this project a reality for over 23 years. . . . We all want the project to move forward." The council passed the bill, but the mayor vetoed it.

Walmart agreed to paint an Arizona store the color of the desert. It built a store in Long Beach in an Art Deco style, and it opened a Middlefield, Ohio, store with hitching posts for Amish customers. Perhaps its biggest challenge was Monsey, about halfway between New York City and West Point. More than half of Monsey's 28,000 residents were Hasidic Jews, and as a patient Walmart official said, "The rabbis have a lot of concerns. . . . There's no question our outreach has been greater than usual."

Walmart's Limits

Even in parts of the country where Walmart was popular, it had a tough time attracting wealthy customers. Late in 2005 the company bought a six-page spread in *Elle Girl* and eight pages in *Vogue*. The ads made no mention of low prices. This was out of character, but an analyst explained, "Walmart is frustrated by not being able to penetrate the upper income market as much as they would like, because that's what is providing growth for some of their competitors, including Target."

A fashion consultant rubbed salt in the wound: "Target is so good. I really believe that they have revolutionized mass merchandising on fashion. Target created an image and then moved the merchandise up into that image." What about Walmart? The consultant said, "I think Walmart and fashion is such an oxymoron. I admire them for taking a crack at it." Would it work? He thought not. Walmart, he said, meant "good value for very little money. And that isn't what fashion is about. They can sell apparel. I don't think they can sell fashion."

"All retailers have a formula," another analyst said. "They grow as far and as fast as they can with that formula." And Walmart? His verdict was that "they have hit the wall." Walmart's same-store sales in 2006 increased only 1.9 percent over the previous year, much less than the increases at Target, Costco, and Best Buy. By 2011 same store sales had decreased for eight consecutive quarters. By 2014 they had declined for five. One observer said, "Maybe it's possible to fatten the bottom line with improvements to the supply chain. But they've pretty much accomplished what they're going to accomplish here." An analyst said, "The glory days are over."

New Tricks

Was the company so gloomy? Not a chance: gross profit margins on clothes approached 50 percent, twice the average for the rest of the store. In 2006 the company hired 340 "fashion merchants" to help tailor inventories to local markets. "It is one of the most important positions we have created," said an executive. Yet 20 percent of Walmart customers did not have a bank account, 40 percent had an annual household income under $50,000, and 70 percent had annual household incomes under $70,000. Walmart's customers spent 18 percent of all the food stamps in the country. Would fancy stuff drive them away?

Perhaps it was smarter to focus on "action alley," the wide aisles in which the company could build huge stacks of laundry detergent or tortilla chips. The physical arrangement of goods could always be improved. Shoppers typically spent twenty-one minutes in a Supercenter but found only seven of the ten things on their lists. Walmart hoped to get that number up to eight or even nine.

The company also set out to "de-homogenize" stores, by which it meant tailoring stock to the neighborhood. The new store in Garland, Texas, set out to serve its heavily Latino neighborhood and sold five-pound bags of fresh, moist, tamale masa. Signs at the meat counter were not only bilingual but used the same font size for both Spanish and English. A "de-homogenized" store in wealthy Plano had a sushi bar, a coffee shop with wireless Internet access, and $500 bottles of wine positioned with cheese at the front of the store. Similarly, Walmart developed stores for Jews who kept kosher, stores for empty nesters, stores for suburbanites, and stores for rural populations. The predominantly black shoppers at the Walmart in Evergreen Park, Illinois, could browse ninety-two feet of gospel, rhythm and blues, and hip-hop music, four times as much as they would find in the average Walmart.

The company announced in 2006 that it hoped to build fifty stores in troubled neighborhoods and would fund economic-opportunity programs for small businesses there. Those businesses would get free newspaper advertising and a place in Walmart's in-store advertising. The CEO said, "We see we can be better for communities than we have been in the past." An opponent dismissed the program as "another P.R. stunt in a litany of P.R. stunts."

In 2011 Walmart announced that it would open stores in America's "food deserts," defined by the USDA as places where at least 500 people live more than a mile from a supermarket. Walmart planned to build 300 stores in such areas, some rural, some urban.

Walmart took on Best Buy too. That company had become the biggest consumer-electronics retailer in 1996, when it overtook the doomed Circuit City. Walmart might not beat Best Buy on price, but it would sell much cheaper extended warranties. Best Buy fought back with what it called "customer centricity," by which it meant stores adjusted to local demographics. It would open stores for business users, for early adopting young men, for older men, for affluent professionals, and for busy suburban women. This amounted to "de-homogenizing," but Best Buy had some other tricks. For one thing, its employees were on salary, not commission, which made salespeople less pushy. Best Buy also invested heavily in its Geek Squad, which by 2007 had sales of about a billion dollars.

Best Buy struggled against "showrooming," shoppers fondling the merchandise, then going home and buying it online to save close to 10 percent in states that did not collect sales tax on online purchases. By 2013 all but five states collected taxes on those sales. Best Buy then set out to match Amazon's prices. It also welcomed Samsung stores within Best Buys, which gave Samsung a strong incentive to resist undercutting on Amazon.

Walmart faced the same showrooming pressure and encouraged shoppers to buy at walmart.com. Salespeople in Walmart stores resisted this policy because they got bonuses based on in-store sales. Rather than fight the salespeople, Walmart credited online sales to the physical store closest to the online buyer's home address.

Amazon remained a challenge for both Best Buy and Walmart. Walmart was by far the biggest of the companies, with revenues of almost $500 billion, compared to Amazon's $60 billion and Best Buy's $40 billion. Amazon was growing faster than Walmart, however, and it was by earthly measures a huge operation, shipping about 600 million packages in the United States in 2013—a third with the post office, a third with UPS, and a third divided between FedEx and smaller shippers. Amazon offered same-day delivery in eleven cities. To serve customers of its subscription service for household paper products, Amazon opened a distribution center next door to Procter & Gamble's huge Mehoopany Paper Products factory near Tunkhannock, Pennsylvania. The move annoyed Target so much that for a time it wouldn't stack P&G products on its stores' "endcaps," the coveted shelves at the ends of aisles.

Walmart's online sales were less than $10 billion annually, but the company had little choice but to join this battle between "bricks and clicks." Bricks weren't doing so well, after all. In the years around 2005, the United States had opened about 300 million square feet of new retail space annually; in 2010 and the next few years, it opened fewer than 50 million. Foot traffic was way down too, declining steadily from about 33 billion store visits in 2010 to fewer than 18 billion in 2013. A consultant said, "Retailers have got to be asking themselves what they are going to do if shoppers only go to the mall once a month," and even that frequency sounded optimistic. One analyst warned, "Thousands of supercenters are going the way of the horse and buggy."

To fight Amazon, Walmart offered its own subscription service. It also offered free shipping on purchases from the company's website, provided that the buyer pick up the package from either a Walmart or a FedEx store. In California it experimented with home delivery for a service charge of five or ten dollars. Amazon went one better and introduced Amazon Tote, a grocery service with free home delivery, no minimum purchase required. Walmart's head of e-commerce said that developing online shopping would "take the rest of our careers and as much [money] as we've got. This isn't a project. It's about the future of the company." Walmart's budget for e-commerce jumped from $400 million in 2013 to a billion dollars two years later. There seemed little choice. An analyst said that online grocery shopping in particular was "the next frontier." He put it simply: "Once you get people hooked, that's it."

Grocers

By 2012 Walmart had grocery sales of $145 billion. That was twice as much as runner-up Kroger and four times as much as tied-for-third-place Supervalu, Safeway, and Ahold. Between 2000 and 2011 the share of the grocery business held by conventional supermarkets fell from two-thirds to barely over half. Albertsons in 2004 promised handheld scanners to help shoppers keep running totals. A year later it gave up and sold itself mostly to Supervalu, which sliced off chunks of the business and tried to run the remaining stores more profitably.

A&P, which operated 16,000 stores in the 1930s, was down to 400 when it declared bankruptcy in 2010. Its onetime national rival, Safeway, tried to survive by converting its 1,750 stores into high-end "Lifestyle" stores. It didn't work, and in 2014, when Safeway had a 9 percent share of the supermarket business in the United States, it was acquired by Cerberus, a private-equity company that intended to merge Safeway's 1,300 stores with Albertsons' 1,000. Combined, they'd still be smaller than Kroger or Walmart.

The biggest of the supermarket chains, Kroger focused on what it called "the center of the store," by which it meant selling standard items at low prices. The company was also deeply involved in market research aimed at producing booklets of coupons sent to customers and tailored to their shopping tastes. Other companies did this too, but the boss of Frito-Lay said, "I've been in this business 32 years, and this is the best blend of customer data and retail insight I've ever seen. I'm blown away. It's given me new hope."

Who was likely to do best against Walmart? One possible answer was Whole Foods, which with a bit over 300 stores had a stock-market valuation larger than Kroger, which had 2,400 stores. Another possibility was Target, founded in 1962, when the Dayton Company, based in Roseville, Minnesota, opened a bargain basement without the usual upstairs department store. Target would survive where wannabes, including Woolco, Ames, Bradlees, and Caldor, would fail. Part of Target's success lay in its locations: more than 80 percent of Target stores were in urban or suburban—and therefore wealthier—communities. The figure for Walmart was slightly more than half. A third of all retail sales in the United States came from California, Chicago, and the Boston-to-Washington corridor. Fewer than 2 percent of Walmart's Supercenters were in those areas.

Target had brilliant advertising too. Its annual ad budget was about $400 million, less than Walmart's and much less than Sears'. But whose logo did people remember? Then there was the lure of "Tarzhay" chic. A consultant said, "The strategy is to lure its customers with a few wow-'em products and then sell them doughnuts on their way to the register."

Still, there were only about 200 Super Targets in the United States, compared to almost 3,000 Walmart Supercenters. And not everyone admired Target. One analyst said that the company, with its new emphasis on food, was "going through an identity crisis." He explained: "All the emphasis they put now into food is a diversion from the hip, trendy, designer-focused brand personality that they worked so hard to develop." There was a populist line of criticism too. An advocacy group, Jobs Now, said, "We feel they are worse than Walmart because they are masquerading as this benign employer." Target had no unionized employees, and a union official said, "They have gotten this pass because they have set up this foundation and have this chic look, and that's more cruel than Walmart. Walmart doesn't pretend." Worst of all, the company began to look more and more like Walmart. Perhaps a tough economy left Target no choice, but an analyst said that the company had "lost a lot of what used to make it unique."

Another challenger—and perhaps one that posed a bigger threat to Walmart—was dollar stores. Prices were even lower at these stores than at Walmart because dollar stores offered only a few thousand stock-keeping units, instead of the tens of thousands found at Walmart and full-service supermarkets. Dollar stores didn't waste money making themselves look pretty either. As the head of Aldi in the United States put it, "Our customers aren't paying for someone to stack each jar of peanut butter on top of each other and turn the labels just so."

One analyst said that dollar stores had "the best business model for retail in the world," and if Europe was any guide, there was lots of room to grow. There, hard discounters had 40 percent of the market, while in the United States they might have 2 percent. The business in the United States was divided primarily among Dollar General, with 10,000 stores; Family Dollar, with 6,600; and Dollar Tree, with 3,800. All were based in the South. Their target customers, as Family Dollar described them, had household incomes under $40,000 and were "poor to just getting by." Between 2008 and 2013 the compounded five-year annual growth rate for same-store sales at Dollar General was 5.9 percent; for Walmart, it was 0.3 percent.

Dollar General experimented with a format called Dollar General Market, twice the size of the usual store and stocking fresh and refrigerated foods. Breaking with traditional supermarket practice, these stores put bread and milk up front, maximizing convenience for shoppers in a rush. Would it work? The CEO said, "We're trying to be analytical and thoughtful, eating the elephant one bite at a time instead of swallowing the whole thing." Meanwhile, Dollar General was fighting Family Dollar for control of Dollar Tree.

Then there was Aldi, a German hard discounter with sales exceeding $60 billion. Aldi was determined to grow its American business from 1,300 stores in 2013 to almost 2,000 by 2018. A money-saving 90 percent of its stock-keeping units were house brands. (The same thing was true at Trader Joe's, a different kind of store but one controlled by another branch of the Albrecht family.) Aldi might prove a major threat not only to the other dollar stores but to Walmart.

Who else would dare to swim in these waters? Tesco, Britain's largest and the world's number-three grocer, decided to jump in. The company's boss, Terry Leahy, envisioned a chain of 10,000 American stores, often located at highway junctions. Success depended, he thought, on keeping prices as low as Walmart's, offering top-quality fresh food, and making shopping easy. Where to begin? Tesco picked Los Angeles, partly because Walmart was weak there and partly because Californians seemed constitutionally eager for new things.

The Tesco stores were called Fresh & Easy. They were small—about 10,000 square feet—and as the name suggested, they emphasized fresh and prepared foods. To save money, much of the produce section wasn't refrigerated, and all checkouts were self-serve. Tesco set up its American headquarters in Riverside, east of Los Angeles, and it brought with it two of its UK suppliers, Wild Rocket Foods for vegetables and 2 Sisters Food Group for cooked poultry. Tesco ran its own kitchen for prepared foods, with ingredients supplied largely by these two neighbors. Cooking started at 2:00 each morning.

Tesco's Leahy said, "Walmart is a great retailer, but America is a big place. The part of the market that we are addressing, which is convenience, is an underinvested part of the market. And I think there is plenty of room in the market now." Tesco soon opened another supply center. This one was in Stockton and served Northern California.

Walmart responded with urban convenience stores; first a few stores called Marketside, then another group under the name Walmart Express. Each covered about 15,000 square feet. These were the first new kinds of store for Walmart since the Neighborhood Market, introduced in 1998. Walmart had been cautious with that smaller format, but 400 Neighborhood Markets were open in 2014, and same-store revenues were rising at over 5 percent annually while superstore revenues were flat.

And Fresh & Easy? By 2010 there were 170 stores scattered over California, Nevada, and Arizona. Five years after the experiment began, and perhaps for reasons outside Tesco's control, Fresh & Easy was still losing money. By 2011 it had lost $900 million. Tesco bought the American operations of its two suppliers. It closed a dozen stores in mortgage-battered Arizona and Nevada. Still, the company continued to open a store a week. A new CEO in 2012 seemed determined to stay the course, though he admitted, "We are playing in a playground with some very big and very old retailers who are very wise." Later that year, Tesco announced that it would open no more Fresh & Easy stores until the existing ones became profitable. Still later, it announced cumulative losses of $1.6 billion. Pushed to the wall, Tesco decided to close all 191 stores. In 2013 the Yucaipa Companies agreed to take 150 of the stores off Tesco's hands in exchange for a payment from Tesco of £150 million. Some 4,000 employees might yet keep their jobs.

Manhattan was a special case, with large-format supermarkets almost unknown decades after they were ubiquitous in most American cities. Residents of converted Wall Street office buildings needed more than the Hermès store in the old J.P. Morgan building at 15 Broad Street. They needed more than the Tiffany store in the former offices of Trust Company of America at 37 Wall Street. One option was FreshDirect, an online grocer with 150,000 customers and about 8 percent of Manhattan's grocery bill, or $160 million annually. For downtown customers who wanted to see what they were buying, there was Gourmet Garage in SoHo and Greenwich Village. They too delivered.

The dam broke in 2006, when both Whole Foods and Trader Joe's opened Manhattan stores. By 2012 Whole Foods had five stores on the island. Soon there would also be a half million square feet of shops and restaurants in the redeveloped World Trade Center. More startling than any of these new choices was East River Plaza, a long-delayed shopping center with a Home Depot and Costco Wholesale Club. What was so startling? The location was on the East River between 116th and 119th. This was Harlem. Target arrived in 2010.

Clothing Stores

Shoppers meanwhile needed clothes, and for this they often turned to specialty stores. The biggest was Gap, which had almost 3,000 stores,

150,000 employees, and annual sales of $16 billion. Gap had a problem, however: same-store sales in April 2006 were down for the seventeenth consecutive month. The next year, a consultant compiled a ranking of customer loyalty to 362 brands. Gap came in 355th. Was Gap too big, too sluggish, to compete with smaller rivals like Abercrombie & Fitch, American Eagle, and Aéropostale? Was it losing business to Walmart and Target? The company opened Forth & Towne to reach women between Abercrombie and Ann Taylor, but eighteen months later the company shut it down, perhaps with the thought that the experiment was a distraction from more important things. One analyst, echoing many, said, "There is nothing exciting or interesting on the sales floor." Even a Gap executive admitted, "We've disappointed our customers for several seasons and we know it will take us time to win them back."

Early in 2006 the company announced a new store design. Good-bye, white; hello, warmer colors. Think "at home." Think Starbucks. The next year, the company parted company with its ex-Disney boss. Five years later, though reporting increased revenues, Gap announced that it would close a fifth of its stores in the United States. By 2013 its stock price was up sharply, but an analyst said, "They seem to be doing better, but they are still not operating in a leadership position." The company's chief executive, adopting the language of a military commander on the battlefield, said, "There's business to be had, there's traffic to be taken, there's market share to be gained and that's the attitude we have to take." Brave words, but the company lost money in five of the six years between 2007 and 2012. The next year was better; the following year, not so much. The CEO resigned.

Meanwhile, Ann Taylor, with annual sales under $2 billion, hired a software company to install the Ann Taylor Labor Allocation System, or ATLAS. ATLAS monitored performance, including sales per hour and dollars per transaction, and it used the numbers to make sure that the most productive employees worked during the busiest hours. An executive said that the name was important "because it gave a personality to the system, so [employees] hate the system and not us." L Brands, Williams-Sonoma, and Gap began using similar systems.

Abercrombie too was in trouble. With revenues about the same as Ann Taylor's, the company stuck to its high-price strategy. A consultant warned that the company "keeps working to protect their brand. But when you see 30% sales declines, you're going to protect your brand into oblivion." Another observer said, "Once you lose your brand loyalists—and you have to do a lot to piss them off—you don't get them back." Could news be worse? It could. Surveys at Talbots revealed that customers of every age bracket, including women over sixty-five, believed that Talbots clothes were best suited to women older than they.

The Lucky Few

Ralph Lauren operated a piddling 160 or so stores of his own but sold Chaps at Kohl's and American Living at JCPenney. Under the labels Ralph Lauren, Lauren by Ralph Lauren, RRL, RLX, Polo Sport, and Rugby, he sold clothes at many other stores too, and somehow, despite the dilution, he retained an aura of luxury. An admiring competitor said, "Ralph Lauren is the king of public perception." A consultant said, "All the Lauren labels are feeding off the same aspirational image." It was a dramatic contrast with Armani, which operated 2,500 stores and, according to analysts, was "losing its exclusivity." Prada's chief executive knew the problem: "It's important not to turn too mass-market," he said.

Another exceptional operation was Sweden's cheap-chic H&M, which opened its 3,000th store in 2013. A third was Zara, founded in 1975 and based in tiny A Coruña, in the northwest corner of Spain. From this remote corner of a corner, Zara—or, more precisely, its owner Inditex—ran 6,000 stores in eighty-seven countries. They were stocked every two weeks, which meant that shipments were small but styles hot. Half of Zara's merchandise was made close to A Coruña, which also helped get new ideas into stores fast. Still not content, in 2014 the company was spending over $200 million on a cluster of four warehouses at Cabanillas del Campo, 30 miles northeast of Madrid's airport. The warehouses would ship almost 500,000 garments every day and begin making deliveries to each of the company's stores twice a week. Perhaps the most striking of the company's innovations was that it did not advertise. Even so, Inditex had become Spain's biggest company, and Zara was the world's largest fashion retailer.

SHOPPING CENTERS

Between 2000 and 2008 the United States opened about 300 million square feet—or almost 11 square miles—of retail space annually. The number plunged to under 50 million square feet annually between 2010 and 2013, and depending on the future of Internet sales, it might never return to its older level. Still, the existing inventory of retail space wasn't going anywhere, at least for a while, and there was lots of it. Between 1970 and 2010 retail space had grown 126 percent, more than twice the 52 percent growth in the population of the United States.

This retail space comprised corner stores, larger convenience centers, still larger neighborhood centers, community centers, and—biggest of all—regional centers. The minimum population need to support each class of shopping center increased from 1,000 households to 2,000, 7,000, 25,000, and 75,000. The regional centers, which generally measured a million square feet or more, included about a thousand enclosed shopping malls, a form developed chiefly by Victor Gruen, an Austrian architect fleeing the Nazis. Once on the lucky side of the Atlantic, Gruen began dressing display windows. After the war he designed Detroit's Northland Center. His Southdale, the prototype of the enclosed mall, opened near Minneapolis in 1956. Shoppers could see the stores below them by looking over low balconies or through transparent escalator side panels. Trees lured eyes to higher floors. To calm customers, lighting simulated a perpetual mid-afternoon, and it was 75 degrees round the clock.

An architectural critic wrote of Southdale, "It does not seem like a historic building, which is precisely why it is one." Only 5 percent of Southdale's first tenants were chains, however. Malls developed in other unexpected ways too. Gruen wanted them to have artwork because, as he wrote, "as art patrons, merchants can be to our time what the church and nobility were to the Middle Ages." Gruen also wanted low-cost housing near shopping centers, but even less came of that. He returned to Vienna and wrote of "land-wasting seas of parking. I refuse to pay alimony for those bastard developments."

With a good location, malls could do very well. The Beverly Center, just outside Beverly Hills, was nobody's idea of a handsome building. Wandering around the food court, its owner said, "This just isn't that nice. We have to figure out what to do here." Still, location, location, location: the mall had Louis Vuitton, Prada, Gucci, Fendi, Tiffany, Jimmy Choo, and more. Similarly, the King of Prussia Mall, where the Pennsylvania Turnpike approaches Philadelphia, had Bloomingdale's, Nordstrom, Neiman Marcus, and Tiffany. Its annual sales of $750 per square foot of leasable area were almost twice the national average of $370. A few malls earned more still, among them the Ala Moana in Honolulu, the Forum Shops in Las Vegas, and the Bal Harbour Shops in Miami Beach. Those locations weren't half bad either.

Good locations for new malls were getting hard to find, but Taubman Properties in 2012 took a chance on City Creek, adjacent to Salt Lake City's Temple Square. The plan was a conventional dumbbell, with Nordstrom at one end and Macy's at the other, but the mall was in a market where customers had plenty of choice. Something special was needed, and Taubman hoped a retractable glass-and-steel roof might do the trick, along with a central fountain with both fire and water. The goal was to create an aspirational space, not merely a functional one. Two years later, in 2014, Taubman opened another entirely new mall, the University Town Center in Sarasota. An analyst said, "They're really the only one building malls from the ground-up in the U.S. right now."

South Gate, a couple of miles south of downtown Los Angeles, did not have such a wealthy hinterland but was, as a developer said, "a huge untapped market. The area is totally unserved by major retailers." Plans were developed for a $175 million open-air center at Firestone Boulevard and Atlantic Avenue. It was to be called The Gateway. Despite the site's potential, the developers could not get financing. Six years later, in 2012, the site was still "in development," though it now had a new name, Azalea.

Shopping Centers on Life Support

Jaded shoppers might recall Fran, the girl in 1978's *Dawn of the Dead*. She and her friends had gone to the mall in the hope of avoiding zombies. They failed, of course, and Fran told her friends, "You're hypnotized by this place, all of you. It's all so bright and neatly wrapped that you don't see that it can be a prison." As a nervy department-store manager once told Mel Simon, a pioneer mall developer, "I can tell it's your mall because the plastic plants died."

One developer said that shopping centers were dinosaurs "ready to fall into a pit." He had moved on to open-air power centers, basically big-box strip malls. Power centers appealed to tenants because space could be leased for half the price of space at malls. Power centers appealed to shoppers too because they could park at the entrance to a store and not have to walk half a mile to get what they wanted. As one shopper said, "I'm busy and I want to get right to the point. I'm not strolling around most of the time." Fifty years after Southdale, a realtor discussing enclosed malls said, "We're overbuilt." He predicted that 15 percent of the nation's malls would fail by 2018. Other forecasts were grimmer, anticipating the closure of twice that many. Still, one mall developer cautioned, "People have been predicting the death of the mall ever since it was born, practically."

Owners of troubled malls looked for help. Some malls were converted to outlet centers. There were about 150 of these around the country, and there was room for perhaps 100 more. Simon Property Group, which owned or had an interest in over 300 malls, had about 70 outlet centers. Taubman converted its Great Lakes Crossing near Detroit to an outlet center. It did the same thing with its Dolphin Mall in Miami. Some major retailers liked the outlet format so much that, like Saks and Nordstrom, they had more outlets than full-price stores.

Another solution for malls in trouble was to welcome discounters. A spokesman for the International Council of Shopping Centers said,

"Department stores used to be the 800-pound gorilla." No longer: a mall could easily be anchored by a Walmart or Target, even in combination with Nordstrom or Neiman Marcus. The spokesman himself could hardly believe it. "Who would have ever thought?" he asked. There were plenty of opportunities for these newcomers too because the collapse of Montgomery Ward in 2000 by itself created 207 large, dark spaces. Walmart perked up. Sometimes moving into an abandoned building was less controversial than starting from scratch. An old mall became Walmart's first store in El Cajon, California, as well as the company's first multistory store.

By 2006 Walmart had twenty-six stores in malls, with eighteen more on mall outparcels. Contrary to expectations, sales in the other stores in the mall often went up after the Walmart opened. At the Grossmont Centre in San Diego, sales by existing tenants rose 26 percent in the year after Walmart arrived, and vacancies declined from 18 percent to almost nothing. The Beast of Bentonville turned out to be a shopper magnet. Costco began locating in malls too, not by choice but for lack of alternatives. Was this company also a magnet? It seemed not, perhaps because Costco shoppers were exhausted by the time they got out.

Big-Splash Centers on the East Coast

Some developers were especially creative. The Lab opened in 1993 around an old military night-goggle factory in Costa Mesa, California. The developer explained what he had tried to do. "If anyone blindfolded you and dropped you in a typical mall across the country," he said, "you would not have any idea where you are. Here, we tried for something different, not the old fountain-and-marble formula. We tried to put some excitement in retailing." No chain stores; instead, stores included Eye Five, Carve, and Black & Blue. Across the street, the same developer built The Camp, a sporting center for cyclists, surfers, skaters, and skiers. For lunch, there was the Native Foods Café, a vegan restaurant.

A few years later, and on a much larger scale, the Mills Corporation became famous for "shoppertainment" malls such as Potomac Mills near Washington and Sawgrass Mills near Fort Lauderdale. Ambitiously, it began to develop Xanadu Meadowlands, a 2.2 million-square-foot mall in the New Jersey Meadowlands, only 5 miles from Manhattan and with a planned rail link to Penn Station.

One merchant admitted that Mills was "the most creative of any developer out there," but he questioned whether it was "possible to be that creative and be financially successful." Construction of Xanadu began in 2004, but after investing $800 million, Mills lost control of the project to Colony Capital Acquisitions. Colony planned to invest another $1.5 billion but made its offer conditional on the Xanadu developer continuing to work on the project. In 2009, and with the project 80 percent complete, work stopped. By 2011 Xanadu was on its third developer, who promised to invest another billion dollars. This third developer, Triple Five, was controlled by the developer of the huge Edmonton Mall and the Mall of America, near Minneapolis. Xanadu got a new name: American Dream Meadowlands.

What impact would Xanadu or Dream have on Paramus, a few miles to the north? With only 27,000 people, Paramus had four big malls— the Garden State Plaza, Fashion Center, Paramus Park, and Bergen Town Center. Together, these four had a total of 320 stores, each with annual sales exceeding a million dollars. That was more than any zip code in the country, except for Manhattan's East Side 10021. The four malls together had 20 million shoppers a year. They drew 200,000 cars daily in December. Was Xanadu overkill? One local planner said, "I always thought it was a crazy idea." Vornado Realty, which owned the Bergen Town Center, decided not to wait and see: it converted its mall to an outlet center.

One state north, Destiny, near Syracuse, called itself a "visionary initiative" and was budgeted at $20 billion. Its modest developer, Robert Congel, declared that Destiny would run entirely on renewable energy and "produce more benefit for humanity than any one thing that private enterprise has ever done."

Back on Planet Earth, town planners in suburban DC watched the continuing expansion of Tysons Corner. Macerich of California, which owned Tysons Corner Center, added a theater and a bunch of restaurants. The ads read, "Blackened mahi-mahi with Cajun remoulade. Hungry? Tysons, where the restaurants are." Across the road, Tysons Galleria, a General Growth Properties mall, was planning high-rises. Not wanting to be left behind, Macerich added the twenty-two-story Tysons Tower. The company's CEO said, "I see our residential strategy as being an ornament on a great retail town center." Both of these centers were part of what the president of the local chamber of commerce called "the world's most successful office park." Every day, 120,000 workers converged at this mighty crossroads, and a 2010 master plan anticipated 200,000 workers by 2050. "What we want," the chamber president said, "is a downtown" for Northern Virginia. The key was the construction of the Silver Line, extending the Washington Metro from East Falls Church through Tysons. Four stations opened there in 2014, which meant that housing densities could be legally doubled, increasing the residential population at Tysons from 17,000 in 2013 to 100,000 in 2050. The chamber president warned that it was now or never for Tysons Corner: "There are no do overs after this point."

Caruso's Wars

Rick Caruso was the big-splash builder of The Grove, an open-air center in LA that boasted of having more visitors than Disneyland. He explained, "We have stories. We have story lines of all of the projects." Caruso explained that the story line for The Grove was based on Charleston, South Carolina. Then he decided to build something twice as big. Americana at Brand was in Glendale and included a hundred condos and almost 300 rental apartments. Caruso said, "I've been influenced by the fact that I don't like malls." What he did like—and what the public apparently liked too—was the neo-traditional architecture of an imagined American past. Caruso said, "The idea is to put people in a place that transports them to a better time and reminds them of a village square or old American town."

At Glendale, Caruso bumped into GGP, the biggest mall operator in the country after its acquisition of the Rouse Company. GGP was determined to protect its Glendale Galleria, which was literally across the street from Americana, and it fought Caruso at city hall, in a referendum, and in the courts. It warned Cheesecake Factory that if it opened at Americana it would be blacklisted by GGP malls nationwide. Caruso fought back and won a settlement of $89 million from GGP. Americana opened in 2008, the same year that GGP declared bankruptcy. Americana had a Cheesecake Factory too. Shoppers were reluctant to spend much, but Caruso said he was patient. Even GGP was happy. The marketing director of the Galleria said, "I think we're seeing good cross-shopping that's really facilitating both properties." As for past hostilities, GGP's marketing director said, "We've moved on."

Caruso set out to build The Shops at Santa Anita, an open-air center on part of the Santa Anita racetrack in Arcadia. Westfield Corporation, the Australian owner of a hundred malls, including the nearby Santa Anita Mall, called out the lawyers. Caruso said, "It will get nasty." The project went ahead, forcing Westfield to expand its own mall and upgrade several of its other Los Angeles properties, including the Topanga Canyon Mall, Fashion Square in Sherman Oaks, and Century City.

Dallas

What city had more retail space per capita than Southern California? The answer was Dallas. Its first enclosed mall was Mesquite's Big Town Mall, which opened in 1959. Big Town thrived until upscale NorthPark opened in 1965. Big Town's Foley's quit in 1989, Woolworth closed in 1993, and Montgomery Ward turned off the lights in 2000. Finally, in 2006 Big Town was demolished, leaving behind a seventy-seven-acre parking lot enclosing a block of weeds that puzzled anyone who happened to notice.

Up on the city's booming north side, Frisco's Stonebriar continued to grow, along with The Commons on Legacy and, around it, the huge Legacy Business Park. In the New Urbanist mode, The Commons had hundreds of homes and apartments. Residents could walk between home and office, as well as to eighty shops and restaurants. Who needed downtown Dallas anyway? A customer at the Main Street Bakery and Bistro said, "There's too much riffraff down there." Public transit? Forget it. Public schools? The nearest elementary was 3 miles away. You still needed a car if you wanted a supermarket or a hardware store.

Stonebriar had more conventional competitors too, including Alliance, a 17,000-acre development at the north end of Fort Worth. Some 140 businesses had built 25 million square feet of office and warehouse space around the Alliance Airport, which the Hillwood Development Company opened in 1990. Those buildings had 24,000 employees served by a raft of residential and commercial developments. Hillwood, which was run by Ross Perot Jr., was working on an additional 4 million square feet of commercial space to be called Alliance Town Center. A local realtor said, "It sure looks like this is going to be the next super regional shopping hub in North Texas."

Venerable NorthPark emerged from a huge expansion. As if that weren't enough, Harvest Partners had gone across the street, imploded a ten-story building, and begun Park Lane, with 2 million square feet including a mall, hotel, 330,000 feet of office space, and 650 apartments. A realtor involved with the project said that, along with NorthPark, Park Lane would make the intersection of Park Lane and the North Central Expressway "the No. 1 retail destination in Texas."

Manhattan and San Francisco

Malls, like supermarkets, were latecomers to Manhattan. Ferdinand Marcos of the Philippines—he whose wife never saw a pair of shoes she didn't like—bankrolled in 1985 the conversion of the defunct E. J. Korvette at Herald Square. This was Herald Center, whose tenants included Ann Taylor, Brookstone, and Caswell-Massey. The project failed, however. The upper floors were abandoned, and JCPenney occupied the rump that remained.

The Time Warner Center had much better luck. Opened in February 2004, it was a Related Companies project designed by the same David Childs who a few years later would design 1 World Trade Center. Business boomed at the center's Whole Foods, Manhattan's top-selling grocery store. Other merchants in the center included Williams-Sonoma, apparently willing to pay an annual rent of $300 a square foot.

The Time Warner Center was part of a broader change. National retailers had always avoided New York's outer boroughs. Now there were five Victoria's Secrets just in Brooklyn and Queens. By 2014 at least five shopping centers were under construction in the Bronx. The Mall at Bay Plaza, an expansion of the Bay Plaza Shopping Center near Pelham Bay Park, would be New York City's first enclosed center since the failure at Herald Square in the 1980s.

San Francisco remained determined to keep malls out. Stonestown had opened in the 1950s and established itself before the portcullis dropped. No other mall got in, at least none with acres and acres of open-air parking. Even formula retail had a hard time. A city planner said, "The predominant view in most parts of the city is, 'We've got enough; if we want to go to Starbucks we know where to find one.'" In the entire Richmond District there was only one. It felt creepy, like the streets of Pyongyang.

2 Making

BEVERAGES AND SNACKS

The average American in 2007 drank forty-nine gallons of soda pop, the equivalent of 789 eight-ounce glasses. Coca-Cola had 17 percent of that market, or 25 percent if you included Diet Coke. Pepsi and Diet Pepsi together trailed at 14 percent. Though consumption was close to its historic peak, sales in recent years had slipped 1 or 2 percent annually. By 2012 consumption was down to forty-three gallons per capita annually. That was still more than enough to overtop a good-sized bathtub, but the trend was clear. A worried bottler said, "There are a lot of bottlers who realize now that it's innovate or die." There was no time to waste, especially with sales in 2013 falling another 3 percent—and twice that much for Diet Coke and Diet Pepsi.

Both Coke and Pepsi began shifting from carbonated soft drinks to "liquid refreshment beverages." In 2011, for example, Pepsi sales by volume declined over 5 percent, but Aquafina thrived. The quickest way to build volume was to buy existing companies, so Coke didn't bother developing a competitor to Odwalla juices; it just bought Odwalla. Pepsi bought Naked Juice. Between them, Coke and Pepsi came to own two-thirds of the American orange-juice market, including Simply Orange, Minute Maid, Tropicana, and Dole. Unfortunately for the companies, American consumption of orange juice had fallen from almost 6 gallons per capita at the peak in 1998 to 2.8 gallons in 2012. In response, Coke bought Monster Beverage. Nestle, which had purchased Juicy Juice in 2006, went the other way: it decided to stick with coffee and sold the company.

Globally, the picture was more complicated. Seventy percent of Coke's beverage revenues came from overseas, where Coke was available in every country except Cuba and North Korea. That kind of penetration took time, and Coke had begun exporting in 1912, when it began selling Coke in the Philippines. Coke left China in 1949 but returned in 1979. It left India in 1977, when the government demanded that it release the Coca-Cola formula, but it returned in 1993, when the government changed its mind. Coke returned to the former East Germany on the day in 1990 of German reunification. As its Turkish American CEO said, "Coca-Cola has always stood for optimism at times of change and progress around the world."

Coke dreamed of selling Coke around the world the way it already sold Coke in Mexico. There, people drank an average of 700 glasses annually. In China the figure was thirty-eight; in India, a pitiful twelve. To boost sales in China, Coke began offering six-ounce returnable bottles for the equivalent of ten cents.

It had little choice: Coke got 80 percent of its revenues from beverages. Pepsi, on the other hand, earned only 20 percent of its revenues from drinks and relied instead on its Frito-Lay division, which just about owned the chip section of any supermarket you could name. Not just supermarkets either. Holidays were crowded at Mahabaleshwar, a hill station southeast of Bombay. On holidays a small truck took advantage of the crowds and set out a display of Frito-Lay snacks.

Wed to salty snacks, Pepsi became China's biggest potato grower, with 3,000 acres under cultivation in Dalata Banner in Inner Mongolia. A Pepsi manager said, "PepsiCo is not a farming company. But to build a market we had to take extra steps like this." The company helped Russian farmers grow potatoes for a Frito-Lay plant in Kashira, 65 miles south of Moscow. (Russians ate twice as many potatoes as Americans, but chips were new to them.) The plant, which opened in 2002, employed 1,200 people and drew workers from 40 miles around. Far to the south, in Azov, Pepsi in 2007 began building a second potato-chip factory. Cost: $170 million. Meanwhile, on a different continent, Pepsi entered long-term supply contracts with South American farmers who could supply exotic potato varieties for the company's Andina-brand chips.

Working with Peasant Producers and Consumers

The same logic drove many different kinds of companies to venture far from their normal methods of doing business. South African Breweries bought grain from 28,000 smallholders. Cadbury operated twenty South Indian nurseries where cocoa saplings were grown and then given to farmers along with technical advice. Mondelēz, which bought Cadbury in 2010, set up a $400 million program to help African cocoa growers and a $200 million program for Southeast Asian coffee growers. Starbucks began helping farmers in Yunnan raise coffee, even though the beans would be sent to the United States for roasting and then sent back to China. McDonald's helped farmers grow lettuce and tomatoes in Guatemala and Panama. Walmart contracted with Central American farmers accustomed to selling through informal channels. The company had forty agronomists giving them advice. A farmer with seventy-five acres of vegetables in Guatemala said, "Their pickiness has helped me improve." That was the good news. The bad was that farmers with fewer than seventy-five acres had a tough time finding their way into an increasingly organized market.

Many people thought that the expansion of global brands was bad for locals, but Unilever had the courage to find out if this was true. Allowing Oxfam to study the company's operations in Indonesia, Unilever's CEO explained, "We needed to increase understanding of the impact of the operations of a business like ours on the lives of poor people." Oxfam's analyst said afterward, "We were all just amazed at the scale of the value added that is generated in the distribution chain, and the number of people who may not be full-time but are getting a first taste of what the formal economy is like." Unilever, it turned out, had 5,000 employees in Indonesia, but its operations generated the equivalent of 300,000 full-time jobs, including hawkers and people selling Unilever products in 1.8 million shops and kiosks.

Unilever was pushing into Africa too, especially with Lifebuoy, an antibacterial soap. There was money to be made, but there were also health benefits if the company could persuade Africans to wash with soap before eating. A truck rolled into Muko, in southwestern Uganda, and the crew set up a stage. A campaign coordinator said, "If it becomes the 'in thing' to wash your hands with soap because it has status, or because people think you're civilized, or because it's the best thing to do for your kids, it will be more effective than saying: 'If you don't you'll get sick and die.'"

The same approach worked in rural India, where Interpublic Group, a French mega-agency, ran Linterland Rural Communication. Company vans went from village to village and staged shows promoting motor oil, noodles, soaps, toothpaste, and condoms. One salesman said, "Stick to the countryside if you want to be successful. When we arrive, the whole village comes out."

Dr Pepper

For many years Cadbury Schweppes owned Dr Pepper and 7UP, plus Snapple, Sunkist Soda, A&W Root Beer, and Canada Dry. A Cadbury officer said, "Our portfolio is a non-cola portfolio. That's what differentiates us." Still, in 2008 Cadbury spun off its drinks division into a new company called Dr Pepper Snapple Group.

The biggest challenge for stand-alone Dr Pepper Snapple was finding a way into stores. The company promptly arranged for Pepsi Bottling Group to distribute another old Cadbury brand, Orange Crush. This was startling because PBG, which handled more than half the Pepsi sold in the United States, normally distributed only Pepsi products. Now it was distributing a competitor's product—and dropping Pepsi's Tropicana Twister. A spokesman for Pepsi put on a brave face: "Of course we would prefer our bottlers to carry our products over anyone else's, but we have no objection to PBG's orange-soda decision." In another surprising change, Dr Pepper agreed to pay Coke over $100 million for the right to be the only non-Coke product sold in Coke's Freestyle vending machines.

Brewers

Germans made fine beer and drank a lot per capita, but the country had too few people to become the biggest beer market in the world.

The United States was first for a while, but it was overtaken—here as in so many things—by China. SABMiller and Anheuser-Busch were locked in combat there. Miller had a local partner, CR (for China Resources), with whom it made a beer called Snow. Anheuser-Busch had interests in several brands in China, including Harbin 1900, Harbin Ice, and Tsingtao, a premium brand created in 1903 by brewers at the German treaty port of Tsingtao (now Qingdao).

In 2006 an unhappy Anheuser-Busch saw Miller's Snow become China's leader, by both volume and revenue. By 2008 analysts reckoned that Snow was, or was about to be, the biggest brand in the world, measured by gallons brewed. SABMiller, which had been formed by a merger of South African Breweries and Miller, was also expanding in Africa. In Uganda it sold Eagle beer, brewed with sorghum instead of corn. It aimed to develop a beer made from cassava. In 2011 it bought Australia's Foster's for $10 billion.

Worldwide, Anheuser-Busch was number two not after SABMiller but after InBev, a company created in 2003 by the merger of Belgium's Interbrew and Brazil's AmBev. InBev's leading brands in Europe were Stella Artois, Beck's, and Bass; in Latin America, Skol; in North America, Labatt and Rolling Rock. Speaking of his strategy in the United States, InBev's boss, a Brazilian working for a company domiciled in Belgium, said, "We're not going head-to-head with Budweiser, Miller, and Coors. That would be suicidal." Rather than trying to develop a global brand, InBev relied on different brands in different markets but sought global sourcing efficiencies. For example, the company no longer used Belgian hops in Belgium's Hoegaarden beer. Instead, it bought hops in bulk from Australia and the United States.

Rumors swirled in 2008 about a merger between Anheuser-Busch and InBev. The American company had a lock on the United States, but growth in that market was very slow—and mostly from imports—so Anheuser had some incentive to do a deal. It already imported several InBev brands, including Stella Artois and Beck's. Together, Anheuser-Busch and InBev would have 300 labels and brew 10 billion gallons of beer annually, almost twice as much as SABMiller.

InBev offered $46 billion for Anheuser-Busch. Despite resistance from within the Busch family, August III overruled the ambition of his son, August IV, and the deal was done after the offer had been raised to $52 billion. The new company called itself AB InBev. For another $20 billion AB InBev bought Mexico's Grupo Modelo.

Spuds MacKenzie might be in trouble. The Clydesdales too. AB InBev had big ambitions for Budweiser, however. The CEO—still Brazilian and still working for a company domiciled in Belgium but now headquartered in New York—was soon calling Bud "America in a bottle." The beer was launched in Russia, Ukraine, Brazil, and—most important—China. By 2013 Budweiser was coming from eight Chinese breweries. That was far from the eighty breweries making Snow, but AB InBev's CEO didn't seem worried. "The potential is so huge," he said, "I don't see us [exhausting it] anytime soon."

The CEO of SABMiller meanwhile was cool to the idea of building a global brand. "We remain convinced beer is fundamentally a local business," he said, and he was eager to expand by buying nationally established brands. "There's plenty of room" for acquisitions, he said. Between them, AB InBev, SABMiller, Heineken, and Carlsberg had only 60 percent of the world market.

Wine

It's time to put our shirts on.

Americans loved the cachet of foreign wine, which is why California's share of the domestic market slipped from 72 percent in 1998 to 57 percent in 2013. Decades earlier, the state had supplied 90 percent of the domestic market. What to do? Gallo, the world leader by volume, had once sold only cheap wine. After all, Brother Ernest had said that his goal was to make Gallo "the Campbell Soup Company of the wine industry." No longer. Gallo annually sold about 70 million cases of wine in the United States (almost a quarter of the national total, 300 million), but it also marketed wines made by foreign partners under new labels, like Italy's Ecco Domani and Bella Sera, Australia's Black Swan, and France's Red Bicyclette. There were plenty of other opportunities. As droll Brother Joe once said, "Americans love Chianti. They just don't like the way it tastes." Wrapped in straw, the bottle was irresistible. Not so the bitter contents, with an aroma of the maquis, the Mediterranean scrubland of juniper and sage. Maybe the taste could be softened.

CLOTHES

In 1945 Americans spent 13 percent of their disposable income on clothes. By 1970 that figure was down to 7 percent, and in 2012 it was 3 percent. Americans weren't simplifying their wardrobes. Instead, clothes were now made overseas by workers who, by American standards, were paid next to nothing. That's why the percentage of clothing made domestically slipped from 56 percent in 1991 to 2.5 percent in 2012. That's why clothing prices between 1990 and 2013 rose only 10 percent while food prices rose over 80 percent.

The End of the Road in North America

James W. Cannon in 1887 founded the company town of Kannapolis, 20 miles northeast of Charlotte, North Carolina. Kannapolis became the home of Cannon Mills, later renamed Fieldcrest Cannon and, still later, Pillowtex. In 2003 the company shut down, throwing 4,800 people out of work. Some found new jobs; some were still looking; some went to school; some retired. One laid-off worker said, "Some days I'm pissed off, some days I'm not. It's like a roller coaster." He was one of 1.2 million workers in the textile and apparel sectors who lost their jobs between 1990 and 2012—more than three-quarters of the workers in the industry.

Kannapolis was banking now on Biopolis, officially the North Carolina Research Campus. It had a deep-pocketed angel, David Murdock, who among other things owned Dole Food and Lanai, Hawaii's pineapple island. Lanai no longer grew pineapples, and Murdock eventually sold almost the whole island—88,000 acres of it—for $300 million to Oracle's Larry Ellison.

Murdock invested half a billion dollars in Biopolis and was said to hope that if things went well, he would profit from the sale of nearby property he owned. Everyone wanted to play the biotech game, however. The old Kayser-Roth plant in Pittsboro, near Chapel Hill, used to have 400 workers making hosiery. No more. The building had survived, but now it was occupied by Biolex Therapeutics, which had ninety well-paid workers developing a drug for hepatitis. Would it succeed? The industry was full of companies with promise but no profits. Besides, the business was already concentrated in Boston, San Diego, and the San Francisco Bay area. Those places had a huge advantage in their existing pool of expertise, and they weren't going to step aside politely for newcomers.

Of all the products made by American textile mills, socks survived longest, mainly because their production was almost completely mechanized. Still, American sock makers saw their market share slip from almost 80 percent in 1999 to about 30 percent in 2004. Imports between 2001 and 2003 rose 2,200 percent. Fort Payne, Alabama, which had 125 sock mills in 2000, had 14 a decade later. Renfro Socks of Mount Airy, North Carolina, was determined to survive, which meant making socks in China, Pakistan, Mexico, Turkey, and India. Thanks to protectionism, the company still made socks at home, but the boss, a Republican, felt betrayed by the federal government. He said, "You're either for a global economy or you're an isolationist—take your pick."

Ceaseless innovation saved a few survivors. Glen Raven Custom Fabrics of Norlina, North Carolina, stayed alive by quitting pantyhose and turning to the manufacture of special fabrics for outdoor furniture, boats, and awnings. In 2006 it exported $52 million worth of fabric to China, where the fabric was made into products like sun umbrellas, which were exported back to the United States.

Another survival strategy was to automate, automate, automate—if possible while making high-end products. That's what happened when Parkdale Mills reopened its Wellstone plant in Gaffney, South Carolina. Wellstone in 2013 made 2.5 million pounds of yarn a week with 140 workers. That was less than a tenth of the 2,000 workers that would have been employed making the same amount of yarn in 1980. A customer, American Giant, came along and began buying Wellstone yarn rather than poorer-quality and more expensive yarn from Pakistan. The yarn had to be woven into cloth, then cut and sewn into garments, but American Giant did it all in the United States. Sewing here cost more than three times as much as in Asia, but "Made in America" worked for American Giant because its sweatshirts sold for eighty dollars.

The UK

Textile employment in the UK fell from a million people in 1970 to fewer than 200,000. The pioneering mills of Manchester's Ancoats district were converted into stylish apartments, their prices enhanced by recognition of the district as the world's first industrial suburb. Up in neighboring Blackburn, the aptly named Perseverance Mills made parachutes, as well as fabric for outdoor clothing for The North Face. The boss talked about the need to be nimble. Whatever you do, he said, "They [Asian competitors] will be copying you in 12–18 months' time."

Mexico

In 2002 the president of Mexico inaugurated Textile City, 65 miles east of Mexico City. The plan was to cluster makers, suppliers, and 4,500 workers in one spot, the way China did. Three dozen companies said they would build. Seven actually did. The owner of one said, "We were going to make a beautiful textile city like those in China and Korea. It didn't work and it's not going to. . . . This industry is leaving Mexico, and quickly." Between 2000 and 2005 Mexico lost a third of its textile jobs.

Would the curve turn? By 2012 Chinese wages, measured by production, were higher than Mexico's. Labor costs were only a part of total manufacturing costs, however, and China had an incomparable network of suppliers. It also offered a comparatively safe environment. Even though factories were generally left alone, investors considering Mexico had a hard time ignoring a murder rate of 18 per 100,000 residents. The rate in China was 1 per 100,000.

China

An hour or two south of Hangzhou, Datang—or Sock City—made 9 billion pairs a year. The business was highly concentrated, with Huafang Group alone employing 30,000 employees. This was great for buyers who wanted to place huge orders. If buyers wanted a zillion neckties, they went to Shenzhou, Necktie City, four hours south of Beijing. If they wanted children's clothing, they headed to Huzhou, two hours west of Shanghai. Sweaters? The dominant source was Jiaxing, midway between Shanghai and Hangzhou, or possibly nearby Honghe, where 50,000 workers made 200 million sweaters annually. Counterfeiters clustered too. Buyers wanting knock-off Nikes headed to Putian, midway between Shanghai and Hong Kong.

Even companies that made expensive clothes headed to China. Helen Morley, a British designer working in the United States, made $3,000 dresses for Saks Fifth Avenue and Neiman Marcus. She had only twenty employees but in 2005 began making most of her clothes in China and shipping them by UPS air freight. She said, "All the designers are looking to China now. The small business ties to Chinese industry are going to explode."

Sun Hong Garments in Hangzhou made hand-sewn garments for Armani Collezioni. The garments carried a Made in China label, proof that Armani customers no longer assumed that Chinese products were shoddy. Louis Vuitton was headed down the same road. Its shoes might have Made in Italy labels, but by 2008 the uppers on some of those shoes were sewn to the soles at a plant near Pondicherry, south of Chennai.

China didn't just make Western-style clothes. Chinese factories made the billowing gowns, or *thobes*, worn by Saudi men. So much for the mystique of the desert kingdom. It was the same story with kaffiyehs, the checked scarves worn by Palestinians. Herbawi Textile had woven them in Hebron, but Herbawi's price to merchants—about thirty dollars a dozen—was twice the China price. Herbawi lost most of the market.

Rather than risk American and European reprisals, China would probably cap the rise of its clothing exports. Buyers were sensitive too.

A sourcer with Hong Kong's Li & Fung said, "We're being very cautious about China." In 2009 the company actually reduced its procurement in China by 5 percent, while increasing its business in Bangladesh by 20. Still, unless rising wages in China spoiled the party, clothes would probably follow the pattern of shoes, for which quotas had been eliminated in 1983. Since then, China's share of the global shoe market had risen from 4 percent to 80 percent. The only sneakers still made in the United States were about a quarter of New Balances. That company's several factories, all in New England, were protected by a tariff and by the fact that New Balance had a sole owner who could do what he liked, without regard for pesky stockholders.

India

India's clothing manufacturers were much smaller than China's. One of the biggest was Bangalore's Gokaldas Exports, with 33,000 employees— almost all women. They made clothes for Gap, Abercrombie, and dozens of other brands. The boss explained the brutal choice facing American and European companies. "The moment your competition shifts production to India or China," he said, "you have no choice but to follow, otherwise you would go out of business." India's labor laws and its tariffs on imported materials, however, forced Gokaldas to concentrate on higher-value garments. The boss said, "We couldn't possibly compete on price with China by making the cheaper garments." A Delhi manufacturer added, "If you are going to buy a $4 blouse, India's not the place to make it."

India had foreign-owned big operators too. MAS Holdings of Sri Lanka, sometimes called the secret behind Victoria's Secret, employed 3,000 women. The company, which also sewed for Nike, Banana Republic, Gap, Old Navy, Reebok, and Triumph, was South Asia's biggest clothing manufacturer, with sales in 2010 of $700 million. It set out to hire 30,000 production workers for a cluster of twenty plants near Gudur, in the Nellore District on India's southeast coast. Similarly, Brandix Lanka opened Apparel City farther north, near Visakhapatnam. In both cases, the strategy was to hire rural women eager to work without having to leave home. This was a strategy commonly used by the textile industry in Sri Lanka.

Bangladesh

Between 1974 and 1994 an international multi-fiber agreement had slowed China's growth by dividing imports into dozens of streams, each one coming from a country assigned a quota. The system had been a boon to Bangladesh, and the expiring agreement was replaced by an agreement allowing clothing from Bangladesh to enter Europe duty free. In 2005 the country had been the world's eighth-largest clothing exporter, by value; by 2011 it had become the world's third largest, following China and (surprise!) Italy. No wonder: with a minimum wage of thirty-nine dollars a month, workers in Bangladesh cost only a quarter as much as workers in China.

Clothing remained the country's only significant manufactured export, with products worth close to $20 billion annually in 2010. Epic, a Hong Kong–based company, bought 70 million yards of denim and had its 20,000 Bangladeshi employees make jeans sold for $450 million to Levi Strauss, Abercrombie, and Walmart. Walmart alone purchased a billion dollars' worth of clothing that year from Bangladesh, though by 2013 Sweden's H&M was the country's biggest customer. To keep labor costs down, the government banned unions. Despite the ban, workers demanded a pay hike from the minimum wage of 3,000 taka, roughly $40 a month, to 5,000 taka, about $70. It seemed a modest request, given the ferocious pace of the work, with seamstresses expected to sew buttons on shirts at the rate of ten a minute.

A factory owner warned, "If it's 5,000 taka, I would close all my factories." Perhaps he was exaggerating because 5,000 became the legal minimum wage in 2013. Yet rent cost workers forty dollars, and simple food for an adult cost thirty dollars. If a seamstress was married to a rickshaw puller and had a child who drank five dollars' worth of milk every month, the family could not live within its budget. Yet the company for which the seamstress worked might have a contract to deliver shirts for $6.75 each. Almost five dollars went for cotton cloth of the right quality. Another dollar went for buttons, labels, and other accessories. Fifteen cents per shirt went for a final washing and preparation, eleven cents went for building rent, eleven cents went for marketing and head-office costs, and twenty-five cents went for repaying bank loans. There wasn't much room for higher wages. The only solution appeared to be higher productivity.

A fire in 2013 destroyed the eight-story Rana Plaza and cost the lives of over 1,100 textile workers. One owner worried that if there were another fire, "Bangladesh will be history for garments." Within a month there was another fire, killing ten in Ghazipur. Both American and European buyers quickly joined organizations that set fire and safety standards. Some buyers might want no part of Bangladesh, even though the departure of the industry would consign thousands of workers to destitution, but there was no other country except China able to handle big orders so efficiently, and most big buyers already sourced heavily enough from China that they didn't want to become even more dependent on that country.

Next Collections, whose 4,500 Bangladeshi workers sewed for Gap, VF, and Tommy Hilfiger, prepared pay slips showing workers putting in forty-eight hours weekly, plus twelve hours of overtime. A duplicate set of slips showed that the workers were actually putting in more than a hundred hours weekly. A spokeswoman for VF said, "We are planning to exit the facility." The seamstresses were sticking it out, however. A teenager injured in the collapse of the Rana Plaza said, "As soon as the pain gets better, I will go back to work. There really isn't any choice."

Africa

With the expiration of the multi-fiber agreement, Walmart quit sourcing in Lesotho. That small country now leaned precariously on Gap, which bought half of Lesotho's exports. Labor in Lesotho was cheaper than in heavily unionized South Africa. Lesotho also had the advantage of the African Growth and Opportunity Act, an American law allowing African-made garments to enter the United States tariff free, even if the fabric was made in Asia. The biggest fear for Lesotho's manufacturers was that the Growth and Opportunity Act was due to expire. American congressmen said they were in favor of its extension, but they were having difficulty passing bills of any kind. An industry official in Lesotho said, "It's an industry at the crossroads. It's 200,000 families . . . and time is not on our side." Other countries wanted a share of the American business too. Walmart in 2012 sourced over half a million sets of hospital scrubs from Ghana. Godiva ordered cloth tote bags from Liberia. Most Africans, of course, couldn't afford the clothes they made. As Pietra Rivoli wrote in *The Travels of a T-Shirt in the Global Economy*, they wore T-shirts that had been made in China from cotton grown in Texas. The T-shirts were first sold in the United States, then discarded and sold again in one of Africa's many "bend-down boutiques," where piles of old clothes were heaped on the ground to await a second buyer.

FURNITURE

In the early 1990s an American who wanted a good four-poster bed probably considered buying one made by Henredon, which had a factory in Spruce Pine, North Carolina, and made bed frames that retailed for about $5,000. Then the Philippines started exporting similar beds retailing for about $2,000. By 2007 the same bed cost $800 and came from China. Workers in the huge furniture factories owned there by companies such as Lacquer Craft, Markor, and Shing Mark made forty cents an hour, compared with fourteen dollars at Henredon. In 2004 Henredon closed the Spruce Pine plant. A thousand jobs, with benefits, were lost. A JCPenney executive said, "The reason practically all home furnishings are now made in China factories is that they simply are better suppliers. American manufacturers aren't even in the same game."

Statistics backed him up. In 2002 China supplied about 42 percent of the furniture market in the United States. By 2011 China supplied 63 percent. Of six firms that had until recently made furniture in Galax, Virginia, only one was still in business in 2012. It was Vaughan-Bassett, which employed over 600 workers. They earned between nine and fifteen dollars an hour, plus benefits. The owner said that his workers understood the Chinese threat. He said that they had told him, "You all tell us what you need and we'll work with you."

Ethan Allen also stuck it out. It made furniture mostly in Vermont and North Carolina, plus some in Mexico. The owner was not a Yankee; he was an ethnic Kashmiri. He explained that his furniture was almost entirely custom made and so it could not easily be manufactured offshore. On the other hand, he knew that the Chinese appreciated imported luxuries, and by 2013 Ethan Allen was operating seventy-seven furniture stores in China. Meanwhile, Furniture Brands, maker of Broyhill, Thomasville, and Drexel, declared bankruptcy. In a previous incarnation Furniture Brands had been International Shoe Company. Failing in that business, it now failed in another.

MOTOR VEHICLES

Furniture was nice and clothing was important, but both were trivial compared with the industry that kept America on wheels. The United States had about 130 million automobiles and over 100 million trucks. California alone had 33 million motor vehicles; Texas, 17 million. Over 90 percent of all American households had a vehicle, though Manhattan was once again an outlier, with three-quarters of its residents getting by without.

The industry was so important that when it got into trouble in 2008, government came to the rescue. As one analyst said, "Governments have tipped lots of money and prevented Darwinian selection. It has been a good reminder of what this industry is: a government-supported job creation scheme." He was talking about the European industry, but he might almost as well have been talking about the United States. Used to selling 16 million passenger vehicles annually, in 2009 it sold only 10 million. It hadn't sold that few since 1982. Globally, things were no better: an industry capable of producing 90 million cars and light trucks sold 55 million.

The American Industry on Life Support

For General Motors, Ford, and Chrysler, the big question was not whether the market would recover—in fact it had nearly recovered by 2013, when it sold 15.6 million vehicles—but whether, when it did, Americans would buy American. As far back as 1971, a wiser-than-he-knew Henry Ford II had said, "I frankly don't see how we're going to meet the foreign competition."

Between 1997 and 2008 GM shrank from 608,000 employees to 255,000. Ford went from 364,000 to 246,000. Chrysler went from 119,000 to 54,000. The results showed up most dramatically in Michigan, which by mid-2009 had an unemployment rate exceeding 14 percent, the highest of any state in the country. House prices in Michigan fell 13 percent in 2006, well before the national decline began. An unusual number of summer cottages came on the market. An economist said that the plight of the domestic auto industry marked "the end of an era of middle-class prosperity when you could get a high-paying job in the auto sector without a college education."

Membership in the United Automobile, Aerospace and Agricultural Implement Workers union, or UAW, declined from over a million to about 340,000. In 2007, even before GM entered bankruptcy, the UAW agreed that salaries for new hires would be cut in half. Assembly lines now had old-timers earning over twenty-eight dollars an hour while standing next to new workers earning fourteen dollars. One of those old-timers said, "I hate my job. And there is no way I would do this for $14 an hour. These new cats are getting screwed." A new worker was more accepting: "You gotta be grateful," he said. Another GM worker, who had once earned twenty-eight dollars an hour, had taken a bonus to retire at age sixty. Now he was looking to top up his pension. He applied at the new locomotive plant opened by Caterpillar in Muncie, Indiana. Nonunion, it paid twelve dollars an hour. "I'm able to adapt to that," he said.

The workers at the efficient GM plant in Moraine, Ohio, had the bad luck to be represented by non-UAW unions. Once GM and the UAW worked out their post-bankruptcy arrangements, there was no room for GM to hire non-UAW workers. The Moraine plant closed, and its workers were not given the option of moving to a GM plant represented by the UAW. One of the workers transitioned to street cleaning, which meant going from twenty-nine dollars an hour with benefits to eleven dollars without. He said that his friends and relatives were shocked. "Mitch," they said, "why are you doing this? You're better than that." His reply: "It's a job and it pays the bills."

Dealers

For Americans far from assembly plants, the industry's pain was most visible along auto row. Nationwide, there had been 30,000 dealerships in 1980. By 2008 there were 20,000. About 900 more closed that year. The next year GM announced that it would close a thousand. Chrysler said it would close almost 800.

Most of the dealerships to be closed were small: half of the GM dealerships to be closed sold fewer than three new cars a month. Still, not all were tiny. AutoNation had forty-one GM dealerships, and six of them were on the hit list. AutoNation also had seventeen Chrysler dealerships. Seven closed. Meanwhile, a $75 million Lexus dealership opened in Newport Beach in 2006. It was just across the street from the number-one Mercedes dealership in the country, Fletcher Jones Motorcars, which sold 600 to 1,000 cars every month. Customers in the waiting room there got free shoe shines and manicures. Down in the mass-market trenches, the average GM dealer sold 586 cars annually; the average Toyota dealer sold 1,800.

A Buick dealer in Columbus, Ohio, recalled that in the 1960s he sold 200 Buicks a month. By mid-2008 he was down to ten. The showroom, with space for twenty-five cars, now had a mix of new and used cars, and the general manager said, "I don't think we're going to be here in five years." An analyst said, "One side is trapped with excess capacity and legacy costs, and the other side is in hog heaven trying to build plants as quickly as they can."

The biggest Chevrolet dealer in the country, Bill Heard Enterprises, had revenues in 2007 of $2.1 billion spread over eight dealerships. All eight closed in 2008. Two were bought by Classic Chevy, from the Dallas suburb of Grapevine, and with that purchase Classic moved into first place. Talk volume: Classic's Grapevine lot had between 1,500 and 2,000 vehicles in stock, four times the inventory of most big Chevy dealers. Classic tried to keep so many vehicles on hand that customers could walk onto the lot, find exactly what they wanted, and take it home that day.

Lemmon Avenue, near the moneyed part of Dallas, had an auto row. Eagle Lincoln Mercury had once been on it. For a time, Eagle had been the top Lincoln Mercury dealership in the country. As recently as 1999 Lincoln itself had been the top-selling luxury brand in the country, but by 2011 it ranked eighth. Eagle tracked that decline. In 2006 its owner said, "In the 70s, we sold 450 cars a month. Now, we're selling 65 a month and we do not see our volume growing at any appreciable rate." Late that year, the dealership closed.

Out nearer Dallas–Fort Worth airport, McDavid Honda sold 3,047 vehicles in 2006; next door, McDavid Pontiac-Buick-GMC sold 465. A McDavid official said, "We'll use the space at the dealership for our other dealerships. We'll also use it for office space." In 2008 Prestige Ford of Dallas, once the country's number-one seller of F-series pickups, was stocking its new-car lot with used vehicles. The owners of Big Billy Barrett Chrysler-Jeep by 2010 were selling only high-mileage used cars; they handled their own financing too and sold those cars on four-year contracts at 18 percent.

By 2006 fifteen of the twenty biggest dealerships in Dallas sold foreign cars. Back on Lemmon Avenue, customers could buy a Bentley or a Rolls-Royce, a Maserati or an Aston Martin. A new Mercedes and Porsche dealership, Park Place Motors, spent about $35 million on its showroom and shops. Zoom zoom: the service department had 146 bays. Profits were confidential, but the average Lexus dealer in the United States netted $5 million annually. Meanwhile, BMW-Mini of Dallas opened in the space previously occupied by Eagle Lincoln

Mercury. Nationwide, sales at the surviving 17,700 dealers in 2014 were up from $25 million in 2009 to $41 million by 2014, but pretax profits hovered at about 2 percent of revenues.

General Motors

Between 1932, when it overtook Ford, and 2008, when it was briefly overtaken by Toyota, GM was the world's biggest manufacturer. In 1954 it sold fifty-four out of every hundred cars sold in the United States. Approximately fifty years later, it sold twenty. Its stock in 2006 was at a twenty-three-year low, and the company was worth less than Harley-Davidson. Two years later, its stock declined to a fifty-three-year low. During the second quarter of 2008, the company lost $181,000 a minute. By 2009, when it was forced into bankruptcy, GM had made a grand total of 450 million cars and trucks, but it had shrunk to 91,000 employees in the United States. It provided benefits to 493,000 retirees.

GM's average profit per vehicle was $2,400 less than Toyota's, Honda's, and Nissan's. Half of that difference came from GM's higher labor costs, and of that, half came from health care for retirees. As the company emerged from bankruptcy, a consultant said that GM was "like an Olympic swimmer trying to compete with two bowling balls around his neck. Those bowling balls—health care costs and too much production capacity—are being removed. But now he's got to swim."

He meant make cars somebody wanted to buy. As of early 2007 the three most popular cars in the United States were the Camry, Accord, and Corolla—all Japanese. The most popular American vehicles were pickup trucks, especially the Ford F-150 series, which sold about 60,000 trucks monthly, or about 750,000 annually. Ford grew understandably dependent on a model that had been the best-selling vehicle in the United States for thirty-two years running. A company executive said, "We took our eye off the ball and got intoxicated with just making trucks."

General Motors could tell a similar story for SUVs. The breed had been created at GM's plant in Janesville, Wisconsin, the company's oldest assembly line. For a while that plant produced 20,000 Suburbans, Yukons, and Tahoes monthly. Then the sky fell. Fuel got expensive, and GM no longer needed two plants making big SUVs. GM ran three shifts at its Arlington plant, between Fort Worth and Dallas. The Janesville plant closed.

Bob Lutz, GM's charismatic vice chairman, said, "We did bring it on ourselves, having built products twenty-odd years ago, which in many cases were well below best international standards in design, dynamics, craftsmanship, and reliability." Alfred Sloan, GM's pioneering boss, had ranked his models—"a car for every purse and purpose"—but his Chevy-to-Cadillac spectrum had been thoroughly jumbled, with the same vehicle often produced for several GM brands and distinguished by little more than a badge. Now the company had to downsize, but even this was expensive. In 2000 GM spent a billion dollars closing Oldsmobile, including buying back parts and cars from dealers. In 2009 Pontiac closed, and GM moved to sell Saturn, Hummer, and Saab. Even the surviving models were often ghosts of their former selves. Sales of Chevy's Impala fell from over 1 million in 1965 to 170,000 in 2011—and three-quarters of those went to fleet buyers.

"We are working feverishly to get this thing turned around as fast as we can," GM's boss said. Through bankruptcy the company shed $40 billion of debt. The American market recovered, but more than half the vehicles sold in it were foreign. GM's business in China was good, but the company had big problems in Europe, which was beyond the reach of American bankruptcy reorganization. The company also remained a long way from its goal of fourteen global platforms—cars whose core components were standardized worldwide. It was also still a long way from getting rid of its old regional organization and replacing it with global units for functions such as purchasing, manufacturing, and marketing. "Ford is light years ahead of GM," one analyst said.

Ford

The president of Ford's North American operations, however, had no illusions about regaining the company's historic market share. "Those days are gone," he said. "This is not a cyclical change. This is a secular change." A few years earlier, working at Mazda, he had delivered the same message in Japan: "I told the Mazda team very directly—change or die."

The head of Ford's largest UAW local said, "Ford is in a desperate situation." Bill Ford watched his company's share of the American market fall from 25 percent in 2000 to 18 percent six years later. He wrote, "The business model that sustained us for decades is no longer sufficient to sustain profitability." He passed control of the company to a Boeing executive, who in his previous job had cut the Boeing workforce from 120,000 to 50,000.

Ford now set out to shed over 40 percent of its hourly North American workforce. One worker said, "I knew it would come, but I didn't think it would be this soon." Shedding workers was expensive, and Ford lost $12.7 billion in 2006. With union acquiescence, many Ford workers now worked four ten-hour shifts weekly without overtime, even if one of those shifts fell on a weekend. But what did Ford have for sale? Between 1992 and 1997 the Taurus was North America's best-selling car, but sales fell from 410,000 in 1992 to 145,000 in 2005. By then the company wasn't even advertising the Taurus, let alone improving it. Production stopped after the 7 millionth car came off the line in 2006.

The company was banking now on the Fusion, which was doing well, and the Ford Five Hundred, which wasn't. In 2009 it restored the Taurus, redesigned but too expensive to sell in large numbers. Things got so bad that the company mortgaged its famous blue-oval logo.

The Ford Fiesta was built on the company's first global platform. The car was made first in Cologne for sale across Europe, but production was planned also for Spain, China, and Thailand. Fiestas for the American market would be made in Mexico. Ford's CEO called it "the start of a new era for our fabulous Ford Motor Company."

Next up was the Focus, designed in Europe but conceived from the start as a global car. Along the way Ford sold Aston Martin to Kuwaitis and Jaguar to Tata of India. Jaguar had earlier launched the 420-horsepower XKR, which proved to be a hit, but Jaguar was such a small company that a "hit" in its case amounted to annual sales in the

United States of 6,000 cars. Next to go was Volvo, sold in 2010 to China's Geely. Without a trip through bankruptcy, Ford went in four years from losing almost $15 billion in 2008 to earning $20 billion in 2011.

Chrysler, Daimler, Cerberus

Daimler-Benz bought Chrysler in 1998 in hopes of spreading the cost of new technology over a bigger base, but integrating the companies was such a big job that problems began appearing back in Germany. One analyst said, "The market is less and less forgiving. People don't have to wait for Mercedes to sort itself out. They're going to buy a BMW or Lexus." Sure enough, BMW in 2001 began outselling Mercedes in the United States. With an eye on Japan, one analyst warned that "Mercedes is getting squeezed on all sides by very high-quality cars produced at half the price."

Mercedes lost a billion dollars in the first half of 2005. The mastermind of the Chrysler merger had already been sacked, and the new boss returned to Germany from the thankless task of heading Chrysler in the United States. He promptly cut 8,400 jobs, even though the cost of doing that in Germany averaged $134,000 for every job. He then announced the loss of 6,000 administrative jobs in Germany. This was a 20 percent cut of Daimler's worldwide administration. He said, "There's no politics. It's very straightforward. This is the kind of culture we want to have—no [expletive], no politics—just working together to improve this company as fast as we can." Progress came painfully slowly, and in 2012 Mercedes slipped to third place among luxury-car makers, with sales behind not only BMW but Audi.

In 2007 Daimler sold Chrysler. This was great news for Daimler but not so good for Chrysler, which wasn't selling enough cars to get unit costs down to competitive levels. The new owner, private-equity giant Cerberus, appointed a boss who had previously headed Home Depot. In a bravura demonstration of high-stakes headhunting, the new boss promptly hired Toyota's head of North American operations. Next, he hired the boss of GM's operations in China.

Even these people weren't magicians, however, and within a few months Chrysler announced plans to shut down production of about half the company's thirty models. An executive warned against false hopes: "There's no huge [increase in sales] volume around the corner. We need to give up that dream and face reality." One possibility was for Chrysler to let Asian companies build some of its cars. Sure enough, the company signed an agreement with Nissan in 2008 to make a small Chrysler for sale in the United States, starting in 2010.

It never happened. The Cerberus boss was rueful. "It kills us," he wrote to his investors, "that we have lost money and been part of the problem for you." Mulling over his bruises, he said, "I don't know what we could have done differently. From the day we bought [Chrysler], we worked hard to improve it." As for Chrysler's workers, he continued, "You couldn't think of a worse storm for an employee to have to live through." In 2009 Chrysler sold fewer than a million vehicles, the fewest it had sold since 1962. It made an average profit of $1,000 per vehicle, half or less what GM or Ford made.

Amazingly, a shaft of light struck the factory floor. Forced into bankruptcy in 2009, Chrysler was taken over by Fiat, whose fantastically rumpled but energetic boss said, "Our reputation and credibility is at stake. We've put the whole damn thing on the line." He dismissed some of the top people Cerberus had hired, and by 2012 a Chrysler assembly-line worker said, "There's a primal, real, tangible sense of optimism here now." A twenty-one-year-old unemployed worker in Detroit jumped on a bus when he heard about jobs at a Chrysler plant in Belvedere, Illinois. "This is just a blessing," he said. "I've always wanted to work in an auto plant since other members of my family had worked in plants. I just can't believe I'm here." Outside the plant a café owner kept her fingers crossed. "If I could just get 15 more people in here a day, I could make it," she said.

An analyst warned that the company needed new products. "Chrysler needs something that moves the needles for them," he said. "It is like water. You have to have this to live." One new product was the

Chrysler 200, which had last been redesigned in 2006, when it was called the Sebring. Another was the Ram pickup, a perennial also-ran in the truck market but now much improved and an average of $3,000 cheaper than the competition.

Fiat and the European Industry

Between 2001 and 2004 Fiat had lost about $10 billion. In 2004 the energetic Sergio Marchionne was appointed, and between 2005 and 2006 Fiat swung from a loss of $332 million to a profit of $384 million. By 2007 Fiat's market value of $33 billion was greater than GM's and Ford's combined, even though those two companies together built more than six times as many cars as Fiat.

Marchionne said, "The single most important thing was to dismantle the organizational structure of Fiat. We tore it apart in 60 days, removing a large number of leaders who had been there for a long time and who represented an operating style that lay outside any proper understanding of market dynamics. We flattened out the structure and gave some relatively young people, in terms of both age and experience, a huge amount of scope."

The old Fiat had nineteen vehicle platforms that shared few parts. It produced seventeen different heating and cooling systems. The new engineering boss said, "The customer is interested in a fuel-efficient and well-functioning HVAC unit. Whether it's the same between four cars, he doesn't care." By 2010 the company made 85 percent of its cars on only four platforms. A new engine, the MultiAir, had no camshafts or valve gear and produced an exceptionally low level of carbon dioxide.

Then the bad news arrived, and by 2013 Fiat's European plants were running at under 50 percent of their capacity. It wasn't just a Fiat problem, or an Italian one. In 1999 Europe's car makers had sold 15 million vehicles in Europe; in 2012 they sold 9 million. Sales crept back up so slowly that one analyst said, "Flat is the new up." The head of Ford Europe said, "You can't fight gravity," and if there was any doubt about his meaning he said, "We have a catastrophe here."

GM had owned Opel since 1929. It was the cheapest car made in Germany, though, as the joke went, it was sold mostly to the French. The company's chairman said, "Listen, there's a new economic reality in Europe—we can't deny it, we can't hide from it, we can't hope that it's going to get better." Rumors circulated that the Opel plant in Bochum was going to close. Rumor was right: GM announced that Bochum would close in 2016, making it the first major German auto plant to close since World War II. The company also announced that it would stop making Chevrolets in Europe, with the exception of a few Corvettes. The good news was that a reorganized Opel might yet become profitable, especially if it could sell more cars in Russia and Turkey.

GM proceeded to form a joint venture with Peugeot, which sold about 12 percent of all the cars sold in the European Union but was in a distant second place to Volkswagen, which had 25 percent of that market. Peugeot's financing arm got a €7 billion guarantee from the French government. Even with the guarantee, the best Peugeot could do was offer buyers loans at 6 percent. Even loyal Peugeot customers were sorely tempted by the VW dealer across the street. The German company was in such strong financial shape that its dealers offered financing at zero.

Fiat's Marchionne said, "The fact is that, today, very few manufacturers make money in Europe. This isn't sustainable, and it has to change." Fiat's Italian operations were an extreme case, running at under 50 percent of their capacity. It took three times as many people to make a car at the company's Pomigliano plant, near Naples, than it did at the company's Polish plant in Tychy, near the Czech border. One laid-off worker at the Montefiori plant near Turin, where production was down from 300,000 cars annually to fewer than 50,000, knew the facts of life: "I see no prospects for the future," she said. On top of everything else, Marchionne knew that he was up against Toyota. He said, "The standard of reference for all we do is Toyota. It is a flawless execution machine." His conclusion? "Let's just go out there and fight . . . it will be a fight."

BMW

The head of BMW said almost the same thing. With sales of about 1.4 million cars annually, BMW had overtaken Mercedes to become the world's best-selling premium brand. Still, the company was not immune to global recession, and in 2008 BMW laid off 8,000 of its 107,000 workers. And then there was the longer term. The company's boss said, "We will be challenged—no question. We have to take Lexus seriously."

Hoping to avoid Germany's high labor costs, BMW expanded its plant in Spartanburg, South Carolina. An executive said, "This is about globalisation and where the demand and production of the future will be." Spartanburg would now be, by number of workers, the biggest assembly plant in the United States, but 70 percent of the 240,000 vehicles it made annually would be exported.

VW

Europe's biggest car manufacturer baffled many Americans. They remembered VW as the iconic Beetle, but VW sales in the United States had collapsed from 577,000 cars in 1970 to 49,000 in 1992. In 2005 the company's American boss ruefully admitted, "One of our buyers could have leased the exact same Jetta three times on two-year leases." What was the problem? American assembly-line workers, pre-bankruptcy, averaged thirty-four dollars an hour. The European average was forty-four dollars. VW paid its German workers an amazing sixty-nine dollars an hour. The workers were not even especially productive. The company's assembly lines at Wolfsburg—the world's biggest automotive-assembly plant—took fifty work hours to build a compact car, twice the average for the competition.

As if this weren't bad enough, VW's labor contracts prohibited layoffs. A VW union official declared that his workforce was "not a rabbit that cowers in fear and paralysis in front of the snake." In 2006 VW did manage to negotiate a concession from its workers: they would increase the number of hours they worked from 28.8 weekly to 33—and do it for no extra money. In return, the company agreed to guarantee job security for all factory workers until 2012. The company did manage to shed 20,000 German workers through early retirements and subsidiary spin-offs.

vw made strategic mistakes too. Sales of the new Beetle slumped by half between 2000 and 2005. The ferocious vw Phaeton—12 cylinders, 444 horsepower—was a disaster, pulled from the American market in 2006 perhaps because Americans just weren't willing to spend $100,000 on a car badged vw. Far and away the company's most profitable unit was Audi, whose $60 billion in sales in 2011 was less than half vw's.

Despite everything, vw remained a giant. The company's secret sauce was the remarkable practice of *mitbestimmung,* "codetermination." The American translation might be worker empowerment. The result, vw's CEO said, was "quality, strong motivation and extreme flexibility." The company had succeeded in reorganizing operations so that the Golf, Passat, Jetta, Beetle, and Audi shared the same platform. Additionally, 90 percent of its stock was owned by three shareholders: Porsche, the government of Lower Saxony, and Qatar Holding. An analyst said, "vw does not want to be ultra-profitable. But no one expects it to be. What one does expect is a sustainable strategy and not a double-digit margin."

vw had closed its American assembly plant in Westmoreland, Pennsylvania, in 1988. The company returned in force two decades later with a billion-dollar plant on the east side of Chattanooga. The plan was to sell a million cars annually in the United States by 2018 and to do it with cars made in North America, largely to avoid currency-exchange problems. With the Chattanooga plant initially scaled to build 150,000 cars annually, and even with vw's huge plant in Puebla, Mexico, which annually produced over 500,000 cars, the United States would require additional plants.

Chattanooga welcomed an initial contingent of 2,500 vw workers and 20,000 new workers in support jobs, and it began negotiating with the UAW not only to create unions but to create the kind of *mitbestimmung* that worked so well back home. The only thing vw forgot was to keep new models coming. While the rest of the industry had a good 2013, VW sales in the United States fell. The company's boss said, "The U.S. is the cornerstone of our 2018 strategy. For sure it won't be a walk in the park." The company's top labor representative wasn't so circumspect. He said, "The situation in the U.S. is a disaster." Then the plant's workers voted against forming a union. Pushing back, the company announced that it would invest $900 million to make SUVs in Chattanooga. The company's CEO said, "The VW brand is going on the offensive again in America."

Toyota

High praise from the competition might have made Toyota nervous. Sure enough, in 2010 Toyota recalled 20 million vehicles for safety defects. The company's rating in the Initial Quality Surveys published by J.D. Power slipped that year from seventh to twenty-seventh place.

A former head of the company's North American operations explained, "The root cause of their problem is that the company was hijacked, some years ago, by anti-family, financially oriented pirates." Those pirates had been phenomenally successful, however, gradually reducing the Big Three to the Detroit Three. An observer said, "The last thing Toyota wants is for any of those guys to collapse. [A collapse would be] completely worthless to Toyota in the market. They're selling all the vehicles they can make already. What they actually want is just continuous, slow decline—decline at the same rate that they have the ability to organically expand. That's the ideal world for them." He summed it up this way: "The most important management task at Toyota these days is to manage the decline of the domestics."

In 2006 Toyota overtook Ford to assume second place in the American motor vehicle market. A year later, its global sales overtook GM's. By then Toyota's market capitalization was ten times GM's. Toyota ran forty-seven plants in twenty-six countries. It estimated that the global market would expand from 65 million cars in 2006 to 73 million in 2010. Toyota wanted 15 percent of that total. Most of the growth was going to come in Brazil, Russia, India, and China, which was why Toyota either had or was building plants in all of them.

Toyota's boss compared his job to "trying to pull a handcart up a steep hill: there's always tremendous danger that if we relax, even for a moment, we could lose momentum and be thrown to the bottom." He said that he wanted *kakushin*, revolutionary change that would cut the cost of producing a vehicle by $1,000 every three or four years. "I am told," he said, "a CEO should worry about big-picture stuff and shouldn't be concerned about minute details. I am obsessed with details, I will be an irritant, and I am persistent."

"Wringing drops from a dry towel," as the company put it, Toyota reduced the variety of interior-assist grips from thirty-five to three. It cut air-conditioning vent types from twenty-seven to four. In 2007 Toyota opened an assembly line at its Takaoka plant that cranked out a dozen vehicle models at the rate of one a minute or faster. Searching for efficiencies, in Miyagi the company set up an assembly line so the vehicles moved not bumper to bumper but side to side, which reduced the number of steps workers had to make.

Like its competitors, Toyota was making vehicles such as the Hilux, a small pickup that it intended to sell everywhere except in the United States. There, Toyota in 2007 introduced a full-sized pickup, the Tundra, manufactured both at Toyota's Indiana plant and at a new $1.3 billion plant in San Antonio. The timing was bad. Sales were so poor that the Indiana plant stopped making the truck. The San Antonio plant, working at 70 percent capacity despite Toyota's offering buyers five-year, zero-percent-interest loans, began exporting trucks to Latin America. Perhaps Ford executives smiled when they remembered Toyota's introduction of the Tundra at the Detroit auto show in 2007. The Tundra display models had all been painted Ford blue.

When an earthquake struck Fukushima in 2011, Toyota's global sales slipped to third place. The next year, the company regained the top spot, but its share of the American market was still down from 17 percent in 2009 to 14.4 percent in 2013. A less obvious problem was the company's tremendous investment in its seventeen Japanese plants. More than half of Toyota's vehicles were made in its home country, even though only half its domestic production found domestic buyers.

The surplus might have been exported, but the strong yen was a huge problem. When the yen-to-dollar rate fell from 80 to 79, for example, Toyota's operating profit fell $440 million. The company's president said bluntly, "If you look at it logically, it doesn't make sense to manufacture in Japan." The chief financial officer said, "The destruction of Japan's industrial base is proceeding apace. I find that very shocking." He cannot have been happy when Toyota decided to begin making the Lexus ES 350 in the United States. The model had always been made in Japan, even though it was sold almost exclusively in North America.

The Japanese government set out to push the yen lower. It succeeded within a few months in pushing the yen down by 20 percent. The chairman of Suzuki was not impressed. He said, "We won't suddenly bring production back to Japan just because the yen is cheaper." Perhaps he feared a reversal of government policy. It had happened before.

Nissan

Nissan faced the same exchange-rate problem. Its CEO called the exchange rate "extremely unrealistic and uncompetitive." There was, he said, "no way we are going to continue to position our Infiniti cars only in Japan—no way."

Like so many other manufacturers, Nissan was consolidating platforms. Its boss, Carlos Ghosn (the name rhymed with "phone") said, "Today we know how to make two completely different cars from the same platform by sharing the basics . . . but everything important to the customer is different." Like many of its competitors, Nissan had also developed flexible assembly lines. The one in Canton, Mississippi, was the only plant in the United States where rear-wheel-drive trucks and front-wheel-drive minivans came off the same assembly line. There they were: Titans, Armadas, Infinitis, Quests, Altimas. When oil prices in 2008 rose high enough to push buyers away from SUVs, the Canton factory adjusted by putting one whole shift on production of Altimas.

There were slips. Nissan missed its performance targets in 2007, for example. It was the first time this had happened since Ghosn had taken over in 1999, and Ghosn knew that the problem was a shortage of new models. He said, "For the next five years we will have a steady flow of new products. We have learned the lesson of having a gap." As one expert outside the company explained, the process of building cars had been "thoroughly optimized" across the industry. "Where the real work of making a car company successful suddenly turns complex," he said, "and where the winners are separated from the losers, is in the long-cycle product development process."

Meanwhile, Ghosn was pushing for a billion-euro assembly plant near Tangier. Cars for Africa? No, the plant would make 200,000 vehicles annually for buyers in Europe, Asia, and North America. Tangier was a way for Nissan to keep costs down, because the average monthly wage in Morocco was about $320. For Morocco, it was a big bump up—and especially good news for the Tangier Mediterranean Special Agency, which was trying to develop a major port and transportation hub 25 miles east of the city.

Hyundai

"I worry about them a lot." The speaker was an American executive, and he was talking about a Korean upstart that only began making cars in 1967. Hyundai waited until 1986 before entering the American market, but by 1990 the company ranked thirteenth among global producers. By 2010 it ranked fifth, after GM, VW, Toyota, and Nissan/Renault. In Jangjin, west of Seoul, Hyundai made its own steel. It was the first and only global maker to do this since the days of Henry Ford's River Rouge steel plant. Hyundai made unusual concessions to its workers too. In 2012 it agreed not only to a pay hike but to ending night shifts, which workers at its huge Ulsan plant insisted were unhealthy.

Early in 2012 Hyundai's European sales were rising even while sales for almost every European producer were declining. The company's chief designer said, "Hyundai was a fast follower, now we are becoming a leader." A worried American executive called Hyundai "a bigger threat right now than anyone else." Hyundai's CEO insisted that sales volume was not his primary concern. He said, "We don't know what size is optimum. But bigger, bigger, biggest is always good? We don't think so."

The Boeing Company estimated that between 2012 and 2031 the world's airlines would order 34,000 big planes, those with more than a hundred seats each. That was almost three times as many planes as the 12,600 that flew in the world's commercial fleets in 2006. Airbus made similar projections. It and Boeing had the market to themselves, and they were neck and neck, measured either by planes delivered or planes on order.

Boeing

Boeing's chief executive said, "Huge sums in the beginning and then an annuity for the next 25 to 35 years. That's the business model we have." He might have had in mind the 737, introduced in 1968 but still selling well in 2014. By then the company had sold almost 8,000, and it had orders for 2,100 more.

In a textbook case of lean manufacturing, Boeing could now assemble a 737 in eleven days. (General Electric, the leading producer of railroad locomotives, boasted that in Erie, Pennsylvania, it could assemble one in twenty-two.) A 737 assembly line in Renton, south of Seattle, kept planes moving forward at two inches a minute. It wasn't fast enough to meet demand; from fifteen planes a month in 2001, Boeing raised production to thirty-one a month in 2011 and forty-two monthly by 2014.

In 2011 Boeing weighed a painful choice: put a new engine on the 737 to compete with the new and very successful Airbus A320neo or wait and produce an entirely new plane. A huge order from American Airlines nudged Boeing to choose the re-engined plane, dubbed the 737 MAX. Engineers might lament the loss of an opportunity to make bigger improvements, but the American sale was so large that Boeing couldn't afford to lose it.

Despite a precarious first few years, the Boeing 747 had been another great success. Pan American, the first airline to fly the jumbo, was long gone, but in 2014 the 747 was still in production, and Boeing had built more than 1,500 of them. For decades the 747 had appealed to airlines with long-haul networks, which helped explain why British Airways, Japan Airlines, Korean Air, and Cathay Pacific had the biggest 747 fleets. Each had about fifty of the planes, more than twice as many as United and Delta, the American carriers with the most. The newest version of the plane, the 747-8, had room for 467 passengers. By mid-2014 Boeing had orders for 120, though most were freighters.

By now the plane was very profitable, but the 747 was gradually being replaced by Boeing's twin-engine 777, introduced in 1995. In 2011 Boeing delivered over 200 of these more fuel-efficient planes, and by 2013 fewer than 700 of the four-engine 747s remained in service, down from over a thousand in 1998. In 2011 longtime stalwart Japan Airlines retired the last of its 747s. A year later Singapore Airlines did the same thing. More than sixty 747s had been delivered in 1990, but in 2012 only thirty were delivered, and that year was better than most of the previous decade.

The 777 was also annihilating the four-engine Airbus A340. In 2011 Airbus gave up and canceled production of that model. By that time Boeing had delivered 900 777s, while Airbus had delivered only 375 A340s. As one analyst said, "The A340 is dying slowly and horribly. It is one of the more colossal failures in aviation. With higher fuel prices, no one wants four engines." The 777 did well even against Airbus's new double-decker, the A380. There were many reasons for this, but one was that the huge plane had only one deck to hold luggage. Cathay Pacific, which relied heavily on air freight, said it didn't want planes whose holds were full of suitcases.

Boeing by 2013 also had orders for over 900 787s, or Dreamliners, a twin-engine, wide-body plane with a carbon-fiber fuselage capable in its first version of carrying 250 passengers 8,200 miles. Though sales were usually discounted, the planes on order had a nominal value of $163 billion. Good-bye, 1,200 aluminum sheets and 40,000 rivets. The technology was so promising that Airbus in 2007 decided to follow suit with its A350, which had originally been planned with carbon-fiber sheets attached to an aluminum frame.

Good-bye, American jobs, too. Boeing would make the 787 tail but assemble the plane mostly from parts sent by global suppliers—wings from Japan, wing tips from Korea, the center of the fuselage from Italy, passenger doors from France, and cargo doors from Sweden. Boeing's Seattle workers were furious. One said, "They're basically going to try to train just about anybody to come in and do our jobs. That's not right." Others said that there would be the devil to pay when, years in the future, maintenance problems arose and nobody at Boeing knew how to fix them.

Boeing then bought two factories owned by Vought, one of its suppliers. The factories, one in North Carolina and the other in South, made fuselage parts for the 787, and by controlling them directly, Boeing could tighten its supply chain. Not only that: the North Charleston plant would become a second assembly line for the 787.

This was the first time in Boeing's history that it had assembled planes outside Washington State and the first time it had a nonunion assembly line. Workers on the new line averaged fifteen dollars an hour; those back in Washington averaged twenty-six dollars. The workers in Seattle brought a complaint before the National Labor Relations Board. The company responded, "Customers don't want production delays caused by strikes." An administrative law judge warned that he might be "retired or dead" before the matter was finally decided. Airbus, whose European workers were unionized, was paying close attention. Boeing won the right to operate the nonunion plant, and it wasn't long before Airbus opened an assembly plant in Mobile, Alabama.

Boeing began calling itself a "systems integrator," not a manufacturer. Not that this made its task any easier. When the company brought together the parts for the first 787 (the bigger pieces arrived by Dreamlifter, a modified 747), it found that it had 30,000 pieces to put together, not the 1,200 it had expected. Just to help the various Dreamliner manufacturers communicate, the company needed translators for twenty-eight languages.

Delays arose, and by early 2009 the plane was two years behind schedule. Was it the Dream-on Liner? The Seven Late Seven? Orders for seventy planes were canceled. The company backtracked on its "systems integrator" approach and decided that two-thirds of the parts of the first variant of the plane, the 787-9, would be designed by Boeing, up from 40 percent.

In 2011 Boeing delivered its first three 787s more than three years behind schedule. In 2013 it delivered its 150th. Boeing's thousand firm orders at the end of that year would take until the end of the decade to fill. The breakeven point for the 787 was 1,100 planes, a long way off. One analyst summed up the high stakes this way: "If the 787 works out as planned, or close to it, then Airbus will be lucky to regain 50 percent of the market. . . . But if something goes wrong with the 787 in terms of its operating economics and performance, then Airbus would certainly overtake Boeing."

Airbus

Hurrying the A380 to market, Airbus shortened the interval between first flight and first delivery to only a year, far shorter than the normal two or three years. Problems were almost inevitable, especially with a plane that among its statistical bragging points had 100,000 separate pieces of wire. As of late 2006 eight of the giants sat unfinished on the ground in Toulouse; nine more sat unfinished on the ground in Hamburg. Airbus managed to finish and deliver only one of those planes during 2007. It went to Singapore Airlines. A dozen planes were delivered the next year, and fourteen in 2009. By mid-2010 twenty-eight were flying. The wiring in all or nearly all of them had been done by craftsmen, and only by plane number twenty-six did Airbus even hope to have a digital mock-up. The wiring plan varied for every customer because the planes were all configured differently. One of the 2,000 German electricians slaving away in Toulouse said, "Normal installation time is two to three weeks. This way it is taking us four months."

Frustrated by the delay, FedEx canceled its order for ten A380 freighters and instead ordered fifteen Boeing 777s. FedEx's CEO said, "The last thing we need is a large hub in Guangzhou without the aircraft capable of serving it." A few months later, Airbus lost its last customer for the A380 freighter when UPS canceled its order, also for ten planes.

By 2012 Airbus had 257 A380 orders—including forty-seven for Emirates, twenty for Qantas, nineteen for Singapore, and fifteen for Lufthansa. British Airways finally made up its mind and ordered a dozen—mostly for flights between London and Hong Kong and Singapore. Emirates came back in 2010 and ordered another thirty-two planes. The airline didn't know how to fill the seats; what it really wanted was permission from the German government to increase flights to Germany. With steadfast opposition from Lufthansa, the only way Emirates knew how to get that permission was to create jobs in Germany by ordering Airbus planes.

By the end of 2013, Airbus had delivered 122 A380s, but the company would not begin making money until it had sold more than 400. Airbus was counting for help from the carbon-fiber A350, which the company said was so superior to Boeing's 787 that customers should wait. Some did. The first big order came in 2007 from Qatar Airways, which agreed to buy eighty.

Meanwhile, to generate the $15 billion needed to develop the A350, Airbus was building the single-aisle A320 at a terrific rate. Assembly lines in Germany and France produced thirty-two a month, and output rose to forty-two a month with the opening of an assembly line in China. Airlines had ordered 3,290 of the A320s, but discounts were so large that profits were slim.

To cut costs, Airbus in 2008 announced that it would begin sourcing parts from Tunisia and Mexico. In 2012 it announced that it would build A320s in Mobile. Boeing was not amused, but the head of General Electric said that the deal was proof that "U.S. manufacturing can compete with anyone in the world." GE was not an innocent bystander, however. Half the cost of an A380 was in its engines, and many airlines, including Air France and Emirates, ordered A380 engines made by a joint venture between GE and Pratt & Whitney.

The Outcome

Final victory in the Boeing-Airbus contest depended not only on the performance of the planes but on whether the future belonged to point-to-point flights flown by smaller planes or hub-to-hub routes flown by monsters and fed by shorter, connecting flights. Boeing, with its Dreamliner, was betting on direct flights, like the nonstop London Heathrow to Austin, Texas, flights that British Airways introduced in 2013. Airbus with its A380 was betting on hubs, especially crowded ones like London Heathrow, where landing slots were very expensive. Some airlines, however, even big ones flying to crowded hubs, preferred several daily flights with smaller planes to a single flight with a huge one. An executive at American Airlines put it this way: "Our best corporate customers demand that we have frequency of service in key markets because they want to fly when they want to fly. They don't want to fly when we tell them to fly."

WAR BY ANOTHER NAME
A Stroll in the Industrial Cemetery

The owner of a small clothing factory in Bangladesh said, "I always keep this in my mind. Today my business is doing well, tomorrow my business may fail." The failed-business graveyard, as he knew, was crowded. Among the tombstones was one for Fairchild Semiconductor. That company had been created when a small group of scientists learned in 1957 how to make silicon chips and then the integrated circuit. The name came from Sherman Fairchild, who provided a $1.4 million loan and had an option to buy the company for $3 million. He exercised it. The company within a year was making planar chips, followed by integrated circuits with transistors, capacitors, and resistors on a silicon crystal. Great news: within a decade Fairchild had 11,000 employees. Bad news: many were restless under Fairchild's profoundly conservative management. Some set out on their own. Among the dozens of "Fairchildren" was Intel, established in 1968. Fairchild Semiconductor disappeared in 1979.

RCA was in the corporate graveyard too. George Heilmeier had been a researcher there when he invented the liquid-crystal display in 1964. RCA didn't want to abandon its profitable color-TV technology, so it sold the LCD patents to Japan. Acknowledging its debt, Japan in 2005 gave Heilmeier a $425,000 Kyoto prize. RCA's failure, he later recalled, was "a shame. But our wounds were self-inflicted." RCA went out of business in 1986, though the trademark lived on under French ownership.

One Foot in the Grave

Fujifilm estimated that about 100 billion photographs were taken in the year 2000; thirteen years later, the number had skyrocketed to 1.6 trillion. It was a fantastic increase but did no good for the makers of film and film cameras. Between 2010 and 2013 sales of point-and-shoot cameras fell worldwide from 132 to 80 million, and a parts supplier warned, "Inexpensive cameras are dead, just like PCs." Kodak in 1988 had employed 145,000 people worldwide. By 2012 it employed 13,000. The company, which had invented digital cameras, outsourced its manufacture to Singapore's Flextronics. In 2012 it quit selling cameras altogether. In 2009, only ten years after Kodak's peak year for roll-film sales, the company stopped making Kodachrome, the color-slide film it had introduced in 1935.

Meanwhile, Sony was in trouble, and not just with money-losing televisions. Costs were rising for the PlayStation 3, which faced Nintendo's very successful Wii console. In 2006, struggling against Apple's iPod, Sony's boss said, "I tell everybody, don't call anything an iPod killer because Steve Jobs is always thinking." The next year, Jobs introduced the iPhone.

More broadly, consumer durables had constituted 30 percent of Japan's exports in 1986, but by 2013 they were down to 13 percent. Help came from the manufacture of special materials, like carbon fiber for the Boeing 787, and from high-value parts. Americans didn't buy Sony cameras, for example, but Sony supplied the image sensors in Apple phones. Still, it probably wouldn't take China very long to replace Sony there, too.

The CEO of Corning said that his company had "spent 14 years working on LCD glass without making any money out of it." By 2010 Corning had a nearly 60 percent share of the $7 billion market for the flat panels used in LCD screens. This was glass so pure and flat that it sold for about eighty times the price of common window glass. The technology was now mainstream, and the price of flat-panel TVs was dropping.

Unfortunately for American workers, Corning's panels were made in Japan and Taiwan. This should not have come as a surprise because it was part of a much larger story. Toledo, 50 miles from Detroit, had once been Glass City, but between 1973 and 2010 the number of workers in the city's glass industry fell from 10,000 to 2,500. By 2010 the United States had only forty-four float lines, the glassmaking equivalent of assembly lines. The Chinese city of Shahe, in Hebei, alone had that many. China as a whole had 150 lines and made almost half the world's glass.

American experts were impressed when a Chinese company made the glass panels for the Beijing and Shanghai airport terminals. They were surprised when a Beijing manufacturer proved that it could make the eight-by-forty-foot panels of ultra-clear tempered glass needed to clad Apple's flagship store in Shanghai. They were shocked when the same company supplied the blast-resistant glass used in New York City's 1 World Trade Center. They were stunned when Chinese companies were the only ones able to provide the hundreds of 1,300-pound glass plates needed for the glass pavilion in Toledo's Museum of Art.

At least Corning wasn't sitting still. Its new products included bend-insensitive optical fiber, clad in such a way that the fiber could carry a signal around tight curves, even if it was wound in loops around a pencil. Telecom companies took note; finally they had a way of bringing optical fiber into millions of apartments around the world. Corning was also busy with filters for diesel engines. It had spent $500 million developing these filters from aluminum titanate, a ceramic paste that could be shaped into a dense, tough honeycomb.

The retired longtime boss of Southwest Airlines put it to the airline's employees this way: "What we're talking about here is your future. If we don't change, you won't have one." That was positively benign in comparison to the metaphor chosen by the CEO of Starbucks, who said, "Any business today that embraces the status quo as an operating principle is going to be on a death march." The chief executive at Sears boiled it down to five words: "You don't change, you die." The managers of a Daewoo shipyard on Koje Island got it down to four: "No change, no future."

Together with Hyundai and Samsung, Daewoo had fifteen shipyards that built 40 percent of the world's ships. New players were entering the game, however. They included India and Vietnam, but the giant was China, which rose from also-ran in 2000 to being the world's top shipbuilder, by tonnage, a decade later. South Korea had built 212 LNG supertankers, far more than the 102 built in Japan or the 13 built in China, but China's banks had been told to lend to this industry, and the Chinese government wanted LNG shipments to come to China in Chinese-built ships. What could Korea do to avoid being pushed aside, just as it had once pushed Japan aside?

The answer, of course, was innovate. Hyundai built a drillship that Noble Corporation would rent to oil companies for over $600,000 a day. Daewoo built for Chevron the $1.8 billion Agbami floating production, storage, and offloading vessel, a portable tank farm to be anchored offshore. It would be handy in Nigeria, where onshore tanks drew insurgents. Daewoo was swept up in bigger changes too. It became part of POSCO, the Korean steel company whose boss explained the logic behind the purchase: "If we can tailor our ship plates to a specific ship, their costs can be saved."

Even so, the South Korean companies could not rest, because similar ships were being built in Shanghai by Keppel Shipyard, a Singapore-based company. At the request of Lukoil and ConocoPhillips, Samsung built a tanker able to force its way through ice five feet thick. Samsung went to work building for Shell and partners the 1,600-foot-long *Prelude*, a vessel capable of producing 3.6 million tons of LNG annually and eliminating the need for onshore facilities. Estimated price: over $11 billion.

Another Path: Buying the Competition

When innovation was in short supply, acquisitions might do. Buying Gillette for $57 billion, the boss of Procter & Gamble said, "We believe we can build a juggernaut." A couple of years later, Nestlé bought Gerber for a mere $5 billion. An American icon gone? Not quite: Gerber was already foreign-owned, acquired in 1994 by Sandoz, another Swiss company.

Richemont made Montblanc pens and Alfred Dunhill leather products. It also made Baume & Mercier, Cartier, Jaeger-LeCoultre, Montblanc, and Piaget watches. Swatch made Blancpain, Breguet, Jaquet Droz, Omega, and Rado. Think of all those glossy ads—and half the competition in-house. And sunglasses! You could buy Ray-Bans, Bulgari, Dolce & Gabbana, Prada, Tiffany, Versace, Chanel, and half a dozen more. No matter: they all were made by Luxottica, an Italian company that also owned Sunglass Hut, not to mention LensCrafters and Pearle Vision.

Reckitt Benckiser didn't search out glamorous acquisitions: it owned Clearasil, Mucinex, Veet, d-CON, Lysol, Durex—and nothing for the kids at Christmas.

Back in the kitchen, Kraft was second to Nestlé in the global food business. It wasn't good enough, and Kraft's CEO was replaced in 2006 by an executive from Frito-Lay. She didn't want anything to do with tobacco and soon separated Kraft from Altria. (Philip Morris had bought Kraft in 1988 and then camouflaged itself behind a new, supremely bland name.) The domestic market for processed cheese like Velveeta wasn't what it used to be, and Kraft Singles had lost a lot of their once widespread appeal, despite the company offering an organic variant. Better, the boss thought, to pay more attention to foreign markets, including Russia, Ukraine, Brazil, and Mexico. With foreign markets in mind, and bludgeoning her way past parliamentary opposition, she engineered Kraft's purchase of Cadbury for almost $20 billion. Having built a giant, she then cut the company in half, one busy with grocery items like Miracle Whip and Kraft Macaroni & Cheese. The other would get snacks and another puzzling new name, Mondelēz.

Entering Global Markets

Not so long ago, Campbell's Soup had been in deep trouble, propped up by subsidiaries such as Pepperidge Farm and Godiva. The CEO said, "We are in 85% of households with an average of six units apiece. [But] people forget it is in the pantry. Except for a blizzard."

Could Campbell's make a comeback? At home, under attack from dehydrated products, the company introduced microwaveable containers, pop-tops, four packs, and a supermarket shelving system that simulated cans dropping from a vending machine. (New packaging helped other manufacturers, too. Heinz boosted ketchup sales with its Dip & Squeeze packets, and Kraft did so by switching from oval containers to round ones, meaning it could fit more packages of Philadelphia cream cheese on store shelves and keep them in place, words to the front.) Packaging wasn't enough, however, and Campbell's set out to open markets in China and Russia. Perhaps it had no choice. The CEO of P&G said, "You're either active everywhere or nowhere. There can be no in-between."

Campbell's boss said that at first he thought his company "could just take our existing products and ship them to other parts of the world." Not so. Even though soup was a traditional part of the diet in both China and Russia, he said, "You can't just say, 'Well, we like chicken noodle here so they'll like it in China.'" Instead, he said, Campbell's "put teams on the ground in Russia and China for three years, just living with consumers and studying how they eat soup.... We discovered they weren't prepared to accept ready-to-serve products. We basically have soup-starter concepts."

Other companies had similar stories. Kraft's head of global biscuits said, "You have to understand how the consumer operates at a really detailed level." Hitachi's president told his employees, "It's not enough to simply take the services and products we sell in Japan and bring them to our overseas customers. In order to really find out what they need, you can't do it sitting at your desk in Japan and studying it, you have to go to the local market, learn the languages and sense it for yourself."

A P&G executive said, "There really is no substitute for being there in consumers' homes watching what they do. It helps you get to a very smart formulation that meets their needs at the cost that they can pay." Targeting consumers with only a few pennies to spend on treats, Cadbury in India began selling four-cent packages of Dairy Milk Shots, sugar-coated chocolate balls. Nestlé sold stock cubes one at a time in Nigeria and single-serving sachets of coffee in Peru. Danone sold tiny packages of yogurt for ten cents in Senegal and Indonesia; in Mexico, the price was fifteen cents. Urban Chinese could buy Crest toothpaste branded as Icy Mountain Spring or Morning Lotus Fragrance, but villagers got simpler, cheaper tubes of Crest Salt White. They could also get four-cent sachets of Pantene and buy China Tide, which lacked water softeners but came at the right price. Tailoring products to local markets worked for bigger purchases too: Samsung's DuraCool refrigerators were designed for the African market and insulated to stay cool even with protracted power cuts.

Companies that skipped consumer ethnography often came to regret it. Mattel closed its Barbie stores in China after discovering the hard way that Chinese mothers wanted their daughters to be studious, not flirtatious. Home Depot shut its last China store in 2012 after the company had decided that China had a "do-it-for-me" culture, not a do-it-yourself one. Best Buy shut down its China stores after concluding, as its Asia manager said, that "we were stupid and arrogant." The company now ran a chain called Five Star, with 200 stores targeting customers who were more interested in washing machines than home-entertainment systems.

Sometimes the variants developed for overseas markets found their way back home. Concentrated detergents had been introduced to Japan in the 1980s. There they appealed to customers who lived in tiny apartments. A generation later, the same smaller bottles were introduced in the United States, where consumers had begun deploring plastic waste. Seeing American shoppers counting pennies, P&G also brought basic versions of Charmin and Bounty back home. Tide Basic was next. It was pulled in 2010, perhaps because it cannibalized sales from the premium brand, but in 2013 Tide Simply Clean & Fresh was introduced and was about a third cheaper than regular Tide.

At the same time, and at the upper end of the market, P&G introduced dissolvable capsules called pods. The industry had long relied on housewives using too much detergent in every load. Pods might help the company hang on to its share of over 40 percent of the American detergent market, but they reduced the amount of excessive detergent consumers used. That couldn't be good for the industry. One of Tide's competitors said, "If you decided to go to a format that eliminated all the consumers overdosing, you have a shareholder issue on your hands." At least momentarily, pods were good for Tide because they drew customers away from other brands, but an executive at one of Tide's competitors said, "Pod is killing the laundry detergent category."

Shorter Supply Chains

What else could companies do to survive? GM made its Tahoe and Yukon SUVs in Arlington, between Fort Worth and Dallas. The doors, fenders, and hoods, however, were made in stamping mills in Ohio and Michigan. They often arrived damaged. It made no sense, and in 2013 the company opened a $200 million stamping mill next to the assembly plant in Arlington. The shorter supply chain was expected to save $40 million annually.

Similarly, the 3M Company began consolidating its 214 manufacturing plants. Adhesive for picture-hanging hooks had for years come from a 3M plant in Springfield, Missouri. The adhesive was shipped to Indiana, where it was applied to foam. The foam was shipped 600 miles to Minneapolis, where the logo was added and the foam was sliced into desired sizes. Finally, the sliced bits of sticky foam went 200 miles to a contractor in Wisconsin who put hooks on the foam and packaged the product. In 2009 all these steps were consolidated at a hub plant in Hutchinson, Minnesota.

Michelin had planned new tire plants in Mexico, but in 2012 its head of operations said, "We can't tolerate the level of instability there." China was another possibility, but labor costs were rising there, and Michelin feared that its industrial secrets would not remain secret in China. Result? Michelin opened new car and truck tire factories in South Carolina. That state offered tax incentives, skilled workers, right-to-work laws, and the Interstate 85 corridor. South Carolina was about to become the number-one tire-producing state.

Shorter supply chains came with losers, of course. Heinz had an efficient frozen-food plant in Pocatello, Idaho, but what sense was there in trucking enchiladas from San Diego to Pocatello, combining them there with rice and sauce, then shipping the product to warehouses on the East Coast? The Pocatello plant closed, to the shock of 400 workers who had been told that the plant was a model operation. A former executive said that Heinz's new owners, 3G Capital, "didn't do it with malice. It's all business."

Last but Not Least: Cutting Labor Costs

Electrolux, which made Frigidaire appliances in L'Assomption, just downstream from Montreal, decided to close the plant in 2014 and move operations to Memphis, Tennessee. Workers there, nonunionized, would get thirteen dollars instead of the nineteen dollars an hour paid in Canada. Besides, Tennessee was offering to pay for Electrolux's new $190 million factory.

Half the Canadian plant's 1,300 workers were age forty or more. They weren't going to find jobs as good as those they were losing, and Canada had more than one such story. Caterpillar told its unionized workers at a locomotive assembly plant in London, Ontario, that it wanted to cut their pay in half, reduce benefits, and cancel the pension plan. The Canadian Auto Workers, representing 465 workers at the plant, declined the offer. Caterpillar closed the plant in 2012 and moved operations to a new, nonunion plant in Muncie, Indiana. Wages there averaged about fifteen dollars an hour. The Canadians had been making thirty-five.

Caterpillar was equally draconian at its Joliet plant, where a strike collapsed in 2012 after more than two months. Workers accepted reduced pension and health benefits. An older worker said, "I feel sorry for the younger people still trying to make a living." Meanwhile, Caterpillar's chief competitor, GE, from Erie, Pennsylvania, announced that it would shift workers, to a nonunion plant in Fort Worth.

Perhaps Caterpillar's workers were lucky to have jobs at all. In Amboise, on the Loire River just upstream from Tours, Pfizer made 70 million packages and bottles of Viagra every year. The product was labeled in forty-four languages, but hardly any languages were heard in the eerily quiet factory, which was staffed with robots and conveyors. Then there was JCB, a heavy construction-equipment manufacturer based in Derby, England. JCB built a dozen low-emission diesel engines every hour in a factory with thirty employees. That was a thousand engines a year from every one of them. Meanwhile, in 2014 Mars opened a new candy factory in Topeka. There were two manufacturing lines in the plant, one for miniature Snickers bars and the other for peanut M&Ms. The first produced eight million bars daily; the second, 39 million M&Ms. Each line employed a total of two workers.

3 Moving

TRUCKING

Most of the things Americans bought came to them by trucks belonging to one or more of the country's 200,000 for-hire trucking companies. Most of those companies were very small, but the combined revenues of UPS and FedEx were half again as large as those of the next ten companies.

The logistics world had become a time-driven place for all of them. A FedEx Freight executive said, "For a long time, the trucking industry did not know what a customer was." No longer. The boss of YRC, the number-four trucker, said, "The days of getting it there when it's convenient for the carrier are gone. Customers need to know exactly when deliveries are going to arrive because they no longer keep stockpiles of inventory."

UPS was a master at this. It had taken over the distribution of Ford cars and put barcodes on every one of them. A Ford dealer recalled, "It was the most amazing transformation I had ever seen. My last comment to UPS was, 'Can you get us spare parts like this?'" A UPS official confessed, "We're obsessed about efficiency." Perhaps he had in mind the rule that drivers on delivery calls should walk at 2.5 paces per second.

UPS had opened its Chicago Area Consolidation Hub in 1995. A million packages—a tenth of the company's domestic ground business—soon passed through the hub's 126 inbound doors and 1,000 outbound ones. There were four "sorts" daily—ticktock, ticktock—and the average package was in the building for all of fifteen minutes. If a package was going to a destination farther than 400 miles from Chicago, it went next door to the Willow Springs Intermodal Facility, built by the BNSF Railway in conjunction with UPS. A dozen trains loaded with

trucks arrived every day; another dozen headed west. For all the preci-
sion, however, the company was still under intense pressure, perhaps
most of all from Amazon, a huge customer that not only negotiated
discounts but went into the delivery business itself. UPS revenues had
been flat from 2008 to 2014, and the company was casting about for
ways to cut costs. One might be to reduce household deliveries and
deliver instead to local businesses. Customers wouldn't have to wait
around to sign for packages, businesses would see new faces, and UPS
wouldn't have to drive so much.

Both UPS and FedEx provided almost worldwide door-to-door
intermodal service from manufacturer to retailer. An executive at Red
Wing Shoes recalled the time when "we would have a container from
factory A and another from factory B arriving in the U.S. at different
times." They'd be consolidated in Salt Lake City and repackaged. Now
UPS, which had fifty warehouses in China, did the final packaging in
Yantian, just across the border from Hong Kong. The Red Wing executive said, "We never even touch the inventory."

FedEx took a different approach. An executive said, "We believe the
solution is to get rid of the warehouse completely. Every day a piece of
inventory sits on a shelf is a bad day no matter where the warehouse
is. We want to keep goods flowing from the production line to consumer without stopping." Motion Computing, in Austin, Texas, would
send an order to its plant in Kunshan, near Suzhou. The computer was
trucked to Shanghai, flown to the United States, and sent by truck to
the customer. The company's boss said, "We have no inventory tied up
in the process anywhere. Frankly our business is enabled by FedEx."

From Freeways to Toll Roads

During the first quarter of 2010 Americans paid over $50 billion in gas
taxes, but federal gas taxes hadn't been raised since 1975. Adjusted for
inflation, they now produced less than half as much money as they
had raised then. Over the space of forty years, for example, Oregon's
gas tax receipts, adjusted for inflation, declined from 3.2 cents per
mile driven to 1.3 cents, and though this wasn't enough to maintain a

good road network, legislators who liked their jobs would not vote for a hike. The federal transportation secretary in 2008 summed up the situation. "Our federal approach to transportation is broken," he said. "And no amount of tweaking, adjusting or adding new layers on top will make things better." The chair of California's Senate Transportation and Housing Committee talked about freeways as though he was giving a history lesson. "That is a 1950s model," he said. "If we want to move forward, we are going to have to head in a different direction."

What to do? An assistant secretary for transportation policy called private toll roads "the next step." Oklahoma, New York, and Pennsylvania each had between 500 and 600 miles of toll road, more than any other state. The roads were run by state agencies, but the key to expanding them and building others was privatization, which insulated elected officials from the political heat of higher tolls.

The first big deal was the 2005 lease for ninety-nine years of the Chicago Skyway to a partnership between Cintra, a Spanish toll-road operator, and Macquarie, an Australian fund manager. The same partners next leased the Indiana Toll Road. The leases allowed the companies to raise tolls after 2010 by whichever was highest: 2 percent, the rate of inflation, or the rate of economic growth. Another Spanish consortium agreed to build and operate toll lanes along Interstate 595 south of Fort Lauderdale. Generally, buyers of existing roads were willing to pay forty times the annual revenues of the property.

Led by an enthusiastic governor, Texas had 163 miles of toll roads built and operated by the state when it announced a $175 billion program for new ones, privately built and operated. The roads would roughly parallel the interstates but bypass the cities. The first road to be built would be the 370-mile Dallas–San Antonio section of the proposed Trans-Texas Corridor. Cintra, the Spanish company already operating in Illinois and Indiana, was discussed as a possible owner, with tolls of about fifteen cents a mile for cars and four times that much for big trucks.

Communities near the roads feared that, with exits far and few between, the roads would isolate them. These communities had some clout, and in 2007 the legislature passed a two-year moratorium. A representative said, "We need to put the brakes on these private toll contracts before we sign away half a century of future revenues." By 2009 the governor had backed off. He said, "The name Trans-Texas Corridor is over with, it's finished up." He wasn't abandoning new toll roads, however, and one soon opened parallel to Interstate 35 near Austin. The consortium running the new road included Cintra, and it paid the state $100 million for the right to post a speed limit of 85 MPH on the new road. Perhaps to nudge drivers to take the new road, the speed limit on I-35 was dropped from sixty-five to fifty-five.

Pennsylvania hoped to turn the Pennsylvania Turnpike over to a partnership between Spain's Abertis and Citigroup. That deal fell through. So did a plan to impose tolls on the 21 million drivers who used Pennsylvania's part of Interstate 80. The state had hoped to collect almost a billion dollars annually from that road and then divide the money between roads and mass transit, but truckers were unhappy. They used I-80 to avoid the Pennsylvania Turnpike, which charged them over a hundred dollars. People in Lock Haven, DuBois, and other towns along I-80 were unhappy, too, because they thought they'd lose business not only from motorists and truckers but from companies lured by the free road and eager to build warehouses close to it.

California began planning one toll road for trucks heading inland from Long Beach and another for cars and trucks going north from the Mexican border. Work continued despite the state's bad experience with California Private Transportation. That company had developed toll lanes on Southern California's 91 Freeway on the condition that the state not invest in other roads within 1.5 miles of the company's toll lanes. When those other roads grew congested, the state bought out the private company for $207 million.

By 2013 private companies had invested $27 billion in toll roads in the United States, but traffic projections were too high. Investors, especially in the projects undertaken before 2008, began seeking relief, and states considered alternatives, such as contracting with private investors to build and maintain toll roads for a flat fee. That was the approach taken by the Port Authority of New York and New Jersey, which hired Macquarie to replace the obsolete Goethals Bridge, linking Staten Island to New Jersey.

Asian Highways

China's minister of communications might have had the United States in mind when he said, "Democracy sacrifices efficiency." In the space of seventeen years starting in 1990, China built 33,000 miles of controlled-access highways. The ministry published a map showing a bridge crossing the 90-plus miles of the Taiwan Strait, and if that was unlikely to be built soon, other huge works had already been completed, including a twenty-two-mile bridge across Hangzhou Bay. A few miles to the east, the barely shorter Donghai Bridge connected the north shore with Shanghai's new Yongshan Port, on an island in the bay.

As usual, India lagged behind. For fifty years the country acted as though the old British network was good enough, with two-lane roads everywhere, all routed straight into the middle of villages, towns, and cities already choked with traffic—wheeled, footed, hooved, or pawed. India belatedly began a modern network, with four-lane divided highways connecting its four biggest cities. The highways minister in 2009 hoped to entice private investors. He called it "a paradigm shift, not merely an increase in spending." He added, "I see a huge amount of money coming in."

An observer demurred. "The investment opportunity," he said, "is not great by any stretch of the imagination." Sonia Gandhi came to Mumbai in 2009 to open Sea Link, a three-mile-long bridge that would ease congestion in the city. It had taken almost a decade to build, and when it opened, there were still no proper access roads. The result was new bottlenecks. By 2011 India was opening 4 miles of road daily, not the twelve promised by the minister, who had been reassigned. Meanwhile, the Yamuna Expressway connecting Delhi to Agra was bogged down in farmer protests, some of which became savage. Protests subsided when the government promised landowners not only a purchase price but an annuity. Call it a better mousetrap.

Both India and China were pushing to rebuild the 1,100-mile road built during World War II from Assam, in northeastern India, to Kunming, the capital of Yunnan. The Indians were behind schedule on the two-lane highway they were building to the Burmese border, and they had not yet begun on their 300-mile section of the road in Burma. The almost 600-mile-long Chinese part of the road—nicknamed the Southern Silk Road—was already a six-lane highway, with a new bridge across the Irrawaddy at Myitkyina. The Chinese planned on dredging that river so ships could use it year-round as far upstream as Bhamo, about a hundred miles downstream. Separately, the Chinese were building a highway south from Kunming to Bangkok via Laos, with a branch to Cambodia's Sihanoukville Port, and they were working with the Vietnamese to build another road—four lanes—from Kunming southeast to Hanoi. The road into Vietnam cut what had been a three-day trip to just nine hours.

The Asian Development Bank funded the 150-mile-long Vietnamese section of the road, Asian Highway 14. This highway was part of a much bigger project, the Asian Highway Network, a United Nations–sponsored road planned since 1959. The network would be a long time coming, but in 2008 a caravan of trucks left Beijing's port city, Tianjin, and drove all the way to Istanbul. Additional trucks joined the parade from branch roads coming from both Bangkok and Delhi.

Farther north, Russia in 2010 completed a paved road running from Saint Petersburg 7,000 miles east to the Pacific. It wasn't a freeway, and when the World Economic Forum rated road systems around the world, Russia's came in at 130th place, behind Angola and Tajikistan. Still, the 1,200-mile Amur Highway, the last link of the trans-Siberian road, opened from Chita, east of Baikal, to Khaborovsk, on the Pacific. Americans had little interest in this or most other Russian roads, but the Northern Distribution Network was an exception. When Pakistan refused to allow the United States to ship supplies from Karachi to Afghanistan, the Russian network, in conjunction with Kazakh highways, was a precious alternative to the exorbitant expense of air freight.

Meanwhile, the airline industry served 37,000 city pairs but had a tough time making money. The director general of the International Air Transport Association put it this way: "The flags on the tails of our aircraft are so heavy they are sinking our industry.... The only way to be successful is to run the industry as a real business. Who cares who owns an airline as long as markets are served with safe operations?" The answer, unfortunately for airlines, was lots of people.

Domestic consolidation was easier. During the 1980s National Airlines had gone out of business. So had Braniff Airways and Western Airlines. During the 1990s Eastern Air Lines and Pan American disappeared. Trans World Airlines followed in 2001, and it was joined in the next decade by Continental Airlines and Northwest Airlines. That left four legacy carriers—Delta, United, American, and US Airways—and in 2013 US Airways merged with American.

Southwest Airlines

The three survivors had been severely battered by Southwest, the pioneering budget or low-cost carrier. Based in Dallas but prevented by federal law from building a hub there, Southwest chose Las Vegas and Phoenix.

In Las Vegas Southwest soon offered over 200 flights daily and wrecked the business previously enjoyed by US Airways. Then Southwest looked at Baltimore. US Airways had more than half the traffic there. Within a decade, it had less than 10 percent, while Southwest had more than half. Strong enough now to fight fare wars, Southwest increased flights to Philadelphia and Pittsburgh. In both cases it tripled its traffic from 5 to 15 percent within three years. That was about the rate at which it had decimated US Airways in Baltimore.

In 2006 Southwest landed in Denver, where United Airlines had 60 percent of the airport's business. A local travel-agency executive explained that Southwest immediately "carpet-bombed Denver with ads." With over a million Denver passengers by 2013, Southwest had the most passengers originating or terminating in Denver. United was down to 40 percent of the airport's traffic and survived on international and passengers-in-transit business.

Meanwhile, Southwest went after US Airways on the Philadelphia–Boston route. Early in 2010 the average fare on US Airways from Philadelphia to Boston, 300 miles apart, was $684. Two months later, with Southwest flying the route, the highest fare on US Airways was $281. Other budget carriers began to play the same game. Between 2008 and 2011 JetBlue Airways raised its share of traffic at Boston's airport from 14 to 23 percent. American's share fell from 17 to 12. Southwest in 2012 turned fearlessly to Atlanta, where Delta had a fortress hub with over a thousand departures daily.

As the legacy carriers went through bankruptcy and cut costs, Southwest's advantage became, in the words of one researcher, "a shadow of what it once was." There was no relief for the legacy carriers, however, because a group of ultra-low-cost carriers emerged to drive prices lower still. Spirit Airlines and Allegiant were first, followed by Frontier Airlines. A Frontier executive said, "There's no point in trying to be another Southwest." The new formula was fees for everything. An analyst said, "This is the direction of the industry."

Cities Losing Service

Both American and United abandoned Oakland to Southwest, and the city saw its traffic decline from 14.8 million passengers in 2007 to 9.4 million in 2011. Other cities could tell similar stories. With the collapse of Mexicana, for example, Portland, Oregon, lost its only flight to Latin America. The city also lost its Lufthansa flight to Frankfurt. There remained one Asian connection—Delta to Tokyo—and Portland committed up to $5 million to offset Delta's losses on the route. Boston was luckier. Although it wasn't a hub, by 2014 it offered nonstop flights to Tokyo, Beijing, Dubai, and Istanbul, and it had service to London on at least eight carriers, including not only British and American carriers but Iberia, KLM, and Finnair. Even so, Boston's director of route development said, "You hear the word 'no' in many, many languages."

Former hubs suffered perhaps the most. After American took over Trans World Airlines, departures from TWA's St. Louis hub fell from 475 to 256 daily. Cincinnati had been a Northwest hub, but in the five years after Delta absorbed Northwest in 2008, daily departures from Cincinnati fell from 670 to 200. The same thing happened in Memphis. At the time of the Delta and Northwest merger, Northwest operated 240 flights daily there. Five years later, the merged company had cut back to 60 Memphis flights daily.

Expansion of International Networks

An airline executive said, "We make all of our money, when we're making it, offshore and not onshore." The result was that in 2006 Delta started a dozen new routes to Europe, including service to Nice, Venice, and less tourist-friendly Kiev. (Serving tourist destinations was an easy way to sell seats but a hard way to make money, because few tourists bought the expensive up-front seats that were most profitable for airlines.) Continental in 2007 began flying from Newark to Oslo, Bristol, Belfast, and Copenhagen. Call them experiments. The Bristol and Copenhagen routes quickly died.

For years after the collapse of Pan Am, and with the exception of Delta's flights to Cairo, no American airline flew to Africa, yet British Airways' most profitable route, according to one consultant, was its Nigerian service. Delta now tested the water with flights from New York to Accra and from Atlanta to Lagos and Johannesburg. In 2009 it planned to begin service to Nairobi, Monrovia, Abuja, Luanda, and Capetown via Dakar. None of those got off the ground, in part because the Transportation Security Administration refused to allow the airline to fly to Nairobi and Monrovia until airport security at those places improved. Delta persisted. A company executive said, "We're going to continue to invest in Africa. It's more expensive to operate, but you do get more for it." Delta was happy to find that it could sell 80 percent of the seats on its African flights. United was watching, and in 2011 it started flights from Houston to Lagos. Still, the American companies were far behind the market leaders, which built on old colonial ties.

Air France–KLM served forty-two destinations in Africa. Lufthansa, along with its subsidiary Brussels Airlines, served thirty-six.

American Airlines over the years had abandoned flights from Dallas to Osaka, Brussels, Manchester, and Zurich. It had dropped service from Chicago to Buenos Aires and from San Jose to Tokyo. It introduced service between Chicago and Moscow with a fanfare but soon scaled back to summer-only and then dropped service completely. Chicago–Delhi failed. So did Delta's Newark–Mumbai flight. Delta openly blamed the Export-Import Bank, which provided cheap loans for foreign buyers of American products. Delta claimed that its annual payments on a Boeing 777 were $4 million higher than Air India's payments for the same plane, thanks to the bank. Still, the carriers kept experimenting. In 2014 United began flying nonstop between San Francisco and Chengdu.

European Carriers

In the 1980s KLM became the first European carrier to adopt a hub-and-spokes network. Then, in partnership with Northwest, it pioneered code sharing. These changes weren't enough, and in 2003 KLM agreed to a takeover by Air France. Thinking of the competition he faced from BA and Lufthansa, KLM's president said, "We were middleweight champions in a heavyweight contest." Operating profits rose sharply after the merger, although pressures to keep costs down remained intense. By 2012 the combined company was insisting that staff work more hours without a pay raise. The finance director said, "We won't back down because the survival of the group is at stake." Scandinavian Airlines staff faced similar demands, and an official at the pilots' association said, "The union had no alternative but to settle."

In 2009 Air France bought a 25 percent stake in Alitalia. Lufthansa gradually took over Swiss International Air Lines and then began buying control of Brussels Airlines, British Midland, and Austrian Airlines. It had an eye on SAS too. A few years later, it sold its stake in British Midland to International Airlines Group, the holding company for BA and Iberia, but went on to consider acquiring TAP, the

Portuguese airline, which was the major connector between Europe and Brazil.

Despite consolidation, the future was still cloudy for Europe's legacy carriers. A seat mile cost BA, Lufthansa, and Air France–KLM about seventeen cents. Most of the legacy carriers in the United States had bludgeoned their cost below thirteen cents a mile. Southwest's costs only crossed the ten-cents-a-mile threshold when 2008 brought spectacularly high fuel costs.

In 2005 the exasperated boss of BA said, "America, the land of the free, is turning itself into the land of the free ride." He was objecting to bankruptcy laws that could be very advantageous to a carrier. Both American and United, for example, had for years flown Boeing 767s coast to coast. These planes used a lot of fuel, but a lease is a lease and the airlines were stuck with them. United declared bankruptcy, broke its leases with no penalty, and put 757s on the route. American was left to hemorrhage until it too declared bankruptcy and migrated to Airbus planes for the same routes.

Several European airlines experimented with ultra-long flights, which appealed to travelers eager to cut travel time but were costly to operate because planes had to carry so much fuel. As the CEO of Air France–KLM said, "You get . . . a flying tanker with a few people onboard." Thai Airways dropped its New York-to-Bangkok nonstop, as well as its nonstop from Los Angeles. Delta dropped Detroit to Hong Kong. Singapore converted its eighteen-hour Newark-to-Singapore nonstop to all-premium class in an Airbus A340, but this left the airline with a lot of expensive seats to fill. After a four-year run the flights were abandoned, and the planes flying them were sold back to Airbus. Singapore's New York passengers now refueled in Frankfurt. The longest surviving flight was the 8,600-mile Qantas nonstop from Sydney to Dallas, though the return flight refueled at Brisbane.

Many carriers experimented with service to secondary cities. Thai Airways tried nonstop flights from Bangkok not just to India's biggest cities but to the pilgrimage centers of Varanasi and Gaya. Japan Airlines announced plans to expand its China destinations to include

Dalian, Qingdao, and Hangzhou. Hangzhou failed, but the company came back with service to Boston and San Diego. Air France meanwhile offered oil workers nonstop flights from Paris to Point Noire, Congo (Brazzaville). The economy fare was $2,300, far higher than most economy seats sold to Africa.

Budget Carriers in Europe

The Southwest model had meanwhile been exported to Europe. Ryanair's publicity-hound boss, Michael O'Leary, demanded, "What part of 'no refund' don't you understand?" Refusing refunds was company policy, even if a flight was canceled. In high gear O'Leary mocked the fussbudgets who dreaded the racket. "If you want a quiet flight," he said, "use another airline. Ryanair is noisy, full, and we are always trying to sell you something." Passengers had to pay to check bags or get drinking water. They paid if they wanted an assigned seat or priority boarding. O'Leary planned to offer in-flight gambling, once a phone system was in place. By that time seat-back trays would have become mini billboards.

Ryanair flight crews bought their own uniforms and office workers bought their own pens. O'Leary declared his intention of charging for toilets, not to make money on them but to reduce the number of toilets and squeeze in more passengers. Perhaps uncomfortable in the role of straight man, Boeing ventured to say that it would not build such planes because they would probably fail to pass certification requirements. Straight-faced, O'Leary told reporters that he had contemplated ripping out seats and substituting standing room only for those willing to stay on their feet during short flights. He also proposed operating short flights with only one pilot. He argued that after millions of flights Ryanair had only once had a heart attack in the cockpit, and on that occasion the pilot still landed the plane.

O'Leary called EU commissioners "communist morons" and officials at the British Airport Authority "overcharging rapists." He was honest about it: "We specialize in cheap publicity stunts." Perhaps he was thinking of 2003, when he declared war on easyJet by hanging a sign saying "Ryanair Fare Buster" on an old army tank that he tried to drive to easyJet's base at Luton Airport.

Ryanair gave away 25 percent of its seats, but O'Leary hoped to double that number and ultimately make all the seats free. The profit was in the peripherals, and Ryanair was very profitable, with 2012 profits exceeding €500 million on revenues of €4.3 billion. O'Leary said, "Look, this is a stupid business. With the exception of Southwest and Ryanair—well, easyJet to a lesser extent—nobody makes a lot of money at it." A rare patch of modesty emerged when O'Leary talked about Southwest and its longtime boss: "All we've done is copy Herb Kelleher's successful model." But the result put O'Leary back in his customary high spirits: "Nobody else can compete with us. They're all screwed." When asked if he was interested in expanding Ryanair by buying other airlines, he dismissed the idea: "There's nothing out there for sale; it's all rubbish." He wasn't entirely serious because in 2012 he made his third bid for control of Aer Lingus, which he promised to operate separately from Ryanair but which would give him control over almost the entire Irish airline industry.

Apart from the racket on its planes, Ryanair also forced passengers to fly to and from secondary airports. Most of Ryanair's London flights used Stansted or Luton, not Heathrow, which in 2012 charged airlines about twenty pounds for every arriving or departing passenger. Ryanair's flights to Frankfurt actually went to Hahn, 70 miles to the west. Its flights to Vienna actually went to Bratislava, 40 miles east in Slovakia. When Ryanair began service from Manchester to airports like Brussels-Charleroi and Paris-Beauvais, easyJet couldn't resist taking a poke. A spokesman said, "Ryanair continues to unveil yet more low frequency routes to airfields in the middle of nowhere."

Yet Ryanair remained exceedingly efficient. Lufthansa and Air France annually carried about 600 passengers for every employee. BA managed 900. Ryanair carried over 8,000. True, Ryanair flights were generally shorter than those of the legacy carriers, but employees accounted for

11 percent of Ryanair's operating costs. For Lufthansa and BA the figure was over 20 percent, and for Air France it was 30 percent.

Europe's budget carriers did wonders for underused airports and nearby businesses. Tiny Bergerac, on the Dordogne River east of Bordeaux, greeted 16,000 passengers annually. In 2005, thanks to service by Buzz Airways, another budget carrier, it welcomed 250,000. Londoners could now fly Ryanair to Lake Balaton in Hungary and easyJet to Split, Croatia. Poland in 2003 had flights connecting a total of three airports with three British airports; a few years later, it had flights connecting twelve Polish cities with twelve British ones. Norwegian Air Shuttle built a network offering 400 routes, more than any European legacy carrier. It then proposed to begin long-haul international service from Ireland to both the United States and the Far East.

Southwest began looking at international markets, too. In 2010 it had acquired AirTran, which flew mostly from Atlanta to Mexico and the Caribbean. Soon Southwest sought permission to begin developing its own Mexican and Caribbean network from Houston's Hobby Airport. United, which had inherited Continental's Latin American network, was not amused. Appearing before the Houston City Council, United said that its ninety daily flights were in jeopardy, but the council sided with Southwest and approved the construction of five international gates at Hobby. By 2014 Southwest was flying as far south as Aruba, and Southwest wasn't the only threat. Between 2005 and 2010, American's share of all seats flown between the United States and the Caribbean fell from 56 to 35 percent. JetBlue's share of those seats rose in the same period from 3 to 15 percent.

The European legacy carriers, like the American ones, tried to defend themselves by creating their own low-cost subsidiaries. Delta had tried this with Song and had failed. United's short-lived Ted had failed. Nevertheless, Air France, Lufthansa, and Iberia all decided to try for themselves. Air France would send its nonconnecting and intra-European traffic to its subsidiary Hop! Lufthansa would do the same thing with Germanwings. Would it work? The chief operating officer of Ryanair thought not: "You couldn't start from a worse place," he said.

The North Atlantic Route

On both sides of the water, airlines struggled in the ultracompetitive North Atlantic market. BA operated ten of the twenty-four daily flights between London and New York but had more than half the premium-class seating. Almost 60 percent of BA's profits came from that route— and nearly all of that that profit came from premium-class passengers. Catering to this market, BA began flying a small plane fitted with only thirty-two flatbed seats. It flew from London City Airport to John F. Kennedy International Airport with a quick stop at Shannon Airport to clear American customs.

This was bad news for American carriers. So were the comparable business-class-only flights offered by Lufthansa, Air France, and Swiss. A former CEO at Continental said that the European carriers were "going to trash the profitability of the international routes, which are the only thing the major [U.S.] carriers make money on." That's why he thought the American carriers were on the edge of a wave of mergers. "They've got to come together and combine their own international networks or get chewed up by the Europeans." Mergers did not solve the carriers' problems, however. In 2014 Norwegian Air began flying daily nonstop 787s from Los Angeles to London Gatwick. More cheap flights would follow.

The Special Case of London Heathrow

Between 1977 and 2008 flights between the United States and London's busiest airport were restricted to only a few airlines. In the last years of the arrangement, those few were BA and Virgin on one side and United and American on the other.

The monopoly of the so-called Heathrow Four was finally broken in 2007, when the EU and the United States signed an Open Skies agreement that allowed EU-based carriers to connect any airport in the EU to any airport in the United States. It gave American operators reciprocal privileges. The chief American negotiator said that the old Heathrow arrangement had been "a cash-generating machine for these [four] carriers. They make money by gouging customers at Heathrow." He called the 1977 Bermuda II Agreement, which created the arrangement, "one of the greatest crimes in the history of aviation," and he added, "We can now put an end to this abomination." BA's chairman responded in kind: "So there you see it. . . . The greedy Americans want Heathrow."

With Open Skies, Heathrow service to and from the United States was likely to jump 20 percent to about 10,000 seats a day. There was a big catch for Open Skies at Heathrow, however. The airport was already full, which meant that any airline wanting to start Heathrow service had to find an airline willing to sell gate rights or, more accurately, slot pairs. The sale involved not merely literal access to a gate but, more important, two minutes of runway time, one for takeoff and another for landing. BA in 2007 paid British Midland about $60 million for six daily slot pairs. Seeking prime-time slots, Continental paid $209 million for four slot pairs so it could fly twice a day to both Houston and Newark. In 2012 Delta, which at the time had two daily slot pairs, bought 49 percent of Virgin—not for its planes but for its 155 Heathrow slot pairs. Delta might rent them outright from Virgin or, alternatively, set up a code-sharing agreement that had Delta's passengers flying on Virgin's metal. If the deal went through, on this crucial route Delta would be far ahead of United and American, which each had about a hundred slot pairs weekly. All three carriers would still be far behind BA, which had 270 slots or about 40 percent of the airport's capacity.

Instead of selling slot pairs, owners sometimes swapped slots. Delta in 2009 picked up 125 pairs at LaGuardia from US Airways; in exchange Delta gave US Airways 42 pairs at Reagan National, plus Delta's rights to fly to Tokyo and São Paulo. Airlines might also use slots more efficiently. KLM for many years flew small planes from Heathrow to Eindhoven, 70 miles southeast of Amsterdam. With Open Skies it assigned those slots to its partner Northwest, which began flying big planes from Heathrow to Detroit, Minneapolis, and Seattle. Similarly, Air France dropped a Heathrow–Paris flight and replaced it with a Heathrow–Los Angeles flight. The competition on the route was so intense, however—not only from Virgin, United, and American, but from Air New Zealand—that Air France quit after six months.

BA was already looking beyond Open Skies. With Northwest absorbed by Delta, the next move might be Air France's takeover of Delta. Could that kind of consolidation happen, despite decades of restrictions on foreign ownership of American airlines? The CEO of BA not only thought so but demanded it. He said, "We want Stage Two [of Open Skies] to sweep away the anachronistic restrictions on the ownership and control of airlines, so that EU investors can take majority stakes in U.S. airlines and vice versa. . . . If the negotiations [for this] do not succeed by 2010, we shall press for the termination of the Stage One deal." He retreated, but when plans stalled for a third runway at Heathrow, he said that his company might channel future growth through Madrid. BA had completed its merger with Iberia and the airport there had plenty of spare capacity.

The Emirates Threat

Both American and European carriers were nervously watching a newcomer. "We've never seen anything like it before. We've never seen growth at this rate," said a consultant talking about Emirates, a newcomer founded in 1985. The Emirates boss did not hide his ambition: "What we are witnessing today," he said, "is the rewriting of the world's aviation history and the beginning of a new era of global aviation." By 2003 the airline was carrying 18 million passengers annually; nine years later that figure had more than tripled to 57 million. By 2006 Emirates had a fleet of 112 planes, all wide-body. It also had $37 billion worth of planes on order, far more than anyone else and including forty-five A380s. The airline was so important as a customer that the engines and wings of the forthcoming Boeing 777X were modified to accommodate the climate of Dubai, whose high temperatures reduced aerodynamic lift. Emirates ordered 150 of the planes.

Why was Emirates doing so well? For starters, the government owned it, so it paid no taxes in Dubai and could, with its implicit sovereign backing, borrow money cheaply. It also bought cheap fuel, had no pension obligations, paid low wages, and ran its hub twenty-four hours a day. But there was still another reason. The president of Emirates said, "Look at a map of the world, with the Americas down one side and China and Japan down the other. If you balance that all on a point, that point is Dubai." (He might have added that two-thirds of the world's population lived within reach of an eight-hour flight from Dubai.) A BA executive came close to agreeing. "Forty years ago," he said, "the busiest airlines in the world flew across the north Atlantic and a bit beyond." Today, he continued, "the growth is in Asia, and the emerging markets, and BA is simply unable to exploit those opportunities like airlines such as Singapore, Emirates, and Cathay can."

His argument applied with special force to Qantas, an "end of the line" carrier with little traffic at that end. Qantas had two-thirds of the domestic traffic in Australia, but only a fifth of all Australians flew Qantas when they headed overseas because the airline had so few overseas destinations. Qantas had already dropped service to Beijing and Seoul, Delhi and Mumbai, Paris and Amsterdam, and Chicago and Atlanta. What to do? A consultant said, "The logical thing to do would be to focus on a couple of routes like London and Los Angeles out of Melbourne and Sydney and link up with Emirates for everything else." As if to prove him right, the company in 2012 formed a joint venture with Emirates and let that airline fill up its new airplanes with Qantas passengers heading to Europe. As a former chief economist for Qantas said, "Qantas doesn't go anywhere anymore." The only European destination that Qantas would serve with its own metal was London Heathrow.

Singapore was in pain too. It had long been the leading stopover for passengers between Heathrow and Sydney, but in 2013 Dubai took the lead, with 55,000 passengers compared to Singapore's 40,000. Passengers looking for a real bargain might instead choose China Southern with a stopover in Guangzhou and savings of $1,000 on a return economy ticket.

Not content with serving Asia, Europe, and Africa, Emirates in 2005 introduced nonstop service from Dubai to New York. Houston followed in 2007. Next up was service to Los Angeles, San Francisco, and Seattle. Emirates also had flights to São Paulo and contemplated other South American cities. By 2014 Emirates was flying two A380s daily from New York and was planning to add a third. Most worrisome to American and European carriers, Emirates won permission to offer nonstop flights between New York City and Milan; tickets were a third cheaper than the other nonstop choices.

In 2013 Dubai's airport handled 66 million passengers and was about to overtake Heathrow as the world's biggest international terminal. A BA executive complained that Emirates was "sucking our U.K. long-haul traffic over their heavily subsidized hub airport." Goldman Sachs reported "an inevitable erosion" of revenues "as the long-haul business model begins to implode." A few years later, BA's CEO said, "I do not take this threat lightly. I think it is a very significant threat." Lufthansa's chief executive had a similar complaint and admitted that European "airlines are fairly weak to defend their interests."

Not content with ramping up the numbers at Dubai International, Dubai began building another airport a short drive to the west at Jebel Ali. With six parallel runways and a capacity of 120 million passengers a year, it might become the world's biggest airport. Initial service began in 2010. Originally named World Central International Airport, by the time it opened the airport had been renamed Al Maktoum International. As for the resentment brewing in Europe, Emirates didn't seem too worried. Its CEO said, "The last thing they [Europe's governments] want is to upset Emirates because we're the only ones buying airplanes."

Emirates did have weaknesses. One of them was that nearly all the airline's flights began or ended in Dubai. This was not a big problem for budget travelers, but it was a major one for passengers who paid top dollar for seats at the front of the plane and wanted nonstops. There wasn't much Emirates could do to win their business, even though they were prized customers.

Another problem was more easily solved. It had in fact already been neatly solved by Etihad Airways, an Emirates copycat. The boss of Etihad, based in Abu Dhabi, explained his company's success this way: "We are seven years old; we are not a legacy carrier. I am not bound by union agreements that may be 25 or 30 years old." Then he got back to another page from the Emirates storybook: "Whereas the European hubs were at the center of the aviation world, today they are at the end of it." Like Emirates, however, Etihad had no European network to feed traffic to its long-haul operations. While Lufthansa could pick up passengers from twenty German airports, in other words, Etihad could pick them up from five. Solution: Etihad bought a third of Air Berlin, not for its planes or its people but for its market. It bought 49 percent of Alitalia. It was in discussions with the Irish government to buy that government's 25 percent stake in Aer Lingus.

Asia

Seven million passengers had flown in China in 1985; by 2007 the figure was 185 million. In 2014 the country had ninety-seven civil airports, but that number was expected to double by 2020. Such ambitions might be unrealistic elsewhere, but China had built the huge new Beijing terminal—1.8 miles long and bigger than all five Heathrow terminals combined—in the period that it took Britain to conduct public hearings on whether or not to build Heathrow's Terminal 5. Perhaps the biggest threat to the Chinese airline industry came from the country's high-speed rail lines. In all likelihood, China's airlines would drop routes shorter than 300 miles and see substantial traffic declines on routes of between 300 and 500 miles. Even so, the air-travel market would grow hugely.

India was growing more slowly. It rose 40 percent between 2006 and 2007. Air India, a state-owned carrier no longer enjoying a monopoly on domestic travel, fell to third place, shoved aside by Jet Airways and Kingfisher Airlines. The boss of short-lived Air Deccan, which merged with Kingfisher, said that a visit to Phoenix had got him thinking: "This tiny airport in the desert, in the back of beyond, was handling 1,200 flights a day, twice the number of flights in all of India." By 2012, however, Kingfisher had halted operations, and financial problems had crimped Jet's plans. As late as 2012 the country had 3 million people for every airplane in its commercial fleets; the United States had about 40,000.

The leading budget carrier in Asia was Air Asia. Based in Kuala Lumpur, Air Asia with its subsidiaries operated a hundred aircraft. It aimed to keep them in the air 18.5 hours daily, well above the industry norm of 15. The company's CEO said, "We will strive to make Malaysia the world's biggest low-cost hub." Sensing a winner, Richard Branson's Virgin Group bought 20 percent of the airline.

Other budgets started up. Sharjah's Air Arabia began operating in 2003 with six planes. Destinations included Khartoum, Istanbul, Almaty, and Colombo. Jazeera Airways began operating a year later and soon had flights to Egypt and Pakistan. Flydubai began operating in 2009 and within a year had thirty destinations.

Legacy carriers decided to get in the game. Singapore Airlines took one of its own planes with 285 seats, reconfigured it with 400, and began flying it as Scoot. Thai started Smile, and All Nippon Airways started Peach. Unable to make money on its flights to Japan, Qantas quit the market but began serving it with Jetstar Airways, its own budget airline. The chief executive of Cathay Pacific was skeptical. "The fact that people are setting up a lot of [budget] airlines," he said, "doesn't necessarily mean that they are successful." Even Ryanair hit occasional bumps. One was its aborted service to Deauville, a snobbish resort on the coast of Normandy; there had been many supporters of this route, but local opposition had been intense. Many residents didn't want *that* kind of visitor.

The Southern Hemisphere

Calling Africa "the last frontier for aviation," the former chief executive of easyJet set out in 2012 to build Fastjet, a pan-African budget carrier grafted onto a Kenya-based carrier, Fly540.

On the other side of the Atlantic, Brazil's flag carrier, Varig, was sold in 2006 for all of $24 million to a former air-cargo subsidiary controlled by an American consortium. The new owner agreed to invest almost $500 million in the company, which in its last incarnation had been reduced to a fleet of thirteen planes. More than half the company's 10,000 employees were to be sacked. Some might work for TAM, which became Brazil's biggest carrier. With forty-four domestic destinations, TAM was building an international network—New York, Miami, London, Frankfurt, Paris, Milan. Its boss said, "The first thing Brazilians want to do if they have money is to have a better meal. The second thing, when they have a better meal at home, is to have a cellular phone. And the third thing is to travel. Flying. It's interesting. It's magic."

He wouldn't have the magic all to himself. In 2008 the former CEO of JetBlue began running Azul, a Brazilian budget carrier with a hub at tiny Campinas, an hour northwest of São Paulo. By 2014 low-cost carriers were flying a third of all the airline seats in Latin America. In Mexico, Volaris priced its tickets to compete with bus fares.

Air Freight

By weight air freight remained trivial, accounting for 2 or 3 percent of global shipments. The port of Rotterdam handled in one day as many tons of freight as Schiphol, Amsterdam's main airport, handled in a year. On the other hand, air freight accounted for 40 or 50 percent of the world's freight bill. Cathay Pacific in 2005 started flying a freighter from Hong Kong to Dallas–Fort Worth and Atlanta. The company's cargo manager said, "Everyone wants it now. It's less acceptable to have something in 48 or 72 hours." The value of the merchandise shipped this way was enormous: London Heathrow, which handled only a quarter as much air freight as Hong Kong, was still annually shipping £133 billion worth of merchandise.

Korean and Cathay carried more air freight than any other passenger airline, but the business was important for all of them. Delta maintained daily flights from Cincinnati to Paris, not to carry people but because General Electric had a jet-engine plant in Evendale, 15 miles north of the Cincinnati airport. Delta's flight carried more than 4 million pounds of GE engine parts annually.

Some customers balked at the cost. With air freight costing five or six times more than a trip by ship, rail, and truck, managers at Abercrombie & Fitch between 2008 and 2012 cut the fraction of their merchandise arriving by air from 60 to 12 percent. The company still flew in hot items that would sell for top dollar, but its supply-chain manager said that shipping more than half its inventory by air was "crazy."

Some businesses did not have that choice. Every day, Alaska Airlines carried 3,000 pounds of fresh basil north from Puerto Vallarta. Delta often carried twenty-two tons of asparagus north from Lima. Such dependence on air freight could be painful for shippers. BA in 2005, for example, canceled its weekly 747 freighter from Lusaka, Zambia, to Spain. It had been used heavily by shippers of fresh flowers, who were told that they could now send flowers in the hold of BA's passenger flights. Space wasn't always available there, however, and an unhappy shipper said, "If it is the high cost of fuel that is the problem, they could simply have increased the freight rates." BA replied obscurely that "changing its prices would have had little effect."

The biggest producer of roses worldwide was probably Karuturi Global. By 2009 it had over a thousand acres of greenhouses producing over a million stems daily, mostly from Ethiopia and Kenya despite the company's roots in India. The challenge came from China. The industry there was based in Kunming, which had an ideal climate for roses. China's labor was so cheap—about twenty-five dollars a month—that growers could afford to hire women to clip the thorns on each stem. That way the roses could be tightly packed for air shipment. China planned to export a billion rose stems annually by 2010. Commercial growers of tulips and lilies were lucky that their flowers were too delicate for tight packing and so did not face Chinese competition. Meanwhile, a woman in Kunming who used a kind of pliers to strip thorns from the stems complained that her hand went numb after a while.

Emirates threatened to disrupt the flower industry as thoroughly as it had already disrupted the passenger business. Replacing the discontinued BA service, Emirates offered Zambian growers nonstop flights to Dubai, where the new (and prodigiously cooled) Dubai Flower

Centre had just opened as a hub for flowers headed to the Middle East and Asia. A director of the Cool Chain Group in Amsterdam said, "If it [Dubai] also becomes an auction house, then that will be a disaster for people here."

An auction house is exactly what Dubai had in mind, but challenges lay ahead. One was the development of shipping flowers by sea. It sounded improbable, but if flowers were chilled to just a degree or two above freezing, they withstood a two-week sea voyage well. A large part of the business might be lost, not only to Emirates but to Dubai.

UPS, FedEx, and DHL

In North America the UPS Worldport at Louisville International Airport handled a million packages daily—everything from Louisville Slugger baseball bats to Nova Scotia lobsters. On a typical night, 5,000 employees—mostly women—oversaw a river of packages moving on 17,000 conveyor belts linking a hundred arriving with a hundred departing flights. The company also had nearby warehouses where it did much more than handle freight. UPS employees fixed Toshiba computers returned for factory service, refurbished cell phones and printers, maintained stocks of spare parts for Bentley and Rolls-Royce, and repackaged cameras shipped in bulk from the Far East. No longer only a parcel-delivery service, UPS changed its name from United Parcel Service to three letters.

FedEx's ant farm in Memphis was even bigger. With 200 flights daily, FedEx probably had the world's biggest air-cargo operation, with 6 million packages every day carried by almost 700 planes and 90,000 vehicles. "I believe we engineer time," the chief information officer said. One hundred thirty foreign companies had offices near the Memphis airport to take advantage of late pickup times. Flight 24 arrived nonstop every night with seventy-seven tons of electronics from Shanghai.

To the dismay of many Filipinos, FedEx announced in 2005 that it would close its Asia hub at Subic Bay, northwest of Manila, and move to a $150 million hub in Guangzhou. With an initial capacity of 24,000 packages an hour, the new hub was twice the size of unlucky Subic.

Each week, 136 flights would arrive or depart, making this FedEx's biggest hub outside the United States. A Filipina who had worked years before to get FedEx to come to Subic said, "I'm totally devastated. This brings us back to almost square one." Taiwan was another victim of this shift to China. An analyst there said, "Taiwan's airports are being marginalized, and a large part of our freight forwarding, trucking, warehousing and logistic industry is going to die."

More bad news came in 2008, when UPS announced that in 2010 it would close its regional hub at Macapagal International Airport and move to Shenzhen. Macapagal was America's former Clark Air Base, not far from FedEx's station at Subic Bay. Over 700 companies, including Texas Instruments and Samsung Electronics, employed 60,000 workers in the adjacent Clark Freeport. That was almost three times as many people as the U.S. Air Force employed before it left in 1991. Plans existed for Clark Green City, a Singapore-lookalike of four million people, but the loss of UPS wouldn't help make those plans a reality.

DHL, originally an American company but owned by Deutsche Post since 1982, bought Airborne Freight in 2003 and began operating globally with three service centers. One was in Prague; one was in Cyberjaya, outside Kuala Lumpur; and one was in Scottsdale, Arizona. Each operated eight hours a day, handing off to the next as the sun set. It sounded highly efficient, and the company was handling 1.2 million parcels daily in the United States, but the competition from UPS and FedEx was strong. After it had lost almost $10 billion, DHL in 2008 abandoned its operations in the United States; closed the hub it had acquired from Airborne at Wilmington, Ohio; and contracted with UPS to handle DHL's shipments in the United States.

Instantly, DHL was UPS's biggest customer. Almost half of DHL's biggest customers, however, were American, and the company put a foot back in American waters by developing a hub in Cincinnati, not far from its old hub in Wilmington. By 2012 DHL's American operation was handling about 115,000 international packages daily. Most of them went through Cincinnati, with about forty DHL flights arriving and departing daily. Many were picking up or delivering from other airports in the United States, but two Boeing 777s were kept busy providing daily long-haul service eastbound to Bahrain, Hong Kong, and back. Another pair provided daily service westbound from Los Angeles to Leipzig and Hong Kong.

RAILROADS

The CEO of America's second-largest railroad admitted that for a time his industry had been "given up for dead." No wonder. In 2011 more than 80 percent of America's intercity freight bill was spent on highway transport. Yet railroads excelled at moving freight inexpensively. They advertised that with a single gallon of fuel they could pull a ton of freight 410 miles. A truck, in contrast, could pull it only 120 miles. The higher the price of diesel, the better railroads looked, which was why trucking companies often put trailers on flatcars, especially for long journeys when fuel prices were high. Seeing the logic, Berkshire Hathaway in 2009 paid $26 billion for the 77 percent of the BNSF Railway that it didn't already own.

Despite the larger and larger slice of the nation's freight bill carried by trucks, the tonnage carried by railroads kept increasing. In 1900, American railroads had carried 142 billion ton miles. In 1950, in their postwar decline, they carried 592 billion ton miles, and in 2000 they carried 1,534 billion ton miles. A few years later they carried over 40 percent of all intercity ton-miles; trucks carried less than 30.

At least 40 percent of the railroad tonnage was coal. Carried very cheaply, it produced about 20 percent of all railroad revenues. Most of the coal was on its way to generating stations. Plant Scherer, near Macon, Georgia, relied on coal delivered by thirty-five unit, or dedicated, trains, their cars permanently connected. The coal arrived after a five-day trip from Wyoming on the BNSF and Norfolk Southern. (Crews handed over control at Memphis, but the cars and BNSF locomotives ran all the way through.) At any one time there were about seventeen loaded trains on the line and seventeen empty ones. Each train, carrying 15,000 tons of coal in a line of gondolas over a mile long, carried enough coal to run Plant Scherer for eight hours. The fires of hell could hardly be more impressive.

Track Improvements

Railroad enthusiasts might recall that railroad investments had surged around 1900, when the Union Pacific under Edward Harriman double-tracked its route across Nebraska and Wyoming. Harriman did the same thing on another of his properties, the Illinois Central from Chicago to New Orleans. One of his competitors, James J. Hill of the Great Northern Railway, electrified his tracks over the Cascades. The New York Central developed a four-track route between New York and Chicago along what it called its water-level route, a slap at the Pennsylvania Railroad and its up-and-down crossing of the Appalachians.

A century later the American railroad system had been almost entirely consolidated into four lines, and each had just completed major upgrades. The Norfolk Southern, formed by the 1982 merger of the Southern Railway and the Norfolk and Western Railway, rebuilt its Heartland Corridor to handle double-stacked containers from Chicago to Norfolk; the work required raising the height of many Appalachian tunnels. CSX, formed in 1986 by the merger of the Chesapeake and Ohio Railway with the Seaboard System, upgraded its Southeast Corridor from Chicago to Florida. BNSF, formed by the merger in 1996 of the Burlington Northern and the Atchison, Topeka and Santa Fe Railway, double-tracked the Santa Fe mainline between Chicago and Los Angeles. The Union Pacific, which took control of the Southern Pacific also in 1996, rebuilt the Southern Pacific mainline from Los Angeles to New Orleans. The bill for all four systems was $10 billion, and investment didn't stop. In 2012 and again in 2013, the industry spent over $12 billion.

The Union Pacific and BNSF shared a hundred miles of Wyoming track from Donkey Creek to Shawnee Junction. This was the Powder River railroad, and though the station names sounded quaint, the line carried a third of all the coal mined in the United States, over a million tons daily, or a hundred trains with a hundred cars each. The Powder River railroad was so crowded that a new company, the Dakota, Minnesota & Eastern Railroad, got into the act with plans to restore and put back into service the track of the once-upon-a-time Chicago and North Western. People joked that the old track was in such poor condition that it derailed locomotives standing still, but the Canadian Pacific was enticed in 2007 into buying the still-unfinished 850-mile system for $1.48 billion. The CP knew coal. Back home its biggest customer was Teck Resources, whose coal the company dragged from the Rocky Mountains to Point Roberts, near Vancouver. Something went wrong in Wyoming, however, and in 2012 the CP abandoned its plans to extend track into the Powder River Basin. Shortly after, it sold its existing tracks to a short-line operator.

All these improvements did nothing to ease the Chicago bottleneck, where all the continent's major railroads converged. In 2009 the Canadian National overcame community resistance and bought the Elgin, Joliet & Eastern, an old, little-used beltline around Chicago. Improving it would reduce but not eliminate congestion, which was so severe that perishable goods arriving from the West Coast were sometimes taken off one train, trucked across Chicago, and then loaded on a second train to continue their journey east. The Canadian Pacific once again stepped forward and in 2014 proposed the radical step of merging with the much larger CSX. Freight would move straight through Chicago, the CP said, without sitting there for a day or more. The proposal went nowhere but something like it would probably return.

Changing Traffic Patterns

A map showing railway-freight traffic in the United States in 1929 resembled a trident with its base at Chicago and its points heading east on the New York Central, Pennsylvania, and Norfolk and Western railroads. There were no comparable flows in either the South or the West. By 2010 the heaviest traffic flows originated in eastern Wyoming, crossed Nebraska, and then diverged. One branch went east to Chicago and beyond, and another pointed southeast to Kansas City and from there branched east to St. Louis and south to Texas. It was a coal story of course, which is why CSX parked a hundred locomotives in April 2012. The power plants that once kept them busy were shifting to natural gas, and CSX was losing $400 million a year in coal revenues.

The old mainline of the Santa Fe from Los Angeles to Chicago was now a BNSF property and was critical to the handling of containers from Asia. The Northern Pacific Railway, the pioneer line across the northern tier of western states, was also part of BNSF, which sold much of the old Northern Pacific track in Montana and redirected freight farther north to the gentler grades of the Great Northern. Meanwhile, the old Central Pacific, which had been built east of Sacramento as part of the first transcontinental railroad, had been downgraded by Union Pacific, which sent more West Coast traffic along a line running from Salt Lake City through Las Vegas to Los Angeles.

Alternative Routes for Container Traffic

The Kansas City Southern opened in 1897 between Kansas City and Port Arthur, Texas, which was named for the railroad's builder, Arthur Stilwell. Faced a century later with the four goliaths of American railroading, the KCS dared to expand into Mexico with a track to the small West Coast port of Lázaro Cárdenas, north of Acapulco. The idea was to steal business from Los Angeles and other West Coast ports. The rationale came in two parts: first, Los Angeles was crowded; second, the rail trip to Houston was over 500 miles shorter from Lázaro than from Los Angeles. Hutchison Port of Hong Kong invested $200 million in a terminal at Lázaro. Daily container trains began running in 2006, despite warnings from a spokesman that the longshoremen's union did "not plan to take this lying down."

The KCS headed from Houston to Beaumont and then north to Shreveport and Kansas City. Dallas was on a branch line, but that city had its own ambitions. The Union Pacific in 2005 opened a new intermodal terminal in Wilmer, 12 miles south of downtown. Built to move a thousand containers daily from railcars to trucks, most of Wilmer's containers came from Southern California. So did the containers coming to the larger BNSF terminal in Alliance, northwest of Dallas–Fort Worth Airport. Three thousand containers were loaded or unloaded daily.

Dallas was meanwhile waiting for work to finish on the expansion of the Panama Canal. Many more container ships would then come to Houston. That port was crowded, and Dallas hoped to catch the spillover. Six thousand acres were assembled for the Dallas Logistic Hub, conceived by the Allen Group of San Diego and wedged south of Interstate 20 and between the spokes of Interstates 35 and 45. The project was forced into bankruptcy and lost all but 2,000 acres of its land. Still, work on the hub continued, stimulated by the fact that Dallas–Fort Worth in 2008 added more warehouse and distribution space than any other city in the United States—nearly 19 million square feet of it. In 2013 alone, Quaker Oats, Ace Hardware, BMW, and L'Oréal all built distribution centers along the local section of Interstate 20.

The Union Pacific and BNSF weren't overjoyed by the prospect of traffic coming through Mexico or the Panama Canal. Another idea appealed to them more. Instead of going south to Lázaro, ships might instead unload at Punta Colonet, a tiny place of 2,500 people about 150 miles south of Tijuana. The plan was to build a $4 billion port there, entirely new and requiring hundreds of miles of new railway construction to join either the Union Pacific or BNSF. Supporters hoped that Punta Colonet in 2014 would handle 2 million containers annually. Unlike most Americans, the residents of Punta Colonet were delighted at the prospect of a container port in their backyard. One said, "What we need is employment for our kids. Everyone is excited."

Passenger Traffic and High-Speed Tracks in the United States

Created in 1971, Amtrak, a federally subsidized company, took over the nation's notoriously unprofitable rail-passenger traffic. Amtrak now ran trains on 22,000 miles of track that it rarely owned and for which it paid the nation's freight railroads a user fee. Three-quarters of its passengers took short trips that were profitable for Amtrak, but the company lost an average of $125 on every long-haul passenger. The federal government made up the difference by pouring $2.6 billion annually into the company and justifying it because Amtrak reduced national fuel consumption, traffic congestion, and carbon emissions.

The California High-Speed Rail Authority wanted trains to run faster. The impatient governor, a man of action, said, "Look at the train system. They're running the same speed as they were 100 years ago. Is that what No. 1 does? Live in the past?" For the moment, federal law capped Amtrak at 125 MPH on tracks belonging to the freight railroads. Those railroads themselves lowered Amtrak's cap to 79 MPH. Faster than that, the companies argued, freight operations would be impaired. Lots of money was needed for dedicated high-speed lines, which would require curves of much greater radius than those on existing tracks, and resistance to new tracks came from many quarters, including farmers, who objected that high-speed trains running through the San Joaquin Valley would create such powerful airflows that bees over a wide area would be unable to pollinate crops. The farmers said that they were ready to file suit.

European Passenger Trains

Europe was a famously different story. High-speed trains were introduced there in 1981, when the French ran the first Train à Grande Vitesse from Paris to Lyon. Germany began high-speed service in 1988. Twenty years later, the leader, measured by miles of high-speed track, was Spain. It had even nudged aside world leader Japan and now operated a high-speed line from Malaga, on the Mediterranean coast of Andalusia, through Madrid to Zaragoza and Barcelona. Across Europe additional high-speed lines, operating at 150 MPH or more, opened in 2007 from Paris to Strasbourg, Antwerp to Amsterdam, and Brussels to the German border. The Russians offered trains running 155 MPH between Moscow and St. Petersburg. Prompted by the 2018 World Cup, they were also planning a $20 billion upgrade of the country's rail network, including a high-speed line at least as far east as Kazan. Perhaps most surprising was Britain's High Speed 1, which linked the Channel Tunnel to London's spectacularly renovated St. Pancras Station. The new line cut the stately peregrination from London to the Channel by over twenty minutes.

Seeking to integrate rail networks across its member states, the European Union set out to build a high-speed network from Budapest to Paris via Vienna, Munich, Stuttgart, and Strasbourg. There, the track would cross another high-speed line running from Hamburg to Lyon via Frankfurt. The lines would be run by Railteam, an alliance of seven railway companies, and might prove very profitable. The existing high-speed trains of France made two round-trips daily from Paris to the south of France—four trips total, with a thousand passengers on each. Ticket prices were dynamic, modeled on the yield management system developed by American Airlines. Paris to Marseilles was sometimes as little as thirty dollars. The French railway boss said, "We are the French low-cost carrier." A subsidiary called Keolis operated rail or bus systems not only in Europe but in India, Australia, and Canada.

Perhaps as important as the development of high-speed systems was the decision to allow privately owned companies to run trains over state-owned track. Italy was the pioneer, with the arrival in 2010 of Nuovo Trasporto Viaggiatori, which ran a new generation of French-built high-speed trains from Naples to Venice and Milan. Alstom built what NTV called the Italo train, which promised Rome-to-Milan service in three hours—no faster but much more comfortable than the existing trains.

European Rail Freight

The EU was also planning a new network for rail freight. One major line began in Lisbon and ran to Madrid. There it split, with one branch running to Bordeaux and Paris while the other went to Barcelona, Lyon, Milan, Venice, Ljubljana, and Budapest.

The Alps were a problem. More than 1.4 million trucks drove across Switzerland in 2000. Traffic was especially bad following Alpine rockfalls, and in 2006 one such rockfall, along the highway approaching the

Gotthard Tunnel south of Zurich, forced 3,500 big trucks every day to find other routes over the mountains. Some went to less-used Swiss passes, including the San Bernardino, Simplon, and Grand St. Bernard. Some went farther west to France and the Mont Blanc tunnel. Some went east to Austria's Brenner Pass, south of Innsbruck. With 4.5 million trucks annually, this six-lane route was by far the busiest Alpine crossing.

The Swiss decided to impose road tolls high enough to persuade trucking companies to send their trucks through rail tunnels. To make the tunnel trains faster, in 2007 the Swiss opened the twenty-one-mile Lötschberg Tunnel, a $3.5 billion project that replaced the higher-elevation Simplon Tunnel and carried about seventy freight and thirty passenger trains daily between Bern and Milan. On the same principle of flattening the continent, the Swiss were working on the world's longest rail or road tunnel, the thirty-five-mile-long Gotthard Base Tunnel. The original Gotthard Tunnel was finished in 1880 and involved spiral curves; in 1980 a road tunnel opened, parallel to the rail one. By 2017, however, the thirty-five-mile Gotthard Base would connect Zurich and Milan with a straight and nearly level route, a big plus for locomotives pulling heavy trains.

Plans were creeping along for a twenty-mile rail tunnel between Lyon and Turin, and the Austrians hoped to open by 2025 the even longer Brenner Base Tunnel, which required hundreds of miles of approach track, much of it in Italy. This line was part of an EU project to improve the rail line from Berlin to Naples via Munich, Innsbruck, Florence, and Rome. The scheme was so huge that it made the Betuwe Line—a mere $6 billion, hundred-mile line from Rotterdam across the Netherlands to the German border—seem small.

European freight operations had previously been operated by national rail companies whose crews and engines changed at every border. Private companies were now able to run trains and crews internationally. British Rail's freight services had been reformed first, in 1994. By 2010 state-backed Network Rail maintained UK tracks. Companies then bid for the right to run trains in various parts of the country, and the network was divided among the dozen or so winners. Virgin operated the west coast mainline. Railfreight Distribution handled freight coming into the UK through the Channel Tunnel.

In 2003 the British freight service English Welsh & Scottish Railway received authority to run trains in France, much as American railroads ran trains over their competitors' tracks. Consolidation came quickly, with the purchase of EWS in 2007 by Deutsche Bahn, which also ran Euro Cargo Rail and PTK, a Polish rail-freight operator. DB changed the name EWS to Schenker Rail. It also ran freight trains through the Channel Tunnel in a joint operation with France's SNCF. In 2009, however, only a million tons, or 1 percent of all cross-channel freight, used the tunnel. In a bid to attract more traffic, Groupe Eurotunnel in 2010 bought GB Railfreight, an independent British operation whose business it hoped to reroute from rail ferries. France's SNCF meanwhile took over an Italian rail-freight outfit, Ferrovie Nord Cargo.

In the midst of this reform, the huge Russian system remained stuck. State-owned Russian Railways had a million employees and handled 83 percent of the freight in the country, excluding oil. So much for Russia as a modern economy. Until 2010 the government's only concession to reorganization was allowing private companies to license freight cars and run them on the system for a fee. Then the government decided to sell a third of its railway company. A cautious analyst said, "Nobody knows what kind of shareholder Russian Railways will end up being."

Chinese Railroads

Chinese railways had been slow to develop: the link from Beijing to Shanghai did not open until about 1910, and the link to Guangzhou did not open until 1933. Now, however, the system covered about 100,000 miles. That was less than half the length of the American network, but the Chinese system carried more ton-miles. China hauled 24 percent of the world's rail traffic over 6 percent of the world's track mileage.

To ease congestion, the Chinese government spent $160 billion on new railroads between 2006 and 2010—by one calculation $45 million every day. The work employed 6 million men. Far from content with conventional track, the Chinese planned to build 10,000 miles of high-speed passenger track by 2020. By 2012, 5,800 had been built. The new track not only speeded travel but reduced freight-train congestion on the older, slower lines. Built at a cost of $33 billion, a high-speed line cut travel time between Beijing and Shanghai from ten hours to five. Tickets were three times as expensive as on slower trains, but business was so brisk that ninety trains ran daily in each direction—and they were often full, with a thousand passengers.

In 2008 a high-speed line opened between Nanjing and Hefei. The next year, it pushed farther west to Wuhan. Another high-speed link opened between Taiyuan and Shijiazhuang, provincial capitals southwest of Beijing. Travel time between those two cities was cut from five hours to one. The Wuguang High-Speed Railway, linking Wuhan and Guangzhou, opened at the end of 2009, and trains began making the 600-mile trip in three hours. Every day, twenty-five trains ran in both directions. Three years later, the route was extended north to Beijing; the 1,400-mile journey between Beijing and Guangzhou now took eight hours and cost $140.

A professor in Shanghai said, "Physically they are good assets. Financially they are black holes." To fix the numbers, some trains slowed from 350 to 200 kilometers an hour. Operating costs declined because running a train at 350 kilometers an hour took twice as much power as running one at 200. Ticket prices came down.

But were the lines in fact physically "good assets"? The Beijing–Shanghai train was officially named *Hexie*, or "harmony." Brave bloggers began calling it *Hexue*, or "drinking blood." Someone dared to widen the theme to the precarious status of the country as a whole. "China today," this person wrote, "is a train traveling through a lightning storm. None of us are spectators; all of us are passengers." Work on a dozen projects was suspended after an accident in 2011 at Wenzhou. The accident was blamed on a Japanese signaling system that the Chinese did not understand and that the Japanese, fearful of losing their intellectual property, did not explain.

The spectacular Tibet railroad opened in 2006. Known in China as the Qingzang because it linked the province of Qinghai with Xizang (the Chinese name for Tibet), the train's cars were made by Canada's Bombardier and were pressurized like an airplane because the track over the Kunlun reached an elevation of 15,700 feet. A passenger said, "Aren't we Chinese great? They said it couldn't be done. And yet, we've not only done it, we've done it ahead of plan. No other country in the world could do this. Chinese people are so clever."

The railroad carried tourists, but that wasn't its only purpose. An extension was already planned to continue the line west from Lhasa to Shagatze and points beyond. A billion tons of iron ore—three years' worth of imports—lay there, half of it in the Nyixung seam, near Coqen, several hundred miles west of Lhasa. There was also a lot of copper in the valley of the Yarlung Tsangpo, or Upper Brahmaputra. Oil, gas, and oil shale awaited development in the vast Qiangtang Basin of northern Tibet. All of these discoveries came from a geologic survey conducted in secret by the Chinese government and involving over a thousand researchers. The Chinese did not ask if Tibetans approved.

Mongolia was watching. As a mining-equipment company employee there said, "If China closed the borders, we would starve to death." Yet, as a banker said, "Mongolians see what's happening in Tibet and Xinjiang. They know the Chinese don't have their best interest at heart." (Perhaps some Mongolians had heard the startling Burmese proverb, "When China spits, Burma drowns.") What to do? Mongolia decided to build a thousand-mile track northeastward to the Trans-Siberian Railway, even though shipping coal from the huge resource at Tavan Tolgoi to Russia's Pacific ports would be far more expensive than shipping it 140 miles south to China. Perhaps Mongolia's decision was influenced as well by the United States. American companies were eager to buy Mongolian coal. The diplomatic message was "We can't be your best friend and primary third neighbor if all the goodies go to China." With coal heading north, in 2012 the Aluminum Corporation of China (Chinalco) abandoned its plan to buy Mongolia's SouthGobi Resources.

India

Between 1990 and 2004, while China added 10,300 track miles, India added 400 miles. True, the existing Indian network was huge, with 7,000 stations and 60,000 miles of track. With 1.4 million people on the payroll, Indian Railways might claim to be the biggest utility in the world. Still, the network was of colonial vintage, and more than half of all the freight and passengers ran along just seven routes, all so crowded that they ran at 150 percent or more of their design capacity.

Four of those routes formed a quadrilateral connecting the country's four main cities. Two formed diagonals connecting opposite corners of that quadrilateral, and the last paralleled the Delhi-Kolkata line but ran farther north, still within the heavily populated Indo-Gangetic Plain. Congestion would be relieved when a new freight line between Delhi and Mumbai opened in the next few years. The new line would support a chain of industrial zones coordinated by the Delhi Mumbai Industrial Corridor Development Corporation. In the meantime, private companies were allowed to run container trains on public tracks. One of these new carriers, IndiaLinx, was owned by Singapore's APL Logistics and specialized in refrigerated goods.

Integrating Asia's Rail Systems

Only 100,000 containers a year passed between Russia and China. Border formalities at Zabaikalsk-Manzhouli were slow, and Chinese and Russian railways had different gauges, which meant that containers had to be moved at the border from one car to another. Still, in 2007 European Rail Shuttle, a subsidiary of container giant Maersk, ran a train from Shenzhen to Prague. It made the trip in seventeen days, half the time of the journey by sea. In October 2008 DB Schenker Rail began a weekly service. The timing was bad, and as Schenker's chief executive said, "That was almost exactly the date that there was no longer any business on it." Service was terminated but was soon back. By 2012 a container train left Leipzig every day. Twenty-three days later, it pulled into Shenyang to unload auto parts for an assembly plant run jointly by BMW and Brilliance.

Kazakhstan projected its own rail-bridge service expanding from 2,500 containers in 2012 to 7.5 million by 2020. That total would still be only a tenth of the number of seaborne containers, but it was an ambitious goal. In 2013 Hewlett-Packard sent a trainload of computers made in Chongqing west to Duisburg via Kazakhstan, Ukraine, Belarus, and Poland. Gauge changes forced reloading the forty-three containers twice, first on leaving China and again when entering Poland, but the whole journey took nineteen days. The journey by truck to the Chinese coast and then by container ship would have been 25 percent cheaper but taken twice as long. Chongqing had a major airport, but air freight would have cost seven times as much.

Hewlett-Packard and its contractors employed 80,000 workers in Chongqing, where they made 20 million laptops and 15 million printers annually, but HP wasn't the only potential rail customer in the area. Hon Hai/Foxconn employed twice that many people in Chengdu, and DHL in 2013 began catering to a range of shippers with a weekly train from Chengdu to Poland. An HP manager said of other companies watching HP's experiment, "They were all highly interested, but wanted to see someone else prove it."

There was talk of a southern route running from Kazakhstan to Greece via Turkmenistan, Iran, and Turkey, but political obstacles were in the way. So was the earthquake-prone Bosphorus. Two bridges crossed the strait, including one that was part of the Trans-European Motorway. Neither carried a track. For that, the Marmaray Tunnel was completed in 2013 with financing from the Japan Bank for International Cooperation. With the tunnel's completion, attention would shift back to Iran. In theory, railroads could run from Turkey not only to Turkmenistan but also to India. A likelier rail project would run from Gwadar, on the west coast of Pakistan, north to Kashgar. Always looking for alternatives shortening its links west, China was also building a rail line south from Kunming via Laos to Bangkok. From there it might continue west to Burma's proposed new port and industrial center at Dawei.

Track had long ago reached from Istanbul south to Medina. The southern half of the line had been destroyed in World War I, but the Saudis now pushed the line south to Riyadh. Passing through extensive dunes, it was partly elevated. Plans called for it to join a track running from Jeddah to Damman via Riyadh. The Saudis also planned to build a high-speed passenger line between Mecca and Medina.

Africa

Apart from South Africa, Morocco, and Algeria, Africa mostly had "lunatic lines," stubs starting on the coast and dead-ending hundreds of miles inland at locations that made little sense. A track, for example, ran from Port Sudan hundreds of miles west to Nyala, in Darfur. There it stopped, without connecting to any other railroad and with minimal potential for attracting freight. The same thing happened with the Nigerian line ending at Kaura-Namoda, just short of the Niger border.

Some dead ends had once, it is true, made more sense. The French had built a line east from Dakar to Bamako, where freight could be loaded onto ferries on the Niger. The Belgians had built a line northwest from the copper mines of Katanga to Port-Francqui (now Ilebo), where freight could be loaded onto ferries running down the Kasai toward Kinshasa. The British built a railroad north across Rhodesia to the western shore of Lake Tanganyika, where a ferry connected to a track continuing to the coast at Dar es Salaam.

There had probably never been an economic justification for the famous Cape-to-Cairo railroad. The idea was resurrected from time to time, and the infrastructure commissioner at the African Union Commission insisted that only a few links remained to be filled. Even he admitted that there were higher priorities. One was a road and rail bridge across the Congo to connect Kinshasa and Brazzaville. (Two bridges already crossed the river, but one was at Matadi, near its mouth, and the other was 1,700 miles upstream, at Kongolo.) Another priority was a line to landlocked South Sudan. The Lamu Port–South Sudan Transport Corridor was intended to link the new country to the Kenyan coast with both a railroad and a highway. Rift Valley Railways intended to renovate the railroad from Mombasa to Kampala, via Nairobi, and branches might be added not only to South Sudan but south to Kigali, the capital of ambitious Rwanda. Still another possibility was a line from Nigeria north to the Mediterranean. An enthusiastic consultant said that if Africa were "one country, this railway would have been built a century ago and would be carrying 50 million tons of traffic a year." What, precisely, it would be carrying he did not specify.

The Chinese in the 1970s had built the Tazara Railway from Lusaka northeasterly to Dar es Salaam. Now, in exchange for Angolan oil, they were rebuilding the Benguela Railway, originally constructed by the British to provide an all-rail route from the copper mines of the Congo to the Atlantic coast. After a gap of twenty years, a passenger train was operating from Benguela east as far as Huambo, and service was planned through to the Indian Ocean.

The Chinese were busy in Nigeria, too. Rail freight there had collapsed from 3 million tons in 1962 to 52,000 tons in 2009. The China Railway Construction Corporation, an offshoot of the People's Liberation Army, set out to rebuild the 700-mile line from Lagos to Kano. Work was suspended when a new Nigerian government objected to China getting an offshore oil block in exchange. Work resumed when the China Civil Engineering Construction Corporation and a Nigerian partner signed a contract for $153 million, and late in 2012 passenger service resumed with a journey scheduled to take thirty hours. The CCECC was also building an entirely new and faster track between the same destinations. Another Chinese consortium, this one including a Turkish partner, set out to refurbish Nigeria's Eastern Branch, running from Port Harcourt to insurgent-wracked Maiduguri.

MARINE TRANSPORT

Forty thousand commercial vessels sailed the seas. More than half were tramp steamers, wanderers going where business took them.

About 10,000 were tankers, of which most were small though about 500 were very big. That left 6,000 container ships; 3,600 dry-bulk carriers for grain, coal, and ores; and about 600 car carriers.

Greeks owned many of these ships. Call it the Homeric legacy, but a more immediate explanation was that Greece offered shipowners an almost complete exemption from taxes. In exchange, Greece got thousands of jobs.

The shipowners weren't named Onassis and Niarchos. Those families were out of the business—the children disinterested—but George Economou's DryShips in 2010 owned thirty-eight vessels, and Economou privately owned another fifty-two dry-bulk carriers and twenty-three tankers. Many of the world's other big fleets were owned by Japanese or Germans. Americans came in fourth. American President Lines was now simply APL, for the very good reason that since 1997 it had been owned by Singapore's Neptune Orient.

Whiplash Prices

A dry-bulk freighter with a carrying or deadweight capacity of 60,000 to 80,000 tons rented in 2005 for $10,000 a day. The next year, driven by Chinese demand, the rent was $25,000 a day. By 2007 it was $58,000. Rent on a capesize carrier, exceeding 80,000 tons, peaked in 2008 at $234,000 a day. Later that same year, the price collapsed to $2,400. A few months later, it ran about $90,000. By 2012 it again was less than $3,000.

Price volatility hit container ships too. In July 2009 a forty-foot container could be shipped from Hong Kong to Los Angeles for $871. A year later, the price was $2,600. Price fluctuations like these helped explain why in 2011, with prices declining, the China Ocean Shipping (Group) Company, known as COSCO, which leased about half of the 400 ships it operated, announced that it would no longer pay the agreed lease rates. It demanded negotiations and dared the lessors to refuse.

Excess capacity kept pushing prices down while spiking fuel costs kept pushing them up. At normal speeds, a ship carrying 7,000 containers burned about 217 tons of fuel daily. A return journey from

Shanghai to Los Angeles took twenty-eight days of sailing time, which meant that in 2008, with bunker oil at its peak price of $767 a ton, fuel for the return trip cost over $4.6 million.

Container Ships, Fleets, and Routes

The container-ship pioneer had been Sea-Land, an American company. Its *Ideal X*, a converted tanker, made its maiden voyage in April 1956 with fifty-eight containers sent from Newark to Houston. Sea-Land now belonged to the biggest container-ship operator in the world, A.P. Moller-Maersk of Denmark. That company's ships used more oil than all other Danish users combined. The company was secretive, keeping even the capacity of its biggest ship, the *Emma Maersk*, secret as long as possible. Eventually, the statistics leaked: the ship turned out to be 397 meters long and 56 meters wide, with a capacity of 11,000 containers.

In 2011 Maersk ordered a dozen even bigger ships from Daewoo; they were the biggest ships afloat, each with a capacity of 18,000 containers. The lure of such giants was simple: they could carry a container for a third less fuel than a ship with a capacity of 13,000 containers. The giants—so-called triple-E vessels—would join a Maersk fleet of almost 600 ships, 243 owned and 350 chartered.

The first triple-E ship began running from South Korea to Europe in 2013, but it wasn't smooth sailing. Only sixteen ports were certified to handle ships this big, and several of them lacked cranes able to reach high enough to fully load the ships. For a time, it seemed, the ships would be limited to loads of 14,000 containers. With loads like that, their profitability was in question.

China Shipping promptly ordered some giant ships of its own. The number-two operator, Mediterranean Shipping Company, launched its own so-called ultra-large, the *Daniela*. Maersk's CEO said, "It is a really stupid, stupid strategy to deploy more capacity." In 2011 Maersk lost over $500 million on its container operations.

Responding to surging capacity, Maersk that year began operating what it called the "conveyor belt," with ships picking up and dropping off containers every day at Shanghai, nearby Ningbo, Yantian (Hong

Kong), and Tanjung Pelapas (Johor Bahru). At the other end, ships stopped daily at Felixstowe (London), Rotterdam, and Bremerhaven. Maersk took the additional step of forming an alliance with the companies operating the second- and third-largest container-ship fleets. Sharing ships and ports with the Marseilles-based CMA CGM Group and the Swiss-based Mediterranean Shipping Company, the P3 Alliance would pool operations of 255 ships in much the way airlines operated code shares. Between them the three companies in the alliance would handle 43 percent of the traffic on the Asia-to-Europe route. In reaction, APL, Hyundai Merchant Marine, Mitsui, Hapag-Lloyd, Nippon Yusen Kaisha, and Orient Overseas formed the G6 Alliance and advertised ninety ships calling on forty ports arranged in seven loops between East Asia and Western Europe. Chinese and Japanese carriers, including COSCO, "K" Line, Yang Ming, and Hanjiu, also announced their own joint operation. In 2014 the Chinese government refused to approve the P3 alliance, but within a few months the companies were back with a looser arrangement called 2M.

Container Ports in the Eastern Hemisphere

For many years Singapore had been the world's busiest container port, with about 25 million containers handled annually. In 2010 Shanghai overtook it. By gross tonnage Shanghai had already been in the lead for years, but about 2,000 of Shanghai's 3,000 annual sailings were domestic, mostly moving iron ore, coal, oil, and sand on the Yangtze. That river was also busy with container ships and barges loaded with motor vehicles, like the Fords made in Chongqing and sent downstream for export. Eager to see more traffic, the Chinese invited foreign port operators to build terminals at Nanjing, Wuhan, and even Chongqing, 900 airline miles inland.

Shanghai's international tonnage included freight handled at the new port at Xiao Yangshan, 50 miles southeast of the city. This $1.5 billion development opened in 2005, right on schedule. Four thousand people living on the mainland side of the bridge were moved out ahead of schedule; those who objected were either jailed or sent to labor camps. The Chinese didn't allow foreign ships to transfer cargo between Chinese ports, but they were eager to attract business to Yangshan. Solution: they designated Yangshan as outside China, so ships could berth both there and at another Chinese port.

Down the coast a bit, more than a dozen container ships entered the Hong Kong harbor every day. Serving them, over 26,000 trucks crossed daily to or from China. The turnaround time of the ships was so fast—just a few hours—that sailors didn't have time to go ashore. The chaplain from Mission to Seafarers used a motor launch to go to them.

Why didn't more exporters use cheaper Shenzhen or other Pearl River Delta ports? The chairman of the Hong Kong Container Terminal Operators Association knew the answer. "If tomorrow Chinese customs changed to be as good as Hong Kong customs," he said, "I think Hong Kong's logistics business would be dead the next day." He was putting his finger on an essential advantage that Hong Kong had over the rest of China. As one banker said, "Hong Kong's legal system is the best asset it has."

Over on the other side of Eurasia, the three biggest container ports were Rotterdam, Antwerp, and Hamburg, all located close to the mouth of navigable rivers. Rotterdam, at the mouth of the Rhine and the biggest of the three, ranked third in the world, but its Maasvlakte 2 project, at the mouth of the river, would almost double the port's capacity from 10 to 17 million containers annually. The new docks were on land newly created in the sea, which put them at risk from storms but also made them easy for giant ships to approach.

Looking for room to increase capacity at Antwerp's docks, Dubai's DP World and Singapore's Port of Singapore Authority jointly built the new Deurganckdok, or Antwerp Gateway, with a container-handling capacity equal to that of all UK ports combined. DP World also built London Gateway on the site of a former Shell refinery about 25 miles downstream from the City of London. The plan was to build a logistics center here and replace the Midlands as the UK distribution hub, but it would take years for this to happen, especially because other terminal operators, especially Hutchison Port, which controlled Felixstowe, the UK's largest container port, were unlikely to sit back idly.

Farther south, about 200 container ships passed daily through the Strait of Gibraltar. Many stopped at the Spanish port of Algeciras, which had become the biggest container port on the Mediterranean. The port was run by Maersk's APM Terminals, and it was primarily a transshipment point handling containers moving between East Asia and the South Atlantic. A shipment from China to Angola would be dropped off here and transferred to a smaller ship for the last part of the journey. Algeciras was so crowded that APM was building a terminal on the other side of the strait, at Tangier. Other shipping companies developed their own transshipment facilities. The Mediterranean Shipping Company, which had once relied on Piraeus, the port of Athens, built its own terminal at Gioia Tauro, on the top of Italy's toe. China's COSCO in 2008 bid more than $6 billion to take over Piraeus. It pledged to triple the business there to 4.5 million containers annually. Looking for the best way to serve the east coast of Africa, Maersk developed a major transshipment port at Salala, on the south coast of Oman.

Terminalization

Harbors had once been public works, operated by local government agencies. The Port of Marseilles was still run that way, which is probably why it closed for three hours every day to accommodate the workers' seven-hour shifts. A third of the containers destined for France went past France for unloading at Rotterdam and Antwerp, where privately run terminals were cheaper.

Privatization made terminal operators highly competitive. Malaysia thought that its new low-cost port at Tanjung Pelapas could compete with nearby Singapore. Tanjung won Maersk's business, and for a while it looked as though Singapore would be in trouble. Then Singapore refused to give customary discounts to any feeder line that called at Tanjung. Its growth slowing, Tanjung managed to handle 7 million containers in 2011.

Singapore faced a stronger competitor in deep-pocketed DP World, which had grown as fast as Emirates Airline. In 2004 it had bought the ports operated by CSX. (The American railroad company had acquired them in 1987 from Sea-Land.) With that single acquisition DP World expanded from Dubai to China, Australia, Venezuela, Germany, and the Dominican Republic. The company then announced its intention to build new container terminals at Qingdao and Istanbul.

DP World also bid on the terminals operated by P&O, the old British shipping line. The Port of Singapore Authority made a counter-bid, but DP kept raising the stakes until, at $6.8 billion, PSA dropped out. A question arose: Could DP World operate P&O's terminals in the United States? Port operators, railroads, and shippers saw nothing wrong with it, but American politicians of both parties objected. DP World agreed to divest itself of the American properties, even though it would continue to run ports where millions of containers were put on ships heading to the United States.

The biggest terminal operator of all remained Li Ka-Shing's Hutchison Port, which operated in thirty countries and included among its ports both Mexico's Lázaro Cárdenas and the UK's Felixstowe. Second place was a tie between DP World, PSA, and Maersk's APM Terminals. In the longer term the emergent leader might be none of the above. Instead, it might be the Shanghai International Port Group, which had already partnered with APM at Zeebrugge, Belgium.

Terminalization came to Africa's ports, too. Traffic at Apapa, the port of Lagos, tripled once Maersk's APM took over. The port remained hugely inefficient, however, because Nigerian Customs insisted on inspecting every container. They weren't quick about it, and on average a container sat for three weeks before being allowed into the country. A Maersk official said, "Everybody has been living with congestion for years. For them, it's just life." Farther west, APM also ran Tema, the port of Accra. Space was so constricted that the standard practice of "berthing windows," or scheduled times of unloading and loading, was replaced by a policy of first come, first served.

Container Ports in North America

In 2011 American ports handled about 40 million containers. Three-quarters of them went through one of the ten biggest ports, led by conjoined Los Angeles and Long Beach. Together, these two handled almost $400 billion worth of imports in 2012, almost twice as much as the runner-up Port of New York. Between them, the California twins handled the equivalent of 14 million twenty-foot containers. New York handled fewer than 6 million, which was almost twice as many as Savannah, the third-busiest container port.

To relieve congestion, Los Angeles began working nights and weekends and charging lower rates for vessels loading or unloading at those times. Still, congestion prompted shippers to seek other ports. One such port was Lázaro Cárdenas, which handled a million containers in 2013, but there were others, including the Fairview Container Terminal at Prince Rupert, 500 miles north of Vancouver. The port opened in 2007 and handled half a million containers in 2013. Rupert was ninety-nine hours by train from Chicago—forty hours longer than expedited shipments from Los Angeles—but ships got to Rupert two days before they got to Los Angeles. Besides, Rupert wasn't jammed. By 2012 it was handling almost 50,000 containers monthly, most to or from the Midwest. The terminal had been developed by Brian Maher, whose Maher Terminals had been the biggest terminal operator in New York before selling itself to Deutsche Bank in 2007 for about $2 billion. Brian Maher remembered community opposition so strong that the acronyms NIMBY (not in my backyard) and LULU (locally unwanted land use) fell short. He proposed a new one: BANANA, for build absolutely nothing anywhere near anything.

Vancouver was another option. Its managers, like those at Long Beach, wanted to lengthen port hours, but labor unions were still potent in Canada, and almost half of the port's 2,500 truckers refused to pick up cargo through the summer of 2005. A port authority official said, "Fish plants were laying off people. Sawmills were shutting down. There were stores with nothing on the shelves." The result:

Canadian drivers were now paid eighty dollars for local handling of a container. Drivers at Los Angeles got fifty-five dollars. Chalk one up for the Vancouver Container Truckers' Association. The drivers went on strike again in 2014, leaving the province's forest products stuck in warehouses. The head of an industry organization said, "This is grinding us down to a trickle of exports coming out of the province. We're sort of strangled here."

New York's position as the country's second-biggest container port was surprising because, although it had been the world's biggest port until 1984, containerization had then just about killed it. The old docks in Brooklyn and Manhattan had been more or less abandoned—destined for conversion to residential, commercial, and recreational uses—while what was left of the shipping business moved west a few miles to Port Elizabeth. It was only logical. The Pennsylvania Railroad had once barged a thousand cars across the Hudson daily. It had quit that business in 1969, and shippers who insisted on landing in New York City could get west of the Hudson only by sending their freight north almost to Albany, where there was a bridge across the river. The alternative was the single barge operated by the miniscule New York New Jersey Railroad. It ferried about 5 railcars daily between Jersey City and Brooklyn.

So why was New York back as a major port, even if its port was actually mostly in New Jersey? Why did shippers not unload on the West Coast and send their containers rolling east on railroad flatcars? One reason was that container ships could now cruise at twenty-five knots, not the sixteen typical in 1970. Sending goods to New York by ship through Panama, in other words, took only three days longer than using rail—even less than that if Los Angeles was congested. Another reason was that shipping by rail was $1,200 more expensive per container. As a result, the percentage of Asian goods reaching New York by train from California declined from 86 percent in 1999 to 65 percent in 2004. Walmart, which had routed 80 percent of its incoming shipments through Los Angeles in 2002, was down to 15 percent in 2009. The Panamanians were happy, although for the moment they couldn't handle anything larger than a Panamax-class ship—about a thousand feet long and a hundred wide. New York's longshoremen were happy too, although there were only 5,000 of them, far fewer than the 39,000 on the docks in 1954, the year of *On the Waterfront.*

Longshoremen were still the highest paid blue-collar workers in America. Auto mechanics made about $40,000. Old-scale UAW members on a GM assembly line averaged $75,000, assuming 2,000 hours of work. Longshoremen averaged $124,000, including benefits. That was why the Port of Los Angeles in 2004 had 300,000 applications for 3,000 jobs. Thank the country's two unions—one on each coast.

The Panama Canal, increasingly important with the resurgence of New York, was about to become even more so. Back in 1980, almost all the traffic through the canal had been between North American ports. Now, more than 40 percent of it was to or from Asia. As recently as 2000, container ships constituted only a quarter of the canal's traffic; now they constituted more than half. A tug captain said that the canal had "just got busier and busier. It doesn't matter what time of day or night." Transit fees were steep too. A container ship with 4,000 containers paid over $270,000 for the nine-hour trip.

The third lane of the Panama Canal was soon to open. Instead of a dozen locks, this new channel had only six. Instead of using huge amounts of water from Gatun Lake, the new channel would recycle water. Best of all, the third lane would handle ships up to 49 meters wide and 366 meters long—ships carrying 12,000 containers, a few more than the *Emma Maersk.* By a vote of 78 to 22 percent, Panamanians had approved the expansion in 2006. Many Nicaraguans were disappointed. They had hoped the Panamanians would vote no so Nicaragua could build the $20 billion Nicaragua Interoceanic Grand Canal.

Navigation Opportunities and Hazards

At twenty-one knots a ship required twenty-nine days to go from Rotterdam around Africa to Yokohama. Passing through the Suez Canal shaved a week off the journey, but the trip would take only fifteen days if ships could pass north of Russia. Could it be done? Gazprom in 2012 chartered a Greek ship, the *Ob River*, and had it carry 13,000 cubic meters of liquefied natural gas from Hammerfest, Norway, to a Japanese terminal near the Strait of Shimonoseki. Gazprom said that the savings on the shorter route were greater than the cost of the ice-breaker escort.

The *Ob River* wasn't alone; a total of forty-six ships in 2012 took what shippers were calling the Northern Sea Route. The next year, the figure was 71. Most of the ships began and ended their voyages within Russia, but the Chinese freighter *Yong Sheng* sailed at fourteen knots from Busan to Rotterdam. The voyage took twenty-one days; at that speed the Suez route would have taken an additional fourteen.

Maersk's chief executive remained cautious. The Northern Sea Route might "in a very far, very distant future" be a major route, he said, but not "within the next 15 to 20 years in our opinion." Russia had only five icebreakers available, and there were other problems. Some were political. One executive said bluntly, "One thing that makes me nervous is that this route is in Russia's hands. If they suddenly want to triple rates or impose this condition or that condition, they can."

Canada was watching too. Its defense minister in 2005 said, "I don't see the Northwest Passage as something for another 20 years, but at the rate of present global warming, we know that it will be within 20 years and we have to get ahead now." A Manitoba transport minister said, "We look to be the gateway, the logistical hub of the world for circumpolar navigation." OmniTRAX, the port owner at Churchill, on Hudson Bay, had already spent $50 million upgrading its port. The premier of Quebec in 2011 got in the act too. "With global warming," he said, "a northern route is going to open up just on the tip of northern Quebec in 2030 or 2040." The transport minister for Sakha, a Siberian republic with its capital at Yakutsk, anticipated a steady flow of ships bringing Siberian resources down the Lena River and straight to Canada.

Going beyond words, the Canadian Coast Guard in 2013 provided a free escort to the *Nordic Orion*, which carried 15,000 tons of coal from Vancouver north through the Arctic to Pori, Finland. The journey saved four days, 1,500 miles, and about $200,000.

Meanwhile, piracy had declined in the Strait of Malacca, through which 50,000 ships passed annually. The daily oil traffic alone amounted to 11.7 million barrels, which was more than two-thirds of the 17 million barrels coming out of the Persian Gulf. In July 2006 there were only four attacks, and Lloyd's, the insurer, dropped its war-zone premium. As if to keep shippers on their toes, pirates became exceedingly busy off the coast of Somalia and the adjoining Gulf of Aden.

Piracy began there as fishermen saw their business stolen by big East Asian fish boats whose crews no longer had to worry about a Somali government. The Somali fishermen decided to become tax collectors. Then they moved up the food chain and in 2009 tried to board over 300 ships. They actually boarded about fifty, and late that year they held fourteen. In 2010 there were forty-nine hijackings, but the number was cut to twenty-eight in 2011, not because of fewer attacks but because of stronger resistance. Armed guards became especially important as shipowners disregarded the advice of security experts. No ship had ever been hijacked in these waters if it sailed at speeds over eighteen knots. Yet by sailing slower than that, shipowners could save $50,000 a day in fuel costs, more than enough to pay for guards. Attacks declined from 237 in 2011 to 75 in 2012, and the pirates began looking for other occupations, such as charcoal smuggling. Shippers might feel relieved, but they also had to deal with a Suez Canal operating at capacity, with 300 ships passing daily.

4 Fueling

Worldwide, oil companies in 2013 produced over 90 million barrels of oil daily. That quantity was impossible to visualize, but 1 million barrels, the daily production of North Dakota in 2014, would fill sixty-six Olympic-size swimming pools. Over the course of a year, the world yielded about 30 billion barrels of oil, enough to fill 2 million Olympic pools. A handier image was a single tank, cubic, and a mile square.

BIG OIL ADAPTS

The Squeeze on Oil Companies

Until the 1970s a handful of investor-owned companies dominated the oil industry. They were British Petroleum (later known simply as BP), Shell, Gulf, Texaco, and three fragments of John D. Rockefeller's Standard Oil Company. Those fragments were Esso, Mobil, and Chevron, more formally Standard Oil of New Jersey, of New York, and of California. These seven companies dominated the petroleum industry everywhere except the Soviet Union and Mexico.

In the 1970s, however, oil-rich countries around the world followed the Soviet Union and Mexico, nationalized their oil industries, and assigned development rights to a group of new state-owned oil companies that now controlled about 75 percent of the world's reserves. These companies included Saudi Aramco, National Iranian Oil Company, Iraq National Oil Company, Petróleos de Venezuela, China National, Gazprom of Russia, and Petrobras of Brazil. The world's dozen biggest government-controlled companies were now all oil companies, with the exception of Japan Post.

A consultant called this shift in power "the issue the chief executives of the major oil companies think about before they go to sleep and when they awake." The chief executive of BP conceded, "National oil companies are the future of the oil business." Another executive added that the old giants, squeezed between state-owned producers on one hand and service companies such as Schlumberger and Halliburton on the other, were being forced "to question what it is we bring to the table."

The answer to that question was that it was getting very hard to find oil, and nobody could find it better than the old giants. Even they had to fight for it. Exxon in 2013 produced about 4 million barrels of oil daily, but its production had been declining for the two previous years. That same year, Exxon spent $38 billion as part of a plan to increase production by a million barrels a day by 2017. Other companies faced similar difficulties. Despite world oil prices tripling between 2003 and 2013, world production rose only 12 percent. A banker said, "Anytime price goes up and supply doesn't really follow, it's getting damn hard to get it out of the ground."

The companies were also paying more for drilling rights. Back in the early 1990s, bids of under $100 million were enough to secure rights to a 5,000-square-kilometer block in deep water off the coast of Angola. (This was entirely separate from royalties; it was an extra amount called a signature bonus.) In 2006, however, the Italian company Eni bid $902 million for a similar block. Then China's Sinopec came along and bid $2.2 billion for two blocks. A consultant called the bids "the highest ever offered for exploration acreage anywhere in the world." An oil-company official called the bids "insane" and added, "I can't figure out how anyone is going to make money." Auctions continued, though the bonuses were secret. Indirect evidence suggested that in one case a consortium including BP won a block for $2.2 billion spread over four years.

Bulking Up

One way oil companies survived was by swallowing their competition. The first major to do this was Chevron, which acquired Gulf in

1985. Thirteen years later, in 1998, Exxon merged with Mobil, British Petroleum with Amoco, and Total with Petrofina. In 2001 Chevron took another gulp and swallowed Texaco. Life became harder than ever for midsize companies. In 2006 Anadarko Petroleum acquired Kerr-McGee for $16 billion. A great deal of high-rise office space was suddenly available in downtown Oklahoma City, Kerr-McGee's hometown.

Taking Political Risks

The bigger the companies became the greater the risks they dared to take. The Iraqi pipeline from Kirkuk west to the pipeline junction at Baiji, north of Tikrit, was protected by ditches on both sides, a dirt barrier, fencing with coils of razor wire, and guard posts at road crossings. The oil companies could live with the hazards. As a former Iraqi oil minister explained, "The international oil companies are short of reserves and opportunities and countries control almost 88 per cent of oil reserves. The only real opportunity is Iraq." A consultant said, "Iraq may be at the bottom of any scale ranking investment climate," but "it is at the top of any scale ranking the attractiveness of its oil reserves." By mid-2008 Iraq was producing about 2.4 million barrels a day, and export revenues from oil were over $5 billion monthly.

Farther north, Iraqi Kurdistan contained at least 45 billion barrels of oil. The former chief executive of BP, obliged to resign after the Deepwater Horizon disaster in the Gulf of Mexico in 2010, set out to get some of it. He called Iraqi Kurdistan "almost the only place in the Middle East where the private sector can explore virgin territory" and added, "Kurdistan is the oil exploration capital of the world." He didn't sound worried.

Superior Technologies

A third strategy was to develop or acquire new technologies. XTO Energy had used a new technology to drill about 5,000 wells in Colorado's Piceance Basin, with an estimated 35 trillion cubic feet of gas— more than a year's domestic consumption. The technology captured small pockets of gas, as many as fifty for every well. Rather than reinvent the wheel, Exxon bought XTO for $31 billion and with that purchase moved ahead of BP and Anadarko to become the country's biggest gas producer. Its timing wasn't great, because gas prices soon fell in the midst of a national glut caused in part by the fact, as one of Exxon's competitors said of the new technology, "This stuff doesn't remain proprietary."

Exxon had other tricks. Oil is an electrical resister, so rocks containing it reflect electromagnetic waves. Drillers had been using technology based on this fact for many years. Exxon's Remote Reservoir Resistivity Mapping, or R3M, now used a ship to skim the seafloor and check for oil-bearing strata below. This technology lay behind a meeting of Exxon's CEO and Libya's Muammar Gaddafi in 2007. Exxon's CEO emerged to say, "It was a great meeting. He was a very gracious, cordial host." The Libyans, he explained, were "interested in our technology set. And we can show them what we've already done in other fields around the world."

Again the timing wasn't great. One oilman, commenting on Libya's new receptivity to foreign companies, cautioned, "The Libyans will no doubt be the big winners in this. . . . The international oil companies will only be there at the margin." Another cautioned that working in Libya was "like kissing a porcupine." By 2011 a consultant said, "Libya has gone from the world's most exciting oil-exploration hot-spot in 2005 to another geologically, politically and fiscally risky also ran."

Like Exxon, Shell worked to extract oil from pockets too small to justify a well to each one. Instead, the company drilled snake wells, which twisted laterally for several miles. Tapping pockets along the way, Shell in this way produced 70,000 barrels of oil daily from Brunei's Champion West Field. The company planned on introducing the technology to Oman, the North Sea, and Nigeria.

Midsize companies had specialties too. For Anadarko, it was deep water. The company's Independence Hub floated on 10,000 feet of water in the Gulf of Mexico. Around it 125 miles of seafloor tubing— "umbilicals"—gathered a billion cubic feet of natural gas daily from ten fields, including one 30 miles away. Such technology explained how deepwater wells, which in 1990 produced almost nothing anywhere, by 2010 were producing almost 6 million barrels of oil daily, more than half of it from Brazil and Angola, followed by the United States and Norway. A consultant warned that deep water involved "extraordinary uncertainty, immense levels of information processing, [and] staggering amounts of capital." Shell's head of major projects said, "You have to have the idea, you have to have the engineering solution, and you have to have the guts to put it into reality."

THE UNITED STATES AND CANADA

Throughout the first half of the twentieth century, the United States produced more than half the world's oil. Starting in 1971, however, production began slipping from almost 10 million to less than 5 million barrels daily. That was less than a tenth of world production, even though the United States had a phenomenal 500,000 producing wells, approximately half the oil wells in the world. For a time, the most productive onshore well in the lower forty-eight was owned by Swift Energy. It was in Louisiana and produced a pitiful 1,600 barrels a day, a quarter of the average yield of a Saudi well.

Onshore Public Lands

What to do? For many years a popular answer within the industry was to open public lands to exploration and leasing. Republican administrations obliged, leading a Trout Unlimited employee to say, "Farmers and ranchers are fit to be tied about what they consider their administration is doing." ("Their" because they mostly voted Republican.) A Bureau of Land Management employee chimed in on the ranchers' side: "We're told to follow new deadlines that are totally driven by industry. We're not given time to do adequate [environmental reviews] and to consider the consequences of our decisions." One Republican rancher concluded, "It's going to cost us the freedom that the West stands for." A BLM director, charged with caring for these lands, denied it. "I absolutely reject the premise that the BLM ignores the bulk of its mission to promote a single use," he said.

Alaska

Alaska's North Slope, fronting the Arctic Ocean, was the most promising area for conventional production anywhere on the public lands, but for years the state government struggled over the financial package for a gas pipeline that Exxon, BP, and ConocoPhillips might build alongside the Alaska Highway. This was a $30 billion project, with a pipe more than five feet in diameter. Exxon watched Sarah Palin, Alaska's newly elected governor, rejigger the previous governor's plans for controlling the pipeline and dividing its revenue. "I don't really know where we are," Exxon's chief executive said. "I don't think it looks like Alaska knows where it wants to go, either." Slap! Canada's Mackenzie Pipeline showed how these projects could get bogged down. It was still in the planning stage some twenty years after right-of-way negotiations began with native peoples.

In 2008 BP and ConocoPhillips announced their intention of building an Alaska gas pipeline on their own, without Exxon. The Denali Pipeline, as they called it, would run from the North Slope down past Anchorage, over to the fuel-hungry Athabasca tar sands of Alberta, and then on to Chicago. Exxon sat on its hands, saying it needed time to study the proposal, which it called "among the largest, costliest, and most complex projects ever undertaken." Then, in 2011, BP and ConocoPhillips pronounced the pipeline dead, a victim of low gas prices. A better choice might be exporting Alaskan LNG, but that would require an investment in Alaska of at least $40 billion. An analyst said, "There's only one country in the world that can do that, and that's China." By 2012 Exxon was back in the news with BP and ConocoPhillips. The trio announced that they intended to build a $65 billion gas pipeline from the North Slope to a marine-export terminal 800 miles to the south.

The American Gulf

The public lands also included the Outer Continental Shelf, and by 2010 federal lands in the Gulf of Mexico produced almost a third of all the oil produced in the United States. Here was an unexpected turn of events. As late as the 1980s, the Gulf was commonly dismissed as a second Dead Sea. Looking back, an engineer recalled what petroleum engineers thought at the time. "All the elephants were gone," he said, "and we were pursuing field mice."

Shallow-water production, which generally came from state-owned lands, had a long history, but deepwater production—production in waters over 600 feet deep—began in 1994. Shell's Auger platform floated in 2,900 feet of water 140 miles off the coast of Louisiana. By 2012 Auger had produced 300 million barrels of oil. In 2006 Exxon spent $200 million drilling the Blackbeard Prospect. It was only 30 miles off the coast of Louisiana, but the drillers went down 30,000 feet. They found nothing and quit. Despite Exxon's failure, McMo-Ran Exploration in 2008 took up the same lease and was soon down to over 32,000 feet. The McMoRan boss said, "We're very optimistic. But remember: I'm a geologist, and I have to be optimistic to do this job." By 2012 the company was down to over 33,000 feet with nothing to show for it.

Despite the risks, everybody wanted in. Chevron had five projects in the Gulf of Mexico, including Tahiti, a $3.5 billion platform shared with minority partners Norway's Statoil and France's Total. Its manager warned, "Every deepwater field is unique." After delays caused by trouble with the shackles intended to immobilize the platform, production began in 2009 and stabilized at a bit over 100,000 barrels a day.

A partnership between Chevron, Devon Energy, and Statoil reported in 2006 that Jack 2, a well 175 miles off the coast of Louisiana, was producing 6,000 barrels of light, sweet crude daily from a depth of almost 30,000 feet under the sea floor. A few months later, Shell Offshore announced that it was going to spend billions developing several fields in the Perdido Foldbelt, also under 7,500 to 10,000 feet of water.

BP pushed hard—too hard—in the Gulf. An observer said that the company thought "of itself as the teenager of the oil industry. . . . It thinks fast and furious won't kill them." Mad Dog, which was supposed to produce 100,000 barrels daily by 2007, was by then producing only half that much. Thunder Horse, 150 miles south of New Orleans, was the company's biggest platform but nearly sank in 2009 because of a design failure. Two years behind schedule, it was producing 250,000 barrels daily from only seven wells. Three years later, BP announced the discovery of a field with 3 billion barrels of oil. The discovery well, called Tiber, lay 400 miles southeast of Houston in 2 miles of water. The well itself went down another 35,000 feet and was "the deepest well ever drilled by the oil and gas industry," according to a BP spokesman. The rig that drilled the well was the doomed *Deepwater Horizon*. Towed to its next job, at the Macondo well, the rig was destroyed in 2010 by an explosion that caused the biggest oil spill in American history. About 5 million barrels of oil went into the Gulf of Mexico—about 300 Olympic-sized swimming pools of the stuff.

The Macondo well had been drilled with a rig owned by Transocean. The company, which had merged with its competitor GlobalSantaFe in 2007, operated fifty-three floating rigs, so-called semisubmersibles. It also operated about seventy jack-up rigs in shallow water and a score of drill ships. A smaller company, Seadrill, was also at the party. A Seadrill executive said, "I have oil companies that are coming to us and saying: 'Please help us with a rig in 2008; we're going to lose the license because we can't drill.'" He meant that in the Gulf of Mexico, federal lessees had ten years to drill. If they didn't, the leases expired, and the blocks—usually 3 miles square—went back on the market.

Competition was especially intense for the ten rigs capable of drilling in water more than 10,000 feet deep. In 2006 the official daily rate for the one used by Chevron's Tahiti—the *Discoverer Deep Seas*—was $245,000 a day. To make sure its owners didn't send it elsewhere when the lease expired, Chevron agreed to pay double that, plus the cost of a crew of 350. By 2012 the going rate for the biggest rigs was $600,000 daily, plus labor.

The North American Arctic Ocean

Eighty miles north of Barrow, Shell in 2012 tried to drill six wells in the Arctic Ocean. A resident of nearby Point Hope said, "We're kind of torn apart between development and sustaining our lifestyle." The mayor of the North Slope Borough said, "It's a tough, tough call to make." Despite spending $6 billion on permits, people, and equipment, Shell announced that not a single well had been completed and that it had abandoned plans to drill in 2013. The declining price of natural gas had a lot to do with the decision, but the federal government didn't help when it soon issued a report questioning Shell's "ability to operate safely and responsibly in the challenging and unpredictable conditions offshore Alaska."

The CEO of Total, thinking of the damage an Arctic oil spill would do to the reputation of an oil company, recommended no drilling for Arctic oil at all. (Drilling for gas, he thought, might be all right.) Conoco, too, puts its Arctic plans on hold, and Norway's Statoil said it would wait until 2015 before proceeding in the Chukchi Sea. ExxonMobil, through its subsidiary Imperial Oil of Canada, announced, however, that it was planning a tremendously deep exploratory well—between 5 and 6 miles deep—at a location 110 miles north of the Canadian coast at Tuktoyaktuk. A consultant for the company said that the well, which would probably take three years to drill and which would probably not get started until 2020, "could be the most expensive well ever drilled."

Secondary and Tertiary Recovery

New technologies meanwhile breathed life into old, often senescent fields. For generations the industry had recovered no more than about 10 percent of the oil in a reservoir. Beginning in the 1960s, however, secondary recovery, usually involving the injection of steam or water, pushed recovery to about 30 percent.

A classic example came from the oil fields in California's San Joaquin Valley. One of the fields there was Kern River, just north of Bakersfield. A giant, it had produced 15 million barrels annually around 1906, but by the 1960s production was down to 3 million. Steam injection boosted production by the 1980s to 50 million and for a time helped California produce more than a third of the oil the state used. Each well at Kern River produced only about ten barrels a day, but the field had 8,500 closely spaced wells. Production cost about sixteen dollars a barrel, including the costs of drilling and maintaining the steam-injection wells, then of generating the steam for them. That figure might decline if solar power was used to produce the steam. Bright-Source and Chevron were experimenting with solar power at nearby Coalinga. An analyst had advanced recovery in mind when he said, "Ironically, most of the oil we will discover is from oil we've already found." Experiments were being conducted with steam in other countries, including the Wafra Field, shared by Saudi Arabia and Kuwait.

Companies were also experimenting with tertiary recovery, in which carbon dioxide or carbon-dioxide-generating microbes were injected. The gas dissolved in the oil, made it less viscous, and caused it to expand and move toward production wells. The method had been a brilliant success in the Permian Basin of West Texas, near Midland-Odessa. After that field peaked in 1974 at 1.9 million barrels a day, production fell by 2008 to 1 million barrels. Now it was up to 2 million, which was more than the existing pipelines or local refineries could handle. A consultant called it a "major, major modern boom." A few years earlier, companies had paid no more than fifty cents to send a barrel of oil by pipe 500 miles to Cushing, Oklahoma. Now, with all the pipelines full, companies were being asked to pay ten or even twenty dollars a barrel, at which point it was cheaper to ship by truck.

Fracking for Gas

Then came fracking, soon the best known of all these advanced recovery methods. The idea of shattering tight sandstones had a long history, including some experiments with underground nuclear explosions in the 1960s. That approach went away, but the gas locked up in the rocks did not.

Some 27 trillion cubic feet of recoverable gas—a bit more than a year's consumption for the United States—was locked up in the very tight Barnett Shale, which underlay 5,000 square miles of fifteen Texas counties but was thickest under Fort Worth.

In the 1980s George Mitchell began experimenting with fracturing this rock with water, chemicals, and sand pumped underground at high pressure. This was not a delicate operation. About twenty-five railcars full of sand had to be injected with each fracking—and wells could be fracked repeatedly. Mitchell made the process work, however. In 2002 Devon Energy, an Oklahoma City company specializing in horizontal drilling, bought Mitchell out and combined its expertise with his. Barnett production soared from 300 million cubic feet in 2002 to 4 billion cubic feet. From 400 wells in 2004, the Barnett rose to over 10,000 in 2010. By then it was the most productive onshore gas field in the United States. In 2006 Devon completed more than a well a day there. The company's CEO said, "Devon has drilled 4,000 wells in the Barnett and is planning 4,000 more, at least. And we have not drilled a dry hole." Fort Worth homeowners were delighted with signing bonuses of $22,000 an acre, plus royalties of 25 percent of the value of the gas produced from their land. Chesapeake Energy paid Dallas–Fort Worth Airport a signing bonus of $185 million.

In 2000, 2 percent of America's gas came from fracked shale; by 2012 the figure was 40 percent. The CEO of Chesapeake Energy said, "It's the one thing we have seen in our adult lives that could take us away from imported oil." He explained the simple strategy that kept him close to his Oklahoma home. "We don't take foreign political risk," he said. "We don't take hurricane risk. We're not trying to pick fights with environmentalists." Instead, the company was casting an eye toward northwest Louisiana's Haynesville Shale, which had an estimated 75 trillion cubic feet of recoverable gas, three times the amount in the Barnett. Chesapeake spent $2.5 billion leasing over half a million Haynesville acres, where it anticipated drilling almost 7,000 wells. A person with intimate knowledge of the company said that its philosophy was simple: "More. More." The sheriff of Mansfield, Louisiana, said, "I'm going to get me one of these $70,000-a-month personal checks, and it's going to change my life."

Chesapeake and others also took shares of the even vaster Marcellus Shale, stretching from New York to West Virginia. A fifth of the population of Bradford County, Pennsylvania, smack in the Marcellus, sold leasing rights to Chesapeake for about $5,000 an acre. Times were good for truck dealers and motel and restaurant owners in Towanda, the county seat. They weren't so good for renters, who saw apartment rents jump in two years from $400 a month to $1,500.

It was an extraordinary turnabout for the gas industry, commonly said in the 1960s to be within a decade of exhaustion. BP's chief executive summarized the situation: "The United States is sitting on over 100 years of gas supply at the current rates of consumption." The head of the U.S. Energy Information Agency said, "This is a new era of thinking about market conditions, and opportunities created by these conditions, that you wouldn't in a million years have dreamed about."

What to do with the gas? An economist said, "The U.S. is now going to be the low-cost industrialized country for energy." Dow Chemical announced a multi-billion-dollar plant at Freeport, Texas, to make plastics. Shell, with an eye on the Marcellus Shale, proposed to replace an obsolete zinc plant at Monaca, downstream from Pittsburgh, with a factory making ethylene, a foundation chemical for the plastics industry. Orascom, an Egyptian company, proposed a billion-dollar fertilizer plant downstream from Burlington, Iowa. It would convert gas into ammonia—a source of nitrogen—and be the first new fertilizer plant in the United States in twenty years. Voestalpine, an Austrian steel producer, announced that it was planning to use American gas to process iron ore on the American East Coast and then ship that iron to Europe for final processing. Sasol of South Africa planned to invest $20 billion in a gas-processing plant on Lake Charles, Louisiana.

Shell announced its intention to build small LNG plants in Louisiana and Ontario to supply gas as fuel for ships and trucks. FedEx calculated that four-dollar diesel could be replaced by fifty cents worth of natural gas, and it began switching its truck fleet. The Union Pacific, which spent $3.6 billion on diesel fuel in 2012, began experimenting with gas-fired locomotives. So did the BNSF, the nation's largest user of diesel after the U.S. Navy.

Power companies, the biggest of all gas users, slowly shifted from coal. Exxon predicted that by 2025 gas would replace coal as the nation's chief source of energy for electrical generation.

It didn't take long before rising production pushed prices down. In 2006 gas sold at the wellhead for about six dollars per thousand cubic feet; by 2012 it was under three dollars. One exasperated producer said, "You're kind of giving your own stuff away, and it's stupid to do that." Exxon's boss said, "We are all losing our shirts today. We're making no money. It's all in the red." A banker said, "We just killed more meat than we could drag back to the cave and eat."

The predictable result was that the number of rigs drilling for gas in the United States was cut in half between 2011 and 2012. Late in 2012 only 429 were still at work, the fewest since 1999. Chesapeake, which had kept 44 rigs working in the Barnett in 2008, was down to 2 rigs four years later. In the Haynesville it was down from thirty-eight to two. Producers began pumping gas into depleted oil wells, where it could be stored until prices rose. Other industries began to hurt too. Coal prices fell sharply, and the head of General Electric warned that low gas prices meant that "it's just hard to justify nuclear, really hard." A Citigroup analyst put it this way: "In the geopolitics of energy, there are always winners and losers."

By early 2010 the bonuses on Barnett leases had fallen from $25,000 to $5,000 an acre. Royalty checks shrank as gas fell from over $15 per million BTUs late in 2005 to under $2.50 four years later. To the dismay of landowners who had signed leases on land not yet drilled, Chesapeake insisted on renegotiations to cut the number of wells it would eventually drill. On top of all these problems, some landowners found that production declined sharply after a couple of years, far more quickly than they had been led to believe. The head of Russia's Gazprom said that the shale boom in the United States was "a bubble that will soon burst."

Perhaps he was right, but there was far more gas in this shale than was economically recoverable today. In the case of the Barnett Shale, there was ten times as much. An engineer reminded skeptics that fracking technology would improve. "We are at the dawn of this new age," he said. Chesapeake's CEO was another optimist, even about low prices. "This sets up," he said, "I kind of think, the mother of all price recoveries." He himself sailed too close to the financial wind and was forced out of the company, which was so indebted that its new boss spent several years selling off properties. Some went to Norway's Statoil, whose American boss said of the Marcellus shale, "We're here for the long term, and the resource potential is very great."

The United States Becomes a Gas Exporter

Since the early 1970s the United States had imported liquified natural gas. Until fracking, the conventional wisdom was that it would import more and more LNG as the years went by. By 2014 the United States had a half-dozen LNG terminals on the Gulf Coast, three on the East Coast, and plans for dozens more.

Tankers full of explosively flammable material made people nervous. Anticipating crippling delays in the construction of onshore terminals, Exxon proposed tethering a floating storage vessel 20 miles off the New Jersey coast. (Looking around for a good name for the project, the company came up with BlueOcean Energy.) Australia's BHP Billiton and Woodside wanted to build LNG terminals at Malibu, while ConocoPhillips and Mitsubishi wanted to build at Long Beach. Sempra Energy had a better idea and actually built the Costa Azul plant, 15 miles north of Ensenada. The permitting process in Mexico was much, much simpler.

Four of the six Gulf Coast terminals were clustered near the Texas-Louisiana border, either on the Sabine River or on nearby Lake Charles. Then shale gas came and turned the tables. A Cheniere Energy executive said simply, "We underestimated the magnitude of shale gas." By 2010 the United States became the top natural gas producer worldwide, and late that year Cheniere used its import terminal to export a tanker full of American LNG. Cheniere began building an export terminal, with a first shipment scheduled in 2015. Buyers lined up from the UK, Spain, India, and Korea. The head of Cheniere said, "This is the beginning. It is the dawn of the global significance of North America as a gas exporter."

Japanese buyers, accustomed as they were to paying more than three times the American price for gas, were thrilled, and Mitsui and Mitsubishi joined Sempra in building an LNG-export terminal on Lake Charles. Sumitomo, it was said, hoped to begin importing LNG from Chesapeake Bay's Cove Point Terminal, which had opened in 1972 to import LNG from Algeria. By 2012 fifteen LNG export terminals awaited Department of Energy approval. The average cost of those terminals was $5 billion, though some were bigger. Exxon and Qatar Petroleum planned a $10 billion plant at Port Arthur.

Without federal approval, gas could be shipped only to countries with which the United States had a free-trade agreement. The lines were soon drawn. On one side were power companies and their residential customers. They were joined by manufacturers, including Dow Chemical, Alcoa, and the steel producer Nucor, which formed a coalition opposing exports. They were supported, if silently, by Australia. Chevron, Exxon, and Shell were involved there with the development of a huge offshore field called Gorgon, and they announced that the field's start-up date, planned for 2014, would be postponed because Asian customers were likely to buy LNG from the United States.

On the other side of the debate, gas producers lined up with overseas buyers. They "came from everywhere," in the words of one Department of Energy official. Free-trade agreements were suddenly popular, not only with foreign buyers of American LNG but with American businesses that saw new opportunities coming with free-trade agreements.

The Department of Energy finally concluded that the benefits of exporting LNG outweighed the costs. It estimated that by 2027 the United States would export 4 billion cubic feet of gas annually, or 6.6 percent of its production, and in 2013 the department approved export permits for Freeport LNG and another for Lake Charles Exports. Analysts estimated that ten export terminals would finally be built. Canada was entering the game, too. Under the name Pacific NorthWest LNG, Petronas of Malaysia was planning to export LNG from near Prince Rupert.

Fracking for Oil

It didn't take long before fracking technologies came to oil. Drillers had known for decades that there were several billion barrels of oil in the Eagle Ford Shale, which lies in a two-hundred-mile-long expanse southeast of San Antonio. Now the oil companies knew how to get it, and by 2014 the field was producing 1.5 million barrels daily. A retired pharmacist who owned about 600 acres said that ConocoPhillips had "been very, very super-good to me."

Chesapeake's CEO meanwhile called the oil-bearing Utica Shale the "biggest thing to hit Ohio since the plow." One landowner received a bonus check of $280,000 for the right to drill on her seventy acres. She said, "It doesn't seem real. We haven't planned much about what to do. The most important thing is I want to make sure my grandkids do well." The industry took another look at the Mississippi Lime, a formation straddling the Oklahoma-Kansas border. This wasn't shale, but carbonates held oil too, and they were easier and cheaper to drill than shale.

In the 1990s Shell, Gulf, and Texaco had all given up on the Williston Basin, which underlies the western part of North Dakota, as well as eastern Montana and southeastern Saskatchewan. Montana's state geologist later said, "I thought my job was going to be turning out the lights." Then a wildcatter discovered that the Bakken Shale, the lowest layer in the basin, was productive with fracking. Production by 2010 was 400,000 barrels daily. A state official said, "We'll probably get 150 new wells a year at this rate, and there are very, very few dry holes."

The sheriff of western North Dakota's McKenzie County said, "We don't have the quiet, tranquil county we had, but a lot of people are working." One county away, motel rooms in Williston ran $200 nightly for basic accommodation. Housing was so short that Kohlberg Kravis Roberts bought 160 acres in Williston and set out to build 800 apartments and homes for 4,000 people—this in a town of 25,000. The state's budget director said, "It makes the job a lot more fun." By 2012 the state overtook Alaska, where production was declining, to become the second-biggest producer in the country, though still far behind Texas. In 2014 the state had 10,000 wells, each producing a hundred barrels daily.

Pipelines could handle only half the state's production, but the BNSF had a line through North Dakota. ConocoPhillips bought 2,000 tank cars. Norway's Statoil, which in 2011 paid $4.4 billion for Brigham Exploration's North Dakota properties, leased a thousand more. In 2008 American railroads had carried fewer than 10,000 carloads of crude oil, but in 2012 they carried 200,000, or slightly over a tenth of all crude oil shipments. One terminal, the Bakken Oil Express, could load 200,000 barrels a day, or well over 2,000 tank cars. At the other end of the line, an old refinery in Bakersfield became an import terminal receiving 150,000 barrels daily. The railroads also carried fracking sand, about 200,000 carloads of it in 2013 for the Union Pacific alone. The BNSF, too, was in the sand business and even built a sand distribution hub south of San Antonio. Most of the sand came from Wisconsin and neighboring states, and along with the tank-car traffic, it helped counterbalance declining coal traffic.

By 2020 the United States might once again be the top hydrocarbon producer worldwide, and the talk in Texas was of the United States exporting oil as well as gas. The deputy director of Port Corpus Christi shook his head in amazement. "It's unbelievable," he said. "Imported crude was our mainstay cargo for decades." Net import requirements might fall so low that they could be met in their entirety by Canada and Mexico. The United States might not need so much even from Mexico. Between 2008 and 2014 imports from that country fell from 1.8 million barrels to half that, and Mexico began looking for buyers in both Europe and Asia.

Athabasca Tar Sands

Which raised the subject of a friendly northern neighbor. More than 90 percent of Canada's oil was buried in northern Alberta's oil or tar sands, and $100 billion was likely to be spent retrieving it between 2006 and 2016. By 2030 production might double again. An estimated 175 billion barrels of oil were recoverable even with current technology. That was enough to meet global demand for seven years.

About half the oil from the sands was mined with huge shovels filling huge trucks with 400 tons of oily grit, about the weight of a loaded Boeing 747. The yield was about 200 barrels of oil per truckload. The other half of oil-sands production came from steam-assisted gravity drainage, pioneered by Total. Two wells would be drilled, vertically but curving to horizontal. The upper one injected steam through perforations along its horizontal length, while the lower one extracted oil made liquid by the heat above. The steam was produced by burning natural gas, but if the producers got lucky, it could be produced as a by-product of refining the oil itself. "The steam goes down," people said, "money comes up." Some companies experimented with electrical heating of the sands and hoped that this would greatly boost recoverable reserves.

By 2006 eleven tar-sands projects were running and another twenty were under construction. They were mostly in American hands, chiefly Chevron, Exxon, and Devon. The scale of the projects was breathtaking, with Exxon's Kearl Project including an $11 billion processing plant that produced 170,000 barrels of oil daily—and that was only Kearl Phase 1. Sinopec pumped billions of dollars into a stake in Syncrude, PetroChina spent billions for a piece of Athabasca Oil, and CNOOC agreed to rescue OPTI Canada, a bankrupt producer, for billions more. One investment adviser said, "It's like you've got one door frame and the Three Stooges trying to get through at the same time." Why such a push? The boss of Suncor said, "You've got one of the biggest oil reserves in the world adjacent to the biggest market in the world—and the political climate is stable."

There was plenty of opposition to tar-sands development, not only from Al Gore but from Peter Lougheed, a longtime Conservative premier of Alberta. Closer to the ground than any environmental activist, one elder in an indigenous community said of the Athabasca River, "The river used to be blue. Now it's brown. Nobody can fish or drink from it. The air is bad. This has all happened so fast. It's terrible. We're surrounded by the mines." He might have added that the incidence of bile-duct cancer at Fort Chipewyan had been reported to be 500 times the Canadian average. That number was disputed, but now when villagers wanted to eat fish, they bought it frozen from a store. The chief of the Fort MacKay First Nations Council found jobs for his people in the industry. He said, "There is no other economic option. Hunting, trapping, fishing is gone."

None of these objections stopped development, and a former Canadian environment minister, Stéphane Dion, believed he knew why. "There is not a minister of the environment on earth," he said, "who will stop this oil from getting out of the sand. The money is too big." An environmental campaigner fighting the companies said, "The oil industry has more money than God." A consultant said, "It's mind-boggling that people think that crude won't get produced." So much was likely to get produced that a lot would likely be pipelined to the Gulf Coast and reexported from there. Federal laws prohibiting export of American crude oil didn't apply to the Canadian stuff, and a researcher predicted that "reexports are going to change the industry." Even if the United States had refused to take Alberta's oil, other buyers stood ready— and not just in Asia. In 2014 two shipments of Canadian oil arrived in Europe—the first ever. No distinction was made there between oil from a conventional field and oil from the tar sands.

LATIN AMERICA

Mexico

Petróleos Mexicanos, or Pemex, was Latin America's biggest company. It operated every oil well in the country, as well as every gas station. Its biggest field, an offshore giant called Cantarell, was named for Rudesind Cantarell, a fisherman who brought geologists to see an oil slick in 1971, Cantarell had only 208 wells spread over 70 square miles, yet for a short time it had been the second-most productive field in the world, after Saudi Arabia's Ghawar. For many years Cantarell produced about a million barrels of oil daily. Nitrogen injection increased oil production to a 2003 peak of about 2.3 million barrels daily, but production then slumped. By mid-2010 it was under 600,000.

Cantarell was in water about 200 feet deep, and Mexico had much more oil farther out. One consultant called its deep water "probably the largest untapped play that's out there." The problem was that it lay under water 3,000 feet deep, and Pemex didn't know how to get it. As a result, Pemex now found only one barrel of oil for every four it pumped.

Pemex might have turned to Exxon or others for help, but the Mexican constitution proudly declared all subsoil resources to be the inalienable right of the state. Polls showed a large majority of Mexicans liked it that way. Mexico denied foreign companies the right even to refine oil. The ironic result was that Mexico exported crude oil to the United States and then imported gasoline from a refinery at Deer Park, near Houston. Pemex owned it jointly with Shell.

In 2006 Pemex made a profit of $97 billion, which might have gone a long way toward an exploration and development program, but 79 of those billions went straight to Mexico's budget, which would otherwise have been deeply in deficit. Pemex was simultaneously starved for investment capital and prohibited from tapping the private market.

The head of Pemex's exploration department said, "You have to not underestimate Pemex." He had in mind the company's intention in 2012 of drilling in 9,000 feet of water. Still, at current rates of decline, the country would be a net oil importer by 2016. The CEO of Canada's Encana, for a time North America's biggest gas producer, had little doubt about which way things would go. He said, "We've given up on Mexico." He might have noted that oil production at Pemex had fallen from 3.4 million barrels per day in 2004 to 2.6 million in 2013. Over that same period Pemex grew from 138,000 to 160,000 employees.

The country's political elite began quietly considering the return of the private sector. An Exxon executive said, "We think that would be a win-win if ever there was one." The Mexican Congress in 2013 voted 354 to 123 to end Pemex's seventy-five-year monopoly, and the Mexican President signed the bill into law. Mexico, he said, could "achieve more, grow more, and do more through alliances with the private sector." A new chief executive at Pemex said, "We can't do it alone." It remained to be seen if Pemex could control its labor unions, quick to defend refineries with three times as many workers as comparable refineries in other countries.

Venezuela

Stepping out of a time warp, Hugo Chávez said, "All of the power to the Communal Councils, power to the people." It was only a hop, skip, and jump before Chávez said, "Capitalist Venezuela is entering its grave and socialist Venezuela is being born." By 2011, $30 billion of Petróleos de Venezuela's earnings that year of $35 billion was spent on social programs, prompting critics to call the Oil Ministry the Ministry of Poverty Alleviation.

The head of PDVSA welcomed the accusation. He said, "The PDVSA that neglected the people and indifferently watched the misery and poverty in the communities surrounding the company premises is over. Now the oil industry takes concrete actions to deepen the revolutionary distributions of the revenues among the people." Cameras recorded a woman in Barinas, Chávez's hometown, being given the keys to an apartment in a new building. "We've struggled for many years," she said, "but today the Bolivarian revolution has made my dreams come true."

Spending its earnings this way, Venezuela saw its oil production fall from 3.4 million barrels a day in 1999, when Chávez came to power, to 2.4 million ten years later. Production would have been lower still, had it not been for the huge reserves of tar-heavy crude in the Orinoco Belt, near Ciudad Bolívar.

The Orinoco Belt contained over a trillion barrels of oil, half of which was estimated in 2009 to be recoverable with current technology. Production had begun in 1998 at a project involving Total, whose chairman, thinking of the upgraders that processed the tarlike oil, explained, "New technology really changed the picture." By 2012 Venezuela's oil production had returned to 3 million barrels, with 1 million coming from the Orinoco Belt. That figure could double by 2020 but required an investment of $80 billion.

Total, ConocoPhillips, Exxon, Chevron, BP, and Statoil had already invested some $17 billion in exchange for which Venezuela had set taxes and royalties very low. With the fields in production and oil prices high, Venezuela not only raised taxes and royalties but demanded majority control of the fields, just as it had earlier done in its conventional oil fields west of Caracas. An oil-company executive commented, "It's naïve to expect stability in a developing country." Another, with a bit more edge, said, "You think Iraq is any better?"

Chevron, Total, BP, and Statoil accepted the new terms. ConocoPhillips and Exxon did not. The argument for accepting the terms, as one analyst put it, was that "when all the oil in the world has run out, Venezuela will be one of the last countries turning its taps off." The argument for refusing was that a contract was a contract. Exxon began seeking compensation in American courts.

Meanwhile, in 2008 Italy's Eni stepped in to replace ConocoPhillips and Exxon. It agreed to invest $4.5 billion in a joint venture in which PDVSA retained a 60 percent interest. The next year, the world's major companies were competing to drill in the Carabobo block, a $40 billion project. A consultant explained, "The Orinoco Belt is just too large to be ignored, with no geological risk but huge potential."

EURASIA

The North Sea

Production from Britain's side of the North Sea declined from a 1999 peak of 2.6 million barrels daily to 1.4 million eight years later. Britain used 1.7 million daily and was now a net importer.

Norway was in better shape. Its recoverable reserves were almost twice the UK's 2.8 billion barrels, and more was likely to be found. With Norway in mind, a staffer at the World Wildlife Fund said, "Finding more oil is the only political idea this country has. If you want more childcare, find more oil. If you want a new road, find more oil. That's politics in Norway." By 2012 the country's sovereign-wealth fund, the world's biggest, was sitting on $600 billion and growing at $50 billion annually. The fund's managers were frugal and spent only 3 percent of their assets annually. They owned 1 percent of all global equities but were forbidden by the Norwegian government from investing in Walmart and tobacco companies.

Russia

A Kremlin economic adviser said, "Natural resources should belong to the state . . . [and] any decision by foreign investors to acquire natural resources is expected to be discussed with the state." After all, Vladimir Putin had written a doctoral dissertation in which he recommended the creation of "financial-industrial corporations . . . able to compete on an equal basis with the West's transnational corporations." Putin was already seeing, in the words of one analyst, that energy was Russia's "key to being a great power." It was the key because Russia had little else to sell. Its entire economy was a tenth the size of the economy of the United States. Its per capita GDP was only about a third as large as that in the United States.

Enter Kremlin, Inc. As soon as Putin had the boss of private giant Yukos behind bars for tax evasion, that company was broken apart and sold to Rosneft, a state oil company. The state then increased its stake in Gazprom, the state-controlled natural-gas company. Gazprom in turn bought Sibneft for $13 billion from Roman Abramovich, who celebrated by buying, among other things, the Chelsea Football Club.

And so the Russian government came to control a fifth of the world's gas production and a third of Russia's oil production. It also controlled the pipelines, which gave it control over everything else. As a banker said, "If you have a gas project, you have to work a deal with Gazprom for access to the pipeline. Otherwise you will end up with a very bright gas flare."

Russian consumers paid about $40 for a thousand cubic meters of gas, but Europeans buying from Russia paid about $150, plus another

$100 in transport fees. Gazprom wanted to raise its domestic price, but how? Its first step—no doubt with Kremlin approval—was to make Ukraine, which was paying about $90, buy gas at the European price. Ukraine balked, so Russia turned off the gas. The two countries soon negotiated a compromise figure of $130, but Russia's tactics unsettled Europe and undermined Putin's broader intention of positioning Russia as a reliable supplier of energy.

In 2006 Russia unnerved Europe again, this time demanding that Belarus pay $200 per thousand cubic meters instead of its existing bargain-basement price of $50. The Belarus president told Russian journalists that Belarus would survive this price hike but that Russia would lose its "last ally." Gazprom's CEO didn't help when he walked into a Moscow meeting of European diplomats that year and said that any European plans to impede Gazprom's expansion into Europe "would not lead to good results." The not-so-subtle threat was that Moscow could ship energy east instead of west.

Russia's deputy prime minister defended his country's actions. "There is no energy imperialism," he said. "Oil and gas have a price. In the mid-1990s you taught us how to be a . . . market economy. We learnt our lesson." He switched to English to twist the knife a bit: "Now we hear criticism that 'you are acting wrongly—you are using energy prices for political aims.' [But] we're selling to everyone according to market prices." Exxon or Saudi Aramco couldn't have said it better.

Russia added new pipelines to serve its European customers. The $5 billion North European Gas Pipeline (NEGP, or Nord Stream) went offshore near St. Petersburg and came onshore in Germany. This added cost to the project and risk, because unexploded World War II munitions lay in the pipeline's underwater path, but it also saved the Russians the trouble of paying transit fees to the Poles and made it impossible for the Poles to shut the pipe down. "Sometimes we Poles are too naïve," one angry Polish politician said. "We believed too much in European solidarity."

With American gas production rising, however, the United States was importing less natural gas. Qatar needed new customers and found them in Europe. Russia, which had supplied a quarter of Europe's gas, saw its sales there fall 9 percent in 2012. A former Bulgarian finance minister said, "They can't bully us in the way they could before." His country negotiated a 20 percent price cut.

Back home, a Russian official in 2007 said that BP had to begin production from the Kovykta gas field in three months, despite the lack of accessible markets. The alternative? The official said, "The conditions can be changed only one way. You tear up the license agreement and the state sells it off at an auction now." Predictably, BP sold its interest in Kovykta to Gazprom for about $800 million, about as much as BP had already invested. BP's boss put on his brave face: "I consider this issue to be no more than one of those bumps in the road." With Gazprom in charge, there was at least a chance that gas from Kovykta, near Lake Baikal, could find its way to a pipeline to China or South Korea.

BP could dance even faster if it had to. Defunct Yukos owned about a tenth of Rosneft, which wanted to buy back those shares. Russian law required at least two bidders at an auction. BP placed one bid, slightly above the floor price, and then politely withdrew. One observer said, "It appears BP was trying to curry favor with the Kremlin and Rosneft by conferring legitimacy on the auction." Another said, "In Russia, these are the rules. If you have an opportunity to do a favor for one of the state companies you'd be foolish to pass it up."

Things got a lot worse for BP in 2008. It had been operating in a partnership with several Russian oligarchs. An observer said, "We go over a cliff at the end of July. This is the drop-dead time. The permits will expire and then it's game over. All the foreigners will be out of the company and the Russian shareholders win." Another observer said, "I've been here for five years and sometimes you forget. There have been a lot of improvements. But really you have to remember it's a jungle still." Sure enough, BP's boss in Russia had to leave because he could not get his residence visa renewed. A British board member described himself as "mystified" that the government "cannot see that these shareholders' actions are inimical to Russia's national interest."

The company managed to keep its half share of the operation but lost management control.

Undaunted, BP was back in 2011 to sign an agreement with Rosneft that gave the British company a share of the 35 billion barrels of oil that potentially lay under the South Kara Sea. BP's Russian partners objected that they were being ignored, and the new deal fell apart. BP shortly announced that it was willing to sell its stake in the partnership, only to have the partners say that the company was contractually prohibited from sharing financial details with any potential buyer. That meant there would be no buyers. A banker warned that BP "needs to be in Russia if it wants to remain a supermajor." A former executive at the company agreed and said that the country's reserves were so large that "you just have to be there." The head of BP Russia could only say, "We remain committed to Russia, and I'm optimistic we will have a future there. I just don't know yet what the future looks like."

Rosneft stepped in and, with the implicit support of the government, suggested that it might like to buy BP's share of the partnership. Now the Russian partners started to squirm. They did not want to partner with the Russian government, even if it was disguised as Rosneft, yet they were not eager to sell their own interest. On the contrary, as one executive said, "There is no way to get those guys to exit at the right price unless they've got a gun put to their heads." Guns were not hard to find, and in 2012 Rosneft expressed an interest in buying out the Russian partners. The choreography was stunning because Rosneft then expressed an interest in selling a fifth of itself back to BP, which, if all went well, would find itself once again firmly connected to Russia. The oligarchs finally got $27 billion for their half of the company, and BP got $14 billion plus a fifth of Rosneft. One observer cautioned, "It's not risk-free. This is Russia." Rosneft was now the world's biggest publicly traded oil producer, even if the Russian government owned 75 percent of it.

Over on the other side the country, Shell was having a nightmare at Sakhalin-2, Russia's first LNG project. Shell had a production-sharing agreement under which it divided its profits with Russia once the project's development costs had been reimbursed. Shell then announced that development costs had doubled to $20 billion, which pushed far into the future the date at which Shell would start paying the Russian government. Suddenly, Shell's pipeline permits were withdrawn on environmental grounds. An analyst said, "Everyone understands why this is going on." Back in London, a financial columnist said, "When it comes to rewriting history, the Kremlin is a past master." A few months later, Shell and its Japanese partners, Mitsui and Mitsubishi, agreed to sell control of the project to Gazprom for $7.45 billion. The Kremlin's concerns about the project's environmental impact vanished.

What choice did Shell have? An analyst summarized the situation: "Give me half of what is in your pocket, or I shoot you and kill you." One of Shell's contractors, however, said that Shell had acted stupidly. "Instead of accommodating, they come out with lawyers and try to prove their case. You can run a project in Russia and have a win-win deal—even a project of this size. But it takes engaging with these people, and Sakhalin Energy [Shell and its partners] hasn't been real good at it." One Sakhalin resident said, "The company did everything that was good for them and not good for us."

Exxon too was active on Sakhalin. Its Sakhalin-1 project had so far escaped reorganization, but Gazprom in 2007 attacked the company's plans to export LNG to China. The company insisted that it could sell the gas wherever it liked. A year later, the CEO of Exxon was characteristically blunt. Speaking in St. Petersburg, he said, "There is no confidence in the rule of law in Russia today."

A consultant said, "He has obviously decided he doesn't ever want to do any more business in Russia." Apparently the consultant underestimated Exxon, whose CEO said that Exxon's position of strength "never changes, and typically survives even when you have changes of government." The Russian budget was predicated on oil selling for $120 or more a barrel. With current production and oil at $80, Russia would quickly exhaust its rainy-day fund. Russia couldn't do much about prices, but with foreign help it could certainly step up production. And so the harsh words from Exxon were forgotten and in 2012 the Russian government approved an agreement between Exxon and Rosneft. Exxon would get a share of the oil and gas in Russia's Black and Kara Seas, while a Rosneft subsidiary would get a 30 percent stake in the development of the La Escalera Ranch near Fort Stockton, Texas. This was a project in which Exxon was using its most sophisticated exploration technology; it was also the first time a Russian company had taken a stake in an American energy project.

Gazprom meanwhile set out to develop Shtokman, a 4-trillion -cubic-feet gas field 300 miles offshore just east of Norway and in more than a thousand feet of water. In 2005 Gazprom narrowed its proposed partners to Statoil, Norsk Hydro, Total, Chevron, and ConocoPhillips. Development costs were estimated to be at least $15 billion. Gazprom planned to extract Shtokman's gas with a floating device that could be moved out of the way of icebergs. The gas would then be pumped 300 miles to a terminal at Teriberka, near Murmansk.

Work at Shtokman came to a halt in 2012, however. Work also stopped on the Bovanenkovo Field, whose reserves, on the Yamal Peninsula, were large enough to supply Europe for decades. The problem was that Russian gas was expensive. Worse, Russia demanded long-term contracts. European buyers found other suppliers.

China

The United States consumed twice as much oil as China, but China was now the world's biggest petroleum importer. China's biggest field— Daqing, or "Great Celebration"—had begun producing in 1959, and it was a big field, with 14 billion barrels of oil. It was also a declining field, with production falling from a million barrels daily in 1997 to about 100,000 in 2011. What to do?

PetroChina announced in 2007 that it had found 7 billion barrels of recoverable oil in shallow waters off the coast of Tianjin. That was the good news. The bad news was that the new field, called Jidong Nanpu, would yield about 200,000 barrels daily, which was just about the amount that China's imports increased annually.

That same year, PetroChina partnered with Chevron to develop a gas field in Kai County, 150 miles northeast of Chongqing. Almost a tenth of the gas in this 2-trillion-cubic-foot field was hydrogen sulfide, and a blowout in 2003 at a well called Luojia 16 had killed 243 people and injured 2,000. (Didn't read about this in the news? Nobody else did either.) The Chinese were counting on Chevron to show them how to handle the stuff safely.

Sinopec did a $2.5 billion deal with Devon Energy, and CNOOC invested $2 billion in Chesapeake's holdings in South Texas. The investments might be profitable, but perhaps their greatest value would be helping the Chinese learn how to extract shale gas back home. The shale in China was deep, geologically tricky, and not well connected to pipelines. The overlying ground, especially in shale-rich Sichuan, was densely populated. There was another problem. An expert said, "Technology is not the real issue. Neither is capital. The key is water.... The reserves estimates aren't realistic, because without water how can you develop them?" Still, Shell in 2013 won a contract to develop shale gas in Sichuan. It was the first company to do so, and its eagerness to get a foothold in China reflected the fact that Shell had been late investing in American shale gas.

China also kept an eye on the sea-lanes from the Middle East, which carried almost half of China's oil. To watch more closely, China began building a "string of pearls" around the Indian Ocean, including ports at Gwadar, in western Pakistan; Hambantota, on the south coast of Sri Lanka; and Kyaukpyu, on the northwest coast of Burma. Gwadar and Kyaukpyu had the special attraction for the Chinese of offering shortcuts from western and southern China to the Middle East. The distance from Kashgar to Gwadar, for example, was half the distance from Kashgar east to Shanghai.

India, which got two-thirds of its oil from the Middle East, felt encircled. This pleased the Pakistanis. Gwadar also gave Pakistan a new port hard for the Indian navy to attack. Then India lost to China in the competition to develop Burma's A-1 Block in the Shwe or "Golden" Field. Burma's generals, it seemed, wanted China's support in the UN Security Council. Pipes in due course brought gas from the Shwe Field to the mainland at Kyaukpyu, where an 800-kilometer pipeline to Kunming opened in 2013; an oil pipeline was expected to open the next year, and a road and rail line would follow. The volume of oil heading to China through the Strait of Malacca would likely decline by a third.

Hungry for more, China hoped for an oil pipeline from Siberia. The 2,550-mile East Siberia–Pacific Ocean pipeline already carried 1.5 million barrels daily and reduced Japan's Middle East imports by 15 percent. The pipeline was part of a broader pattern of cooperation between Russia and Japan, which included Toyota agreeing to build 50,000 Camrys annually at a new plant in St. Petersburg.

Was China shut out? Not a chance. One analyst described the competition as "like being tied to someone during a knife-fight." In 2010 China won a round with the opening of a branch on the same pipe. The branch ran south from Skovorodno to the most northerly point of the Chinese border and from there to Daqing, the old, declining oil center. The line would deliver 300,000 barrels daily. China would now, it seemed, also receive LNG by tanker from the Yamal Peninsula. The Russians knew, in any case, that they had better not play games with the Chinese the way they did with the Europeans. The West might worry about Russia turning off the gas; not so the Chinese, who saw a huge and mostly empty Siberia closer to Beijing than Moscow. In 2014 the Russians agreed to invest over $50 billion in a project that for 30 years would deliver to China 38 billion cubic meters of gas annually from fields near the north end of Lake Baikal.

Farther afield, China tried to buy control of Unocal, the old Union Oil Company of California. A firestorm of opposition arose from American politicians who said that no American oil company should be controlled by the Chinese government, even if that control was nominally in the hands of a private company. Rebuffed, China went out and bought PetroKazakhstan.

Kazakhstan

Thinking of the Chinese and the Americans in Kazakhstan, one observer said, "You've got two very large consumers competing over the same sandbox." Chevron had entered the sandbox in a consortium called Tengizchevroil, which spent $6 billion developing the Tengiz Field, close to the northeastern shore of the Caspian. Production rose very slowly, from 60,000 barrels daily in 1993 to over 500,000 in 2012.

Ultimately, Tengiz might produce a million barrels daily, but getting that oil to market was a challenge. In 2001 a 900-mile pipeline—the Caspian Pipeline Consortium—linked Tengiz to Novorossiysk, on the Black Sea. The Russians weren't happy that foreigners owned the CPC, the only foreign-owned pipeline in Russia. When Chevron proposed increasing the pipeline's capacity to about 1.3 million barrels a day, Russia said no. Looking for alternatives, Tengizchevroil and the Kazakh government spent over $500 million improving the rail system. Meanwhile, Chevron was deep in talks with the Kazakh government about a $609 million fine imposed for improperly handling the mountain of sulfur produced along with the oil at Tengiz.

Along came China in 2006 with the East-West Pipeline, originally carrying oil from wells drilled by PetroKazakhstan. The pipeline was subsequently extended west to the Caspian, where its owners hoped to capture some of the oil going into the CPC.

Both these pipelines could be kept busy carrying oil from slow-to-awaken Kashagan, a huge field 50 miles offshore in the northeast Caspian. With about 13 billion barrels of recoverable oil, Kashagan was the fifth-biggest pool in the world. Kashagan's oil was 12,000 feet under the floor of the Caspian, however, and it was dangerously laced with hydrogen sulfide. The Caspian annually piled mountains of shifting ice against obstacles such as oil wells. The consortium developing the field, originally led by Eni of Italy, decided that oil rigs could not survive there, so Eni built rock islands and surrounded them with protective reefs. It installed high-pressure pumps to reinject the poisonous gas and bought several high-speed boats with which to evacuate in case of a leak. All these things drove costs up, up, up to $136 billion for development and operating through 2040.

Not entirely humorously, Kashagan was sometimes referred to as "Cash-all-gone." An analyst said that the field had been "a nightmare for almost 10 years." Some $30 billion had been spent without any oil production, and the start-up date had slipped repeatedly, first from 2005 and then from 2010. The government of Kazakhstan had learned from watching Russia deal with Western oil companies, and the prime minister said, "We are very disappointed with the execution of this project. If the operator can't resolve these problems, then we don't exclude their possible replacement." No soft edges there, but the minister acknowledged that "without foreign investment and the sanctity of contract, Kazakhstan can't develop." The government finally settled for an additional payment of several billion dollars, along with an 8 percent increase in its stake in the project.

Work proceeded, but BP and Statoil eventually bailed out and Eni lost its lead role. ConocoPhillips sold its interest for about $5 billion. The Chinese bought it, but ConocoPhillips had no regrets. An executive said, "It feels good to be out of it." Production started in 2013 but, plagued by pipeline leaks, was stopped within a month.

Saudi Arabia

Saudi Aramco wanted to raise its production capacity from 12 to 17.5 million barrels daily by 2030. To do this, the company was experimenting with steam-assisted secondary recovery. It also tried waterflooding at Khurais, a field to the west of giant Ghawar. Where would the water for 125 injection wells come from? The Saudis invested billions to pipe in seawater. If the technology worked, the water would drive 1.2 million barrels of oil daily into the field's 300 production wells.

If the Saudis met their target, they would produce 15 percent of the oil exported globally. The oil minister emphasized that this investment showed his country's "responsibility toward the international community." He was really saying that Saudi Arabia had more to lose than anyone else from a decline in world demand for oil. Depending on the calculation method, the country's GDP was between $700 billion and $900 billion. Oil sales provided more than half that amount and over 90 percent of state revenues.

A few Saudis worried, as one prince wrote, that "rising North American shale gas production is an inevitable threat," but for the time being the more immediate question was how to invest a budget surplus that in 2011 ran to $80 billion.

An executive at Ma'aden, a state-controlled mining company, explained that Saudi Arabia would build at Ras az Zwar, on the coast north of Jubail, "the largest sulfuric acid plant in the world, the largest phosphoric plant and the largest ammonium plant." Then there was the King Abdullah Economic City, north of Jeddah. It would be the home of Saudi Aramco's $10 billion King Abdullah University of Science and Technology. For Saudi Arabia, KAUST was radical, even allowing women to drive on campus. This was big news in a country where women made up more than half the country's new college graduates but only 5 percent of the workforce. Women could go to law school, but they couldn't appear in court because the judges were men. At the nation's other universities women entered lecture halls through a door reserved for them and sat in a section screened off from male view.

Jobs were a problem for Saudi men, too. One said, "We spend our time on the streets. Saudi Arabia is rich but you need connections to get a job." He meant the kind of job he wanted. The government announced that it would issue 750,000 immigrant visas in 2007, more than twice the 350,000 issued two years earlier, yet Saudi unemployment ran about 12 percent—double that among the young.

Social pressures were building alongside economic ones. Tawfiq al Saif was a Saudi Shia who happened to be that rare bird, a Saudi author. He said, "My father wanted only freedom to practice his religion. I want religious freedom and political rights. And my son wants the kind of life he has lived as a student in Britain." Could he have it? An imam in Riyadh told a visiting American, "Your leaders want to bring your freedom to Islamic society. We don't want freedom. The difference between Muslims and the West is we are controlled by God's laws, which don't change for 1,400 years. Your laws change with your leaders." He added, "We are waiting for the time to attack. Youth feel happy when the Taliban takes a town or when a helicopter comes down, killing Americans in Iraq."

Iraq

In the 1970s Iraq produced 3.5 million barrels of oil daily. After the collapse of Saddam Hussein's government, production fell to 2.5 million. By 2012 production had recovered to over 3 million, and early in 2014 it at least momentarily reached a record high of 3.6 million. The government planned on 8 million by 2035, but there was a lot of work to do before that would happen.

Forty-one companies qualified in 2008 to bid on contracts to renovate eight major fields, including the country's giants, Kirkuk in the north and the North and South Rumaila in the south. Among the applicants were BP and Shell, which had both been part of the Iraqi consortium nationalized in 1973. For them, Iraq was familiar ground—BP had discovered Rumaila in 1953—which explained why BP offered to bring the field back into production for only $3.99 a barrel. Iraq's oil minister said he would pay no more than $2. As an analyst said, "The maximum service fee the Iraqis were willing to pay blew a lot of bids out of the water." BP accepted the deal, even with the requirement that the company invest $15 billion in the field.

Who would actually do the work? Once BP won the Rumaila contract, it promptly issued $500 million worth of subcontracts. One of the subcontractors was a partnership between Schlumberger and the Iraqi Drilling Company. Another was China's Daqing Oilfield Company. Production soared, with some wells producing 50,000 barrels daily. Security remained a problem, along with water shortages and a sluggish Iraqi bureaucracy.

In the north the Kurdistan Democratic Party signed an agreement with a private oil company, DNO of Norway, to drill for oil near Zakho. Baghdad announced that no company signing a deal with the Kurds would do business in the rest of Iraq and that those who already had contracts in the south would find payments delayed. Exxon decided that the lure of Kurdistan was greater than the potential of continuing in the south, and so it signed a contract with Kurdistan and put its stake in the West Qurna Field up for sale. Total and Gazprom followed. Kurdistan would likely build a pipeline west through Turkey and no longer be dependent on Iraqi ports. In the meantime, it began shipping oil through Turkish pipelines. Tankers were loaded at Ceyhan. Iraq threatened legal action again anyone buying the oil, and the tankers for a time hunkered down in international waters. Would a buyer be found? The answer of course was yes, possibly through intermediaries. The first buyer proved to be Israel.

Iran

Iran's oil production, over 6 million barrels daily in 1974, collapsed to 1.3 million in the early 1980s. Slowly it climbed back to almost 4 million in 2007 and then slipped back to 3. Like Mexico and Venezuela, Iran bled its oil profits, skimped on investment, and let its equipment age. A former National Iranian Oil Company official said simply, "The industry is in a crisis."

Other Iranians were more optimistic. The Chinese, after all, hoped to import natural gas from the huge South Pars Field, an extension of Qatar's North Dome. They also negotiated a half-interest in the 17-billion-barrel Yadavaran oil field. In 2005 an Iranian said, "U.S. sanctions [against Iran] will pale into insignificance once the China energy arrangement takes off." Cheerily, he continued, "The whole mood around here is to look thataway [eastward]."

A few years later, Iranian officials celebrated the completion of a gas pipeline to the Pakistan border. From there plans called for the pipeline's continuation to Karachi and Jaisalmer, India. Would it get built? One analyst said, "The Iranians have never really been able to do these deals. They have talked about all sorts of projects but never really been able to follow through." The pipeline put Pakistan at risk of American ire for violating the existing sanctions on Iran. Pakistan hoped to gain an exemption such as had already been given to Turkey and India. "Pakistan needs gas very badly," said its prime minister. "There is an acute shortage of gas in Pakistan, so we have to import gas from somewhere."

For fear of jeopardizing their business in the United States, Chinese banks declined to finance deals in Iran. Statoil, Total, and Shell all stayed away. Even Iran's own Revolutionary Guard Corps was scared off because its construction department, Khatam al-Anbiya, worried that company assets held abroad could be frozen. The EU in 2012 tightened the screws on Iran further by prohibiting the issuance of insurance policies on shipments of Iranian oil. The governments of China and Japan did a workaround, issuing sovereign insurance to their shipping companies, but Iran's exports still suffered. The Iranian government ordered maritime tracking devices turned off so tankers could sail unmonitored to customers willing to buy, but customers were still hard to find. The Iranians began using their fleet simply for storage.

Using most of its production for domestic consumption, Iran should have had low fuel prices. For many years in fact, Iran did have delightfully cheap gasoline, rationed at thirty-five to forty cents a gallon. Even with rationing, however, Iran had to import 40 percent of its gasoline. A dozen tankers arrived with gasoline monthly. Then, late in 2010, the fuel subsidy was cut. Gasoline prices tripled, and diesel prices rose over 800 percent. Exports fell from $110 billion in 2011 to $60 billion in 2013. The big question was whether the decline made Iran's leaders any more willing to yield in their quest for nuclear status.

Kuwait

A few oil-rich countries in the Middle East remained stable. Sometimes it seemed that the biggest problem for Kuwait was deciding what to do with the money piling up in the treasury. Ninety-six percent of Kuwaiti nationals of working age were already on the government payroll. That left private-sector jobs to foreigners. What would happen if oil prices came down? A Saudi economist warned, "The surge in religious extremism we witnessed in the past is a direct result of the lack of foresight by the government during oil booms. When prices dropped, they couldn't give the people the subsidies they expected. They were left with a youth population that was jobless. That translated into anger."

Kuwait's huge Burgan Field was sixty years old. Some 28 billion barrels had been extracted from it, and between 1 and 2 million barrels a day continued to flow. The Kuwait Oil Company was as secretive as Saudi Aramco but claimed that Burgan would continue producing at that rate for another thirty years. If that were true, there were only two problems. One was the price of oil, which had to stay high. The other was that a lot of the field equipment had been installed by Gulf and Anglo-Iranian Oil in the 1930s. It wouldn't last forever.

Qatar

Established as the world's biggest LNG exporter, Qatar's per capita income rivaled that of Luxembourg, long the world leader. What to do with the loot? The Qatar Investment Authority owned 18 percent of Sainsbury's, the supermarket company; 16 percent of Barclays Bank; and 12 percent of Volkswagen. It owned Harrods in London and Printemps in Paris. It had so much money that it didn't even use its own money to fund these investments; instead, bankers fell over themselves to lend it money almost interest-free. An observer said, "You won't even get a meeting with the Qataris unless you have a financing package to go with it."

Qatar wasn't Norway, however. A court sentenced poet Mohammed al-Ajami to life in prison for reading aloud a poem with the line, "We are all Tunisians in the face of the oppressing elite." On appeal, his sentence was reduced to fifteen years. Still, Qatar had a great deal of gas. Working with Exxon, the emirate pushed ahead on Qatargas 2, at $13 billion the world's biggest LNG plant. Tankers with a capacity of up to 265,000 cubic meters would transport the gas to Milford Haven, at the southwest corner of Wales, where 700,000 cubic meters of would flow hourly into the UK's National Transmission System.

Qatar decided to place a huge bet on a colorless, odorless, clean-burning diesel called gas-to-liquids fuel. There was nothing radically new about the technology. Instead, as an analyst explained, "The game-changer here has been the oil price." GTL cost about fourteen dollars a barrel to produce, and almost half of the gas entering the plant was used as fuel during the conversion process. Still, when the cost of oil exceeded thirty dollars a barrel, selling GTL became more profitable for Qatar than selling gas.

Qatar had partners on each of its two GTL projects. Sasol of South Africa was behind Oryx, and Shell was behind the other even bigger project, called Pearl, a $19 billion investment. At the run-up to its opening in 2011, Pearl employed 52,000 construction workers. On the assumption that prices would stay over thirty dollars, Chevron and Sasol bravely embarked on another GTL plant. Why brave? This project was at the Escravos Terminal, on the coast of Nigeria.

AFRICA

Singapore's Lee Kuan Yew once said, "Supposing we had oil and gas, do you think I could get the people to do this [work, save, and prosper]? No. If I had oil and gas, I'd have a different people, with different motivations and expectations." Many Middle Easterners, including King Idris of Libya and Sheikh Yamani, for over twenty years the Saudi oil minister, were credited with saying that they wished their countries had instead discovered water.

It was hard to find a better example of the resource curse than Equatorial Guinea, three-quarters of whose population lived on less than two dollars a day. Theodoro Obiang, the president's son, spent $315 million between 2004 and 2011. His shopping list included a Gulfstream jet, diamond-studded watches, five Rolls-Royces, and the glove Michael Jackson wore during his Bad tour. A former president of Ghana, whose offshore Jubilee Field was discovered in 2007, said, "For once, I am almost tempted to believe it when people say that oil finds are a curse." Contemplating Mozambique's huge reserves of offshore gas, the president of that country said, "Countries, when they have this sort of resource, instead of being a source of social harmony, it becomes a source of problems, social convulsions." A Ghanaian chief said, "We all have our fears about oil, because we have seen what happened in the Niger Delta."

Nigeria

Shell relied on Nigeria for 16 percent of its global production of 2 million barrels daily. Shell was more vulnerable than the other foreign companies working in the country because they tended to work offshore. Shell, on the other hand, had been in Nigeria for fifty years and a lot of its production came from the onshore Niger Delta, where the company had over a thousand wells and 4,000 miles of pipeline. It was easy to sabotage Shell, in other words, as well as kidnap its employees (about sixty were snatched in 2005). One analyst said, "I think it's worrying everyone. It's a substantial part of Shell's production." Another said, "The situation has sharply deteriorated in the Nigerian delta over the past few months. Where we are at the moment is unprecedented in terms of the level of unrest."

Early in 2006 Ijaw insurgents captured four oil workers and demanded $1.5 billion from Shell, along with the release of their jailed leaders. After nineteen days the militants released the four, while warning that the Movement for the Emancipation of the Niger Delta aimed to cut Nigeria's export capacity by a third. A lecturer at Nigeria's national war college said, "Hostage rescue capacity is just not there." In 2002 the premium for $5 million of kidnap insurance for Nigeria was $10,000. By 2007 it was $100,000.

When MEND in March 2006 released the last of a batch of hostages, it explained that it had done so to free up its fighters from guard duties. It warned that oil company "workers should not be deceived into a false sense of relief." A MEND e-mail in 2008 stated that the organization's "goal remains to paralyze 100 percent of Nigeria's oil export in one swipe." Residents were told "to avoid milling around army checkpoints and armored personnel carriers as they have become targets for attacks by explosive devices." The organization was armed with machine guns and rocket-propelled grenades sold by Nigerian soldiers.

Oil companies that felt safe in Nigeria because their operations were miles offshore got a shock in 2008 when MEND used speedboats to attack a huge floating production and storage vessel anchored 60 miles at sea. MEND said that it had "decided against smoking out the occupants by burning down the facility to avoid loss of life." The vessel, which handled 200,000 barrels a day, a tenth of Nigeria's output, was shut for three weeks.

But who was MEND? It didn't exist until late 2005, when a speedboat attacked a Shell offshore facility. The organization claimed credit through an e-mail from a Jomo Gbomo, whose Yahoo account was routed through South Africa and who admitted that his name was fictitious. Gbomo wrote, "We are not communists or even revolutionaries. Just a bunch of extremely bitter men." One British hostage, released after nineteen days, said, "The main demand was that all [foreigners] would have to leave the Niger Delta, and they had to have some sort of control over their resources."

MEND could push world oil prices up a dollar a barrel simply with an e-mail like one it sent in February 2006: "All pipelines, flow stations and crude loading platforms will be targeted for destruction." Early in 2007 a large part of Shell's Nigerian operations were still shut down, yet hundreds of thousands of barrels of Nigerian oil were exported illegally every day. Two foreign observers wrote, "This level of theft could not take place without official collusion at many levels, weaving an alarming web of corruption, violence and gangsterism."

Shell's executive vice president for Africa said, "There were 100 bunkering [pilfering] boats out there [at the Soku natural gas plant near Port Harcourt] at one point, stealing condensate." A MEND e-mail boasted, "We are like mosquitoes, and come out only at night and suck the blood from the oil majors." A Nigerian general estimated that he was fighting 2,000 to 3,000 gunmen and said, "That's my endgame. Arrest them, or if that's not possible kill them, or chase them out of Rivers State." Undaunted, MEND attacked the Atlas Cove Jetty in Lagos itself. Five dockworkers died.

The governor of Cross River State said, "There is complete, total breakdown of the social contract." In an effort to fix the problem, the oil companies began generating power and distributing it for free in the hope that this would calm communities and help create jobs processing palm oil and cassava. Free power might even reduce the practice of drying cassava by putting it near gas flares. Warning signs were posted at a flow station at Eriemu: "Danger!!! Entering of the flare area by unauthorized persons and tapioca drying at your own risk." Despite the sign, wooden racks were arranged in a circle around the flare, and strips of cassava were hung on it. A woman said, "We are aware that there may be some health implications."

The government announced its intention of dividing a tenth of its net oil and gas revenues among the communities atop the oil fields. It wasn't a lot—perhaps twenty dollars a year for each of the 28 million residents of the delta—and the plan assumed that the money wouldn't be stolen by the notoriously corrupt provincial governors or the Niger Delta Development Commission, one of whose heads was reported to have literally burned almost $5 million in cash as part of a virility ritual.

Russia arrived in 2008 with an offer from Gazprom to create a new joint venture, Nigaz, which would use Nigerian gas to fire new power plants and possibly fill a trans-Sahara pipeline to Europe. A Nigerian official said, "What Gazprom is proposing is mind-boggling. They're talking tough and saying the west has taken advantage of us in the last 50 years and they're offering us a better deal. . . . They are ready to beat the Chinese, the Indians, and the Americans."

The Chinese stepped forward through an agency called Sinosure, which was ready to guarantee $50 billion in private investments in a refinery in Kaduna, a railway from Lagos to Kano, and a hydro project in Mambilla. Nigeria's finance minister was ecstatic. "The possibilities are endless," he said. "Which other country has made that kind of money available?"

In exchange, of course, the Chinese wanted offshore oil blocks. Worried Shell officials met with Nigeria's president and told a parable about "us building the foundation, us building the house, us living in the house and others knocking on the door." The president "got it," a Shell official said. A new Nigerian government suspended the Chinese contract.

By 2012 kidnapping had decreased because of a remarkable amnesty offered, along with cash, to 26,000 militants. One of those militants was appointed head of Nigeria's maritime security agency. Another was paid $9 million annually to stop stealing fuel and instead use his 4,000-man force to protect pipelines. "I don't see anything wrong with it," he said. "How much money is involved in this interview," he asked a reporter before hanging up.

In 2011 alone over 4,000 deliberate pipeline punctures were recorded, and this didn't count theft from wellheads or from tampering with flow meters. The government estimated that 400,000 barrels a day were being stolen, either diverted to small, illegal refineries or sent by canoes to tankers waiting to carry it abroad. For the Nigerian military, a delta posting was considered a prize because, as the saying went, "You will never find a poor admiral." A businessman at the smuggling port of Abonnema said, "Every family has someone involved."

In 2013 Shell reported that the company was losing 60,000 barrels a day to theft. In April it decided to shut down the Nembe Creek Pipeline, where theft was especially rampant. Eni shut down its onshore operations because 60 percent of its production there was being stolen. ConocoPhillips sold its Nigerian holdings to Nigeria's biggest oil company, Oando, which paid $1.8 billion on the brave assumption that it could reduce theft. Still, thefts in 2013 were estimated at 150,000 barrels a day, with a loss to the government of a billion dollars monthly.

Angola

At independence in 1975 half a million Portuguese left Angola. Now, Portuguese were returning, not as rulers but as workers. One newcomer, looking at apartments priced at $12,000 to $15,000 a month, complained, "It has to be the highest rental market in the world." Local Chinese didn't have to worry about the cost of living. Their quarters were hidden behind an eleven-foot wall topped with eight strands of barbed wire. A Chinese contractor said, "My workers don't have a chance to go out. They just stay here. They have no energy to think about other things; they are too tired."

A reporter wrote that Angola was "a country that could really make it, and there are not a lot of countries in Africa that could say that." Would it make it? The minister of economic coordination told a skeptical reporter, "It doesn't work if you are OK and the people around have nothing to eat. You don't feel comfortable." Yet three-quarters of Luanda's 4.8 million people lived in slums, and Angola's president, José Eduardo dos Santos, was the richest man in the country. The head of a local human rights organization said, "The ruling elite is a parasite on the state," and Transparency International put Angola in its top ten for corruption, worldwide. The International Monetary Fund posted on its website a paper about Angola with the headline, "The Main Institution in the Country Is Corruption," but Angola complained, and the page was removed.

Both Chevron and Exxon had major investments in the country, and the United States had a spanking new embassy. Angola's state-owned oil company paid Atlas Air to fly the "Houston Express," three times weekly between Houston and Luanda. An opposition party member said, "The west legitimises this mockery of a democracy because of its own interests," but China too was interested in Angola, which was its top source of imported oil. China Southern ran direct flights between Luanda and Beijing.

5 Mining

COAL

The United States in 1990 relied on coal to produce over half the nation's electricity. By 2013, with natural gas abundant and cheap, coal was down to less than 40 percent. Southern Company, a major generator, as recently as 2008 used coal for 70 percent of its electricity. Four years later, it used coal for less than 35 percent. The Tennessee Valley Authority, which used coal for 80 percent of its electricity in 1970, was down in 2013 to 38 percent.

With natural gas under three dollars per million BTUs, electricity could be generated for two cents a kilowatt hour. That was half the price of coal-fired power, which is largely why coal prices fell 30 percent from 2011 to 2012. Consol, the biggest operator of underground mines, sold five of its West Virginia mines in 2013 and contemplated going into the gas-production business. One coal-company executive said, "The U.S. market for coal is going to be smaller going forward. It doesn't take a rocket scientist to figure it out. The question is, 'How much smaller could it get?'"

One pipeline executive said that the situation was, "without question, unprecedented." The manager for Oklahoma Gas & Electric said that its gas plants were "pushing coal out of the way and the customer is benefiting." GenOn, a power wholesaler, took the unprecedented step of declaring force majeure. The chief executive explained, "We have given *force majeure* because our coal piles are full. We just can't physically take it right now." The reason he couldn't take it, of course, was that he had shifted to gas for 39 percent of his fuel.

Although U.S. coal production was nearly flat, at a billion tons annually it was four times higher than it had been in 1900. Jobs were a different story. The number of coal miners in the United States peaked at about 700,000 in 1919. By 1994 the nation had fewer than 100,000 coal miners, and their numbers never again rose above that level.

Wyoming, meanwhile, hardly produced any coal in 1970, but by 1980 it was producing 100 million tons annually, and its production kept rising. One county alone, Campbell County, in 2012 produced over 354 million tons, all from eleven mines. That one county produced more coal than the 342 million tons produced by all 488 underground mines still struggling to stay open in the United States.

The nation's four biggest coal-mining companies—Peabody, Arch Coal, Alpine, and Cloud Peak—between them produced over half the country's coal, but none of them operated big mines east of the Mississippi. Instead, they ran mines like Campbell County's North Antelope Rochelle, a surface mine whose thousand or fewer workers used draglines and shovels to produce 111 million tons of coal in 2013, enough to supply electricity for 6 million American homes.

Kentucky's Harlan County, famous for labor strife in the 1930s, produced all of 7 million tons from its forty-five operating mines. A laid-off miner there said, "Obama's starving us out." You could see what he meant. Anticipating federal rules requiring carbon capture, Southern built a clean-coal generating station north of Meridian, Mississippi. The plant was designed to capture two-thirds of its carbon dioxide and pipe it to customers who wanted to inject it into oil fields, but the cost of the plant rose from a planned $2.9 billion to $4.7 billion even before construction was finished. "War on Coal" or not, Kemper had been built on the assumption that gas would sell between seven and twenty dollars per million BTUs. With gas well under five dollars, power companies were unlikely to prefer coal, no matter what environmental regulations the president imposed.

Coal exports rose to levels last seen twenty years earlier. The UK and the Netherlands were the leading importers, mostly because the other exporters were farther than the United States. The bad news was that Europe, like the United States, was shifting away from coal, so the export boom would be brief. There was hope for coking or metallurgical coal, which was used in steelmaking and in the United States was found almost entirely in Pennsylvania and West Virginia. Free of impurities, coking coal sold for three times the price of thermal coal, the kind used in power stations. The bad news was that fading demand from China pushed the price of coking coal down from $330 a ton to $110 a ton in 2014. There were many victims, including the Grand Cache mine in the Rockies west of Edmonton. Investors had paid $900 million for that mine in 2012. With their coal now worth $30 a ton less than it cost to mine, they sold the mine for exactly $2. Other Canadian mines, such as Peace River Coal, suspended operations. Worldwide, India was likely to replace China as the big buyer of coking coal, but Australia, conveniently nearby, was likely to be the dominant seller.

Until 2000 the United States and China had each produced about a billion tons of coal. Five years later, U.S. production had hardly changed, but coal production in China had doubled. By 2012 American production remained almost unchanged, but Chinese production had almost doubled again, to 3.8 billion tons. China consumed everything it produced and wanted more. It got it mostly from Australia and Indonesia. Australia for years had been the biggest supplier, but Indonesia was gaining fast because of Australia's strong dollar and high wages and taxes.

Trying to control the country's notoriously dirty and dangerous coal mines, the Chinese government in 2006 shut down about 8,000 of the 10,000 mines operating in Shanxi Province, sometimes called China's Wyoming. There was no decline in output. The survivors simply grew larger.

Ten power plants in Inner Mongolia had been built without central-government permission. The vice chairman of the National Development and Reform Commission said, "It is impossible for our central government to go everywhere to see, when the small power plants start building." That was hard to believe, but local governments had every reason not to help the central government: they were investors in both the mines and the power stations burning the coal from the mines. Miners and construction workers came from across China to work in Inner Mongolia. One remembered when his Hunan village got electricity in 1990. Now his house there had a TV, a washing machine, a refrigerator, and an air conditioner. He just wasn't there to enjoy them.

China's biggest coal producer was Shenhua, which sold about 170 million tons of coal in 2007, about two-thirds of the amount sold by Peabody. The company was planning to expand into Mongolia, Vietnam, and Australia. "We are very good at coal," the CEO said. Good enough that Shenhua and Peabody joined forces to build a power plant in the United States that would sequester the carbon dioxide it produced. The companies were doing the same thing at Tianjin with a plant they shared with Huaneng Power.

In 2011 Peabody entered a partnership with the government of Xinjiang. The goal was to develop a surface mine producing 50 million tons annually. The coal might be burned at a mine-mouth power plant. It might be converted to gas and pipelined east. It might be sent east by rail. Meanwhile, Shenhua in Inner Mongolia was building China's first coal-to-liquids plant.

And Europe? In the 1920s Britain had employed more than a million miners. When nationalized in 1947, the industry still had 718,000 workers at 958 mines. Almost fifty years later, a newspaper published a story that began: "British Coal announced today that it would close 31 of its remaining 50 mines and lay off 30,000 miners, nearly three-quarters of the industry's dwindling work force." The surviving nineteen mines had fewer than 13,000 miners. Power-plant operators in Britain were shifting from coal to natural gas and, within coal, away from expensive domestic coal, produced underground, to coal that was cheap, foreign, and surface mined. Still, coal wasn't quite dead in Britain. Yorkshire's Hatfield Colliery reopened in 2008. Was it a struggle finding workers? Not in the least: the boss said that his advertisements got a response "like an opening at Ikea."

The German industry traced the same curve. In the 1950s it employed 500,000 miners in a hundred underground mines centered in the Ruhr Valley. Five decades later, eight mines survived. Northwest of Essen, the Wolsum Mine at Voerde worked coal faces 2,500 feet underground. The only thing that kept the industry alive was the $200 billion in subsidies paid since the 1960s. Deutsche Steinkohle, the owner of all the surviving mines, earned $2.9 billion from the sale of coal in 2007 but received $3.3 billion in subsidies, or about $100,000 for each of the company's 32,000 employees. In 2007 the government announced that the subsidies would end in 2018. The last mines would then close. As part of the deal, no miner would be left unemployed. In practice, many by then would have retired on pension, which they were allowed to do at age forty-nine if they had worked underground for twenty-five years.

Germany's soft coal, or lignite, mines would continue operating. These were surface mines—and profitable. Many of the dozen power stations that Germany would build by 2020 would run on soft coal—a lot of it mined near Düsseldorf. Grevenbroich, a few miles away, called itself Germany's energy capital.

More coal miners lost their jobs in Ashibetsu, on the island of Hokkaido in Japan. With encouragement from the central government, the local townspeople tried to reinvent their town as a tourist attraction with simulated ethnic communities—Canadian, German, and so on. No luck. Nearby Yubari, another coal-mining town, set itself up as the History Village, but its population crashed from 120,000 in the 1960s to 12,000, of whom 40 percent were sixty-five or older. Thanks to all the encouragement they got from the central government to develop tourist facilities, the townspeople now carried a collective debt of $500 million, over $40,000 per person. The museum was for sale.

Oddly enough, the world's biggest coal-mining company, both by production and number of employees, was Coal India. India was also the number-three coal producer worldwide and had huge reserves. Yet India was unable to meet its coal needs, which was why a coal terminal was rising at Mundra on the Gujarat coast. Next to the terminal was a four-gigawatt coal-burning power station, bigger than anything in the United States. The problem was that Coal India was besieged by lawsuits, protests, and bureaucratic inefficiency. Cutting the knot, Gautam Adani, a Gujarati magnate, developed the Mundra terminal and bought an Indonesian coal mine and dry-bulk carrier to feed it. An observer said, "It's probably the fastest, most likely way to succeed approach in the current environment." India's coal imports were likely to double to 300 million tons annually by 2020.

IRON ORE

In 1900 the United States had been the world's top iron-ore producer, mining more than twice as much as the runners-up, Germany and the UK. U.S. production had continued to rise to a peak of a bit over 100 million tons in the early 1950s. Sixty years later, it was half that. For every ton of ore produced in the United States, Russia produced two, India produced five, Brazil produced seven, Australia produced eight, and China produced an astonishing twenty-six. Despite its enormous dominance as a producer, China was also the world's biggest importer, receiving 800 million tons of ore annually, or 60 percent of all seaborne shipments of iron ore. The imported ore was added to the 1,300 million tons produced domestically.

Seventy percent of the world's seaborne ore came from three companies, one in Brazil and two in Australia. Vale, the Brazilian company, produced almost a million tons of ore daily and intended to up its production 50 percent in the next few years. Its Brucutu Mine near Belo Horizonte produced 30 million tons of ore annually, more than half the ore produced by all the mines operating in the United States. Carajás, a Vale mine in the Amazonian state of Pará, was three times as large as Brucutu and was soon to be expanded from 100 million tons annually to almost 200 million. The mine, originally developed in the 1980s with a loan from the World Bank, was embedded in rain forest and connected by a proprietary railroad to the Atlantic port of São Luís. Vale had meanwhile paid $17 billion for control of Canada's Inco, formerly the International Nickel Company, which meant that the Brazilian company produced the key materials of stainless steel. Vale was additionally developing Goro Nickel, a $3.2 billion mine planned for New Caledonia, 900 miles northeast of Brisbane, Australia.

The two operators in Australia were BHP Billiton and Rio Tinto. BHP operated a huge mine at Mount Whaleback, near the town of Newman in the Hamersley Range of Western Australia. The mine began production in 1968, and its ore was 68 percent iron. Every hour, 14,000 tons of ore, broken up by crushers, went by train about 300 miles to Port Hedland, mostly for export to China. Annual production was 22 million tons but BHP produced an additional 20 million tons from nearby mines and was developing two mines 60 miles to the northwest. Each would produce over 40 million tons of ore annually.

Rio, less diversified than BHP, ran mines around Mount Tom Price, about 100 miles to the northwest of Mt. Whaleback. To keep costs down, Rio began experimenting with remote-controlled trucks, including Komatsu monsters with 3,500 horsepower engines. Rio claimed that it could operate its mines profitably even if ore prices fell to $50 a ton. At that level, the company claimed, many Chinese mines would close.

It cost seven or eight dollars to ship a ton of ore from Australia to China. From Brazil it cost twenty dollars. A Vale engineer said, "Logistics are always the challenge." One answer for Vale was to sell to Europe. Another was to build Valemax bulk carriers with a capacity of about 375,000 tons, the equivalent of 3,750 railcars. Thirty-five Valemax ships were built, twenty-five of them in China with funding from Chinese banks. The first ship uploaded 350,000 tons at Dalian in fifty-five hours, but the Transport Ministry blocked further shipments as hazardous. Vale was forced to unload in Malaysia or the Philippines and reload on smaller ships for the short hop to China. Curiously, another Valemax shipment was allowed in 2013 to unload at Lianyungang, in Jiangsu. Observers speculated that the ships would eventually be sold to Chinese buyers and would then, miraculously, be allowed to unload in China.

Across the Atlantic from the Vale mines, Guinea's Simandou iron deposit was described by one executive as "fabulous, unlike anything else in the world." It was no mystery; the two landmasses had once been joined. Simandou had originally been awarded to Rio Tinto in 1990. Eighteen years later, nothing had happened, and Rio was ordered to relinquish the north half of the deposit, which was awarded at no cost to Benny Steinmetz, an Israeli investor who put $160 million into developing the property. He then sold a 51 percent interest in it to Vale for $2.5 billion.

The transaction was judged the "best private mining deal of our generation," at least for Steinmetz. It was so good that suspicions arose. The government launched an investigation. To minimize risk to its remaining property, Rio in 2011 paid the government $700 million. One observer said, "I have absolutely no doubt that if they [Steinmetz and Vale] paid $1 billion, like Rio, then Vale would have no trouble." Instead, Vale set Simandou aside and concentrated its efforts closer to home. Alpha Condé, the president of Guinea, was philosophical: "Looking at the iron ore, the grade is world-class. The quality is world-class. Yet, in so many years, we haven't been able to benefit from any of these tremendous resources. How can we be so rich and yet so poor?"

Nippon Steel merged with Sumitomo in 2012 not simply to become the world's number-two steel producer but to negotiate lower ore prices. China meanwhile was determined to secure its own foreign mines. In 2006 it won the right to produce iron-ore tax free for twenty-five years from the Belinga Mine in Gabon. In return, the Chinese agreed to build a 300-mile railroad, power stations, and a deepwater port. The Chinese were also negotiating to buy the Iron Ore Company of Canada, now mostly owned by Rio Tinto.

American production limped along. In Minnesota's Mesabi Range, which for generations had been the most important iron-ore region of the United States, Cleveland-Cliffs managed United Taconite, the Northshore Mine, and Hibbing Taconite. United States Steel owned the nearby Minntac and Keetac Mines. Together, these two companies produced about 80 percent of the country's ore.

The most interesting American operation may have been the United Taconite Mine in Eveleth. This was the mine depicted in *North Country*, a 2005 film starring Charlize Theron. The mine was bankrupt and idled in 2003, when China's Laiwu Steel came by in partnership with

Cleveland-Cliffs, bought the mine, and reopened it. Cleveland-Cliffs took all the pellets from the mine but in exchange gave Laiwu Canadian pellets produced in Labrador and sent by rail to the Gulf of St. Lawrence. That way, Laiwu didn't have to ship pellets so far to a coast. A café operator in Eveleth said she liked hearing the trains running again. "It's comforting," she said, "knowing people are going back to work." Cleveland-Cliffs soon got into trouble in Canada, however, where in 2011 it paid $4.9 billion for the Bloom Lake Mine. Three years later the company wrote off $6 billion of that investment and decided to stick to its American mines. There, in Minnesota, there was another glimmer of hope around Hoyt Lakes, where investors were piling into companies interested in the extraction of nickel and copper from the very low grade but now economically recoverable ores of the Duluth Complex. The reserves were huge, though there was stout opposition from environmentalists worried about water pollution.

Meanwhile, Lakshmi Mittal, the steel magnate of magnates, was determined to double to 70 percent the fraction of his iron-ore requirements that came from his own mines. "Ensuring a reliable source of raw-material supply is more important than ever," he said. In 2005 Mittal won the right to a billion-ton ore deposit near Liberia's Mount Tokadeh, less than a hundred miles south of Simandou. He agreed to rebuild the railroad constructed in the 1950s by Lamco, the Liberian-American-Swedish company that had first tackled the ore in these mountains. (The old company town at Yekepa was sometimes called "Little New York.") He also agreed to rebuild the port at Buchanan and build a power plant.

Steel production, however, was paralyzed in 2008. Sales, which had been running at about a trillion dollars annually on output of 1.3 billions tons, took their biggest drop in sixty years. U.S. production fell that year from 98 to 58 million tons. Mittal halted work on the Liberia project and slowed work on another project, the Baffinland Iron Mine, 1,500 miles from the North Pole. The deposit there contained $450 billion worth of ore, but getting it into production would cost about $6 billion.

If the financial troubles of 2008 and 2009 were steel's short story, its epic novel was the rise of China. That country jumped from about 5 percent of world steel consumption in 1980 to 30 percent in 2005. In 2009 China's 568 million tons of steel almost equaled the 622 million tons made by the rest of the world. China that year made four times as much as Japan, the second-place producer. Two years later, China made more than six times as much.

Looking for a bargain, Shagang Steel went to California and took apart a Kaiser Steel mill at Fontana, east of LA. The mill had been built in 1979 at a cost of $287 million. It produced high-grade steel but never could compete successfully with Japanese and Korean producers. The mill was sold in 1983 to California Steel Industries for a knockdown $120 million. Shagang knocked the price down to only $15 million but then spent $400 million disassembling the mill, shipping the pieces to China, and putting them together again.

Shagang also went to Germany, where it bought a ThyssenKrupp mill at Horde, near Dortmund, and put it back in business at Jinfeng, near the mouth of the Yangtze. Before the decline of 2008, the company's boss said, "I needed a horse that would run fast and not eat much hay. When the next crash in world steel prices comes, and it will certainly come in the next few years, a lot of competitors who have bought expensive new equipment from abroad will go bust or be so weighed down by debt that they will not be able to move." Ironically, the old mill in Germany had supplied high-grade steel to Volkswagen, and so did the new mill, this time a vw in China. A pastor back in Horde said, "Our identity is lost. And that is the most important thing that can be taken away from somebody."

Mittal Again

The Chinese industry was fragmented among 800 producers of whom the largest, Shanghai Baosteel, produced less than 5 percent of the country's total. In contrast, Korea's largest producer, POSCO, produced

60 percent of Korea's steel. The biggest producer of steel worldwide, however, was neither Chinese nor Korean but British-based Arcelor-Mittal. In 2006 it produced 117 million tons of steel, more than the combined production of Nippon Steel, JFE Steel (also Japanese), and POSCO, its three closest competitors. By 2012 Lakshmi Mittal had 112 plants in twenty countries.

Lakshmi Mittal began his ascent in Indonesia. He then bought a plant in Trinidad and others in Mexico, Canada, Kazakhstan, and Poland. In the United States Mittal bought International Steel Group, a group of companies including the old Bethlehem Steel mills at Indiana's Burns Harbor and Maryland's Sparrows Point. Antitrust officials forced Mittal to sell the Sparrows Point mill, and he did, to a Russian company, Severstal, which was launching its own North American invasion.

In a 2005 auction, Mittal bought Ukraine's huge Kryvorizhstal mill for $4.8 billion. The losing bidder was a consortium including Belgian-French Arcelor, then (briefly) the world's biggest steel producer. The next year, Mittal set out to acquire Arcelor. He wanted it for a special reason: Arcelor's Sidmar mill in Ghent was super-efficient, "one of the best mills in the world," according to a consultant. Mittal said he hoped that it would teach his other mills to improve. He wasn't kidding. Once he had acquired Arcelor, he sent a hundred Burns Harbor engineers and managers across the Atlantic and said, "Do as the Belgians do." Between 2004 and 2012 productivity at Burns Harbor doubled to 900 tons of steel per worker annually. Production rose from 4.2 million to 5.1 million tons, with fifty 300-ton "heats" daily.

Getting Arcelor had been a battle. French politicians had sprung to its defense, with one calling the proposal "totally absurd." After all, he said, "the laws of a modern, liberal economy are not those of a jungle." A former Mittal employee explained, "This is the biggest battle Lakshmi has faced but he won't be put off." An observer said simply, "You can't say no to that man." An Indian industrialist added, "If you look at his ambition and persistence, it blows your mind." The head of the French Senate's Finance Committee was fatalistic. "It is time," he said, "that we, the French, acknowledge what globalization of the economy is about."

Despite management's determination to resist the takeover, Arcelor's shareholders liked Mittal's offer. A desperate effort to merge instead with Severstal failed. Looking forward after the takeover, a Mittal employee said, "What we can bring is management know-how in commercial areas. Mr. Mittal knows the world market as no one else."

Management know-how included bunching the American mills to run as a unit, buying supplies in bulk, and prohibiting competition among the plants. That was Mittal's softer side. His harder side included asking his 12,000 workers in the United States to accept a 36 percent pay cut. He was not prepared to continue paying them an average wage-and-benefit package of $170,000 annually.

Mittal made half his steel in Europe, but European steel consumption was slowing, probably permanently. Mittal ordered nine of his thirty-four European blast furnaces idled or permanently closed. In 2012 he proposed to permanently close two already idled blast furnaces at Florange, on the Moselle just south of Luxembourg. A newly elected French government threatened to nationalize Mittal's operation, then backed off after Mittal reassigned the workers to process high-strength steel for the auto industry. Still, between 2006 and 2012 Mittal managed to cut his European workforce by 30 percent to 130,000.

Mittal struggled to gain control of a mill in China. He bought a majority of the shares in China Oriental, only to be forced by the government to reduce his holdings to about 30 percent. Without success, he tried to convince the Chinese government that allowing him to own a Chinese mill would help improve efficiency across the rest of the industry. In 2008 Mittal tried the back door and announced that he would spend $5 billion expanding production from the Kazakhstan plant he had bought early in his career. The mill would produce steel primarily for export to China. In 2014 Mittal finally got his way with the opening of a joint venture between Mittal and Hunan Iron and Steel. The plant, at Loudi, 70 miles southwest of Changsha, would make high-grade automotive steel.

"I have not stopped making history," Mittal said. "I love steel. There are changes in the economic environment, but steel is important and it will always come back." Mittal hoped along the way to invest $20 billion in two mills and associated coal and iron-ore mines in India. The logic of investing there was simple. Americans and Europeans annually used over 800 pounds of steel per capita. The comparable figure for booming China was about 500 pounds. For India, it was about seventy. The head of India's Tata Steel saw the same potential and said, "The opportunities are huge." His own company planned on increasing production from 5 million tons in 2005 to at least 20 million in 2020.

Consolidation Pro and Con

Some people argued that there was plenty of room for more consolidation in the steel industry. After all, ArcelorMittal made just 11 percent of the world's steel, and the five biggest producers together made only 20 percent. Apparently in agreement, India's Tata in 2006 spent $12.2 billion on Corus, an Anglo-Dutch company that made three times as much steel as Tata but was much less profitable. Tata had its own iron-ore and coal reserves—this was probably its major advantage as a global competitor—and it planned to ship semifinished steel to Europe for final processing into high-strength steel for car bodies.

Other experts weren't so sure about the value of consolidation. The chief executive of POSCO said that he didn't see "any obvious synergy effects that would result from a merger between us and any other large steelmaker." The head of United States Steel, which by 2013 ranked thirteenth globally, agreed. He said that he wasn't interested in expansion "purely to add to the number of tons we produce." He went on to say, "In my view the steel industry still adds up to more of a regional business than a global business." His successor was ready to consider a radically reduced future, including one in which the company abandoned its heroic steel mills in favor of minimills that recycled scrap.

United States Steel, in short, wouldn't seek to invest in China. The company would invest, however, in its already big Slovakian operations. In 2007 it also paid over a billion dollars to buy Canada's last domestically owned steel company, Stelco. The prize was Stelco's Lake Erie Works, at the time the most efficient integrated mill on the continent. Much like Tata shipping Indian steel to Europe for further processing, United States Steel would ship Canadian slabs to American plants for upgrading into steel for cars and appliances. That was the plan, at least. Seven years later, and after continuing losses, U.S. Steel Canada filed for bankruptcy and announced that it hoped to restructure.

Missteps by Others

Severstal—its name meant "northern steel"—had been created from the wreckage of a mill built in the 1950s at Stalin's command. Not content with Russia, Severstal came to the United States in 2004 to attend a bankruptcy auction. For $285 million the company bought Henry Ford's River Rouge steel plant in Dearborn. The sign now said Severstal North America. The next year, Severstal announced plans for a mill in Columbus, Mississippi. Hyundai and Kia were nearby. So were Honda and Mercedes. Severstal intended to save a hundred dollars in shipping cost for every ton of steel it sold to the fourteen automotive plants within a 250-mile radius of the plant.

A couple of years later, at the top of the market, Severstal bought three other plants, including the old Bethlehem mill at Sparrows Point, the one that Lakshmi Mittal had been forced to sell. Sparrows Point, at the entrance to Baltimore Harbor, had once been the world's biggest steel mill. It had made girders for the Golden Gate Bridge and cables for the George Washington Bridge; it had operated ten blast furnaces and employed 32,000 men. Still, the timing of the Russian purchase was bad, and Severstal, which paid $850 million for the plant, sold it within three years for $225 million. Within a year RG Steel, the new owner, went bankrupt, blaming cheap imports. By 2013 the plant was closed, though it might reopen. In 2014 Severstal beat a full retreat, deciding to concentrate its efforts back home in Russia. It sold the Rouge plant at a loss.

The Russians weren't alone in making mistakes. Germany's ThyssenKrupp in 2010 opened perhaps the most advanced steel mill in the United States. It was the Calvert mill, near Mobile, and it annually processed over 3 million tons of steel slabs shipped from a company mill in Brazil. The market was weak, however, and competition stiff. It cost twenty dollars a ton to ship the slabs from Brazil and another fifty dollars a ton to ship the mill's finished steel to Michigan. There were customers nearer than that, but ThyssenKrupp apparently couldn't find them. After having lost $11 billion, the company announced in 2012 that the two mills were for sale for about $4 billion. One potential buyer said that the mill produced a "wonderful, world-class product, but unfortunately, the freight cost is insurmountable." Mittal disagreed and in partnership with Sumitomo bought the Calvert mill for $1.5 billion. ThyssenKrupp was stuck with the Brazilian mill, although Mittal agreed to source raw steel from it for six years. Mittal now controlled 40 percent of the U.S. market for automotive steel.

ALUMINUM

Primary production of aluminum worldwide ran a bit over 30 million tons annually, almost trivial in comparison to the 1.5 billion tons of crude steel. Still, aluminum fought for a place at the table. The industry fretted over the rise of carbon fiber in airplanes but had won the battle of beverage cans and was elbowing into the automotive industry.

This was hard to do because aluminum was twice or three times as expensive as steel and steelmakers were now making high-strength steel that tended to offset aluminum's weight advantage. Still, Ford in 2014 began making its F-150 series trucks with aluminum bodies that cut the weight of a 5,000-pound truck by 700 pounds. The cost of the materials in the truck rose about $1,500, but fuel economy rose about 7 percent. Paying Ford the ultimate compliment, General Motors began signing contracts for the aluminum it would need to build its own aluminum truck bodies, starting with the 2018 model. Alcoa, which had lost over $2 billion in 2013, now invested almost $600 million in mills in Iowa and Tennessee to produce rolls of aluminum sheet for the auto industry.

For many years Alcoa—its Pittsburgh headquarters rising across the Allegheny River from the headquarters of United States Steel—had been the world's biggest aluminum producer. It was so big that even when it was broken into two pieces, those pieces—Alcoa and Alcan of Montreal—remained the world's two biggest aluminum producers, challenged only by Norsk Hydro.

Unlike United States Steel, which remained anchored in North America, Alcoa reached much farther afield, both for the bauxite that was the raw stuff of aluminum and also for the cheap power needed in abundance to process it. The two countries with the largest reserves of bauxite were tiny Guinea, with 8.6 billion metric dry tons, and big Australia, with 7.9 billion. Between them they had more than half the world total of 32 billion tons. It was a long way down to the next-in-line countries, Brazil and Jamaica, each with reserves of 2.5 billion tons. The United States came in at thirteenth place, with 40 million.

On the production side the rankings were different. Towering over everyone else, Australia produced 70 million tons of bauxite in 2010. That was a third of the world total and almost twice as much as the number-two producer, China. All of Australia's bauxite came from only five mines. The biggest was Alcoa's Huntly Mine in the Darling Range, east of Perth.

Alcoa fell off its top-of-the-world perch when Russian newcomer Rusal merged in 2006 with Sual, another Russian company. Rusal had a twenty-five-year supply contract with Guinea's Compagnie de Bauxite de Kindia. It also had huge hydroelectric plants at Bratsk, Krasnoyarsk, and Sayanogorsk—all on branches of Siberia's Yenesei River—and it had the two biggest smelters in the world, at Bratsk and Krasnoyarsk. Sual had two bauxite mines in the North Urals. For an industry that gobbled electricity—as a rule of thumb, 25–40 percent of the cost of finished aluminum came from buying the electricity to make it—United Company Rusal was a marriage made in heaven. Until low prices put plans on hold, Rusal planned big new smelters at Sayanogorsk, Taishet, and Boguchansk.

Good-bye to the world of 1980, when the United States and Western Europe produced half the world's aluminum. They were already down to less than a quarter. South Africa was another loser. The problem was Eskom, the state-owned power utility, which for years sold power at dirt-cheap rates to BHP Billiton, which had two smelters in South Africa and a third in Mozambique, which got its power from South Africa. Eskom wanted to escape from its industrial power-supply contracts, mainly because in post-apartheid South Africa the number of Eskom's customers had almost quadrupled, from 1.2 million to 4 million. The country intended to double its generating capacity of about 40 gigawatts, but that wouldn't happen until 2025. In the meantime, South Africa generated as much power as Illinois but had four times as many people. In 2008 Rio Tinto scrapped its plans to build a major smelter at Port Elizabeth. (The comparison with Illinois made South Africa look bad, but Nigeria's generating capacity was equal to Montana's, and the Democratic Republic of the Congo's equalled Hawaii's.)

Power costs were forcing Alcoa, too, to rethink its operations. There was still money to be made rolling and recycling the metal in the United States, but not in producing it. The company even closed its smelter at Alcoa, Tennessee, where it had been making aluminum since 1913 with hydropower from the Little Tennessee River. The company blamed the Tennessee Valley Authority, whose price for industrial power rose 78 percent between 2001 and 2011. Alcoa's biggest smelter, in Warrick, Indiana, relied on power produced in company-owned power plants burning coal from nearby, company-owned mines, but Alcoa weighed closing smaller smelters in Intalco and Wenatchee, which both relied on power from the Bonneville Power Administration.

Meanwhile, Alcoa moved ahead with a huge new mine at Juruti, upstream from Santarém on the Amazon. The company hoped here to produce about a tenth of all the bauxite mined globally. The ore would be barged down the Amazon and sent about 500 miles east along the coast to São Luís, the same place to which iron ore went by rail from Carajás. Alcoa and BHP Billiton had a joint venture at São Luís called Alumar, which both refined alumina and smelted aluminum. The company also had new smelters in Iceland, Trinidad, Brunei, and China.

In the same search for cheap electricity, Norsk Hydro was a partner in Qatalum, whose smelter ran on electricity from Qatar's immense reserves of natural gas. Norsk would source its bauxite from Brazil, where it bought Vale's huge Paragominas Mine, about 250 miles from São Luís.

Who else had cheap power for sale? The Bakun Dam in Malaysia's Sarawak State generated 2.4 gigawatts. For a long time nobody knew where the power would go, but Rio Tinto announced in 2007 its plan to build the company's biggest smelter and run it on Bakun power. BHP Billiton, China's State Grid, and Alcoa had said they, too, were interested in Bakun power, but none had the political clout to make it happen. Rio Tinto had already offered 40 percent of the smelter to a construction company whose major shareholders included Sarawak's chief minister.

In the midst of this game of musical chairs, it was easy to forget that China had become the world's leading aluminum maker. In 1996 it had produced less than half as much as the United States. Since then, it had jumped from 1.5 to 9.3 million tons, while American production had declined from 3.6 to 2.3 million. The Chinese government wasn't entirely happy with the aluminum boom because aluminum production used 6 percent of all China's electricity. Better to import the metal, which is why Brazil was building a big power station at Belo Monte on the Xingu. The power would go to Chinese-Brazilian alumina plants being built near Belém. Chinese companies were involved also with a nearby steel mill using iron ore from Carajás.

GOLD

Unlike iron and aluminum, gold was mostly a fetish. Still, its production generated all the social and environmental problems that came with mining of the serious metals, and gold by its allure generated lots of publicity, mostly bad.

As late as 1970 South Africa produced a thousand metric tons of gold, or 80 percent of the world's supply. By 2013 South African production was down to 180 tons, which, with rising production from other countries, left South Africa producing less than 1 percent of the world's supply. As late as 1996, 340,000 men were working in South Africa's gold mines. Ten years later, there were only 137,000.

The country continued to hold some impressive records. South Africa's biggest gold company, AngloGold Ashanti, was working 13,000 feet underground at the Mponeng Mine. A competitor called Goldfield operated 11,000 feet underground at its Driefontein Mine. In comparison, the deepest American mine was the Homestake Mine in South Dakota. Before it closed in 2002, it had been operating slightly over 8,000 feet underground. AngloGold now looked, however, not to South Africa for its future but to the Obuasi and Ahafo open-pit mines of Ghana. With them in mind, AngloGold merged with Ashanti Gold in 2004 and became AngloGold Ashanti.

The country producing the most gold now was China, closely followed by Australia, South Africa, and the United States. The top gold-mining companies worldwide were Barrick and Newmont, both Canadian companies with major operations in Nevada. In 1994 Barrick's Nevada mines had been patented, or deeded to the company by the federal government, for a total of $9,764—quite a bargain for 1,949 acres holding 30 million ounces of gold. Interior Secretary Bruce Babbitt, hemmed in by federal law, called it "the biggest gold heist since the days of Butch Cassidy."

So how were things at the company's huge Goldstrike Mine in Nevada? The pit would eventually be abandoned and flooded. No longer trapped underground, the water would evaporate in the desert sun. Natural groundwater feed to the Humboldt River would be reduced if not eliminated. A former Interior Department lawyer said, "Nevada is being written off as a sacrifice area for gold." Still, late in 2008, when jobs were disappearing almost everywhere else, they were on offer at Elko, the town at the center of Nevada's gold.

The problems at Freeport-McMoRan's Grasberg Mine in Papua, or western New Guinea, were more serious. Jane Perlez of the *New York Times* was unable to get so much as a simple tour of this gold and copper giant, but she managed to document a web of corruption, including $20 million in payoffs, largely to the Indonesian military. The mine produced 700,000 tons of tailings every day. According to a company consultant, those tailings had left 90 square miles of wetlands "unsuitable for aquatic life." The nearby town of Timika had grown, Perlez wrote, from a village to a city of 100,000 people "in a Wild West atmosphere of too much alcohol, shootouts between soldiers and the police, AIDS and prostitution, protected by the military." The mine had thirty-five years to go.

A movie producer might try telling the Grasberg Mine's story by beginning with two American teachers who had been working there until they were killed in 2002. Four years later, a dozen men were detained in connection with the murders. The men, from the Free Papua Organization, were lured by the FBI to a meeting to discuss going to America to present their grievances. Their attorney said that the men were being sacrificed by the Indonesian government in the name of better relations with the United States.

In 2006 the mine was briefly closed after hundreds of men blocked its entrance in a protest against Freeport-McMoRan's attempt to evict them. One of the men, who like the others survived by panning in tailings, said, "To us, you take, take, take and never give back. We don't see any benefits coming back to our island.... That's why we are out there calling for Freeport to be closed." It didn't help that Freeport's chairman, Jim Bob Moffett, personally netted $59 million in 2005. Moffett called it an "apples and oranges comparison." He said, "If you look at the support we've provided for the Papuan community, it's far beyond what would be expected of a mining company in any situation." He might have added that in 1970 American CEOs were paid twenty-eight times more than their average workers; by 2006 the ratio was 369:1.

Perlez also went after Newmont's Yanacocha gold mine in Peru, which the company took over in 2000 after it had driven off French competitors. The mine operated tax and royalty free, a beneficiary of a desperate Peruvian government in the 1990s, and though the mine had to pulverize thirty tons of rock to get a single ounce of gold, it was very profitable. It was also environmentally heavy-handed. A com-

pany executive resigned after writing that the company had "eliminated many environmental safeguards that were in the construction
and environmental management plans."

BIG BOOTS

A Rio Tinto executive said, "The mining industry is judged by its worst
performers and there are some real cowboys out there." Perhaps he
had Robert Friedland in mind. "Toxic Bob" had been the promoter of
Colorado's Summitville gold mine, which was run by modestly named
Galactic Resources. After it had dumped 6 million tons of cyanide-
laced waste in a convenient canyon, Galactic declared bankruptcy and
left the EPA to put the waste back in the hole it came from and to do
it before the cyanide entered the Rio Grande.

Friedland, a billionaire, changed horses and began developing Ivanhoe Mines. That company was busy at Mongolia's Oyu Tolgoi, where
Friedland hoped to develop a gold and copper deposit worth $300
billion and located next door to the world's biggest market. Seeking
cover, he drew in Rio Tinto as a partner and hired an executive from
Freeport-McMoRan as Ivanhoe's CEO. Rio Tinto gradually increased
its share in the project to over 50 percent; the name Ivanhoe was
changed to Turquoise Hill, the translation of Oyu Tolgoi. In the meantime Friedland had already invested in, and then quit, a copper project in toxic Burma.

The Chinese, too, had a terrible reputation. An official at a Zambian
copper mine admitted that they "must learn something new when
we are operating a company in a foreign country, to meet the cultural
gap." Would they? A South African who knew something about British rule said, "The Chinese are far more ruthless than the Brits ever
were." A Zimbabwean engineer said, "That's how they run things at
home, after all—and on top of that, they despise blacks." A Zambian
politician said of the Chinese, "Their interest is exploiting us, just like
everyone who came before. They have simply come to take the place of
the West as the new colonizers of Africa." The head of Human Rights
Watch's Africa division said, "Wherever there are resources the Chi-

nese are going to go there. They see no evil. They hear no evil. That's very bad for Africans."

A government minister in Zambia took a tour of the Chinese-owned Collum coal mine and came out to weep on national television that the mine's Chinese bosses treated their workers like animals. One of those workers said, "We are seen as nonentities. The mine management is just concerned about profit, not human life." A reporter came by in 2010 and was told by one of the mine managers, "You know, they are kind of lazy." One of his workers said, "In Zambia the Chinese can get away with anything." The reporter noted that the workers walked a thousand steps underground to get to the active mine face. The only light came from their helmets. The men earned four dollars a day.

Late in 2008, with prices falling, many of the Chinese entrepreneurs who were operating small copper smelters in the Democratic Republic of the Congo fled the country, leaving their workers unpaid. The local governor said, "Katanga is not a jungle. They [the Chinese] worked as if it was a jungle." Meanwhile, cheap Chinese clothes had forced the closure of the Zambia China Mulungushi Textiles factory at Kabwe, north of Lusaka. The head of the local chamber of commerce said, "Sending raw materials out, bringing cheap manufactured goods in. This isn't progress. It is colonialism."

In defense of the Chinese, a South African official said that the loss of the textile industry was less important that the development of a market for mineral exports. He insisted, "With China we have a relationship as equals. They don't look down on us. They are not condescending." A copper mine at Letpadaung, Burma, might signal a change for the better. Villagers were protesting the mine and costing the mining company money. The company was a subsidiary of a Chinese-government-controlled arms manufacturer, but in 2013 the CEO said, "Talk of financial returns is the language of the past. Now the focus is on social returns." His company was investing in schools, clinics, and electrical hookups.

Skeptics would mock that claim, but there was no doubting that the companies were growing larger very fast. Vale's boss said, "You have got to be big. Small and medium can't grow production at the rhythm demand is growing." Another executive said, "I think it will be difficult for single-metal companies to survive." The boss of BHP Billiton explained, "Consolidation is unstoppable. It is increasingly difficult to be of scale with one product."

Canada's premier nickel producer, Inco, attempted in 2006 to take over its smaller rival Falconbridge. Falconbridge's owners preferred a cash deal offered by newcomer Xstrata of Switzerland, which quickly vaulted from nowhere into the top ranks of global mining companies. The Falconbridge boss said of the government, "We could have been manufacturers of potato chips as far as they were concerned."

Rio Tinto in 2007 bid $37 billion for Alcan. Its intention was to deliver Australian alumina to Canadian smelters. One analyst said, "Alcoa certainly looks like the fish flopping on the beach right now." Alcoa fought back by putting about a billion dollars into Rio Tinto stock, reportedly with the thought that Rio Tinto was about to be taken over by BHP Billiton and that Alcoa's price for agreeing to this would be regaining control, once again, of Alcan.

Things went awry when BHP Billiton failed to gain control of Rio Tinto. That left Alcoa with Rio Tinto stock but still without Alcan. To pay for Alcan, Rio Tinto tried selling an 18 percent stake in itself to Chinalco, the China Aluminum Company. Angry stockholders killed that deal, poisoning Rio Tinto's customer relations in China and doing absolutely no good for the career prospects of Chinalco's chairman. An insider said of the Chinese, "These executives are political appointees and at the end of the day they have to consider their political careers in government, which can be badly damaged by a high-profile failure."

Manufacturers of mining equipment expanded too. In 2010 Bucyrus, the heavy equipment manufacturer that had built the excavators for the Panama Canal, paid a billion dollars for the mining-equipment operations of Terex, a major competitor. Later that year, Caterpillar bought Bucyrus for $7.6 billion. Together with competitor Komatsu, Caterpillar made 85 percent of the huge trucks used worldwide by the mining industry. About a thousand of these haulers were built annually. Each sold for about $5 million.

The tires used by some of these trucks were twelve feet high and weighed 13,000 pounds. They lasted a year, and sometimes less than half that. They could easily cost $70,000 each, and during an industry peak in early 2008, a set of six hit $900,000. The tire makers—Goodyear, Michelin, Bridgestone, and Yokohama—were slow to build capacity because they rightly anticipated that prices would fall. That left retreaders and casing hustlers looking for old tires. A retreader in Ohio in 2006 said, "This has never happened in the 35 years I've been in this business. . . . Right now the entire mining industry is going berserk, and we're feeding into it." The mining companies, forced to wait two years for the delivery of new tires, told their drivers to take it easy on the bumps. Rio Tinto went a step further and opened its own retread shop in Perth. The effects rippled across the country, with life becoming difficult for automotive-repair shops in Sydney and Melbourne. Experienced mechanics kept leaving to take jobs with the mining companies. "We can't compete with the wages they offer," one shop owner said.

Perhaps the day would come when these mines would join Utah's Bingham Canyon, less than an hour's drive from Salt Lake City's Temple Square, and become tourist destinations. At Bingham Canyon, visitors came to gawk at the parade of trucks that every day hauled 450,000 tons of rock from the mine. Ninety-nine percent of it was waste, but the remaining 1 percent included 795 tons of copper, 12,000 ounces of silver, and 1,400 ounces of gold. The mine had produced 19 million tons of copper since the Utah Copper Company opened it in 1906. Like a titan's game of jacks, the property had been scooped up over the years by Kennecott Copper, then by Standard Oil of Ohio, BP, and, most recently, Rio Tinto. The hole in the mountain just kept getting bigger.

6 Farming

During the twentieth century the population of the United States quadrupled from 75 million to 300 million. Over that same period the number of farmers fell from 6 million to 2 million, and more than half of those 2 million were part-timers. The average farmer reported a farm income of about $30,000. He was growing older too, from an average age of fifty in 1982 to fifty-seven in 2007.

Crop acreage was declining as well. The nation's premier crop by acreage, corn, peaked in 1917 at 116 million acres. By 1987 it had sagged to under 60 million. Ethanol came to the rescue and pushed the acreage to over 97 million in 2013. Ethanol couldn't do much for wheat, however. The staff of life covered over 70 million acres in the United States in 1890. In 2013, it covered 56. Cotton, once an icon of American agriculture, had come under attack chiefly from polyester, which was almost exactly tied with cotton at just under half of the fabric Americans used. Cotton's acreage collapsed in the United States from a peak of 43 million in 1929 to 10 million in 2013.

On the other hand, there *was* another hand. China had 200 million farm families—a hundred times the American total—but the United States had more cropland than China. Not only that: production of most of the leading crops in the United States was up, not down. With higher-yielding varieties and increased use of fertilizer and irrigation, corn production had jumped 500 percent since 1929. Wheat production had almost tripled. Cotton production was up by a third. Farms had been mechanized too, which is why, over the course of the twentieth century, the acreage of the average farm in the United States tripled to over 400 acres. James G. Boswell II, until his death in 2009 one of the biggest cotton producers in the United States, had once employed

5,000 cotton pickers. In his lifetime they were replaced by a hundred machine operators who picked Boswell's 150,000 California acres.

CORNUCOPIA

To grow its corn crop, the United States devoted an area a bit larger than twice the size of Iowa, which happened conveniently to be the leading producer. A quarter of the land area of the state was planted in corn, whose chief rival was the soybean. Iowa was also one of the two leading producers of that crop, which was the country's second-most widely grown. (Now *there* was a story. In 1900 China produced 70 percent of all the soybeans on the planet, but now it produced less than 10 percent. The United States, whose soybean acreage had risen from 2 million in 1929 to about 70 million, had grown accustomed to being the top soybean producer worldwide. In 2014 it was nudged aside by Brazil.)

Together, corn and soybeans were the mainstays of the most intensively farmed part of the United States, an arc stretching from eastern North Dakota southeasterly through Minnesota, Iowa, Illinois, and Indiana to northwestern Ohio. Within this arc, more than three-quarters of the land was cropland. California earned far more money from agriculture than any other state, but Iowa and Illinois each had about triple the cropland of their fancy sister with her almonds and artichokes, pomegranates and pistachios.

For many years corn prices had been a sorry story, with grain piling up unsold even when it was almost given away at a miserable two dollars a bushel. Corn continued to be grown because of federal subsidies, which totaled $41 billion between 1995 and 2004. It was time, some said, to speak of the midwestern blue states as red-ink states.

Ethanol changed all that. Federal law required that increasing quantities be blended into gasoline. Some 85 million tons of American corn were fermented into ethanol in 2005, but the figure in 2012 was 128 million tons, far above the 30 million exported that year as grain and about two-fifths of the entire crop of 293 million tons. In 2007, demand pushed the price of corn to a ten-year high: $4.31 a bushel. This was twice the average price of corn during the preceding decade.

Even at $3.50, a farmer producing 180 bushels per acre could net $270 an acre, ten times the profit of a few years earlier. Prices continued to rise to a peak in 2012 of over $8 a bushel.

"Farmers tend to be pessimists," one Minnesota farmer said. Then he added, "Around here, that's starting to change." A few years later, another farmer said, "This is the best we've ever had it, financially speaking." The USDA's chief economist was cautious. He said, "We are embarking on a profound change in our agricultural economy."

The boom pushed the price of farmland in Iowa from about $2,000 an acre in 2003 to $8,300 in 2012. In central Illinois good land rose in five years from $3,000 an acre in 2002 to $5,000. There was hardly a farmer in Iowa who hadn't heard about the Sioux County sale in 2011 of seventy-four acres at $20,000 an acre. A year later, that price was topped with a sale of 770 acres at $10,900 an acre.

A realtor in Nebraska said, "For the young farmer to get in, the amount of capital required is almost prohibitive." Farmers raising corn-fed hogs were in serious trouble, too. One Iowan had about 3,000 sows that produced 75,000 piglets annually. He needed about 75,000 bushels of corn every year and called the situation dire. "Nobody predicted this kind of rising grain prices," he said. Tyson's boss said that with the diversion of corn to ethanol, the cost of producing a pound of chicken rose from twenty-five to thirty-five cents.

The head of Smithfield Foods, the world's biggest pork producer and processor, said, "You eat eggs, you drink milk, you get a loaf of bread, and you get a pound of meat. Those are the four staples of what Americans eat in their diet. All of these are based on grain." In his own business, he explained, two-thirds of the cost of raising hogs was the cost of buying feed grain, which was mostly corn and which had tripled in cost. As an observer said, "One farmer's high output price is another farmer's high input cost." The head of Prestage Farms, a turkey and pork producer, said, "These high feed prices are absolutely killing us."

About 10 percent of the world's sugar went to ethanol, much more than the 3 percent of the world's corn, but that 10 percent doubled the world sugar price, which in 2010 stood at a thirty-year high. It didn't last, but the implication for corn worried the boss of Cargill. He said, "There are unintended consequences of this euphoria to expand ethanol production," and continued, "Unless we have huge increases in productivity, we will have a huge problem with food production." An economist added this warning: "As the corn price reaches up above $3 a bushel, the livestock industry will be forced to raise prices or reduce their herds. At that point the American consumer will start seeing rising food prices." By 2012 the director general of the UN's Food and Agriculture Organization was calling for a suspension of the ethanol mandate to "allow more of the crop to be channeled towards food and feed uses." Perhaps nobody was more pointed than an economist with ConAgra, who said that federal law now "mandated burning of our food."

The consequences of high American corn prices reached south of the border, where the market price of tortilla flour rose in 2006 from 61 cents to about $1.50. The average Mexican family of four ate a kilo of tortillas daily, which at market rates cost about a third of Mexico's minimum wage of $4.60 a day. Such prices were driving Mexicans from tortillas to imported and less nutritious instant noodles. Grupo Gruma, far and away Mexico's biggest tortilla producer, was safe because two-thirds of its $3 billion in sales in 2007 came from outside Mexico. Unfortunately for many Mexicans , the price of instant noodles went up by about a third in 2007. Blame the price of palm oil, a key ingredient that was itself a biofuel. Its price had doubled in the previous year.

THE END OF THE BOOM

The government might command the blending of billions of gallons of ethanol into the nation's gasoline, but there was no forcing consumers to buy more and more gasoline, with or without ethanol. Fuel demand tapered, and as early as 2009, 24 of the country's 180 ethanol plants had closed. Many were sold at huge losses. The nation's first big ethanol plant, built in 1984 in South Bend, Indiana, was sold at a bankruptcy auction to a bidder who planned to sell it for scrap. Another refinery, the Bionel plant in Clearfield, Pennsylvania, had been built for $270 million. A new owner bought it for $9 million. Valero, the country's biggest oil refiner, bid successfully at a bankruptcy auction and won seven VeraSun Energy ethanol plants for $477 million, less than half their replacement cost.

A cynic at the Environmental Working Group had in 2006 commented that all "incumbents and challengers in Midwestern farm country are by definition ethanolics," but lower oil prices and lower gasoline consumption undermined political support for ethanol. By 2014 the EPA proposed to relax the requirement to produce 15 billion gallons by 2015. Ethanol producers hoped for export markets, but the European Union imposed a tariff to encourage its own biofuel producers. Corn prices stayed high for the moment—over six dollars a bushel during 2013—but land prices stopped rising. By 2014 corn prices had fallen under the breakeven price of four dollars a bushel. Over twelve months, shares of Tyson Foods rose 47 percent.

FARM SUBSIDIES

The politics of ethanol were a long way from opening a straight furrow on a crisp spring morning, but American farmers were accustomed to keeping a close eye on Washington. The 1996 Freedom to Farm Act had been conceived as a way of phasing out crop subsidies. Under its program of so-called direct and countercyclical payments, landowners would be paid an amount determined by the acreage they planted in subsidized crops in 1981. Participants were under no obligation to continue farming, so some landowners got checks for land that in 1981 grew rice but now grew trees. Land developers around Houston subdivided old cropland into ten-acre plots and then advised buyers to build a house on one acre and claim a payment for the remaining nine. Between 2000 and 2006 the federal government paid $1.6 billion to landowners who did not farm at all.

A farmer living in Kansas said his farmer neighbors were "living off their welfare checks." Another farmer said, "Washington unbundles the money, opens the window and turns on the fan." All told, about 15 percent of American farm income in 2005 came from subsidies.

Seeking to justify this, some pointed to Canada, where the figure was over 20 percent; to the EU, where it was almost 40 percent; to Japan, where it was almost 60 percent; or to South Korea, Switzerland, Norway, and Iceland, where it was over 60 percent. Expressed another way, American farmers received $29 billion, but tiny South Korea paid its farmers $25 billion. Japanese farmers got $41 billion, and EU farmers received a breathtaking $138 billion.

With high corn prices, payments declined to $11 billion in 2011. The percentage of farm income coming from subsidies declined from 15 percent in 2005 to 7 percent less than a decade later. "We don't envision farmers here ever seeing a price-support check again," said an economist in Illinois. That left other subsidy programs in place, but as the secretary of agriculture said, "There are no sacred cows. Everything is on the table." The Agricultural Act of 2014 put an end to price supports for grain but also greatly expanded the federal crop-insurance program, which now guaranteed farmers 85 percent of the average price for corn and soybeans. About two-thirds of the nation's producers signed up, with the government paying 60 percent of the premiums. One beneficiary of the program, grateful that he was reimbursed for the failed corn crop of 2012, said, "I live to get to play another day."

SUBSIDIZED IRRIGATION

Crop subsidies had begun in the 1930s, but agricultural subsidies went back much further, all the way to the cheap or free land offered to settlers in the nineteenth century. Another kind of subsidy was built into the government's irrigation program, which since 1902 had sold water to farmers at prices that would never repay the government's investment in dams and canals.

The irrigation mystique withered in the 1960s, but almost fifty years later, the Bureau of Reclamation was renewing about 200 contracts with irrigation districts in California's Central Valley Project. The new prices were higher than the old ones—up from two dollars an acre-foot in 1950 to twenty dollars—but they still didn't cover the cost of providing the water, which not only had to be stored and conveyed but usually lifted by pumps.

Reclamation law had originally limited farmers to the quantity of water needed to irrigate 160 acres. Subsidies would at least be limited to farmers of modest means. Farmers were smart enough to find ways around the limit, even after the limit was raised to 960 acres by the Reclamation Reform Act of 1982. The justification for the amendment was that 160 acres was too little for modern farming, but many farmers found 960 equally bothersome. By dividing land between family members, Woolf Farming and Processing, near Fresno, got bureau water for 20,000 acres. George Miller, a California congressman from a district where the rivers of the Central Valley meet San Francisco Bay, said of these subsidies, "It's a great gig if you can get it."

It got better because the irrigation districts signing the new contracts were free to sell their allocations to cities. The going price was about $500 an acre-foot. Congressman Miller went to town. "This isn't about farming," he said. "It's about building an annuity for people who want to sell government-subsidized water to Southern California or whoever needs it." Such sales were almost inevitable, simply because the new contracts covered the volume of water the districts received in the past, even though the districts irrigated less land than they used to. The Westlands Water District, on the west side of the San Joaquin Valley, was the poster child, having been forced by poor drainage to take half of its 570,000 acres out of production. Still, its water allocation was not reduced.

If irrigation subsidies helped some farmers, they hurt others. As late as the 1940s, for example, the leading potato-growing state had been Maine, but farmers there often suffered droughts. The federal irrigation program brought assured water supplies to the Snake River Plains of Idaho and the Columbia Basin of Washington. Those states became the leading potato producers. The town of Othello, in Washington, was the world center of french fries, with ten factories making 6 billion pounds of them annually. Production in Maine fell from over 200,000 acres in 1945 to barely over 50,000.

ORCHARDS

Fruit growers had to be either huge or tiny. The fatal in-between size was from 300 to 600 acres, which left growers too big to sell locally but too small to have their own packinghouses. With 12,000 acres near Reedley, southeast of Fresno, Gerawan Farming was perhaps the biggest peach, nectarine, and plum grower in the world. It produced 5 million boxes of fruit annually from three houses that could pack 6,000 boxes an hour. The owner said, "Processing and marketing always make money, while farming might or might not."

California sold over $30 billion worth of agricultural products annually, more than 10 percent of the nation's total. The state's most valuable agricultural export, surprisingly, was almonds, whose acreage in the state rose from a bit over 100,000 acres in 1960 to over 800,000 in 2013. California by then produced 80 percent of all the almonds grown on the planet. Investors bought groves for somewhere between $8,500 and $15,000 an acre. A realtor with a side play in almonds compared the crop to what he knew best. "Almonds are like Las Vegas," he said in 2007. "It keeps growing, people keep thinking it's gotten too big, but still there aren't enough rooms." A couple of years later, Vegas had all the rooms it needed—and more—but almonds were still on the rise.

DAIRY

Americans didn't drink as much milk as they once had, but consumption of other dairy products increased enough that per capita milk production stayed constant. The number of milk cows should have risen along with the American population, but in fact it fell from over 20 million animals in 1950 to fewer than half that, mainly because milk production per animal skyrocketed from an average of 5,000 pounds annually to 20,000. The number of dairy farms fell from 334,000 in 1980 to about 60,000.

California already produced more milk than Wisconsin and was catching up with it in cheese production. Both states produced over 2 billion pounds annually, and California was likely to push Wisconsin aside just as Wisconsin pushed New York aside in 1910. Wisconsin's producers were becoming more efficient as the years went by; the state had 130 cheese factories now, down from 2,807 in 1922. California was more efficient still, however, with all of its cheese coming from fifty-five factories. Their owners worked hard to make sure that California's milk price, regulated by the state, was lower than the federal average. Raise the price, they said, and they would leave. The price stayed low, which at least partly explained why a hundred of the state's 1,600 dairy farms failed in 2012.

POULTRY

Between 1962 and 2002 U.S. turkey production soared from 6 million to an incredible 283 million birds grown annually. Broiler production merely quadrupled, but the numbers were much larger, rising from 2 billion birds in 1962 to 8.5 billion in 2002. Tyson, producing 2 billion chickens annually, owned those birds even when they were kept in houses run by contract farmers. The corporation supplied the feed and antibiotics and stayed with its property right up the production chain to the sale of finished products. Brazil's JBS decided to join the party. It already owned Swift & Co. Now it added Pilgrim's Pride, at one time America's biggest poultry processor. Tyson in turn moved into hogs and cattle and slaughtered 20 million pigs and 2 million head of cattle annually.

In 1962, 83 percent of the chickens sold in America had been sold whole, with only feathers and blood removed. That number declined to 10 percent, although customers in New York's Chinatown could buy Buddhist-style chicken, a USDA classification for chickens sold with head and feet. They came from a company called Bo Bo, whose birds lived thirteen weeks, seven more than conventional commercial chickens, whose diets included animal fats. The Bo Bo birds were sold fresh, though not quite fresh enough for buyers who wanted live birds, killed at the time of purchase. Chinatown had those too.

SHEEP

Sheepherders, meanwhile, were nearly extinct. ("Shepherds"? The word belonged to poets and folktales. "Flock" was gone too, replaced by "band.") In the entire country there were only about 825 sheep-herders. The reason was simple: the U.S. sheep population had peaked at 51 million animals in 1884. By 1962 there were only 30 million, and by 2007 there were fewer than 6 million, including lambs. Americans relied mostly on imports for both the wool they used and the small amount of lamb they ate. The herders meanwhile came mostly from Peru, Chile, Bolivia, and Mexico, and they were unhappy when they compared their lives in California, Texas, and Wyoming—the leading sheep states—with their expectations on arrival. Many quit to work in construction or landscaping.

GENETICALLY MODIFIED ORGANISMS

Genetically modified crops rose worldwide from zero acres in 1995 to 365 million by 2010. More than 13 million farmers now grew these crops in at least twenty-two countries. Herbicide and insect resistance were the most common traits, but drought, flood, heat, and salt toler-ance were on the way.

More than half the world's GM acreage was in the United States; Argentina followed in a distant second. More than two-thirds of all GM acreage was planted to seeds from Monsanto—"Mutanto," as its friends called it. The company had sold its first GM seed, Roundup Ready soybeans, in 1996. Driven more by politics than science, the company shelved research into wheat, tomatoes, potatoes, and bananas and focused instead on crops that people didn't eat, including alfalfa, cotton, corn grown for grain or forage, and sugar beets. There was one important exception: sweet corn, for which Monsanto developed a GM variety that came to American markets in 2012. Shoppers might be pleased to learn that Cheerios and Grape-Nuts had no GM ingredients, but those same shoppers were already getting plenty of GM calories because half the sugar they ate came from sugar beets, and more than 90 percent of that crop in the United States was genetically modified.

Although Monsanto developed GM seeds, it didn't grow them. That task was contracted to outside suppliers like Tom Farms, a big Indi-ana producer of seed corn. Tom harvested 10,000 acres of seed corn annually. Usually Tom fell short on the quantity it had contracted to deliver, and so it relied on a farm in northwestern Argentina, where it harvested roughly 2,000 acres during the Northern Hemisphere's winter.

Monsanto had competition. Switzerland's Syngenta sold enough GM seed in 2005 to plant almost 8 million acres. DuPont, which was tied with Monsanto in the production of corn seed, tried a different tack. Its Pioneer Hi-Bred corn, a conventional hybrid, had fallen from 40 percent of the seed market in 2001 to 29 percent in 2006, while Monsanto's share jumped from 11 to 29 percent. DuPont signed a cross-licensing agreement with Monsanto to create a family of corn varieties that were to be sold under the umbrella name SmartStax. The seed incorporated eight genes developed to resist weeds and insects, four from each of the two companies. Farmers would be able to buy different varieties of SmartStax from either Monsanto or Dow, which had a comparable arrangement with Monsanto. DuPont signed a similar cross-licensing agreement with Syngenta.

Keeping its lead, Monsanto in 2007 paid $1.5 billion for Delta and Pine, a cottonseed producer. Monsanto also collected patent-infringement fees averaging $100,000 from about a hundred American farmers. The company's aggressive policy prompted one justice of the U.S. Supreme Court to say from the bench, "Seeds can be blown onto a farmers' farms by wind, and all of a sudden you have Roundup seeds there and the farmer is infringing, or there's a 10-year-old who wants to do a science project of creating a soybean plant, and he goes to the supermarket and gets an edamame, and it turns out that it's Roundup seeds. . . . So it seems as though—like pretty much everybody is an infringer at this point, aren't they?" Monsanto's attorney replied, "Your point about the ubiquity of Roundup Ready's use is a fair one. I mean, this is probably the most rapidly adopted technological advance in history."

Canada's courts, too, sided with the company, specifically in the case of a farmer whose fields were contaminated with GM canola, a kind of rapeseed, drifting in from neighbors' fields. The seed survived herbicide, so the farmer harvested the crop and planted it the following year. Against the law, the court held.

Arkansas farmers produced almost half of the nation's rice and were fit to be tied over the contamination of their crop with escaped GM varieties. The farmers weren't opposed on principle to GM rice, but they sold heavily to Europe, where buyers refused conventional rice contaminated by even a few errant GM grains. The problem began with LibertyLink rice, a GM variety developed by Aventis Crop Science and unaffected by Liberty, an Aventis weed killer. Although LibertyLink was no longer being produced commercially—there was no point in growing something buyers wouldn't touch—a strain of it popped up, somehow, in rice from Arkansas fields in 2006. The USDA declared it fit for human consumption, only to find that other strains of LibertyLink were mysteriously present in Arkansas rice fields. How did it happen? A rice breeder said, "I have been dealing with this for nine months, and I still can't give you a definitive answer."

A critic from Friends of the Earth (you didn't expect an admirer, did you?) assailed the industry: "The most widely grown GM crop, soy, is grown mostly as high-protein animal feed for export to the UK and Europe. GM soy monocultures in South America are wiping out forests, causing massive climate emissions and forcing communities off their lands." Roundup-resistant superweeds were appearing too, along with insect pests, such as corn rootworms, that had acquired immunity to the toxins that Monsanto and Syngenta had built into GM corn. One remedy was to rotate corn with other crops. Another was to return to the use of older pesticides that had been on the verge of obsolescence. "Companies like Monsanto," a critic said, "are now telling these farmers to use really toxic chemicals. It is a joke." Dow, DuPont, Bayer, and BASF were suddenly back in the game, at least until pigweed, horseweed, and Johnson grass developed resistance to the herbicides those companies made. By 2012 over half of the soybean acreage in the United States was treated with one of these non-Roundup herbicides. In 2014 Texas sought permission for the state's cotton growers to spray propazine on up to 3 million acres of cotton, half the state's crop. The problem was pigweed, which had developed resistance to Roundup. Meanwhile, citing budget constraints, the USDA in 2013 stopped collecting data on the matter. Americans unhappy about this lack of information might be surprised to learn that the government did not even have a technical definition of genetically modified organisms. It left the matter to a private organization, the Non-GMO Project.

ORGANIC AGRICULTURE

The virtuous alternative was organic agriculture. Despite its "small is beautiful" aura, five farms produced half of California's organic produce. One of them, Greenway Organic Farms, farmed 2,000 pesticide-free, synthetic-fertilizer-free acres next to 24,000 acres that it farmed conventionally.

Paul Keene's Walnut Acres, a pioneer organic marketer established in the 1940s near Penns Creek, Pennsylvania, now belonged to Hain Celestial, whose sales in 2011 exceeded a billion dollars. Cascadian Farm belonged to Small Planet Foods, a company taken over by General Mills, whose revenues exceeded $15 billion. Trudging along with slow-growing Cheerios and Green Giant, General Mills added Annie's Homegrown in 2014 for $814 million. Kellogg's bought Bear Naked, Kashi, and Wholesome and Hearty.

To help the industry grow, the USDA allowed foods to carry the organic label even if they contained baking powder, pectin, ascorbic acid, carrageenan, or other products on a government-issued list. A rule also allowed the makers of prepared organic foods to use conventionally grown ingredients when organic ones were not commercially available. An official at Earthbound Farm, a consortium of 150 growers of organic produce, said, "We see this as opening up a Pandora's box. Any company that can't compete because something is too expensive could go to the Secretary [of Agriculture] and claim they need an exemption."

Then there was organic milk, which accounted for about 4 percent of the nation's milk supply. Of the country's 9 million dairy cows, only 150,000 produced it. That was too few to meet the demand. Organic Valley stopped supplying Walmart in 2005 because the dairy company simply couldn't get its hands on enough of the stuff. Danone, the French company that owned Stonyfield Farm, turned to organic powdered milk from New Zealand for the yogurt it sold in the United States. (Customers didn't see *that* on the label. Nor, for that matter, did they learn that Silk soymilk was made with beans from China and Brazil.) Stonyfield's boss said, "It would be great to get all of our food within a 10-mile radius of our house. But once you're in organic, you have to source globally." For flavored yogurts he used Chinese strawberries, Turkish apples, Canadian blueberries, and Ecuadorian bananas.

Like everyone else, the producers of organic milk were growing larger. Dean Foods owned both Horizon and WhiteWave. Horizon got 20 percent of its milk from a 4,000-cow dairy in Paul, Idaho, midway between Twin Falls and Pocatello. Aurora Organic Dairy had two farms that produced a third of the organic milk in the country. A reporter visited one, in Platteville, east of Longmont, Colorado, and found 5,200 Holsteins in pens. The owners insisted that the cows were "very healthy and happy." The USDA disagreed and cited the company for fourteen violations of organic standards, including insufficient pasture. The case was settled in 2007, with Aurora cutting the herd to a thousand cows.

Meanwhile, the head of Syngenta attacked the common belief that organic products were ecologically preferable to GM crops. Arguing that organic farms had lower yields than conventional ones—and therefore required more land—he said, "Organic food is not only not better for the planet. It is categorically worse. . . . If the whole planet were to suddenly switch to organic farming tomorrow, it would be an ecological disaster."

LATIN AMERICA
Brazil

For a time the ethanol boom brought many would-be ethanol investors to Brazil. In 2007 they spent $17 billion on new sugar or ethanol mills there. An executive at Archer Daniels Midland, the biggest American producer of ethanol, said, "We're devoting a lot of time and energy to this area. We're not talking about something 10 years down the road. It's on the front burner." In 2009 ADM found what it wanted and invested $370 million in Grupo Cabrera, a large Brazilian producer. An analyst said, "What ADM really understands is the global nature of green fuels."

Brazil was not an easy place for ethanol investors, however. Its biggest producer was Cosan, but together with its four biggest rivals, Cosan produced only 17 percent of Brazil's ethanol. Many of the mills were privately owned, and rife with family rivalries. One frustrated investor from India kept his sense of humor when asked to sum up his experience of fruitless months spent shopping. "I have been to a lot of nice houses," he said. Still, ADM's wasn't the only deal. Shell formed Raízen, a $12 billion joint venture with Cosan. The plan was to make cellulosic ethanol from bagasse, or cane waste.

The ethanol fever would cool, but between 1990 and 2010 Brazil's cultivated acreage more than doubled from 24 million to 60 million acres; yields nearly doubled too. The country was already the world's biggest producer of coffee, orange juice concentrate, sugar, and tobacco. With new varieties of wheat and corn, Brazil might become a major producer of those crops. It was also the world's biggest or second-biggest beef producer, and it was a major beef exporter, especially to Russia, Egypt, and the UK. Beef productivity had risen after the introduction of more nutritious grasses and the application of crushed limestone to neutralize soil acidity. A rancher near Cuiabá said, "The sky's the limit."

Perhaps the biggest threat to the industry was consumers who worried about rainforest destruction. Tesco, the British supermarket chain, had already quit buying beef from giant JBS, despite the insistence by that company's boss that "we don't buy cattle from farmers who are not compliant" with Brazil's forest code. That code had been created to quell the international uproar over the "Arc of Fire," the zone of forest clearance in the Amazon and the savanna to its south. The rate of clearing fell from 4.5 million to 1.5 million acres annually between 1995 and 2010, but clearance continued. About 2,200 square miles of Amazon forest disappeared in 2013. One farmer said simply, "Wherever a combine can go, soybeans will grow."

In 2005 Greenpeace awarded its Golden Chainsaw—for the Brazilian who most contributed to rainforest destruction—to Blairo Maggi, governor of the state of Mato Grosso. Personally, Maggi had 400,000 acres under cultivation, but he was not South America's biggest producer. Grupo Los Grobo farmed 670,000 acres spread over Brazil, Paraguay, and Uruguay and had sales exceeding $800 million. Meanwhile, the head of Brazil's National Confederation of Agriculture and Livestock was a widow known not so affectionately among conservationists as "Lil' Miss Deforestation." Katia Abreu wasn't intimidated. She said that Brazil had "built one of the biggest, low-cost and high-quality agricultural industries on the planet and still managed to preserve 61% of the forest, a thing that no other country in the world can claim."

American soybean farmers spent $6.70 growing a bushel of soybeans. A Brazilian spent $5.05. That wasn't the end of the story either, because the Brazilian got two or, with irrigation, three crops annually. Americans got one. The only advantage Americans had was in transportation. Half of all Brazil's agricultural exports crowded into the Port of Santos, and they arrived there over terrible roads, which is why Brazilians shipping to Santos paid five times as much, per ton, as Americans shipping to New Orleans. The port was expensive, too, charging shippers $2,000 to handle a container.

Eike Batista, for a moment Brazil's richest man, said that investors came to him. "I love your country," they said. "I love Brazil, but I don't know how we can get stuff in or out of it." Batista was working to fix the problem by having his logistics company, LLX, build the Superporto do Açu, east of Campos. Batista had a lot more than agriculture in mind. Among the superport's many planned components were a $3 billion fertilizer plant and docks big enough to accommodate Valemax bulk carriers. In 2007 he sold mining rights around Conceição do Mato Dentro to Anglo American for $4.6 billion, and the company spent an addition $9 billion developing a mine and a 320-mile pipeline to ship 90 million tons of iron ore annually to Batista's docks. Eventually Batista lost control of LLX but work continued under EIG, a Houston-based private-equity firm.

Foreigners Jump In

A group of American farmers toured Brazil in 2001. They did some calculations and came away saying, in the words of one, "Can this be true? If so, I am screwed." A number of them decided it would be smart to move south. In western Bahia, plow-ready land near Barreiras, population 130,000, sold for $750 an acre. Raw scrub on the endless plains went for $100. "*Deadwood* with malaria," some called it. Buyers dealt with shaky land titles and merchants who saw them as easy pickings. An immigrant from Missouri said, "I'm learning lessons that I didn't necessarily want to learn. But it's an adventure." He continued, "In the Midwest you take people at their word. Here, you don't know who to trust." He remained optimistic. "I rearranged my whole life to farm in Brazil," he said. "I'm not coming home empty-handed."

The soybean acreage in Mato Grosso fell in 2006 from 5.9 to 5 million hectares. International soybean prices were down, while the Brazilian real was up, raising the price of seeds, machinery, and chemicals. Car sales in Rondonópolis were slow, and the manager of Rondonópolis Plaza said, "The soybean crisis has been a disaster for us. Many stores closed and the ones that survived saw their sales plummet. Commerce in many parts of the state has been destroyed." A year later, in 2007, a farmer with 17,000 acres near Rondonópolis said, "Just because we're producing a lot of beans here doesn't mean we're making money." His summary was gloomy: "Even when you do everything right, you still lose." In Querência, a boomtown in Mato Grosso's northeast, the John Deere and New Holland dealerships both closed.

Conditions improved, and between 2007 and 2012 the value of uncultivated land in western Bahia rose to about $3,000 an acre. Cultivated land was worth twice that, and the boom town of Luís Eduardo Magalhães, west of Barreiras, was surrounded by soybean and cotton fields, many irrigated by center-pivot sprinklers. Big foreign investors were interested, including Genagro of Britain, Louis Dreyfus of France, and both Mitsubishi and Mitsui of Japan. Hong Kong investors bought into Agrifirma, a Brazilian company on its way to farming 250,000 acres in

Bahia. Chongqing Grains tried to buy land for a soybean empire but was steered by the Brazilian government into investing instead in a soybean processing plant, a $2.4 billion deal.

The transportation system was meanwhile getting better. In 2011 the Interoceanic Highway was completed, linking the ports of Brazil with those of Peru. It had been a long time coming, but the distances were huge; a sign at Puerto Maldonado, near the border, gave the distance to Rio de Janeiro as 4,373 kilometers. The road's completion was welcomed by Brazil's soybean exporters and also by pulpwood producers. It wasn't such good news for the primary rainforest through which the road ran.

Mexico

Proponents of GM crops argued that with GM corn Mexico could meet its domestic requirements. No luck. The country in 2010 grew 250,000 acres of GM cotton, alfalfa, and soybeans but only thirty-five experimental acres of GM corn. A defender of traditional varieties said, "We are the children of corn." Perhaps the loyalists could hold out.

The news was bad, however, for Mexico's dairy producers, even those of Cuenca Lechera, "Dairy Valley." This was Tizayuca, not far north of Teotihuacán. The industry opened in 1976 as a government-sponsored dairy center serving Mexico City. Subsidies disappeared in 1990, however, and the ninety-six remaining dairy farmers, each with herds averaging 250 cows, lost their tariff protection against American milk in 2008. One producer said, "We're not even covering our costs of production. We can't compete with [U.S.] subsidies."

St. Lucia

Once upon a time St. Lucia, a speck of an island just south of Martinique, had produced sugar for Britain. With independence in 1979, farmers shifted to bananas, for which Britain gave the island a preferential tariff. Production rose from almost nothing to 132,000 metric tons in 1992. Then Ecuador, the most important source of Chiquita bananas, complained to the World Trade Organization. St. Lucia defended its preferential tariff in vain. The director of its Chamber of Commerce said, "I don't think the Windward Islands ever accounted for more than .5 percent [of the global banana trade]. . . . That's why the WTO has been such a bitter pill for us to swallow. We were never talking about market-distorting quantities."

No matter. St. Lucia in 2004 grew only 42,000 tons. World's Finest Chocolate, from Chicago, stepped in and agreed to buy a half-million pounds of cocoa beans annually for a few years. Other than that, there was the tourist business, for which local farmers could supply organic vegetables and exotic fruit. The island already had sixty-eight hotels, up from seven in 1986, but their profits went mostly to foreign investors. The idealistic director of the Windward Islands Banana Development and Exporting Company nursed his bitterness: "The United States was wrong in pursuing this in the way it did, inflicting dire consequence on these small islands. . . . Why can't things work out in a way that doesn't hurt us? We're not a threat to anyone. . . . The international community has to understand that we are each other's keeper."

EUROPE

Sick of the way he was treated at home, one British farmer moved to France. "Here," he said, "people care about food and the system takes care of farmers." Even in France, however, off-farm jobs provided 31 percent of farm-household income by 2003, up from 19 percent in 1997.

EU farm subsidies were generous, but 80 percent of the money went to the largest fifth of Europe's farmers. More than 700 of them in 2008 collected more than a million euros each. The single biggest payment, €140 million, went to Italia Zuccheri. Another sugar producer, the conglomerate Südzucker, collected with its many subsidiaries almost three times that much. In 2009 Groupe Doux, a French poultry processor, collected €63 million. The EU in 2004 paid £700,000 to the Duke of Buccleuch, reportedly Britain's largest nonroyal landowner, with holdings of 207,000 acres. The royal family owned three times that much, and Queen Elizabeth got £546,000 to help with expenses at Windsor and the 20,000-acre Sandringham Farm. Prince Charles got £225,000.

A brave EU farm commissioner proposed in 2006 that no landowner should receive more than €300,000. If that were the case, about 2,000 landowners would see their payments cut. A spokeswoman in the UK maintained with a twinkle, "There is no clear link between wealth and the size of a farm." Big farms, she continued, could be more efficient than small ones and more environmentally benign. Then she pulled out the big guns, for which she might have thanked American farmers on federal irrigation projects. Cut subsidies for big holdings, she warned, and the owners would split their farms into chunks owned on paper by compliant accountants and lawyers.

European Farmers in a Cold World

Farmers in Sardinia came in 2007 to a meeting to protest the EU's insistence that they were not entitled to concessionary loans from the Italian government. What did they hear? A sample: "Europe will be a continent of consumers, fed by outsiders, by exploited workers in Egypt paid $2 a day, in joint ventures. This is the destiny prepared for you."

The threat wasn't just from Egypt. A farmer near Baoding, Hebei, grew strawberries on eight acres leased from the government. He sold the berries in the local market for $180 a ton. What he couldn't sell there he sold for $60 a ton to Binghua Food, which froze the berries and sold them to a Belgian jam company, Materne Confilux. In 2004 Materne ordered 360 tons of berries from Binghua—and cut its purchases of Polish berries, which were more expensive because Polish growers got $600 a ton. The value of Chinese frozen strawberries shipped to the EU rose from $6.2 million in 2002 to $26.4 million three years later.

(Impressive? The value of China's apple exports to Europe jumped from $4 million in 2000 to $46 million in 2005. It was the same story in the United States. In 1996 China sent 4.5 million gallons of apple-juice concentrate there; by 2005 the figure was 250 million gallons, or two-thirds of the market. The jar might read, "Fruit we've grown ourselves," but the fine print told the truth.)

The EU responded to the strawberry invasion by imposing a 34 percent tariff. Materne, the jam maker, objected. So did European yogurt

and ice-cream makers. The EU's trade commissioner said, "Agriculture will be an area of tremendous growth." Most likely, he anticipated
China shipping commodity products to Europe, while Europe sent
specialty products the other way. He couldn't promise much to Polish strawberry growers.

Genetically Modified Organisms Again

Only one in twenty Americans worried that foods made from GMOs
were dangerous. The figure in Europe was one in two. A European
supermarket executive said that selling GM food would be "almost
commercial suicide." The Austrian health minister added that her
country remained dead set in opposition. "Our vision of a good society," she said, "is certainly not one where everybody is allowed to do
whatever is technologically possible." Prince Charles said that "clever
genetic engineering" would "cause the biggest disaster environmentally of all time."

Swiss voters in 2005 approved a five-year ban on GM crops. The Poles
approved a similar measure. The Greek Parliament's ban of 2004 was
overturned by the EU, but all fifty-four Greek prefectures promptly
passed their own bans. One Greek legislator had a sense of humor about
it. "All political parties," he said, "are opposed to GMOs, which is odd
because we disagree on everything else." The boss of a Greek farmers'
union said, "The environment minister who gives in and allows GMOs
into this country will never be minister again."

French wine growers were worried about GM vines, introduced
by Moët & Chandon as part of a project to fight fan-leaf virus, which
affected a third of French vineyards. As a result, GM vines were grown
under tight security by the National Institute of Agronomic Research.
A hostile grower said, "There needs to be a multitude of organisms in
the soil for the land to express itself in the vine. . . . The more diver-
sity, the greater the character of the wine, but there will be no diver-
sity if you use a clone."

The boss of Syngenta chose not to beat his head against the wall.
"Let's just say the outside environment in Europe helped persuade

Syngenta that focusing first on leadership in crop protection was the right thing to do." Result: Syngenta was the world's biggest producer of herbicides, insecticides, and fungicides. Still GMOs were too big for the company to ignore, and so Syngenta developed GM corn for the American market. The boss said, "All that scientists have been doing since the late 1990s is replicating in the laboratory what nature has been doing for thousands of years. The European Union represents an area of resistance. But Europe is increasingly an island." Echoing that view, BASF, the chemical giant, shut down its GMO research station in Germany and moved its labs to Raleigh, North Carolina.

Still, GMOs were cats with many lives. In 2004 the UK published a ban on GM crops, and an observer said, "This is the end of GM in Britain." Fast-forward to 2007, and the government reported, "The ability to have drought-resistant crops is important not only for the UK but for other parts of the world. And the fact that some GM crops can produce higher yields in more difficult climatic conditions is going to be important if we're going to feed the growing world population." Enter the Amflora, a blight-resistant GM potato developed in the UK by BASF. The EU approved the potato in 2010. As observers might have guessed, the Amflora was intended not for human consumption but as a source of industrial starch. It joined a Monsanto GM corn that the EU had approved in 1998 for industrial uses.

Despite opposition from nineteen of the EU's twenty-eight members, the European Commission in 2014 approved the planting of DuPont's GM corn variety called 1507. It had taken DuPont thirteen years to secure approval for the seed, which was at least momentarily resistant to corn borers. Meanwhile, many European governments were keen on a comprehensive trade agreement with the United States. They hoped that it would allow them to bid on government contracts in the United States that were presently restricted to American companies. The price demanded by the United States for that agreement was likely to be free entry to Europe of American crops, genetically engineered or not.

The director of a French winery said, "The trade in wine is like the trade in Coca-Cola or in washing powder." So Cordier Mestrezat Grands Crus, which made wines that sold for over $3,000 a bottle, also sold wine in eight-ounce juice boxes. They came with a special straw with four holes, so the wine sprinkled in the mouth. The company didn't dare market the boxes in France. Another producer, Boisset, dared to sell wine in recyclable plastic bottles.

After twenty years of negotiation, ambassadors in 2006 signed the U.S.-EU Wine Trade Agreement. Under its terms the United States agreed to ask Congress to prohibit new American brands from using semi-generic terms such as Chablis, champagne, Chianti, claret, port, and sherry. The name *burgundy*, for example, would be restricted to European wines and existing American brands. The Europeans, on the other hand, conceded that wine labels would not have to carry information about production processes unrelated to health or safety. Customers wouldn't be able to distinguish between wine aged in oak barrels and wine aged in steel tanks containing oak chips.

(Devious? No more so than shipping grapes from the San Joaquin Valley to the Napa Valley, processing the grapes there, and labeling the wine Napa. That was part of the reason that the biggest vineyard owner in the United States, Bronco Wine, with 45,000 acres, was able to sell Charles Shaw wine as Two Buck Chuck from Napa. Don Sebastiani wines played the same game with Chilean grapes.)

Despite the treaty, vineyard acreage in the EU was likely to continue its decline. It had already fallen from 14 million acres in 1960 to 9 million in 2008, but that was still too much. The EU's agriculture commissioner forecast that the EU would soon become a net importer of wine, with consumers shifting to wines whose taste they preferred and whose labels they could understand. In 2006 she said, "I think we can all see that we are heading for a crisis." Accordingly, she announced a plan—compensated and voluntary—to destroy a million acres of European vineyards. The next year, that figure was cut in half. Growers of low-quality vines would be encouraged by payments of several thousand dollars an acre to grub them out. In 2009, 180,000 acres were cleared; in 2010, 130,000 more. In theory, the surviving producers would be more competitive with foreign growers.

Champagne growers were luckier because France restricted production to an area of 80,000 acres already in full production. Sales were up, mostly in the hands of Moët Hennessy–Louis Vuitton. The company produced almost 20 percent of the world's champagne and over 60 percent of the champagne sold in the United States. It owned about 4,000 acres but also bought grapes on long-term contracts from hundreds of small growers. Its brands included Veuve Clicquot, Moët & Chandon, and Dom Pérignon.

Russia

With the collapse of the Soviet Union, Russian farmers were told, "You are free now; do it by yourself." They generally assigned their share of a defunct state farm to a new private association. Short of capital, the associations couldn't afford new equipment or fertilizer. The result was that the amount of cultivated land in Russia declined from 276 million acres in the late Soviet period to 182 million. The country's record grain harvest, 127 million tons, occurred in 1978, back in the distant days of Leonid Brezhnev. Thirty years later and two decades after the collapse of the Soviet Union, the harvest was 105 million tons. Russia imported half of its meat and two-thirds of its sugar. Its neighbors were often equally prostrate. The rate of fertilizer application to wheat fields in Ukraine fell from 149 kilograms per hectare in 1990 to 24 kilograms in 2000. The harvest was so protracted that almost a fifth of the grain spoiled before it could be gathered.

Optimists argued that Russia might again become, as it once had been, the world's biggest grain exporter. "Perhaps above and beyond anything else," one minister said, "Russia is a major agrarian power." In 1998 the countries of the former Soviet Union exported 3.4 percent of the world's wheat; by 2009 they exported 23 percent, a sliver more than the 22 percent exported by the United States. From Novorossiysk, the chief grain-exporting terminal, grain headed mostly to Egypt, Turkey, and Pakistan.

Investors saw an opportunity. Black Earth Farming claimed control of almost 800,000 acres. An executive predicted that in a decade or so, "Russia will be the leading force in world agriculture, just because of its mass." Black Earth had competitors. One was Richard Spinks, an Englishman whose company, Landkom, leased 165,000 acres from farmers around Bilyi Kamin, or White Stone, a village 500 miles west of Kiev. His first harvest, in 2008, was from 25,000 acres planted to wheat, barley, and rapeseed. The next would be from 100,000 acres.

There were ways around inadequate storage and poor transport, Spinks said. Corruption was a tougher problem. Three-quarters of Russia's farmland was still controlled by former collectives, and transferring control to outside investors wasn't straightforward. One investor said, "Unless you agree with the governor, you can't register any land." The rule of thumb was to set aside a third of your capital for bribes. As one journalist wrote, "In Russia, there is usually only one winner." A McKinsey study concluded that the cost of building a distribution center in Moscow was a third more than building it in London; a power plant was a third again as expensive in Russia as in the EU. The McKinsey analyst said, "There is no good reason for the cost of building in Russia to be this high." The explanation, offered tactfully, was "leakage."

Ironically, conditions were improving around the Aral Sea, a salt lake that not so long before had been a poster child for environmentally disastrous rural development. The Amu Darya and Syr Darya, huge rivers, had been diverted to grow cotton in what had then been the Turkmen and Uzbek Soviet socialist republics. This had nearly eradicated the sea, which depended on the rivers for replenishment. Nearby cotton fields, inadequately drained, were in trouble, too. Looking at one field turned into a salt flat, a farmer said, "It's like standing on a graveyard."

The good news was that the Aral Sea had been divided by the Kok-Aral Dam into two parts, a small northern lake and a much larger southern one. Almost beyond redemption, the southern part was fed—or not—by the Amu Darya, but the northern part was fed by the Syr Darya and with the dam had risen twenty-five feet. The old fishing town of Aralsk, once on the northeastern shore of the sea, was now only 7 miles from the water, not 43. There was talk of a second dam that would raise the lake enough to reach Aralsk, and water was even spilling over the existing dam into the southern lake, though there was little prospect of restoring it to its historic level. If both countries quit irrigating altogether and allowed the Amu Darya and Syr Darya to flow at their natural rates, the Aral Sea would not be restored for forty years.

Poland

Poland's aristocratic estates had been reorganized after World War II as state collectives. With the collapse of communism, the state farms were broken up and their lands divided among members of each collective. A few very large farms were consolidated, so that by 2008 about 6 percent of all the cultivated land in Poland was in farms exceeding 2,500 acres. Most of the country's farms, however, remained small. An owner of ten acres said, "Of course, I have my land and I am a farmer, but are you kidding? Living off it, I couldn't support my family. I wouldn't be able to cover production costs for a start." Perhaps his farm would survive as a part-time operation, but restrictions on foreign ownership of Polish farmland were scheduled to end in 2016, and the more fertile parts of the country were probably destined for consolidation into large, technically sophisticated farms. Young Poles weren't waiting. In the decade after 2004, 2.5 million of them emigrated. Of those, only 300,000 chose to return.

AFRICA
Better Seeds

The CEO of Agral Export Senegal wasn't so sure that big farms were necessary. He ran a cooperative with 200 small farmers who in 2007 shipped $750,000 worth of chili peppers, pineapples, and other produce to Europe. The CEO said he could expand if he could get money for irrigation, seeds, and fertilizer.

The head of DuPont's seed business in Africa was ready to help. The way to higher production, he said, was "through the use of better technology, genetics, and agronomic practices." The man in charge of the company's business in Ethiopia was hugely excited by the possibilities. "When I heard that only 1% or 2% of the U.S. population are farmers, and they feed the whole country, I couldn't believe it," he said. "I started dreaming that if every farmer in Ethiopia increases production, we can change the whole country. We can change Africa." He was thinking of GMOs, but for the moment most of Africa's governments were keeping them at bay. One exception was Egypt, which in 2008 allowed the planting of GM corn; another exception was Burkina Faso, which allowed the planting of GM cotton. At the same time there was still plenty of room for conventional plant breeding. Cassava yields had been greatly improved after 1977, when plant breeders in Nigeria developed bulbs resistant to the mosaic virus.

Fertilizer

Africans were charged six times the world price for fertilizer, which is why African farmers used an average of thirteen kilograms of fertilizer per hectare. The average in East Asia was 190 kilograms. A large part of the reason for the high price was that African roads were terrible, which meant that truck deliveries were expensive. A good example came from South Sudan, where SABMiller opened a brewery in Juba, 1,100 miles by truck from Mombasa. The journey took a week and freight charges for one load were $15,000 to $20,000. Often it was cheaper to ship a ton of fertilizer from the United States to an African port than it was to truck that same ton 60 miles inland.

Seeking to cut transport costs, Rwanda encouraged Tanzania to rebuild the colonial-era railroad that ran from Dar es Salaam to Kigoma, on Lake Tanganyika not far from the Rwandan border. Rwanda dreamed of becoming a transport hub and of the day when shipping a container from Mombasa to Kigali, Rwanda's capital, did not cost three times as much as getting it from the United States to Mombasa.

Disregarding outside advice, Malawi in 2006 began spending about $75 million annually on fertilizer subsidies. About half of the country's farmers that year got 220 pounds of fertilizer for fifteen dollars, instead of the usual forty-five. Corn production doubled and then tripled, rising from 1.2 million tons in 2005 to 2.7 million in 2006 and almost 4 million tons in 2011. The extra production was worth twice the cost of the subsidy, but many small producers needed cash and sold their fertilizer to larger growers.

An American NGO, the One Acre Fund, lent subsistence farmers in Kenya seventy-five dollars to buy sufficient seed, fertilizer, pesticide, sacks, and crop insurance for a bit less than one acre. It provided training, too, and claimed to help farmers double their yields and income. The organization began with 40 families in 2006 and by 2012 had grown to 130,000. One of its American founders said, "I believe fertilizer is the world's most important humanitarian product." A similar organization, Doreo Partners, had huge ambitions to reduce Nigeria's food imports by providing farmers with inputs, credit, machinery on loan, and training.

Capitalist Alternatives

Foreign investors occasionally tried to run a big African farm in a way that benefited nearby smallholders. That was the case with Jon Maguire, a British fund manager who invested $16 million in Malawi and put 2,500 acres in cultivation. He also began buying peppers on contract from 9,000 nearby families. Maguire said, "The whole basis of agricultural development has been: how do we help the small farmer? You will never solve Africa's problems like that. You need small and medium enterprises rotating around massive farms that will plug them into the global economy." It sounded plausible, but Maguire quit Malawi in 2009.

A simpler alternative was to establish big commercial farms. In southwest Kenya, Dominion Farms set out to grow rice on 17,000 acres it leased in Siaya District, on the eastern shore of Lake Victoria. Despite Dominion's agreements with local and national authorities, nearby villagers weren't happy. They accused Dominion of failing to deliver promised jobs and services. The company's owner, based in Oklahoma, was short on public-relations skills. He shot back, "The area was a malaria-infested swamp before we got here." And now? "When you try to help these people," he said, "all they do is complain." Should traditional ways be kept intact? He didn't think so. "I disagree when people say, 'Oh, you have to preserve the local culture.' If you preserve it, people will starve, and you won't have a culture to preserve."

The World Bank argued that large-scale farming in Africa could be a good thing, provided that biodiversity and the rights of indigenous occupants were protected. The bank calculated that Africa had almost half the world's uncultivated land that could produce crops without irrigation. Others remained skeptical. Kofi Annan said, "We have seen a scramble for Africa before."

The World Bank calculated that between 2004 and 2009 Sudan alone signed almost 4,000 contracts allotting a median of 20,000 acres each. Citadel Capital leased 260,000 acres for $125,000 annually. That was chicken feed compared with the deal struck by Philippe Heilberg, who, like many before him, looked at Sudan's White Nile plains and saw tremendous potential. In 2009 he leased a million acres in Jonglei State. He appeared to be confident that his lease would be honored by the government of the emergent state of South Sudan.

Down in Madagascar, Daewoo in 2008 announced that the government had allotted it 3 million acres of forest free of charge. The land was to be cleared and planted to corn and palm oil grown for export. For Madagascar, the only benefit was some jobs. The plan was never implemented.

Mali leased 250,000 acres to a Libyan company for the Malibya Project. Over 2,000 residents had to move from Soumani, between Segou and Mopti. The villagers resisted—"Le Mali n'est pas à Vendre!"—but officials at Mali's Office du Niger were enthusiastic; over the space of eighty years they had reclaimed only 200,000 of the 3 million acres they controlled in the Niger's inland delta. Then both the Libyan and Malian governments were overthrown.

Cameroon leased 200,000 acres to Herakles Farms in 2009. The plan was to establish an oil-palm plantation for which Herakles would pay the government one dollar a hectare annually for ninety-nine years. Work was suspended in 2013 with villagers' complaining about loss of their rights and the Cameroon president's refusing to sign the lease.

At least two Nigerian states offered thousand-hectare blocks on free, long-term leases to dispossessed white farmers from Zimbabwe. The plan of the Shonga Farms in Kwara State was to grow irrigated rice and reduce Nigeria's rice imports, but irrigation was never provided, and transport was a perpetual problem. Corn and soybeans failed, though cassava did well; so did poultry. Most of the farmers quit, but a few soldiered on. By 2012 only one of nineteen farmers remained on a similar scheme in Nassarawa State. Problems with transport, power, and finance had driven the rest away.

Perhaps the Dangote Group would be more successful. Aliko Dangote, reputed to be Africa's richest man, had built a fortune on a huge cement plant at Obajana, about 100 miles southwest of Abuja. Now he proposed to invest $1.5 billion in farming 740,000 acres in northeastern Nigeria. The area was plagued by insurgents, but a spokesman for Dangote said that the project would bring such wealth to the region that "Boko Haram will not have guys to recruit."

Competing against Subsidized Americans

It cost Ghanaians about $230 to produce a ton of rice. That was only a bit less than the $240 it cost an American grower, but the American rice industry received $780 million in subsidies in 2006, so American rice could be sold in Ghana at $205 a ton and still make money for the American grower. Ghana had previously subsidized its farmers too, but in 1983 it adopted free-market policies that helped the economy overall but left farmers in deep trouble. Ghana's rice producers concluded that the best solution for them as individuals was to move to

Europe. American producers defended themselves by saying that they needed subsidies to compete with rice from Vietnam and Thailand. Ghana's urban poor, they added, were grateful for cheap rice, whatever its source.

Stories about the United States tilting the playing field abounded. Egypt's famous long-staple cotton, for example, had lost ground to subsidized American growers of pima. In 2009 Egyptian production fell to its lowest level in a century, even though, as an exporter said, "If the U.S. were to remove its cotton subsidy, they would not be able to compete with us."

Oxfam calculated that the elimination of cotton subsidies for American farmers would raise world cotton prices 10 percent. With the elimination of American subsidies, farmers in Chad, Benin, Burkina Faso, and Mali, who on average earned $2,000 a year, could earn an additional $100 annually. (Another hundred would go to middlemen.) One observer said, "Fifty or a hundred bucks is a lot of money to these people." Another disagreed and said that with normal price fluctuations, "I'm not sure the effect will be large enough for farmers to really notice." Some help came from Victoria's Secret, which pledged to buy organic cotton from Burkina, but the country's production of organic cotton in 2007 was about 240 tons. That was much less than 1 percent of its 700,000-ton harvest. African producers might hope that Brazil would be successful in the action it had brought in the World Trade Organization to force an end to American subsidies, but news to the contrary came in 2014 when Brazil, in exchange for payments totaling $750 million, instead agreed to drop the matter.

ASIA

Gold-Plated Agriculture

The Abu Dhabi Organics Group sold locally grown produce at prices no higher than the imported competition. To do that, the company grew its crops under 1,700 acres of cloth-topped greenhouses and irrigated them with water provided free by the government.

Years earlier, center-pivot irrigation systems had created green circles in Saudi Arabia. The water pumped by those systems was worth more than the wheat it helped grow, and in 2008 the Saudi government decided to import wheat and keep the water underground. The biggest problem now was finding jobs for the farmworkers. Water continued to be pumped to produce feed for the 67,000 dairy cows producing for Almarai. Based at Al Kharj, southeast of Riyadh, Almarai had sales exceeding $2 billion annually, but it had to keep the cows cool, which meant shade structures and misters, which required more water and electricity.

India

For decades after independence, the government of India could not shake Mahatma Gandhi's ideal of an India of village republics, each almost self-sufficient and satisfied with what it could provide for itself. As late as 2014 a Delhi economist would say, "People who formulate policy in Delhi have a very, very romantic image of what it is like to live in a village." The villagers themselves had no such delusions, and their wholesale rejection of the Congress Party in the election of 2014 revealed a deep impatience not only with Gandhi's party but with his view of what India should be.

One indicator of the pace of change was that the world's biggest tractor manufacturer, Mahindra & Mahindra, was an Indian company. How could this be, in a country where half the labor force worked in agriculture? A farmer explained, "I can't find enough people to do the hard work in the fields anymore." He meant that there were plenty of local villagers who needed to make money, but they preferred working for the Mahatma Gandhi National Rural Employment Guarantee Scheme, which promised them a hundred days of easier work annually.

The new government of 2014 was unlikely to kill that program, but if it had a hope of satisfying the electorate, it would have to encourage investors like FieldFresh, a joint venture between Del Monte and Bharti Enterprises that farmed 4,200 acres in the Punjab and exported beans, snow peas, carrots, and okra via Chandigarh Airport to Europe.

FieldFresh also supplied the sixty Easyday stores run by Bharti in partnership with Walmart. The boss of FieldFresh said, "To my mind, the next big wave—which will be bigger than telecoms or outsourcing—is in agriculture. India's strength lies in its huge area of arable land, with great weather conditions. For three, four or five months Europe doesn't grow a fig—but we can grow anything. I want to connect India's farms with the world."

Fast-forward nine months. "We have sent over the first 30–40 shipments, but it has been much tougher than we thought." Mushrooms were a "wash-out." Mangos were "OK." Pomegranates were "mixed." What went wrong? One problem was Indian Customs, which was so slow that produce awaiting inspection rotted on the scorching tarmac. In the future, the Bharti boss said, "The cargo will be allowed to go straight to the aircraft where customs will stamp it on the spot." Not so fast: a few months later, FieldFresh reported that it grew eighty tons of snow peas, of which only 15 percent were of export quality. In 2013 Walmart announced its withdrawal from the partnership.

China

The Chinese prime minister in 2013 visited a farm of about a thousand acres and, instead of calling for the owner's arrest, said that increases in farm production "can only be done through concentrating the land into large farms." Unregenerate cadres must have muttered to themselves, but the central government declared that consolidation of farmlands should be encouraged, and in 2013 a government survey found that about 13 percent of the country's arable land had already been organized into what the government called "family farms." There were 877,000 of them, averaging a bit over thirty acres each. That might seem small, but it was huge compared to the Chinese average of about 1.5 acres.

The chairman of Chengdu's New Hope Group said, "The gap between the modern industrial and urban economy and the small peasant economy is getting larger and larger. We need to modernize farming, and that means scale. . . . How can we supervise a system with 200 million production units that each raises four or five pigs?" He planned to run a vertically integrated operation that would grow feed grain at one end and sell pork at the other.

He had competition from Shuanghui, a pork producer that in 2013 paid almost $5 billion for Smithfield Foods in the hope that American methods might help the Chinese firm bolster its reputation among Chinese consumers worried about contaminated foods. Tyson wasn't in the pork business in China yet, but it was deeply involved in chicken production there. It already had about twenty farms near Shanghai and was planning another seventy. Each had over 300,000 birds, and the plan was to produce 300,000 birds weekly, again with American methods that might reassure Chinese consumers that the product was wholesome.

China Modern Dairy had 130,000 dairy cows spread over fifteen farms. It aimed to nearly triple that herd within a few years and to import cows in a breeding program that would double milk yields and make them equal to yields in the United States. China Modern had competitors too. Mengniu, or "Mongolian cow," which was also based in Inner Mongolia, operated fourteen farms, each with over 10,000 cows. Nestlé's head in China said, "Farms of two or three cows have melted like snow in the sun."

LongDa Foodstuff Group was another "dragon head," as the Chinese called these huge firms. It had 23,000 employees working 4,000 acres in Shandong, Henan, and Inner Mongolia. They produced green beans, broccoli, and strawberries, largely for export to Japan.

Chinese wine? Per capita consumption was only 1.4 liters per year, but China's population was so large that wine revenues in 2012 came to $41 billion. China was France's biggest customer for Bordeaux, but domestic production was growing fast. At Donglia, a village 30 miles from Taiyuan, a Hong Kong businessman built Grace Vineyard. He said, "It's my dream to introduce good wine into China." Rémy Cointreau and Swarovski both invested in the industry. Even largely Muslim Xinjiang was in the wine business, especially in the grape-rich Turfan Depression, southeast of Urumqi.

In Anhui, farmers accustomed to growing wheat and beans leased their land, saw it pooled into an operation covering 200 acres, and watched as it yielded green peppers, eggplants—and ten times as much money for the farmers as wheat and beans. Annual farmland rents doubled between 2005 and 2008, by which time they averaged $267 an acre. About 15 percent of the country's 200 million farmers rented out their land this way, some for periods of years and others for only a season. During the rest of the year, those farmers could grow a crop for their own use.

Water Transfer Schemes

In many parts of China, irrigation water was short and getting shorter. A small but vivid example came from Gansu's western edge, where the famous Crescent Lake at Dunhuang was surrounded by desert dunes. The lake level had dropped twenty-five feet since 1975, when nearby farmers began irrigating with groundwater. Flanked by a Buddhist shrine, Crescent Lake now held about a third of its historic volume.

Farther east but still in Gansu, the Shiyang River once flowed north through the Great Wall and into Inner Mongolia, where it died in the desert. Mao Zedong had ordered construction of irrigation works near the town of Minqin, but officials calculated that the surrounding desert was burying 1,500 square miles of land annually. In 2004 the project reservoir, called Hongyashan, went dry. Villages were abandoned, and farmers were relocated.

Top heavy with civil engineers, the Chinese leadership called for more engineering. Officials in Xinjiang began pushing for a scheme to pump seawater all the way to China's westernmost province and up to a height of over a kilometer. They wanted to desalinize some of that water and let the rest fill dry lakebeds. Their idea was to let the water evaporate and bring rain to the surrounding, barren countryside. They insisted it could be done for a dollar a cubic meter.

Perhaps that was a pipe dream, but the government had long ago decided to import Yangtze water to the North China Plain. A western route would divert water upstream in Sichuan. A middle route passed from the Three Gorges Dam north to the Danjiangkou Reservoir and then, with a tunnel under the Yellow River, through Henan and Hebei to Beijing. The eastern route, following the Grand Canal, brought water north from the lower Yangtze—again with a tunnel under the Yellow River. One of the project managers said, "I've been to the Hoover Dam, and I really admire the people who built that. At the time, they were making a huge contribution to the development of their country. Maybe we are like America in the 1920s and 1930s. We're building the country."

Maybe so, but many farmers on the North China Plain, the most densely settled part of rural China, weren't going to be happy, because the government had decided that the water should go to the cities of the Plain, not to the farmers. It might have been better to raise water rates in those cities—and some Chinese cities, including Shanghai, did just that—but water in most of China's cities remained exceedingly cheap by world standards. Australians paid 8.6 percent of their disposable income for water. Americans paid 2.8 percent. Chinese paid half of 1 percent.

The central canal opened in 2014, but the western one was postponed and the eastern one delayed. With forty pumping stations along the line of the Grand Canal, it had already cost $2.5 billion, including the expense of dredging the Grand Canal through the provinces of Shandong, Jiangsu, and Zhejiang. When project water finally arrived, it would be sent to the busy port city of Tianjin, with a population over 7 million. Meanwhile, something would have to be done about the unanticipated pollution of the water as it passed through the ancient waterway.

Organics and GMOs

Nervous consumers pushed the value of certified organic produce in China from less than $1 million in 1999 to $142 million four years later. Exports were an even bigger market, reaching $350 million in 2005—about 5 percent of the global trade in organic produce. China had twenty-one agencies claiming to certify organic foods. Only one, the Organic Food Development Center in Nanjing, was recognized by the International Federation of Organic Agriculture Movements.

A consultant said, "1,000 pounds in an envelope will get you the certificate you need."

China meanwhile spent 20 percent of the world's GMO research budget. Monsanto's watchful chief technology officer said, "My long-term competitors are going to be from India and China. They are putting in massive research and development investment." Like Monsanto, China was cautious with GM food crops, but in 2007 it approved GM varieties of tomatoes, peppers, and papaya. Two years later, it declared certain strains of GM rice and corn safe to grow and eat. It had no intention of developing GM soybeans, not when it could export conventional ones at a premium price to frightened consumers in Europe, South Korea, and Japan. One Japanese producer said that his customers would "never tolerate GM soybeans in their tofu and nobody's brave enough to try to change that."

7 Developing

In 2006 a fifth of the Russian population got by on thirty-eight dollars a month or less. At a village near Irkutsk, near Lake Baikal, a young woman sat drunk in a potato field. She said, "People drink, and they drink a lot, and they drink for a long time, because they can't help but drink." Her mother, also drunk, added, "This is our life; we call it normal. We plant potatoes, we dig them out, and that's it. There's nothing for people here."

An administrator explained that the communist "system was such that you were punished for mistakes rather than encouraged to correct them." Along came an ex-teacher with a grant from the Soros Foundation. In the near-arctic Pinega District, east of Archangel, he set up the Institute for Social and Human Initiatives. A villager said of the teacher-turned-organizer, "To be honest, nobody really understood what he was saying." But with persistence and a small amount of pump priming, the villagers rebuilt their collapsed bridge. Another village built a home for the elderly. A third created a guesthouse. Then the ex-teacher was charged with tax evasion, and his office building was seized. He said, "I was told by regional bureaucrats they no longer required my services." One of those bureaucrats said, "The authorities do not like it when someone tries to change the mentality of people and make them more independent-minded."

AFRICA

Western Europeans had almost forgotten such poverty, but many Africans had not. A dozen countries there had an average per capita GDP of less than $1,000. One of them was Tanzania. Forty years after independence and 10 miles inland from Lake Malawi, the villagers in the Bulongwa Forest Reserve survived on subsistence plots of wheat and corn. For cash—an average of ten dollars a year—they grew peas. They could not afford the two-dollar fare for the one-hour jeep ride to Makete, which was the nearest place with a market. They could even less afford the four-hour trip to Njombe, the nearest town. A local politician said, "Quality of life here is good because most people don't need more than they can get." A villager disagreed: "I'm not content, but there's nothing I can do."

Tanzanian villagers close to Lake Victoria, 500 hundred miles to the north, welcomed a proposed highway linking Musoma to Arusha and bringing with it cheaper prices in shops, easier access to medical care, and perhaps electricity and cell-phone service. The proposed road ran through the Serengeti, and wildlife advocates opposed the road. The government's response was, "You guys always talk about animals, but we need to think about people."

Nigeria, with oil and gas, ought to have been in better shape, with a per capita GDP well over $2,000. Half an hour's drive south of Makurdi, however, the village of Ullam had about a thousand people. Typically, each family had three or four fields cultivated in a sequence of yams, sorghum, and cassava, followed by several years of fallow. These people were Tiv, and the Tiv were careful farmers. A man could not be circumcised or married until he was strong enough at about age sixteen to take a hoe and build a straight line of sixty thigh-high earth heaps on which a wife could plant yams.

Rising population had put the system at risk by reducing the fallow period from ten years to two or three. For a time it seemed as though the Nigerian government would come to the rescue by distributing fertilizer, but with the general collapse of the civil administration, fertilizer was now unobtainable. The villagers' yams, once the king of crops, became physically smaller.

INDIA

The Indian Ministry of Finance reported in 2007 that the country had 100 million farms. The average size was 2.5 acres—and shrinking. In

1960 there had been only half that many, but holdings were split at each generation.

One result was that India's farmworkers constituted half the country's workforce but contributed less than a fifth of the country's GDP. One study concluded, "We are in a very critical situation. It has reached what you might call epidemic proportions." A senior government secretary said, "We need to move some people out of agriculture. I don't think that a 17 percent share of GDP and a 50 percent share of employment are viable in the long run."

Where would they go? A McKinsey consultant, considering India's population over the twenty years between 2010 and 2030, said, "Close to 270 million people will be entering the workforce. Yet the real job creation will be closer to 120–150 million. That means the rest of the people will have to stay in agriculture."

Those people wanted *bijli, sadaak,* and *paani*—electricity, roads, and water. The lack of those things in 2004 cost the Indian People's Party reelection. The succeeding prime minister was intelligent, highly educated, incorruptible, and hardworking, but he faced passive resistance from the bureaucracy. And worse. *Time* magazine in 2004 praised Gautam Goswami, the top administrative officer in Bihar, for his work in emergency relief. Late in 2005 he was jailed for owning property he could not have purchased on his salary. Ten years later, failure to provide *bijli, sadaak,* and *paani* once again decimated the government, this time led by the Congress Party.

Electricity, roads, and water also topped the to-do list for the Naxalites, the estimated 20,000 guerrillas of the Communist (Maoist) Party of India. An analyst said, "Unless something radical is done in terms of a structural revolution in rural areas, you will see a continuous expansion of Maoist insurrection." A few months later, Naxalites attacked a remote police station in Chhattisgarh State and killed fifty police.

India, the Naxalite leader said, was now in an "excellent revolutionary situation." More than 17,000 Indian farmers had committed suicide in 2003. Between 2001 and 2005 the total was 90,000. Debt was the usual cause. Loans from banks and cooperatives carried an annual interest rate of between 10 and 20 percent per annum, but in several big states, including Rajasthan, Punjab, Bihar, Andhra Pradesh, and Tamil Nadu, moneylenders provided over 30 percent of all loans, and they almost always charged more than 20 percent. A common arrangement was 5 percent per month, along with the farmer's signature on a blank form that gave the moneylender the right to take the farmer's land without notice. The average debt of the farmers who committed suicide in 2007 was $835.

One of those farmers was Boya Madhiletti, a farmer in Andhra Pradesh's Mahbubnagar District. Madhiletti had twelve acres, which he planted with sunflowers, cotton, and corn. He ran up agricultural debts, came to the end of his tether, and was advised to phone a government help line. He did so, pleading for assistance in getting a bank loan to be secured by his land. A meeting was set up with the local revenue officer, who demanded a bribe of about fifty dollars. Madhiletti declined and, debt taking no holiday, finally drank pesticide. Rushed to the hospital, he ran up $200 in medical bills. Released, he was promptly jailed for attempting suicide. After two weeks his neighbors bailed him out. One of them said, "None of this would have happened if he had paid that bribe. He would have had no problem." With the publicity given the case, he finally got a bank loan of $400.

India had its own unique shame too. The caste system had sustained Hindu society for centuries but had also trapped Indians in the fatalistic acceptance of misery. Perhaps the day would come when high-caste villagers didn't sprinkle holy water on a dirt road just crossed by a Dalit. Maybe the day would come when parents didn't burn the clothes of a child if they were touched by a Dalit.

That day hadn't yet arrived. Bhaiyalal Bhotmange, a Dalit from a village near Nagpur, had had the nerve to prosper enough on his five acres to have his children educated. Bhotmange lived now with a police guard an hour's drive from his village. There, he imagined his former neighbors having said to one another, "Let's finally cleanse our village of the mahars [carcass handlers]." Bhotmange explained what happened next. "I thought that if I weren't in the house, they wouldn't touch the womenfolk." He fled, but the mob killed his wife and three children. The youngest, seventeen, was the last to die. Her last words were, "Mamma, they killed me. Mamma, I am dead." Bhotmange concluded by saying of the villagers, "I think they're happy. They got what they wanted."

A twenty-four-year-old mother near Varanasi, that most sacred Indian city, went to a hospital to get a card that would entitle her to free milk for her children. She said that the doctors told her, "We don't want to see you Dalits here bothering us." Her two children died of starvation. A government investigation followed, but its sole result was a three-foot-high dais, built at the insistence of government officers who would not talk to Dalits except while standing above them.

Another Dalit went fishing in a pond. Upper-caste villagers "told me I couldn't take any big fish out of the water. They surrounded me from all sides and beat me. When I hobbled home, my life's work [two huts, including food stores] was on fire. Even my daughter's dowry was burnt." An upper-caste villager said the man's family members had "burned down their own huts to get money from the government. You see they're not smart people. To be very frank, they're very dirty." A lifetime had passed since Dr. B. R. Ambedkar, himself an Untouchable, as Dalits were then known, had famously called the Indian village "a den of ignorance, narrow-mindedness and communalism."

CHINA

The other behemoth was India's none-too-fraternal northern neighbor. About 130 million people lived in China on less than a dollar a day. Worse, their incomes instead of rising seemed to be falling. Many of these people were in the province of Gansu, on the upper Yellow River. A woman there said, "Life here is so miserable, no one wants to marry the men. For girls, the ideal is to marry someone in the city or in a better village." A mother fixed a meal of steamed bread, served with a bowl of cabbage and potatoes. That was her menu, day in and day out. She said that the children "don't ask for anything else because that's all they know."

The agricultural potential was higher in Anhui, just west of Shanghai, but the average Anhui family subsisted on a third of an acre. The province was so crowded that young adults usually had to leave. One said, "There's no way not to leave the village. The conditions here are too poor and there's nothing for us to do."

Even those who wanted to stay often found themselves landless as local governments reclassified farmland for urban use, took it at whatever price the government determined it was worth as farmland, then sold it at market rates—with the difference going either to the local government or the pockets of local officials. Land sales generated a quarter of local-government revenue, but farmers got only a sliver of the proceeds—by one estimate, 2 percent.

Since 1990 some 16 million acres had been taken and some 40 million farmers wholly or partly dispossessed in this way. This kind of land confiscation was an increasingly frequent cause of "mass incidents," which by the Chinese Academy of Social Science's count jumped from 10,000 in 1995 to 58,000 in 2003, 74,000 in 2004, and 87,000 in 2005. Chinese farmers knew that the legal system was stacked against them, and in 2004 only 5,400 complaints were filed with the Chinese legislature.

In the village of Dongzhou, west of Shanghai, police opened fire the next year on farmers protesting a power plant planned for land taken without compensation. "At about 8 p.m. they started using guns, shooting bullets into the ground, but not really targeting anybody. Finally, at about 10 p.m. they started killing people." About twenty died.

A year later, farmers at Aoshi, near Yunfu City in Guangdong, lost thirty-six acres. It wasn't much, but it was the economic anchor of 144 families. The land was then sold, with one two-acre parcel going to a Honda dealer who paid the city $250,000. The farmers were offered $25,000. Their efforts to get more were in vain, despite petitioning Beijing. An American reporter wrote that when he "returned a couple of weeks later, he was swiftly surrounded by four unmarked vehicles and taken by plainclothes police to North Yunfu District headquarters. There he was interrogated and lectured on the need for authorization from provincial authorities for any reporting in Yunfu, before being escorted to the city limits and sent on his way." One farmer did manage to catch the reporter's ear to say, "We can't afford to buy those cars. The only ones buying them are government officials."

News of such events spread despite the government's best efforts. Late in 2010 the Internet carried photos of the crushed body of Qian Yunhui, a former party representative in Zhaiqiao Village, Zhejiang. Witnesses said that security officials held Qian down while a heavy truck rolled slowly over his body, apparently because he had refused to remain silent after officials in nearby Yueqing took the village's farmland, without compensation, to make way for a power plant.

Two years later a villager died in police custody following a protest over land confiscation in the village of Wukan, Guangdong. A survivor warned, "If all the farmland is sold, we will be slaves." To the consternation of many officials, the government of Guangdong decided to allow the Wukan villagers to run a genuine, unscripted election for village leaders. Pictures soon appeared on the Internet of the simple voting booths the villagers set up. A blogger wrote, "This is a picture that will be recorded in history." A year later, perhaps a fifth of the 3,200 acres taken from the villagers had been returned to them. The old village party chief had been expelled from the party for corruption, but higher officials still impeded the work of the newly elected leaders. They understood very well that if they paid higher prices for land they would have to find other sources of income.

Yu Keping, of Beijing University's Center for Chinese Government Innovations, gave out prizes in 2004 to Shenzhen for "market-oriented reforms of public utilities," to Buyun Township in Sichuan for "direct election of a township leader," and to Wenling City, Zhejiang, for "democratic consultation." Yu then published a book called *Democracy Is a Good Thing*. A reporter came by for a chat. Yu declined: the issue was too sensitive, he said. Another critique came in 2007 with *Will the Boat Sink the Water?* Chen Guidi and Wu Chuntao argued that in the years following the breakup of agricultural communes, local governments turned into voracious collectors of taxes and fees of every description, beggaring the farmers of Anhui while enriching government officials and urban Chinese. The book was banned within two months of pub-lication, but 10 million copies were sold, mostly illegally.

Partly to counter rural anger, the Chinese government in 2006 announced that it would increase spending on rural health, educa-tion, and welfare, while abolishing fees for the first nine years of school. By 2012 almost all Chinese villages had seen improvements in their roads, electricity supplies, and water systems. The government side-stepped the politically explosive question of whether it would allow farmers to sell the land they cultivated.

LAND REFORM

The government of Hugo Chávez proposed reorganizing Venezue-la's rural economy around state-financed cooperatives established on ranches confiscated from private owners. It would then move slum dwellers out to the countryside. An official said, "We will conduct, con-vince, have them [the relocated slum dwellers] fall in love and seduce them with successful alternative proposals showing that one can live, under 'X' conditions, in rural areas." The program, originally named Misión Vuelvan Caras, or "Mission About-Face," was renamed Mis-ión Che Guevara. The new name sent a clear signal, but just to make sure the message wasn't lost, Chávez added, "The revolution is here." A new settler had a message for a nearby rancher: "Why so much land owned by one man and so many others dying for land? Tell Lecuna [the rancher] we are going to take everything. We are coming his way."

Many Africans too believed that land reform was the key to bet-tering their lives. A Masai guide lamented the loss of Masai lands to whites in colonial times. He said, "We're now squatters on our own land. I'd rather spend my days in prison than see settlers spend their days enjoying my motherland."

The South African government set out to acquire for redistribution to blacks about a third of the country's farmland, of which more than four-fifths had gone into white ownership after the Natives' Land Act of 1913. The target date was 2014, but as of 2007 only 5 percent had been redistributed. Five years later, the total was about 9 percent. Since 1994, ironically, more blacks had been evicted from white-owned farms than had acquired land under the redistribution program.

A founder of South Africa's Landless Movement said, "Land reform is going nowhere. People are being patient but they are being fooled. Market-led reform has failed in many countries. Land invasions are the only way." The head of the African National Congress Youth League agreed and said, "We must take the land without payment." (He wanted to take back the country's mines too.) A white farm operator, mindful of experience in other countries, responded, "Economic empowerment isn't about handing out land. That's not going to help anybody." The Recapitalization and Development Program offered financial help to about 1 percent of the new owners, and Walmart, through its Massmart subsidiary, offered one new owner a test contract for delivery of 50,000 cabbages.

All but 250 of Zimbabwe's 4,500 white farmers in 1999 were forced off their land within a decade. Some 60,000 smallholdings were created. One of the surviving white farmers commented on a neighboring farm now shared by fifty families. "They're producing nothing," he said. "With that many people on the land, it doesn't work." An economist agreed. "If you are going back to small-scale pre-colonial traditional farming," he said, "you are subjecting yourself to the same constraints that those people suffered from, that kept the population of this country at a few hundred thousand for thousands of years. The country has become poorer because of what's happened, much, much poorer."

Was it inevitably so? From a peak in 2000 of 522 million pounds, Zimbabwe's tobacco production fell to a low of 108 million in 2008. By 2012, however, it was back to 330 million. Instead of 2,000 producers, nearly all white, the crop now came from 60,000, nearly all black. One of those producers said, "All the big guys who got land, they are doing nothing. But the small guys are working hard and really producing." Conflicting reports suggested that much of the confiscated land had been sold back to its white owners.

Integrated rural development programs, package programs of innovations less threatening than land reform, had been around since the late colonial era. The United Nations undertook its own version in 2002, shortly after the signing of the Millennium Declaration. Kofi Annan announced that the Millennium Development Project sought to cut in half by 2015 the number of people living on a dollar a day.

The cost of reaching this goal was calculated to be $150 billion annually for ten years, less than the 0.7 percent of global GNP that the industrialized countries had repeatedly pledged they would spend. Jeffrey Sachs, the perennial or millennial gadfly, said, "You can't have a civilized world in which the rich aren't even willing to live up to this tiny commitment." He was particularly critical of the United States. "My country," he said, "spends nearly $450 billion on its military and only $15 billion in development aid per year." That aid figure was about 0.2 percent of GNP. At the Monterrey Summit in 2002, the United States announced the creation of the Millennium Challenge Account and pledged a 50 percent increase in its foreign aid by 2006. As of 2006 the United States gave more than any other country, but per capita it lagged behind not only Sweden, which gave over 1 percent, but Norway, Ireland, Britain, France, Switzerland, Germany, Spain, Australia, Canada, and Japan.

Sachs wrote, "Slowly, fitfully, the voices of the world's poor are breaking through the protective shield of the rich and mighty." Elsewhere he wrote, "I reject the plaintive cries of the doomsayers who say that ending poverty is impossible. I have identified the specific investments that are needed; found ways to plan and implement them; shown that they can be affordable; and addressed the counsels of despair who claim that the poor are condemned by their cultures, values, and personal behaviors."

Sachs's program began with a dozen "millennium villages," soon increased to eighty. One was Sauri, a collection of settlements with 65,000 people living on the Kenya side of Lake Victoria. Its farmers received fertilizer and hybrid corn seed. Everyone in the village got a mosquito net. There was a school lunch program, an electric line, and a water main. The cost was estimated at $350,000, which worked out to $70 per person annually over five years, with the villagers contributing the equivalent of $10, the government contributing $30, and foreign donors the rest. The plan was to scale up to 1,000 villages, then 100,000.

But would the program meet its goals, even given more time? The World Bank in 2010 concluded that it would be impossible to undertake a formal evaluation of Sauri because its "before" status had not been measured. That problem could be corrected with better preparation at the next stage of the project, but skeptics anticipated that replication would be difficult without a highly trained and expensive staff that was likely to feel marooned if told to live in the places they were supposed to help. Another critic warned that expansion of the program would run "into the problem we've all been talking about: corruption, bad leadership, ethnic politics."

Sachs admitted, "What we're focusing on is about one-third of the problem." The good news, as he pointed out, was that the percentage of people in sub-Saharan Africa living on less than $1.25 a day declined from 58 percent in 1999 to 49 percent in 2010. That was a much less dramatic decline than in the world as a whole, where the percentage of people living at the same level fell in the same period from 34 to 21 percent, but it was still a major change. Sachs pointed out as well that the percentage of children dying in sub-Saharan Africa before the age of five declined from 177 per 1,000 in 1990 to 98 per 1,000 in 2012. The nagging question was whether the change was the result of improved rural conditions or the tide of urban migration.

AGRICULTURAL RESEARCH AND MICROCREDIT

Norman Borlaug, the wheat breeder who had won a Nobel Peace Prize for his work, hated the politicizing name Green Revolution. Bestowed by William Gaud, the administrator of the U.S. Agency for International Development, the name stuck anyway.

The amount of money allocated to agricultural research did not stick. It declined steeply after the 1960s, and crop yield increases slowed. Still, work continued in the Philippines at the International Rice Research Institute, which hoped to develop a genetically modified rice that would photosynthesize the way corn did, with four carbon atoms instead of three. If IRRI succeeded with this so-called C4 rice—a big if—rice yields could go up 50 percent, even with reduced irrigation and fertilizer. Another blockbuster would be water-efficient maize that didn't need heavy irrigation in semiarid locations.

Such plants might be part of a second generation of genetically modified organisms, developed not for their resistance to herbicides and insects but for their resistance to drought, flood, heat, salinity, or acidity. Syngenta announced its development of a sugar beet suited to the hot, dry parts of India. The beets were being grown in the Baramati District, southeast of Pune. They were tricky to grow and labor intensive, but they yielded twice as much sugar per acre as cane, did it in half the time, and used only a third as much water. India grew about 11 million acres of sugarcane (more than ten times the acreage in the United States), so a shift to beets could free up a lot of land and water for other uses. The biggest problem was that sugarcane growers might lose their markets. They would have a hard time finding a new crop as profitable as cane.

Another big production boost might come from the System of Rice Intensification. Supporters claimed that yields doubled if the spacing between transplanted rice plants was increased and if the ground was kept damp but not flooded. The method had many passionate supporters, along with many passionate doubters, but the balance of opinion was tipping in its favor. One senior Indian scientist said, "I would say to them [the skeptics], 'go to the fields and see the evidence.' There are now close to a million hectares under SRI and that cannot be regarded as a delusion. It is real."

Improvements were urgently needed because India's rice yields were falling. Paradoxically, this was because India subsidized urea, or nitrogen fertilizer. Instead of applying nitrogen and potassium in the recommended ratio of four to one, farmers were applying it in a soil-damaging ratio of twenty-four to one, or even more. It was a vicious cycle. A government officer said, "One farmer sees another's field looking greener, so he adds more urea. A farmer will become bankrupt, but he will not stop using urea." A farmer in the famously progressive Punjab said, "The soil health is deteriorating, but we don't know how to make it better. As the fertility of the soil is declining, more fertilizer is required."

There were other development strategies, too. For creating an alternative to traditional moneylenders, Muhammad Yunus won the Nobel Peace Prize in 2006. His Grameen (or "of the village") Bank went on to lend $5.3 billion in Bangladesh. The money was divided among 6.5 million borrowers, 95 percent of them women borrowing an average of $150. Grameen had no provision for legal recovery of losses, but it had a 99 percent recovery rate, mostly because borrowers were grouped and further loans blocked to all members of a group in which a single member defaulted.

Worldwide, 1,800 microcredit lenders like the Grameen Bank had $65 billion in outstanding credits by 2010. The average loan was $520. Outstanding loans in India alone jumped from less than $1 billion in 2006 to $6.7 billion in 2010. That money was spread over 30 million borrowers, more than half the 54 million clients of India's conventional banks.

Much more could be done. That was the view of Vikram Akula, founder of Swayam Krishi Sangham Finance, the "Farmers Self-Help Group." Akula argued that nonprofit organizations doing microfinance were "incredibly inefficient and hopelessly unscalable." SKS borrowers, in contrast, had to repay a fixed amount each week in exact change. That way, a loan officer could visit three villages in a morning, not one, and could meet fifty borrowers at each meeting, not twenty. By 2006 SKS had lent $57 million to 200,000 borrowers. The loans averaged $285 with an interest rate of 25 percent. Citigroup and HSBC took notice and were happy to lend SKS millions of dollars. Akula said, "This can work driven only by greed. That's the magic of it."

Problems? Peer pressure to repay was so great that borrowers sometimes resorted to traditional moneylenders for the money needed for the next microloan payment. A backlash began in Andhra Pradesh, the Indian state with the most microlending—a third of the national total. There were stories of harsh collection tactics, and government officials began telling farmers to delay payment or to make payments monthly instead of weekly. Andhra reported fifty suicides from borrowers in 2010, and SKS reported a 20 percent drop in collections.

PHONES AND COMPUTERS

In 1984 AT&T employed over a million people. Management wondered about the threat posed by the emerging wireless technology. It hired McKinsey. The eminent consultant told AT&T not to worry. By 2000, it reported, America would have only 900,000 cell-phone users. McKinsey turned out to be wrong by a factor of 100. By 2007 there were 3 billion mobile phone subscriptions worldwide. Pay phones weren't quite an endangered species, but in the United States their numbers fell from 2.6 million in 1998 to 1 million in 2007. Globally, the number of calls from pay phones dropped by half between 2002 and 2007. Sales of cell phones in Europe, Japan, and the United States eventually maxed out. NTT Docomo's boss said, "Mobile-phone growth has reached a limit." An executive at Dutch KPN added, "The industry is maturing, that's what you get."

There was still a lot of room for growth elsewhere. The boss of China Mobile, China's biggest wireless provider, asked, "Can an elephant as big as China Mobile still run fast? My answer is, 'This elephant will still run.'" In the first half of 2006, his company signed up 26 million new subscribers, and by the end of the year, it had 300 million subscribers. By June 2007 it had added another 30 million and had made mobile coverage available to 97 percent of all Chinese. By early 2008 China Mobile had 370 million customers; in 2009 it had 464 million, and a year later it had 564 million. Still, the elephant had a long way to run. China Mobile said it was working on a cheap solar-powered recharger for users too remote to have electricity.

About 85 percent of Kenyans had no electricity in their homes, but many had phones anyway. One woman was tired of the three-hour ride by motorcycle taxi to her nearest power source, in the town of Mogotio. She invested eighty dollars in a solar panel. "My main motivation," she said, "was the phone, but this has changed so many things." She was thinking of her four bright LED lights. Now her older children could study at night without the danger of kerosene fires or burns. She saved about thirty-five dollars monthly in kerosene, transportation, and battery-recharging costs. By 2010 more than sixty of her neighbors had also bought solar panels and developed their own power supply, far from the national grid.

In 1993 eight of the top ten phone companies in the world, by capitalization, had been American. The other two were Japanese and British. Fifteen years later, in 2008, only two of the top ten—AT&T and Verizon—were American. China was top dog. Chasing it were Vodafone (UK), Telefónica (Spain), France Telecom, Deutsche Telekom, NTT with NTT Docomo (Japan), and América Móvil (Mexico).

The cell-phone business was booming in India too. Service was divided among Bharti Airtel, Reliance, Hutchison Essar, Bharat Sanchar Nigam, and Idea Cellular. Together, by the end of 2005, they had 143 million subscribers and more than 6 million new accounts every month. By mid-2007 the figure was 218 million, with 7 million new accounts monthly. A year later, there were 347 million subscribers, approaching ten times the country's 40 million landlines. By early 2010 the figure was over 600 million. By 2012 it was 900 million, including about 300 million in rural areas. These astronomical numbers were exaggerated because they included SIM cards no longer in use or activated; even so, the number of actual cell phones was very large.

The biggest Indian provider was Bharti Airtel, up explosively from 3 million subscribers in 2003 to a claimed 120 million in 2010. How did the company grow so fast? The company's founder, Sunil Bharti Mittal, explained that he was meeting with European companies. "I saw that these were huge companies, hugely resourced. And it began to dawn on me: I have to be like them. But could I afford to be like them?

We'd need to hire 10,000 people, maybe 20,000, within two years. Did we have the resources to do that? Were we the best company to attract that kind of talent? The answer, clearly, was no."

So, reversing the familiar pattern of companies outsourcing to India, Mittal outsourced from India, handing his network to Ericsson, Siemens, and Nokia and then paying them for their services. "People gasped in horror," he recalled. "I got calls from around the world saying, 'You've gone nuts, this is the lifeline of your business, it's something you can't afford to lose.'" Mittal replied, "If something goes wrong with my switch, there's no way anyone from Bharti can do anything about it. An Ericsson guy is going to have to come and fix it. I don't manufacture it; I can't maintain or upgrade it. So I'm thinking, 'This doesn't really belong to me. Let's just throw it out.'"

Bharti concentrated on marketing and developing new services. With 55,000 retailers just in the two poor eastern states of Bihar and Jharkand, Bharti sold handsets for as little as forty dollars and prepaid cards for as little as twenty-five cents. Thousands of his retailers were cigarette and betel-nut sellers, and many of the buyers were illiterate, registering their phones with a thumbprint. Often, they charged their phones off car batteries owned by some enterprising villager who let them do it for about a dime. The phone masts themselves—Bharti had 50,000 in 2007 but was adding more furiously—were up to 15 miles from the nearest electricity supply, so diesel was trucked in weekly for the generators that kept them going. Bharti and other providers watched as Vihaan Networks Limited experimented with solar-powered masts. Power consumption would be about a hundred watts instead of the 600 or 700 required by Ericsson and Alcatel-Lucent towers. There would be no fancy controls; the towers had only one button: on/off. The station beeped until the villagers setting it up pointed it correctly.

Cell phones changed lives as surely and probably more noticably than any rural-development program. A Chinese farmer who had a cell phone said, "Before, we had to travel 20 kilometers to make a phone call. Now we contact the buyers, and they come to us." Visiting Shanghai, the CEO of Kodak saw a man fishing with a bamboo rod and said, "All of a sudden he reaches in his pocket and takes a picture of the fish. Immediately he makes a call, sends the picture and then he's talking to someone to make a deal. He gets the fish on his bike and goes to deliver the fish. He broke five different generations of supply chain in the West!"

In India porters once had to wait for a chance to carry shopping bags. Now regular customers called them to make an appointment. Cab drivers and even rickshaw pullers made appointments too. A peanut farmer 300 miles south of Mumbai had a tractor that he rented on demand. With a phone, he said, "I can run my business even from the field. When I had problems with the tractors before, we would just have to leave it where it was for a day, now I can call and get it fixed right away."

Babu Rajan, a fisherman in South India, said that in the past he had sailed into port and sold his fish to buyers who had the market to themselves and could offer what they liked, knowing that the fish would spoil if Rajan held out for a higher price. Worse luck, Rajan might come into port late and find the buyers gone. Now, while still at sea Rajan called buyers in different ports and let them bid for his fish. He said, "Even if it takes us one or two hours to get there, they will still be waiting for us. It was never like that before." If other fishermen saw him throw his big net into the water, they knew he had found fish, and they mentioned this to their own buyers, who phoned Rajan. "When I have a big catch," he explained, "the phone rings 60 or 70 times before I get to port." Engine problems? In the past Rajan drifted until another fisherman saw him and sent help. Now Rajan called a mechanic, who of course had his own phone. Rajan's income had tripled to $150 a month. He said, "When I was a kid, we never had enough money for clothes and books, so we never really went to school. Now everything is different."

Phones changed African lives, too. A reporter visited Congo (Brazzaville) and wrote, "One woman living on the Congo River, unable even to write her last name, tells customers to call her cell phone if they want to buy the fresh fish she sells. She doesn't have electricity—

she can't put the fish in the freezer. So she keeps them in the river, tethered live on a string, until a call comes in." She charged her phone off a neighbor's car battery. The neighbor had no car but periodically took the battery by bus to town to get it recharged. This had become his business. How many people had the same business? The fish lady said, "Oooh, a lot of people. Too many."

Across the river, Congo (Kinshasa) in 2006 had 20,000 landlines but 3.2 million cell-phone customers—about one phone for every twenty people. The two biggest providers were the British company Vodafone and Dutch-owned Celtel. Along with three smaller providers, they had erected 700 towers reaching about 70 percent of the country's people. At twenty-six cents a minute, calls were expensive, but the benefits in a country otherwise falling apart were huge. A truck driver could call a mechanic or a doctor. A resident in Kinshasa could call a parent who couldn't be seen in person without a week's hard traveling.

The boss of Safaricom, a Vodafone partner with 8 million subscribers in Kenya, demonstrated the power of phones by sending a text message and getting a response from the Kenya Agricultural Commodities Exchange. He said, "So a 126 kg bag of cabbage is 1,000 shillings in Nairobi and 2,200 in Mombasa. So you'd better go and sell your cabbage in Mombasa."

With banks far and few between, Africans also used phones as money-transfer devices. If they wanted to send money back to parents in a distant village, they went to a phone lady and gave her the money. For a fee she transferred the balance as airtime to a phone lady in the parents' village. The second phone lady took a fee and handed the rest of the value of the airtime to the parents. Goods could be bought the same way. One man said, "It has totally changed life in Congo." It was the same story in South Africa, where Wizzit provided financial services by phone. A barber in Soweto said that half his customers paid with their phones.

Kenya's Safaricom set up its own money-transfer business. Customers gave cash to one of the company's 625 tellers in places like gas stations and supermarkets. The teller—referred to as an HTM, for "human teller machine"—sent a text message with a PIN to the recipient, who went to another HTM and, with the PIN and ID, collected the money. Safaricom had 2.3 million subscribers who had taken the next step and signed up for its M-Pesa payment systems. A company agent added a menu to the phone. It allowed the phone's owner to send money to anyone with a phone. The system handled several million payments monthly.

New ways to make money: in 1996 Grameenphone, Grameen Telecom, and Grameen Bank started Bangladesh's Village Phone Program. It grew to provide 250,000 impoverished women with phones and logged annual revenues of a billion dollars. Participating women sat in their local markets with two, three, or four phones and waited for rural customers who needed phone service. Some of the women had small generators that powered a board with thirty plugs. For a fee customers could recharge their phones.

There were losers, of course. The ancient work of scribes was in terminal decline. One lingering practitioner in Mumbai had a daughter in the United States. An American reporter volunteered to hand-deliver a letter to her, to which the scribe replied, "Why would I send her a letter? I'll just call her on the phone." Meanwhile, he might, for two cents a minute, listen to dial-up radio. About 20 million Indians did that in 2009. They chose from Bollywood tunes, soccer matches, or live prayers from major temples.

The Internet, too, changed the lives of the poor. As of 2007, 22 million Indians accessed the Internet; five years later, the number had quintupled to over 120 million. Some of them used Karnataka's Bhoomi, or Land, Project, which by 2004 had digitized and posted on the Internet 20 million land-ownership records. A farmer said, "The village accountant was corrupt. He'd delay making any changes, and he made mistakes, too." Bhoomi's director said, "With equal access to information, a lower-caste person now has the same privileges as an upper-caste person." The company that contracted to digitize the records, Comat, later set up 800 kiosks called Nemmadi, or "peace of mind." The kiosks offered other services. For thirty cents or so, a villager could get a copy of a birth certificate or a pension document or a caste and income certificate that allowed children to attend private schools without charge.

Comat was handling 50,000 such transactions daily. As for the land records, they weren't useful only to farmers. A tractor manufacturer used them to find landowners with more than ten acres. They were potential customers. Meanwhile, Babajob gave illiterate Indian laborers web pages much like those of Facebook. It paid about two dollars to "connectors," people who successfully linked employers to employees—gardeners, drivers, housepainters—through a network of mutual acquaintances.

In Vietnam 200 community centers were set up in Bac Ninh Province, near Hanoi. Each was equipped with five PCs, a printer, and an Internet connection so farmers could check crop prices and land-allotment maps. China meanwhile sold 414,000 PCs under a subsidized program that provided farmers with computers built to handle power fluctuations and loaded with software for inventory management.

Court records were coming online too. The Southern African Legal Information Institute posted decisions from sixteen countries. A judge said, "People are always talking about African states and the rule of law. But you can't have the rule of law without the law." Now, with the Internet, villagers could see the law for themselves. Another judge said, "Ordinary people in the region will benefit if the law is open and judges can be held accountable. . . . It's hugely empowering and enriching of democracy if that is the case."

VOTING WITH THEIR FEET

Along with their more immediate uses, cell phones and the Internet reinforced the message that life was better in cities. The tide of migration reached every country on every continent. About a fifth of all Mexican men between twenty-six and thirty-five, for example, now lived in the United States. Many were legal residents, but many were not. Could they be stopped? Before becoming secretary of homeland security, the governor of Arizona had said, "Show me a 50-foot wall and I'll show you a 51-foot ladder." A Border Patrol agent on the Rio Grande agreed: "We're never going to stop them," he said, "never. This was happening before I was born, and it will be happening long after I am gone. There is no way to shut the river down." Another agent added, "It's like catch-and-release fishing." Another critic said, "I see so much waste. Ray Charles could see it."

A woman who had lived in Fresno for six years was stopped for a traffic violation, then deported. Taking the long view, she said, "They can't stop us." She might have added that out of every twenty people who tried crossing the border illegally, nineteen made it. The government spent an average of $12,000 deporting the twentieth, which was why some critics said that border-control measures were really job programs for Americans.

A weaker American economy and a stronger Mexican one finally slowed the tide. A Mexican who had worked as a trucker found himself driving a cab in 2008. He said, "To live in America these days is to suffer. I'm not recommending to my friends back home that they come here. I'm thinking of leaving myself." A laborer in Los Angeles said, "Life is very difficult. No one is hiring."

Border Patrol statistics suggested that Mexicans back home heard the message. The number of Mexican arrivals fell from a peak of 700,000 in 2000 to 150,000 in 2009. In the five years after 2005, about 1.4 million Mexicans entered the United States, but as many left. By 2012 border arrests were down to a forty-year low, and detention centers were reportedly almost empty. "We have turned the page in terms of immigration," one analyst said. "We haven't turned the page yet in terms of the politics."

Mexicans working on construction jobs around Los Cabos, at the tip of Baja California, meanwhile earned about $800 a month, three or four times the usual Mexican wage. One man who came to Los Cabos as a driver built a business selling coconuts to tourists. Now he had a house of his own. He said, "I know it sounds strange, but this is the Mexican dream made right here in Mexico." Another man, whose family ran a nopal bottling operation in Oaxaca, remembered his own

American past and said, "In our village, the land is ours and we will soon have everything we need. We won't have to be up before the sun. In my house, nobody will say, 'Get up. Hurry. It's time to work now.'"

There was a similar story at Rosarno, a town of 15,000 at the toe of the Italian boot 7,000 miles away. Every morning, migrants gathered and hoped for work in the nearby orange and olive groves. They came from Morocco, Romania, Egypt, and—at the end of the hiring line, just after Gypsies—sub-Saharan Africa. Wages ran about ten dollars a day, and living conditions were so bad that Caritas and Médicins Sans Frontières offered clinics and free meals. The mayor recognized what he called the "inhuman conditions" facing the workers but said, "Officially I can't help them, they are here illegally and I should call the police and get them sent home." Without them, he said, the town's economy would collapse.

A college graduate who had abandoned a job teaching in a Gambian high school was now squatting on forest land near the strawberry fields of Huelva, on Spain's Atlantic coast. He said, "I cannot go home empty-handed. If I went home, they would be saying, 'What have you been doing with yourself, Amadou?' They think in Europe there is money all over."

A resident of Khouribga, 70 miles south of Casablanca, said, "Everyone here talks about migrating. Here, even if you have a job, you make little money." And so there was a continuing exodus of migrants— "candidates," they were called—who set out in long, motorized pirogues for the Canary Islands, 950 miles away. From there the plan was to enter the EU and find a job. In Spain these people could earn seventy dollars a day—at home, two dollars. About 31,000 attempted the trip in 2006, but many of them—some said a tenth, others a sixth or a third—died in the attempt. Some wore talismans with Quranic quotations; some bathed in holy water before the journey. The motto was "Barça ou Barzakh" (Barcelona or the afterlife).

A mother of three sons in Europe said, "Everyone wants to have a son there. It's a source of advancement.... Nicer houses and more money. That way people respect you and think highly of you." A mother of a son who wasn't so lucky said, "My other sons will never try it. No, a thousand times no. No more sea."

In 2003, 504 Africans died while attempting to cross to Spain. Others continued to make the attempt. Some who stayed behind were reduced to desperation. A twenty-one-year-old Moroccan who had lived in France legally for seven years returned home for a summer vacation. "I went back to the area I grew up in. It's a very poor district of Fes. At a bend in the road this guy pulled a kitchen knife on me and demanded my bag and my t-shirt. I gave them to him but then I said, 'Hey, Essrine, don't you recognize me? It's me. Issam. We played football together for 10 years in the street just over there.' Suddenly he realised who I was and he put down his knife and my things and started to cry."

A leader of Malta's anti-immigrant Republican National Alliance said bluntly, "We don't want a multicultural society." A Sudanese among the immigrants on Malta said, "I see the way people look at me on the bus. Some people make you feel so sad." A government adviser said, "We've got to live with it. We've got to adapt to it. We have got to make it work." He meant that there was no way to stop the flood. One migrant journeyed from Libya to Sicily on a small boat loaded with forty-five other men—Palestinians, Moroccans, Tunisians, Iraqis. He said, "We were already dead when we were in Sudan and Libya. If we died on the boat, it's all the same."

THE CHINESE WAY

Few countries had been as successful as China in finding a path out of poverty. A Pew Research Center survey in 2008 found that 20 percent of respondents in the United States said economic conditions were good. In India the figure was 62 percent. For China the figure was 82 percent. The results were inflated because the survey counted only urban households, which in China earned more than three times as much as rural ones. Still, urban incomes in China, which averaged over $2,000 annually, had jumped an extraordinary 4,000 percent from the average household income in 1987 of $50. A retired senior official echoed the famous remark of Deng Xiaoping and asked, "What's wrong with everyone in China becoming rich?"

China's growth rested on exports, and in 2010 the country exported in a day what in 1978 it had exported in a year. By 2010 China had a 14 percent share of global manufacturing, far ahead of Germany's 7 percent and lagging only the United States, which still had a commanding 25 percent. An Indian importer said, "Anything you can think of comes from China these days—that's how it is." By 2012 China had become even India's top source of imports, up from seventh place in 2001. The UK, India's old master, was no longer even in the top ten.

The Shanghai representative for Malaysia's Kerry Group spoke about setting up a plant in China. "It's a mistake to try to do it yourself," he said. "You pay a lump sum, and the government does it all for you—very smooth." Did a potential manufacturer need a bit of road? A logistics expert said, "When the Chinese government talks about building infrastructure, they will do it on time and on a scale that defies belief." The number-two man in Longnan County, 200 miles north of Guangzhou, said, "We treat the companies that invest in our industrial park as gods. We assign a government official to serve each big company, helping it prepare administrative documents. Companies in our park don't waste their time and energy on paperwork."

There was no trouble getting land: the government took it, by force if need be. And so Dongguan, on the east side of mighty Guangzhou, went in the space of twenty years from a small town to a city of 7 million with 6,000 registered companies. The pioneer was Taiping Handbag Factory of Hong Kong, which opened in 1978. Twenty-five years later, the city made a third of the world's disk drives and 40 percent of its magnetic heads. Think shoes, furniture (giant Lacquer Craft was here), purses, and toys. The city's motto was "One Big Step Every Year, a New City in Five Years."

Foreign companies working in China typically had to share trade secrets with a Chinese partner. Airbus was so happy, for example, to get an order for 150 jets in 2006 that it agreed to build the planes on an assembly line in Tianjin. Sure enough, China in 2007 announced that it planned to begin making a regional jet of its own, for sale in its own huge market. By 2010 China's Commercial Aircraft Corporation put a mock-up on display and promised deliveries of the C919 by 2016.

How had the Chinese learned to make engines for those jets? General Electric had been so eager to get a $900 million Chinese contract for gas turbines that it had agreed to build them in China with a partner to whom it agreed to reveal the secrets of the 9F turbine. GE had spent half a billion dollars developing that turbine. The same turbine-blade technology was used in jet engines.

Alstom, a French company, wanted to sell 500 heavy freight locomotives to the Chinese. It agreed to build the locomotives in a joint venture with Datong Electric Locomotive, even though Datong in a few years might begin exporting locomotives to Europe. Why would the French do this? An indirect answer came from an executive at Bombardier, the Canadian manufacturer building the pressurized passenger trains running to Tibet. Those trains had been made with a Chinese partner. The Bombardier executive said, "The short answer to why we do it is we wouldn't get the work if we didn't do it that way."

Alstom and Siemens, along with Kawasaki, thought they were the only suppliers of high-speed train sets. Kawasaki's partner, China South Locomotive and Rolling Stock, begged to differ. A Kawasaki official asked, "How are you supposed to fight rivals when they have your technology and their cost base is so much lower?" Sure enough, Chinese manufacturers were now bidding on high-speed-rail jobs in Venezuela, Turkey, Brazil, and Russia.

A manufacturer of synthetic diamonds said, "Operating in China is like being in a leaky sieve." GE's boss said, "I am not sure that in the end they want any of us [foreigners] to win, or any of us to be successful." His views were echoed by the head of the German chemical giant BASF, who said that Chinese behavior "does not exactly correspond to our views of a partnership." Still, companies continued to bring their industrial secrets to China. Until 2010, for example, nobody in China could make large LCD panels. Then Samsung announced its intention to build a factory in Suzhou; LG Display made a similar announcement for

Guangzhou. Both offered the latest technology. The Chinese still weren't satisfied and began buying foreign companies outright. Putzmeister, a German manufacturer of concrete pumps, was now Chinese. So was Nexen, a Canadian oil-sands, shale-gas, and offshore oil company.

One Set of Chinese Problems

China sometimes seemed like a juggernaut, but its ascendancy wasn't assured. As early as 2006 an economist said, "We're seeing an end to the golden period of extremely low-cost labor in China." Seven years later, a textile manufacturer in Shenzhen said, "Operating in Southern China is a breakeven proposition at best."

By 2012 wages at Jiangxi Creative Knitwear Garments had doubled in four years to $309 monthly. The manager said, "We already give them free room, free meals and cake on their birthdays, but they want more." In 2004 the minimum wage for workers in Shenzhen had been a twelfth that in the United States. By 2012 it had risen to a quarter, or about $240 monthly.

China's population growth was beginning to slow too, with the labor force predicted to begin shrinking in 2016. Already, fewer young Chinese were available to work in factories. Older workers were an alternative, but they had a tough time handling eleven-hour days, six- or seven-day workweeks, and dormitory crowding.

Some Chinese manufacturers hired couples and offered housing in apartments instead of the usual same-sex dormitories. Other companies headed to other countries. The average cost of labor in Vietnam was fifty cents an hour in 2010, about a quarter of the $1.84 average in China. That's why the chief financial officer of Coach said, "We are looking to move production into lower-cost geographies, most notably Vietnam and India."

On the other hand, fabric and shipping costs accounted for 60 percent of the cost of a garment—three times the cost of labor. Few countries could match China on fabric availability and infrastructure, which is why one Hong Kong retailer said, "Consumers will have no choice but to accept the new reality." He meant higher prices.

An officer at a leading Hong Kong firm had another solution. "The answer to high prices in China is more China," he said. He meant that companies should invest in western China, where wages were lower. This had been official policy since 2000. Probably no more than 5 percent of foreign direct investment was actually going west, but Chengdu had Intel, Dell, and Motorola. Chongqing had Ford, BP, Ericsson, Carrefour, Isuzu, and Suzuki. By 2011 Chongqing also had Hewlett-Packard, Acer, Asustek, and Quanta, and a proud city official said, "We will become the world's largest notebook manufacturing base within a year." Chongqing's municipal boundary had been extended far into the countryside, and its leaders were determined to make their city into another Shanghai. Since 1990 the city proper had doubled to over 6 million people. Part of the region's appeal for manufacturers was that salaries in Chongqing averaged about $200 a month in 2014; in Shanghai, they averaged almost $300.

Another manufacturing center emerged in the provinces of Hunan, Jiangxi, and especially Anhui, 250 miles west of Shanghai. Call it the Chinese Midwest. Here, too, salaries were a third less than in Shanghai. Anhui had another thing going for it: high-speed trains now ran to Shanghai in less than half the eight hours the journey used to take. In 2009 alone, companies based elsewhere in China invested $70 billion in Anhui. Walmart, Carrefour, and Tesco all opened stores to serve the middle class emerging in Hefei, the provincial capital.

As early as 1998, however, Nike's CEO had been obliged to admit that "the Nike product has become synonymous with slave wages, forced overtime, and arbitrary abuse." The manager of Zhi Qiao Garments in Panyu said he knew that he was supposed to pay time and a half for shifts over eight hours. He was supposed to pay double time on Saturday, Sunday, and holidays. He said that the price he got from Nike, however, "never increases one penny."

Nike was far from alone. In 2005 Walmart conducted 13,600 inspections of 7,200 factories and, as a result, dropped 141 factories from its list of suppliers. Were the other 7,000 companies treating their workers well? Foreigners had a hard time finding the truth. They were shown fake records, while underage workers hurried out the back door and the rest were coached about what to tell the inspectors.

The Yue Yuen shoe factory at Gaobu, a suburb of Dongguan, was the world's biggest shoe factory, with 70,000 workers scattered over 173 production lines, each line making 2,000 pairs a day. The workers were paid seventy-two dollars a month, plus room and board. They worked sixty-hour weeks and bunked ten to a room. About 85 percent of them were young women. A worker in Shenzhen said that the city "may seem prosperous, but it's a desperate place."

Up in Wenzhou, on the coast of Zhejiang, 400,000 people worked in or were suppliers to shoe factories. The city exported 438 million pairs of shoes in 2005, but although there were some big firms— Aokang had 10,000 workers—most of the companies made only a few hundred thousand pairs annually. Profits were low—by one calculation thirty-seven cents a pair—but a factory owner boasted, "We work from 8 a.m. to 11 p.m. We Wenzhounese work harder than anyone else in China." The results showed. From a tiny core of narrow lanes, the city had grown hugely and now had a forest of high-rises, as well as flashy Mercedes and Cadillac dealerships. A furniture maker in town earned $200 a month and said, "We won't stay here forever. Our dream is to make enough to build a big new house and lead a quiet life back in Shaanxi."

Across China an estimated 22 million children had been left behind by parents who had migrated to factory jobs. One ten-year-old said of her parents, "I think they are suffering in order to make my life better." One elderly man and his wife cared for five such children. He said, "Most of the children are still too young to know the difference, but the oldest one cries every New Year when they [her parents] leave. There's no choice in this matter. This is the way things are these days." By one calculation, almost a third of China's rural children were growing up with at least one parent away in a city. More than half of those children had both parents away.

Eventually, many of the parents returned, driven by the Chinese government's insistence that they could collect social benefits only from the place where they were formally registered as residents. Researchers found that 37 percent of China's rural residents had left those places to work in cities at age twenty-five; ten years later, half that group had returned home. This created a big problem for the manufacturing centers, yet the city's residents couldn't build their lives there because they could not get schooling or medical services for their children anywhere except in the place where they were legally registered. A Yantian official said of the departing workers, "We really need them but from a political point of view we cast them out." Blame the residential *hukou*, the system of permits intended to control the movements of China's people.

Labor unrest came to a climax at a company established in 1974 in Taiwan. With an initial investment of $7,500, the company set out to make television control knobs. By 2000 this company, Hon Hai or Foxconn, had 30,000 people on the payroll and revenues of $3 billion. By 2006 revenues were $40.6 billion. By 2010 revenues were $85 billion. In 2012 they were $130 billion

By 2012 Hon Hai was China's biggest private employer, with over 920,000 workers in China and an additional 100,000 elsewhere. More than 390,000 were on the company's payroll at the Longhua Science and Technology Park in Shenzhen. Within a few years the company planned to have 500,000 workers in Chengdu, Wuhan, and Zhengzhou. Half of Hon Hai's business came from Apple, and by 2012 Hon Hai had 192,000 employees making iPhone 5s in Zhengzhou. Another 110,000 were making iPads in Chengdu.

"It's the prices," said one observer. "Their prices are lower for high-quality work." To compete, Flextronics in 2007 paid $3.6 billion for Solectron, another contract manufacturer. Combined, the new company was still smaller than Hon Hai, which by now was busy making not only iPods and iPhones but PCs for Hewlett-Packard, video-game consoles for Nintendo, cell phones for Nokia, and computer parts for Dell.

Hon Hai's chairman, Terry Gou, said that with inland wages a third lower than wages on the coast, more than half of China's manufacturing workers would in a few years be located inland. At least for the next twenty years, he said, "China won't have a competitor." Vietnam? Too small to be a threat, he said.

Ten workers at Hon Hai's Longhua plant committed suicide in 2010, however, apparently because the hours and working conditions drove them to despair. Another employee said, "I do the same thing every day. I have no future." A former employee said, "I believe it was the first time Terry Gou started seriously thinking about the workers as human beings." Gou himself, sounding like a Victorian mill owner, said that "a harsh environment is a good thing."

Trying to calm its workers, Hon Hai doubled their wages to almost $300 a month. Early in 2012 the company announced another increase, one that would lift salaries to about $400 a month. Aware of simultaneous troubles at Honda's Chinese suppliers, Gou said, "This is a watershed. You can no longer rely on China's cheap labor." It wasn't quite as bad as it sounded for American consumers, because labor accounted for only about 5 percent of the retail cost of consumer electronics.

Doubtful that higher salaries would stop suicides, Hon Hai strung netting around its dormitory stairwells. In the long run Gou said he wanted to get out of running what amounted to company towns. He said, "Today we are going to return these social functions to the government."

A riot broke out at a company plant in Taiyuan in 2012. Gou had already raised the minimum wage there to $285 a month; with overtime, workers could make twice that much. Then a guard beat a worker. It was the match that started the fire. A worker said, "It is so rare in China that you can demonstrate when you're unhappy about something. It felt like the right moment."

Worker shortages had forced Gou to hire men to work on the assembly lines, and men weren't as docile as women. Gou would have liked to automate, but product cycles were so short that automation was often uneconomic. Besides, robots were expensive, and though they worked without protest twenty-four hours a day, seven days a week, they couldn't be laid off when orders were slow. By 2013 Hon Hai was looking to increase its profits by making its own branded devices or by producing content for the devices it assembled.

A Deeper Set

Thirty years after Mao's death, the forty-year-old party secretary at Silver Dragon Village, in Guizhou, said, "I worship Chairman Mao; he was great and wise." A steelmaker at Xingtai, south of Beijing, could still say, "Chairman Mao is infallible, and humankind will have to wait a long time until another man as great as him will be born." A professor at the Central Party School insisted, "The more pressure placed on Chinese culture and the Communist party, the more united and cohesive they become." Even among the faculty at that school, however, there were doubts. Another professor said, "We just had a seminar with a big group of very influential party members and they were asking us how long we think the party will be in charge and what we have planned for when it collapses."

By 2025 half of all urban Chinese families would have incomes over $20,000 a year. Would they tolerate one-party rule? What would happen as wealth percolated through this society? Would it bring a Western idea of individuality and a refusal to accept the government's word as final in all things? If that happened, could the government repress an increasingly willful population?

"Americans," a journalist wrote, "have rights; the Chinese have duties. Americans worship freedom; the Chinese cherish stability. American governments are accountable to the people; Chinese governments are responsible for them." On the face of it, this arrangement had worked, with periodic breakdowns, for millennia. The Chinese had come to believe that as human beings they were first and foremost parts of a social network. That's why when the "diamonds are forever" advertising campaign came to China, it had nothing to do with romance. Instead, the stones symbolized the permanence of marriage.

To make matters worse, by 2011 a third of the wealthiest people in China held official political positions. A journalist wrote, "Many entrepreneurs have given up on gaining wealth from normal business activities. Instead, they rely on cultivating special relationships." Another observer was blunter: "China is controlled by an interconnected, mutually dependent but mistrustful and faction-ridden plutocracy focused on a single purpose: the creation and consolidation of wealth in their own hands." A Mao loyalist said that Deng Xiaoping had pushed China to "the worst of all worlds: hyper-capitalism, corruption, and fascism." A party member said, "The fundamental problem is that there are no real rules in this country. The party makes the laws but then says it and its members are not subject to them. This is unsustainable." A foreign expert said, "When you get down to the most important aspect of the legal system—does it protect its citizens— almost nothing has changed."

A British journalist wrote that China's combination of an authoritarian government and a tightly controlled market economy was "unstable, monumentally inefficient, dependent upon the expropriation of peasant savings on a grand scale, colossally unequal and ultimately unsustainable." He continued, "The country has made progress to the extent that communism has given up ground and moved towards Western practices," but he called the Communist Party "one of the most corrupt organizations the world has ever witnessed." He anticipated that in the next decade "the growing Chinese middle class will want to hold Chinese officials and politicians to account for how they spend their taxes and for their political choices."

Was the government open to self-criticism and reform? One critic argued that China's elite had "little interest in real reforms." The party, he wrote, "no longer imperiled, is smug and complacent." A senior official in the Education Ministry dared to say that there used to be "a lot of indoctrination." Now, he said, "We stress a lot of traditional virtues, like respecting teachers and respecting the elderly. Especially now, we stress honesty." And what did students actually learn? The same official said that students "don't believe in God or communism. They're practical. They only worship the money." The *China Daily*, arch-defender of the status quo, carried an op-ed by a retired head of the Institute of World Economics and Politics at the Chinese Academy of Social Science. There, in public, one could read, "Meritocracy has been eroded by a political culture of sycophancy and cynicism."

A former vice minister of civil affairs expressed the new outlook concisely: "The core content of communism," he said, "is for everyone to get rich." A railway minister learned it so well that he lost his job and party position while being accused of accepting $159 million in bribes. He disappeared into the *shuanggui*, the punishment system intended to curb official corruption and run by the Central Commission for Discipline Inspection. A Chinese lawyer, talking about *shuanggui*, said, "The word alone is enough to make officials shake with fear." "Once called in," a professor explained, "you almost never make it out a free man." Was it effective? A young official thought not: "*Shanggui* is useless because corruption is everywhere."

For the moment, the solution was repression. Two hundred thousand security cameras in Shenzhen weren't enough to watch the city's residents. The government experimented in this city of almost 11 million with residency cards containing computer chips recording patterns of travel and purchases. The technology came courtesy of China Public Security Technology, a Florida company.

A foreign observer didn't pretend to know if the Communist Party would survive, but he noted, "Tiananmen is the event that cannot be discussed in China." The luckless staff of the *Chengdu Evening News* in 2007 published a one-line want ad that read, "Saluting the strong mothers of victims of 64." The clerk who accepted the ad was too young to know that "64" referred to June 4, the date of the Tiananmen crackdown. She was told and believed that it referred to a mining disaster. Too bad. The deputy editor in chief and two others got the ax. Contacted about the episode, surviving staff had only a "no comment."

The government's nerves were revealed when Falun Gong followers attempted in 1999 to organize a sit-in at Zhongnanhai, the walled and unmarked compound where China's leaders live next to the Forbidden City. The sit-in, which was called to protest a magazine's unflattering description of the movement, was no threat, but the fact that the secret police had no warning of the event alarmed the government. Surely

Falun Gong must be a highly organized, deeply secret organization. As such, it could not be tolerated, no matter how peaceful its adherents.

Since 1957 China had run, parallel to its judicial system, labor reeducation camps with a capacity of perhaps 300,000 people. Falun Gong members and drug addicts had been incarcerated in these places without charge for up to four years. A reporter wrote that "menstruating women were shackled standing against a board and then prevented from sleeping or going to the bathroom for several days."

In 2005 alone about 8,000 Chinese were executed, although the exact number was a state secret. The number of capital offenses had risen from thirty-two in 1983 to sixty-eight; now they included smuggling and tax evasion. In 2004, 99.7 percent of all criminal prosecutions ended in conviction. Conviction of the innocent—even execution—was tolerated as a justified sacrifice for the nation. As one official put it, "If you go after legal justice, it might cause more harm to social stability."

A UN report in 2005 found—in a reporter's paraphrase—that guards were "pushed to extract admissions of guilt and are rarely punished for using electric shock, sleep deprivation and submersion in water or sewage." One account of a man falsely charged went as follows: "On the fourth day, he broke down. 'What color were her pants?' they demanded. 'Black,' he gasped, and felt a whack on the back of his head. 'Red,' he cried, and got another punch. 'Blue,' he ventured. The beating stopped." When the suspect was proven innocent, the police still did not want to release him. A brother of the accused said of the police, "Their attitude was that if my brother was released, 20 officials would suffer. But if he was executed, only one person would suffer."

The novelist Ma Jian, prudent enough to stay abroad, wrote of the Chinese Communist Party: "Now they are riding on the back of the tiger and the tiger is the people. And if they fall off the tiger's back, they will be eaten." An observer who wisely chose anonymity said of China's new leader in 2013 that most probably he had "no fresh ideas so he just quotes Mao and tries to hold on tight to power." One of the new Chinese leader's most dramatic demonstrations of tiger riding came the next year, when he ordered the arrest of Zhou Yongkang,

China's retired security chief and a former member of the Politburo Standing Committee. The presumed charge was corruption. Who was next? A newspaper editor said, "Everyone is corrupt. You can't go on flipping over every rock."

JUST POSSIBLY THE TORTOISE TO CHINA'S HARE

The head of Bharat Forge said, "Manufacturing jobs will get created but it will not be like before, when unskilled laborers from rural areas got work. They will need to find jobs in construction, building roads, ports and power infrastructure. . . . What makes Indian manufacturing competitive today is technology, not cheap labor. We tried it the other way around before and it didn't work."

There was a similar story at Bajaj Auto, which used to have 810 people on an assembly line in Chakan, near Pune. They had made 244,000 motorbikes annually. Now Bajaj had 900 on that line, but they were making almost three times as many bikes. The company's Indian workforce as a whole was down from 23,000 to 10,000, but production was up. "Low-cost workers do not provide consistent products," said Sajjiv Bajaj. He wasn't shy about fighting Honda, Suzuki, and Yamaha either and planned to build bikes in Indonesia and Nigeria.

American buyers of generic drugs were likely to know the names Ranbaxy and Dr. Reddy's. Now Eli Lilly, Wyeth, and GlaxoSmithKline outsourced some of their research to Indian companies. Merck did the same, contracting with Advinus Therapeutics, also in Pune. Advinus— the name was compounded from Advantage India United States—was run by an Indian who had spent twenty years working for Bristol-Myers Squibb in New Jersey.

Americans were even more aware of American companies outsourcing jobs to India. The snowball began when American Express in 1993 set up a data-processing office in India. The office soon had 4,000 employees. GE followed in 1997 with the creation of Genpact. It grew to 17,000 employees before being spun off in 2004 as a separate company, Gecis Global. By 2011 the company was India's biggest provider of business processing, with revenues of $1.6 billion.

Freestanding, Gecis itself became a multinational, offering Spanish-language services in Mexico. Standard Chartered had meanwhile joined the parade. Perhaps it could better be called a stampede. Convergys had 5,000 employees in India. In 2004 IBM paid $150 million for Daksh, a Delhi call-center operator with 6,000 workers. IBM's Indian workforce jumped from 9,000 in 2004 to 53,000 in 2007. Over those years IBM shed 20,000 jobs in the United States, Europe, and Japan.

An American economist warned, "Tens of millions of *additional* American workers will start to experience an element of job insecurity that has heretofore been reserved for manufacturing workers." He called it the Third Industrial Revolution, following the original Industrial Revolution and the subsequent shift to services.

A good example? Try TNQ Books and Journals, which produced international scientific journals. Based in Chennai, the company had over 600 employees and was expanding. The woman who ran the company said, "The lowest qualification in this office would be a first-class Bachelor's degree in science. The rest would be Masters or MPhils. We're recruiting so frantically right now. It needs English, it needs science, it needs IT and it needs low wages, and you can't get it anywhere except India."

There was room for expansion in much simpler jobs, too. Wages in small towns ran $60 a month instead of big-city $150. One entrepreneur said, "We thought, 'Why not take the jobs to the village?' There is a lot of talent there, and we can train them to do the job." A young woman was hired to process time cards. She came from a village near Bagepalli, 60 miles north of Bangalore. She told a visitor, "I am the only person in the village to have an office job. I never thought it would be possible."

How far would outsourcing go? Nandan Nilekani of Infosys said, "Anything that can be sent over a wire can be outsourced. . . . The sky is the limit. . . . It's an inexorable trend." The interview finished, the reporter wrote, "Nilekani moves purposefully towards a nearby office, presumably to plot the disaggregation of a grotesquely inefficient supply chain somewhere near you." Infosys had 3,000 people on its payroll in 1999; by 2007 it had more than 72,000. An overwhelming share of its revenues, which were about $7 billion, came from American clients.

Were these Indian workers cybercoolies, "productively docile workers"? That was the charge in a study from the V. V. Giri National Labour Institute. Gecis Global's boss called it "hogwash." A university student eager to get in the door was equally dismissive: "Nobody wants arts or history anymore. All of my friends want IT."

JPMorgan Chase announced plans in 2005 to hire 4,500 graduates in India. It was part of the company's strategy of offshoring a third of its back-office staff. The company's head of operations said, "The quality of the people we hire is extraordinary and their level of loyalty to the company unbeatable." ABB, the Swiss-Swedish electrical engineering giant, must have agreed; the company had over 100,000 workers, but its biggest research center was in Bangalore.

Americans knew Indian call centers firsthand, but India's market share fell from 80 percent in 2004 to less than 40 percent by 2009. This was still big business, with Indian call-center revenues running about $11 billion, but business was shifting to other countries, sometimes because customers were frustrated with Indian accents and sometimes because clients didn't want to rely on call centers in only one country. In 2011 the Philippines overtook India, with 400,000 agents compared to India's 350,000. Filipino "voice service exports" were worth $7.6 billion that year, while India lagged at $7 billion. The Filipino agents earned $300 a month, $50 more than Indians, but their English was easier for Americans to understand.

Tata, Wipro, and Genpact all compensated by heading to China. Dalian, once part of the Japanese Empire, still had Japanese-language speakers, and so the city became especially attractive as a call center handling Japanese customers. Meanwhile, the same Indian companies outsourced work to America. Perhaps it was temporary. As one Indian executive said, Americans in hard times were "open to working at home and working at lower salaries than they were used to."

The boss of GE India in 2006 said, "We're convinced that India's time has come. I think the underlying fundamentals are really there this time." Perhaps he was thinking of Bangalore and its 150,000 IT engineers. Maybe he was thinking of billion-dollar investments from Cisco, Intel, and Microsoft.

IBM had left India in the 1970s, but its CEO came to Bangalore in 2006 to announce that he was going to invest $6 billion in India. "I am not going to miss the opportunity," he said. Ears perked up. Even the state government of West Bengal, which had been run by elected Communists for many years, welcomed the foreigners. No longer calling computers "job-killing devices," the state government supported the development of Rajarhat New Town, with a 250-acre IT zone. The government declared IT industries to be an "essential service," which made strikes illegal. The IT minister, a dedicated Marxist, said, "We have to play the same capitalist game as everywhere else. But we will use the gains to help our poor."

A nonresident Indian returning to Kolkata said, "When I left Calcutta, I was a pessimist. I didn't think the situation here would change so fast and so radically." Wipro's chairman agreed: "It is Kolkata which has the potential to become the second IT hub of India after Bangalore." An Infosys director was even more effusive and said, "India's renaissance in the 21st century will come from Calcutta, like it did in the 19th century." The modern economy was beginning to reach all the way down to the countryside. Some villagers near Jaipur commuted two hours each day to and from jobs in Delhi. Others in the village complained about the poverty of the village, but one of the commuters scolded them: "I go out and work, why don't you?"

Problems

Skeptics had a long list of objections, beginning with the caste system, Hindu-Muslim relations, and the status of women. All of these impeded India's economic development, and there were many more mundane and less tragic but still very real problems. India invested 1.4 percent of its GDP in transport infrastructure, for example. China invested 4.3 percent. An executive at GE India said that India's 8 percent GDP growth rate could be 2 to 4 percent higher if you "dropped in China's infrastructure." A real-estate executive put it this way: "The bad news is, it's really bad. . . . This is one big problem that could end the party before it's even begun."

Most of India's ports were government-run disasters, not only inefficient but so small that they couldn't handle big ships, which meant that containers were shipped to Colombo or Salala for reloading onto bigger vessels. India's most efficient ports were at Navi (New) Mumbai and Gujarat's Mundra. At Navi Mumbai's Jawaharhal Nehru Port Trust, one terminal was owned by the government, one by DP World, and one by Maersk of Denmark. Together, they could handle 4 million containers annually and could turn a ship around in two days. That was exceptional for India but light years behind Singapore, which handled five times that many containers and could unload and load a ship in a few hours.

Once landed at Mumbai, a container might be put on a flatcar for the journey north to Delhi, but the train crawled at an average speed of 15 MPH. That's why a new, 900-mile-long freight line was under construction, with a planned extension to Kolkata. This new line would allow not only higher speeds but also double stacking of containers, precluded on the existing track by drooping power lines.

Much to the amazement of passengers accustomed to sweaty scrums, Delhi's airport was rebuilt by Germany's Fraport, which operated Lufthansa's hub at Frankfurt. Airports Company South Africa was bringing Mumbai's airport into the new century. New airports were in the works for Bangalore and Hyderabad. Yet India's civilian aircraft fleet in 2007 consisted of 310 planes, with 480 planes on order for delivery by 2012. That was a big jump, and it meant that India's airports would have a tough time meeting demand. In one classic case, thousands of Nokia cell phones were ruined at Chennai International Airport in October 2006, when, for lack of warehousing, crates full of them were stored outside and then drenched in a heavy rain.

By 2014 observers were sure that the Nokia plant, which for a time had employed 8,000 people, would either close or be sold, not because of the airport bath but because the company was hit with retroactive tax bills totaling over $300 million. One investor said, "Any major electronics manufacturer looking to open a big plant in India would only have to look at Nokia and think: 'Why would I take that risk, when there are other places to go?'"

Unpredictable taxation was bad. Worse was the law that any company with more than a hundred workers had to get government permission to lay anyone off—permission that was almost impossible to get. An economist pointed to Gujarat as proof of the harm done by this policy. "Gujarat has fantastic ports," he said, "responsive officials, the power and roads are good, but no one is rushing to set up textile or basic electronics operations there. So this proves labor reforms are what matters." They were especially important because IT generated less than 1 percent of India's GDP and employed only about a million people. This might well double, but 2 million jobs were still trivial in a labor force of 450 million.

In the wake of a national scandal over the allocation of coal-mining leases, one businessman said, "In this country, it's difficult to survive. Whoever has a master key wants to eat up all of India. Whoever doesn't have a key is struggling to survive." The master key was connections to the right people in government, connections maintained if not by outright bribery then by discreetly helping officials who needed a bit of support and letting them know that they could count on such support in the future if they were sympathetic now.

One businessman concluded, "China has world-class manufacturing, India has third-world manufacturing. I have been in a lot of auto plants, textile factories and metal foundries and was not impressed. I've been in foundries where there are sparks flying around and the operators don't even have eye protection."

In a concentrated attack on at least some of these problems, the government of India in 2006 authorized special economic zones modeled on those that had been so successful in China. Within a year over 400 SEZs were announced, although only sixty-three had received final approval. Nokia already had a plant running in an SEZ near Chennai. (That plant had been the source of the cell phones with the airport bath.) So did Flextronics of Singapore. Thinking of the contrast between the village bazaar and the modern buildings at Hinjiwadi, an SEZ north of Pune, one analyst said, "You drive up to it and think: 'Oh my God, are we in India?'" One SEZ, planned for Haryana by Reliance Industries, was to cover 25,000 acres and have its own inland container port, cargo airport, and power plant. It was also supposed to generate half a million jobs.

India's SEZs, however, faced a distinctly Indian problem. An executive said, "If you have to build a road in China, just a handful of people need to make a decision. If you want to build a road in India, it'll take 10 years of discussion before you get a decision." An Indian official put it this way: "India is a democracy. People own the land. If we wanted a zone the size of Shenzhen it would take us 30 years." It didn't help that India's laws for acquiring land for SEZs dated from 1894.

The government in 2012 proposed fresh legislation offering four times the market value of land and allowing compulsory purchase only if 80 percent of the landowners agreed. Would they? One owner on the outskirts of Delhi said, "I enjoy the natural surroundings, pure milk and pure food. How much money would I need from my land to get this life again?"

Tata wanted to build its micro-car, the Nano, on a thousand-acre SEZ near Singur, about 25 miles northwest of Kolkata. The plant was going to create almost 20,000 jobs—1,000 directly at the plant, 7,000 more at nearby parts makers, and 12,000 in piggybacking businesses. The plant site, however, was divided into 3,900 plots with ownership shared by 11,000 people. Many were happy with Tata's offer. In one case the company paid $24,000 for two acres. That was five times the land's market value. Tata also gave one of the owner's sons a year of training so he'd be ready to work in the factory. The young man said, "I am 100 percent satisfied with my new job."

Other owners, however, refused the company's offer. A comparatively moderate opponent said, "There can be no industry on fertile land. We are opposed to that." Smelling votes, a politician with a tongue of vitriol told a rally, "When the police come to force you out, skin them alive." Tata was growing impatient. Didn't West Bengal want the plant?

The chief minister of West Bengal was steadfast. "The Tatas will get their land," he said. Early in 2007 work began on the site with 500 police and a site blessing, a *bhoomi puja*. The owners of one plot were still holding out, however. By the next year Tata's chairman was warning that protests might force the company to move to a new site in a more welcoming state. If that happened, he warned, he didn't "know how many 15-billion-rupee ($345 million) investments would come to West Bengal." People may have thought he was bluffing, but he wasn't, and in 2008, seeing no end to the resistance, Tata gave up and moved operations to Sanand, near Ahmedabad, capital of Gujarat.

Meanwhile, an Indonesian chemical company wanted to build a plant near Nandigram, also near Kolkata. Early in 2007 at least fourteen villagers were killed, either by the police or by agitators. In China this would have been insignificant, but the killings brought work at Nandigram to a stop. The state's chief minister said, "We did not understand that there would be such a huge resistance in Nandigram. Our assessment of the situation is wrong. I did not know that police excess would be to such an extent. I am shocked. I am sad." The leader of another political party toured Nandigram and reported what he heard people saying about the chief minister: "Wherever I went people cried hang that man."

Reliance Industries found its plans for a power plant on the outskirts of Delhi blocked by a judge who held that farmers had not been consulted. Lafarge, the giant French cement manufacturer, saw its proposed plant in the Mandi District, in the Himalaya foothills, blocked on environmental grounds.

Lakshmi Mittal said, "There's no way I can ignore India, and I am not giving up on these projects." Yet India was no longer a top priority for him; it presented too many problems. Ratan Tata explained, "You may have the prime minister's office saying one thing and maybe one of the ministers having a different view. That doesn't happen in most countries. You wouldn't have a seven- or eight-year wait to get clearance for a steel mill."

POSCO hoped to build a $12 billion steel mill in an SEZ at Dhinkia in Odisha (until 2010, Orissa). This was India's single-biggest foreign direct investment, and POSCO breathed a sigh of relief when in 2008 India's Supreme Court allowed the company to take 3,000 acres of government-owned forest. The forest was used, however, by villagers cultivating betel-nut vines. They protested, and two years later, twenty-five were injured by rubber bullets. POSCO offered to pay each family $10,000 to vacate the land, and it guaranteed a job to one person in each family. Still, some of the villagers objected. The prime minister said, "The government is keen to move forward with the POSCO project," but the National Green Tribunal in 2012 ordered a "fresh review." POSCO had already been delayed five years from its first environmental approval, and the tribunal's assertion that the earlier approval had been done "casually, without any comprehensive scientific data" suggested further delays.

Plans for a huge bauxite mine in Odisha—a million tons a year at Lanjigarh—were stopped by India's environment minister, who accused the developer, Vedanta, of illegally occupying tribal land belonging to the Dongria Kondhs, a group of 8,000 hunters and gatherers. Vedanta had invested $4.5 billion in a nearby aluminum refinery whose feedstock would now have to be sourced elsewhere. The minister was taken to task by businesspeople who urged him to be "pragmatic, not dogmatic." The minister shot back, "I am being pragmatic, just not automatic." He admitted that he hadn't always been so willing to stop industrial developments, but he defended his new position. "Where you stand," he said, "depends on where you sit."

FAST-FOOD PLANET

Militant Indians in the early 1990s had condemned fast food as poison, but by 2007 Pizza Hut had 134 restaurants in India. Domino's had 149. McDonald's had only 56, but they were wall-to-wall in Delhi and busy from open to close. McDonald's had been in Lahore since 1998, and by 2011 Islamabad had McDonald's, Pizza Hut, KFC, and Domino's. Dunkin' Donuts and Starbucks both opened their first Delhi restaurants in 2012.

South Asia was a slowpoke compared with East Asia. KFC sales in the United States, where the company had 5,300 restaurants, were almost flat, but the company had expanded to Japan in 1970 and become an essential part of Christmas for many Japanese children. China came later, but KFC by 2011 had 3,700 restaurants there, and Pizza Hut had 600. More than half the profits of Yum! Brands, the parent of both KFC and Pizza Hut, now came from China, where the company opened the country's first drive-through in 2002. A decade later, opportunities there were still vast, with three Yum! restaurants for every million Chinese, compared with sixty for every million Americans.

The company's chief executive said, "China is the restaurant opportunity of the 21st century." He added that Chinese parents fifteen years ago had introduced their children to KFC, "and now, the biggest thing that I see and the biggest difference when I go to China is that the kids are buying the food themselves. . . . The business is exploding because of it." It was an odd contrast with the United States, where KFC was so sluggish that an executive at Popeyes wrote KFC off. "Our largest competitor is abdicating the US market," he said. To keep its lead in China, however, KFC would have to work hard. One adult customer there said that the company's food was "just not healthy. We all went because it was so new. But there are many other options with better food now."

McDonald's by 2010 had 1,400 stores in China, including 105 with drive-throughs. Under the terms of a twenty-year agreement signed in 2006, many new restaurants would be attached to Sinopec gas stations. The mayor of Beijing wasn't applauding. "This is something of great difficulty for us," he said. "The contradiction of population and the environment—for us and the whole of China."

The vice minister of the State Environmental Protection Administration echoed him: "If we follow the current track of consumption patterns to develop the automobile in China, the world will not be able to support [it]." Perhaps he shook his head at the opening in Beijing of the Feng Hua Yuan drive-in theater, where waitresses wore roller skates and ponytails. Perhaps he applauded in 2010 when the Beijing city government decided to issue only 240,000 license plates in the coming year. The result, predictably, was a rush late that year to buy a car while plates were still available.

Huang Huahua, the governor of mighty Guangdong, had no time for such environmentalist nonsense. "You are a fool if you don't make cars," he said. "If we still depend on color TVs and a few similar industries, then Guangdong's 9 percent GDP growth can no longer be assured." He got his wish, with assembly plants from Toyota, Nissan, Honda, and Volkswagen, as well as Chinese brands such as Foton. China had made only 5,000 cars in 1980. Twenty years later, it made 5.8 million, and production was rising 30 percent annually. By 2010 China made 6 million more cars than the United States and planned to double production to 33 million vehicles by 2018.

Starbucks too was eager to expand in China. By 2012 it had 700 stores there and planned many more. The president of Starbucks Greater China summed up his schedule by saying, "In China, there's only one speed: faster." The company's China boss, an American-trained lawyer, called his target customers "little emperors." He meant that they were the pampered offspring of prosperous parents with only one child. Prosperous indeed: a medium coffee in China cost about $3.50. The average annual salary in Shanghai was $3,800, so a cup of Starbucks coffee was the equivalent of a $50 coffee for an American earning $50,000 annually. Ironically, the Chinese didn't much like coffee—per capita consumption averaged three cups annually—but Starbucks offered status, which the Chinese liked very much.

Formal Retail Expands

Before setting foot in Europe, Walmart had gone to Mexico, where it operated three brands: Walmex, Suburbia, and downscale Bodega Aurrera. Together, sales came to $21 billion in 2007, about a quarter of Walmart's foreign revenue and half of Mexico's supermarket business.

Bodega angered many Mexicans in 2004 by opening a store close to the pyramids at Teotihuacán. One local resident said, "It's like having Mickey Mouse on the top of the Pyramid of the Moon." Detailed investigations by the *New York Times* in 2012 pointed to Walmart's bribing, through intermediaries, numerous officials whose approval had been needed before that store could be built; recipients included not only Teotihuacán's mayor but officials at the National Institute of Anthropology and History. The *Times* reporters wrote that Walmart had secured many other Mexican sites in the same way and that the company was "an aggressive and creative corrupter, offering large payoffs to get what the law otherwise prohibited."

The only Mexican state without a Walmart was Baja California Sur. A Los Cabos liquor-store owner hoped it would stay that way. "When the small-business owner goes out of business," he said, "the middle class gets smaller." The mayor disagreed. "I can understand that some businesses might be hurt by Walmart," he said, "but the fact is that the people here want it. It increases the purchasing power of people with very little money." He might have pointed to a Bodega in Juchitán, Oaxaca. Sales were so strong at that store's opening that, according to its manager, "the place looked like it had been looted." Juchitán's deputy mayor added, "The ones who have benefited the most are the poorest. I hope another one comes."

Walmart hoped to be equally successful in Europe. Its UK subsidiary, Asda, contributed a third of Walmart's international sales, even though it struggled against Tesco, whose sales were twice as large. Tesco's boss, Terry Leahy, was described as "very unusual in that he is very, very simple and very, very focused. . . . If you say to him, why is Tesco successful, he will say 'because we sell what consumers want.'" Germany was a different story. Walmart collided there with Aldi, the dollar store. "Aldi literally ran Walmart out of continental Europe," a consultant said. In 2006 Walmart sold its eighty-five German stores to Metro, another German chain.

One analyst called that sale "a brilliant decision." He intended no sarcasm and meant only that the sale allowed Walmart to focus on Asia, but sailing was rough there too. Walmart gave up on South Korea, a tough market abandoned as well by Carrefour, the French chain. Tesco was sticking it out in South Korea with Homeplus, a joint venture with Samsung. In 2008 Tesco even bought thirty-six ex-Carrefour stores near Seoul. That left South Korea with two big chains, Homeplus and Shinsegae, which operated a chain called E-mart.

Late in 2005, and after four straight years of losses, Walmart took full control of its Japanese subsidiary, Seiyu. Walmart wanted to bypass middlemen, but this was so contrary to Japanese practice that by 2010 Walmart was ordering shipping containers of cream cheese and mineral water direct from the United States. Looking for ways to cut costs, it moved 80 percent of its store employees to part-time positions. It downgraded its inventory too, a dangerous step in quality-conscious Japan. One of the company's Japanese managers whispered, "Seiyu became a completely different store after it came under Walmart management. National-brand food product prices have definitely come down, but high-quality merchandise has disappeared from the shelves, and customers have left."

A Japanese analyst said, "They need to completely change their strategy, but it's too late. They are doing it totally wrong. They should pull out of the country and focus on China." Walmart's Japan boss retorted that the company "cannot just ignore a market of this particular size." He took refuge in the belief that the Japanese consumer was finally becoming price conscious.

Walmart entered China in 2003. The first store, in Shanghai, broke company records, with 40,000 customers on some days. One of them said that Walmart "makes everyone feel our living standards are rising." The company expanded to seventy stores in thirty cities but sought a still bigger footprint. In 2007 it agreed to buy a third of Trust-Mart, a Taiwanese-owned chain of 101 high-volume stores in thirty-four Chinese cities. By late 2008 Walmart had 217 stores in the country, and two years later, it introduced a new-format "compact hyper," less than half the size of the standard store and modeled after the Bodega Aurrera.

Tesco meanwhile partnered with a Taiwanese company and in 2008 opened China's first Tesco Express. Two years later, Tesco had ninety-three stores in Shanghai alone and ventured at Qingdao into opening a mixed-use development including offices and apartments. Tesco hoped to open more. Instead, the company began talks to merge its 131 stores into the 3,000-store China Resources chain, an arm of the Ministry of Commerce. Tesco might continue supplying its stores, but the name of the British company was likely to disappear.

Carrefour, which had abandoned Mexico, Japan, and Switzerland, decided in 2010 to quit Thailand, Malaysia, and Singapore. With China, however, it dug in. The company had more than 170 stores there by 2010, as well as several hundred hard-discount stores operating under the name Dia. Some of the hypermarkets—the French equivalent of supercenters—were in unexpected places, including Urumqi, way out west in Xinjiang.

The manager of the Urumqi store admitted he had a hard time selling French wine at twelve dollars a bottle. Shopping carts were full of products unknown in North America, and the average checkout total was the equivalent of five dollars. Stocking the store was a bigger challenge because China had few big suppliers. A Carrefour manager explained, "We have one centralised structure [for stores] in Shanghai and then we decentralise elsewhere." For a while, at least, that was likely to be the general practice. (And not just in China. As the CEO of Metro Cash & Carry in India said, "Stores are just the tip of the iceberg—90 percent of the work is under water.")

There were big Chinese-owned chains too. Among them was 240-store Gome Electrical, a Chinese equivalent of Best Buy. The owner was a young accountant named Huang Guangyu. His nickname was the "Price Butcher." When he opened his biggest Beijing store, in 2005, 100,000 people crowded in to buy things like twenty-one-inch color TVs for seventy-nine dollars. Huang said he worked all the time. Candidly, he added, "I don't know what else to do."

Late in 2008 Huang vanished. Two years later, he and his former chief financial officer turned up in Beijing's Number One Detention

Center. A dozen prisoners there shared cells measuring twenty-five feet by forty. Beds? Not a chance. Prisoners were forced to sleep on a plank and to sit upright on it during the day. Someone who had been held in one of these cells said, "Leaning too far forward, leaning too far back, and even crossing your legs was forbidden." Huang, he continued, "was taken out for questioning much more than other inmates and he was even taken out on weekends and in the middle of the night, sometimes from around 2am until 6am. [Zhou Yafei, the former chief financial officer,] told me they just kept asking the same questions over and over." Finally, in 2010, Huang was sentenced to fourteen years. His offense remained secret.

Formal retail lagged in India but was not out of the race. Ermenegildo Zegna, who had fifty stores in China, said, "The India of 2005 is the China of 1991." He based his opinion on luxury watches and cars. "They," he said, "are the two signs [of consumer readiness]." Hong Kong alone imported more Swiss watches than the United States. The government of India, however, was reluctant to open the door to global retailers. It was an elected government, and it knew that 95 percent of the country's retail trade was handled by the country's 12 million *kirana* stores, open-fronted, family-owned groceries usually no bigger than an American bedroom. The backlash to companies like Walmart could be huge. One analyst estimated that 8 million people would be out of work if stores like that took even 20 percent of India's retail trade.

As a compromise the Indian government insisted that foreign retailers work as junior partners to Indian companies. Walmart formed a partnership with Bharti Enterprises and opened the first of over 200 Easyday retail stores. In 2009 Walmart also opened a wholesale store in Amritsar called Best Price Modern Wholesale. At 50,000 square feet, it was less than half the size of an American supercenter, but 75,000 *kirana*-store owners came by every month. Amritsar itself had 35,000 *kirana* stores, so either local owners were stocking up twice a month or the store was drawing customers from farther afield.

For decades Indian farmers had been required to sell their produce in one of the country's 7,000 government-approved wholesale markets.

Those markets had some 413,000 traders buying and selling, and they had 214,000 commission agents who negotiated with those traders on behalf of the farmers. Walmart wanted to bypass the markets, agents, and traders. It contracted directly with 7,000 farmers and planned to have contracts with 35,000 by 2015.

State legislators feared a voter backlash, but the central government understood the need for change. India had only 10 percent of the refrigerated warehouses and trucks it needed. For lack of that infrastructure, a third of all perishable crops spoiled before reaching consumers. As one member of the Central Planning Commission said, "We can't solve this problem. It's something the private sector has to do."

In 2011 the government proposed to allow foreign retailers to open wholly owned retail stores provided they stayed in big cities and sourced a third of their merchandise from small, local producers. The proposal died in the face of opponents such as one who threatened to "set fire to the first Walmart store whenever it opens here." The law was eventually enacted, but Walmart wasn't prepared to operate retail stores if it had to source so much locally from small producers. In 2013 it announced that it would take over the 20 wholesale stores it operated in partnership with Bharti Enterprises, expand their number to 50 by 2018, and let Bharti have the partnership's 212 Easyday retail shops. Supercenters would have to wait.

Tesco partnered with Tata. Carrefour, choosing to act without a partner, opened a wholesale market in Delhi in 2010. Ikea, eager to open in India and to invest almost half a billion dollars, was discouraged by the government's insistence on local sourcing. The company retreated. Three years later, the government modified the rules to allow the 30 percent to come from larger suppliers.

Staples found a partner in Pantaloon, with which it planned to open Staples Future Office warehouses in India's major cities. Pantaloon was a Mumbai-based chain that ran department stores. Clerks made about $1,600 a year, more than twice what they would have made in a garment factory. Speaking of his customers, one of the clerks said,

"I will spend money like them someday." His words were important because the press frequently reported protests over the opening of modern stores in India. The usual story line was that these places destroyed jobs, which was true, but not that they created new and often better ones, which was also true.

Pantaloon also had about a hundred crowded and successful supermarkets called Big Bazaar. The owner, Kishore Biyani, explained his business. "The Indian model of shopping is theatrical," he said. "There is buzz and haggling. If you have wide aisles you have a problem." He hadn't understood this at first, when he designed his original Big Bazaars to resemble stores in the West. He found that "customers never stopped. They kept on walking on and on so we had to create blockages"—make the stores crowded, messy, and noisy. "We all have to discover by doing," he said. He had learned to make "shouting, the untidiness, the chaos . . . part of the design."

Biyani spent $50,000 replacing the long wide aisles of a Mumbai store with narrow twisting ones. He said, "Making it chaotic is not easy." On purpose, Big Bazaars were not air-conditioned. On purpose, they included some spoiled produce so shoppers could pick and choose and "get a sense of victory." Some of the stores had on-site grain mills, so picky customers could buy wheat in the store and be assured of fresh, clean flour. Biyani's hero, of course, was Sam Walton.

Another Indian chain was My Dollarstore, which sold goods for less than ninety-nine rupees, or about two dollars. The twist here was that My Dollarstore was created by an Indian living in California. Beginning with an online company in 1996, he opened his first brick-and-mortar store three years later. Now he had fifty stores in California but 200 abroad, including forty in India and plans for at least 400. The walls were decorated with posters of the Statue of Liberty.

Reliance Industries, a huge petroleum and chemical company, announced in 2007 that it would open a hundred Reliance Fresh stores in Delhi during the first four months of the year. The second step was to open stores in 784 Indian cities and towns. The third step was to open in 6,000 smaller places. The first four Delhi stores opened in January, with prices a third lower than at *kirana* stores. Those first stores were perhaps twice the size of an American convenience store.

Reliance stopped work in Kolkata after some of its stores were physically attacked by supporters of the Forward Bloc, a left-wing political party. Stores in Uttar Pradesh were ordered closed after some were ransacked. A Reliance Industries spokesman spoke soothingly. "This is a temporary crisis situation," he said, "and things will be normal soon." Perhaps. The Movement for Retail Campaign set out to repeal a law passed in 2003 that allowed retailers to buy directly from farmers. The big retailers wouldn't be happy if the campaigners were successful, forcing the retailers to buy only from wholesalers buying from state-regulated co-ops buying from farmers.

By 2014, Reliance Fresh had 550 stores in operation. Biyani had almost as many, and there were other chains. All faced tough competition from India's millions of small traders, all of whom were closer to home for most Indians, had longer hours than many stores, and were clustered in groups offering as much selection as the shiny new stores. Surveys suggested that a majority of customers preferred the small traders, not only for produce but for staple products as well. Big Bazaar still had plenty of customers, but Biyani concluded that it was more profitable, per square meter, to operate convenience stores.

Shopping Centers

Another global frontier was disappearing too. By 2011 only one of the world's fifteen biggest malls was in North America. That was the West Edmonton Mall. The other fourteen, scattered from Dubai to China, were located mostly in East and Southeast Asia. The biggest of them all was the badly located and nearly empty South China Mall in Dongguan. Even it seemed small, however, compared to the wholesale mall in Yiwu, a city 200 miles south of Shanghai. There, the International Trade City had 18 million square feet and 30,000 stores grouped by kind of product. The owner, Zhejiang China Commodities City Group, intended to double the size of the place. Who was there? Not just

Chinese; the city had 8,000 foreign residents. Tourists were welcome to visit and pick up a crate of 160 teddy bears or 500 rolls of ribbon.

Surprisingly, a consultant called Shanghai "a dreadful retail market" for luxury goods. Plaza 66—much more expensive than its name suggested to American ears—was a *gui gouwu zhongxin*, "a ghost mall," with people coming in just to find a quiet corner in the crowded city. The Shanghai rich shopped mostly in Hong Kong, where prices were a lot cheaper and variety a lot greater.

Why was Saks Fifth Avenue planning to open on the Shanghai Bund? Why were Cartier and Armani already there, along with Dolce & Gabbana and, hiding around the corner, Hugo Boss? Perhaps they wanted to get in on the ground floor. Or, as some suggested, perhaps they merely wanted to add another exotic name to shopping bags already banded with New York, Paris, and Milan. That probably had something to do with the opening of Japan's prestigious Mitsukoshi store in Beijing in 2007. Despite such warnings, Shanghai got its first high-end suburban mall in 2008 with the opening of Friendship Shopping in Xinzhuang. The mall had a Costa Coffee and shops selling Brooks Brothers shirts and Rolex watches. Maybe it would prosper.

The Chinese were busy developing malls in Southeast Asia too. They were prominent among the mall owners of Bangkok, for example, where malls were a part of social life for people who lived in close quarters, usually without air-conditioning.

The dominant chain in the Philippines was Chinese-owned Shoemart, which operated eighteen malls. People across the Visayas island group took an overnight ferry trip to the Cebu SM, which drew 113,000 visitors daily. An ecstatic shopper in Baguio, in the mountains north of Manila, said of her new SM, "I don't even crave a trip to Manila. I have the mall here, and it's beautiful." In mid-2006 SM opened its biggest mall, the 4-million-square-foot Mall of Asia, on the Manila waterfront. In addition to the mall, the project included office space, condos, and a convention center. Dell used the second floor of one building for a call center.

Late to the party, as usual, India had only three shopping centers in 2002. By 2008 it had an amazing 250. Most shoppers did not arrive by private car, and those who did usually had chauffeurs, so parking was typically in a dark and congested basement. Upstairs, the typical Indian shopping center had five or six stories, with a food court up top, along with a multiplex theater. India allowed foreign retailers to operate on their own in India, as long as they sold only a single brand, so Nike, Tommy Hilfiger, and Mango all opened stores in Indian malls. Levi Strauss allowed customers to spread payment over three months on any pair of jeans selling for thirty-three dollars or more.

A real-estate expert called these malls "the biggest growth story in organized retail ever witnessed on Planet Earth." The boss of Aditya Birla had a soberer view. "The Indian consumer," he said, "is a damn tough customer." He meant that Indians, unlike Chinese, weren't prepared to pay more just for a famous brand. The boss of Pantaloon tempered his enthusiasm, too. "I was an eternal optimist; now I have become a realist," he said. By 2012 the vacancy rate in Delhi malls was 30 percent. For a while, India's biggest mall was likely to be the Sobha Global Mall in downtown Bangalore. It was small by Chinese standards—only 2 million square feet—but the Oman-based developer, P. N. C. Menon, sounded like an American developer when he promised "a one of a kind experience for the shopper—never to be forgotten, always to be relived and to come back to again and again."

8 Building

Hong Kong's chief executive remembered 1982, when he was a district officer responsible for building the new town of Shatin: "It was wonderful. That was my best job in public service. . . . I did not have any environmentalists in my hair in those days. We were pulling down mountains. We were reclaiming seas. We were building our new town."

Who had such fun now? Until a family feud and corruption charges spoiled the party, one contender might have been the Kwok brothers. Through their Sun Hung Kai Properties, the brothers built what briefly was Hong Kong's tallest building, the International Finance Center. It sat on filled land adjoining Central, the city's financial district. Central itself was jammed, however, and it was expensive, with office rents at fifteen dollars a square foot monthly. In most cities the pressure would have forced the clearance of older buildings and their replacement with bigger new ones, but ownership of office buildings in Hong Kong was divided floor by floor between different parties. Sometimes the ownership of a single floor was divided.

Looking elsewhere, the Kwok brothers in 2007 topped the IFC with the 1,588-foot International Commerce Center across the harbor in Kowloon. Most of the people working in Central didn't want to move, but ICC rents were a third lower, and soon Morgan Stanley, Deutsche Bank, and Credit Suisse moved across the water. The new building had a great location for people in Guangdong, too; it was atop Kowloon Station and only fourteen minutes from Shenzhen, with trains every three minutes. It was soon to be forty-five minutes from Guangzhou.

The developer of The Cullinan, an apartment building near the ICC, claimed to have sold a 4,000-square-foot apartment for $38 million. Promotional literature for another tower, The Arch, read, "You are master, and the sky is your kingdom." A realtor said, "If you count the lights at night you won't see many. It's sold out, but it's pitch dark." He explained that the buyers were usually from the mainland, which explained why the neighborhood had begun to be called Chinatown. "They just want to park some of their money in Hong Kong," he said. They also wanted prestige. A sales manager said, "They're buying face."

They were buying face over on Victoria Peak too. A developer there sold a $46 million apartment at 39 Conduit Road to the Shanghai founder of an online gaming company. On the south shore of Hong Kong Island, a shipping magnate from Hebei paid $85 million for a house at 11 Headland Road. A record was set in 2011, when a house on humbly named Pollock's Path sold for $103 million, or $11,000 a square foot. The Frank Gehry–designed Opus Hong Kong, on Stubbs Road, had twelve apartments with prices starting at $58 million. Hoping to avert a bubble, the government imposed a 15 percent tax on all purchases by nonlocal buyers. They hardly blinked.

Shanghai

Up the coast 500 miles, the government of China's financial capital worried about housing prices. The city had less than 200 square feet of residential space per capita, but prices were prohibitive for most residents, with the average Shanghai apartment selling for about $275,000, or $3,500 a square meter. A Millionaire Fair was held in 2006, and the displays included advertisements for a $31.2 million mansion. The result was a ban on the construction of large, detached houses, so-called villas. The government also decreed that 70 percent of the housing built in new residential areas had to be for low- or middle-income buyers and no larger that ninety square meters. Would the rules hold? An earlier ban on villas was flouted, apparently because the Chinese were no longer afraid to display wealth. Rolls-Royce had dealerships not only in Shanghai but in Chengdu. Not one American in 10,000 had heard of Dalian, but its residents were rich enough and confident enough to support a Ferrari dealership. (Dalian Wanda, primarily a real-estate company, reached across the Pacific Ocean in 2012 to buy AMC Theatres, with over 5,000 screens in the United States.)

Meanwhile, an American architect named Benjamin Wood had been gutting and renovating workers' housing into the upscale, mixed-use Shanghai development called Xintiandi. Working for Vincent Lo of Hong Kong, Wood was upfront about his business. The people in the surviving bits of the old housing, he said, "know me pretty well in this neighborhood, because I like to ride [a motorcycle] through here a lot. What they don't know is that I'm also the guy who is going to make this way of life disappear." He had similar plans for Chongqing and Hangzhou. But what was the alternative? "The biggest problem in China," Wood said, "is that the Forbidden City is burned into every brain. It's symmetrical, monumental, and out of scale." Without projects like Wood's, the old buildings would simply be demolished and replaced by symmetrical, monumental, and out-of-scale high-rises. "The real tragedy," Wood concluded, "is not the disappearance of the [old buildings], but of life on the streets."

The Rockefeller Group was redoing the north end of Shanghai's famous waterfront, the *wai tan*, or "Bund" in English. (The term *bund* arrived from India, where it denoted the artificial rim of a water body, most commonly the edge of a rice paddy.) The Shanghai Bund became the Shanghai Bund de Rockefeller. Local officials were thrilled at first but then angry when they learned that the Rockefeller Group was owned by Mitsubishi. They wanted *real* Rockefeller money. A few blocks upstream, Bund 18, which once housed the Chartered Bank of India, Australia and China, and Bund 3, which used to be Union Assurance, were open again, this time with fancy restaurants and Cartier and Armani shops. The Shanghai Club was now a Waldorf Hotel, part of the Hilton chain. Renovation had become a respected alternative to clearance; as an engineer working for the city said, "It's not like the past, when we just cried 'chai!' [raze]."

Beijing

Between 1998 and 2002 Beijing demolished 15 million square meters of floor space and replaced it with 80 million. Between 2002 and 2005, 315,000 households were relocated, some willingly, some not. By the first quarter of 2010, 1.87 billion square meters of residential space were under construction in the city. A Dutch architect said, "No other city has this level of ambition."

Pan Shiyi and Zhang Xin had become the city's most visible developers. The white walls of their high-rise complex, called soho China—for Small Office, Home Office—stood out on Beijing's southeastern skyline. Up near the northeast corner of the old city wall, however, Steven Holl had designed the even more eye-catching Beijing Looped Hybrid, eight residential towers joined by corridors at the twentieth floor.

Beijing had other icons, including a national center for the performing arts, an Olympic stadium, and—higher than either—the China Central Television Tower, which had almost as much floor space as the Pentagon and was a lot more visible. Despite the tower's celebrity architects, a critic observed that the building would "remind you of how small you are, and how big the state." Call it the Forbidden City of the new millennium. Was the critic Chinese, living in China? Take a wild guess.

Near Beijing's airport, the 150-acre Palais De Fortune had 173 houses for sale, each measuring about 15,000 square feet. Prices started at about $5 million, and every house came with a guard. Panic rooms were available for $25,000 and up. Once again, the government worried and in 2007 embarked on an "urban reorganization exercise" to "reorder the urban landscape"? Reorganization meant pulling down every billboard within the perimeter of the Fifth Ring Road. The mayor explained that the billboards "use exaggerated terms that encourage luxury and self-indulgence which are beyond the reach of low-income groups and are therefore not conducive to harmony in the capital." He was talking about signs like the one that read, "Indulge your heart by spending a small indulgence on a villa."

Most Beijing residents lived in small apartments privatized in 1998. An analyst described that process as the "largest one-time transfer of wealth in the history of the world." That was the good news; the bad was the poor quality and crowdedness of the apartments. Residents wanted something better, but in the second quarter of 2010, Beijing prices were 37 percent higher than they had been a year earlier. It was probably a world record, although Shanghai was close behind at 36 percent. Hong Kong came in at 28 percent. The only other big cities to see prices jump over 20 percent that year were Singapore and Mumbai.

Speculators were kept at bay by a policy prohibiting ownership of more than two apartments, even if buyers were prepared to pay cash. Still, prices kept rising, in part because the two-apartment limit was circumvented by buyers using surrogates such as their own chauffeurs. In the United States the ratio of home price to income had peaked at 5:1 in 2005. In China as a whole, the ratio was close to 8:1. In Beijing and Shanghai it was 30:1. Satirical e-mails began bouncing around the country. One, based on the fact that a 1,000-square-foot apartment in Beijing cost about $450,000, calculated that peasants could afford to buy such a place if they could get mortgages with terms of 1,100 years.

If this was a bubble, it was a bubble whose pop would be felt acutely by Australia, Brazil, and Chile, the countries supplying China with cement, iron, aluminum, and copper. Another potential victim was Caterpillar, which earned almost a tenth of its revenues in China and which had relocated its president to Hong Kong in 2010. "We have got to win in China," he said. The Chinese had plenty to worry about too. A salesperson in a furniture store said, "If they don't buy homes, we don't sell sofas."

Then there were the construction workers. A third of metropolitan Beijing's 19 million people were migrants, and 2 million of them slaved away on at least 10,000 structures in 2008. They were part of an army that by 2011 numbered 250 million low-wage migrant Chinese who lived in cities but had no legal right to live there. Most of them left family members back in the village where their *hukou* allowed them to live.

Sharp-eyed observers noted that because of this tight control, China's cities did not have the squatter settlements that migrants so often built on wasteland in the cities of more loosely governed countries.

One of these builders of Beijing sat on a bed in a room that housed a dozen men. He said, "Men don't want to cry, but we have cried many times." The men bought used clothes, wore them until they fell apart, and then sold them and started again. Baths? Maybe once a month. If the men were lucky, their meals were tofu and rice; if not, steamed buns. Work hours: fifteen a day or longer. In exchange the men sent home a hundred dollars a month, twice that if they had a skill like bricklaying. One of those bricklayers said, "We're very well respected in my home." His wife back home had a five-room house with only a thatched roof but a twenty-one-inch color TV. Half the money he sent home kept his daughter in a public but expensive high school. "We're not that close," he said. "I don't know what she likes." His wife said, "We keep being separated for such a long time, and I can hardly count how many days we've been together in the past 19 years." Back in Beijing her husband carried a ring of keys. He had found them and had no idea what they opened.

Off the Map

Although the foreign press lavished attention on a few Chinese cities, China had over a hundred with more than a million people. (India had forty; the United States, nine.) Wenzhou was one of them. There, an apartment tower called the Versailles Residentiel de Luxe La Grand Maison offered almost 200 apartments at up to $11,000 per square meter. A nervous salesman said, "Prices are dropping fast and everyone is waiting for them to fall further before they think about buying."

Shangqiu was another. In the eastern corner of Henan, its population jumped from 170,000 in 1980 to 1.65 million in 2005. In 2008 the mayor said, "We are a new, emerging city, and we need a lot of infrastructure . . . , but the speed at which we can build this infrastructure can't keep up with the expansion of the city." He wasn't thinking just about concrete either. "How do we provide social services to rural migrants who come to cities? This is a problem." Not just for him. In another decade more Chinese would live in cities than in the countryside. Already the country had 225 million urban households. A third of them lacked kitchens and plumbing.

By 2020 the country would likely have 140 cities with more than a million people. The government began allowing villagers to transfer their *hukou* to most cities, except the biggest ones. In anticipation of urban growth, 80,000 developers had already acquired long leases to enough land for a hundred million apartments. Trying to bring down average prices, the government set out to build 36 million subsidized apartments in the incredible space of three years. Chongqing alone planned to build 690,000 like those of the Xiyong Micro-Machinery Industry Park Low-Cost Housing Project. A realtor discussing that project put his finger on a more serious problem than the name: the apartments, he said, were "all very poor quality and in terrible locations." The Xiyong Project was 25 miles from central Chongqing.

Near Tianjin airport, Huaming was another planning disaster, poorly built and offering few jobs. A dozen villages with a total of 41,000 people had been relocated on one square mile. In exchange for some of the village lands, a developer had built gated compounds, each with half a dozen mid-rise apartment buildings. The villagers moved in reluctantly. One of them, who came only when the utilities to her old village were cut, said, "I have anxiety attacks because we have no income, no jobs, nothing. . . . We never had a chance to speak; we were never asked anything, I want to go home."

New Mousetraps

In Changsha, the capital of Hunan, the Broad Group set out to build a 2,750-foot building, Sky City, planned as the home of 30,000 residents and designed with offices, schools, hospitals, and shops. The entire building was to be assembled from identical, prefabricated steel modules. The company's boss said, "Lots of industries are very high-tech these days but not construction and we wanted to fix that."

China's biggest property developer, China Vanke, had a different solution to the housing crisis: micro-homes. The company often sold units of between 400 and 500 square feet, but in 2012 it displayed in Dongguan an apartment measuring only 160 square feet, with a folding bed and built in fixtures. The price was $21,000, or about $160 a foot. The company's chairman said, "Urban residents in China have no right to live in large houses." He proposed to begin selling micro-homes in Xian. Working on many fronts, China Vanke also announced a partnership with Tishman Speyer to build a pair of condominium towers in San Francisco.

Mumbai

With 12 million people in the city proper and more than 22 million in the metropolitan area, Mumbai was so infernally crowded that during 2006 more than 3,400 people died in accidents on the city's commuter trains and tracks. First-time visitors were sometimes horrified on the drive in from the airport, but a resident was quick to point out that "everyone has a job, no matter how small, they are all earning." Many Mumbai slum dwellers had certainly done well enough to replace their sheet-metal shacks with small but two-story concrete buildings with electricity, telephone, and TV. Falling short, others returned to an emaciating ancestral village. One young man, returning to his village, looked back at his time in the city: "Whenever someone leaves his village for the city, he thinks, 'I will earn money.' Everyone has dreams, but it's not always in their power to turn them into reality."

The director of the Bombay Stock Exchange still maintained that "Bombay is the sunrise city of the 21st century. The creative energies of this city have been held back too long." He was thinking of the license raj, that bureaucratic tangle that choked Indian business for decades after independence. A McKinsey report, "Vision Mumbai," imagined a Shanghai on the Indian Ocean. A new financial center emerged at the Bandra Kurla Complex, on the waterfront overlooking Mahim Creek. Two miles to the south, the Lodha Group began building World One, a residential tower 1,450 feet high, with 117 stories. In the surrounding neighborhood of Worli-Lower Parel, apartments were selling for $2,000 a square meter.

The architect Charles Correa wasn't buying it. He said, "There's very little vision. No one really knows. They're more like hallucinations." What would he have said about Antilia, the twenty-seven-story house built on Altamount Road by Mukesh Ambani, India's richest man? It replaced the mere fourteen floors of Sea Wind, the Ambani family's previous home.

A school superintendent was discouraged. He said, "We grow so selfish when we become wealthy. We lose all sense of community. We come home and we lock the door; we say 'I want my car, I want my house, I want, I want . . .' We are losing our humanity, our social sense in the process."

In 1995 the government adopted a slum-eradication plan. Instead of building public housing, the government would turn the land over to private developers to build whatever was most profitable, provided that at the same time they provided free apartments for the displaced slum dwellers. A consultant said, "The moment you put them [the slum residents] in a tower, you're releasing 90% of the land." Provided that each displaced family got a free apartment, the government allowed the developer to sell the rest at market rates. The policy was that if 70 percent of a slum's residents agreed, the slum could be cleared and replaced by apartment buildings.

For women who had never had access to a private toilet and for schoolchildren who had never had a quiet place to study, this was a great deal. On the other hand, who would maintain these buildings properly, and how would vendors survive when they could no longer wander through narrow lanes and call out for customers? One tenement resident said, "Before, there would always be four guys around your shanty. We sat, we chatted. Now it's like being caged in a poultry farm."

In 2007 the state government of Maharashtra set out to redevelop Mumbai's biggest slum, Dharavi, where 600,000 people crowded into 57,000 buildings on 345 acres. Free housing for the slum residents would use 30 million square meters but leave 40 million for market-priced housing and commercial buildings. That wasn't a 90-10 split, but it was enough to entice developers.

The chief impediment to all these clearance schemes—and over a thousand had been authorized by the Slum Rehabilitation Authority—was the hundreds of court cases brought on behalf of slum residents complaining that their signatures had been forged or coerced. Other residents complained that the apartments were poorly built and had running water only one hour a day. Some said they had been forced out of their new apartments because they could not afford the maintenance fees. By 2014, nearly twenty years after the programs' implementation, 127,000 slum dwellers had been rehoused, far short of the originally planned 800,000. They lived next to but physically separated from the residents of the luxury apartments in the same development. Hafeez Contractor, a prominent builder, defended the segregation: "If you had it combined, neither the slum guys nor the prospective clients would like it."

Mumbai's old textile mills, clustering in or near Worli, offered another opportunity for developers. Once there had been sixty of them. They had all closed. Should they be made into parks for this city almost without parks? Impossible: the land was too valuable. The 17.5 acres of the former Bombay Textile Mills came up for auction in 2006, and the winning bid was $160 million. It came from DLF, originally Delhi Land and Finance and now India's biggest real-estate company. DLF was also the chief force behind modern Gurgaon, a southern satellite of Delhi. Gurgaon had shot from 30,000 people in 1990 to 800,000 by 2001 and 1.5 million by 2011. Along with Noida, on the east side of Delhi, Gurgaon was ground zero for companies looking for modern office space in India. With 3.6 million square feet of Grade A office space, Gurgaon had five times as much as Delhi proper. Tishman Speyer, Goldman Sachs, Citigroup Venture Capital, and Emaar from Dubai all came to the party. Another magnet was Faridabad, on the highway to Agra. Business Park Town Planners built a forest of residential high-rises there called Parklands Pride.

Speaking of the prices paid for Mumbai's textile-mill land, the CEO of a private equity fund said, "It's madness." The day after DLF's winning bid for the Bombay Textile Mills, the five-acre Kohinoor Mills tract was sold for $100 million. Nobody was going to put parks there. More likely, the result would be something like Mindspace, a $1.4 billion, 5-million-square-foot, multiuse project built in Hyderabad. Or maybe something like Bangalore's Adarsh Palm Meadows, an eighty-five-acre blend of offices, apartments, and shops. DLF was also involved in Bangalore, where the regional development authority was eager to build five integrated townships covering about 90 square miles on a site 22 miles southwest of the city. The contract for the first township, Badadi, with an intended population of 750,000, was awarded in 2007 to DLF in partnership with Limitless, a subsidiary of Dubai World.

Three years later, in 2010, the eight-acre site of Bharat Mills was sold at auction for $330 million to a company called, appropriately enough, Indiabulls. Other developers set out to sell single-family suburban houses to slum dwellers. Tata Housing Development offered 300- to 400-square-foot houses, complete with electricity and plumbing. It certainly wasn't an easy commute: the first development, Shubh Griha or Auspicious Homes, had 3,000 houses in Boisar, 60 miles north of Mumbai. The houses were priced at about $10,000, or five years' income for target purchasers.

Dubai

In the space of a century, Dubai went from being a village to perhaps the world's most publicity-hungry city. A brave South African developer said, "Dubai has been able to achieve so much so fast because it is not a state, it is a corporation, Dubai Inc., which practices pure capitalism. People living here are employees, not citizens. . . . Everything here takes a back seat to profits."

Some observers dared to go further. Faisal Devji, a historian apparently with no intention of visiting again, argued, "The small number of Dubai citizens makes a national culture there impossible." Devji's knife was especially sharp when it came to the sheikhs: "Having been granted their titles by the British in India, the UAE's rulers derive their glamor from the vanished world of the Raj, while functioning like presidents of corporations."

Nakheel, a state-owned property developer, had built the heavily promoted Palm Islands on fill just off the coast. (The company's name meant simply "palm.") The company's boss was also a cabinet minister. The project sold out, and the boss was ready with a follow-on project, a set of 300 artificial islands shaped to resemble a crude world map and intended to attract 250,000 residents. He was also building a second Palm Island.

In 2008, 50,000 residential units were completed in Dubai. The next year, 70,000 were under construction. What would happen when the waterfront was fully developed? Dubai had already answered that question with the Palm Islands—make more waterfront—but in 2007 Limitless announced the $11 billion Arabian Canal. Land along half of this forty-mile seawater ditch would be developed over fifteen years into housing for a million people; the other half of the canal would pass through existing developments. (Tides and locks were supposed to keep the water moving.) On the theory that it should live up to its name, Limitless was also building not only Badadi, near Bangalore, but a new town for 14,000 people near Moscow's Sheremetyevo Airport.

Tired of bath-warm seawater? Dubai's Arabian Ranches offered a sand sea chopped into thousands of villas on lots so small residents could smell whatever was cooking next door. If that didn't appeal, there was always the opportunity to buy one of the thousand apartments in the world's tallest building, begun in 2004 as the Burj Dubai, or Dubai Tower. The head of Emaar, the company that built the tower, originally planned something smaller, but Sheikh (or shall we say CEO?) Mohammed, the prime minister, was unhappy. He wondered aloud why Dubai should build something shorter than Taiwan's Taipei 101 Tower, the world's tallest building at the time. A few years later, Emaar's boss was reminiscing. He recalled, "The sheikh asked me, 'Why is it taller—are people there smarter than you?'" And so Adrian Smith, an architect at Skidmore, Owings & Merrill, raised the roof. The spire now exceeded 2,700 feet. As completed in 2009, the building had 160 stories and overlooked a 500-acre, $20 billion project imaginatively named Downtown.

Burj Dubai apartments sold, furnished, for almost $2,500 a square foot. Residents on high floors had to make two elevator transfers to get to their apartments, but looking through the nonexistent clouds they could make out in the near distance the Dubai Mall, with 9 million square feet—200 football fields—and 14,000 parking places. Huge, it was not as big as the proposed Mall of Arabia, which was to be built in Dubailand, a theme park three times the size of Manhattan and budgeted at $110 billion. Plans called for Dubai to have the world's first Tiger Woods golf course, and Woods reportedly was paid $55 million for his help, though by 2011 the project had been abandoned, and dunes were invading the few greens that had been built. Dubailand survived, at least on paper, as Mohammed Bin Rashid City, and the Mall of Arabia was now the Mall of the World.

Nearby, Dubai Waterfront occupied over 7 miles of beach west of Dubai and was supposed to have homes for 700,000 people. The Lagoons, much closer to the city center, was a $17 billion, 70-million-square-foot project being built by Sama Dubai, an arm of state-owned Dubai Holding. The Lagoons was planned as the home of 140,000 people, with another 120,000 coming to work in offices or one of fifty shopping centers. There were celebrity-branded projects too, including an Armani hotel occupying ten floors of the Burj Dubai and a Palazzo Versace on Dubai Creek. Absurd? Not for those pleased to be met at the airport by a chauffeured Bentley. Not for those excited to open an office in Business Bay or in buildings named Boris Becker or Michael Schumacher.

A prominent architect surveyed the city and said, "It makes me ill. Some of these buildings are going to the absurd." The sheikh's defense was simple: "Does anyone ever remember the second man who landed on the moon or the second man who climbed Mount Everest?" The government now entertained a proposal for a 3,300-foot building to be built by Nakheel and called simply the Burj. Nakheel's boss, an Australian, had no inkling of what lay ahead when he spoke in 2008.

"You'd be mad not to question it," he said of the Burj, but he went on to assure his listeners that all was well. "The fundamentals in the market are too strong," he said. "There won't be a crash."

A crash promptly arrived, but even in the heady days preceding it, Dubai had problems. A talk-show host lamented, "The city is losing its authenticity. It's losing its past. Maybe in globalization, identity is irrelevant. That's what the government says. But in reality, hell no, you're losing something very precious." The government responded by declaring Arabic to be Dubai's official language.

Well and good, but Dubai had a population of about 1.5 million, and fewer than 10 percent were citizens. Over a million were contract workers from non-Arabic-speaking countries, especially in South Asia. They had come to help build Dubai. They were also not quite as powerless as they thought when, on arrival, they had turned over their passports to their employers, and gone to work—twelve hours a day, six days a week—for $175 a month. In 2006 the workers at Burj Dubai downed tools and tore up the construction office. Workers across town at the new airport stopped and demanded better conditions.

The government had eighty inspectors overseeing the 200,000 companies employing these workers. Of thirty-six camps inspected in the first five months of 2005, twenty-seven were judged "well below" government standards. A worker in one said, "I thought this was the land of opportunity, but I was fooled. . . . I wish the rich people would realize who is building these towers. I wish they could come and see how sad this life is."

The Middle East director for Human Rights Watch said, "If the U.A.E. wants to be a first-class global player, it can't just do it with gold faucets and Rolls-Royces. It needs to bring up its labor standards." The government imposed summer sun breaks and shut down a company that wasn't paying its workers. Beyond this, the Minister of Labor said smoothly, "We don't force people to come to this country." To which the director for Human Rights Watch replied, "That's what exploitation is—you take advantage of someone's desperation." There was no end of that; 350,000 workers arrived in Dubai during 2008. They owed agents an average of $2,500. With the economic collapse of 2008, things got worse. One worker said, "Every day, more people are losing their jobs, but they can't go home yet because they haven't paid off their debt." These people bunked ten to a room and hoped for day jobs.

It wasn't just the laborers building the city who were in trouble. By the time the Burj Dubai opened, debt had forced Dubai to turn to its richer neighbor, Abu Dhabi. In return for a $25 billion loan, Sheikh Mohammed renamed the Burj Dubai the Burj Khalifa, for Abu Dhabi's ruler. The loan did nothing for the thousands of buyers of property in the Burj or elsewhere in Dubai. They saw prices fall 50 percent in 2009, with expectations for another 30 percent drop. Residents at the Burj Khalifa fretted that their property values had suffered more than most in Dubai. They had paid 20 to 30 percent more, per square foot, than buyers on the first Palm Island, and they had to pay service fees of $15,000 annually for a 1,000-square-foot apartment.

Remembering 2008, when Dubai completed 54,000 apartments, a consultant said, "The economy just stopped in the middle of November." The global recession had much to do with this, but secrecy made things worse. A bank economist said, "At the moment there is a readiness to believe the worst. And the limits on data make it difficult to counter the rumors." There were reports, denied by the government, that 3,000 cars had been abandoned at the Dubai Airport by people fleeing the country to escape debts they could not repay. One investor, detained by the government for two months, said later, "I used to believe in the miracle of Dubai. But now I see it all as a mirage." While held, he said, he had been stripped of his properties.

The value of Emaar shares fell 90 percent between 2008 and 2009 before bouncing back. In 2012, 5,000 hotel rooms opened, half again as many as opened in Manhattan. In 2013 Dubai completed about 13,000 new apartments, though thousands of empty ones remained unsold.

Saudi Arabia

Over on the other side of the peninsula and north of Jeddah, Emaar was developing the King Abdullah Economic City. The Kingdom Tower, a kilometer tall and complete with a Four Seasons hotel, would be designed by Adrian Smith, the same architect who had designed the Burj Khalifa. Five other new cities were planned. They were Knowledge City in Medina; the Prince Abdulaziz Bin Mousaed Economic City in Hail (north of Riyadh); New Tabouk, in the far north near Jordan; and Jazan Economic City, near the Yemeni border.

The new cities were part of Saudi Arabia's attempt to diversify its economy so the next oil bust wouldn't be as painful as the last. Oil revenues had more than tripled to over $150 billion annually since the late 1990s, but even the Saudis didn't expect this windfall to last. The six new cities were supposed to house 4.5 million people and create 1.3 million jobs—500,000 of them in the King Abdullah Economic City alone.

Then there was Mecca. A Saudi architect was appalled. "If a stone moves in Jerusalem the whole Muslim world shouts up and down," he said, "but if a mountain [is destroyed in Mecca] nobody says anything.... It's the only place in the world you send bulldozers and then you plan. If you see the view inside Mecca, the Kaaba is getting smaller all the time. Eventually it will be looking like the center of Manhattan."

Mecca had 3 million pilgrims during the Haj season of 2010, but planners expected to accommodate five times that many. Millions came outside the season too. Catering to their needs, a banker said, was "pretty much recession-proof. More Muslims are becoming affluent and they have a spiritual side to their life which includes more frequent visits to Mecca." Where to stay? Between 2008 and 2012 the government anticipated investments of $30 billion on land within 1.6 miles of the Grand Mosque. The iconic building was the 1,300-foot-high clock tower copied from Big Ben, then enlarged to be the biggest clock in the world, 140 feet across its face. One of the clock hands weighed 7.5 tons.

At night the clock was rimmed with a circle of lollipop green that would have embarrassed a casino operator in Vegas. A critic said, "It is the commercialization of the house of God." He added, "They are turning the holy sanctuary into a machine, a city which has no identity, no heritage, no culture and no natural environment." The minister of tourism dismissed the criticism: "When I am in Mecca and go around the kaaba," he said, "I don't look up." It was an odd comment for a tourism minister, but then Saudi Arabia had no tourists. It did have plenty of pilgrims, however, and to accommodate 130,000 an hour circling the Kaaba, the government demolished the arcade encircling the courtyard. This was the oldest part of the Grand Mosque, and it was the work of Sinan, the most famous of Ottoman architects. The government had no qualms about demolishing it—indeed, it welcomed the demolition—because the arcade was inscribed with the names of the prophet's companions and therefore qualified, under the Saudi interpretation of Islam, as idolatrous.

Meanwhile, the Saudi Binladen Group presented sky-high plans for what it called a hundred Cities of Light. The first two were to be built on either side of the Bab al-Mandeb, the twenty-mile-wide strait at the southern end of the Red Sea. On the principle of no plan too outrageous, a spokesman promised an investment of $200 billion in the pair, which would be linked by a bridge and connected by rail across Arabia to Dubai, possibly also with a railroad and highway heading west from Djibouti to East Africa's big cities.

EUROPE

London

The British decision to stay out of the euro zone should have killed London. The city depended on finance—fewer than 3 percent of London's 4.2 million jobs were in manufacturing—and the number of jobs in finance had already fallen from 500,000 in 1945 to 220,000 by the time the euro was introduced in 1999.

Contrary to expectations, London's financial sector bounced back to 330,000 jobs by 2005, and the figure predicted for 2015 was 400,000. London handled 36 percent of all foreign-exchange trades—more than twice as much as runner-up New York—and 30 percent of all international bond issues. Why? Because the UK made it easy to fire people. "You can do it here," one businessman said, "but in France and Germany it is incredibly expensive." Not only expensive but time-consuming. The chief executive of Whirlpool, frustrated after three years of trying to cut his Italian workforce, called Europe "the slowest place in the world." Peugeot Citroën, struggling with sales that collapsed from 300,000 vehicles in 2007 to 120,000 in 2012, tried to close its assembly plant at Aulnay-sous-Bois, between Paris and Charles de Gaulle Airport. The French government finally agreed, provided that the company found jobs for the plant's 3,000 workers.

London not only retained its preeminence as Europe's financial center; it became an exceedingly expensive place in which to live. While the price of homes across the UK declined 10 percent between 2008 and 2013, in London it rose 20 percent, and in top London neighborhoods it rose 30. A shipping magnate who owned Chelsea's Old Rectory turned down an offer of $200 million for the house and its two acres. Next door, developers in 2011 paid £85 million for an old schoolhouse on one acre. They called it The Glebe and planned to develop it into six apartments and a penthouse. In 2008 the British government sold a 5.7-acre tract known as the Chelsea Barracks for the astronomical price of £959 million. Six years later, planning permission was finally given to build the first seventy-four apartments on the site. The patient developer was Qatari Diar, one of Qatar's sovereign-wealth funds.

Few English families could afford to buy homes in Mayfair, Belgravia, or South Kensington, where in 2014 homes sold on average for £1,700 a square foot; in Knightsbridge, the average was £2,400. Professionals struggling to survive in the market were soon nicknamed "cling-ons." None of this was a problem for property developers because 60 percent of the buyers in central London were foreigners. They were drawn to London, as an estate-agency executive said, because the city had become "the global center for wealth preservation in all its forms," including real estate. Of the seventy-six apartments at One Hyde Park, built with Qatari financing, only seventeen were registered as primary residences.

The dominance of foreign buyers wasn't evident on the street, because these owners were in town only occasionally. Additionally, the UK government spent $34 billion annually on housing subsidies, including not only the provision of 823,000 government-owned apartments in London but subsidies for a lucky 150,000 families who were able to live in privately owned London apartments and houses they could never afford on their own. The government announced in 2011 that it intended to cap all benefits at $41,000 per family annually, which was the average before-tax household income in Britain. Housing experts estimated this would force 82,000 families out of central London.

Where could they go? On the city's east side, the old warehouses at Canary Wharf had been replaced by 16 million square feet of office space occupied by 100,000 workers. Major tenants included Credit Suisse, JPMorgan Chase, and Barclays. Their stability attracted foreign investors looking for steady income. The South Korean National Pension Service paid £772 million for 8 Canada Square, which housed HSBC's headquarters, and Qataris paid almost as much for One Cabot Square, occupied by Credit Suisse. Now, however, Canary Wharf was turning into a mixed-use development. Ten million more square feet of space was planned, along with 100,000 more jobs, but residential development was also on the way, particularly at Wood Wharf, on the east side of the already developed area. The secretary of the Canary Wharf Group explained, "No one wants to commute anymore."

Few Londoners could afford apartments in Canary Wharf, but the redevelopment of old docks and warehouses there set developers and planners to work on cheaper projects away from the Thames but near picturesque old canals. The largest of these canal-side projects was King's Cross Central, a sixty-seven-acre site that by 2020 would have 20,000 residential units, along with a lot of commercial space, including Google's UK headquarters. The site was just north of King's Cross railway station and bordered on two sides by the Regent's Canal.

Another area of housing for the middle class was Stratford City, a 180-acre mixed-use project built by Westfield of Australia in conjunction with the 2012 London Olympics. The company boasted that this would become the metropolitan heart of east London, but Stratford was only one of four centers planned for the Thames Gateway. By 2016 the Gateway was planned to add 160,000 new homes between the Docklands and Sheerness, 50 miles downstream on the Thames Estuary.

High-rises were on the way, too. Until 1950 London's height limit had been 300 feet, a bit less than the height of the dome of St. Paul's Cathedral. Centre Point, a slab at Tottenham Court, was one of the first buildings to break free. A few years later, in 1963, the twenty-six-story Shell Center opened on the south side of the Thames. Then Lloyd's got a new and controversial office tower in the City of London, and in 1987 Prince Charles famously complained that builders had "wrecked London's skyline and desecrated the dome of St. Paul's."

An estate agent explained, "For decades the very mention of a high-rise sent shudders through everyone. Now there have been a number of pressure points. The shortage of land, the need to put higher densities into developments and the desire for more glamour have all brought changes. Actually, glamour is one of the main drivers. On a big site you can create an iconic identity that can add to the image of the whole site—and indeed the whole city." Nicknames like The Shard and, earlier, The Gherkin were powerful tools in consolidating popular recognition of these buildings. A tower at 122 Leadenhall became The Cheesegrater; another, at 20 Fenchurch, became The Walkie-Talkie. Critics dubbed other buildings Darth Vader's Helmet and The Stealth Bomber.

Charles stuck to his guns. Decades after castigating what he called the "monstrous carbuncle" of a building proposed as an extension of the National Gallery, in 2008 he made a speech in which he said, "For some unaccountable reason we seem to be determined to vandalize these few remaining sites which retain the kind of human scale and timeless character that so attract people to them and which increase in value as time goes by." Thanks in some measure to Charles, the British began to pay more attention to heritage buildings. When the Battersea Power Station, Europe's biggest brick building, was decommissioned about 1980, it was not demolished. What to do with it was less clear, but Malaysian developers came along in 2012 and offered £400 million for the thirty-nine-acre site, on which they planned an

£8 billion, mixed-use complex that would preserve the power station with its four stacks rising like white spires at each corner of the huge building. It would be surrounded by 2,500 apartments. The first 866 apartments were already priced at £588,000 for units of 413 square feet.

Royal complaints were no longer royal commands, and design professionals battered Charles, more or less telling him to go cut some ribbons. Soon after the Tate Modern opened in a stylishly renovated power plant, its director objected to a twenty-story high-rise proposed for a nearby site. No luck. Other tall buildings followed. In 2005 Deputy Prime Minister John Prescott allowed work to begin on the forty-nine-story Vauxhall Tower, next to the Vauxhall Bridge. The curator of New London Architecture called it "Prescott's Monster," but a report from the London School of Economics said that London had to "accommodate or die."

Other high-rise projects in London included Bishopsgate Tower and a sixty-story residential tower near the south end of Blackfriars Bridge. The fifty-floor Pan Peninsula rose near Canary Wharf. The tallest of all was the Qatari-financed London Bridge Tower or Shard, designed by Renzo Piano. Slightly over a thousand feet tall, it had sixty-six stories, including a Shangri-La Hotel in its upper floors. Upstream from The Shard and around the bend, the United States was building a new embassy. Within a decade it would be surrounded by 16,000 new homes on about 480 acres—the "New South Bank"—fronting the Thames between Battersea Park and Vauxhall Bridge. All this was impressive, but London in 2013 still had fewer than a dozen buildings over 500 feet tall. That was fewer than Brazil's Curitiba or China's Wuhan.

Moscow

In 2011 London built 6 million square feet of office space, more than any American city. Yet Moscow added 26 million. The space was desperately needed because the capital of Europe's biggest country had only about 50 million square feet of office space. Paris and London, both of which were smaller cities, each had six to eight times as much.

A lot of Moscow's space was old too, without air-conditioning, parking, or modern communications. That's why good office space rented for as much in Moscow as in New York. Morgan Stanley Real Estate, Austria's Meinl European Land, and other outsiders noticed the shortage and took stakes in big developments.

Opposition? Plenty. The head of Russia's Art Research Institute said, "Moscow is being deliberately destroyed. In the 1920s and 1930s this was happening for ideological reasons: there was no place for old buildings in the new Soviet utopia. Today it is happening for purely commercial reasons. The Bolsheviks hated old Moscow. The current Moscow government does not hate it, it simply does not recognize it." The mayor, Yuri Lushkov, disagreed. He said he'd do more than restore, he'd create. So the historic Moskva Hotel was destroyed and then rebuilt with underground parking.

Stalin had deliberately blown up the Cathedral of Christ the Savior. He planned to build the Palace of the Soviets on the site, but war intervened. The church had now been rebuilt in replica, again with underground parking. Cynics called it the "Savior of the Garages." The director of the Shchusev State Museum of Architecture remembered the rebuilding of the church. "When they wanted to rebuild the cathedral," he said, "the architects from [Moscow's chief government architect] Mikhail Posokhin's office came to us. We had all the drawings in our archives. They used the exact plan, but all of the details are wrong: they put the church in the wrong spot, it is clad in a veneer of marble instead of limestone, the reliefs are in fake bronze instead of plaster. It could not be more tasteless." The cathedral was capped by a fake-gold dome.

A professor summed up the changes she saw coming to Moscow. "They have no idea what history is," she said. "In the past 10 years, we have built up this strong feeling that life exists only in money. It is the most horrible thing that happens to people." Meanwhile, the city's old Ostozhenka neighborhood was wiped out and replaced with the Golden Mile, where modern flats started at $1,000 a square foot. The work of the early Soviet architects barely survived. Moisei Ginzburg's

Narkomfin, built in the 1920s as an idealistic experiment in communal living, was decrepit. For how long would it be suffered to stand at all?

Construction activity rose and fell in phase with world oil prices. During one of the price peaks, Norman Forster designed the 2,008-foot Russia Tower. This was to be a vertical city for 25,000 people and part of the Moscow International Business Center or Moscow City, a 148-acre complex of twenty-five high-rises along the Moscow River. Then oil prices fell, and the Russia Tower was never built. Other parts of the project managed to get built, however, including the Mercury City Tower, which topped out in 2012 as Europe's tallest building. It was soon to be eclipsed by the nearly 1,200-foot Federation Tower.

Another icon that stalled in 2009 was Crystal Island, proposed for the Nagatino Peninsula. On this site Russian Land and Norman Foster planned the biggest building in the world. Four times the size of the Pentagon, Crystal Island would contain not only almost a million square feet of office space but 900 apartments and 3,000 hotel rooms.

Both the Russia Tower and Crystal Island had been the brainchildren of Chalva Tchigirinski, a self-made oil billionaire who fell out with his business partner, Elena Baturina, the mayor's wife. Baturina also controlled Inteko, the city's biggest construction company, and was described as the richest woman in Russia. Tchigirinski's lawyers maintained, "No major projects can proceed in this city without her backing." With it, the lawyers continued, "she would ensure that any planning or other bureaucratic issues did not get in the way." When her husband, the mayor, was dismissed in 2010, Baturina sold Inteko for a billion dollars.

Petersburg

Unlike every other ruler of post-czarist Russia, Vladimir Putin liked St. Petersburg. So much money was coming into the city that there was a joke about the eight-lane highway to Moscow—one lane to the capital and seven the other way.

Along came Gazprom City, renamed Okhta Center. Plans called for a 1,299-foot riverside high-rise opposite the Smolny Cathedral. The director of the Hermitage warned that the tower, designed in the shape of an inverted icicle, would destroy the "unique aura" of the city and, in turn, "the economic foundation for our existence." Perhaps he was right, but the tower would also symbolize a new Russia. Meanwhile, as if to say that the government could do preservation if it wanted, plans were drawn up for New Holland, a small Petersburg lake rimmed by warehouses previously turned into an army base. In the hands of Norman Foster—the man never slept—it was becoming a set of concert halls, hotels, and restaurants, including a stage floating in the lake.

Investors on a smaller scale tried to convert the city's old palaces into modern apartments, but work was slow because the palaces were already occupied, not by the descendants of aristocrats but by average citizens, *kommunalkas*, who in the Soviet period had been awarded a few rooms with shared facilities. If a developer could persuade them to leave and if the building were then restored (or perhaps rebuilt behind its historic facade), an apartment could easily sell for $20,000 a square meter.

Berlin

Despite Germany's wealth, in 2010 only 44 percent of Germans owned their homes. In 2001, however, Nomura bought 64,000 railway workers' homes for resale to their occupants. Then a German power and gas company inscrutably named E.on sold 150,000 apartments for €7 billion to Terra Firma and Citigroup. The American firm Fortress came along and bought 80,000 apartments from the state pensions administrator. A Fortress officer said, "This is an unbelievably big structural change for Germany. For 100 years, the government and big corporations have controlled the country's housing stock."

The general approach was to take the current rent, imagine that it was the payment on a thirty-year mortgage, then calculate the principal amount of that mortgage, and call it the purchase price. The tenants loved it, and the sellers were making big money—double or triple what they paid.

Some of these apartment blocks were architectural monuments. One group, bought by the American pension fund Oaktree in 1998, comprised Hufeisensiedlung (Horseshoe Settlement) and Wohnstadt (Residential City) Carl Legien. Both were complexes of modernist blocks designed by Bruno Taut. Built between 1926 and 1932 by Gehag, a joint venture of labor unions, state insurance funds, and private businesses, these *siedlungen* (settlements) were built with an eye to *licht, luft, sonne* (light, air, sun), and they did away with the Wagnerian ornamentation of most big German buildings of the time. Now Gehag was gradually selling the complexes, whose plain facades and flat roofs were legally protected and even inscribed on UNESCO's World Heritage List. The purchasers included architects who loved the unpretentious simplicity of these buildings.

Paris

In the 1960s Paris had allowed the construction of precisely one highrise, the much-reviled Montparnasse Tower. The verdict was Never Again, although there were a few exceptions, most notably the highrise jungle called La Défense, the biggest business center in continental Europe. A smaller exception, which combined a few high-rise towers with many mid-rise buildings, was Paris Rive Gauche, where €3.2 billion were spent building 5,000 housing units, offices, shops, and a university. The site already had the Bibliothèque nationale de France, a signature high-rise complex of François Mitterand, but Rive Gauche was much bigger than that. It occupied about 300 acres of former railway land east of the Austerlitz station and may well have been the city's biggest redevelopment scheme since the work of Georges-Eugène Haussmann in the 1860s. A resident preferred the results to Haussmann's. In an implicit slam at the baron, he said, "Look. There are different colors and shapes, not just buildings that are all calculated to be in exact proportion to the width of the street."

Maybe Paris Rive Gauche would fare better than Les Halles, the famous old food market cleared and replaced in 1977 by the Forum

Les Halles, a mostly underground shopping center. The forum now served as a transit center and meeting point for suburban youth. A teacher said, "I consider myself a true Parisian but Les Halles is nothing now to do with Paris: it is the suburbs in the city. In fact it is now dangerous for Parisians to go there." The mayor, eager to redevelop the site again, said, "Everyone has an ideal. Mine is to imagine how people in Paris can really live together." He said that the new Les Halles "will be a real work of art for the 21st century," but he faced plenty of resistance. A bookseller said, "Parisians don't like change. They will prefer to stay with something they know is bad if it means change in any way." Still, the builders went to work.

President Nicolas Sarkozy meanwhile set his sights on the Grand 8, an eighty-mile-long automated railway shaped like a figure eight. An extension of the city's existing underground railways, it would connect the city's suburbs and cost $25 billion. Cynics might observe that the new lines would allow residents to cross the city without setting foot in the city center, where they weren't wanted. Who was? In 2008 the royal family of Bahrain paid $83 million for the Bourbon-Condé mansion on Rue Monsieur.

Speaking of France's suburbs, an architect said, "It is the suburban location of the estates in France that is the . . . problem. Their physical isolation sustains a sense of alienation, they become dormitory ghettoes." Another architect said, "These isolated blocks are effectively prisons."

Residents were mostly a generation or two from Africa or Turkey and had an unemployment rate of 23 percent, 40 percent for men. The mayor of Evry, where half the population was foreign or born to foreigners, said, "We have been engaged in a form of ethnic, social and territorial apartheid, segregation, for at least 30 years." A job applicant said, "If I say I live in Clichy-sous-Bois, they won't even call me back." The apartment buildings had nice names—The Grove, The Forest, The Pointed Oak—but the trees of Clichy-sous-Bois had been cut down when the apartment blocks went up. A father said, "I will die before I let my kids spend their life here."

As far back as 1971, an American journalist visited the freshly built apartment blocks at Sarcelles, on the northern edge of Paris, and came away calling the place a "nightmare." Another visitor judged Sarcelles an "egg crate world, where a person's individuality counts for nothing, where everybody has sold his soul for uncracked plaster and is sorry he did it." Many of France's leaders agreed. As early as 1983, François Mitterand wrote that the blocks "must disappear from our country." Some banlieues were in fact dynamited. Venissieux, a suburb of Lyon, blew up ten of its fifteen-story buildings—the Towers of Democracy—in the quarter called Les Minguettes. Over a thousand apartments were demolished in Lyon's La Courneuve. Over 2,000 remained, however, and in the first eight months of 2005, the town reported over 2,000 acts of banlieue delinquency, including 1,175 thefts.

Milan

What to do with Italy's obsolete *quartieri industriali*? By 2011 Milan's Santa Giulia Project would house 9,000 people in a mixed-use development on a site that was formerly a Montedison chemical plant and a Redaelli steel mill. No need for the residents to join Milan's 800,000 commuters, but if they wanted to go downtown, 6 miles to the northwest, they'd be there in fifteen minutes by train. They'd also be close to the city's ring road. Norman Foster—Lord have mercy!—explained, "It's a better alternative to suburbia. It's something that seeks to have the qualities and place of the city, but with the benefits of more open space, more green space, more security, less problems with the car, and a good pedestrian experience which is, after all, what we think of when we think about our favorite cities."

Meanwhile, there was Porta Nuova, a $2.5 billion project on some seventy acres of former railway yards close in on the northeast side of the city. The project included Italy's tallest high-rise, designed by Cesar Pelli. The developer was Hines of Houston, and by 2015 the project would include 2.5 million square feet of offices and apartments. The city's former trade-fair grounds were meanwhile being transformed into the €2.2 billion CityLife, which included towers by Zaha Hadid,

Daniel Libeskind, and Araki Isazaki. Apartment prices averaged €8,500 a square meter.

AMERICAN CITIES

So unlike the cities of Asia, half of the biggest cities in the United States lost more than a third of their populations between 1950 and 2010. Chicago, which had peaked at 3.6 million people in 1950, lost almost a million and was back to where it had been in 1920. Explanation? Chicago had once been a manufacturing powerhouse, but despite rising productivity and production, manufacturing jobs in the United States had declined from 19 million in 1980 to 12 million in 2012. Viewed another way, manufacturing was down from 42 percent of the American labor force at the height of World War II to about 10 percent.

St. Louis collapsed from over 850,000 people in 1950 to fewer than 320,000 in 2010. No wonder. Anheuser-Busch was now a subsidiary of a Belgian brewer. Ralston-Purina was now part of Switzerland's Nestlé. McDonnell Douglas had disappeared into Boeing. Trendy apartments were being carved from millions of square feet of empty St. Louis commercial space, and prices were low—about $150 a foot—but demand was limited and the number of condos relatively small, about 2,000 scattered over 125 projects. Two miles northwest of the Gateway Arch, a seventy-four-acre forest stood on the site of a demolished residential neighborhood.

Then there was the poster child. Between 1950 and 2000 the population of Detroit was cut from 1.8 million to 950,000. The 2010 census delivered more bad news: a population of about 800,000. Detroit became the only city in the country that, having risen above a million people, fell below that number. In 2014, with its population reduced to 688,000, the city declared bankruptcy.

In 1970 per capita income in Detroit had been higher than in better-educated Boston. Thank unionized jobs in the auto industry. Then foreign cars arrived, and the median house price in Detroit began declining. It was down to a ruinous $73,000 in 2006 and a catastrophic

$7,100 three years later. By 2009 the city had 200,000 empty lots. Forty of the city's 140 square miles that had once been once residential or commercial were now vacant. In the next four years, the city had over 70,000 foreclosures.

The city's last two national-brand supermarkets—both of them A&P subsidiaries—closed in 2007, which meant that residents chose between shopping in dollar stores or the suburbs. Borders, the bookstore, had headquarters in nearby Ann Arbor, but it closed its last Detroit store in 2009, almost as a prelude to the entire chain's liquidation two years later. Starbucks had only five stores in the entire city. (Little Ann Arbor, 40 miles to the west, had nine.) The city's famed orchestra was threatened with bankruptcy. There was no place within the city limits to buy a Chrysler or a Jeep. Most ominously, enrollment in the city's public schools fell from 190,000 in 2000 to 90,000 in 2009. When the 2009 school year began, 172 city schools opened, but 100 didn't. Consolidation might not be a bad thing, but nobody could defend a dropout rate of 75 percent from the city's high schools.

A resident said, "We are in an economic disaster. There's no help here. There's no hope here." The mayor was slightly more hopeful. "We've got to focus," he said, "on being the best 900,000 population city that we can be and stop thinking about 'We can't turn the clock back to the 1950s and '60s.'"

Michigan offered substantial tax rebates to film producers, and scouts looking for gritty locations had plenty to choose from. The Kresge Foundation was based in the city and actively involved with its future—some said too involved. The foundation called for investment in the more prosperous parts of the city and the restoration of natural conditions in the poorest areas, where forests might be replanted and buried creeks unearthed.

Between 2009 and 2012 the city razed 4,800 homes, and it planned to demolish another 10,000 in 2013. Razing a house cost about $8,000, which inclined the city to consider an offer from Hantz Farms to buy 2,300 parcels west of Chrysler's Jefferson North assembly plant. Hantz offered to pay $300 per acre, raze everything, and convert the land to a tree farm, an orchard, or a vegetable farm. It predicted that this would increase tax revenues by $60,000 annually.

The mayor liked the idea of zoning into "steady," "transitional," and "distressed" neighborhoods. It was a sign of the city's condition that "steady" was the best of the three. One of the steady areas, Midtown, got some good news in 2013 with the opening of a Whole Foods store, even if it floated on a raft of grants, loans, and tax breaks. A few brave employers had by then invested in the city: Quicken Loans had 10,000 employees in Detroit, Blue Cross had 4,000, and Chrysler had moved its headquarters back from Auburn Hills, in the northern suburbs.

The city's thirty-three-story Book-Cadillac Hotel, which opened as the world's tallest hotel in 1924 but closed sixty years later, reopened in 2008 as a 455-room Westin, with an additional sixty-seven condominiums. Four years later, a Canadian company, the Triple Group, paid $5 million for the forty-seven-story Penobscot Building. That amounted to five dollars a square foot, compared to a national average of $200. The building was half empty, but Triple hoped to fill it by dropping rents from fifteen dollars to ten dollars a foot. A Triple officer said, "There's huge upside," which was like saying that a failing student has lots of room for improvement.

Smaller Youngstown, Ohio, dropped even more steeply, from 168,000 people in 1950 to 66,000. The city began demolishing the worst of its abandoned homes. Ten came down weekly. The mayor planned to let homeowners enlarge their yards by taking over now-empty next-door lots. He also wanted to close streets, create parks, and remove sidewalks and streetlights.

Over on the other side of the state, Dayton declined from over 260,000 people in 1960 to 155,000. Hundreds of homes were demolished, and hundreds of residents had been given the choice of taking the empty lot next to their house as a gift or seeing it become a city park. One observer said that the program seemed "un-American. It seems like you're doing something wrong if you're not growing." Another said, "It's really hard to do something like this. The one thing you always run up against is that Americans don't want to be told about decline."

Canton, between Youngstown and Dayton, sagged from 110,000 in 1950 to 80,000. Two thousand houses were empty, and house prices fell more than 11 percent in 2005, well before the national market declined. Many houses were for sale at under $20,000, but realtors wouldn't touch them. One explained that after subtracting marketing costs, "It costs you money to sell a home that cheap."

In 1966 General Motors opened an assembly plant in Lordstown, Ohio, on Interstate 80 a few miles west of Youngstown. People soon feared for the survival of the plant, a union stronghold, but this was the only GM plant in the United States that made compact cars. With Americans hyperventilating over high gasoline prices in 2008, GM announced that Lordstown would get a third shift to make more Chevy Cobalts. The addition of 1,400 jobs was manna not only for Lordstown but for Youngstown. Lordstown, population 3,000, couldn't possibly accommodate the plant's new workers.

Late in 2008, with gas prices down and GM bankrupt, Lordstown lost two shifts and went from 5,000 to 2,000 employees. The mayor said, "There is no Plan B for us, no alternative." An employee added, "If GM is going to survive, this plant is going to survive. The question is whether it will." By 2011 things were looking up again. The plant was turning out Cruzes on three shifts. It wasn't quite the good old days, because new workers were paid only half what the old-timers got. One worker overlooked the disparity and said, "You know now that the plant will be here for a long time."

Youngstown got another boost from a $650 million steel mill built by a French company making pipe for drill rigs working on the nearby Marcellus Shale. The mayor said, "I never imagined a new steel mill in Youngstown." The mayor of Gary, Indiana, must have cast envious glances. Her city over the previous forty years had lost more than half its population. The workforce at Gary's huge United States Steel plant on the Lake Michigan waterfront had dropped over that period from 30,000 to 5,000.

Survival Strategies

A few cities were lucky. Columbus, Indiana, about 40 miles southeast of Indianapolis, was the home of Cummins, which in 2007 exported $1.7 billion worth of engines and engine components. Waterloo, Iowa, 90 miles northeast of Des Moines, had a big John Deere factory. Kingsport, in the northeast corner of Tennessee, had a huge Eastman Chemical factory making plastics and fibers.

Rochester, New York, was not so lucky. Kodak, once the pride of the city, had slashed its Rochester workforce from 60,000 in 1980 to under 5,000. Still, its former workers were highly qualified. They attracted new employers, and the city's unemployment rate stayed 2 percent below the national average.

Adopting a common though almost desperate strategy, Chattanooga attracted a Volkswagen assembly plant by giving the company a thirty-year tax holiday, along with 1,300 acres of free land. To secure a Boeing assembly plant for Charleston, South Carolina offered a package worth $450 million.

Big firms like these could be magnets. The Kansas side of Kansas City had slumped from 170,000 to 150,000 people, for example, and its per capita median income of $16,000 was about $6,000 below the national average. Along came the Kansas Speedway in 2001. The speedway drew Cabela's, a sporting-goods superstore that quickly became the number-one tourist destination in Kansas. The 700,000-square-foot Nebraska Furniture Mart joined the fun, along with other retailers creating a district called Village West, which boosted Kansas City's annual tax revenues by more than $6 million.

Omaha, Nebraska, tried a different approach, building up the city's tax base by annexing suburbs. This didn't please everyone swallowed by the expanding city, but if Omaha had stayed within its 1960 boundaries, it would have had 200,000 people instead of over 400,000. It would also have been a much poorer place, probably deprived of Qwest Center Omaha, which opened in 2003. Two years later, measured by ticket sales, that center was one of the top-ten entertainment venues anywhere.

Sometimes the military came to the rescue. In the summer of 2005, people in Box Elder, South Dakota, thought that Ellsworth Air Force Base, just outside town, was likely to close. Four thousand jobs were at risk, many of them in Rapid City. Could the base be saved? One voter said of Senator John Thune, "Unless he has a cape and tights I don't know how he will pull it off." Thune turned out to like phone booths.

Corsicana, Texas, got a similar break. An old oil town south of Dallas, it was in steep decline. Northrop Grumman, which did a lot of classified work that couldn't be offshored, was based in Los Angeles, where its workers couldn't afford to live. Solution: Northrup moved some of its work into a nearly empty Corsicana shopping center.

Philanthropy could help too. Wealthy donors with the modesty to remain anonymous funded the Kalamazoo Promise, guaranteeing that students whose high-school years were spent in Kalamazoo would have two-thirds of their college tuition paid, provided they attended a public college or university in Michigan. If the students were in Kalamazoo from kindergarten through high school, the Promise guaranteed payment of all college tuition. The program attracted new residents with young children. Employers liked it, too.

No Room for Complacency

In 1950 more people worked in New York City's garment district than in all of Detroit's automotive plants. The jobs disappeared, but the city recovered with the rapid expansion of financial services. Time for champagne? The average salary for people in the securities industry in New York City in 2012 was $343,000. In St. Louis it was $102,000. The result was that between 2007 and 2012 New York City lost 9 percent of its securities jobs. The number in St. Louis rose by 85 percent.

By 2012 the ten biggest banks in New York City had cut their office requirements by 25 percent to 32 million square feet. Deutsche Bank moved most of its operations all the way to Jacksonville, Florida. New Jersey offered Goldman Sachs a package of inducements worth $164 million; in exchange, Goldman transferred 4,000 jobs from Manhattan to the other side of the river. Perhaps there was some satisfaction in New York City when Goldman took New Jersey's money, set up shop, and then left—by 2012 moving a third of the New Jersey jobs to even cheaper states.

Small Towns Cling to Life

Howard, South Dakota, an hour's drive north of Sioux City, had a thousand people. It was also the seat of Miner County, whose population had declined from 8,500 to 3,000. Howard's street names were pure Americana—Park, Washington, College, Farmer, Market—but what were people to do here, except commute 70 miles each way to Sioux Falls? The town was hoping to build on wind-turbine repair and organic beef. It didn't expect to grow but hoped to stay even.

McLean County, north of Bismarck, North Dakota, fell from 19,000 in 1950 to fewer than 9,000. The county seat, Washburn, slipped from 2,000 in 1980 to about 1,300. Along came Headwaters, a Utah company. It wanted the waste steam from Washburn's coal-fired power plant, owned by Great River Energy. The two formed a partnership to build the $90 million Blue Flint Ethanol plant, using waste steam to make ethanol from corn. The project promised 400 temporary and forty permanent jobs.

Not everyone looked on enviously. By a vote of 263 to 136, the residents of Cambria, Wisconsin, rejected a proposed ethanol plant. Their victory was brief because the company got permission from the county to build just outside the town's boundary.

Then there were server farms. Google had perhaps two dozen, though the exact number might as well have been a state secret. Every one of the billion searches Google did daily used a third of a watt-hour, which meant that the company used 260 megawatts continuously just for searches. The company was on the lookout for cheap power, ideally in a chilly climate.

The center for cheap power in the United States was the Northwest, with abundant hydropower from the dams on the Columbia River. Electricity cost about half the national average of six to seven cents a kilowatt hour, and so it was no surprise when what was apparently

Google's biggest data center opened at The Dalles, on the Columbia upstream from Portland. Farther upstream still, at Boardman, Amazon had a data center. At Prineville, a hundred miles south of The Dalles, Facebook had a farm. Microsoft, Yahoo, Dell, and Intuit all converged on modest Quincy, where Microsoft alone signed up for 48 million watts, enough to power 29,000 American homes. A shop owner in Quincy said with only a hint of regret, "We're going to lose the little-town atmosphere. But this will set us up for the next 100 years."

(This was a global quest, and Microsoft in 2009 opened a server farm in Dublin, which was to be the home base for Bing, Hotmail, Windows Live Messenger, and Azure, Microsoft's cloud-computing platform. The center was said to use twenty-two megawatts and, for emergencies, to have its own generators, along with enough diesel to run them for six days. Managers hoped never to use the air-conditioning they had installed for Ireland's rare heat waves. Iceland, with cheap geothermal power and a bracing climate, cast envious glances as it worked to attract customers to Grindavik, south of Reykjavik.)

Google offered another tantalizing opportunity for a few lucky towns. Austin, Texas, offered the highest Internet speed of any major American city—almost a thousand kilobytes per second—but Google Fiber promised speeds 125 times faster than that. Parts of Kansas City, Des Moines, and Omaha were the first to have Fiber, and Internet-reliant start-ups began renting office space in neighborhoods soon called Silicon Prairie.

Tunica, Mississippi, 20 miles south of Memphis, gambled on gambling. In 1990 only a third of the town's high school students graduated. Twenty years later, almost 90 percent did. Thank the town's nine casinos, floating on the river. They had created 15,000 jobs, though many belonged to workers commuting from counties closer to Memphis. Tunica now had 6,000 hotel rooms, including the state's tallest building, the Gold Strike Hotel. It was the fifth-busiest gambling market in the country, after Las Vegas, Atlantic City, Chicago, and Detroit.

Gambling was itself a gamble, however—three Atlantic City casinos closed in 2014, leaving eight survivors—but what would Tunica have looked like without gambling? The answer was probably on display at Shelby, two counties and 60 miles to the south. There was no gambling there—and not much else either. A resident said, "There's no industry, no factories, no hope for the future, nothing to keep the people here. And what the answer is, I don't know." Ironically, the federal government pumped about $40 million a year into agricultural subsidies for Bolivar County, but the payments went almost entirely to whites, though 90 percent of the town's 2,700 residents were black.

One black farmer said, "You're in the Delta. Most of the real economy is controlled by large families. It has been that way for 200 to 300 years." By "large families," he meant white ones. A member of one of those families said, "When I was a kid we had theaters, service stations and steakhouses in Shelby. Now, it's just going down." Another woman agreed: "That's what's happening all over. These Delta towns, they're just folding up." Forty miles southeast of Shelby, residents of Greenwood—"Cotton Capital of the World"—thought they had escaped Shelby's fate by becoming the home of Viking Range, but declining sales of Viking's expensive appliances forced the company in 2008 to lay off workers. Five years later, the company laid off 20 percent of its workforce after selling itself to the Middleby Corporation of Illinois.

Dallas

The collapse of oil prices in 1986 brought downtown Dallas to a halt. For more than a decade, about a third of the city's downtown office space stood vacant, including twenty completely empty high-rises. With 8 million square feet of unoccupied space, downtown Dallas had the highest vacancy rate in the country. A radio host said, "You could shoot off a Scud missile in downtown Dallas on a Wednesday night and not hit anybody." Planners hoped to get 10,000 people living in those empty buildings, but that meant attracting grocers, pharmacists, and dry cleaners. Vicious circle: the merchants wouldn't come if the people weren't there.

In the mid-1990s fewer than 200 people lived downtown, but by 2007 the number was up to 4,400. By 2009 it was up to 7,000. Thank $640 million of private money. It began arriving with two investors who came from Denver in 1997. They converted the abandoned Republic Bank Center into 183 apartments. The city paid one shop owner's rent for eighteen months, plus half his design cost. The city helped on the residential side too. In 2005 it paid $70 million to Forest City Enterprises of Cleveland, which created 840 apartments from nine former office buildings. Gables Residential set out that year to remodel another abandoned Republic National Bank tower into 229 apartments. Rockwood Realty converted an office building into The Metropolitan, with 283 condos.

North of downtown, stacks of money lined the streets. Ross Perot Jr., Tom Hicks, and Estein & Associates were busy with their Victory Park development, which included the Victory Tower condos, the One Victory Park office and retail tower, and the chic-beyond-chic House by Starck. Nearby, the Design District had been developed after World War II as part of the Trinity Industrial District. Now it was shifting to mixed use with the development by Crow Holdings of 240 lofts mixed with retail, showroom, and gallery space. One of the city's winners in the development game built a celebratory mansion and spent half a million dollars on lighting it. He described the house as "the most perfect place that I've ever been in my life."

So things in Dallas were peachy? Try again. Perot and his partners lost control of Victory to their German creditors, and seventeen of the thirty shops and restaurants at the center had closed by 2010. Yet these were far from the city's biggest problems. The *Dallas Morning News* in 2004 commissioned a study from Booz Allen Hamilton. The resulting report compared Dallas to fourteen other American cities. Dallas came in twelfth, with high rates of violent crime, low SAT scores, and slow economic expansion. (The best cities were San Jose, Austin, San Diego, San Francisco, and Phoenix; the three worse than Dallas were Philadelphia, Baltimore, and Detroit.)

The trouble was concentrated south of Interstate 30. Taxable land values in this southern half of the city were a sixth or less of those to the north. The cruel numbers were $27,000 an acre versus $173,000. Median house prices were far apart too: $58,000 in South Dallas and $150,000 in North. As for new homes, builders had fled the Dallas Independent School District as soon as busing became mandatory in 1970. Since then more than 20,000 homes had been built in Dallas, but fewer than a fifth were in the Dallas school district. How was that possible? Simple: the Supreme Court had held that busing had to be confined within the boundaries of a school district. The result was that Dallas developers made sure that their subdivisions were assigned to suburban districts.

South Dallas had 46 square miles of vacant and developable land; North Dallas, which was about the same size, had eight. South Dallas did have industry, but don't applaud too quickly. A retired boss of Trammell Crow pointed out, with sarcastic reference to an affluent corner in North Dallas, "You don't find many lead smelters at the corner of Preston and Forest, do you?" By late 2004 there were thirty-six Starbucks shops in Dallas north of the Trinity River; there was one to the south. More came in the following years, but the imbalance remained.

A South Dallas resident said, "You're not starting out at ground level. You're starting out by having to dig yourself out of a hole." Some readers criticized the *Dallas Morning News* for making things worse by advertising its problems, but two years later, a blunt columnist wrote, "The city is locked in an outdated political stalemate, ostensibly between white, wealthy North Dallas and a poor, mostly minority southern sector." This time one reader wrote back in agreement: "This town makes the top ten list of 'hopeless' towns and cities. You know it, and I know it and so does everyone else." Another said that Dallas was on its way to becoming another Detroit.

Southern California

Politicians kept two cards in their pockets, one with good news and the other with bad. The mayor of Los Angeles had the bad-news card in hand when he called his city "the capital of homelessness in America." He had statistics too: 48,000 homeless in the city proper, about the same number as in the five boroughs of New York City. For metro LA the homeless figure was 88,000.

It wasn't just the homeless who were in trouble. One analyst said that Los Angeles had "more billionaires than any other part of the country. It's also the capital of the working poor." No wonder: the median apartment rent in Los Angeles in 2014 was $1,860 monthly. The Census Bureau, after factoring in the cost of living, calculated that California had the highest poverty rate in the nation—some 9 million people, or a quarter of the state's total. Fewer than 40 percent of the families in Los Angeles owned their homes. The national average was the other way around, with 40 percent renting.

Santa Barbara, up the coast a comfortable distance, offered no help. It forbade the construction of buildings more than sixty feet tall; it also discouraged demolition. This was a great way to push prices up in a popular place, and the median house price in 2006 was $1.2 million. Many of the city's police and firefighters, along with its teachers and nurses, commuted from Santa Maria, 75 miles to the north. The city set out to build affordable housing, but even these homes would be so expensive—about half a million dollars—that the likely buyers were doctors and lawyers. Meanwhile, the city reluctantly began a Safe Parking Program for the homeless, who were to be allowed to park overnight in a dozen lots. The mayor wasn't happy. She didn't want the homeless to "tell each other that it's OK in Santa Barbara, that's not the message we want to give out." Perhaps she had heard that Roseburg, Oregon, had passed a law making it illegal for motorists to give money to panhandlers. Kinder and gentler. A thousand points of light.

Up the coast from Santa Barbara, Monterey County had working-class, heavily Hispanic Salinas. It also had very white and nosebleed expensive Monterey, Carmel, and Pebble Beach. Even in Salinas, median house prices tripled from $175,000 in 1996 to $620,000 in 2006. People coped by packing every room. A nonprofit home developer said that the message to new arrivals was simple: "You can work in our restaurants, hotels, and golf courses. But go home to your crowded conditions in Salinas at the end of the day."

In 2007 the old Robinsons-May department store at 9900 Wilshire, closed for years, sold for $500 million. Despite that price, it was a tear-down, with condos and retail on the way for a project called 9900 Wilshire. A Los Angeles realtor said, "It's of historic proportions in sheer magnitude. This is huge." The seller, New Pacific Realty, had bought the building three years earlier—it's a great country—for $33 million. The buyers this time were Britain's Candy brothers, described by a local realtor as "what Tiffany is to jewelry here." The brothers had shot from obscurity to international prominence after partnering with Qatar's sovereign-wealth fund on London's £800 million One Hyde Park. That building had forty-six apartments selling for an average of £25 million each. A penthouse went for £135 million. A one-bedroom apartment of 989 square feet was offered in 2014 for $11.1 million. Like other apartments in the building, its windows were bulletproof.

In 2008 the brothers and their partners defaulted on a $365 million loan from a Mexican banking group, Banco Inbursa. The problem lay not with the brothers but with one of their partners, the Kaupthing Bank of Iceland. In vain, the brothers gave Kaupthing an interest in another London project in exchange for the bank's share of the Los Angeles project. It didn't work, and a worried observer said of this and some adjacent properties, "These sites are as primo as they come, and even these deals are being dragged down." One of the Candy brothers said, "Construction finance across the world has completely dried up." In 2010 the Wilshire property was given away for $148 million to a Hong Kong company that planned to put up its own version of luxury condos. One of the Candy brothers meanwhile sold an apartment he personally owned in Monaco. Sale price: €240 million.

At the peak of the boom, a 72,000-square-foot Beverly Hills estate, once the home of William Randolph Hearst, went on the market for $165 million. It sat unsold and was rented at $600,000 a month. In 2011 the price was cut to $95 million. Buyers looked as well to Fleur de Lys, a mansion modeled on Vaux le Vicomte. That place—slip of the tongue! I meant palace—had been built by Louis XIV's finance minister. The copycat didn't have the pedigree, but it did have about 45,000 square feet on five acres, and it was on the market for only $125 million. The woman selling the property said, "I'm in no rush."

For decades, LA was said to have no downtown, but things had changed. A planner went so far as to say, "We believe downtown Los Angeles can become a point of destination for the region." Between 1999 and 2007, 9,300 residential units were created downtown. A dip followed, but by 2014 another 5,000 units were under construction.

The last downtown supermarket had closed in 1950. By 2007, however, downtown's population had climbed to 29,000, and Ralphs, a unit of Kroger, opened a high-end market in the ground floor of Market Lofts. Half of that building's 267 apartments were sold in the first five months after the building's completion; prices ranged from $425,000 to $900,000. Realtors said that some of the customers apparently bought because Ralphs was downstairs.

Perhaps the biggest problems for residents were the 13,000 homeless people who also lived downtown. Sued by the ACLU, the city agreed in 2007 to let the homeless lie down between 9 p.m. and 6 a.m. on sidewalks anywhere in the city, provided they stayed at least ten feet from doorways.

The downtown population of Los Angeles rose by 2014 to 52,000. Some of the newcomers had been attracted by the $400 million Staples Center and the encompassing LA Live entertainment complex. Philip Anschutz, who had developed both, also added a nearby, fifty-four-story building with condos and two hotels, a JW Marriott and—on higher floors and with higher prices—a Ritz-Carlton.

A dozen blocks to the north, Related Companies, developer of the Time Warner Center in New York, planned to build the Grand Avenue Development Project. Financing problems intervened, and the project's main tower remained unbuilt, but a smaller, twenty-four-story apartment building was completed close to the Walt Disney Concert Hall.

In between LA Live and Grand Avenue, the forty-two-story Wells Fargo Center, originally the Crocker-Citizens National Bank Building, had been the city's tallest in the late 1960s. A New York firm, the Chetrit Group, bought it in 2005 and announced plans to carve the building into fifteen lower floors of commercial space and, way upstairs, 402 "live-work" condos. (Residents were let out on weekends for good behavior.) Back in 1967 the building's architect, the prominent William Pereira, had said, "Within the next decade, thousands of Angelenos are going to discover the convenience and pleasure of walking to work." He was right, though off by a few decades.

Richard Meruelo marched to a different drummer. The child of Cuban refugees, he now owned over a hundred downtown properties, especially in the gritty area east of Broadway. "I see tremendous opportunity here," he said. "To the extent that everybody else doesn't see it yet, it gives me an opportunity." Among his holdings was the twenty-three-acre block of the Southern Pacific's Taylor Yards, for which he paid $30 million in 2005 and on which he hoped to build the mixed-use Riveredge Village. Meruelo hadn't forgotten where he had come from. "I'm a Latino first," he said. "I'm a Republican second."

Farther out on the city's east side, MJW Investments was planning to turn a huge Sears warehouse in Boyle Heights into a residential-commercial complex. The company was already at work downtown on Santee Court, nine office buildings that were being converted to apartments and condos.

Down in San Pedro, the vacant 1960's Pacific Trade Center—never profitable—was imploded in 2006 to make way for a $175 million, sixteen-story waterfront condo block called Vue. The councilwoman who helped push the button had a great day. "Wow!" she exclaimed. "That was exciting! When's the next one? What else can we blow up?" Her hope was that the new building would help rejuvenate the neighborhood and strengthen a waterfront promenade that was part of the city's $800 million Bridge to Breakwater Master Development Plan.

Big deals like these were hard to do. The president of Anschutz remembered the days when Los Angeles was controlled by men with names such as Baldwin, Otis, Chandler, and Huntington. Since then, he said, the city had become "a little dysfunctional, more spread out and a little more difficult to manage. . . . You have to be prepared to work very hard, and be very patient, to get big projects, big visions completed here. But this is still the land of opportunity." But if the city was more difficult to manage, who was actually calling the shots? The president of Anschutz answered, "Labor. Contractors and vendors and lobbyists who do business with the city. . . . [There has been] more empowerment of communities, neighborhoods, activist groups, constituent groups."

San Francisco

In early 2006 the median house price in San Francisco was $780,000. In 2013 a one-bedroom apartment measuring 862 square feet and carved from an old printing plant sold for $750,000. A city planner said, "More than half of the city's firefighters, police officers, emergency medical workers, nurses, and teachers live outside the city." The city's school system was losing a thousand children annually. The director of the city's Planning and Urban Research Association suggested that San Francisco might turn into Venice, "a beautiful tourist town with few long-term residents and no families."

Cheaper accommodation wasn't easy to find even in the suburbs. Down on the peninsula, the median house price in Atherton was $4.9 million. That was the third-most expensive zip code in the country (after 10065, on Manhattan's Upper East Side, and 07620, around Alpine, New Jersey). Over in scenic Marin, on the north side of the bay, prices in Belvedere averaged $3.8 million, which edged out Beverley Hills and its famous 90210.

Despite its wealth, San Francisco was no longer the West's banking capital, and the Bank of America Building was now just plain old 555 California Street. The bank had sold the building in 1985 to Walter Shorenstein, a leading realtor, and his son had sold it in 2005 to New York investors. Why? The son explained that prices were "staggeringly high." His rule of thumb was simple: "If somebody is willing to pay a lot more than I would pay, then we're a seller."

The title of San Francisco's biggest owner of real estate went to Equity Office. For a time it had been the nation's biggest office-building owner, with 590 office buildings and a total of 100 million square feet of rental space. "For a time"? That's because in 2006 the Blackstone Group offered $20 billion for Equity. Vornado Realty and partners offered more, but Blackstone finally clinched the deal with an offer of $39 billion.

Did Blackstone sit on its new investment? Not a chance. It sold all but 105 of the properties to sixteen other companies. An analyst with a knack for metaphor said, "The carcass keeps being fed upon—first by the lion, then by the hyena and then by the vultures." The following year, many of those buyers found that they owed much more on their new properties than those properties were worth. An analyst said, "Those who bought from Blackstone have not fared well at all." Emerging from the dark years, Blackstone continued selling bits of the Equity portfolio, and in 2014 Oxford Properties, the curiously named property arm of the Ontario Municipal Employees Retirement System, paid, with partners, about $2 billion for several Blackstone office towers in Boston.

Las Vegas

If Los Angeles could have a downtown, so could Las Vegas. The CEO of MGM Mirage was not modest about his ambition. "We view ourselves as patrons," he said, "like the Medicis." His company hired Daniel Libeskind, Rafael Viñoly, Norman Foster, Cesar Pelli, Kohn Pedersen Fox Associates, Helmut Jahn, and a cast of thousands to design a $9.2 billion, seventy-six-acre project called CityCenter, reportedly the biggest privately financed development in the country. Appropriately, Dubai World contributed $2.7 billion toward the financing of the project, which offered 5,000 hotel rooms and 2,440 condos. Some enthusiastic buyers in 2006 and 2007 paid their deposits without even looking at floor plans or mock-ups.

Historically, Las Vegas had never been a shopping town, but it got a high-end and profitable mall with the Forum Shops in 1992. Fast-forward to the Grand Canal Shoppes, with Tory Burch, Chloé, and Christian Louboutin. Oscar de la Renta had a store in Vegas but not in Los Angeles. Vegas had celebrity chefs too: Ducasse, Boulud, Serrano, Keller, Palmer, and Robuchon. It had fourteen master sommeliers, while poor LA had none. Vegas was also buying so many date palms from the nurseries at Indio that the price hit $2,700 each. A fifteen-foot Canary Island date palm could be three times that much. Los Angeles dropped out of the market and downgraded its street trees to cheaper species.

(Time-out for antiquarians. Palms were introduced to California by Spanish missionaries. They were planted on glamorous estates—Lucky Baldwin's in Arcadia, Henry Huntington's in San Marino—and went from there to the streets of Pasadena, Santa Monica, and Beverly Hills. The City of Los Angeles now had 75,000 palms on public property, at least until they died of old age.)

An hour's drive northeast of Vegas, Coyote Springs wasn't much to look at, but Harvey Whittemore, a lobbyist, got his hands on 43,000 acres there and was planning a city of 400,000 people. How had he got so much land in a state where almost everything was federally owned? Simple. He bought it from Aerojet-General, which in 1988 got the land from the government to test rockets. (It never did.) Whittemore said, "The final product is the most environmentally friendly development ever proposed in Nevada. I want people to understand that I am the platinum standard." Whittemore had earlier built Wingfield Springs, a smaller project to the northeast of Reno, but he lost control of Coyote Springs and was soon snarled in litigation with a partner. Work stopped, though a golf course was built, its fairways winding between graded lots.

Whittemore wasn't alone in his grief. Between 2006 and 2012 housing prices in Las Vegas fell 60 percent. Vacant lots at Lake Las Vegas, in nearby Henderson, fell all the way from $250,000 in 2006 to $30,000 in 2012. Housing demand, which had peaked at 35,000 units annually, fell to 3,500. The Veer and Mandarin Oriental projects, both part of CityCenter, had 900 condos, but by 2012 only 292 had been sold, despite Veer's cutting prices on the cheapest units from $500,000 to $315,000. Many people who had bought condos at CityCenter wanted their money back; others had trouble getting financing to close on their purchase. The dismayed chief construction officer for MGM said, "In 28 years in the industry I have never seen anything like it." A real-estate agent said, "They thought the demand would always be there."

It was a similar story at the Trump International Hotel and Tower, a 1,282-unit condo project that sold out in five days. Only a fifth of the buyers closed, and the rest of the building became a hotel. Late in 2010 The Cosmopolitan opened across the street from CityCenter and threw another 2,500 rooms on the staggering market. MGM had already stopped construction at floor 25 of the forty-nine-story Harmon, a CityCenter tower designed by Norman Foster. Now it proposed imploding the built half—and not paying the builder the remaining construction charge of $200 million. Shoddy work, MGM said. The builder said the architect was to blame for any technical deficiencies and that MGM was suffering buyer's remorse.

The Big Apple

Talking about Manhattan, the architect Rafael Viñoly put it bluntly: "There are only two markets, ultraluxury and subsidized housing." In David Harvey's formulation, the city was becoming "a vast gated community for the rich." And not just the American rich; half of Manhattan's luxury condos were sold to foreigners adding another bloom to their property bouquets. Promotional pamphlets for the Sheffield, a renovated building with about 850 apartments close to Carnegie Hall, were printed not only in English but in French, Italian, Spanish, and Chinese.

One disenchanted buyer gave up her search for an apartment even in comparatively cheap Brooklyn. "It was awful," she said. "It feels like buying real estate in New York is something rich people can do, and I was naive to think it was something I could do, too." No wonder. The average apartment in Manhattan in 2013 measured a thousand square feet. At $1,400 a foot, that came to $1.4 million. Early that year, the popular West Village had only one condo priced under $600,000. It was a fifth-floor walk-up, measured 408 square feet, and sold in ten days for $595,000. Even in Brooklyn, the median condo price in 2013 was $651,000. A realtor spoke of hopeful buyers who, leaving Manhattan, "went to Brooklyn first, and now they are getting priced out of there, too."

Most new arrivals to Manhattan would buy or rent a slice of a tall building. Renzo Piano, who had designed a few himself, judged most of these buildings harshly. "Typically," he said, "they are aggressive, arrogant, black, they go up like that—paf! They have a bad reputation and they deserve it. They are full of that desire to tell everybody: 'I am stronger than you.' They are about money and power."

The architecture critic of the *New York Times* wrote that Norman Foster, the architect of a tower proposed in 2006 for 980 Madison Avenue, was "not a social critic; his job, as he sees it, is to create an eloquent expression of his client's values. What he has designed is a perfect monument for the emerging city of the enlightened megarich: environmentally aware, sensitive to history, confident of its place in the new world order, resistant to sacrifice."

Neighborhood objections killed the project, with one man calling it "a glass dagger plunged into the heart of the Upper East Side." As construction funds dried up almost worldwide, other Manhattan projects were canceled. Among them was Santiago Calatrava's 80 South Street Building, also known as Sky Cubes. Proposed for a site near the Brooklyn Bridge, it was to have had only a dozen apartments—one to a floor and each priced at about $30 million.

Despite the failed projects, Manhattan remained a gallery like no other. On the prime site of the Mayflower Hotel and just north of the Time Warner Center, the Zeckendorf brothers built 15 Central Park West. Designed by Robert A. M. Stern and completed in 2008, the building appealed to buyers who no longer felt the need to impress anyone and who were willing to pay more than $10,000 a square foot for immaculate architectural sobriety—limestone from the same quarry that wrapped the Empire State Building.

Frank Gehry's flashier Beekman Tower—its name later changed to 8 Spruce Street and later still to New York by Gehry—rose next door to

City Hall and offered 889 apartments. Charles Gwathmey's Astor Place Tower towered over the Cooper Union. Fifth Avenue had a Michael Graves tower at Thirty-Ninth Street. An Enrique Norten building grew in Tribeca from the chrysalis of an old building at 1 York Street, and lo, there was a public garage under Jean Nouvel's tower at 40 Mercer Street. (Try twenty dollars an hour.) Yoshio Taniguchi had expanded the Museum of Modern Art, and Nouvel's Torre Verre might yet rise above the museum, if its developer could assemble the funding. Costas Kondylis offered the Trump World Tower, and Richard Meier's Perry Street Tower, at about Pier 49, provided fabulous views of the Hudson.

Extell Development spent fifteen years assembling the land and air rights for a site close to Carnegie Hall. One57 then arose, a seventy-five-story structure designed by Christian de Portzamparc. The building had ninety-five apartments, all atop a Hyatt hotel. They were priced at an average of $8,700 a foot, though the building's penthouses were a bit more and offered 10,000 square feet for about $90 million. A realtor said, "The scale of wealth in this building is just unheard of," but a buyer at One57 said, "This type of real estate is where the world is headed." Another buyer said, "With beautiful views and just a block from Bergdorf's I think it doesn't get any better."

An even taller building—1,400 feet and eighty-nine stories—topped out in 2014 at 432 Park Avenue, the site of the demolished Drake Hotel. Designed by Viñoly and budgeted at $1.3 billion, its 121 condominiums would be priced at an average of $10,000 a square foot: a budget-priced 351-square-foot studio was offered for a bit over $1.5 million. If all the units were sold at the asking prices, the developer and his partners stood to make $1.7 billion. The developer said, "There'll never be another job like this one. It's going to live on for a very long time after I'm gone." Yet Extell immediately went on to start Nordstrom Tower a block away and over 1,400 feet high.

Most of the apartments in these buildings, like those in the luxury buildings of Hong Kong and London, were empty most of the time. That was true at the Trump Tower at 1 Central Park West. It was true as well at Eloise's Plaza Hotel. Renovations there had reduced the hotel's 800 rooms to 230, plus 180 apartments. Of those, only six had full-time residents. At night they could wander down to the Demel patisserie in the basement.

Nearby shops mostly catered to people who didn't worry about prices, and shop owners paid rents to match. In 2007 shops of a thousand square feet on Fifth Avenue between Forty-Ninth and Fifty-Ninth Streets rented for $1.5 million a year. Five years later, the price had doubled. A merchant who wanted to buy space was looking at $15,000 a foot, the equivalent of five year's rent.

By 2013 a shop on the east, or sunny, side of Fifth Avenue between Forty-Ninth and Fifty-Ninth Streets rented for $3,500 a foot. That was the most expensive street in the city—and the second-most expensive in the world, after Hong Kong Central's Lan Kwai Fong. From Forty-Ninth down to Forty-Second Streets, rents on Fifth Avenue were $1,000 a foot, and from Forty-Second down to Thirty-Fourth they were only $425. That was still much higher than the average retail space in Manhattan, which rented for $115 a foot.

Who could afford the top prices? The answer par excellence was jewelers such as Harry Winston and Van Cleef & Arpels. Another answer, however, was chain stores seeking to buy prestige. Abercrombie & Fitch didn't sell emeralds, and its 25,000-square-foot store on Fifth Avenue at Fifty-Sixth had annual sales of only a bit over $100 million, or $4,000 a foot. That probably wasn't much above the cost of the space, but the location impressed thousands of passersby and helped persuade them to shop at Abercrombie back home. That's why tourists strolling down the next few blocks passed not only Harry Winston but Hollister, Zara, H&M, Banana Republic, Lacoste, and Benetton. Ironically, people who actually lived in the neighborhood were more likely to shop on Madison Avenue, a block to the east.

Office space was much cheaper, averaging in 2007 about a hundred dollars a square foot annually. The same space sold for $745 a square foot. There were exceptions. In 2011 RFR Holding completed its purchase of the Seagram Building, an architectural trophy. RFR already owned much of the building but for the rest paid almost $2,000 a square foot.

With numbers like that, office-building developers could afford starchitects. Norman Foster had already put up the Hearst Tower, wrapped in a hexagonal web of steel. Cesar Pelli had designed the Bloomberg Tower. Renzo Piano had designed a new building for the *New York Times*, just across from the Port Authority bus station. Santiago Calatrava designed the World Trade Center Transportation Hub, and on the adjoining site of the World Trade Center, cranes were busy on 1 World Trade Center, formerly the Freedom Tower, the tallest of the four buildings planned for the hallowed ground.

Just before the destruction of the twin towers, Larry Silverstein had won ninety-nine-year leases to both of them. Now he hoped to rebuild the entire site. He went ahead with Towers 2, 3, and 4, designed by Norman Foster, Richard Rogers, and Fumihiko Maki, but in 2006 he ceded control of 1 World Trade Center to its owner, the Port Authority. The authority's director of development called the site "the most complex construction project in the world." It was certainly the most expensive, with the price of the heavily reinforced 1 World Trade Center rising by 2012 to almost $4 billion, more than twice the cost of Dubai's much taller Burj Khalifa.

All four buildings were to be ready for occupancy by 2012, but delays set in. For lack of tenants, the construction of Tower 3 was stopped at the eighth floor, seventy-two floors short of the planned height. Tower 2 was postponed indefinitely. Towers 1 and 4 were half leased, with completion dates pushed back. Silverstein had a special reason to be anxious because, despite the destruction of the Twin Towers, his lease obligated him to pay the Port Authority $10 million a month until the year 2100. The Port Authority had its own anxieties and was relieved in 2011 when Condé Nast, the publishing company, leased floors 20–41 of 1 World Trade Center. Even when filled, that building would lose a great deal of money. The Port Authority would have to make up the loss with funds badly needed for other projects under its control, including New York City's airports.

Years earlier, the Metropolitan Transportation Authority had planned a huge development—24 million square feet of office space and 13,000 apartments—on the six blocks of the Hudson Yards, just west of Penn Station. This was the largest block of land available for development in Midtown Manhattan; at one time it had been the site of a failed bid for the 2012 Olympics. Ada Louise Huxtable, a critic with a tongue, predicted that the city would now get "a lot of very, very big buildings that will make someone very, very rich." Work finally got under way in the hands of Related Companies with help from Kuwait, Abu Dhabi, and Saudi Arabia. Related's chairman called the project the "Rockefeller Center—the heart of the city—for the 21st century." More than that, he said, "You're looking at something that will be far greater than Rockefeller Center—that will be the new heart of New York City." He hoped to build seventeen buildings: 18 million square feet of space including not only offices but thousands of apartments, a luxury mall, and a K–8 public school. Major tenants for the first building, on West Thirtieth near Tenth Avenue, included Coach, L'Oréal, and SAP, the German software giant.

Nearby, Vornado Realty secured permission in 2010 to build 15 Penn Place, an 1,190-foot tower two blocks west of the Empire State Building. That building's owners were not amused. Despite its fame, the aging building was only two-thirds occupied, even though it offered modest rents of about forty-five dollars a foot. Incredibly, almost half of the building's income came from tickets to the observatory deck.

Mayor Bloomberg wanted to revise the city's zoning law to allow taller buildings in the fifty blocks around Grand Central Station. More than three-fourths of the 400 buildings in the area he had in mind, stretching from Thirty-Ninth to Fifty-Seventh Street, were more than fifty years old. They averaged only thirty stories. The mayor wanted to allow buildings twice that height, especially near Grand Central Station and Park Avenue. Developers would be allowed to stack air rights from other owners, including the city, and the city would use income from the sale of its air rights to pay for new public space and for improvements to the city's subways, which, with the construction of higher buildings, would carry more people. To alleviate the flood of office space that might come into a market already sluggish from the Hudson Yards and World

Trade Center, the mayor proposed to delay construction several years. The *Times* critic objected that this was not 1965; today, urban designers wanted to make habitable cities, not high-rise jungles.

Old Jersey City waterfront brownstones, unsalable a few years earlier, were now in designated historic districts and going for a million dollars. A few blocks away, Andrés Duany helped design Liberty Harbor North, where 6,000 residential apartments were rising on eighty formerly abandoned acres. Redevelopment also awaited the North Brooklyn waterfront, where 175 acres were rezoned after the departure of the shipping business to New Jersey. Redevelopment was coming to waterfront Queens too. The City of New York announced in 2006 its purchase of twenty-four acres of Queens waterfront opposite the United Nations. The price was $146 million, a bargain price of twenty-nine dollars a square foot. Some 5,000 new apartments would be built for people earning about $100,000 a year and able to pay rents of about $2,000 a month. This was middle-income housing, New York–style.

The city hadn't seen such a big subsidized project since the opening in 1974 of Starrett City, which had been built on an old landfill near Brooklyn's Jamaica Bay. With forty-six towers housing 14,000 residents in 5,881 subsidized apartments, Starrett City had been given a bucolic name, Spring Creek Towers. In 2006 it went on the market. Offering $1.3 billion, Clipper Equity hoped to squeeze some new apartment blocks into vacant spots on the 140-acre tract. The deal fell apart, but the owners began negotiating with a new group of purchasers. Two years later, in a declining market, the new buyers offered about $700 million. One of them said, "It's a unique opportunity to preserve affordable housing at what is already a model community."

There wasn't any waterfront at the intersection of Brooklyn's Flatbush and Atlantic Avenues, but that didn't stop Bruce Ratner from pushing ahead with the Atlantic Yards development. Master planned in 2003 by Frank Gehry, the Yards were to have sixteen towers with a total of 4,000 apartments. Half would be market priced and scheduled to sell for about $900 a square foot, about as much as high-end waterfront condos in Brooklyn. The other half would be subsidized rentals. Along with commercial space, the Yards would also have a $900 million arena that would become the home of the New Jersey Nets.

Then the project came apart, and Gehry's plan was dropped in favor of a cheaper but more conventional one. The disgusted *Times* critic wrote, "Clearly, the city would be better off with nothing." The arena finally opened in 2012, though work had yet to start on any of the residential towers. They were now scheduled to be built over the following twenty-five years. The project had a new name, too—Pacific Park Brooklyn—and it had a new financial backer, Greenland USA, which despite its name was controlled by the Chinese government. The neighborhood was already changing in anticipation of the 220 events planned annually for the arena. Good-bye, hardware store; hello, luxury goods. Rent for commercial space in the neighborhood tripled from about $50 to $150 a square foot.

Meanwhile, Rockrose Development began a forty-two-story build-ing with 709 apartments in Long Island City. Location, location, loca-tion. Although the building was only about five blocks from the East River at Roosevelt Island, apartment prices would be 25 percent lower than on Manhattan. It was the same story on Manhattan itself. Prices at 1280 Fifth Avenue, near 109th Street, were 25 to 50 percent lower than in buildings below Ninety-Sixth Street, even though the archi-tect was Robert A. M. Stern and the building strongly resembled his much more expensive 15 Central Park West.

During the 1980s there had been a wave of conversions of rental units to condominiums, but 75 percent of Manhattan's apartments were still rented in 2000. That number now began dropping. Some of the big con-versions included the immense Manhattan House, with 583 apartments at 200 East Sixtieth Street, and the Sheffield, with its multilingual sales pamphlets. The Manhattan House developers paid $623 million for their project's five twenty-story towers and then set out to spend another $750 million renovating the buildings and selling them for about $1,200 a square foot, or $1.2 million for a one-bedroom apartment.

Across the city, renters were afraid. Vacancy rates were less than 1 percent, and many new rental units were coming in at $3,500 a month for a studio or \$6,000 a month for a one-bedroom. Manhattan had about 250,000 rent-stabilized apartments—about half its apartment stock—but finding one was tough, and even these units weren't cheap. The city's 38,000 rent-controlled apartments were a much better deal but impossible to get without a close family connection to somebody who already had one.

In 2004 a thousand apartments were created from office buildings on Wall Street. Two years later, 36,000 people lived in lower Manhattan, more than three times the number there in 1990. Across from the New York Stock Exchange, the former headquarters of J.P. Morgan at 15 Broad was now an apartment building called Downtown, designed by Philippe Starck. The old Chase Manhattan building at 20 Pine was reopened to a design by Armani/Casa.

One developer, Steven Witkoff, converted the grandly columned Merchants Exchange at 55 Wall Street into the Cipriani Club Residence. These buildings were too good to be torn down, he argued. "Who builds like this any more?" he asked before answering his own question: "Nobody." Witkoff set out to renovate the Woolworth Building too. Early in the twentieth century, this had been the world's tallest building. Now Witkoff planned to develop the lower twenty-eight floors as offices but sell the thirty highest floors to Alchemy Properties, which would develop forty apartments that it hoped to sell for about \$3,000 a square foot.

Conversions could go awry. In 2007 Lev Leviev, a diamond billionaire, paid \$525 million for the massive old New York Times Building, just west of Times Square. He wanted to convert it to retail space, offices, and perhaps a hotel. The previous owner, Tishman Speyer, had bought the building from the newspaper three years earlier for \$175 million. At the time this had seemed like a lot of money. Having spent three times that much buying the building, Leviev spent an additional \$200 million renovating it. By early 2010 it was still unoccupied, and the next year Leviev sold the top eleven floors of the fifteen-story building to the Blackstone Group, which planned to convert the entire space to offices.

There was a much bigger failure. After World War II the Metropolitan Life Insurance Company, supported by Robert Moses, tore down the buildings on eighty acres of Manhattan's Gas House District and replaced them with 11,000 apartments spread over 110 apartment buildings. Stretching east of First Avenue from Fourteenth to Twenty-Third Streets and divided into halves called Stuyvesant Town and Peter Cooper Village, the property went on the market in 2006.

Earlier, in 2004, MetLife had sold the Sears Tower in Chicago for $835 million. The next year, it had sold its own MetLife Building, formerly the Pan Am Building, for $1.72 billion. The Cooper and Stuyvesant sale would be bigger still, but how much bigger? So long as an apartment was occupied by the same tenant, and so long as that tenant's income didn't exceed $175,000 over two years, the rent was capped on average to between a third and a half of market rates. By 2006 only a quarter of the project's 11,000 apartments were decontrolled. Bidders had to guess when the rents on the other units would be uncapped.

A property consultant said, "This is clearly going to be one of the largest property transactions ever to occur in this city, if not the US." The winner was Tishman Speyer, in partnership with BlackRock Realty. The winning bid was $5.4 billion, or $485,000 per apartment. Tishman's president said, "The opportunity to buy 11,000 apartments in a terrific neighborhood doesn't come along very often—maybe once in a generation. You live for opportunities like this one." Another bidder, whose $4.3 billion offer was rejected, said, "It's a great, great transaction for them."

There were worriers from the start because rents covered less than 60 percent of the mortgage. That was bad enough, but two years after the sale, the value of the property had declined by 10 percent. The rating on the bonds used to purchase the property was cut. By late 2009 the project was said to be worth $2.1 billion, with default imminent. Early the next year, the property's value had fallen to a reported $1.8 billion. Rather than face foreclosure, Tishman Speyer returned the property to its creditors. The government of Singapore's famously shrewd investment corporation stood to lose $575 million. The pension fund for California's public employees wasn't far behind. Even the Church of England was involved, facing the loss of $70 million. Tishman itself suffered relatively little, having invested only $112 million of its own money in the $5.4 billion deal. Perhaps the blow to its reputation was more damaging.

Tishman Speyer owned 120 other properties around the world. Among its previous purchases had been not only the MetLife and Chrysler Buildings but Rockefeller Center, which it bought in 2000 for $1.85 billion.

Soon after completing its purchase of Stuyvesant Town and Peter Cooper Village, Tishman turned around and sold an office building called 666 Fifth Avenue. Opened in 1976, the building had originally been called the Tishman Building—it's a small world—and had been sold in 1978 for $80 million. Tishman had bought it back in 2000 for $518 million. That sounds like a bad deal, but when Tishman sold the building again in 2006, the price had almost quadrupled to $1.8 billion. This was the most ever paid for an office building and broke the previous record, set by Tishman itself when it bought the MetLife Building. The buyers for 666 in 2006 were the Kushners of New Jersey. They already owned 22,000 apartments and 5 million square feet of office space. Rob Speyer said, "New York City is the greatest place in the world to own real estate."

Then there was the General Motors Building, at the prized southeast corner of Central Park. General Motors had sold the building for just over $500 million. That was in 1991, when the company was already in trouble. Twelve years later, Harry Macklowe bought it for $1.365 billion. Five years later, in 2008, he had to raise cash fast. Boston Properties offered $2.8 billion. A reluctant Macklowe took it. At that price the building cost about $1,500 a square foot. Rents in the building were about $200 a foot, and many tenants had long-term leases at prices below that. A real-estate expert commented, "Nobody ever made money owning the General Motors Building; they only made money selling it." Four years later, in 2012, 40 percent of the building was sold to two families—one Chinese, one Brazilian—for $1.4 billion. The building's value had risen $600 million since 2008.

9   Escaping

Critics wrote books with titles like *Death by Suburb, Bomb the Suburbs, Little Boxes,* and *The Bulldozer in the Countryside,* but suburbs continued to grow. A developer who knew human nature explained that "people want what everyone else has," but that wasn't the whole story. Homes on the urban periphery were cheaper than comparable homes closer in, and they were also reasonably close to jobs. Yet economics wasn't the whole story either. The suburbs appealed as well to the common belief that a house in the country, even on a quarter acre or less of that country, was better than life on the sixth floor or the twentieth.

In short, the suburbs spoke to the desire to escape the world made for money. Ironically, they also created a big part of it. The United States built about a million new homes annually. In 2013 about 600,000 of them were for single families; the rest, multiple. All told, the country by 2020 would add 250 billion square feet of built space to the 300 billion it already had. Most of the new space would be in outer-ring suburbs. Sometimes that outer ring would be almost as distant as Pluto. The Bridges of Preston Crossing, just east of tiny Gunter, was 30 miles south of the Red River and forty north of downtown Dallas. Bluegreen Communities planned to build homes there for 6,000 people on a 1,587-acre site mocked as Baja Oklahoma. The good news was that buyers might not have to drive 40 miles to work because Dallas jobs had begun migrating north. With the exceptions of New York City and Chicago, every major American metropolitan area had more office space in its suburbs than in its central city.

North, south, east, or west, the average American house in 1950 had been built in the suburbs for a city family accustomed to a rented apartment or flat. The proud new homeowners moved into 1,100 square feet of living space. By 1973 the average new home had 1,660 feet. By 2005 it had 2,400. A peak came in 2007 at 2,507 feet. Two years later, it was down to 2,392, and builders were looking for things to cut. Four bedrooms were still a necessity; granite countertops were important too. Some builders dared to do without fireplaces, at a savings of about $3,500. They usually came to regret it because buyers held tight to this link to the Paleolithic. Housing prices in any case rebounded, and in 2013 the average house size set a new record of 2,642 square feet. Meanwhile, the 1950s California rancher was long gone, replaced by homes with facades meant to impress. There were columns and pediments and, for the certificably ambitious, porte cocheres.

One builder, KB Homes, opened a subdivision called Twin Lakes. It was in Cary, North Carolina. The homes carried a brand: "Martha's Choices." John Nash had, with Blaise Hamlet in 1811, probably created the first named subdivision, but branded houses apparently arrived only with Donald Trump. Speaking of one of Trump's high-rises, a realtor said, "We can sometimes sell over the phone just by saying, 'It's Trump.'" It was only a step from there to Martha Stewart explaining her role at Twin Lakes. "We're helping people," she said. "You could go into a house painted terrible colors or you can go into a house painted beautiful colors. Which would you choose, you know? That's what we're here for." She and KB had plans for "Martha's Choices" in Atlanta and Houston.

Like the houses they built, the nation's homebuilders grew larger. The United States had about 100,000 of them. The vast majority, called custom builders, were small, but a few—the production builders— blazed a new path, with the biggest 200 responsible for 40 percent of all the country's new homes. Top-ranked D.R. Horton peaked in 2006 at almost 53,000 homes. That wasn't so far short of the 70,000 homes sold by Sears, Roebuck over the entire period 1908 to 1940, when Sears sold prefabricated houses that came in as many as 30,000 pieces, the joists mercifully numbered.

Things slowed down after 2006, but Horton was still at the top of the list in 2013, when it built 25,000 homes. Pulte, which had sold 46,000 homes in 2005, sold 18,000 in 2013. Even so, it was big enough to buy building materials in bulk and stock its own regional distribution centers. Product standardization was the rule. The CEO of NVR, another production builder, put it this way: "Our business is like a hamburger stand," he said. "We make hamburgers and cheeseburgers. That's it. We don't customize the designs of our houses; except for the specific options that we offer with each model, they're absolutely fixed."

Toll Brothers slipped in at thirteenth place, with 4,100 homes in 2013, but Toll worked at the high end, selling what it was pleased to call "estate homes," averaging almost $700,000 each in 2013. Toll's boss said, "We're really a marketing company." He meant that contractors did the actual building. A customer wanted French Provincial? Red-brick Colonial? No problem. A model called the Cornell was Toll's most popular. It was available in twenty-two exterior finishes, depending on whether the buyer wanted to look like a French count or a New England sea captain.

Like other builders, Toll was always looking for what builders called "ground." In late 2005 Toll had enough for 80,000 houses. Pulte had enough for 350,000. Builders often had trouble getting building permits, but an economist explained that the builders went ahead and bought the ground anyway. "We have lawyers," they told themselves, "we have experts, we have money, we're going to buy these tracts of land and fight it out." Regional planning might ease the problem, but as Toll's boss said, "It can't be done, unfortunately. In order for you to take power for zoning and planning and put it in a regional council, you would have to take the power from the township. It would be the last move you ever made in politics."

Across the liberal Northeast and the Pacific Coast, developers were demonized. This kept the brakes on construction and in turn kept housing prices high, hurting the very people that the Democratic voters who dominated these places thought government should help. The predictable result, as one demographer put it, was that "if you don't own a piece of Facebook or Google and you haven't robbed a bank and don't have rich parents, then your chance of being able to buy a house or raise a family in the Bay Area or in most of coastal California is pretty weak."

So it was that, of the ten American cities issuing the most housing permits in 2013, seven were in the southern tier. (The exceptions were New York City, the District of Columbia, and Seattle.) The city issuing the most permits in 2011 was Houston, with 25,000 permits. The runners-up were New York City with 17,000, Dallas with 16,000, and Miami with 12,000. At Cross Creek, 30 miles west of Houston, 5,500 homes began to rise on 3,200 acres. On the other side of Sugar land, Toll Brothers spent $78 million on 3,700 acres at Sienna South and planned 6,500 homes for the site.

Phoenix, in 1950 a city of 106,000 people, grew to have 1.5 million by 2013 but over 4 million with its suburbs. On the city's east side, suburban Mesa now had more people than Minneapolis, Cincinnati, Cleveland, Miami, or Pittsburgh. The mayor of Phoenix epitomized the let-'er-rip ethos. "We have property rights in this country," he said. "We stole it from the Indians fair and square, and people feel strongly that if you own land you can build what you want on it. So there is no legal way you can stop the growth. We have zoning, but if you have 20 acres of land, and I said, 'I'm the mayor, and I say all you can do is look at it,' you'd take me to court, and you'd win." That's why the suburbs stretched west 40 miles to 293rd Avenue, somewhere in remoter Buckeye.

The Suburbs of Megalopolis

New York City's western suburbs now included Allentown, Bethlehem, and Easton. In 2004 alone 14,000 New Yorkers moved to these Pennsylvania towns, a two-hour commute. The national rule of thumb was that buyers would save $1,000 in house price for every extra minute of commuting time, but here the cost per minute was much higher. Toll Brothers sold its 4,400-square-foot Coventry for $625,000 in Allentown, Pennsylvania. The same house in Basking Ridge, New Jersey, 60 miles closer to Manhattan, cost not $685,000 but $1.7 million. The savings in Allentown weren't quite as impressive as they looked. Residents who worked in Manhattan would spend $400 a month on bus fares, twice as much as residents of Basking Ridge.

There was a similar story in Loudoun, three counties west of Washington DC. By October 2005 Loudoun had 2,900 houses on the market, more than double the number the year before. The median price had dropped from $506,000 to $480,000. Still, things weren't too bad. The Census Bureau reported in 2006 that at $98,000 Loudoun had the highest median household income of any county in the country. Two-thirds of Loudoun's households included a married couple. That was twice the number in closer-in Arlington.

Still farther west and just inside West Virginia, a planner in Jefferson County said, "The land use regulations in Loudoun and Fairfax have done nothing to stop sprawl. They've only accelerated it. They've pushed it out here." Perhaps he was thinking of 3,200-home Huntfield, west of the Blue Ridge and, in the middle of the night, an hour's drive from Washington. Someone buying here paid $270,000 for a house that would have cost $420,000 if it had been a couple of counties closer to the capital. Of the first hundred buyers, only five worked in the District but thirteen worked in Maryland and seventy-two in the Virginia suburbs. The builder said, "We leapfrogged over Loudoun to find the next logical place to build. We don't like to think of it as exporting sprawl, but it is clearly leapfrogging development." One sardonic buyer said, "I've been enjoying the pastoral setting because I've been put out to pasture by the housing market."

California

Ironically, the state most famous for sprawl was no longer sprawling. California's cities were surrounded by open space, but most of it was public land, off-limits to developers. That made land expensive. At the peak, only one in ten households in Orange County could afford the median house price of $725,000.

Nine of the ten American cities with more than four people per household were in greater LA. Latino families were large, but people were also doubling up. Developers began packing homes onto less land, so that newly urbanized land in Los Angeles had nine people per acre. The comparable figure for Atlanta was two. For Nashville, it was one. Enter Playa Vista, a thousand acres just north of Los Angeles International Airport. It had once been the headquarters of Hughes Aircraft, but in the decade after 2000, it became the site of 3,000 homes and 2 million square feet of office space. The last 110 acres were sold for $250 million to a Canadian company, Brookfield Residential, which planned to squeeze in 700 homes and 1,500 apartments. A developer said, "In the next 10 years the typical single-family subdivision will be a dinosaur." He himself was building attached homes.

Developers in this market planned carefully before picking up a nail gun. Orange County's Ladera Ranch, part of the privately owned Rancho Mission Viejo, had 25,000 people clustered in two villages. The word *village* had been used, a marketing officer said, because "neighboring is one of the biggest concepts in America." Ladera's marketing company had then analyzed thousands of questionnaires before naming the villages Covenant Hills and Terramor. The first targeted social conservatives; the second aimed at what the developer called "cultural creatives."

Ladera's median house price in 2007 was $780,000. Two years later, the median was $530,000. By then a tenth of the mortgages in Ladera were more than a month late, and that wasn't including the 4 or 5 percent already in foreclosure.

Trimark Communities built and sold some 16,000 homes on the west side of Tracy in a development called Mountain House. There was no mountain in sight—this was the Central Valley, after all—but that hadn't discouraged real-estate refugees from the Bay Area, an hour's drive to the west. The sky fell on Mountain House in late 2008, when nine out of ten homeowners in the Mountain House zip code, 95391, owed more than their houses were worth. The average homeowner owed $120,000 more.

Even in good times, Mountain House sounded like a commute from hell, but there were worse places. Every day 175,000 vehicles came south through Cajon Pass on Interstate 15. This was the road between Los Angeles and Victorville, a place with its own suburbs. Victorville was almost a hundred miles from downtown LA, but with its suburbs it was home to 250,000 commuters who never saw their homes in daylight, except on weekends and holidays. Commuters were willing to try even California City, a realtor's 8,000-acre dream from the 1950s. California City was closer to Bakersfield than to Los Angeles.

The combined population of Riverside and San Bernardino Counties grew from 2.6 million in 1990 to 4.1 million in 2007. This was the Inland Empire. One analyst said that it "captures people before they would head to Arizona or Nevada."

A lot of the prisoners were buying homes on land that a couple of years earlier had been part of a dairy farm. The epicenter was Chino, where in 2004 and 2005 more than 160 dairies were sold or in escrow—almost half of the 400 dairies in Chino in the late 1980s. With subdividable land worth $500,000 an acre, San Bernardino County was no longer the nation's top milk producer. Instead, Chino was now the site of The Preserve, with 7,300 homes on 1,000 acres. Many of the dairy farmers took the money and ran to the Central Valley. One, age seventy, said he'd retire. He added, "I will make 10 times in real estate what I did during a lifetime of dairy."

Even Baja was a magnet, attracting retirees to towns like Rosarito, just across the border. A middling condo there went for a few hundred thousand dollars. Buyers didn't go to LA every day, but when they wanted it, the city was three hours away. Shopping? Walmart, Costco, and Home Depot were all in Tijuana. One happy transplant said, "I go to bed at night listening to the ocean, and we're woken up by the birds in the morning and not the helicopters and traffic." A developer said, "We think the [market] is going to explode."

The same thing was happening on the other side of the peninsula. There, in sight of the Gulf of California, or what Mexicans called the Sea of Cortez, Loreto Bay Homes was developing 8,000 acres. Over on the mainland side, the Mexican Worldwide Group, partnering with Arizona's Abigail Properties, was building 1,500 condos and 200 single-family homes. The buyers were overwhelmingly American, pestered by a few excessively friendly Canadians.

Florida

Beyond the fringe of North Tampa, New River was slated to have 100,000 homes. New River was the brainchild of Beat Kahli, a German who had discovered the land of opportunity. East of Orlando, he was also building Avalon Park for a mere 15,000 people. At New River he had turned homebuilding over to KB Homes, for whom New River was only one of 480 projects. Nobody wanted to live so far from Tampa, but it was the old $1,000-a-minute rule. The aphorism was "drive till you qualify."

Back in the 1950s Lee Ratner, founder of the company that made d-CON rat poison, had bought a ranch near Fort Myers. He subdivided it into Lehigh Acres, a stupefying grid of 100,000 rectangular cells. By 2000 only 15,000 had houses, but a boom from 2004 to 2006 saw another 13,000 houses added. Then the ax fell. The median home price in Lehigh Acres collapsed from $320,000 in 2005 to $107,000 in late 2008. By late 2011 the median was under $60,000.

Lehigh Acres had siblings. One was Cape Coral, known until 1957 as Redfish Point. Two brothers from Baltimore bought the land that year. Fifty years later, the place was home to 167,000 people. It sounded like a great success, but one observer saw it differently. "The Florida economy," he said, "has been based on selling Florida. Our growth is all about population growth. When you take that away, what have you got?"

Florida was about to find out. In 2007 an official from Allied Van Lines told a meeting of the Chamber of Commerce in Tallahassee that the company was helping more people leave the state than arrive. "That really got people's attention," one member of the audience said. Between late 2007 and late 2008, the median house price in Cape Coral–Fort Myers fell 51 percent, more than four times the national decline of

12 percent. One house that sold for $850,000 in 2005 was priced four years later at $273,000. Of Cape Coral's 64,000 single-family homes, 18,000 had been foreclosed.

NEW URBANISM

The average American motorist was said to spend over eighteen hours weekly in a car, and without a vehicle most suburban residents might as well have been under house arrest. Critics insisted there was a better way. Often, what they had in mind was a reinvention of nineteenth-century small-town America, this time with modern plumbing. That is how Robert Davis, the pioneering developer of Florida's Seaside, described what he had tried to do.

Between Pensacola and Panama City, Seaside had been built to house 3,000 people. Only fifteen families lived there year-round, leaving the vast majority of the houses vacant or rented. Still, Seaside's physical design, discouraging cars while encouraging walking and affability, appealed to many people, and Davis's architects, Andrés Duany and Elizabeth Plater-Zyberk, went on to apply the formula not only to exurban locations like Seaside but to suburbia, starting with Kentlands, in Gaithersburg, Maryland. From there, urban villages spread across the country. At first sight an oxymoron, the phrase *urban village* on reflection was a reasonable label for mixed-use islands in a single-use sea. Flagstaff got Presidio in the Pines, Charlotte got Birkdale Village, and Kansas City got Zona Rosa. Dayton had The Greene, Atlanta had Atlantic Station, and San Jose had Santana Row.

Mixed-use became a mantra even in Texas, where men gave their love to trucks. Houston's voters, for example, had turned zoning down in 1948, again in 1962, and again in 1993. A few years later, the mayor was still guarding the castle. Bill White said he wasn't about to "have some bureaucrat in City Hall become the taste patrol for the city." "Not on my watch," he added. White stepped down in 2010, but a spokeswoman for his successor said a few years later that her boss "believed it is way too late for zoning in Houston." Still, nearby Galveston got a planned community in Beachtown, a billion-dollar project designed by Duany and Plater-Zyberk. Down the road was $175 million Evia. Corpus Christi had $250 million Cinnamon Shore, not far from the Shores of South Padre. Dallas was awash in these places, all on the north side of town. Southlake, Legacy, Frisco, and Garland all had developments combining mixed-use with public spaces scattered about like speed bumps for the soul.

Some people preferred to call New Urbanism "smart growth," a name that emphasized the virtue of what skeptics might call crowding. One of those skeptics said pointedly, "People pushing high-density themselves live in single-family homes and often drive very fancy cars, but want everyone else to live like my grandmother did." It was a variant on gated Manhattan: an elite might enjoy large-lot living, but everyone else would be packed like sardines. Other New Urbanists spoke of town centers, which emphasized the social nature of these communities. These were places, the advocates said, where people were encouraged to take their time, where they came together to be together, and where landscapes were distinct enough that people felt that they were in a place, not a zip code.

Like India ink, New Urbanism could be almost infinitely diluted. Forest City Enterprises was building Stapleton, a 3,000-acre, 12,000-home development on the site of Denver's old airport. Stapleton had a town center with boutiques but no bus service to downtown Denver, and residents needed a car to shop at the Walmart or Home Depot at Quebec Square, Stapleton's shopping center. Some jobs had been created at Stapleton Business Center South, where United Airlines did staff training, but one planner said, "They make out that it's this really original super place but frankly I don't think it's anything special."

Even undiluted, New Urbanism had many critics, including the many architects who despised the pseudo-historical trappings of most New Urbanist designs. The director of the Southern California Institute of Architecture said, "It is the most pessimistic and unimaginative form of architecture because it does not allow for the possibility that something new could be better than what went before. These people do not believe in the natural evolution of cities." The dean of architecture at Tulane, who in the debate about rebuilding post-Katrina New Orleans was surrounded by New Urbanists, said, "New Urbanism's biggest flaw is its belief that simulation can be as good as the real thing. You cannot create authentic neighborhoods by trying to recreate the past." Other critics were even sharper: the New Urbanists were an "agricultural cult" with "revivalist fervor" and a yearning "for the good old days of the Old South."

Andrés Duany gave as good as he got. "The architecture of the past 20 years has been idiotic," he said. Architects "had almost completely lost their traditions." A sympathetic Renzo Piano suggested that Americans wanted "something European, a more subtle, more humanistic approach. They want to rethink the relationship between public and private space, between the building and the street. We are masters of that [in Europe]. At least we are not too bad. Sometimes we forget."

New Urbanist principles could be applied downtown too, and by 2014 almost eighty rental-apartment high-rises were under construction in various American cities. Some were in Austin; others in Minneapolis. Boston's rundown Four Corners, rebranded as Downtown Country, began attracting investment with a Ritz-Carlton in 2001. It was followed by Millennium Place, along with a Roche Bros. supermarket opening in 2015 in the semi-fabled space of Filene's Basement.

Akridge, a developer in Washington DC, bought the air rights over fifteen acres of the rail yard leading into Washington's Union Station. The tracks would be forever dark after Akridge spent a billion dollars covering them with the offices, apartments, and shops it was calling Burnham Place at Union Station. Two blocks to the west, Property Group planned Return to L'Enfant, another billion-dollar mixed-use project. This one would be built on a platform over Interstate 395 as it ran in a shallow trench south of Massachusetts Avenue. Even the names of these places—Burnham, L'Enfant—evoked the psychologically comforting past.

Washington's convention center, though built only in 1983, was to be torn down and replaced by CityCenterDC, a six-building, mixed-use project funded mostly with $620 million from the ubiquitous Qatar Investment Authority. A few miles downstream on the Potomac, National Harbor had several hotels, along with office buildings, apartment buildings, restaurants—and 4,500 parking spots. The developer, Milt Peterson, was an enthusiast. "Real estate," he said, "is the greatest thing in the world because you're building something that's going to stay." Perhaps he kept an eye on Konterra, a 2,200-acre site straddling I-95 between Washington and Baltimore. There was no Potomac there, but the 500-acre Town Center East was going to have 4,500 residential units and 5.9 million square feet of commercial space. The head of the local planning board said that his county was known "as a suburban bedroom community, but we need more urban dense living."

The production builders, looking up from their suburban haunts, began applying the mixed-use-and-walkable formula downtown. A KB executive said simply, "As land becomes rarer, you have to look for new areas where you can drive growth." In Emeryville, on San Francisco Bay, Pulte replaced a tank farm with $600,000 condos. Lennar, targeting very crowded, very expensive San Francisco, set out to develop 10,000 homes on a 770-acre tract at the old naval shipyard at Hunter's Point, in the southeastern corner of the city. In 2006 Lennar also won a contract, in partnership with a San Francisco firm, to develop 7,000 homes and four high-rises on Treasure Island, a former navy base built on fill in the middle of San Francisco Bay. Work was slow in starting, though in 2012 the China Development Bank offered $1.7 billion to get things moving. In exchange, it wanted jobs for Chinese contractors.

The City Living division of Toll Brothers began investing in Queens, Brooklyn, and Hoboken. The boss said simply, "We are following our people." He was talking about the suburbanites who missed "the sophistication and joy of culture and music that comes with city dwelling— and doesn't come with sitting in the big home in the burbs watching the day go by while puttering, painting, reading, writing, making flies for fishing, customizing your own golf clubs, stringing your own tennis racket, tending your tropical fish." Still, Toll's boss was cautious. "We are not going first, I will tell you that," he said. "It also has to be a great land price. We are not going into this on a 'let's try it' basis. High-rise development is much more dangerous, much riskier than suburban development because you've got to build the whole damn thing." Another builder echoed Toll: "We don't lead parades, we follow them."

At the southeast corner of Victor Gruen's pioneering Southdale Center, near Minneapolis, Simon Properties built a ten-storey apartment block with studio apartment rents starting at almost $1,400 a month; the marketing tagline was "Luxury living with walk-ability." Similar projects were planned for Dallas, Houston, and Atlanta—and not just by Simon but by General Growth Properties and Macerich as well.

Mixed-use appeared along light-rail lines too. The Federal Transit Administration counted a hundred of these so-called transit villages. Dallas had Mockingbird Station, where a phone-company warehouse was turned into shops and apartments at a major junction on the network. The developer said the station would become "one of the most desirable places to live in Dallas." Two stops north was Park Lane Station, attached to the huge Park Lane mixed-use complex.

Out on the West Coast, Los Angeles was encouraging transit villages on the interurban rail system it was building fifty years after the old one had been torn up. One village was near the North Hollywood station; another was at the Del Mar stop in Pasadena. A third was planned for Universal City in the San Fernando Valley and would have 2,900 new homes, plus shops and offices. The city earned about $750,000 annually from leases on its villages, but the mayor's enthusiasm for them went far beyond the money. He called the Universal City village "a transformative project, a city-making project . . . the epicenter of smart growth in the 21st century." The developer, Jim Thomas, who already owned the Arco Plaza downtown, which he had renovated into the City National Plaza, was more matter-of-fact. He said that LA County was growing by 100,000 people annually. They had to live somewhere.

The suburbs might provide some relief from central-city compression, and New Urbanism might provide a bit of refuge from cities built for cars, but people with deep pockets wanted more. Fresh from CNN, Catherine Crier put her 622-acre Wyoming hideaway on the market in 2007. It came with a new house—a "cabin" in the realtor's brochure—built of wood from old Utah farm buildings. Crier said of the builders, "They rusted every hinge, every nail, all of it to make the cabin look as if it had been there for quite some time."

The median house price in Aspen, the most expensive town in the country, was almost $5 million in 2010. It might have been higher, but four years earlier Pitkin County—Aspen's county—had prohibited construction of new houses over 15,000 square feet. Blame Prince Bandar bin Sultan of Saudi Arabia. He had come to town in the 1990s and on a ninety-acre parcel built Hala Ranch, a 55,000-square-foot mansion irreverently called the Garage Mahal. Among its selling points was a six-bedroom children's wing, but if that weren't impressive enough, there were always the building's 243 phone lines. So why the size cap? A county commissioner said, "They've got a masseuse, a caterer, a landscape guy, a hot-tub guy, the lawn people, the plumbers and electricians, the maids and a caretaker." They all used the county's roads and services. It wasn't the first law of its kind. Teton County, Wyoming, had imposed a 10,000-foot cap in 1994. Hardly room for a decent wine cellar.

Hala Ranch went on the market in 2006 for $135 million. No luck. It was pulled in 2007 and sold five years later to a hedge-fund manager for a knockdown $49 million, with an additional forty-acre parcel thrown in. A similar price cut faced Tranquility, with 38,000 square feet on 210 acres in sight of Lake Tahoe's Zephyr Cove. The property belonged to the former CEO of Tommy Hilfiger and was on the market for $100 million. After five years the price was cut to $75 million. In its seventh year on the market, the house sold for $48 million.

Watching from the Caribbean was Tim Blixseth, the developer of the Yellowstone Club, a members-only ski resort that offered 300 homeowners private powder on slopes reportedly guarded by former Secret Service agents. Blixseth set out to build the fanciest house of them all, the Pinnacle, budgeted at $165 million. Then he tried expanding internationally. Bad move. Blixseth lost the club, which filed for bankruptcy. The Pinnacle never got built, and in 2011 the 160 acres on which it was to have been built sold for $10 million, without club membership.

The biggest private landowners in the country had traditionally been ranchers or loggers. Then Ted Turner came along. His 2 million acres were only a bit shy of the 2.2 million of Yellowstone. Turner as top dog was followed by privately owned logging outfits—Red Emmerson's Sierra Pacific Industries and Canada's Irving family, which owned a lot of Maine—but they were followed by the estate of Henry Singleton, the founder of Teledyne Technologies, who put together about a million acres of New Mexican ranch land. Then John Malone arrived in 2010 and bought the 330,000-acre Bell Ranch, north of Conchas Lake in New Mexico. He followed that with other purchases, including almost a million acres in eastern Maine from GMO Renewable Resources. Suddenly Malone was at the top of the list.

A hedge-fund manager in 2007 paid $175 million for the 170,000-acre Forbes Trinchera Ranch, near Fort Garland, Colorado. A land developer who had married a Walmart heiress bought the Broken O Ranch, 123,000 acres west of Great Falls, Montana. The N Bar Ranch, established in 1885 and comprising over 50,000 acres of deeded land near Billings, came on the market in 2010 for $45 million. The Lazy K Bar Ranch, with 8,500 acres on the east slope of the Crazy Mountains, was only $9 million. The huge Waggoner Ranch, with over a half-million contiguous acres about 50 miles west of Wichita Falls, came on the market in 2014 for $725 million.

A small ranch in the right location could be worth a great deal of money. The 1,750-acre Jackson Land & Cattle Ranch came on the market in 2011 for $175 million. The 1,800-acre Walton Ranch, also at Jackson and with miles of Snake River frontage, was priced at $100 million. In 2014 the price was cut to just under $50 million, or about $25,000 an acre. At the other end of the dollar-per-acre scale, the 740,000 acres of the Blue Diamond Ranch, near Ely, Nevada, came on the market in 2012 for a bargain-basement $29.6 million, or about $40 an acre. It offered room to roam the desert on an almost inconceivable scale, along with the right to kick everyone else out.

For decades, visitors had enjoyed dude ranches, which customarily lacked TVs and phones. One of those visitors said, "It sounds very limiting, but it's very freeing. The only thing you can do is hang out." Now, however, there were more profitable things to do with the land. The owners of Colorado's 8,000-acre C Lazy U Ranch, in the habit of offering room and board for about $600 a night, began selling thirty-five-acre lots for between $1 million and $1.5 million each.

A married couple paid $168,000 in 1968 for the 150-acre Skyline Ranch, near Telluride, Colorado. Fast-forward to Meg Whitman, fresh from eBay. She offered $20 million for the place. The wife said, "We would go to bed at night totally exhausted saying, 'What are we doing this for? We're sitting on a gold mine.'" A similar shutdown occurred at Montana's Boulder River Ranch, a dude ranch bought and taken private by Tom Brokaw, Michael Keaton, and Robert Rubin. A few dude ranches soldiered on, such as the Triple Creek Ranch near Darby, Montana. Room and board ran about $1,000 a day.

The New West Drifts Downwind

In 1979 Ted Turner bought St. Phillip's Island, just north of Hilton Head, South Carolina. Three-quarters of the 4,700-acre island was marsh, but that didn't seem to matter very much because when Turner put the island on the market in 2014 the price was $24 million. There were lots of other places by then to park money on the coasts of the lowland south. St. Joe, an old timber company based near Panama City, Florida, had been selling what it called "New Ruralism." (No surprise: Seaside was next door.) Four-acre lots at St. Joe's RiverCamps averaged $340,000. A little steep? A company official said, "We honestly asked ourselves, 'Will people live in this environment? We've got critters, we've got heat.'" The company chairman said, "People are trying to get back to a time they remember." Planning sessions revealed that buyers wanted "wind in the trees," "stars, no lights," and "slamming, squeaking screen doors."

As Florida real-estate sank into the valuation swamp, St. Joe began focusing on selling land close to the Northwest Florida Beaches International Airport, which had been built on company land near Panama City so visitors wouldn't have to drive from Tallahassee. The shift didn't save the company from a takeover in 2011 by Fairholme Fund, which announced a new strategy centered on selling land to defense contractors.

For a while at least, St. Joe had company in the form of Syd Kitson, a retired pro-football player whose organization paid $500 million for the 91,000-acre Babcock Ranch outside Fort Myers. Kitson set out to build 19,500 solar-powered homes on 17,000 acres. The rest of the land would go into a nature reserve. Kitson succeeded in selling that land to the county and state for $351 million. He said, "How many people get to build a new city? This is how I'm going to change the world." Then nothing. A realtor said, "I don't see Babcock Ranch happening for a long, long time."

Nantucket knew no such pain. The Vanderbilts, Mellons, and DuPonts had been here for generations, but now they were jostled by newcomers. The Great Harbor Yacht Club charged an entry fee of $300,000, raised a few years later to $500,000. Working stiffs couldn't afford to live there, but they didn't have to. Every weekday, 400 blue collars—carpenters, gardeners, plumbers—flew in and out.

The nearby Nantucket Housing Office proposed a McMansion tax of eight dollars a square foot on homes over 3,000 square feet. The money would be used to build housing for the poor, defined as households making less than $120,000 a year. A similar program already existed in San Miguel County, home of Telluride, Colorado. Over a thousand homes in that town could only be sold to county residents with a job in the county, and the deed restrictions allowed the houses to appreciate only 3 percent annually. It sounded harsh, but a three-bedroom house in Telluride cost $2 million, which was why half the people who worked in town commuted an hour or two from places like Montrose or Durango.

THE BATTLE FOR THE COASTS

A half-acre waterfront parcel on Emerald Bay, a private bit of Laguna Beach, sold in 1932 for $10,000. With a house assumed to be a tear-down, it went on the market in 2013 for $38 million.

Ordinary people fought to hang on. A member of the California Coastal Commission said, "The public owns this beach. The public has a right to get to this beach." Yet for twenty-two years David Geffen stonewalled rather than unlock the gate to an old public pathway along the side of his house in Malibu. Finally, he capitulated, with conditions. The public got access to the beach from the Pacific Coast Highway, but video cameras scanned the path, which was locked at night. A local mother was happy. She said, "I've lived here 12 years and have never been able to cross the street and go to the beach. We could see and smell it, but we couldn't touch it."

She was luckier than people in Maine and Massachusetts, where landowners could legally close the beach in front of their property. That's why two-thirds of the beaches on Martha's Vineyard were private. Of the 11,684 miles of shoreline on Chesapeake Bay, only a bit over 200 were open to the public, and of the hundred or so beaches in Anne Arundel County—county seat, Annapolis—not one was public. One unhappy resident called the bay "the world's biggest gated community." Oddly, the Open Beaches Act allowed beachcombers in Texas to walk inland as far as the vegetation line. It was a miracle in a state where private property was in the trinity with God and guns.

Next door to Malibu, voters in Ventura County insisted on their right to approve every proposal to build on land designated as open space. The policy had been enacted by voters in 1998, even though opponents had outspent supporters thirty to one. Would the ordinance hold? A Pasadena developer was dubious. "We are in denial," he said, "about the amount of growth that is coming. There is going to be a tremendous struggle to change those boundaries."

One alternative for crowded coastal cities was to go up. Oxnard already had high-rises, and more were in the pipeline. A forty-six-story resort hotel with condos was proposed for adjoining Port Hueneme. It would be the highest building between Los Angeles and San Francisco. An Oxnard resident said, "I don't believe we should be like New York, with people living in 30- or 40-story towers." The developer of Pacific Pointe responded, "High-rise development is the ultimate expression of smart growth, particularly in an environment where people are concerned about preserving hillsides and agricultural resources. It leads you to the inescapable conclusion that if you can't go out, you've got to go up." He may have been right, but in 2007 the project was rejected by the city council.

The director of the California Coastal Commission lamented, "The dot-com boom really changed everything. . . . People with wealth buy 50 or 100 acres just to put a starter castle on it; technology allows them to live remotely and commute electronically." Someone would pay $3 million for a 150-acre tract with an agricultural value of $200,000. Then they would plunk a huge house on the skyline. After one long battle in Mendocino County, the commission gave up and allowed construction to proceed, provided the owners let the commission keep the $90,000 it had already received as fees.

The Coastal Commission wanted at least to impose what it called affirmative farmland easements. A would-be homebuilder would then have to arrange to have the land farmed in perpetuity, if feasible. Such easements were common in Pennsylvania and Massachusetts, where tracts were leased to a nearby farmer while the new landowner enjoyed the view.

The Hearst Corporation agreed to sell to the state 1,400 acres that provided access to 13 miles of Big Sur coast. The price was $95 million, or about $60,000 an acre. The state also got a conservation easement over the 120-square-mile Hearst Ranch. The ranch's owners retained the right to build twenty-seven secluded canyon homes and a hundred-room hotel, as well as rights to 5 miles of coast.

Farther south, the Cojo and Jalama Ranches, about 60 miles north of Santa Barbara, had a total of 25,000 acres and 9 miles of coastline. Fred Bixby had bought the land between 1912 and 1939. His descendants had not been especially eager to sell, but a grandson explained that "the financial decision finally took over." The buyer, Coastal Resources, paid about $155 million but said that it had no immediate development plans. The ranches had already been divided into fifty-seven parcels that could be sold separately.

There was similar pressure on the East Coast. In 1983 Dade County created an urban development boundary. Land inside the line was developable and worth $800,000 an acre; land outside wasn't—and was worth $60,000.

Fifty miles to the north, near Boca Raton, a developer approached the town of Briny Breezes, which consisted of a single trailer park. The developer proposed to buy the whole thing—43 acres with 488 mobile homes—for $510 million. Many of the residents were thrilled. One said, "It's an overly fair price. I know how hard it is to accumulate a million dollars. When you can get it, take it." Others disagreed. One said, "I would still rather spend the rest of my days here. The money is good, but is it enough to buy another place this close to the beach? Not these days." The developer withdrew his offer when complications arose with neighboring communities.

Another deal fell apart at Riviera Beach, 20 miles farther north. Across an inlet from Palm Beach, which had a median household income of $95,000, Riviera had a median household income of $32,000. The mayor and some other elected leaders decided to condemn the homes of 6,000 of the town's residents and let Viking Inlet Harbor Properties, a condo company from Australia, take over. A house painter said, "What they mean is that the view I have is too good for me, and should go to some millionaire." A state representative said, "This is a reverse Robin Hood." The mayor and the town-council members who supported him were voted out, and the project went away.

John McLaren, who superintended Golden Gate Park for over fifty years—he lived to ninety-seven and never quite retired—was determined to keep his park a shrine to nature, and except for the park's boundaries there was hardly a straight line to be seen in the place. McLaren was phobic about statues, too. He could not prevent their installation but would smother them, once installed, in rhododendrons so that they remained almost hidden until his death in 1943. Ironically, a statue of McLaren was then placed in a lawn as meticulously groomed as a golf green and with such perfect corners that they had to have been measured with a protractor.

Fast-forward to 2009, when Manhattan opened a park atop an abandoned elevated railroad track. Instead of knocking down the so-called High Line, the city was inspired by the Promenade plantée in Paris and converted the track into a park thirty feet above the street.

There was an economic justification for creating the park, because within a few years an investment of $153 million for the first two sections of the line generated $2 billion in economic benefits, but the new High Line was not created by the hunger for money. The head of the city planning commission said, "You will be able to walk 22 blocks in the city of New York without ever coming in contact with a vehicle." (She didn't mean it quite the way it sounded.) Her words echoed the actions of Frederick Law Olmsted. In 1811 New York City's commissioners had adopted a plan for Manhattan with an unremitting grid of twelve north-south avenues and 155 east-west streets. Olmsted's plan for Central Park called for the streets crossing the park to be sunk in trenches so visitors couldn't see them.

The High Line had nearly five million visitors in 2013. Eager to catch the wave, groups in Philadelphia started planning a park on the old Reading Viaduct. Groups in Chicago planned a Bloomingdale Trail, and groups in St. Louis dreamed of the Iron Horse Trestle. Meanwhile, the old El Toro Marine Corps Air Station in California had closed in 1999. In 2005 Lennar bought the 3,700-acre site from the navy for

$650 million. The company set out to build 3,400 homes, their value increased by the creation of a 1,300-acre park. To give this Orange County Great Park some topographic relief on its naturally flat but elevated site, planners called for a seventy-foot-deep artificial canyon. An hour to the north, Los Angeles contemplated the restoration of parts of the Los Angeles River. New York City meanwhile pushed ahead with its Fresh Kills Park, three times the size of Central Park and reclaimed from a Staten Island landfill.

Nature on a Grander Scale

Edgar Wayburn was president of the Sierra Club in the 1960s. The club had had more charismatic leaders, but as one staff member said, Wayburn "doubled the size of the [national] park system, he doubled the size of the wild and scenic rivers system, he doubled the size of the wilderness system.... It's mind-boggling." A historian called Wayburn's accomplishments "the greatest act of wilderness creation that we'll ever see on this planet." (High praise but depressing thought.) In a memoir called *Your Land and Mine*, Wayburn wrote, "In destroying wildness, we deny ourselves the full extent of what it means to be alive."

Between 1982 and 1994 Congress added 23 million acres to the federal wilderness system—say, 2 million a year. Then the ball went to the other team, and between 1994 and 2006 Congress added 3.5 million—say 300,000 per year. The National Park Service itself was about ready for the endangered species list. A brave superintendent at Death Valley said, "Any park superintendent who says the national parks aren't getting slighted isn't worth their ... salt." Occasionally, visitors would arrive at smaller parks and find them closed, with a sign apologizing, per Washington directive, for the "service-level adjustment." A few years earlier, a director of the Office of Management and Budget had called the Interior Department the world's biggest lawn-care service.

The San Onofre State Beach, with 2,100 acres in northern San Diego County, drew the attention of a toll-road agency whose engineers were aligning a new six-lane highway. The engineers weren't attracted by the ocean view; they wanted a route that saved them the cost of buying hundreds of homes and businesses. (That's how Yosemite National Park long ago lost the Hetch Hetchy Valley, a reservoir site that came free of charge.) California's Chamber of Commerce wrote, "We understand that parks serve a recreational purpose, but they should not preclude other uses, such as gas lines and highways, where appropriate." The director of the state's Department of Parks and Recreation shot back, "It's beginning to look like the inalienable right to enjoy natural resources isn't so inalienable."

In 2008 the California Coastal Commission said no to the road. The director of the State Parks Foundation responded, "Millions of people who use the coast are issuing a big sigh of relief." The road agency appealed to Washington on the ground that the highway was a matter of national security, but the appeal was denied. That was the end of the matter for the moment, but every acre kept as park today could be lost tomorrow.

The Hualapai tribe meanwhile welcomed visitors to the Grand Canyon Skywalk, a ninety-ton slab of glass cantilevered seventy feet over Eagle Point. The fee to walk this plank for a good scare was twenty-five dollars, plus fifty dollars for access to the reservation. A Las Vegas tour operator had spent $30 million building the Skywalk, and his contract allowed him to manage it for thirty-five years.

A former superintendent of the Grand Canyon National Park said, "It's the equivalent of an upscale carnival ride. Why would they desecrate this place with this? I've never been able to resolve the apparent conflict between the tribe's oft-stated claim that there is no better caregiver and steward of the Grand Canyon than the tribe, and their approach to the land—which is based on heavy use and economics." A tribal official retorted that the national park is "Disneyland in itself." The tribal council chairman was a master of media sparring, and he dismissed opponents of the Skywalk as elitists "eating tofu and pilaf and sitting in Phoenix with their plasma-screen TVs. Our tribe started in these canyons. We've always been here, and we'll always be here."

In the month after the Skywalk opened in 2007, the number of visitors to the reservation quadrupled to 2,000 daily, but the controversy continued. An anthropologist defended the tribe. "Three hundred years of Indian-government relations," he said, "have been all about trying to make the Indians more like the white man. Now that they're doing that, we don't like it." By 2012 almost 2 million visitors had come by. Despite the money, a tribal member said of the Skywalk, "This should never have been done."

Far to the south, Douglas Tompkins, the cofounder of clothing company Esprit, and his wife, Kristine, a former chief executive of the outdoor clothing company Patagonia, brought the parks battle to South America. Tompkins had sold Esprit to his Hong Kong sourcer in 1989, and now he and his wife ran Conservacion Patagonica. They spent $150 million—more than half of it their own money—on 2 million acres. The land included 741,000 acres in the northern Argentinian wetlands called the Esteros del Iberá and 762,000 acres in the Pumalin Park, a private trust that cut Chile in two with a tract east of the island of Chiloé. The Chilean government in 2005 designated the place a national wildlife sanctuary.

Then Tompkins ran into the head of SalmonChile, who said, "We are not going to be intimidated by imperialist boasts or frivolities of the millionaire gringo. We are not going to accept a sub-nation in our own region with rules dictated by a fanatic." An Argentinian congresswoman said, "We don't want our natural resources to be in the hands of foreigners." She hinted that Tompkins could be working for the CIA.

Tompkins headed 900 miles south of Santiago to buy a 170,000-acre sheep ranch, the Estancia Valle Chacahuca. Clearing off the livestock and tearing down fences, he and his wife planned a huge Patagonian park straddling the border with Argentina. "People," Tompkins said, "are destroying the environment for their own ends and the world is coming apart at the seams." He pointed out that he was only trying to block up land so he could donate it as a park. He added, "The Argentine government should look very carefully not at what passport someone carries but at how they behave economically and ecologically." The congresswoman wasn't buying it. "We believe this is a new way of trying to dominate the South American countries," she said.

She had company. For a century International Paper ran a huge mill at Millinocket, a hundred miles north of Bangor, Maine. The mill had relied on the company's 2 million acres of timberland spread to the west and north, but now the mill had closed—the nation was using less office paper than it once had—and the founder of Burt's Bees proposed personally buying 70,000 of those acres and donating them for a national park close to Mount Katahdin, already a state park. Protesters began picketing with signs reading, "Keep Maine Free! No More Government Land."

THE LURE OF EUROPE

For centuries Americans had traveled to Europe almost as soon as they could afford it. It was a status marker, a sign that they were persons of taste, able to appreciate the finer things in life. Developers noticed, and one of them in the 1920s built St. Malo, a subdivision in Oceanside, California, with eighty-three homes built in a rigidly regulated Tudor style. Eighty years later another developer built Brook in Waterland. It sounded like a place for Cheshire cats, but European craftsmen were brought to upstate New York to build a set of twenty homes that copied seventeenth-century Dutch architecture right down to holding the houses together with mortise-and-tenon joints. Sixty miles to the east, the builder of Avery Lane Settlement, in Simsbury, Connecticut, justified his detailed work by saying, "McMansions are bigger with higher ceilings but they're devoid of all the detail which gives a house its soul."

Many Americans could do more than visit Europe. An estate-agent in Shinfield, 30 miles west of London, spoke to them, as well as to locals, in an ad placed in a newspaper. It ran like this: "Stunning, approx. 400 year old 4 bedroom listed barn. Steeped in history. Lots of character combined with modern living standards. A safe, peaceful must see property set in a shared 3 acre rural setting yet close to all amenities." There was no great surprise when the Riba Stirling Prize, the UK's top award for architecture, went in 2013 not to a daring new structure but to a holiday home created in the burned-out shell of Astley Castle, a twelfth-century manor house.

Country Life ran a contest to find Britain's oldest inhabited house. The winner was Saltford Manor, built in 1148 near Bath. In 1997 it was advertised as in need of restoration. The buyer, who paid £300,000, became the house's twenty-seventh owner. He said, "Where others saw holes in the roof, rotting plaster, and collapsed floors, I saw open blue skies, rough creamy stone and honeyed oak beams." In 2008, after a lot of work, the house was offered at £2.5 million. It sold two years later for £1.2 million.

Thirty miles off the southwest tip of England, most of the rocks called the Scilly Isles belonged to the Prince of Wales, but bits of freehold land were available. A Victorian cottage of hewn granite was available on St. Mary's, the largest of the islands, for about a million dollars. For that you got three small bedrooms, one bath, and a little courtyard. Back on the mainland at Penzance, a cottage with a good sea view was £1 million. Closer to London, there was Sandbanks, where waterfront homes, packed in a tight line, went for $11 million or more.

Buyers who wanted castles and room to roam headed to Scotland, where £3 million bought the Carskley Estate with 7,350 acres on the Mull of Kintyre. The Blairquhan Estate had 16 bedrooms and 670 acres and was available for about £5 million. Buyers who wanted a working farm could go 25 miles east of Edinburgh to Dunbar, East Lothian. There, for £25 million, they got not only a house but 2,000 acres of cultivated land. Buyers who just wanted a house with character could emulate the Syrian-Saudi businessman who came to Tusmore, in Oxfordshire, and built his own Palladian mansion with stone imported from France. They could aim higher, as a Russian did in 2011 when paying £140 million for Park Place, a freshly renovated mansion of 30,000 square feet on 200 acres along the Thames at Henley.

In Saint Tropez, a nice fisherman's cottage with a view of the Mediterranean sold in 2007 for between €4 and €5 million. At Cap Ferrat, secluded on France's Atlantic coast, a one-room oyster shack sold for €500,000. Buyers who wanted a bit of established Bordeaux vineyard had to spend $250,000 an acre, more than twice as much as established vineyards in the Napa Valley. Visitors who craved certified style could choose Lacoste, a Provence village an hour's drive from Marseilles. Pierre Cardin had bought and restored forty properties there, about one for every permanent resident. Homes were available for €1 million and up.

Americans were especially fond of Saint-Rémy-de-Provence, Vincent van Gogh's last home. Brits liked the Dordogne Valley. The Chinese bought Bordeaux. Buyers for whom modern plumbing was at the top of the must-have list gravitated toward Domaine Haut-Gardegan. The name sounded like a good bottle of wine, and Saint Emilion was nearby. A Canadian company, Intrawest, was building from scratch a French village with 400 apartments and prices starting at about $400,000.

Mallorca sounded nice, 75 miles off the coast in the Mediterranean, but 180,000 flights arrived annually. Each year they brought 8 million visitors to an island that measured less than 40 miles by 40 miles. That's why property sales early in 2008 averaged over €450,000. The top end had no top end. In 2008 a place called Cielo de Bonaire was on the market for €50 million. Chickenfeed! A castle on a peninsula just off the town of Pollença went on sale for €125 million. Juan Carlos I summered nearby.

Prices were lower on Menorca—a quieter island, with daily flights only in spring and summer. Even so, a simple two-bedroom apartment went for €175,000. Even the Canary Islands, 800 miles southwest of Spain, were swamped with visitors and were pricey, especially Tenerife and Gran Canaria.

Spain's small interior towns were another possibility. They had begun dying in the 1950s but were coming back to life. An architect explained, "People are looking for tranquillity and to feel what their grandfathers felt." At the market peak in 2007, more homes were being built for Britishers in Spain than in Britain. Two years later, Spain was a different country. A million new homes sat vacant, unsold despite price reductions of half or more. Whole neighborhoods sat empty in towns like Seseña, Cuenca, and Yebes, all on the southern or eastern fringe of Madrid. By 2010 Spain had 100,000 repossessed units, with more on the way.

The top end didn't suffer so badly. Marbella, halfway between Gibraltar and Malaga, had zoomed from 900 residents in 1940 to over 100,000 sixty years later. Credit went to Prince Alfonso zu Hohenlohe, who took a liking to the place in 1947, set up the Marbella Club, and ran the Costa del Sol Promoters' Co-operative. By 2011 construction at Marbella had slowed drastically, not only because of Spain's more general problems but because it turned out that 18,000 homes had been built illegally. Penalties had to be paid, either by the developer or, in his absence, the owner. Undaunted, the owner of La Casa Loriana put his house on the market for €50 million.

Italy offered the Abruzzo, two hours east of Rome and centered on L'Aquila. The town was leveled by an earthquake in 2009, and reconstruction was painfully slow, but nearby villages offered houses for as little as €15,000. As a realtor said, "In Tuscany it would cost €150,000—if you could find one." Still farther south, Puglia had *masseria*, stone farmhouses that came with a couple of acres for a bit over a million dollars. For the whimsical buyer, there were *trulli*, with conical stone roofs on cylindrical stone houses. Just to the west of Puglia, Basilicata offered homes in the coastal town of Maratea. They cost half as much as homes 100 miles north, on the Amalfi Coast just south of Naples.

Impruneto—a ten-bedroom castle on fifteen acres 7 miles from Florence—came on the market for €20 million. A bit farther away, near Lake Trasimeno, Perugia's thirteenth-century Castello Cortona came complete with prison, watchtowers, and gun ports for €14.5 million. Not good enough? Just off the Almafi Coast near Positano, three small islands called Li Galli came on the market in 2011 for €195 million. In comparison, Capuccini Island, off the coast of Sardinia, was cheap at €35 million. Not remote enough? There was always Pantelleria, an island closer to Tunisia than to Sicily. It offered the distinctive stone houses called *dammusi*. With a little effort, you could even have Giorgio as a neighbor. His last name was Armani.

TUI Travel, a British company, offered Castelfalfi, a 2,700-acre property with villas and apartments, some new, some renovated, between Pisa and Florence. There was a golf course on the site, and though prices for villas started at £1 million, fractional ownerships were available for buyers wanting only a few weeks a year. Twenty miles away, Timbers Resorts of Colorado invested $325 million in developing a 4,400-acre-property called Casole, with a combination of new and restored units available in fractional as well as whole ownerships.

Italy also had more than forty Cittaslows on offer. The first to be designated was Greve, which became a designated "slow town" in 1999. Bra, Positano, and Orvieto followed. Now half a dozen European countries had national networks of Cittaslows. Towns hoping to join couldn't have more than 50,000 people. They had to discourage cars, typically by installing gates opened by transponders given only to owners and service vehicles. Residents were supposed to eat only local foods. After all, the Cittaslow movement arose from the Slow Food movement. The townspeople were supposed to rely as much as possible on sustainable forms of energy.

Adventurous buyers might try the old communist East, perhaps at Veliko Tarnovo, a Bulgarian town on the north slopes of the Stara Planina. Created by Czar Peter II as Bulgaria's capital, it was protected during the communist era and its houses were now attracting foreigners. Buyers with steely nerves might also consider Cold River, Stalin's old dacha. It was in Abkhazia, the Russian-controlled part of Georgia, and it was up for sale—asking price, $10 million. It had a spectacular location but was too modest to be called palatial. Call it a hideaway for a buyer not easily spooked. Nobody had ever known when Uncle Joe was in residence.

If that was too macabre, buyers might consider Transylvania, where Prince Charles supported the Mihai Eminescu Trust, which was restoring old homes in twenty or more of the villages settled in the thirteenth century by Germans. England itself offered Lacock, a village of 400 residents spread over eighty-nine old houses owned since 1944 by the National Trust. The only trouble was the hordes of tourists and film crews, like those that came to make the Harry Potter movies. An alternative English Heritage selection was Holmfirth, an old mill town between Manchester and Leeds. It had been the set for *Last of the Summer Wine* and offered small cottages for only £125,000. Then there was Stamford, 30 miles east of Leicester. This was the site of Britain's first urban conservation area and a set in both *The Da Vinci Code* and *Young Victoria*.

Everywhere, celebrity connections helped maintain high prices. Elizabeth Taylor bought a Gstaad chalet in 1962, and Julie Andrews and Roger Moore followed. Then the restrictions arrived. A resident said, "We decided to stay small and beautiful. That means no big developments." Newcomers found prices starting at $1,400 a square foot and heading up to twice that and more, higher than already pricey Zurich and Geneva. Chalets had to be made primarily of wood, and they couldn't exceed four stories. Foreigners were even more tightly restricted, forbidden to build houses exceeding 200 square meters, or a bit over 20,000 square feet.

The celebrity effect hit Italy's Lake Como too. The southern end of the lake was only an hour's drive from Milan's airport. Ten miles up the lakeshore, at Laglio, George Clooney bought a villa in 2001. Richard Branson was nearby, at Lenno. A few miles away, at Cernobbio, an old house came on the market in 2010 for about $20 million. The Lakeside Villa, overlooking Bellagio itself, was for sale for €25 million. A cabdriver wasn't impressed. He said, "I have lived here all my life, nothing here changes, nothing." Just up the hill from Laglio and away from the waterfront, there were occupied houses without electricity.

The Sources of Nostalgia

William Blake had written of "satanic mills," and Philip Loutherbourg had painted the hellish *Coalbrookdale by Night*. Wandering around Europe in search of something less bleak, William Wordsworth came upon moribund Bruges and wrote a sonnet speaking of streets as "consecrated ground, The city one vast temple . . . /A deeper peace than that in deserts found." George Rodenbach, keeper of the Victoria and Albert Museum's National Art Library, persuaded the residents of Bruges to preserve the town. A hundred years later, the 40,000 residents of Old Bruges had 2 million visitors annually.

Every European country had its own Bruges. Some were world famous, like Toledo; others less so, like the Czech Republic's Český Krumlov. An unhappy Friedrich Nietzsche for a time fantasized about retreating to yet another relic. "I am once again seriously making plans," he wrote in 1874, "in order to make myself completely independent and withdraw from all official connections to the state. . . . For now, I have selected Rothenburg ob der Tauber as my private castle and heritage. . . . Everything there still continues in an entirely old German manner; and I hate the characterless mixed cities that are no longer whole."

Three-quarters of Rothenburg was destroyed either by Allied bombing in World War II or postwar demolition. The town was then rebuilt with the guidance of the Bavarian Office for Historical Preservation. Plaster was stripped from the town's surviving half-timbered buildings; the Shell and Esso gas stations were evicted. Brand new but old-looking buildings filled the empty spaces, and in 1956 over 100,000 people came and stayed overnight. Many more made day trips.

The novelist Erich Maria Remarque visited in the early 1960s and wrote, "I came to Rothenburg. And here was suddenly peace. The town stood there as always with its nooks and walls and alleys and dreams, undisturbed by all the horrors, like a bastion of hope, of solace, and a second home for the distraught soul." Walter Hass knew the town better: "When bars appear that no Rothenburger wishes to go into; stores in which no locals shop, when Rothenburgers put out decorations, not to celebrate a festival, but in order to feign customs that were never customs, then the preservation of the town is not to be expected." Still the tourists came, drawn by the lure of a world not made for money.

ESCAPING TO THE WIDER WORLD

Emily Eden visited Lahore in 1838, saw Jahangir's tomb, and wrote that it, "like all fine buildings in the country is going fast to decay." No wonder. Ranjit Singh, the Lion of the Punjab, was on the prowl for building materials and had helped himself. He did the same thing with the nearby tomb of Nur Jahan, Jahangir's principal wife. A visitor in 1846 said that Nur Jahan's tomb had been reduced to "a few crumbling arches." The British partially rebuilt the tomb, stopped the further cannibalization of Jahangir's, and created an archaeological survey that went on to protect hundreds of other buildings that otherwise would have disintegrated.

The Turks in 1908 added a European clock tower at Jerusalem's Jaffa Gate. It lasted until 1922, when the British tore it down as an excrescence. Ronald Storrs as governor had already prohibited builders from using modern materials in the Old City, and he insisted on a green belt surrounding the city's walls. He cleaned up those walls, which had become a dump, and opened a path for visitors to walk most of the circumference. He asked Charles Ashby, an important contributor to the Arts and Crafts movement, to bring dead or dying crafts back to Jerusalem. One vestige of Ashby's work was to survive in the Old City's blue-on-white-tile street signs, carefully trilingual. The glass blowers of Hebron were another lingering part of his legacy.

The British had Continental company. The restoration of historic Cairo began with the Comité de Conservation des Monuments de l'Art Arabe, established in 1881. A generation later, the Thai government ceded Angkor to the French, and Angkor's restoration was begun almost at once by the École Française d'Extrême-Orient.

The Dutch were at it too. Nobody knew what Borobudur was until 1901, when the Dutch scholar C. M. Pleyte realized that some of the panels on the first terrace illustrated the *Lalitavistara Sutra*, a Mahayana version of the life of the Buddha. A few years later, M. J. Krom, the director of the Netherlands Indies Archaeological Service, realized that the second and third terraces illustrated the *Gandavyuha Sutra*, which recounts the search for enlightenment of a young pilgrim, Sudhana.

A century later, the monuments that the colonial British, French, and Dutch had cared for were now on UNESCO's World Heritage List. The list had been created in the aftermath of the international effort to rescue the temples at Abu Simbel from the waters rising behind High Aswan. Now the list was a tourist beacon. Fifty thousand visitors had gone to Pingyao in 1997 to see a town, about 60 miles south of Taiyuan, that had escaped Mao's obliterating hand. Pingyao was put on the World Heritage List that year and in 2013 had 1.5 million visitors. Four-fifths of the walled town's residents had been evicted. Did they or the residents of neighboring towns care in the least about heritage?

Until 1970, after all, Tokyo had capped office buildings at a hundred feet, and until 1996 the city had had almost no tall buildings. Then, especially after 2005, high-rise after high-rise rose, especially along the Tokyo Bay waterfront, freshly vacated by shipbuilders. By 2012 the average price for a new apartment of 760 square feet in Tokyo was $515,000. In Roppongi Hills, there were two-bedroom flats renting for almost $16,000 a month.

Roppongi Hills had been Minoru Mori's baby. He explained, "Asia is different from the United States and Europe. We dream of more vertical cities. In fact, the only choice here is to go up and use the sky." Not content with building a dozen high-rises in Tokyo, in 2008 he completed China's tallest building, the Shanghai World Financial Center. It had ninety-one elevators. The Park Hyatt began on floor 87.

Across the Sea of Japan, the Korean steel company POSCO was working with Gale International, a Boston-based property developer, to build New Songdo City on 1,500 acres created on fill near Incheon Port, 30 miles west of Seoul. The budget was $25 billion—upped to $35 billion. The project included the Asia Trade Tower, a convention center, a golf course, a park, the usual Venetian canals, and an anticipated population of 65,000 people, joined daily by 235,000 commuters. By 2009 a hundred buildings were complete or under construction, and the first few thousand people had moved in.

New Songdo City had competition. In 2012 half of the South Korean government moved with much grumbling to Sejong City, a new town an hour from the capital by high-speed train and taxi. The plan was for Sejong City to have 500,000 residents by 2030.

Who had time for heritage preservation? On the other hand, how many New Yorkers had ever visited Ellis Island? People were busy. Still, Lee Myung-Bak, mayor of Seoul and later prime minister of

South Korea, ordered the demolition of a double-decker freeway and, at a cost of $385 million, the restoration of 3 miles of the Cheong-gye-cheon, the river the road had obliterated. Lee said, "Seoul underwent rapid development in just a few decades so you can't say that it developed out of a well-thought-out plan. That is the price we had to pay, and the environment suffered." The restored river wasn't as natural as it looked because water had to be pumped through 7 miles of pipe to the start of the channel, but an assistant mayor said that in this part of the ocean of concrete, "We've basically gone from being a car-oriented city to a human-oriented city."

Seoul's government meanwhile paid up to $30,000 to any resident who preserved or rebuilt a *hanok*, the traditional Korean house with wood-lattice windows set in walls of brick-faced earth and with interconnected rooms around a courtyard opening to the south, ideally with a mountain behind and a river in front. *Hanok* weren't for everyone—there was no parking in Bukchon, the neighborhood where most were located—but residents said they forgot they were close to Jongno, the city's infernally congested main street. One resident said, "It feels so peaceful and like we are close to nature because we have a garden and there are always birds flying around but actually we are in the middle of Seoul." An architect added, "I believe this area will become the Montmartre of Seoul."

Perhaps it was too little, too late. Seoul had only 800 *hanok*, and one of 900 square feet could cost $2 million. Like apartments in the most expensive neighborhoods of New York, London, and Hong Kong, *hanok* were owned now by part-time residents. A preservationist said, "Walk the streets at night, and there's not a single light in any of the houses. No kids. No little old ladies trudging up the hill carrying their cabbages."

Tokyo's Narita Airport needed a third runway but was even less likely than Heathrow to get it. Instead, Narita passengers occasionally noticed high metal walls screening parts of the taxiways. The walls had nothing to do with airport operations. Instead, they marked the boundaries of small farms whose owners refused to sell and were now marooned in a sea of asphalt and concrete, their homesteads accessible only by underpasses built for no other purpose.

At a cost of $350,000 per resident, Japan built the Kuronoseto Bridge to Nagashima Island, in the Kagoshima Prefecture of southern Kyushu. The bridge had cost the equivalent of $350,000 for each island resident, but an official explained, "I don't know that you can criticize these projects just by the logic of numbers." A school at Ichinosetakahashi, near Mount Fuji, had only one pupil and was run, with teacher and principal, at a cost of $175,000 annually. The principal said, "If we just pursued efficiency, the world would become a very dry place, with no sensitivity."

And China?

Armani in 2001 opened a 12,000-square-foot shop on the Shanghai Bund. Deferentially, he installed traditional red-lacquer doors, only to find that his customers hated them. They wanted (and got, pronto) doors that didn't look Chinese. Visitors going to a Shanghai party might look for a Chinese actress in a fitted *qipao*—that tight and sleeveless silk dress. Better luck at Cannes. The Chinese publisher of a fashion magazine explained, "Over here she wouldn't wear it: the Chinese won't wear ethnic costume to a party, they'll wear Dior." No American would use the word *ethnic* to describe blue jeans.

A shopping center at a major intersection in Taiyuan, capital of Shanxi, was wrapped in huge signs advertising Louis Vuitton, Salvatore Ferragamo, Ermenegildo Zegna, and Cartier. The names and taglines were all in English—and only in English. Not one of the larger-than-life-size models was Chinese. Along came Du Juan, perhaps the first Chinese fashion model to make it big internationally. Back home she was a flop. An agent said, "Her look is just plain to most Chinese people." What did they want? The editor of the Chinese edition of *Harper's Bazaar* said, "Chinese people tend to like models with Western-ish looks: wide eyes, high nose and slender figure."

L'Oréal, Estée Lauder, and Japan's Shiseido all pushed into China. They remained small fry alongside Procter & Gamble, which was already on site with Pantene, Cover Girl, and Max Factor. Chinese women had always wanted light skin—it wasn't only a Caucasian prejudice—but now they were trying to get it with Western brands. The East Asia market was so crucial to P&G that in 2012 the company moved the executives in charge of its global cosmetics unit from Cincinnati to a new headquarters in Singapore. Mary Kay had 350,000 Chinese women selling her products. A few made $25,000 a month and were ready for pink Cadillacs.

Bob Toll, the builder of expensive homes in the United States, was asked if his kind of home would do well in China. He replied, "Yes, it would. They [the Chinese] are 100 times more brand conscious than we are, to the point of silliness. The Chinese have to buy the brand." And so Cartier had four stores in New York City but nine in Hong Kong. So too Beijing had a subdivision called Orange County, with streets signed North Star Drive and California Bay—and with those names written first in English, then in Chinese. There was a Palm Beach and, for Francophiles, a Maison de Bourbon.

With a more comfortable life in view at last, the Chinese seemed determined to destroy whatever stood in the way of economic growth. A Chinese historian offered an additional explanation for his country's willingness to demolish old buildings. "There is a whole Western tradition of classical archaeology and visiting the Parthenon," he said. "But there is no such tradition in China."

Liang Sicheng had swum against the tide and written in the 1930s that, "The only objective of past repairs was to replace the old building with a glorious and sturdy new building; if this meant the demolition of the old building, it would be all the more praise-worthy as virtuous achievements of an high order." Mao was in this sense anything but revolutionary. He brushed aside Liang's plea to preserve more of old Beijing than the imperial palace or Forbidden City. Liang was then crushed by the Cultural Revolution. His house, close to the Forbidden City and after Mao's death a designated historic monument, was demolished by a wrecking crew that went to work with anything-but-accidental timing during the 2012 New Year's holiday, when nobody was likely to stop them.

Yet London had demolished its Euston Arch, and New York had polished off its Grand Central Station. Who were the British or the Americans to cast stones when China tried to catch up with them economically? Besides, the Chinese weren't always oblivious of the price they were paying. A vice minister for construction understood, as he said, that "senseless actions" had "devastated" old buildings. Developers, he said, were "totally unaware of the value of cultural heritage" and acted in a "blind pursuit of the large, new and exotic." The result, he said, was "like having 1,000 cities with the same appearance." A deputy director of the State Administration of Cultural Heritage compared what builders were doing to "tearing up a priceless painting and replacing it with a cheap print."

China now had more than thirty cultural sites on UNESCO's World Heritage List. That was twenty more than the United States and only a dozen fewer than Italy, the world leader. China had worked to take care not only of world-famous parts of Beijing, Xian, and Suzhou but also of Chengde, Pingyao, and Lijiang. True, many of these sites, like Pingyao, were overrun with tourists; some included pretend or brand new antiquities; others displaced local people with newcomers in search of a fortune. But historic preservation was never perfect. A photographer might make Tuscany's San Gemignano look medieval, but a visitor on the spot had to follow the traffic signs, park in peripheral lots, and join the crowds streaming past T-shirt and gelato stands.

Gulangyu, a small island close to Xiamen, had hitched its fortune to the tourist trade, even though the island's mansions were built for the Victorian English or in a European style for overseas Chinese. Shanghai's Holy Trinity Cathedral was restored, and the building nearby that once housed the Royal Asiatic Society was displaying its old name. An official said, "This is nothing to do with politics. This is about history and culture. This area is the root of the development of modern

Shanghai." It wasn't so different from the things said by American preservationists. They too fought a lonely battle.

The lakes at Beijing's Yuanmingyuan (Old Summer Palace) were now lined with plastic to save water. It sounded like a good idea, but the surrounding gardens depended on lake seepage. A biology professor protested. "In the last 10 to 20 years of economic reforms," he said, "pollution, environmental problems and the destruction of the ecosystem and cultural relics have been too widespread. *Yuanmingyuan* is the last straw. To save a little water, they have totally destroyed an ancient landscape." A colleague agreed: "They want to turn a heritage site into an amusement park." The government decided to study the situation, and eventually some of the linings were removed. By then Beijing's water shortages were so acute that the lakes were dry half the year.

A world made for money was not so easily escaped.

Postscript

In the months since these pages were written, the street corner near my house hasn't changed perceptibly: Walgreen's and CVS are still there, along with the bank and the dentist's office. Both Walgreen's and CVS have been in the news lately because of national problems or policies. At the counter, however, I'm only asked if I have a loyalty card. At Walgreen's I'm told, "Be well." The female clerks say it with convincing—and surprising—sincerity.

If I widen the field of vision, a great deal has changed. One of the two streets at the intersection is Main Street. It runs east-west, straight as a surveyor could make it. Within the stretch of 2 miles to the west, away from downtown, there used to be three conventional supermarkets. Two were Safeways and the third was an IGA. One of the Safeways died at least ten years ago, the likely victim of a newly built Walmart. The Safeway became a Hastings, which started out as a bookstore but became a place for people bored with turning pages. The other Safeway became a Homeland store and survived until this year, when both it and the IGA closed for good. The local newspaper published a sentimental account of the IGA, which was locally owned, but the paper offered no reasons for either store's closing. Both stores, however, were within 2 miles of Walmart, Target, and a newcomer called Crest. Not only that: in the last year or two, three new grocery stores have opened on Main Street. They include a Sprouts and a Natural Grocers, both catering to the modern consumer's quest for eternal youth and the equally pervasive suspicion that big food is bad food. The third is an Aldi, whose prices are so much lower than everyone else's that it's a wonder the store isn't sued for cruelty. Facing this posse, I think Homeland and IGA decided that the smart thing to do was to fold.

Aldi sits on a fragment of what until a few years ago was a Chevrolet dealership. The dealer moved to a bigger lot at a freeway intersection, but his timing was bad and the dealership has already changed hands. The old lot has been chopped into a half-dozen parcels. Some are still empty, but Aldi bought one. Arby's bought another, and Goodwill Industries bought a third. The trio form a none-too-impressive first glimpse of town for visitors getting off the freeway. On the other side of the street there used to be a Cadillac dealership, but it moved 5 miles up the freeway and has since been replaced by a Mitsubishi dealership, which is odd because I don't think I've ever seen a Mitsubishi car in town. They must be here, and I must just be oblivious.

The Arby's replaces an older Arby's a few blocks to the east. The franchisee is brave, I think, because a nearby Long John Silver's sits empty. A Wendy's is close by and hasn't had a makeover in decades, while farther west, on the other side of the freeway, there's a Burger King where customers eat in solitude. At the same time, there's always a line of cars waiting faithfully at the drive-through for Chick-fil-A. Is this the chain's moment in the sun or will the lines keep going forever? Main Street also has a very busy Panera. I remember when they added a drive-through, which became an instant hit. Down the street a bit there's a Starbucks with a lot of traffic. There's also a drive-in that advertises "Since 1954." Cars park under a metal canopy weathered over sixty years, and a nostalgic signboard advertises hot dogs for 20 cents and hamburgers for 25. The actual price of the hamburgers is now $2.50, an amazingly round figure in a world where everybody else's prices end in a 9.

We have a regional shopping center, too. It's on Main Street but on the far side of the freeway. General Growth Properties owns it, although, so far as I can tell, nobody in town knows or cares about this. Everyone knows, on the other hand, that the mall has a Sears and a JCPenney's. The problem is that nobody shops at either. I went to check yesterday. I understand that Monday afternoons are not prime time at malls, but both stores were almost deserted, and the few customers were old enough to remember what things cost in 1976 when the mall opened. Perhaps the inline stores were doing better, but judging from the parking lots, I doubt it.

A mile north of the shopping center we have a new commercial center. Target is here, along with perhaps forty new businesses, all in new buildings. More are on the way. There's a Kohl's, an Academy Sports, an Office Depot, and a Petco animal supply store. There's an astonishing array of fast-casual restaurants, too: Pei Wei to Zoe's, Chipotle to Cheddar's. You'd think that driving into this commercial precinct—because certainly nobody walks in—would dampen appetites, but apparently it doesn't: the parking lots here are much fuller than those at the mall. I conclude that people have abandoned the mall just as they abandoned the old downtown, with its two- and three-story brick buildings, in the 1970s. The city has spent a lot of money on new sidewalks and lighting for the old downtown. The plan is to create an art space, with galleries and boutiques and workshops. I don't know if it has paid off. People don't talk about these things.

Speaking of things people don't talk about, we have three good-sized factories. A Shaklee factory opened in 1979, and in geriatric circles became famous a few years later for making Flomax. The factory is now run by Astellas which, although you'd never know it from the name, is a Japanese firm. Nearby, Hitachi makes data-storage equipment and has a distribution center. On the other side of town there's a Johnson Controls plant that makes rooftop air conditioners, as it did back when the sign read York. Earlier still, the sign read Borg-Warner. When the plant opened in 1971 the sign read Westinghouse

Developers are still at work platting new lots and building new houses. Construction peaked in 2005 at a bit over seven hundred single-family homes. Building permits sagged to just over three hundred in 2009, but now we're back to well over four hundred. Most are on the fringe of town, of course, and the names of the subdivisions evoke the customary air of bucolic tranquility: Summit Lakes, Eagle Cliff, Montoro Ridge, Cobblestone Creek, Ashton Grove. We also have many new apartments. The number fluctuates a great deal but averages several hundred annually. You can choose from Cedar Lake, Cimarron Trails, Riverbend, and many others.

The town's population has risen from 68,000 in 1980 when I arrived, to about 120,000 in 2014. Perhaps that's good news, but traffic is so intense at rush hour (don't mock!) that I often find myself muttering about Dallas. I don't know how much gasoline we use, but lately I've been filling up at a new station with sixteen pumps spread among eight islands. I have to hunt to find one that's not being used.

This station is a 7-11, which means that the gasoline comes from heaven-knows-where. I saw a tanker-truck recently making a delivery and I should have asked the driver where he picked up his fuel. I didn't. It's easier to play the role of good consumer, which is to say, somebody who hasn't the least interest where the fuel in his tank was refined or whether the crude was domestic or came from a well halfway around the world.

It's the same story about six blocks east of the drugstore corner, where an important BNSF track crosses Main Street. It's a busy line, with about twenty freight trains passing through daily, headed either north toward the main line in Kansas or south toward Fort Worth, Houston, and Galveston. The grade crossing irritates many drivers. Not me: I who hate traffic lights will happily wait for a freight train.

The other day I saw a bunch of flat cars loaded with FedEx and UPS containers. They were headed south but I have no idea where they had been loaded, where they were going, or what they contained. I'm curious about such things, but I imagine that asking questions might arouse suspicion. The other day, in fact, I stopped, bent down, and took a look at an old siding whose rails were stamped 1903 and whose tie plates were embossed with the initials ATSF. They looked as though they had not moved since Teddy Roosevelt was in the White House. The main track, however, had heavier and shinier welded rail with inscrutable markings. I wondered if the rail came from the Arcelor-Mittal plant at Steelton, near Harrisburg, or whether, as could be the case, it had come from China. I didn't have long to reflect, because within a minute a policeman stopped and told me I could not park next to the track.

All of which helps explain why, as I go about my business here in town, I generally ignore what's around me. I try to keep an eye on the traffic; I listen to the radio; I notice signs. That's about it. Call it learning how to not see. I'm good at it. There's almost the sense that I'm obliged to know about sports and celebrities and possibly politics but I'm not supposed to care about why the world around me looks the way it does.

Sometimes I slip up. A little mental switch gets tripped and I wonder what a world *not* made for money would look like. A second later I'm remembering a farmhouse I know on Saltspring Island, one of British Columbia's Gulf Islands. It's a two-story Victorian that nobody would pay much attention to in San Francisco but which is spectacular because on this island it stands alone in a clearing in the dark forest. There are lots of flowers around it (yes, of course it's summer) and the clearing has a few sheep. Usually there's something for sale at a nearby stand run on the honor system: a few bunches of carrots and beets; maybe a few small bags of homemade cookies. Or I think of some arm on Norway's Sognefjord: long-haired highland cattle, raspberries on trellises, dark red apples, farmhouses as immaculate as race cars, barns built for the ages. There are barns like that in Poland, too, relics of an aristocracy wiped out seventy years ago. I think of Oman's Jebel Akhdar, where springwater irrigates terraces carved from cliffs no mountain goat could climb. Or of India's Godavary Delta, a rice garden if ever there was one: flat, heavy with humidity, and with a dendritic maze of canals threading through the fields.

Escapist fantasies, yes, but look on the bright side: people tell me all the time I should be a travel consultant. "You can help us plan our dream vacation, our great escape." I'd better not tell them that over the next several decades their lives will depend on the continued production of fossil fuels. I'd better not tell them that they don't know how good they have it, right here, right now, with security, medical care, and lots of ice cream flavors. Instead, I tell them, "You'd better hurry, these places won't last forever." It's a hustle: I really have no idea what the world will look like in fifty years. I do think it would be nice to write a book about a world *not* made for money. It would have photographs. I even have a little list, a tentative table of contents. I keep it on a card in my wallet.

Notes

Quotations not listed below come from the same source as the previously cited quotation.

ABBREVIATIONS

BW: *Business Week*
DMN: *Dallas Morning News*
E: *Economist*
F: *Fortune*
FEER: *Far Eastern Economic Review*
FT: *Financial Times*
G: *Guardian*
G&M: *Globe and Mail*
HT: *Hindustan Times*
LAT: *Los Angeles Times*
NY: *New Yorker*
NYT: *New York Times*
T: *Times* (London)
TH: *The Hindu*
WP: *Washington Post*
WSJ: *Wall Street Journal*

1. SHOPPING

2 **"I'm amazed at the people"**: Janet Adamy, "McDonald's Sets Wake-up," *WSJ*, July 27, 2007.

2 **"You try to push people"**: Steven Gray, "McDonald's Menu Upgrade . . ." *WSJ*, February 18, 2006.

2 **"In retrospect, I would have"**: Julie Jargon, "McDonald's Taps Former Executive to Turn Around U.S. Sales," *WSJ*, August 22, 2014.

3 **"You've got to measure everything"**: Matt Richtel, "The Long-Distance Journey of a Fast-Food Order," *NYT*, April 11, 2006.

4 **"veto vote"**: Steve Gray, "Flipping Burger King . . ." *WSJ*, April 26, 2005.

4 **"unprecedented decline in mall traffic"**: Patrick Fitzgerald, "Sbarro Files for Chapter 11 Bankruptcy," *WSJ*, March 10, 2014.

5 **"as sophisticated [a] palate"**: Janet Adamy, "A Little Wasabi Ginger . . ." *WSJ*, December 28, 2006.

5 **"That kind of stuff"**: Janet Adamy, "A Shift in Dining Scene . . ." *WSJ*, June 29, 2007.

5 **"What was good enough yesterday"**: Annie Gasparro, Boss Talk, *WSJ*, June 5, 2013.

6 **"If I want to sit"**: Janet Adamy, "Dunkin' Donuts Tries . . ." *WSJ*, May 2, 2007.

6 **"a great regional brand"**: Matthew Boyle, "Can Dunkin' Donuts Go . . ." *F*, September 5, 2006.

7 **"never been more enthused"**: Janet Adamy, "Starbucks Sets Ambitious . . ." *WSJ*, October 6, 2006.

7 **"no nice places to meet"**: James Crabtree, James Fontanella-Khan, and Barney Jopson, "Starbucks Plans $80m Indian Joint Venture," *FT*, January 30, 2012.

7 **"We are not even paying"**: Julie Jargon, "On McDonald's Menu . . ." *WSJ*, December 27, 2010.

8 **"a 10 percent chance"**: Dean Foust, "Krispy Kreme Has That Glazed Look," *BW*, December 5, 2005.

9 **"They've put together two companies"**: Ellen Byron, "A Clothes Horse . . ." *WSJ*, June 17, 2006.

9 **"comparing apples and monkeys"**: Rachel Dodes, "Showdown on 34th . . ." *WSJ*, August 1, 2009.

10 **"If you only deliver"**: Rachel Dodes, "Penney Weaves New . . ." *WSJ*, August 11, 2010.

10 **"People won't tolerate big stores"**: Dana Mattioli, "J.C. Penney to Overhaul Department-Store Concept," *WSJ*, January 26, 2012.

10 **"The Apple store is"**: Barney Jopson, "Apple's Success a Stretch for US Retailers," *FT*, August 10, 2012.

10 **"The entire value"**: Maura Webber Sadovi, "Deal of the Week," *WSJ*, May 21, 2013.

10 **"As I look at"**: Abigail Goldman, *LAT*, "Hundreds of Stores . . ." September 8, 2006.

10 **"We will hit"**: Kris Hudson and Miguel Bustillo, "Malls Face Surge in Vacancies," *WSJ*, April 7, 2011.

11 **"We've spent"**: Dana Mattioli, "Macy's to Ship Online Orders from Stores," *WSJ*, May 14, 2012.

11 **"The Woolworth Corporation said"**: Andrea Adelson, "Woolworth to Shutter . . ." *NYT*, October 14, 1993.

11 **"Some time in the mid"**: Richard Tomkins, "KMart Fails to Beam Out . . ." *FT*, March 28, 1995.

12 **"what every retailer"**: Kit R. Roane, "Last Gasp for Sears," *F*, October 17, 2011.

13 **"They wanted to expand"**: Maria Halkias, "Wal-Mart's Urban Push," *DMN*, November 1, 2005.

14 **"supply and command"**: Constance L. Hays, "What Wal-Mart Knows about Customers' Habits," *NYT*, November 14, 2004.

14 **"The orders are big"**: James T. Areddy, "China's Export Machine . . ." *WSJ*, June 20, 2008.

14 **"It's always hard"**: Gordon Fairclough, "Wal-Mart Sneezes . . ." *WSJ*, May 29, 2007.

14 **"the retailer people love"**: Miguel Bustillo and Ann Zimmerman, "In Cities That Battle . . ." *WSJ*, October 14, 2010.

14 **"Walmart can say they are"**: Miguel Bustillo, "Wal-mart to Go Smaller," *WSJ*, October 13, 2010.

15 **"Walmart does not suit"**: Kris Hudson and Gary McWilliams, "Seeking Expansion . . ." *WSJ*, September 25, 2006.

15 **"bring their lunch"**: Nancy Cleeland and Debora Vrana, "Wal-Mart CEO Takes . . ." *LAT*, February 24, 2005.

16 **"take over everything"**: Ian Lovett, "A Walmart for Chinatown Stirs a Fight in Los Angeles," *NYT*, September 7, 2012.

16 **"stick guns to council members'"**: Mike De Bonis, "Wal-Mart Says It Will Pull Out of D.C. Plans Should City Mandate 'Living Wage,'" *WP*, July 9, 2013.

16 **"The rabbis have"**: Fernanda Santos, "Fearing Wal-Mart Will Bring Too Much of the Outside In," *NYT*, June 25, 2007.

16 **"Walmart is frustrated"**: Jonathan Birchall, "Wal-Mart Fashions a New Marketing Story," *FT*, September 10, 2005.

16 **"Target is so good"**: Teri Agins, "Goodbye, Mainstream . . ." *WSJ*, January 27, 2007.

16 **"All retailers have a formula"**: Gary McWilliams, "Wal-Mart Era Wanes," *WSJ*, October 3, 2007.

17 **"Maybe it's possible to fatten"**: Barney Jopson, "Walmart: A Thinner Thong . . ." *FT*, June 28, 2011.

17 **"The glory days are over"**: Anthony Bianco, "Wal-Mart's Midlife Crisis," *BW*, April 20, 2007.

17 **"most important positions"**: Robert Berner, "Fashion Emergency," BW, July 31, 2006.

18 **"better for communities"**: Michael Barbaro, "Wal-Mart to Offer Help near Urban Stores," NYT, April 5, 2006.

19 **"Retailers have got to be"**: Suzanne Kapner, "Sales at Nordstrom's . . ." WSJ, February 20, 2014.

19 **"Thousands of supercenters are"**: Shelly Banjo, "Wal-Mart Looks to Grow," WSJ, July 8, 2014.

20 **"the rest of our careers"**: Shelly Banjo, "Wal-Mart's E-Stumble," WSJ, June 19, 2013.

20 **"the next frontier"**: Amy Guthrie and Shelly Banjo, "Wal-Mart Cracks Code," WSJ, February 19, 2014.

20 **"I've been in this business"**: Matthew Boyle, "Kroger's Secret Weapon," F, November 27, 2007.

21 **"The strategy is to lure"**: Julie Schlosser, "How Target Does It," F, October 28, 2004.

21 **"going through an identity crisis"**: Barney Jopson, "Target Seeks to Refocus Its Image," FT, January 12, 2012.

21 **"We feel they are worse"**: Jennifer Reingold, "Target's Inner Circle," F, March 18, 2008.

22 **"lost a lot of what"**: Paul Ziobro and Serena Ng, "Retailer Target Lost Its Way," WSJ, June 23, 2014.

22 **"Our customers aren't paying"**: Annie Gasparro, "Aldi to Boost . . ." WSJ, December 20, 2013.

22 **"the best business model"**: "The Germans Are Coming," E, August 14, 2008.

22 **"poor to just getting by"**: Jonathan Birchall, "Shoppers Lift Sales 13% at Dollar General," FT, June 2, 2009.

22 **"We're trying to be analytical"**: Ann Zimmerman, "Dollar General Enters Grocery," WSJ, April 30, 2012.

23 **"Walmart is a great retailer"**: Cecilie Rohwedder, "No. 1 Retailer in Britain . . ." WSJ, June 28, 2007.

24 **"We are playing"**: Andrea Folsted, "Tesco Chief Stands . . ." FT, September 20, 2012.

25 **"There is nothing exciting"**: Michael Barbaro, "Holiday Season . . ." NYT, December 7, 2005.

25 **"seem to be doing better"**: Karen Terlep, David Benoit, and Telis Demos, "At Gap, Sales Gains . . ." WSJ, February 11, 2013.

25 **"There's business to be had"**: John Kell, "Gap Earnings . . ." WSJ, August 23, 2013.

26 **"keeps working to protect"**: Sean Gregory, "Abercrombie & Fitch . . ." *T*, August 25, 2009.

26 **"Once you lose your brand"**: Matthew Boyle, "Abercrombie & Fitch Bargains . . ." *BW*, November 19, 2009.

26 **"Ralph Lauren is the king"**: Teri Agins, "Polo's High-Stakes . . ." *WSJ*, May 31, 2007.

26 **"It's important not to"**: Manuela Mesco, "Giorgio Armani Risks Losing . . ." *WSJ*, May, 17–18, 2014.

27 **"seem like a historic building"**: Paul Lukas, "Our Malls, Ourselves," *F*, October 18, 2004.

28 **"This just isn't that nice"**: Christina Binkley, "Inside the Strategy . . ." *WSJ*, May 26, 2011.

28 **"They're really the only one"**: Robbie Whelan, "Taubman Remains a Mall Believer," *WSJ*, July 8, 2014.

28 **"a huge untapped market"**: Roger Vincent, "South Gate Looks to Shoppers . . ." *LAT*, August 4, 2006.

29 **"You're hypnotized by this place"**: "Birth, Death and Shopping," *E*, December 19, 2007.

29 **"I can tell"**: Stephen Miller and Kris Hudson, "He Built America's First . . ." *WSJ*, September 17, 2009.

29 **"ready to fall"**: Kevan Goff-Parker, "JCPenney Stores Bound . . ." *Oklahoma Journal Record*, August 3, 2006.

29 **"I'm busy"**: Byron, "A Clothes Horse."

29 **"We're overbuilt"**: Barney Jopson, "America's Malls Seek . . ." *FT*, February 8, 2013.

29 **"People have been predicting"**: Binkley, "Inside the Strategy."

30 **"Department stores used to be"**: Ryan Chittum, "Anchors Away . . ." *WSJ*, March 2, 2005.

30 **"If anyone blindfolded you"**: Victoria Griffith, "Generation X Goes . . ." *FT*, November 17, 1994.

31 **"the most creative"**: Ryan Chittum and Jennifer S. Forsyth, "How Mills Corp. Built . . ." *WSJ*, April 14, 2006.

31 **"it was a crazy idea"**: A. D. Pruitt and Lingling Wei, "Dreams of Retail 'Xanada,'" *WSJ*, February 10, 2010.

31 **"visionary initiative"**: Amanda Little, "The Mall That Would Save . . ." *NYT*, July 3, 2005.

32 **"blackened mahi-mahi"**: Ylan Q. Mui, "Old Magnets Just Don't . . ." *WP*, July 23, 2006.

32 **"I see our residential strategy"**: A. D. Pruitt and Dawn Wotapka, "Big Developers Dabble . . ." *WSJ*, December 21, 2011.

32 **"the world's most successful"**: Peter Whoriskey, "Soaring View of Tysons," *WP*, April 22, 2005.

32 **"We have stories"**: Matthew Garrahan, "Wise to Ways . . ." *FT*, April 15, 2008.

33 **"we're seeing good cross-shopping"**: Andrea Chang, "Americana at Brand Is a Hit with Visitors," *LAT*, April 18, 2009.

33 **"It will get nasty"**: Ashra Khalil, "Mall Operates Wages Fight . . ." *LAT*, April 20, 2007.

34 **"too much riffraff down there"**: Thaddeus Herrick, "Fake Towns Rise . . ." *WSJ*, May 31, 2006.

34 **"It sure looks like"**: Steve Brown, "Setting Up Shops . . ." *DMN*, April 14, 2006.

35 **"The predominant view"**: Patrick McGeehan, "Now, Big-Name Retail . . ." *NYT*, January 14, 2007.

2. MAKING

37 **"a lot of bottlers"**: Dean Foust, "Queen of Pop . . ." *BW*, August 7, 2006.

38 **"Coca-Cola has always stood"**: Brooks Masters, "Coke Plans Investment . . ." *FT*, June 15, 2012.

38 **"PepsiCo is not"**: Chad Terhune, "To Bag China's Snack . . ." *WSJ*, December 19, 2005.

39 **"Their pickiness has helped me"**: Marla Dickerson, "Wal-Mart Plants Seeds . . ." *LAT*, March 8, 2008.

39 **"We needed to increase understanding"**: Alison Maitland, "Globalisation's Strange . . ." *FT*, December 8, 2005.

40 **"If it becomes"**: Barney Jopson, "Unilever Looks to Clean Up," *FT*, November 15, 2007.

40 **"Stick to the countryside"**: Eric Bellman, "The Infomercial Comes . . ." *WSJ*, June 10, 2009.

40 **"Our portfolio is"**: Andrew Ward, "Cadbury Shakes Up . . ." *FT*, December 6–7, 2005.

40 **"Of course we would prefer"**: Betsy McKay, "Pepsi Bottling to Distribute . . ." *WSJ*, August 22, 2008.

41 **"We're not going head-to-head"**: Richard Tomlinson, "The New King of Beers," *F*, October 18, 2004.

42 **"America in a bottle"**: Jenny Wiggins, "Thirst to Be First," *FT*, July 24, 2008.

42 **"The potential is so huge"**: Mike Esterl, "'King of Beers' Sets . . ." *WSJ*, July 27–28, 2013.

42 **"There's plenty of room"**: Mike Esterl, "Beer Giant SABMiller . . ." *WSJ*, September 25, 2013.

42 **"the Campbell Soup Company"**: Julia Flynn Siler, "Remembrances," *WSJ*, March 10, 2007.

43 **"Americans love Chianti"**: Corie Brown, "The World According . . ." *LAT*, January 10, 2005.

43 **"Some days I'm pissed off"**: Barbara Hagenbaugh, "Lives Unraveled . . ." *USA Today*, July 30, 2004.

44 **"either for a global economy"**: Greg Hitt and Dan Morse, "Once Close-Knit . . ." *WSJ*, May 27, 2005.

45 **"Asian competitors will be copying you"**: William Hall, "Stitch in Time for Tattered . . ." *FT*, March 27, 2004.

45 **"We were going to make"**: Marla Dickerson, "From Textile City to Ghost Town," *LAT*, December 8, 2005.

46 **"All the designers are looking"**: Paul Magnusson, "Who'll Survive," *BW*, December 20, 2005.

47 **"We're being very cautious"**: Tracie Rozhon, "A Tangle in Textiles . . ." *NYT*, April 21, 2005.

47 **"The moment your competition shifts"**: Edward Luce, *In Spite of the Gods: The Strange Rise of Modern India* (New York: Doubleday, 2007), 52–53.

47 **"If you are going to"**: Alex Frangos, "Remaking India . . ." *WSJ*, October 6, 2011.

48 **"If it's 5,000 taka"**: Vikas Bajaj, "With Lower Garment-Industry . . ." *NYT*, July 16, 2010.

49 **"Bangladesh will be history"**: Shelly Banjo, "Bangladesh Garment Factories . . ." *WSJ*, October 4, 2013.

49 **"As soon as the pain"**: Gordon Fairclough, "Bangladesh Disaster Survivor . . ." *WSJ*, June 22–23, 2013.

50 **"an industry at the crossroads"**: James Politi and Katrina Manson, "African Jobs Face . . ." *FT*, June 21, 2012.

50 **"The reason practically all"**: Pete Engardio and Dexter Roberts, "The China Price . . ." *BW*, November 6, 2004.

51 **"tell us what you need"**: David Wessel and James R. Hagerty, "Flat U.S. Wages Help . . ." *WSJ*, May 29, 2012.

51 **"Governments have tipped"**: John Reed, "Back on the Road," *FT*, June 18, 2009.

52 **"I frankly don't see how"**: Paul Ingrassia, "GM's Plan: Subsidize . . ." *WSJ*, February 23, 2009.

52 **"the end of an era"**: Bernard Simon, "Exodus of Car Workers," *FT*, October 11, 2006.

52 **"I hate my job"**: Peter Whoriskey, "Auto Bailout's Consequence . . ." *WP*, July 25, 2010.

52 **"I'm able to adapt"**: James R. Hagerty and Alistair Macdonald, "In Rust Belt, Caterpillar . . ." *WSJ*, March 16, 2012.

53 **"Mitch, why?"**: Sharon Terlep, "UAW Freezes Rival . . ." *WSJ*, April 29, 2012.

53 **"I don't think we're going"**: Nick Bunkley, "Detroit's Troubles . . ." *NYT*, June 18, 2008.

53 **"One side is trapped"**: Anonymous, "Objects in the Mirror . . ." *FT*, February 27, 2006.

54 **"In the 70s"**: Terry Box, "Lincoln Mercury Dealer Closes," *DMN*, December 16, 2006.

54 **"We'll use the space"**: Terry Box, "McDavid Dealership Folds," *DMN*, December 21, 2006.

55 **"like an Olympic swimmer"**: Terry Box, "Automaker Cutting 30,000 Jobs, Closing Plants," *DMN*, November 22, 2005.

55 **"We took our eye off"**: Jeffrey McCracken, "Desperate to Cut . . ." *WSJ*, March 2, 2007.

56 **"We did bring it on"**: James Mackintosh, "Western Car Jobs . . ." *FT*, February 16, 2006.

56 **"We are working feverishly"**: Jason Sapsford, Joseph B. White, and Dennis K. Berman, "GM Shares Sink . . ." *WSJ*, December 21, 2005.

56 **"Ford is light years ahead"**: Sharon Terlep, "Target at Post-Bailout . . ." *WSJ*, February 6, 2012.

56 **"Those days are gone"**: Micheline Maynard, "Is There a Ford . . ." *NYT*, January 8, 2006.

57 **"I told the Mazda team"**: James Mackintosh and Bernard Simon, "Ford Motor's Mark . . ." *FT*, January 23, 2006.

57 **"in a desperate situation"**: Jeffrey McCracken, "Desperate to Cut Costs . . ." *WSJ*, March 2, 2007.

57 **"The business model"**: Doug Cameron, Kevin Done, James Mackintosh, and Bernard Simon, "Gear Change," *FT*, September 7, 2007.

57 **"I knew it would come"**: Peter Slevin, "Workers Lament . . ." *WP*, January 24, 2006.

57 **"start of a new era"**: Bernard Simon and John Reed, "Running out of Road," *FT*, August 21, 2008.

58 **"The market is less"**: Alex Taylor III, "Mercedes Hits a Pothole," *F*, October 27, 2003.

58 **"Mercedes is getting squeezed"**: Gail Edmondson, "Global Economics . . ." *BW*, November 2, 2006.

58 **"There's no politics"**: News Roundup, *WSJ*, January 24, 2006.

59 **"There's no huge"**: Neal E. Boudette and Terry Kosdrosky, "Chrysler's Unconventional Plan . . ." *WSJ*, February 11, 2008.

59 **"It kills us"**: Peter Lattman and Mike Spector, "Contrite, Cerberus Looks . . ." *WSJ*, July 10, 2009.

59 **"I don't know what"**: Louise Story, "For Cerberus and Chrysler . . ." *NYT*, August 9, 2009.

59 **"Our reputation and credibility"**: John Gapper, "A Long Haul . . ." *FT*, January 13, 2010.

59 **"a primal, real, tangible sense"**: Ed Crooks and Hal Weitzman, "Back in the Game . . ." *FT*, February 11, 2012.

59 **"This is just a blessing"**: Jeff Bennett, "Car Plant Brings . . ." *WSJ*, May 29, 2012.

59 **"Chrysler needs something"**: Christina Rogers, "Chrysler Updates Old . . ." *WSJ*, January 13, 2014.

60 **"The single most important thing"**: "Rebirth of a Carmaker," *E*, April 24, 2008.

60 **"The customer is interested in"**: Stephen Faris, "Behind the Turnaround at Fiat," *F*, May 8, 2007.

60 **"Flat is the new up"**: David Pearson and Nico Schmidt, "Flat Is the New Up," *WSJ*, September 4, 2013.

60 **"You can't fight gravity"**: Henry Foy, "Carmakers Face Battle," *FT*, July 10, 2013.

61 **"Listen, there's a new"**: John Reed and Chris Bryant, "Automobiles: On Course . . ." *FT*, May 21, 2012.

61 **"today, very few manufacturers"**: Vanessa Fuhrmans, "Europe's Car Makers Confront . . ." *WSJ*, March 6, 2012.

61 **"I see no prospects"**: Gilles Castonguay, "No Work, No Pay," *WSJ*, August 10–12, 2013.

61 **"The standard of reference"**: Adrian Michaels and John Reed, "Fiat Chief Sets out Plan to Double Net Income," *FT*, November 10, 2006.

62 **"We will be challenged"**: Gail Edmondson, "BMW's Dream Factory," *BW*, October 16, 2006.

62 **"This is about globalisation"**: Richard Milne, "BMW to Cut Thousands . . ." *FT*, December 22, 2007.

62 **"One of our buyers"**: David Kiley, "Can VW Find . . ." *BW*, January 31, 2005.

62 **"not a rabbit that cowers"**: James Mackintosh, "Western Car Jobs Hit the Road," *FT*, February 16, 2006.

63 **"quality, strong motivation"**: Daniel Schäfer, "Protective Layers . . ." *FT*, June 18, 2010.

64 **"The U.S. is the cornerstone"**: William Boston and Neal E. Boudette, "VW Labor Rep Blasts . . ." *WSJ*, January 22, 2014.

64 **"The VW brand"**: William Boston and Joseph B. White, "Volkswagen to Invest . . ." *WSJ*, July 14, 2014.

64 **"The root cause"**: Norihiko Shirouzu, "What Really Happened . . ." WSJ, April 13, 2010.

64 **"The last thing Toyota wants"**: Jon Gertner, "From 0 to 60 . . ." NYT, February 18, 2007.

65 **"trying to pull a handcart"**: Clay Chandler, "Full Speed Ahead," F, February 7, 2005.

65 **"I am told a CEO"**: Norihiko Shirouzu, "As Rivals Catch Up . . ." WSJ, December 9, 2006.

65 **"Wringing drops"**: Chester Dawson and Karn Nickle Anhalt, "A 'China Price,'" BW, February 21, 2005.

66 **"If you look at it"**: Jonathan Soble, "Japanese Manufacturing in Search . . ." FT, January 4, 2012.

66 **"destruction of Japan's industrial base"**: Chester Dawson and Yoshio Takahashi, "Toyota Slashes Profit . . ." WSJ, December 10, 2011.

66 **"We won't suddenly bring production"**: Jonathan Soble, "'Abenomics' Yet to Convince . . ." FT, May 16, 2013.

66 **"extremely unrealistic and uncompetitive"**: John Reed, "Nissan and Renault Expand . . ." FT, September 14, 2011.

66 **"Today we know how"**: Peggy Hollinger, "Ghosn Steers His Own . . ." FT, May 9, 2007.

67 **"thoroughly optimized"**: Bob Lutz, "Life Lesson . . ." WSJ, June 13, 2011.

67 **"I worry about them"**: Mike Ramsey and Evan Ramstad, "Once a Global Also-Ran, Hyundai Zooms Forward," WSJ, June 30, 2011.

67 **"Hyundai was a fast follower"**: John Reed, "Hyundai Reaps Rewards . . ." FT, May 8, 2012.

67 **"a bigger threat right now"**: Ramsey and Ramstad, "Once a Global Also-Ran."

68 **"Huge sums in the beginning"**: David Kesmodel, "Boeing Revs Up . . ." WSJ, September 27, 2011.

69 **"The A340 is dying slowly"**: Leslie Wayne, "Boeing Bets the House . . ." NYT, May 7, 2006.

70 **"They're basically going to try"**: Kim Murphy, "Boeing's Global Sights . . ." LAT, October 27, 2008.

70 **"Customers don't want"**: Melanie Trottman, "Boeing, NLRB Clash over Non-Union Plant," WSJ, June 15, 2011.

71 **"If the 787 works out"**: Pilita Clark, "Aerospace: A Longer . . ." FT, March 2, 2010.

71 **"Normal installation time"**: Peggy Hollinger and Gerrit Wiesmann, "It's a Tangle . . ." FT, July 16, 2008.

71 **"The last thing we need"**: Andrew Ward, "FedEx Chief Says . . ." FT, November 9, 2006.

72 **"U.S. manufacturing can compete"**: Daniel Michaels, Jon Ostrower, and David Pearson, "Airbus Details Plans . . ." WSJ, July 3, 2012.

73 **"Our best corporate customers"**: Jeremy Lemer, "American Eyes Route . . ." FT, March 5, 2012.

73 **"I always keep this"**: Tripti Lahiri and Christina Passariello, "Why Retailers Don't Know . . ." WSJ, July 24, 2013.

74 **"a shame"**: Otis Port, "Flat-Panel Pioneer . . ." BW, December 12, 2005.

74 **"Inexpensive cameras are dead"**: Daisuke Wakabayashi, "The Point-and-Shoot Camera . . ." WSJ, July 30, 2013.

74 **"I tell everybody"**: Andrew Edgecliffe-Johnson and Michiyo Nakamoto, "Year of Candour and Resolve Starts to Energise Sony," FT, June 21, 2006.

75 **"spent 14 years working"**: Peter Marsh, "A Careful Giant . . ." FT, September 30, 2005.

76 **"What we're talking about here"**: Jack Nicas and Susan Carey, "Southwest Airlines, Once a Brassy . . ." WSJ, April 2, 2014.

76 **"Any business today"**: Alexandra Wolfe, "Howard Schultz: What Next . . ." WSJ, September 28–29, 2013.

76 **"You don't change, you die"**: Miguel Bustillo, "The Plan to Rescue Sears," WSJ, March 12, 2012.

76 **"No change, no future"**: Anna Fifield, "Korean Shipbuilders Struggle . . ." FT, July 27, 2007.

76 **"If we can tailor"**: "Steely Logic," E, August 28, 2008.

77 **"we can build a juggernaut"**: Mure Dickie, Jeremy Grant, Kohzem Merchant, and James Politi, "We Can Build a Juggernaut," FT, February 4, 2005.

78 **"We are in 85%"**: Joann S. Lublin, "Campbell's Chief Stirs . . ." WSJ, May 16, 2011.

78 **"You're either active everywhere"**: Emily Glazer, Ellen Byron, Dennis K. Berman, and Joanne S. Lublin, "P&G's Stumbles Put CEO . . ." WSJ, September 27, 2012.

78 **"just take our existing products"**: Julie Jargon, "Campbell's Chief Looks . . ." WSJ, May 30, 2008.

78 **"You have to understand how"**: Patty Waldmeir, "Shanghai Lights Up . . ." FT, March 6, 2012.

79 **"It's not enough"**: Daisuke Wakabayashi, "Hitachi President Nakanishi . . ." WSJ, May 11, 2012.

79 **"There really is no substitute"**: Jeremy Grant, "Check the Depth . . ." FT, November 16, 2005.

79 **"do-it-for-me culture"**: Laurie Burkitt, "Home Depot Learns . . ." *wsj*, September 15–16, 2012.

80 **"If you decided to go"**: Paul Ziobro and Serena Ng, "Is Innovation Killing . . ." *wsj*, April 4, 2013.

81 **"We can't tolerate"**: John Bussey, "U.S. Manufacturing, Defying . . ." *wsj*, April 23, 2012.

81 **"didn't do it with malice"**: Annie Gasparro, "Tightfisted New Owners . . ." *wsj*, February 10, 2014.

82 **"I feel sorry for"**: Bob Tita and James R. Hagerty, "Caterpillar Union Bows . . ." *wsj*, August 18–19, 2012.

3. MOVING

83 **"For a long time"**: Andrew Ward, "Yellow Roadway Drives . . ." *FT*, June 6, 2005.

83 **"the most amazing transformation"**: Dean Foust, "Big Brown's New . . ." *BW*, July 19, 2004.

83 **"We're obsessed about efficiency"**: Jennifer Levitz, "ups's Latest Efficiency . . ." *wsj*, September 16, 2011.

84 **"we would have a container"**: Andrew Ward, "New Logic to Shipping Merchandise," *FT*, November 7, 2005.

84 **"We have no inventory"**: Dean Foust, "FedEx . . ." *BW*, April 3, 2006.

85 **"Our federal approach to transportation"**: Christopher Conkey, "Bush Calls for New . . ." *wsj*, July 20, 2008.

85 **"That is a 1950s model"**: Evan Halper, "State's Future May Be Paved . . ." *LAT*, February 13, 2007.

86 **"put the brakes on"**: Emily Thornton, "Roads to Riches . . ." *BW*, May 7, 2007.

87 **"The name Trans-Texas Corridor"**: Rosanna Ruiz, Janet Elliott, and R. G. Ratcliffe, "Trans-Texas Corridor Plans Dropped after Public Outcry," *Houston Chronicle*, January 6, 2009.

88 **"Democracy sacrifices efficiency"**: "Rushing on by Road," *E*, February 14, 2008.

88 **"a paradigm shift"**: Geeta Anand, "India's Road Builder . . ." *wsj*, July 6, 2009.

89 **"The flags on the tails"**: Doug Cameron and Kevin Done, "Airline Consolidation . . ." *FT*, November 21, 2006.

89 **"carpet-bombed Denver"**: Scott McCartney, "How Southwest Airlines . . ." *wsj*, June 6, 2013.

90 **"a shadow of what"**: Susan Carey and Jack Nicas, "Rivals Invade Southwest's . . ." *wsj*, December 16, 2011.

90 **"direction of the industry"**: Jack Nicas, "Cut-Rate Future . . ." *WSJ*, July 31, 2013.

90 **"You hear the word 'no'"**: Scott McCartney, "Boston's Charm Offensive . . ." *WSJ*, February 26, 2014.

91 **"make all of our money"**: Mike Esterl, "Smisek Takes the Controls . . ." *WSJ*, December 31, 2009.

91 **"We're going to continue"**: Daniel Michaels, "Airlines Pour into Growing . . ." *WSJ*, March 23, 2010.

92 **"We were middleweight champions"**: Daniel Michaels, "Behind Easing of Airline . . ." *WSJ*, September 5, 2006.

92 **"We won't back down"**: Andrew Parker, "Air-France KLM Reaffirms . . ." *FT*, May 5–6, 2012.

92 **"The union had no alternative"**: Marietta Cauchi and Daniel Michaels, "Europe's Airlines . . ." *WSJ*, December 13, 2012.

93 **"America, the land of"**: James Boxell, "BA Chief Slams . . ." *FT*, September 23, 2005.

93 **"You get . . . a flying tanker"**: Daniel Michaels, "Airlines Cut Long . . ." *WSJ*, July 8, 2008.

94 **"What part of 'no refund'"**: Keith Johnson and Daniel Michaels, "Big Worry for No-Frills . . ." *WSJ*, July 1, 2004.

94 **"If you want"**: Tom Braithwaite and Kevin Done, "If You Want . . ." *FT*, August 31, 2006.

94 **"communist morons"**: Kerry Capell, Global Economics, *BW*, November 16, 2006.

95 **"this is a stupid business"**: Kyle Wingfield, "My 'Stupid Business,'" *WSJ*, September 15, 2007.

95 **"There's nothing out there"**: Pilita Clark and Jeremy Lerner, "AirTran Deal . . ." *FT*, September 28, 2010.

95 **"Ryanair continues to unveil"**: Graham Hiscott, "Ryanair Goes Head-to-Head . . ." *Daily Mirror*, July 13, 2011.

96 **"You couldn't start"**: Daniel Michaels, "Europe's Major Carriers . . ." *WSJ*, March 29, 2013.

97 **"going to trash the profitability"**: Dean Foust, "Survival of the Biggest . . ." *BW*, February 14, 2008.

97 **"a cash-generating machine"**: Kevin Done, "The Heathrow Cash Machine Is Coming up for Grabs," *FT*, March 7, 2007.

99 **"We want Stage Two"**: Willie Walsh, "Soapbox," *FT*, February 4, 2008.

99 **"We've never seen anything"**: Leslie Wayne, "A Flight Plan . . ." *NYT*, July 6, 2007.

100 **"Look at a map"**: Heather Timmons, "After Dubai Uproar . . ." NYT, March 29, 2006.

100 **"Forty years ago"**: John Arlidge, "Fasten Your Seat Belts," *Sunday Times* (London), July 24, 2011.

100 **"The logical thing to do"**: Neil Hume, "Headwinds for Qantas . . ." FT, June 13, 2012.

100 **"Qantas doesn't go anywhere anymore"**: David Fickling, "Boeing Loses Qantas Order," Bloomberg News, August 23, 2012.

101 **"sucking our U.K. long-haul traffic"**: Daniel Michaels, "From Tiny Dubai . . ." WSJ, January 11, 2005.

101 **"I do not take"**: Pilita Clark, "BA Chief Warns . . ." FT, September 15, 2010.

101 **"airlines are fairly weak"**: Andrew Parker and Ralph Atkins, "Lufthansa Loss . . ." FT, May 16, 2012.

101 **"The last thing they"**: Clark, "BA Chief Warns."

102 **"We are seven years old"**: Christian Oliver, "Etihad Chief Hits . . ." FT, December 12, 2010.

102 **"This tiny airport"**: Anita Jain, "Indian Middle Class . . ." FT, July 27, 2005.

103 **"We will strive to make"**: Kevin Done, "AirAsia to Launch . . ." FT, April 24, 2007.

103 **"The fact that people are"**: Enid Tsui, "Cathay Ignores Calls . . ." FT, July 2, 2012.

103 **"last frontier for aviation"**: Simon Zekaria, "Stelios-Backed Pan-African . . ." WSJ, June 13, 2012.

104 **"The first thing Brazilians want"**: Antonio Regalado, "Flying High . . ." WSJ, January 22, 2007.

104 **"Everyone wants it now"**: Suzanne Marta, "Cargo Business Grows at D/FW," DMN, December 5, 2005.

105 **"crazy"**: Maxwell Murphy, "Pitting Costs against Control . . ." WSJ, February 28, 2012.

105 **"high cost of fuel"**: Alan Beattie, "Zambian Exports Hit . . ." FT, August 25, 2005.

106 **"If it [Dubai] also becomes"**: William McSheehy, "Flower Power in Dubai . . ." FT, October 19, 2005.

106 **"I believe we engineer time"**: Geoffrey Colvin, "The FedEx Edge," F, April 3, 2006.

107 **"I'm totally devastated"**: Roel Landingin and Justine Lau, "FedEx Puts a Dent . . ." FT, July 15, 2005.

107 **"Taiwan's airports are being marginalized"**: Kathrin Hille, "Taiwan Flies into Air Cargo . . ." FT, September 13, 2005.

108 **"given up for dead"**: Robert Wright, "Rail Chief Prepares . . ." *FT*, August 14, 2011.

111 **"not plan to take this"**: Ronald D. White, "Mexican Port Gets . . ." *LAT*, June 20, 2006.

112 **"What we need is employment"**: Marla Dickerson, "It's Full Speed . . ." *LAT*, August 28, 2008.

113 **"Look at the train system"**: Jon Gertner, "Getting up to Speed . . ." *NYT*, June 14, 2009.

114 **"the French low-cost carrier"**: "Mr. High-Speed Europe," *E*, February 21, 2008.

116 **"Nobody knows what kind"**: Courtney Weaver, "Listing a Test for Russia's Rail Reform," *FT*, November 8, 2010.

117 **"Physically they are good assets"**: Brian Spegele and Bob Davis, "Beijing-Shanghai High-Speed . . ." *WSJ*, June 29, 2011.

117 **"China today is a train"**: Jason Dean and Jeremy Page, "Trouble on the China Express," *WSJ*, July 20, 2011.

118 **"Aren't we Chinese great?"**: Jonathan Watts, "The Railway Across . . ." *G*, September 20, 2005.

118 **"If China closed the borders"**: Dan Levin, "Mongolia's Coal Deposits . . ." *NYT*, June 26, 2012.

119 **"That was almost exactly"**: Robert Wright, "Transport Choices . . ." *FT*, March 19, 2012.

120 **"They were all highly interested"**: Keith Bradsher, "Hauling New Treasure . . ." *NYT*, July 20, 2013.

122 **"one country, this railway"**: Robert Wright, "Railways: Difficulty . . ." *FT*, November 22, 2011.

124 **"really stupid, stupid strategy"**: Costas Paris, "Overcapacity, Fuel Costs . . ." *WSJ*, May 4–5, 2013.

126 **"If tomorrow Chinese customs changed"**: Robert Wright, "HK's Port Faces . . ." *FT*, April 17, 2007.

126 **"Hong Kong's legal system"**: Paul Davies, "Finance," *FT*, July 27, 2012.

128 **"Everybody has been living"**: Robert Wright, "Road Haulage . . ." *FT*, November 22, 2011.

129 **"Fish plants were laying off"**: Ronald D. White, "Eyeing Vancouver Port . . ." *LAT*, April 11, 2006.

130 **"This is grinding us down"**: David George-Cosh and Ben Dummett, "Canadian National Won't Move . . ." *WSJ*, March 12, 2014.

131 **"just got busier"**: Richard Lapper, "A Post-Panamax Renaissance," *FT*, July 24, 2007.

132 **"in a very far"**: Richard Milne, "Arctic Shipping Routes . . ." *FT*, October 6, 2013.

132 **"One thing that makes me"**: Tom Michell and Richard Milne, "First Chinese Cargo Ship . . ." *FT*, September 6, 2013.

132 **"I don't see the Northwest"**: Clifford Krauss, Steve Lee Myers, Andrew C. Revkin, and Simon Romero, "As Polar Ice Turns . . ." *NYT*, October 20, 2005.

132 **"With global warming"**: Bernard Simon, "Canada Boosts Claim . . ." *FT*, May 11, 2011.

4. FUELING

136 **"the issue the chief executives"**: James Boxell and Kevin Morrison, "Global Oil Companies Face . . ." *FT*, December 9, 2004.

136 **"National oil companies are"**: Guy Chazan, "Rosneft to Pay . . ." *FT*, October 22, 2012.

136 **"to question what it is"**: Carola Hoyos, "Nationals' Champion . . ." *FT*, July 29, 2008.

136 **"Anytime price goes up"**: Daniel Gilbert and Tom Fowler, "Exxon and Chevron Miss Out . . ." *WSJ*, July 31, 2013.

136 **"the highest ever offered"**: Stanley Reed, "Going off the Deep . . ." *BW*, June 26, 2006.

137 **"The international oil companies are"**: Carola Hoyos, "Oil Groups Set to End . . ." *FT*, May 7, 2009.

137 **"almost the only place"**: Guy Chazan, "An Ocean of Reserves . . ." *FT*, December 3, 2012.

137 **"Kurdistan is the oil exploration"**: Guy Chazan, "Kurdistan's Vast Reserves . . ." *FT*, January 8, 2013.

138 **"This stuff doesn't remain proprietary"**: Russell Gold, "Exxon Looks Close . . ." *WSJ*, February 11, 2008.

138 **"It was a great meeting"**: Russell Gold, "Exxon Courts Libya . . ." *WSJ*, March 8, 2007.

138 **"The Libyans will no doubt"**: Boxell and Morrison, "Global Oil Companies Face."

138 **"Libya has gone from"**: Guy Chazan, "For West's Oil Firms . . ." *WSJ*, April 15, 2011.

139 **"extraordinary uncertainty, immense levels"**: Ben Casselman and Guy Chazan, "Cramped on Land . . ." *WSJ*, January 5, 2010.

139 **"Farmers and ranchers are fit"**: Alan C. Miller, Tom Hamburger, and Julie Cart, "White House Puts the West . . ." *LAT*, August 25, 2004.

140 **"I don't really know"**: William Yardley, "With New Pipeline Plan . . ." *NYT*, February 19, 2007.

140 **"among the largest, costliest"**: Russell Gold, "ConocoPhillips, BP Plan . . ." *WSJ*, April 9, 2008.

140 **"There's only one country"**: Ed Crooks, "Gas Pipeline Sparks . . ." *FT*, March 21, 2012.

141 **"All the elephants were gone"**: Neil King Jr. and Keith Johnson, "Oil-Thirsty," *WSJ*, October 9, 2010.

141 **"We're very optimistic"**: Russell Gold, "A Famed Dry Hole . . ." *WSJ*, July 21, 2008.

141 **"Every deepwater field is unique"**: Brian Baskin, "Chevron Bets Big . . ." *WSJ*, June 27, 2007.

141 **"teenager of the oil industry"**: Abrahm Lustgarten, *Run to Failure: BP and the Making of the Deepwater Horizon Disaster* (New York: Norton, 2012), 301.

142 **"the deepest well ever drilled"**: Russell Gold, "BP's Big Oil Find . . ." *WSJ*, September 3, 2009.

142 **"I have oil companies"**: Guy Chazan, Russell Gold, and Jason Singer, "Transocean Merger Deal . . ." *WSJ*, July 24, 2007.

142 **"We're kind of torn apart"**: William Yardley and Eric Olsen, "Point Hope, Alaska . . ." *NYT*, October 25, 2011.

143 **"ability to operate safely"**: Chester Dawson, "Oil Giants Set . . ." *WSJ*, May 18, 2014.

143 **"could be the most expensive"**: Chester Dawson, "Exxon Unit in Canada . . ." *WSJ*, May 18, 2014.

144 **"Ironically, most of the oil"**: Jad Mouawad, "Oil Innovations Pump . . ." *NYT*, March 5, 2007.

144 **"major, major modern boom"**: Sheila McNulty, "US Producers Break . . ." *FT*, June 23, 2011.

145 **"Devon has drilled 4,000 wells"**: Steven Mufson, "An Energy Answer in the Shale Below?" *WP*, December 3, 2009.

145 **"It's the one thing"**: Clifford Krauss, "Oil in Shale . . ." *NYT*, May 27, 2011.

145 **"We don't take foreign political risk"**: David Whitford, "Meet Mr. Combative CEO," *F*, May 2008.

145 **"More. More"**: Russell Gold, *The Boom: How Fracking Ignited the American Energy Revolution and Changed the World* (New York: Simon & Schuster, 2014), 176.

145 **"I'm going to get me"**: Adam Nossiter, "Gas Rush Is On, and Louisianans Cash In," *NYT*, July 29, 2008.

146 **"The United States is sitting"**: Mufson, "Energy Answer in the Shale."

146 **"This is a new era"**: Russell Gold and David Gilbert, "U.S. Is Overtaking Russia as Largest Oil-and-Gas Producer," *WSJ*, October 2, 2013.

146 **"The U.S. is now"**: Ben Casselman and Russell Gold, "Cheap Natural Gas Gives ..." *WSJ*, October 24, 2012.

147 **"You're kind of giving"**: Tennille Tracy, "U.S. Gas Exports ..." *WSJ*, May 30, 2012.

147 **"We are all losing"**: Clifford Krauss and Eric Lipton, "In a Natural Gas Glut ..." *NYT*, October 20, 2012.

147 **"it's just hard to justify"**: Pilita Clark, "Nuclear 'Hard to Justify,'" *FT*, July 30, 2012.

147 **"In the geopolitics of energy"**: John Bussey, "Shale," *WSJ*, September 21, 2012.

147 **"a bubble that will"**: Gold and Gilbert, "U.S. Is Overtaking."

147 **"We are at the dawn"**: Russell Gold, "Oil Drillers Boost ..." *WSJ*, March 13, 2013.

147 **"This sets up"**: Ben Casselman, "U.S. Drilling Activity ..." *WSJ*, December 14, 2008.

148 **"We're here for the long term"**: Ed Crooks, "Statoil Looks to Tap ..." *FT*, June 12, 2012.

148 **"We underestimated the magnitude"**: Guy Chazan, "Shale Gas," *FT*, April 24, 2012.

148 **"This is the beginning"**: Ed Crooks, "LNG Plant to Be First ..."*FT*, April 18, 2012.

149 **"came from everywhere"**: Tennille Tracy, "U.S. Gas Exports ..." *WSJ*, May 31, 2012.

150 **"been very, very super-good"**: Daniel Gilbert, "New Oil Patches ..." *WSJ*, November 13, 2010.

150 **"biggest thing to hit Ohio"**: Daniel Gilbert and Ryan Dezember, "Chesapeake Raises Big Bet ..." *WSJ*, May 23, 2012.

150 **"It doesn't seem real"**: Keith Schneider, "New Value for Land ..." *NYT*, June 4, 2012.

150 **"I thought my job"**: John J. Fialka, "Wildcat Producer Sparks ..." *WSJ*, April 5, 2006.

150 **"We'll probably get 150"**: Gilbert, "New Oil Patches."

150 **"We don't have the quiet"**: Mark Peters and Ben Lefebvre, "Riding the Dakota Oil ..." *WSJ*, November 1, 2011.

150 **"It makes the job"**: Jack Nicas, "Oil Boom Sparks ..." *WSJ*, April 2, 2012.

151 **"It's unbelievable"**: Gregory Meyer and Javier Blas, "Oil Trade in Throes," *FT*, October 18, 2012.

152 **"The steam goes down"**: Steven Mufson, "Steam Goes Down . . ." *WP*, June 30, 2012.

152 **"It's like you've got one"**: Russell Gold, "As Prices Surge . . ." *WSJ*, March 27, 2006.

152 **"You've got one of"**: Bernard Simon, "Canada Can Give the World . . ." *FT*, November 8, 2005.

152 **"The river used to be"**: Doug Struck, "Canada Pays Environmentally . . ." *WP*, May 31, 2006.

153 **"There is not a minister"**: Jim Landers, "Oh, Canada! Oil Companies See a Fuel's Paradise for U.S.," *DMN*, October 17, 2005.

153 **"more money than God"**: Ed Crooks and Bernard Simon, "Opposition Grows . . ." *FT*, November 8, 2011.

153 **"It's mind-boggling that people think"**: Sheila McNulty, "Industry Fights Back . . ." *FT*, October 10, 2011.

153 **"reexports are going to change"**: Chester Dawson, "Canada Aims to Sell . . ." *WSJ*, June 5, 2014.

154 **"probably the largest untapped play"**: Laurence Iliff and Juan Montes, "Mexico Moves to Overhaul . . ." *WSJ*, August 13, 2013.

154 **"You have to not underestimate"**: Ángel González and Laurence Iliff, "Mexico Oil Watchdog Sounds Alarm," *WSJ*, February 15, 2012.

154 **"We've given up on Mexico"**: David Luhnow, *WSJ*, June 15, 2005.

154 **"We think that would be"**: Juan Montes, Laurence Iliff, and David Luhnow, "Mexico Takes Big Step . . ." *WSJ*, December 13, 2013.

154 **"achieve more, grow more"**: Adam Thomson, "Presidential Hopeful . . ." *FT*, April 4, 2013.

155 **"We can't do it alone"**: John Paul Rathbone and Adam Thomson, "Mexican Reforms Set to Boost Oil Flows," *FT*, February 27, 2013.

155 **"All of the power to"**: Richard Lapper and Nonathan Wheatley, "A Serenade in the Backyard . . ." *FT*, March 8, 2007.

155 **"Capitalist Venezuela is entering"**: Simon Romero, "Chávez's Vision . . ." *NYT*, November 17, 2007.

155 **"The PDVSA that neglected"**: Tina Rosenberg, "The Perils of Petrocracy," *NYT*, November 4, 2007.

155 **"We've struggled for many years"**: Benedict Mander, "Crime Rates Pose Threat . . ." *FT*, June 14, 2012.

155 **"New technology really changed"**: Carola Hoyos, "Tough Choices for Oil . . ." *FT*, September 22, 2004.

156 **"It's naïve to expect stability"**: Stanley Reed, "You're Working for . . ." *BW*, May 15, 2006.

156 **"You think Iraq is"**: Benedict Mander and John Paul Rathbone, "Profligacy Puts Chávez's . . ." *FT*, September 12, 2012.

156 **"when all the oil"**: Ed Crooks and Benedict Mander, "Oil Majors Tread . . ." *FT*, June 28, 2007.

156 **"The Orinoco Belt"**: Benedict Mander, "Fears over Chávez . . ." *FT*, August 31, 2009.

156 **"Finding more oil is"**: James Boxell, "Drilling Is about to Resume . . ." *FT*, December 29, 2004.

157 **"Natural resources should belong"**: Stefan Wagstyl, "Kremlin Man but No Fan of State Control," *FT*, October 19, 2004.

157 **"financial-industrial corporations"**: Kim Murphy, "As Gazprom Grows . . ." *LAT*, October 16, 2005.

157 **"If you have a gas"**: Arkady Ostrovsky, "Winners and Losers in Kremlin . . ." *FT*, November 7, 2005.

158 **"last ally"**: Neil Buckley, "Putin Turns on Belarus with Double Energy Blow," *FT*, December 14, 2006.

158 **"would not lead to good results"**: Neil Buckley, "Russia's Shy Man of Energy," *FT*, April 28, 2006.

158 **"There is no energy imperialism"**: Neil Buckley and Catherine Belton, "Ivanov Sets Out . . ." *FT*, April 19, 2007.

158 **"Sometimes we Poles are"**: Jeffrey Fleishman, "Russia Wields Its New . . ." *LAT*, December 30, 2005.

159 **"They can't bully us"**: James Marson and Joe Parkinson, "In Reversal, Neighbors . . ." *WSJ*, May 1, 2013.

159 **"The conditions can be changed"**: Catherine Belton, "BP under Pressure . . ." *FT*, February 28, 2007.

159 **"I consider this issue"**: Guy Chazan and Gregory L. White, "BP Set to Leave . . ." *WSJ*, June 22, 2007.

159 **"It appears BP was trying"**: Guy Chazan, "BP's Rosneft Bid . . ." *WSJ*, March 28, 2007.

159 **"In Russia, these are"**: Catherine Belton, "BP Pulls Out of Yukos . . ." *FT*, March 28, 2007.

159 **"We go over a cliff"**: Catherine Belton, "Russian Roulette," *FT*, June 5, 2008.

159 **"mystified"**: Guy Chazan, "Head of BP Venture . . ." *WSJ*, July 25, 2008.

160 **"needs to be in Russia"**: Guy Chazan, "BP Faces End . . ." *FT*, June 1, 2012.

160 **"There is no way"**: Guy Chazan, "Rosneft Gives BP . . ." *FT*, July 26, 2012.

160 **"It's not risk-free"**: Guy Chazan and Catherine Belton, "Rosneft Deal Marks . . ." *FT*, October 22, 2012.

161 **"Everyone understands why"**: Andrew E. Kramer, "Russia Revokes Approval . . ." *NYT*, September 18, 2006.

161 **"Give me half of what"**: Abrahm Lustgarten, "How Shell Lost Control," *F*, February 1, 2007.

161 **"There is no confidence"**: Andrew Osborn and Gregory L. White, "TNK-BP Tensions . . ." *WSJ*, June 9, 2008.

161 **"He has obviously decided"**: Ed Crooks, "An Embodiment of Exxon's . . ." *FT*, September 2, 2011.

161 **"never changes"**: Daniel Gilbert, "Exxon Says Russian Projects . . ." *WSJ*, March 5, 2014.

163 **"Technology is not"**: Leslie Hook, "China Faces Difficulties . . ." *FT*, March 28, 2012.

164 **"like being tied to someone"**: Brian Bremner, "Asia's Great Oil Hunt," *BW*, November 15, 2004.

165 **"You've got two very large"**: Mark Magnier, "China Stakes a Claim . . ." *LAT*, July 17, 2005.

166 **"a nightmare for almost"**: Justin Scheck, "A $30 Billion Hole . . ." *WSJ*, April 19, 2013.

166 **"We are very disappointed"**: Guy Chazan, "Kazakhstan Toughens Oil-Project . . ." *WSJ*, August 8, 2007.

166 **"It feels good to be"**: Selina Williams, Geraldine Amiel, and Justin Scheck, "How a Giant Kazakh Oil Project Went Awry," *WSJ*, March 31, 2014.

166 **"responsibility toward the international community"**: Javier Blas, "Go with the Flow?" *FT*, November 15, 2007.

167 **"rising North American shale gas"**: Summer Said and Benoît Faucon, "Shale Threatens Saudi . . ." *WSJ*, July 20, 2013.

167 **"the largest sulfuric acid plant"**: Neil King Jr., "Saudi Industrial Drive . . ." *WSJ*, December 21, 2007.

167 **"We spend our time"**: Roula Khalaf, "Gulf States Struggle . . ." *FT*, April 26, 2007.

167 **"My father wanted only freedom"**: Karen Elliott House, "Host of Conflicting Forces . . ." *WSJ*, April 10, 2007.

168 **"The maximum service fee"**: Carola Hoyos, "Oil Groups Resist . . ." *FT*, July 1, 2009.

169 **"The industry is"**: Bill Spindle, "Soaring Energy Use . . ." *WSJ*, February 20, 2007.

169 **"U.S. sanctions [against Iran] will"**: Vivienne Walt, "Iran Looks East," *F*, February 21, 2005.

169 **"The Iranians have never really"**: Amy Yee and Najmeh Bezorgmehr, "Iran Close to India-Pakistan . . ." *FT*, June 30, 2007.

170 **"Pakistan needs gas very badly"**: Saeed Shah, "Iran-Pakistan Cross-Border . . ." *WSJ*, September 26, 2013.

170 **"The surge in religious extremism"**: Yasmine El-Rashidi, "In Kuwait, Gush..." *WSJ*, November 4, 2005.

171 **"You won't even get"**: Camilla Hall and Simeon Kerr, "Global Expansion Puts Qatars..." *FT*, February 10, 2013.

171 **"We are all Tunisians"**: Leila Hatoum, "Gulf States Curtail..." *WSJ*, April 2, 2013.

172 **"The game-changer here"**: Thomas Catan, "'Designer Fuel' Fires..." *FT*, March 6, 2006.

172 **"Supposing we had oil"**: Seth Mydans and Wayne Arnold, "Modern Singapore's Creator..." *NYT*, September 2, 2007.

172 **"For once, I am almost"**: William Wallis, "Curse of Oil Follows Ghana's Former President," *FT*, October 25, 2010.

172 **"Countries, when they have this"**: Alexis Flynn, "Mozambique's Leader Weighs..." *WSJ*, July 29, 2013.

173 **"We all have our fears"**: Sylvia Pfeifer, Xan Rice, and Andrew England, "Energy: Trial by Oil," *FT*, January 11, 2013.

173 **"I think it's worrying everyone"**: Thomas Catan and Dino Mahtani, "Shell's Problems in Nigeria..." *FT*, April 6, 2006.

173 **"Hostage rescue capacity is"**: Dino Mahtani, "Militants Free Oil Hostages..." *FT*, January 20, 2006.

173 **"workers should not be deceived"**: Dino Mahtani, "Delta Militants Release..." *FT*, March 27, 2006.

173 **"goal remains to paralyze"**: Bashir Adigun, "Nigeria's Main Militant Group..." *Pittsburgh Post-Gazette*, January 4, 2008.

174 **"decided against smoking out"**: Matthew Green, "Shell Shuts Oilfield..." *FT*, June 20, 2008.

174 **"All pipelines, flow stations"**: Chip Cummins, "As Oil Supplies Are Stretched..." *WSJ*, April 10, 2006.

174 **"There were 100 bunkering boats"**: "Nigeria, Shell Plan $1.6..." *WSJ*, February 24, 2009.

174 **"We are like mosquitoes"**: Matthew Green, "Fiendish Terrain Presents..." *FT*, September 23, 2008.

175 **"There is complete, total breakdown"**: Matthew Green, "Lagos State Governor Puts Others..." *FT*, July 21, 2009.

175 **"Danger!!!"**: Michael Peel, "Deep Well of Troubles..." *FT*, June 9, 2004.

175 **"What Gazprom is proposing"**: Matthew Green and Catherine Belton, "Gazprom Plans Africa Gas..." *FT*, January 5, 2008.

176 **"us building the foundation"**: Will Connors, "Oil Majors Race..." *WSJ*, November 24, 2009.

176 **"I don't see anything wrong"**: Drew Hinshaw, "Nigeria's Former Oil Bandits . . ." *WSJ*, August 22, 2012.

176 **"You will never find"**: Patrick Dele Cole, "Why Choke the Goose . . ." *FT*, July 24, 2012.

176 **"Every family has someone involved"**: William Wallis, "Bunkering," *FT*, June 27, 2012.

176 **"highest rental market"**: Alec Russel, "Sky-High Rents in Rundown . . ." *FT*, October 9, 2007.

177 **"It doesn't work if you"**: Tom Burgis, "Angola's Vicente Rejects . . ." *FT*, June 15, 2012.

177 **"The ruling elite"**: Alec Russell, "Investors Sign Up . . ." *FT*, August 23, 2007.

177 **"The west legitimises this mockery"**: John Reed, "Oil-Rich Angola Seeks . . ." *FT*, November 14, 2005.

5. MINING

179 **"The U.S. market for coal"**: Kris Maher, "Coal Industry to Fight . . ." *WSJ*, June 27, 2013.

179 **"without question, unprecedented"**: Russell Gold, Rebecca Smith, and Daniel Gilbert, "Gas Glut Rejiggers . . ." *WSJ*, April 10, 2012.

179 **"We have given *force majeure*"**: Javier Blas, "Miners Hit by Coal . . ." *FT*, June 18, 2012.

180 **"Obama's starving us out"**: Kris Maher and Tom McGinty, "Coals Decline Hits . . ." *WSJ*, November 27, 2013.

181 **"It is impossible for"**: Shai Oster, "Illegal Power Plants . . ." *WSJ*, December 27, 2006.

182 **"We are very good"**: Shai Oster, "Big Chinese Miner . . ." *WSJ*, January 31, 2007.

182 **"British Coal announced today"**: William E. Schmidt, "Britain to Shut Most . . ." *NYT*, October 14, 1992.

182 **"like an opening at Ikea"**: Rebecca Bream, "'King Coal' to Reopen . . ." *FT*, April 18, 2006.

184 **"It's probably the fastest"**: Jim Yardley and Vikas Bajaj, "Billionaires' Rise Aids . . ." *NYT*, July 26, 2011.

185 **"Logistics are always the challenge"**: John W. Miller and Paul Kiernan, "Anglo American Miner . . ." *WSJ*, June 10, 2013.

185 **"fabulous, unlike anything else"**: Tom Burgis, Helen Thomas, and Misha Glenny, "Guinea Reignites . . ." *FT*, November 3–4, 2012.

186 **"I have absolutely no doubt"**: Tom Burgis, Helen Thomas, and Misha Glenny, "Guinea: What Lies Beneath," *FT*, November 8, 2012.

186 **"Looking at the iron ore"**: Patrick Radden Keefe, "Buried Secrets," NY, July 8 and 15, 2013.

187 **"It's comforting"**: Evelyn Iritani, "Minnesota Town Sees ..." LAT, July 10, 2006.

187 **"Ensuring a reliable source"**: Robert Guy Matthews, "World's Steelmakers Go ..." WSJ, June 20, 2008.

188 **"I needed a horse"**: James Kynge, "Shock and Ore," FT, March 18, 2006.

189 **"one of the best mills"**: John Miller, "Indiana Steel Mill Revived with Lessons from Abroad," WSJ, May 21, 2012.

189 **"totally absurd"**: John Thornhill, "Forget the Bogeyman, Arcelor Owners Must Decide ..." FT, February 1, 2006.

189 **"This is the biggest battle"**: Peter Marsh, "Ambitious Man of Steel," FT, February 3, 2006.

189 **"You can't say no"**: Stanley Reed, "Mittal & Son," BW, April 16, 2007.

189 **"If you look at"**: Marsh, "Ambitious Man of Steel."

190 **"What we can bring"**: Stanley Reed, "The Raja of Steel," BW, December 20, 2004.

191 **"I have not stopped"**: Peter Marsh, "Mittal Steels Himself ..." FT, April 27, 2009.

191 **"I love steel"**: John W. Miller, "Steel Titan Mittal ..." WSJ, December 15–16, 2012.

191 **"The opportunities are huge"**: Peter Marsh, "Prospects for the Steel Industry Are Being Reignited," FT, March 2, 2006.

191 **"any obvious synergy effects"**: Peter Marsh, "Posco's Chief Rules Out ..." FT, October 5, 2006.

193 **"wonderful, world-class product, but"**: John W. Miller, "ThyssenKrupp Selling ..." WSJ, October 2, 2012.

197 **"the biggest gold heist"**: John H. Cushman Jr., "Forced, U.S. Sells Gold ..." NYT, May 17, 1994.

197 **"Nevada is being written off"**: Kirk Johnson, "Drier, Tainted Nevada ..." NYT, December 30, 2005.

198 **"unsuitable for aquatic life"**: Jane Perlez, "Below a Mountain of Wealth ..." NYT, December 27, 2005.

198 **"To us, you take"**: Shawn Donnan and Rebecca Bream, "Protests Grow over Group's ..." FT, April 11, 2006.

199 **"eliminated many environmental safeguards"**: Jane Perlez and Lowell Bergman, "Tangled Strands in Fight ..." NYT, October 25, 2005.

199 **"The mining industry is judged"**: Rebecca Bream, "Mining Counts the Cost ..." FT, January 16, 2006.

199 **"must learn something new"**: Robyn Dixon, "Africans Lash Out . . ." *LAT*, October 6, 2006.

199 **"The Chinese are far more"**: Craig Timberg, "In Africa, China Trade . . ." *WP*, June 13, 2006.

199 **"That's how they run things"**: R. W. Johnson, "China's Empire-Builders," *Sunday Times* (London), July 16, 2006.

199 **"Their interest is exploiting us"**: Lydia Polgreen and Howard W. French, "China's Trade in Africa . . ." *NYT*, August 20, 2007.

200 **"You know, they are"**: Barry Bearak, "Zambia Uneasily Balances . . ." *NYT*, November 20, 2010.

200 **"Katanga is not a jungle"**: Barney Jopson, "Chinese Copper Entrepreneurs . . ." *FT*, February 19, 2009.

200 **"Sending raw materials out"**: Polgreen and French, "China's Trade in Africa."

200 **"Talk of financial returns"**: Shibani Mahtani, "Chinese Company Launches . . ." *WSJ*, October 10, 2013.

200 **"You have got to be"**: Antonio Regalado, "Brazilian Mining Titan . . ." *WSJ*, April 25, 2008.

201 **"I think it will be"**: Dennis K. Berman, "Alcoa's Stint . . ." *WSJ*, January 29, 2008.

201 **"Consolidation is unstoppable"**: Robert Guy Matthews, "Drought May Spur . . ." *WSJ*, June 6, 2008.

201 **"Alcoa certainly looks like"**: Paul Glader, "Tio-Alcan Deal . . ." *WSJ*, July 13, 2007.

201 **"These executives are political appointees"**: Jamil Anderlini and Sundeep Tucker, "Outmanoeuvred," *FT*, June 12, 2009.

202 **"This has never happened"**: Simon Romero, "Big Tires in Short Supply," *NYT*, April 20, 2006.

202 **"We can't compete with"**: Neil Hume, "Australia: Mine, All Mine," *FT*, June 18, 2012.

6. FARMING

205 **"Farmers tend to be pessimists"**: Jon Birger, "The Great Corn Gold Rush," *F*, March 20, 2007.

205 **"This is the best"**: Gregory Meyer and Hal Weitzman, "US Farm Subsidies Attacked amid Boom," *FT*, February 22, 2012.

205 **"We are embarking on"**: Christopher Swann, "US Thirst for Ethanol Trims Corn for Export," *FT*, May 24, 2006.

205 **"For the young farmer"**: Monica Davey, "Ethanol Is Feeding . . ." *NYT*, August 8, 2007.

205 **"Nobody predicted this kind"**: Joe Barrett, "Hog Farmers Face . . ." *WSJ*, June 20, 2008.

205 **"You eat eggs"**: Mary Kissel, "It's Getting Harder . . ." *WSJ*, August 20, 2011.

205 **"One farmer's high output price"**: Gregory Meyer and Hal Weitzman, "US Farmers Flourish . . ." *FT*, March 30, 2011.

205 **"These high feed prices"**: Gregory Meyer, "US Farmers Reel . . ." *FT*, October 26, 2012.

206 **"There are unintended consequences"**: Alexei Barrionuevo, "Boom in Ethanol . . ." *NYT*, June 25, 2006.

206 **"allow more of the crop"**: José Graziano da Silva, "The US Must Take Biofuel . . ." *FT*, August 9, 2012.

206 **"mandated burning of our food"**: Gregory Meyer, "Commodities: Against the Grain," *FT*, April 22, 2013.

207 **"incumbents and challengers"**: Barrionuevo, "Boom in Ethanol."

207 **"living off their welfare checks"**: Dan Morgan, Gilbert M. Gaul, and Sarah Cohen, "Farm Program Pays . . ." *WP*, October 15, 2006.

208 **"We don't envision farmers"**: Scott Kilman, "Crop Prices Erode . . ." *WSJ*, July 25, 2011.

208 **"I live to get to play"**: Mark Peters, "Drought Hurts Crops . . ." *WSJ*, August 1, 2012.

209 **"It's a great gig"**: Dean E. Murphy, "Water Contract Renewals . . ." *NYT*, December 15, 2004.

210 **"Processing and marketing"**: Jerry Hirsch, "Profits out of Reach . . ." *LAT*, November 13, 2004.

210 **"Almonds are like Las Vegas"**: Malia Wollan, "Looking for Gold . . ." *WSJ*, September 6, 2007.

213 **"Seeds can be blown"**: *Bowman v. Monsanto*, quoted in Brent Kendall, "Supreme Court Hears Farmer's . . ." *WSJ*, February 20, 2012.

214 **"I have been dealing with this"**: Marc Gunther, "Attack of the Mutant Rice," *F*, July 2, 2007.

214 **"The most widely grown GM crop"**: Clive Cookson, "GM Crops Continue . . ." *FT*, February 12, 2009.

214 **"Companies like Monsanto"**: Raphael Minder and Jeremy Grant, "Transatlantic Split Persists . . ." *FT*, January 31, 2006.

215 **"We see this as opening"**: Melanie Warner, "What Is Organic?" *NYT*, November 1, 2005.

216 **"It would be great"**: Gail Edmondson, "The Organic Myth," *BW*, October 16, 2006.

216 **"very healthy and happy"**: Warner, "What Is Organic?"

216 **"Organic food is not only"**: Kate Galbraith, "Agribusiness Chief Slams Organics," NYT, November 25, 2009.

216 **"We're devoting a lot"**: Lauren Etter and Antonio Regalado, "ADM Plans Entry . . ." WSJ, June 22, 2007.

217 **"a lot of nice houses"**: Antonio Regalado and Grace Fan, "Ethanol Giants Struggle . . ." WSJ, September 10, 2007.

217 **"The sky's the limit"**: Jonathan Wheatley, "Brazil Grabs Juicier . . ." FT, July 6, 2007.

217 **"we don't buy cattle"**: Joe Leahy, "JBS and Greenpeace Lock Horns . . ." FT, June 20, 2012.

217 **"Wherever a combine can go"**: Joshua Schneyer, "Brazil's Answer to Global," BW, May 22, 2008.

218 **"built one of the biggest"**: Leahy, "JBS and Greenpeace Lock Horns."

218 **"I love your country"**: Joe Leahy, "Superport Is Brazil's . . ." FT, May 9, 2011.

219 **"Can this be true?"**: Susanna B. Hecht and Charles C. Mann, "How Brazil Outfarmed . . ." F, January 2008.

219 **"I'm learning lessons"**: Marla Dickerson, "Planting Themselves in Brazil . . ." LAT, November 20, 2006.

219 **"The soybean crisis has been"**: Elizabeth Johnson, "Brazil Farmers Find . . ." FT, November 2, 2006.

219 **"Just because we're producing"**: Alexei Barrionuevo, "To Fortify China . . ." NYT, April 6, 2007.

220 **"children of corn"**: Jean Guerrero, "Altered Corn Slowly . . ." WSJ, December 10, 2010.

220 **"We're not even covering"**: Marla Dickerson, "In Mexico, Farmers See . . ." LAT, April 1, 2006.

221 **"I don't think the Windward Islands"**: Carol J. Williams, "Globalization Uproots Island's . . ." LAT, April 9, 2006.

221 **"Here, people care about food"**: Scott Miller, "French Resistance to Trade . . ." WSJ, May 16, 2006.

222 **"There is no clear link"**: Andrew Bounds, "Communists and Royalty Fight Farm Subsidy Cuts," FT, November 21, 2007.

222 **"Europe will be a continent"**: Guy Dinmore, "Sardinia's Farmers Fend . . ." FT, December 4, 2007.

223 **"Agriculture will be an area"**: John W. Miller, "Chinese Fruit May . . ." WSJ, December 22, 2006.

223 **"almost commercial suicide"**: Raphael Minder and Jeremy Grant, "Crop Resistance . . ." FT, January 31, 2006.

223 **"clever genetic engineering"**: Jenny Wiggins and Jim Pickard, "Prince Accused of . . ." FT, August 14, 2008.

223 **"All political parties are opposed"**: Elisabeth Rosenthal, "In EU, Front Lines in a Global War," NYT, May 24, 2006.

223 **"a multitude of organisms"**: Craig S. Smith, "A Project to Remodel . . ." NYT, September 27, 2005.

223 **"Let's just say the outside"**: Haig Simonian, "Seeds of Growth," FT, June 18, 2008.

224 **"end of GM in Britain"**: Alok Jha, "Return of GM," G, September 17, 2007.

225 **"The trade in wine is"**: Stephen Castle, "The EU Wants Farmers . . ." in NYT, August 3, 2007.

226 **"I think we can all"**: Raphael Minder, "Wine Growers to Feel Squeeze under Broad Overhaul," FT, June 23, 2006.

226 **"You are free now"**: Michael Specter, "Crisis of Bread and Land . . ." NYT, September 19, 1994.

227 **"above and beyond anything else"**: Andrew E. Kramer, "Russia's Collective Farms . . ." NYT, August 31, 2008.

227 **"Unless you agree with"**: Catherine Belton, "The Battle to Bring More . . ." FT, September 30, 2008.

227 **"usually only one winner"**: Andrew Peaple, "BP Bows to the Inevitable . . ." WSJ, October 18, 2012.

227 **"There is no good reason"**: Charles Clover, "Better Productivity Is Seen . . ." FT, June 21, 2012.

227 **"standing on a graveyard"**: Sabrina Tavernise, "Old Farming Habits . . ." NYT, June 15, 2008.

228 **"Of course, I have"**: Anna Bochenska, "Smallholders Sit Tight . . ." FT, December 8, 2008.

229 **"through the use of better"**: Roger Thurow, "Agriculture's Last Frontier," WSJ, May 27, 2008.

230 **"I believe fertilizer is"**: Katrina Manson, "Aid Lifts Kenyan Maize Farmers' Fortunes," G&M, August 15, 2012.

230 **"The whole basis of"**: Alan Beattie, "Seeds of Change," FT, June 3, 2008.

231 **"a malaria-infested swamp"**: Jessica Silver-Greenberg, "Land Rush in Africa," BW, November 25, 2009.

231 **"We have seen a scramble"**: Neil MacFarquhar, "African Farmers Losing . . ." NYT, December 21, 2010.

232 **"Boko Haram will not"**: Drew Hinshaw, "Africa's Richest Man . . ." WSJ, December 27, 2013.

233 **"If the U.S. were to"**: Heba Saleh, "Egypt's Cotton Traders . . ." FT, August 3, 2009.

233 **"Fifty or a hundred bucks"**: Celia W. Dugger, "Oxfam Suggests Benefit . . ." NYT, June 21, 2007.

234 **"People who formulate policy"**: Raymond Zhong and Saptorishi Dutta, "India Suffers . . ." *WSJ*, April 13, 2014.

234 **"I can't find enough people"**: Biman Mukherjee, "Farmers in India Start . . ." *WSJ*, October 29, 2013.

235 **"To my mind"**: John Ridding, "Heard It on the Grapevine," *FT*, February 5, 2005.

235 **"We have sent over"**: Jo John and Khozem Merchant, "India's Phones-to-Farms . . ." *FT*, October 19, 2005.

235 **"can only be done through"**: "Bring Back the Landlords," *E*, May 3, 2014.

235 **"The gap between the modern"**: Richard McGregor, "China's Farmers Change . . ." *FT*, May 9, 2008.

236 **"Farms of two or three"**: Louise Lucas and Leslie Hook, "Land of Milk and Money," *FT*, October 15, 2012.

236 **"It's my dream to introduce"**: Frederik Balfour, "Potations from Chairman . . ." *BW*, October 9, 2006.

238 **"I've been to the Hoover Dam"**: Jim Yardley, "Beneath Booming Cities . . ." *NYT*, September 28, 2007.

239 **"1,000 pounds in an envelope"**: Rahul Jacob, "Organic Pork Row . . ." *FT*, October 11, 2011.

239 **"My long-term competitors"**: Doug Cameron, "Rivals Give Monsanto . . ." *FT*, September 5, 2007.

239 **"never tolerate GM soybeans"**: Hiroko Tabuchi, "High Soybean Prices . . ." *WSJ*, May 15, 2008.

7. DEVELOPING

241 **"People drink"**: Kim Murphy, "A Dying Population . . ." *LAT*, October 8, 2006.

241 **"system was such that"**: Arkady Ostrovsky, "An Outsider Strives . . ." *FT*, August 31, 2006.

242 **"Quality of life here"**: Barney Jopson, "Village Life," *FT*, November 7, 2007.

242 **"You guys always talk"**: Jeffrey Gettleman, "Serengeti Road Plan Offers Prospects and Fears," *NYT*, October 30, 2010.

243 **"We are in a very critical situation"**: Joe Leahy and Arush Chopra, "Left Behind . . ." *FT*, August 25, 2008.

243 **"We need to move some people"**: Jim Yardley, "Drought Puts Focus . . ." *NYT*, September 5, 2009.

243 **"Close to 270 million people"**: Joe Leahy and James Fontanella-Khan, "Squeezed Out . . ." *FT*, December 17, 2010.

243 **"Unless something radical is done"**: Somini Sengupta, "In India, Maoist . . ." *NYT*, April 13, 2006.

243 **"excellent revolutionary situation"**: Jo Johnson, "Leftist Insurgents Kill . . ." *FT*, March 16, 2007.

244 **"None of this would have"**: P. Sinath, "Farm Suicides . . ." *TH*, March 16, 2006.

244 **"Let's finally cleanse our village"**: Yaroslav Trofimov, "Brutal Attack in India . . ." *WSJ*, December 27, 2007.

245 **"We don't want to see"**: Emily Wax, "A 'Broken People' in Booming India," *WP*, June 21, 2007.

245 **"a den of ignorance"**: Amy Waldman, "All Roads Lead to Cities," *NYT*, December 7, 2005.

245 **"Life here is so miserable"**: Maureen Fan, "Two Chinese Villages . . ." *WP*, August 1, 2006.

246 **"There's no way not to leave"**: Ian Johnson and Andrew Batson, "China's Migrants See . . ." *WSJ*, February 3, 2009.

246 **"At about 8 p.m."**: Howard W. French, "20 Reported Killed . . ." *NYT*, December 10, 2005.

246 **"returned a couple of weeks"**: Edward Cody, "Bulldozed by Growth . . ." *WP*, March 26, 2006.

247 **"If all the farmland"**: Rahul Jacob and Zhou Ping, "Local Leader Challenged . . ." *FT*, September 25, 2011.

247 **"This is a picture"**: Rahul Jacob, "Wukan Challenges Party . . ." *FT*, February 10, 2012.

248 **"We will conduct"**: José de Córdoba, "To Fix Venezuela . . ." *WSJ*, December 24, 2004.

248 **"The revolution is here"**: José de Córdoba, "The Revolution Is Here . . ." *WSJ*, May 17, 2007.

248 **"We're now squatters"**: Marc Lacey, "Tribe, Claiming Whites' Land, Confronts Kenya's Government," *NYT*, August 25, 2004.

249 **"Land reform is going nowhere"**: Alec Russell, "Fenced In," *FT*, November 5, 2007.

249 **"We must take the land"**: Peter Wonacott, "As Reforms Stall . . ." *WSJ*, June 21, 2011.

249 **"They're producing nothing"**: Robyn Dixon, "Angry and Unyielding . . ." *LAT*, October 3, 2007.

249 **"All the big guys"**: Lydia Polgreen, "In Zimbabwe Land . . ." *NYT*, July 20, 2012.

250 **"You can't have a civilized world"**: Daphne Eviatar, "Spend $150 Billion . . ." *NYT*, November 7, 2004.

250 **"Slowly, fitfully"**: Jeffrey Sachs, "U.S. Leadership May Be Set to Reach a Consensus with the World's Poorest," *FT*, September 13, 2005.

250 "**I reject the plaintive cries**": Jeffrey Sachs, *The End of Poverty: Economic Possibilities for Our Time* (New York: Penguin, 2006), 328.

251 "**into the problem**": Jeffrey Gettleman, "Shower of Aid Brings Flood of Progress," NYT, March 8, 2010.

251 "**What we're focusing on**": Sachs, *End of Poverty*.

252 "**I would say to them**": John Vidal, "India's Rice Revolution," G, February 23, 2013.

252 "**One farmer sees another's field**": Geeta Anand, "Green Revolution in India Wilts as Subsidies Backfire," WSJ, February 22, 2010.

253 "**incredibly inefficient and hopelessly unscalable**": Eric Bellman, "Entrepreneur Gets Big Banks . . ." WSJ, May 15, 2006.

254 "**Mobile-phone growth**": David Pringle, "Slower Growth Hits . . ." WSJ, May 23, 2005.

254 "**Can an elephant**": Dexter Roberts, "China Mobile's Hot Signal," BW, January 25, 2007.

255 "**My main motivation**": Elizabeth Rosenthal, "African Huts Far . . ." NYT, December 24, 2010.

255 "**huge companies, hugely resourced**": Clay Chandler, "Wireless Wonder," F, January 17, 2007.

256 "**Before, we had to travel**": Roberts, "China Mobile's Hot Signal."

257 "**All of a sudden**": Amy Yee, "Banishing the Negative . . ." FT, January 25, 2006.

257 "**I can run my business**": Eric Bellman, "In India, Rural Poor . . ." WSJ, September 24, 2007.

257 "**Even if it takes**": Kevin Sullivan, "Cellphones Dial Up . . ." WP, October 15, 2006.

257 "**One woman living on**": Sharon LaFraniere, "Cellphones Catapult Rural . . ." NYT, August 25, 2005.

258 "**So a 126 kg bag**": Barney Jopson, "How Safaricom Gives . . ." FT, October 9, 2007.

258 "**It has totally changed life**": Kevin Sullivan, "In War-Torn Congo . . ." WP, July 9, 2006.

259 "**Why would I send**": Anand Giridharadas, "The Ink Fades . . ." NYT, December 26, 2007.

259 "**The village accountant was corrupt**": Manjeet Kripalani, "The Digital Village," BW, June 28, 2004.

260 "**People are always talking**": Stephanie Nolen, "African Legal Judgments . . ." G&M, July 18, 2007.

260 "**Show me a 50-foot wall**": Geri Smith and Keith Epstein, "On the Border," BW, February 7, 2008.

261 **"We're never going to stop them"**: Miguel Bustillo, "Agents' Chase Never Ends," LAT, August 13, 2006.

261 **"It's like catch-and-release fishing"**: Timothy Egan, "Border Desert Proves . . ." NYT, May 23, 2004.

261 **"I see so much waste"**: Ginger Thompson, "Desperation on Unforgiving . . ." NYT, May 21, 2006.

261 **"They can't stop us"**: Damien Cave, "Mexican Immigrants Repeatedly . . ." NYT, October 2, 2011.

261 **"To live in America"**: Miriam Jordan, "Crossings by Migrants Slow . . ." WSJ, April 9, 2008.

261 **"We have turned the page"**: Miriam Jordan, "Mexican Immigration Wave . . ." WSJ, April 23, 2012.

261 **"I know it sounds strange"**: Alfredo Corchado, "New Land of Opportunity," DMN, August 25, 2007.

262 **"inhuman conditions"**: Felicity Lawrence, "Bitter Harvest," G, December 18, 2006.

262 **"I cannot go home empty-handed"**: Suzanne Daley, "Chasing Riches from Africa . . ." NYT, May 25, 2011.

262 **"Everyone here talks about migrating"**: Roula Khalaf, "Moroccans Ready to Risk . . ." FT, October 12, 2004.

262 **"Everyone wants to have"**: Robyn Dixon, "A Passage Buoyed by Hope . . ." LAT, March 16, 2007.

263 **"I went back"**: Pierre Daum, "The Summer Return . . ." *Le Monde Diplomatique*, September 2007.

263 **"We don't want"**: Mary Jordan, "An Island Engulfed by Migrants . . ." WP, June 4, 2006.

263 **"We were already dead"**: Ian Fisher, "For African Migrants, Europe . . ." NYT, August 26, 2007.

264 **"What's wrong with everyone"**: Richard McGregor and Krishna Guha, "Paulson Sides with China's . . ." FT, September 20, 2006.

264 **"Anything you can think of"**: Amol Sharma, "Trade Gap Strains . . ." WSJ, August 3, 2012.

264 **"It's a mistake to try"**: Joseph Kahn, "In China's Cities, Growth Takes Its Toll," WSJ, December 22, 1993.

264 **"We treat the companies"**: Tom Mitchell and Geoff Dyer, "Heat in the Workshop . . ." FT, October 15, 2007.

264 **"One Big Step Every Year"**: Leslie T. Chang, *Factory Girls: From Village to City in a Changing China* (New York: Spiegel & Grau, 2008), 42.

265 **"The short answer to why"**: Robert Wright, "For Alstom China . . ." FT, October 26, 2006.

265 **"How are you supposed to"**: Norihiko Shirouzu, "Train Makers Rail against . . ." WSJ, November 17, 2010.

265 **"Operating in China is"**: Peter Marsh, "In Search of Inspiration . . ." FT, June 12, 2012.

265 **"I am not sure"**: Geoff Dyer, "Immelt Hits out . . ." FT, July 20, 2010.

266 **"We're seeing an end"**: David Barboza, "Labor Shortage in China May Lead to Trade Shift," NYT, April 3, 2006.

266 **"Operating in Southern China is"**: Kathy Chu, "China Manufacturers Survive . . ." WSJ, May 1, 2013.

266 **"We already give them"**: Jon Hilsenrath, Laurie Burkett, and Elizabeth Holmes, "U.S. Faces Costlier . . ." WSJ, June 21, 2011.

266 **"We are looking to move"**: Elizabeth Holmes, "Rising Costs Force Apparel . . ." WSJ, June 15, 2010.

267 **"The answer to high prices"**: Dexter Roberts, "China Factory Blues," BW, March 27, 2008.

267 **"We will become"**: Kathrin Hille, "China's Computer Makers . . ." FT, May 23, 2011.

267 **"the Nike product"**: Shelly Banjo, "Inside Nike's Struggle . . ." WSJ, April 21, 2014.

267 **"never increases one penny"**: Dexter Roberts and Pete Engardio, "Secrets, Lies, and Sweatshops," BW, November 27, 2006.

268 **"may seem prosperous"**: Howard W. French, "Chinese Success Story Chokes on Its Own Growth," NYT, December 19, 2006.

268 **"We work from 8 a.m."**: Stephen Glain, "A Tale of Two Chinas," *Smithsonian*, May 2006.

268 **"I think they are suffering"**: Jim Yardley, "Rural Exodus for Work . . ." NYT, December 21, 2004.

269 **"We really need them"**: Tom Orlik, "How China Lost Its Mojo," WSJ, September 17, 2013.

269 **"It's the prices"**: Stephanie Wong, John Liu, and Tim Culpan, "Why Apple and Others Are Nervous," BW, April 26, 2010.

270 **"China won't have a competitor"**: Jason Dean and Peter Stein, "Hon Hai Looks to China's . . ." WSJ, September 4, 2010.

270 **"I believe it was"**: Kathrin Hille, "The Asian Tycoon with . . ." FT, August 5, 2011.

270 **"a harsh environment"**: Sarah Mishkin and Samantha Pearson, "Foxconn Challenged . . ." FT, January 4, 2013.

270 **"This is a watershed"**: Andrew Batson and Norihiko Shirouzu, "Chinese Strikers Win Raises . . ." WSJ, June 7, 2010.

270 **"Today we are going to"**: Robin Kwong, "Foxconn Reviews Factory Town . . ." *FT*, June 8, 2010.

270 **"It is so rare"**: Kathrin Hille, "Foxconn's Supply Chain . . ." *FT*, September 26, 2012.

271 **"I worship Chairman Mao"**: Jamil Anderlini, Patti Waldmeir, Kathrin Hille, and Simon Rabinovitch, "Welcome to the Party!" *FT*, September 29–30, 2012.

271 **"We just had a seminar"**: Jamil Anderlini, "How Long Can the Communist Party . . ." *FT*, September 20, 2013.

271 **"Americans have rights"**: Martin Wolf, "China's Rise Need Not Bring . . ." *FT*, September 15, 2005.

271 **"Many entrepreneurs have given up"**: John Bussey, "Inside China, Getting Rich . . ." *WSJ*, August 17, 2012.

272 **"China is controlled"**: Minxin Pei, "The Chinese Awakening," *WSJ*, July 30, 2012.

272 **"worst of all worlds"**: Kathrin Hille, "China's Maoists Rue Decline . . ." *FT*, September 15–16, 2012.

272 **"The fundamental problem is"**: Jamil Anderlini, "China Reform Drive Boosted . . ." *FT*, April 27, 2012.

272 **"When you get down"**: Jeremy Page, "Chinese Trial Is Test . . ." *WSJ*, August 8, 2012.

272 **"unstable, monumentally inefficient"**: Will Hutton, "Power Corruption and Lies," *G*, January 7–9, 2007.

272 **"little interest in real reforms"**: Minxin Pei, "China Is Stagnating in Its 'Trapped Transition,'" *FT*, February 23, 2006.

272 **"a lot of indoctrination"**: Mitchell Landsberg, "A Low for Marx . . ." *LAT*, June 26, 2007.

273 **"Meritocracy has been eroded"**: Jamil Anderlini, "China's Growth Model 'Unsustainable,'" *FT*, December 23, 2010.

273 **"The core content of communism"**: Maureen Fan, "Confucius Making a Comeback in Money-Driven Modern China," *WP*, July 24, 2007.

273 **"The word alone is enough"**: Andrew Jacobs, "Accused Chinese Party Members Face Harsh Discipline," *NYT*, June 15, 2012.

273 **"Tiananmen is the event"**: Will Hutton, "New China. New Crisis," *Observer*, June 6, 2007.

273 **"Saluting the strong mothers"**: Jonathan Watts, "Chinese Newspaper Editors Fired over Tiananmen Square Ad," *G*, June 7, 2007.

274 **"menstruating women were shackled"**: Jim Yardley, "Issue in China: Many in Jails without . . ." *NYT*, May 9, 2005.

274 **"If you go after legal justice"**: Jim Yardley, "Desperate Search for Justice . . ." *NYT*, November 12, 2005.

274 **"pushed to extract admissions"**: Joseph Kahn, "Torture Is 'Widespread' . . ." *NYT*, December 2, 2005.

274 **"On the fourth day"**: Joseph Kahn, "Deep Flaws, and Little Justice . . ." *NYT*, September 21, 2005.

274 **"Now they are riding"**: David Pilling, "This Is a Painful Kind of Existence,"*FT*, December 12, 2008.

274 **"no fresh ideas"**: Jamil Anderlini, "How Long Can the Communist Party Survive in China?" *FT*, September 20, 2013.

275 **"Everyone is corrupt"**: Jamil Anderlini and Lucy Hornby, "Xi's 'Tiger' Hunt . . ." *FT*, July 29, 2014.

275 **"Manufacturing jobs will get created"**: Jo Johnson, "India Gains Credibility . . ." *FT*, November 30, 2005.

275 **"Low-cost workers do not provide"**: Peter Marsh, "Effort to Transport Domestic Success . . ." *FT*, January 26, 2006.

276 **"Tens of millions"**: David Wessel and Bob Davis, "Pain from Free Trade Spurs Second Thoughts," *WSJ*, March 28, 2007.

276 **"The lowest qualification"**: Victor Mallet, "Welcome to Megacity . . ." *FT*, August 5, 2006.

276 **"We thought, 'Why not'"**: Lydia Polgreen, "Rural India Gets Chance . . ." *NYT*, November 13, 2009.

276 **"Anything that can be sent"**: Jo Johnson, "The Great Leveller," *FT*, July 22, 2006.

277 **"productively docile workers"**: Amelia Gentleman, "Painful Truth of the Call Centre," *G*, October 20, 2005.

277 **"Nobody wants arts or history"**: S. Mitra Kalita, "India's New Faces of Outsourcing," *WP*, January 11, 2006.

277 **"The quality of the people"**: David Wighton, "JPMorgan Steps Up Offshoring," *FT*, December 5, 2005.

277 **"open to working at home"**: James Lamont and Joe Leahy, "US: Call Center Wages . . ." *FT*, August 17, 2010.

277 **"We're convinced that India's time"**: Jo Johnson, "Manufacturing Finally Comes . . ." *FT*, January 25, 2006.

278 **"I am not going to"**: Khozem Merchant, "IBM to invest $6bn . . ." *FT*, June 7, 2006.

278 **"We have to play"**: Aditya Chakrabortty, "Cars Edge out Cows . . ." *FT*, August 29, 2005.

278 **"It is Kolkata"**: Joanna Slater, "Influx of Tech Jobs Ushers . . ." *WSJ*, April 29, 2004.

278 **"India's renaissance"**: Jo Johnson, "Communists under Scrutiny in India Poll," *FT*, April 17, 2006.

278 **"I go out and work"**: Waldman, "All Roads Lead to Cities."

278 **"dropped in China's infrastructure"**: Alex Frew McMillan, "India's Market Lures Many . . ." *NYT*, November 22, 2006.

280 **"Any major electronics manufacturer"**: Victor Mallet and James Crabtree, "India: Industrial Evolution . . ." *FT*, May 5, 2014.

280 **"In this country"**: Vikas Bajaj and Jim Yardley, "Scandal Bares Corruption . . ." *NYT*, September 15, 2012.

280 **"China has world-class manufacturing"**: Jo Johnson, "India Gains Credibility . . ." *FT*, January 25, 2006.

281 **"You drive up to it"**: Joe Leahy, "Dilemmas Hurt the Property Market . . ." *FT*, May 8, 2007.

281 **"If you have to build"**: Steve Hamm, "The Trouble with India," *BW*, March 19, 2007.

281 **"India is a democracy"**: Peter Wonacott, "In India, Clashes Erupt . . ." *WSJ*, May 21, 2007.

281 **"I enjoy the natural surroundings"**: Amy Kazmin, "India Wrestles with Rival . . ." *FT*, August 27, 2012.

281 **"I am 100 percent satisfied"**: Eric Bellman, "Tata Motors Plant Divides . . ." *WSJ*, September 5, 2008.

281 **"There can be no industry"**: Joe Leahy, "Tata Flooded with Offers . . ." *FT*, August 26, 2008.

281 **"When the police come"**: Jo Johnson, "Drive to Develop Singur . . ." *FT*, October 21, 2006.

282 **"know how many 15-billion-rupee"**: Eric Bellman and Santanu Choudhury, "Tata Chairman Threatens . . ." *WSJ*, August 23, 2008.

282 **"We did not understand"**: Aloke Banerjee, "No SEZ at Nandigram . . ." *HT*, March 18, 2007.

282 **"There's no way I can ignore"**: Prasenjit Bhattacharya, "Arcelor Investments Won't Feature . . ." *WSJ*, April 29, 2012.

282 **"You may have"**: James Crabtree, "Tata Raps India . . ." *FT*, December 7, 2012.

283 **"The government is keen"**: James Crabtree, "New Delay for $12bn Posco . . ." *FT*, April 2, 2012.

283 **"pragmatic, not dogmatic"**: Geeta Anand, "India Deals Face . . ." *WSJ*, December 2, 2010.

284 **"China is the restaurant opportunity"**: Julie Jargon, "Yun's CEO Serves Up . . ." *WSJ*, February 21, 2012.

284 **"and now, the biggest thing"**: Alan Rappeport, "Finger Lickin' All Over the World," *FT*, June 4, 2012.

284 **"Our largest competitor is abdicating"**: April Dembosky, "KFC's China Push Sparks US Chicken War," *FT*, June 4, 2012.

284 **"just not healthy"**: Laurie Burkitt and Julie Jargon, "Yum Concedes Missteps . . ." *WSJ*, October 10, 2013.

284 **"something of great difficulty"**: Gordon Fairclough and Shai Oster, "As China's Auto Market Booms . . ." *WSJ*, June 13, 2006.

285 **"In China, there's only one"**: Janet Adamy, "Eyeing a Billion Tea . . ." *WSJ*, November 29, 2006.

286 **"It's like having Mickey Mouse"**: James C. McKinley Jr., "No, the Conquistadors Are Not Back," *NYT*, September 28, 2004.

286 **"an aggressive and creative corrupter"**: David Barstow and Alejandra Xanic von Bertrab, "How Wal-Mart Used Payoffs . . ." *NYT*, December 17, 2012.

286 **"very unusual in that he"**: Elizabeth Rigby, "The Power of the Grocer," *FT*, December 24, 2005.

286 **"Aldi literally ran Walmart out"**: Miguel Bustillo and Timothy W. Martin, "Beyond the Big Box," *WSJ*, April 27, 2010.

286 **"a brilliant decision"**: Parija B. Kavilanz, "Wal-Mart: 'Auf Wiedersehen' Germany, Hello India," CNN Money, July 28, 2006, http://money.cnn.com /2006/07/28/news/international/walmart_international/.

287 **"Seiyu became"**: William J. Holstein, "Why Wal-Mart Can't Find Happiness in Japan," *F*, July 27, 2007.

287 **"makes everyone feel"**: Andrew Browne and Kathy Chen, "A Booming Coast Breathes . . ." *WSJ*, October 17, 2005.

288 **"We have one centralised structure"**: Elizabeth Rigby, "China's Retail Revolution," *FT*, February 13, 2007.

288 **"Stores are just the tip"**: Eric Bellman and Cecilie Rohwedder, "Western Grocer Modernizes . . ." *WSJ*, November 28, 2007.

288 **"I don't know"**: Don Lee, "It Helps to 'Be Rich Silently,'" *LAT*, April 29, 2006.

289 **"Leaning too far forward"**: Jamil Anderlini and Patti Waldmeir, "China: The Jailed Salesman . . ." *FT*, February 12, 2010.

289 **"The India of 2005"**: Peter Aspden, Lunch with the *FT*, *FT*, September 17, 2005.

290 **"We can't solve this problem"**: Amol Sharma and Biman Mukherji, "Bad Roads, Red Tape . . ." *WSJ*, January 11, 2013.

290 **"set fire to the first Walmart"**: Sadanand Dhume, "India's Wobbly Walmart . . ." *WSJ*, November 29, 2011.

291 **"I will spend money"**: Eric Bellman, "Moving Up in Mumbai . . ." *WSJ*, November 17, 2007.

291 **"The Indian model of shopping"**: Amy Yee, "Indian Stores in Search . . ." *WSJ*, December 29, 2008.

291 **"shouting, the untidiness, the chaos"**: Eric Bellman, "In India, a Retailer Finds Key . . ." *WSJ*, August 8, 2007.

292 **"This is a temporary crisis"**: Vibhuti Agarwal and Krishna Pokharel, "India's Populists Resist . . ." *WSJ*, October 9, 2007.

293 **"a dreadful retail market"**: Don Lee, "Illusions on Sale . . ." *LAT*, July 13, 2006.

293 **"I don't even crave"**: Margot Cohen, "Mighty Malls," *FEER*, July 1, 2004.

294 **"the biggest growth story"**: Manjeet Kripalani and Assif Shameen, "Indian Land Grab," *BW*, September 19, 2005.

294 **"The Indian consumer"**: Eric Bellman, "Retailers Take a Slower Road . . ." *WSJ*, August 26, 2008.

294 **"one of a kind experience"**: Sufia Tippu, "The Malling of Bangalore," *F*, May 15, 2007.

8. BUILDING

295 **"It was wonderful"**: Victor Mallet and Tom Mitchell, "Vocal Lobbies Contend . . ." *FT*, June 15, 2007.

296 **"You are master"**: Te-Ping Chen, "Next Stop, Kowloon . . ." *WSJ*, October 19, 2012.

296 **"If you count the lights"**: Candace Jackson, "In Luxury Real Estate . . ." *WSJ*, May 13, 2011.

296 **"They just want to park"**: Jason Chow, "Why Chinese Buyers Want . . ." *WSJ*, May 13, 2011.

296 **"They're buying face"**: Chen, "Next Stop, Kowloon."

297 **"know me pretty well"**: Frederik Balfour, "Shanghai Rising," *BW*, February 8, 2007.

297 **"It's not like the past"**: Patti Waldmeir, "Shanghai Starts Search . . ." *FT*, February 22, 2013.

298 **"No other city has"**: Aric Chen, "The Road to Beijing . . ." *NYT*, August 22, 2007.

298 **"remind you of how small"**: Mei Fong, "CCTV Tower Mirrors . . ." *WSJ*, November 7, 2007.

298 **"urban reorganization exercise"**: Jason Leow, "Beijing Mystery . . ." *WSJ*, June 25, 2007.

299 **"largest one-time transfer of wealth"**: "China's Property Market," *E*, May 27, 2010.

299 **"We have got to win"**: Leslie Hook and Jeremy Lerner, "Caterpillar Builds . . ." *FT*, August 14, 2011.

299 **"If they don't buy homes"**: Laurie Burkitt, "China Property Malaise . . ." *WSJ*, January 5, 2012.

300 **"Men don't want to cry"**: Mei Fong, "So Much Work, So Little Time," *WSJ*, December 23, 2006.

300 **"Prices are dropping fast"**: Jamil Anderlini, "Chinese Property: A Lofty . . ." *FT*, December 13, 2011.

300 **"We are a new"**: Andrew Batson, "On the Move . . ." *WSJ*, April 12, 2008.

301 **"all very poor quality"**: Anderlini, "Chinese Property."

301 **"Lots of industries"**: Simon Rabinovitch, "Lofty Plan Builds . . ." *FT*, August 20, 2012.

302 **"Urban residents in China"**: Tom Orlik and Esther Fung, "In China, a Move . . ." *WSJ*, October 17, 2012.

302 **"everyone has a job"**: Khozem Merchant, "Selling India's Organised Shanty . . ." *FT*, October 10, 2004.

302 **"Whenever someone leaves his village"**: Raymond Zhong and Saptarishi Dutta, "India Suffers as Workers Abandon . . ." *WSJ*, April 13, 2014.

302 **"Bombay is the sunrise city"**: Nicholas Woodsworth, "Down and Out in Highrise . . ." *FT*, April 15, 1995.

303 **"There's very little vision"**: Somini Sengupta, "Dispute Tears at Mumbai: House the Rich, or the Poor?" *NYT*, May 17, 2005.

303 **"We grow so selfish"**: Woodsworth, "Down and Out in Highrise."

303 **"The moment you put them"**: Anand Giridharadas, "Not Everyone Is Grateful . . ." *NYT*, December 12, 2006.

304 **"If you had it combined"**: Daniel Brook, "The Slumdog Millionaire Architect," *NYT*, June 19, 2014.

305 **"It's madness"**: Kripalani and Shameen, "Indian Land Grab."

305 **"Dubai has been able to"**: John Arlidge, "Dubai's Building Frenzy Lays Foundation . . ." *T*, May 21, 2006.

305 **"small number of Dubai citizens"**: Faisal Devji, "Welcome to Dubai . . ." *FT*, February 5, 2007.

306 **"The sheikh asked me"**: Roula Khalaf, "Drilling Minds . . ." *FT*, May 4, 2007.

307 **"It makes me ill"**: Alex Frangos, "Dubai Puts a New Spin . . ." *WSJ*, April 11, 2007.

308 **"You'd be mad"**: Chip Cummins, "In Dubai, Show Goes On," *WSJ*, December 4, 2009.

308 **"The city is losing"**: Megan K. Stack, "In Dubai, the Sky's . . ." *LAT*, October 13, 2005.

308 **"the land of opportunity"**: Hassan M. Fattah, "In Dubai, an Outcry . . ." *NYT*, March 26, 2006.

308 **"If the U.A.E. wants"**: Jason DeParle, "Fearful of Restive Foreign Labor . . ." *NYT*, October 6, 2007.

309 **"Every day, more people"**: Simeon Kerr, "The Hidden Victims of Recession," *FT*, November 4, 2009.

309 **"The economy just stopped"**: Robin Wigglesworth and David Fickling, "Contractors Suffer . . ." *FT*, March 3, 2009.

309 **"a readiness to believe"**: Robert F. Worth, "Laid-Off Foreigners Flee . . ." *NYT*, February 12, 2009.

309 **"I used to believe in"**: Margaret Coker, "A Dubai Deal Called . . ." *WSJ*, February 14, 2009.

310 **"If a stone moves"**: Andrew England, "Developers Drawn to Mecca by Boom in Building," *FT*, February 25, 2008.

310 **"It is the commercialization"**: Nicolai Ouroussoff, "Mecca Development Veers . . ." *NYT*, December 30, 2010.

310 **"They are turning"**: Oliver Wainwright, "Mecca's Mega Architecture," *G*, October 12, 2012.

311 **"You can do it here"**: Graham Bowley, "A Stodgy City . . ." *NYT*, December 31, 2005.

312 **"the slowest place"**: Deborah Ball and James R. Hagerty, "Slow Pace of Labor Change . . ." *WSJ*, May 21, 2013.

312 **"the global center"**: Darren Lazarus, "For London's Office Towers . . ." *WSJ*, January 23, 2013.

313 **"No one wants to commute"**: Anita Likus, "London Developers Shift . . ." *WSJ*, September 25, 2012.

314 **"wrecked London's skyline"**: Christopher Ogden, "Design: Wrecking Wren's London Skyline," *Time*, December 14, 1987.

314 **"For decades the very mention"**: Caroline McGhie, "From Rock Bottom . . ." *FT*, November 19, 2005.

314 **"monstrous carbuncle"**: Ogden, "Design."

314 **"For some unaccountable reason"**: Jeanne Whalen, "London Stalling . . ." *WSJ*, February 27, 2008.

316 **"Moscow is being deliberately destroyed"**: Arkady Ostrovsky, "Capital's Heart Becomes Construction . . ." *FT*, April 13, 2004.

316 **"When they wanted to rebuild"**: Nicolai Ouroussoff, "Russian Icons . . ." *NYT*, May 15, 2005.

317 **"No major projects can proceed"**: Guy Chazan, "Russian Tycoon's Fall . . ." *WSJ*, September 8, 2009.

318 **"unique aura"**: Edwin Heathcote, "Gazprom Design Contest . . ." *FT*, November 28, 2006.

318 **"This is an unbelievably big"**: Patrick Jenkins, "Germans Lay Foundations . . ." *FT*, July 5, 2005.

319 **"Look. There are different colors"**: Phyllis Richardson, "A Quarter Born of Co-operation," *FT*, January 5, 2008.

320 **"I consider myself"**: Andrew Hussey, "Right Bank, Wrong Banlieue," *FT*, January 12, 2008.

320 **"It is the suburban location"**: Edwin Heathcote, "Suburban 'Prisons' for France's Immigrant Poor," *FT*, November 19, 2005.

320 **"We have been engaged in"**: Catherine Field, "The Sickness in France's Heart . . ." *NYT*, November 8, 2005.

320 **"If I say I live"**: Molly Moore, "A Mixed Family Struggles . . ." *WP*, November 21, 2005.

321 **"nightmare"**: Leonard Downie Jr., "The New Towns of Paris: Reorganizing Suburbs . . ." Alicia Patterson Foundation, May 1972, http://aliciapatterson .org/stories/new-towns-paris-reorganizing-suburbs.

321 **"egg crate world"**: Andrew Barnes, http://aliciapatterson.org.

321 **"a better alternative to suburbia"**: Emily Backus, "An Ambitious Makeover in Milan," *FT*, February 19, 2005.

323 **"an economic disaster"**: Dana Hedgpeth and Jennifer Agiesta, "Poll of Detroit Residents . . ." *WP*, January 3, 2010.

323 **"We've got to focus"**: Monica Davey, "As Detroit Mayor, Bing . . ." *NYT*, September 26, 2009.

324 **"There's huge upside"**: Maura Webber Sadovi, "Doubling Down on Detroit . . ." *WSJ*, June 6, 2012.

324 **"un-American"**: Timothy Aeppel, "As Its Population Declines . . ." *WSJ*, May 2, 2007.

325 **"It costs you money"**: Fred Bernstein, "The City the Boom Passed By," *NYT*, June 25, 2006.

325 **"There is no Plan B"**: John Reed, "Lordstown Prays for State . . ." *FT*, February 24, 2009.

325 **"You know now"**: Sharon Terlep, "Secrets of the GM Diet," *WSJ*, August 5, 2011.

325 **"I never imagined"**: Clare Ansberry, "A Steel Town Finds . . ." *WSJ*, August 2, 2011.

327 **"Unless he has a cape"**: David Kelley, "Prairie Towns Brace . . ." *LAT*, June 13, 2005.

329 **"We're going to lose"**: Jim Carlton, "What Slump?" *WSJ*, March 7, 2007.

330 **"There's no industry"**: Gilbert M. Gaul and Dan Morgan, "A Slow Demise in the Delta," *WP*, June 20, 2007.

330 **"You could shoot off"**: Bruce Tomaso, "Lost Opportunity Has Cotton on Shaky Ground," *DMN*, February 25, 2007.

331 **"the most perfect place"**: Christina S. N. Lewis, "The Stampede of White Elephants . . ." *WSJ*, October 31, 2008.

332 **"You don't find many"**: Victoria Loe Hicks, "Failure or a New Foundation?" *DMN*, December 12, 2004.

332 **"The city is locked in"**: Jacquielynn Floyd, "Dallas Descriptions Filled with Cynicism," *DMN*, July 14, 2006.

333 **"the capital of homelessness"**: Randal C. Archibold, "Problems of Homelessness . . ." *NYT*, January 15, 2006.

333 **"more billionaires"**: Nancy Cleeland, "L.A. Area Going to Extremes . . ." *LAT*, July 23, 2006.

333 **"tell each other that"**: Steve Chawkins, "Choosing Their Lots in Life . . ." *LAT*, December 31, 2007.

333 **"You can work in"**: Miriam Jordan, "In Tony Monterey County . . ." *WSJ*, August 26, 2006.

334 **"It's of historic proportions"**: Roger Vincent, "In Beverly Hills, High End . . ." *LAT*, April 11, 2007.

334 **"as primo as they come"**: Jonathan Karp, "Beverly Hills Development Is in Doubt . . ." *WSJ*, October 30, 2008.

334 **"Construction finance across the world"**: Cassell Bryan-Low, "Market Sours for Condo Kings," *WSJ*, February 12, 2009.

335 **"I'm in no rush"**: Ben Casselman and Christina S. N. Lewis, "'Underpriced' at $100 Million . . ." *WSJ*, August 24, 2007.

335 **"We believe downtown Los Angeles"**: Cara Mia DiMassa, "2 Projects, 2 Visions of Downtown's Future," *LAT*, September 15, 2006.

336 **"Within the next decade"**: Cara Mia DiMassa, "Landmark May Make History . . ." *LAT*, January 30, 2007.

336 **"I see tremendous opportunity here"**: Jeffrey L. Rabin, "Taking L.A. in a New Direction . . ." *LAT*, September 20, 2006.

336 **"That was exciting!"**: Marla Cone, "Will This Boom Lead to Another?" *LAT*, August 7, 2006.

336 **"a little dysfunctional"**: Peter H. King and Mark Arax, "As Dynasty Evolved . . ." *LAT*, March 26, 2006.

337 **"More than half of"**: John Pomfret, "Where Did All the Children Go?" *WP*, March 19, 2006.

337 **"staggeringly high"**: Terry Pristin, "San Francisco's Goldilocks Market . . ." *NYT*, March 23, 2005.

338 **"The carcass keeps being fed"**: Jennifer S. Forsyth, "Blackstone's Slick Flip . . ." *WSJ*, July 26, 2007.

338 **"Those who bought from Blackstone"**: Charles V. Bagli, "Sam Zell's Empire . . ." *NYT*, February 7, 2009.

338 **"We view ourselves as patrons"**: Alex Berzon, "The Long, Bumpy Road . . ." *WSJ*, December 13, 2009.

339 **"The final product is"**: Chuck Neubauer and Richard T. Cooper, "Desert Connections . . ." *LAT*, August 20, 2006.

340 **"28 years in the industry"**: Matthew Garrahan, "Strip Hopes Its Run . . ." *FT*, October 20, 2009.

340 **"They thought the demand"**: Berzon, "Long, Bumpy Road."

340 **"There are only two markets"**: Charles V. Bagli, "Sky High and Going up Fast," *NYT*, May 18, 2013.

340 **"a vast gated community"**: David Harvey, "The Right to the City . . ." *New Left Review* 53 (2008): 38.

340 **"It was awful"**: Elizabeth A. Harris, "Words to Start a Stampede . . ." *NYT*, July 8, 2013.

341 **"went to Brooklyn first"**: C. J. Hughes, "For Cheaper Homes, Skip . . ." *NYT*, September 6, 2013.

341 **"they are aggressive"**: Peter Aspden, "High Ideals . . ." *FT*, July 8, 2006.

341 **"not a social critic"**: Nicolai Ouroussoff, "Injecting a Bold Shot . . ." *NYT*, October 10, 2006.

341 **"a glass dagger"**: Nicolai Ouroussoff, "Designing a Building to Preserve . . ." *NYT*, May 14, 2008.

342 **"The scale of wealth"**: Alexei Barrionuevo, "Billionaires' New Digs . . ." *NYT*, September 18, 2012.

342 **"This type of real estate"**: David Kaufman, "Central Park's New Peaks," *FT*, November 10–11, 2012.

342 **"With beautiful views"**: Julie Satow, "Moving In, Slowly . . ." *NYT*, June 27, 2014.

342 **"There'll never be another job"**: Alan Feuer and Charles V. Bagli, "Harry Macklowe Gambles . . ." *NYT*, October 4, 2013.

344 **"the most complex construction project"**: Kris Hudson, "At Ground Zero, Optimism . . ." *WSJ*, January 16, 2008.

345 **"very, very big buildings"**: Ada Louis Huxtable, "The Hudson Yards Proposals . . ." *WSJ*, January 2, 2008.

345 **"Rockefeller Center"**: Eliot Brown, "Manhattan Megaproject . . ." *WSJ*, October 23, 2012.

346 **"a unique opportunity to preserve"**: Charles V. Bagli, "Effort to Sell Starrett City . . ." *NYT*, December 20, 2008.

347 **"Clearly, the city would be"**: Nicolai Ouroussoff, "Battle between Budget . . ." *NYT*, June 9, 2009.

348 **"Who builds like this"**: Christopher Grimes, "Wall Street Discovers . . ."
FT, June 24, 2006.

349 **"This is clearly going to"**: Christopher Grimes and Rebecca Knight, "Manhattan's Largest Apartments Complex . . ." *FT*, August 31, 2006.

349 **"opportunity to buy 11,000 apartments"**: Alan Rappeport and Henny Sender, "East Side Story," *FT*, February 27, 2010.

349 **"It's a great, great transaction"**: Charles V. Bagli, "Megadeal: Inside a New York . . ." *NYT*, December 31, 2006.

350 **"New York City is"**: Charles V. Bagli, "A Big Deal . . ." *NYT*, December 7, 2006.

350 **"Nobody ever made money owning"**: Jennifer S. Forsyth, "Mr. Macklowe's $3 Billion . . ." *WSJ*, February 20, 2008.

9. ESCAPING

351 **"people want what everyone else"**: Witold Rybczynski, *The Last Harvest: How a Cornfield Became New Daleville* (New York: Scribner, 2007), 250.

352 **"We can sometimes sell"**: Joshua Chaffin, "Welcome to Marthaville," *FT*, March 18, 2006.

353 **"Our business is like"**: Rybczynski, *Last Harvest*, 201.

353 **"We're really a marketing company"**: Jon Gertner, "Chasing Ground . . ." *NYT*, October 15, 2005.

354 **"own a piece of Facebook"**: Allysia Finley, "Joel Kotkin . . ." *WSJ*, April 20, 2012.

354 **"We have property rights"**: Matthew Engel, "Forty Acres and a Pool . . ." *FT*, August 25, 2007.

355 **"The land use regulations"**: Peter Whoriskey, "Washington's Road to Outward Growth," *WP*, August 9, 2004.

356 **"In the next 10 years"**: Conor Dougherty, "Land Crunch Hits Builders . . ." *WSJ*, December 26, 2013.

356 **"neighboring is one of"**: Stephanie McCrummen, "Housing Developers Have Values . . ." *WP*, April 16, 2006.

357 **"captures people before"**: Roger Vincent, "Where the L.A. Dream Landed . . ." *LAT*, April 16, 2006.

357 **"I will make 10 times"**: Jerry Hirsch, "Dairies Moving Out . . ." *LAT*, October 9, 2006.

357 **"I go to bed"**: Evelyn Iritani, "They're Building in Baja . . ." *LAT*, February 21, 2006.

358 **"The Florida economy"**: George Packer, "The Ponzi State . . ." *NY*, February 9, 2009.

359 **"have some bureaucrat"**: Kris Hudson, "Houston's Twilight Zone . . ." *WSJ*, October 17, 2007.

359 **"believed it is way too"**: Ana Campoy, "As Houston Grows up ..." *WSJ*, May 17-18, 2014.

360 **"People pushing high-density themselves"**: Allysia Finley, "Joel Kotkin ..." *WSJ*, April 20, 2012.

360 **"They make out that it's"**: Jim Pickard, "As American as Apple Pie," *FT*, November 18, 2006.

360 **"It is the most pessimistic"**: Andrew Ward, "Main Street or Main Chance ..." *FT*, June 24, 2006.

361 **"something European, a more subtle"**: Aspden, "High Ideals."

362 **"is the greatest"**: Anita Huslin, "Grand Vision for National Harbor Takes Form," *WP*, April 22, 2007.

362 **"as a suburban bedroom community"**: Ovetta Wiggins, "Town Center Closer ..." *WP*, August 16, 2008.

362 **"As land becomes rarer"**: Robert Palmeri, "A New Frontier for Suburban ..." *BW*, September 19, 2004.

362 **"We are following our people"**: Michael Corkery, "Mr. Toll Turns ..." *WSJ*, December 13, 2006.

363 **"We don't lead parades"**: Rybczynski, *Last Harvest*, 213.

363 **"one of the most desirable"**: Steve Brown, "Partners to Work on Three Buildings," *DMN*, December 15, 2006.

363 **"a transformative project"**: Robert Vincent, "A Cast of Thousands ..." *LAT*, December 29, 2006.

364 **"They rusted every hinge"**: Christina S. N. Lewis, "Rudin Sells Retreat ..." *WSJ*, August 3, 2007.

364 **"They've got a masseuse"**: Rich Tosches, "Reining in Mega-home ..." *Denver Evening Post*, April 19, 2006.

366 **"It sounds very limiting"**: Conor Dougherty, "The Disappearing Dude Ranch ..." *WSJ*, July 7, 2006.

366 **"We honestly asked ourselves"**: Abby Goodnough, "In Florida, a Big Developer ..." *NYT*, August 22, 2005.

367 **"How many people get to"**: Fred A. Bernstein, "Betting the Ranch in Southwest Florida," *NYT*, July 20, 2006.

367 **"I don't see Babcock Ranch"**: Maura Webber Sadovi, "Developer Lassos Patience," *WSJ*, October 5, 2011.

368 **"The public owns this beach"**: Bob Pool, "And Now the Coast Is Here ..." *LAT*, May 27, 2005.

368 **"the world's biggest gated community"**: Darryl Fears, "U.S. Groups Working to Open ..." *WP*, July 28, 2013.

368 **"We are in denial"**: Catherine Saillant, "Staking New Territory ..." *LAT*, October 10, 2005.

369 **"I don't believe we should"**: Gary Polakovic, "Sky's the Limit . . ." *LAT*, February 23, 2007.

369 **"The dot-com boom"**: Daryl Kelly, "Panel Declares Coast . . ." *LAT*, December 26, 2005.

370 **"The financial decision"**: Ben Casselman, "Coastal California Ranches . . ." *WSJ*, January 12, 2007.

370 **"It's an overly fair price"**: Peter Whoriskey, "Tiny Briny Breezes . . ." *WP*, December 27, 2005.

370 **"What they mean is"**: John-Thor Dahlburg, "An Eminent Domain High Tide . . ." *LAT*, November 29, 2005.

371 **"You will be able to"**: Paul Vitello, "Rusty Railroad Advances . . ." *NYT*, June 15, 2005.

372 **"doubled the size"**: Julie Cart, "Conservationist Answered America's . . ." *LAT*, September 17, 2006.

372 **"In destroying wildness"**: Douglas Martin, "Edgar Wayburn, a Leader . . ." *NYT*, March 10, 2010.

372 **"Any park superintendent who says"**: Janet Wilson, "A New Campfire Song . . ." *LAT*, April 6, 2004.

373 **"We understand that parks serve"**: Dan Weikel, "As State Grows . . ." *LAT*, March 25, 2006.

373 **"Millions of people who use"**: Dan Weikel, "Panel Rejects Toll Road . . ." *LAT*, February 7, 2008.

373 **"an upscale carnival ride"**: Julie Cart, "Tribe's Canyon Skywalk . . ." *LAT*, February 22, 2007.

373 **"eating tofu and pilaf"**: Sylvia Moreno, "Tribe's Canyon Skywalk . . ." *WP*, March 8, 2007.

374 **"Three hundred years of"**: Mark Yost, "The Grand Canyon's Skywalk . . ." *WSJ*, April 10, 2007.

374 **"We are not going to"**: Patrick J. McDonnell, "A Force of Nature . . ." *LAT*, June 12, 2006.

374 **"don't want our natural resources"**: Benedict Mander, "Philanthropist in Battle to Preserve the Wetlands He Wants to Give Away," *FT*, September 20, 2006.

374 **"The Argentine government should look"**: Monte Reel, "Argentine Land Fight Divides Environmentalists, Rights Advocates," *WP*, September 24, 2006.

375 **"Keep Maine Free!"**: Jennifer Levitz, "Mill Towns Now Look . . ." *WSJ*, July 20, 2011.

375 **"McMansions are bigger"**: Christina S. N. Lewis, "Selling History by the Square Foot," *WSJ*, April 4, 2008.

376 **"Where others saw holes"**: James Wynn, "When the Stones Began to Whisper," *FT*, October 6, 2007; see also his *The House That Jack Built: The Story of the Oldest Inhabited House in Britain* (London: Aurum Press, 2007).

377 **"People are looking for tranquillity"**: Al Goodman, "Granadilla Journal . . ." *NYT*, April 22, 1998.

378 **"In Tuscany it would cost"**: Eluned Price, "In the Land of Bears and Castles," *FT*, June 20, 2007.

380 **"We decided to stay small"**: Tom Wright, "Gstadd's Precious, Pastoral . . ." *NYT*, November 18, 2005.

380 **"I have lived here"**: Justine Hardy, "Bellagio on Lake Como," *FT*, October 17, 2009.

381 **"I am once again seriously"**: Joshua Hagen, *Preservation, Tourism, and Nationalism: The Jewel of the German Past* (Aldershot, UK: Ashgate, 2006), 144.

381 **"I came to Rothenburg"**: Hagen, *Preservation, Tourism, and Nationalism*, 260.

381 **"like all fine buildings"**: F. S. Aijazuddin, *Lahore, Illustrated Views of the 19th Century* (Karachi: Vanguard Books, 1991), 34.

383 **"Asia is different from"**: Martin Fackler, "The Builder Who Pushes Tokyo . . ." *NYT*, March 27, 2008.

384 **"Seoul underwent rapid development"**: Anna Fifield, "Pulling Down a Concrete Jungle," *FT*, November 16, 2005.

384 **"We've basically gone from"**: Andrew C. Revkin, "Peeling Back Pavement to Expose Watery Havens," *NYT*, July 16, 2009.

384 **"It feels so peaceful"**: Anna Fifield, "New Life for an Old Way . . ." *FT*, October 6, 2006.

384 **"Walk the streets at night"**: Mark McDonald, "Saving a Korean District . . ." *NYT*, December 13, 2010.

385 **"I don't know that you"**: Nicholas D. Kristof, "Japan Is Torn . . ." *NYT*, October 26, 1998.

385 **"Over here she wouldn't wear"**: Peter Howarth, "In Search of the Real Shanghai," *FT*, October 16, 2004.

385 **"Her look is just plain"**: Vanessa O'Connell and Cui Rong, "Model's Chinese Looks . . ." *WSJ*, September 8, 2006.

386 **"Yes, it would"**: Corkery, "Mr. Toll Turns."

386 **"a whole Western tradition"**: Geoff Dyer, "China Bulldozes . . ." *FT*, June 16, 2007.

386 **"only objective of past repairs"**: S. Li, "Memory without Location . . ." *Fabrications* 19, no. 2 (2010): 134.

387 **"senseless actions"**: Geoff Dyer, "Beijing Minister Critical . . ." *FT*, June 12, 2007.

387 **"This is nothing to do"**: "Restoration Drama," *E*, May 27, 2010.

388 **"last 10 to 20 years"**: Kathy Chen, "Activists Say Makeover Hurts . . ." *WSJ*, October 26, 2005.

Index

A&P, 20, 323

Abercrombie & Fitch, 25, 26, 47, 48, 105, 343

Abu Dhabi, 102, 309, 345. *See also* United Arab Emirates

Abuja, Nigeria, 91, 232

Accra, Ghana, 91, 128

advertising, 9, 16, 18, 21, 27, 94, 298, 385

Africa: airlines in, 91–92, 94, 101, 103; African Growth and Opportunity Act, 49–50; African National Congress Youth League, 249; auto industry in, 67; beer in, 41; cell phones in, 257–58; farming in, 228–33, 242, 248–51; foreigners' behavior in, 199–200; French residents from, 320; iron ore in, 186; legal system in, 260; migrants from, 262–63; oil in, 122, 136, 139, 172–77, 242; poverty in, 241–42; production in, 39–40; railroad in, 121–22; refrigerators in, 79; roads in, 121, 122, 229, 242, 311; shipping in, 105–6, 127, 128, 131, 133; textiles in, 49–50. *See also* South Africa

Agra, India, 87, 304

agriculture. *See* farming

Airbus, 68, 70–73, 93, 264; the 350s, 69; the 380s, 72; the A320neo, 68; the A320s, 72; the A340s, 69, 93; the A350s, 72; the A380s, 71–73, 99, 101

air freight: and Asian roads, 88; cost of, 120; from India, 235; overview of, 104–8; planes for, 69, 103–4. *See also* airlines; shipping; transportation

airliners: author's coverage of, xiv; Boeing, 68–74, 92–93, 99, 105, 108; for budget carriers, 94, 95; for freight, 69, 103–4, 106; in India, 103, 279; on international routes, 92, 99, 101; manufacture and sales of, 68–73, 193, 264–65; in United States, 103

airlines, 89–105, 125; Aer Lingus, 95, 102; Air Arabia, 103; Air Asia, 103; Air Berlin, 102; Airborne Freight, 107; Air Deccan, 102; Air France, 72, 92, 94–99; Air France–KLM, 92, 93; Air India, 92, 102; Air New Zealand, 99; AirTran, 96; Alaska Airlines, 105; Alitalia, 92, 102; All Nippon Airways, 103; American Airlines, 68, 69, 73, 89, 90–93, 97–99, 114; American President Lines, 123, 125; Austrian Airlines, 92; Azul Airline, 104; Braniff Airways, 89; British Airways, 69, 72, 73, 91–93, 95–101, 105–6; Brussels Airlines, 92; China Southern Airline, 100, 177; Continental, 89, 91, 96–98; Delta Airlines, 69, 89–91, 93, 96, 98, 99, 104; easyJet, 95, 96, 103; Frontier Airlines, 90; Iberia Airline, 90, 92, 96, 99; Japan Airlines, 69, 93–94; Japan Airways, 69, 93, 94; Jet Airways, 102, 103; JetBlue Airways, 90, 96, 104; Kingfisher Airlines, 102–3; KLM Airline, 90, 92, 98; National Airlines, 89; Northwest Airlines, 89, 91, 92, 98, 99; Norwegian Air Shuttle, 96, 97; Pan American Airline, 68, 91; Peach Airline, 103; Qantas Airline, 72, 93, 100, 103; Qatar Airways, 72; Ryanair, 94–95, 96, 103; SAS Airline, 92; Scandinavian Airlines, 92; Scoot Airline, 103; Singapore Airlines, 69, 71, 72, 100, 103; Smile Airline, 103; Song airline, 96; Southwest Airlines, 76, 89–90, 93–96; Spirit Airlines, 90; Swiss International Air,

airlines (cont.)
92, 97; TAM Airline, 104; TAP Airline, 92–93; Ted Airline, 96; Thai Airways, 93, 103; Trans World Airlines, 89, 91; United Airlines, 69, 89–93, 96–99, 360; US Airways, 89, 9-0, 98; Volaris Airline, 104; Western Airlines, 89. *See also* air freight; transportation

airports: in Africa, 91; Al Maktoum International, 101; Brussels-Charleroi, 95; budget carriers at, 95–97; Chennai International, 279; in China, 102, 120, 298, 301; Dallas–Fort Worth International, ix, 112, 145; in Denver, 360; in Dubai, 101, 102, 308, 309; in Florida, 367; freight at U.S., 107–8; in India, 279, 302; in Italy, 380; in Japan, 384–85; John F. Kennedy International, 97; London City, 97; London Gatwick, 97; London Heathrow, 73, 95, 97–102, 104, 384; Los Angeles International, 356; Louisiana International, 106; Macapagal International, 107; Narita Airport, 384–85; in New York City, 344; and North Atlantic flights, 97; Northwest Florida Beaches, 367; of Reliance Industries, 281; in Russia, 306; Schiphol, 104; in Taiwan, 107. *See also* airlines

air rights, 342, 345, 361
Alaska, 140, 143, 150–51
Alberta, Canada, 140, 152
Alcan (mining company), 194, 201
Alcoa, 149, 193–96
alcoholic beverages, 5, 17, 40–43. *See also* beer; wine
Aldi, 22–23, 286, 389–90
alfalfa, 212, 220
Algeria, 121, 149
Alliance TX, 34, 112
almonds, 204, 210
Alstom, 114, 265
aluminum, 193–96, 201, 283, 299. *See also* bauxite; mining
Aluminum Corporation of China (Chinalco), 118, 201

Amazon, 18, 19, 20, 84, 329
Amazon rainforest, 184, 217–18, 220. *See also* forests
Amsterdam, 98, 100, 104, 106, 113. *See also* Netherlands
Amu Darya River, 227, 228
Anadarko Petroleum, 137–39
Andhra, India, 244, 254
Angola, 88, 122, 127, 136, 139, 176–77
Anheuser-Busch, 41, 42, 322
Anhui, China, 236–37, 246–48, 267
Annan, Kofi, 231, 250
Ann Taylor, 25, 26, 34
Anschutz (company), 336–37
Antwerp, 113, 126, 127
apartments: in China, 288, 299–302; in Dubai, 306, 307, 309; in France, 320–21, 377; in Germany, 318–19; in Hong Kong, 295–96; in India, 303–4; in Italy, 321, 378–79; in Russia, 317, 318; in South Korea, 384; in United Kingdom, 312–13, 315; in United States, xiii, 322, 331, 333, 335–37, 340–52, 356, 361–63. *See also* housing
A. P. Moller-Maersk, 119, 124, 125, 127, 128, 132, 279
Apple, 10, 74, 75, 269
apples, 4, 216, 222
appliances, 12, 79, 192, 330
Aral Sea, 227–28
Arcadia CA, 33, 339
Arcelor (steel company), 189–90
ArcelorMittal, 189, 191, 392
Archer Daniels Midland, 216–17
architects: in France, 320; in Germany, 319; of Grand Mosque, 311; in Las Vegas, 340; in Los Angeles, 336; in Moscow, 316–17; on New Urbanism, 360–61; in New York, 341, 344, 347
architecture and architectural preservation, vii, 307, 343–44; in Asia, 297, 382–88; in Europe, 380–81; in Germany, 319; and New Ruralism, 366–67; and New Urbanism, 360–61; in New York, 346–48; in Pakistan, 381–82; in Russia, 316–18; in Spain, 377; in Transylvania, 379; in United Kingdom, 312, 314–15,

Best Buy, 17–19, 79, 288
Bethlehem Steel, 189, 192
beverages. *See* alcoholic beverages; coffee
Beverly Hills CA, 28, 334, 337, 339
Bharti Enterprises, 234–35, 289, 290
BHP Billiton, 148, 185, 195, 196, 201
Big Bazaar stores, 291, 292
Bihar, India, 243, 244, 256
biotech industry, 43–44. *See also* pharmaceutical companies; health care
blacks, 18, 199, 330
Black Sea, 162, 165
Blackstone Group, 338, 348
Bloomberg, Michael, 345, 346; and Bloomberg Tower, 344
Bloomingdale's, 9, 28
BMW, 58, 62, 112, 120
BNSF Railway: in author's hometown, 392; deliveries through, 83–84; fuel use, 146; in North Dakota, 151; and oil industry, 151; ownership of, 108; terminal of, 112; tracks of, 109–11
Bodega Aurrera, 285–87
Boeing Company, 57, 68–73, 94, 322, 326
Bombardier, 118, 265
Bombay, India, 38, 302, 304, 305
Bombay Textile Mills, 304, 305
bookstores, 323, 389
Bordeaux, France, 96, 114, 376, 377
Boston: airlines in, 90–91, 94; developer from, 383; economy in, 322; New Urbanism in, 361; office towers in, 338; pharmaceuticals in, 44; retail sales in, 21; Walmart in, 13–15
BP. *See* British Petroleum (BP)
brands: in China, 386; of clothing stores, 25, 26; global, 39, 42, 79–80; of homes, 352; house, 13, 22; loyalty to, 5, 26; personality of, 21–22; and Philip Morris, 77; regional, 6
Branson, Richard, 103, 380
Brazil: airlines in, 93, 98, 103–4; aluminum industry in, 194, 196; auto industry in, 64; beer in, 41, 42; Brazil National Confederation of Agriculture and Livestock, 218; farming in, 216–20, 233; high-rise buildings in, 315; high-speed

rail in, 265; housing in, 299; iron ore in, 184, 185; oil industry in, 135, 139; poultry farming in, 211; processed foods in, 77; property in New York, 350; soybean production in, 204, 216; steel industry in, 193
Brazzaville, 94, 121, 257–58
Brisbane, Australia, 93, 184
British Columbia, 129–30, 133, 393
British Midland, 92, 98
British Petroleum (BP): in China, 267; and Deepwater Horizon, 137; dominance of, 135, 136, 138; drilling in Gulf of Mexico, 141–42; and gas production, 140; in Iraq, 168; in Kazakhstan, 166; merger of, 137; property of, 202; in Russia, 159–60; on U.S. fracking, 146; and Venezuelan oil, 156
Brooklyn NY, 35, 130, 340, 341, 346–47, 362
Brunei, 138, 195
Brussels, 92, 113
Bulgaria, 159, 379
Burger King, 2–4, 390
Burj Dubai. *See* Burj Khalifa
Burj Khalifa, 306–10, 344
Burma, 88, 118, 121, 163–64, 199, 200
buses, 104, 114, 332, 344, 355

C4 rice, 252. *See also* rice
cabbages, 249, 258. *See also* vegetables
Cadbury, 39, 78, 79
Cadillac, 56, 268, 390
Cairo, Egypt, 91, 121, 382
Calatrava, Santiago, 341, 344
California: automobiles in, 51, 53; economy in Southern, 332–37; farming in, 204, 208, 210, 215; fast food in, 3; high-speed rail in, 113; housing styles in, 375; Indian entrepreneur in, 291; Krispy Kreme in, 8; lettuce from, 4; LNG terminals in, 148; New Urbanism in, 362; oil industry in, 135, 143; palm trees in, 339; parks in, 371–73; property in New York, 349; property values in, 354, 368–69; roads in, 85, 86; sheepherders in, 212; shipping in, 129, 130; steel industry in, 188; stores in, 15, 16, 19–21,

Delhi: airlines in, 92, 100, 279; employment in, 276, 278; living conditions in,
234, 281, 304; McDonald's in, 283–84;
power plant in, 282; production in, 47;
roads in, 87, 88; stores in, 290–92, 294;
trains in, 119, 279
Dell, 267, 269, 293, 329
Democratic Republic of the Congo, 195, 200
Deng Xiaoping, 264, 272
Denmark, 91, 124, 279
Denver CO, 89–90, 331, 360
department stores, xiv, 8–10, 30, 290
detergents, 79–80
Detroit: airlines in, 93, 98; auto industry
in, 59, 65, 327; economy in, 322–23, 329,
331, 332; glass industry in, 75; stores in,
13, 27, 29
Deutsche Bank, 129, 295, 327
Devon Energy, 141, 145, 152, 163
DHL, 107–8, 120
diamonds, 265, 271, 348
discounters, 9, 11–12, 22, 29–30, 288. See
also dollar stores
diseases, plant, 223, 229
DLF (Delhi Land and Finance), 304, 305
Dolce & Gabbana, 77, 293
Dole Food, 37, 43
dollar stores, 22–23, 286, 323. See also dis-
counters
Dominion Farms, 230–31
Domino's Pizza, 4, 7, 283, 284
Dongguan, China, 268, 292, 302
doughnuts, 8, 21
Dow Chemical, 146, 149, 214
Downtown (building), 306–7, 348
downtowns, 321, 335, 336, 338, 360–62, 391.
See also community centers; mixed-
use development; urban areas
DP World, 126, 128, 279
drive-throughs, 2, 3, 7, 284
Duany, Andrés, 346, 359, 360, 361
Dubai, 90, 99–101, 105–6, 126, 128, 292,
304, 305–9, 344. See also United Arab
Emirates
Dubai World, 305, 338
Dunkin' Donuts, x, 6, 7, 284
DuPont, 213, 214, 224, 229

earthquakes, 65, 378
East Coast (U.S.), 30–31, 148, 368–70
Easyday stores, 235, 289, 290
economy, farming, 203–9, 219, 232, 235–36
economy, global: and Africa, 230–33, 250;
and air freight, 104; and auto industry,
62, 65–66; and Dubai, 308, 309; green
fuels in, 217; and oil industry, 137, 138,
157, 158, 166–67; and organic foods,
216; processed foods in, 77–78; production and distribution in, 44, 78–82;
and steel industry, 189–91; in United
Kingdom, 312; and U.S. fracking, 146
economy, local: in Africa, 241–42, 249; in
Angola, 177; in Australia, 181; in Brazil,
219; in China, 245, 246, 263–64, 266,
271–73, 285, 386–88; in Dubai, 307–9;
and immigration, 261, 262; in India,
243–44, 263, 278–81, 289–91; in Mexico, 286; in Nigeria, 175; in Qatar, 171;
in Saudi Arabia, 166–67, 310; in United
Kingdom, 311, 312; in United States,
322–40, 351, 358, 369, 371, 373; in Venezuela, 155–56, 248
Ecuador, 216, 220
education: in China, 248, 269, 272, 300;
in farming, 230; in India, 276, 277; in
Japan, 385; in United States, 323, 327,
329, 331, 332, 337
Egypt, 91, 103, 146, 217, 222, 227, 229, 233,
262
electricity: in Africa, 242, 251; for aluminum processing, 194–96; in Burma,
200; and cell-phone users, 254–55; in
China, 248, 260; coal for, 179–82; on
Columbia River, 328–29; foundation
of, xii; and gas, 146, 149, 180; in India,
243, 256, 275, 302, 305; in Italy, 379, 380;
for Saudi Arabian farming, 234. See
also public utilities
electronics, 18, 73, 106, 107, 264, 269–70,
280, 288, 391. See also specific products
El Toro Marine Corps Air Station, 371–72
Emaar, 304, 306, 309–10
Emirates, 72, 99–102, 105–6, 128
Emma Maersk (ship), 124, 131
Empire State Building, 341, 345

employees: in Africa, 231; in airline industry, 57, 70, 72, 92, 94–96, 104; in Angola, 176; in Asian farming, 234; in Australian mining industry, 181, 202; in auto industry, 51–53, 55, 58–64, 67, 131, 322, 325; at Best Buy, 18; in biotech, 44; in China, 105, 266–70, 285, 299–301, 362; in coal industry, 179–83, 200; cost of, 81–82; in Dubai, 308–9; in Egypt, 222; of Emirates, 100; in Europe, 311–13; at Fairchild Semiconductor, 73; in France, 221, 320; in furniture industry, 50–51; in Germany, 318; in glass industry, 75; in gold industry, 196–98; in India, 234, 243, 260, 275–81, 283, 289–91, 302; in Japanese Walmarts, 287; at Kodak, 74, 326; in Kuwait, 170; migrants as, 261, 262, 268–69; in Mississippi, 329; and New Urbanism, 360; in Nigeria, 175; in oil industry, 150, 153, 155; of phone companies, 254, 256; and production automation, 44–45; productivity of sales, 25; of railroads, 116, 119; in Saudi Arabia, 167, 310; at Sears, 11; in shipping industry, 83, 106–7, 111, 112, 120, 123, 127, 129–31; of Southwest Airlines, 76; in steel industry, 189, 190, 192, 325; in suburbs, 351; at Target, 21; of Tesco, 24; in textile industry, 43, 45–49, 51; of Unilever, 39; in United States, 322, 324, 326–28, 330, 333–34, 337, 349, 367–68; at Walmart, 19, 21. See also unions, labor; wages

engines, xii, 60, 82, 104, 257, 265, 326. See also airliners; automobiles; locomotives

English language, 277, 385, 386

Eni (oil company), 136, 156, 165, 166, 176

entertainment venues, 326, 335, 347. See also shoppertainment; theaters

environment: in Brazil, 217; in China, 284–85, 388; and coal vs. gas use, 180; and construction, 295; costs to, x; and farming, 222; and gas production, 161; and GMOs, 214, 223; and gold mining, 196, 198, 199; in India, 282, 283; and iron-ore mining, 187; and oil pro-

duction, 139, 145, 152–53, 156–57; and organic farming, 216; in Russia, 227; in South America, 374; in South Korea, 384; in Tanzania, 242; in United States, 323, 367, 369–70. See also forests; parks; water

Erie PA, 68, 82

Ermenegildo Zenga, 289, 385

Essen, Germany, 182–83

Esso, 135, 381

ethanol, 203–7, 216–17, 328. See also corn; fuel

Ethiopia, 105, 229

Eurasia, xi, 126

Europe: airlines in, 91–102; aluminum industry in, 194; architecture in, 314–15, 361, 375–81; auto industry in, 51, 56, 57, 60–62, 67; beer in, 41; cell phones in, 254, 255; Chinese locomotives in, 265; cities in, xv, 379, 383; coal in, 180, 182; coffee shops in, 7; construction in, 311–22; dollar stores in, 22; employment in, .70, 276; farming in, 221–26, 233; food exports in, 214, 234, 239; gas in, 158–59, 162, 164, 175; GMOs in, 214, 223–24; iron ore in, 185; migrants in, 262–63; office space in, 315, 319; oil in, 151, 153, 157–58; poverty in, 241; shipping industry in, 124, 125; steel industry in, 146, 190, 191, 192; textiles in, 47–49; trains in, 113–16; Walmart in, 285, 286; wine in, 225–26. See also specific countries

European Union: biofuel in, 207; on budget airline, 94; building costs in, 227; farm subsidies in, 208; on food imports, 222–23; on GMOs, 224; and Iranian oil, 170; on land subsidies, 222; migrants to, 262; and Open Skies agreement, 97–99; and trains, 114–16; wine agreement of, 225

exports: from Africa, 231, 233; of almonds, 210; from Brazil, 217, 218, 220; from China, 105, 125, 222, 223, 236, 238, 239, 264, 265; of coal, 180; of ethanol, 207; of gas, 140, 148–49, 151, 158, 161; of GMOs, 214; from India, 234–35; from

government enterprises (cont.)
83; and computer use, 260; in Dubai,
306–8; in European farming, 221–22,
226–28; European railroads as, 115–16;
in Germany, 318; and GMOs, 215, 224;
in gold mining, 197; harbors as, 127; in
Hong Kong, 296; and illegal immigration, 261; in India, 234, 242–43, 245,
254, 278–81, 283, 289–90, 292, 303–4;
and iron-ore mining, 186; in Korea,
383; in Kuwait, 170–71; in Mexico, 220;
in Mississippi, 330; and oil and gas
industries, 135–36, 154–55, 157–62, 164,
166–68, 175–76; in Russia, 316, 318; in
Saudi Arabia, 167, 310; in Singapore,
349; in South America, 220, 248, 374;
in South Korea, 384; in steel industry, 190; in suburban planning, 353–54;
in Thailand, 382; in United Kingdom,
312–13; in United States, 207–9, 232–33,
339. See also politics; public lands
grain, 205, 208, 212, 226–27, 236, 291
Grameen Bank, 253, 259
Grand Canyon National Park, 373–74
Grand Central Station, 345, 387
Grand Mosque, 310, 311
grapes, 225–26, 236
Grasberg Mine, 197–98
Great Northern Railway, 109, 111
Greece, 120, 123, 127, 132, 223
grocery stores, 15, 20–24. See also food;
supermarkets
Gruen, Victor, 27–28, 363
Guangdong, China, 246, 285, 295
Guangzhou, China, 71–72, 100, 106, 116,
117, 264–66, 295
Guinea, 172, 185, 194
Gujarat, India, 183, 279, 280, 282
Gulf (oil company), 135–37, 150, 171
Gulf of Mexico, 137–42, 148, 153
Gwadar, Pakistan, 120, 163

H&M, 26, 48, 343
Hadid, Zaha, 321–22
Hamburg, 71, 114, 126
Hangzhou, China, 46, 94, 297
Hanoi, 88, 260

Hantz Farms, 323–24
Haynesville Shale, 145, 147
health care: in Africa, 39–40, 175, 242; for
auto workers, 55; in China, 248, 269;
for factory workers, 81, 82; in India,
244; as money-making venture, x; at
Sears, 11. See also pharmaceutical companies
Hefei, China, 117, 267
Heinz, 78, 81
Henan, China, 236–38, 300
herbicides, 212–14, 252
Hewlett-Packard, 120, 267, 269
high-rise buildings: in Asia, 295–96, 298,
383; in Dubai, 306–7, 344; in France,
319, 321; of General Growth Properties,
32; in India, 302–4; in Italy, 321–22; in
London, 314, 315; in Russia, 317–18; in
Saudi Arabia, 309–10; Trump brand,
352; in United States, 302, 329, 330, 335–
36, 341, 342, 344–48, 361–63, 369
Hindu society, 244, 278
Hitachi, 79, 391
hogs, 205, 211
Holmfirth, England, 379–80
Home Depot, 12, 24, 58, 79, 357, 360
Honda, 55, 192, 246–47, 270, 275, 285
Hong Kong: airlines in, 72, 93, 104, 108; Brazilian investments of, 219; Cartier stores
in, 386; Caterpillar president in, 299;
Chinese wine producer in, 236; construction in, 295–97; handbag manufacturer in, 264; housing in, 299, 342;
investment in China, 267; and LA property, 334; Red Wing Shoes near, 84; rents
in, 343; shipping in, 123–26, 128; shopping in, 289, 293; textiles in, 46, 47, 48
Hon Hai/Foxconn, 120, 269–71
hosiery, 44, 46
hotels: in California, 334, 335, 369, 370; in
Detroit, 324; in Dubai, 309; and fracking boom, 146; in Las Vegas, 340; in
London, 315; in Mississippi, 329; in
Moscow, 316, 317; near shopping centers, 34; in New York, 342–43, 348; in
Saudi Arabia, 310; in St. Lucia, 221; in
Washington DC, 362

housing: in Angola, 176–77; in author's hometown, viii–ix, 391–92; in California, 333–37, 362, 363, 368–72; in China, 266, 296–302, 386, 387; in Colorado, 364–68; in Detroit, 322–23, 324; in Dubai, 306–7, 308–9; European style of, 375–81, 387; in former industrial areas, 45; in France, 319–21; in Germany, 318; in Hong Kong, 295–96; in India, 302–5; in Japan, 383; in Las Vegas, 338; in Maine, xii–xiii; in Manila mall, 293; in Massachusetts, 367; in Michigan, 52; near shopping centers, 28, 32, 33, 34; in Nevada, 339–40; in New York, 340–49; in Ohio, 324–25; for oil industry workers, 150; permits in American cities, 354; on Saltspring Island, 393; in South Korea, 384; in St. Louis, 322; in Texas, 207, 331, 332; in United Kingdom, 312–15; in U.S. suburbs, 351–59; in U.S. urban areas, 359–63; in U.S. West, 364–66. *See also* apartments; construction industry; foreclosures; real estate; villas

Houston TX: airlines in, 91, 96, 98, 101, 177; and Brazilian shipping, 218; cropland in, 207; developer in, 321; housing in, 352, 354, 359–60, 363; rail shipments in, 112; refinery near, 154; shipping in, 124; trains in, 111, 392

HSBC, 253, 313

HTMs (human teller machines), 258–59

Hudson River, 130, 342

Hudson Yards, 345–46

Human Rights Watch, 199–200, 308

Hunan, China, 267, 301

Hungary, 96, 114

Hutchison Port (Hong Kong), 111, 127, 128

Hyderabad, India, 279, 305

hypermarkets, 287, 288. *See also* supercenters

Hyundai, 67, 76, 125, 192

IBM, 276, 278

Iceland, 195, 208, 329

Idaho, 209, 216

Illinois, 85, 195, 204, 205, 208, 330

illiteracy, 256, 257–58, 260. *See also* social problems

immigration, 167, 260–63. *See also* migration

imports: to Asia, 233; of automobiles, 54; in China, 51, 118, 162, 169, 264; of coal, 180, 184; of food to Europe, 222–23; of food to Nigeria, 230, 232; of food to Russia, 226; of gasoline to Mexico, 154; in Hong Kong, 289; of iron ore, 184; of LNG, 148–49; of oil to Japan, 164; of oil to U.S., 151; of sheep and lamb products, 212; of steel, 192–93; of textiles, 48; of wine to Europe, 225. *See also* exports; tariffs

Inco, 184, 201

India: airlines in, 92, 93, 100, 102–3; auto industry in, 57, 64; and Brazilian ethanol, 217; *bund* in, 297; bus service in, 114; Cadbury products in, 79; caste system in, 244–45, 259, 278; cell phones in, 255, 257, 259; Chinese imports to, 264; coal industry in, 181, 183–84, 191, 280; coffee shops in, 7; Coke products in, 38; consumers in, 40; development in, 242–45, 252–54, 275–83, 302–5; economy in, 243–44, 263, 278–79; farming in, 234–35, 239, 242–44, 252–53, 257, 259, 260, 289–90; Frito-Lay in, 38; gas in, 169–70, 175; iron ore in, 184, 191; landscape of, 393; LNG to, 148; oil industry in, 163–64; outsourcing to, 256, 275–77; population in, 300, 302, 304, 305; production in, 39, 44, 47–48, 266, 280; rail service in, 114, 119; roads in, 87–88, 243, 275, 281; roses in, 105; shipyards in, 76; steel industry in, 189, 191, 192; stores in, 288–91, 293–94

Indiana: 3M in, 80; aluminum industry in, 195; auto industry in, 65; corn production in, 212–13; declining cities in, 325–26; ethanol in, 206; primary crops in, 204; steel industry in, 189, 325

Indian Ocean, 122, 163

Inditex, 26–27

Kinshasa, 121, 258
kirana stores, 289, 292
Kirkuk, Iraq, 137, 168
Kmart, 11–12
Kodak, 74, 256–57, 326
Kohl's, 8, 10, 26, 391
Kok-Aral Dam, 227–28
Kolkata, India, 278, 279, 281, 282, 292
Komatsu, 201–2
Korea, 45, 67, 70, 76, 132, 148, 188–89, 383
Korean Air, 69, 104
KPN, 254
Kraft, 77–79
Kroger, 12, 20, 21, 335
Kuala Lumpur, 103, 107
Kunming, China, 88, 105, 121, 164
Kurdistan, 137, 168–69
Kuwait, 57, 144, 170–71, 345
Kyaukpyu, Burma, 163, 164

Lacquer Craft, 50, 264
Lagos, Nigeria, 91, 122, 128, 174, 175
Lahore, Pakistan, 284, 381
Laiwu Steel, 186–87
Lake Baikal, 159, 164, 241
Lake Charles LA, 146, 148, 149
Lake Malawi, 241–42
Lake Tanganyika, 121, 229
Lake Victoria, 231, 242, 250–51
land: for African farming, 231–32, 248–50;
    for Brazilian farming, 217, 219–20; in
    California, 355, 357, 369–70; for Chi-
    nese farming, 222, 235, 236–37, 246–
    48; for Chinese manufacturers, 264;
    in Dallas, 332; digital records of own-
    ership, 260; for European farming,
    221–22, 225–28; in Florida, 367–68;
    of Hualapai tribe, 373–74; for Indian
    farming, 235, 244; in Michigan, 323–
    24; and mixed-use developments,
    362; ownership in India, 281–83, 303,
    304; rights in New York, 342, 346,
    363; rights in United States, 354, 368–
    70; for Russian farming, 226, 227; in
    suburbs, 351, 353, 355; in Tennessee,
    326; in United Kingdom, 314, 376; for
    U.S. farming, 203–4, 205, 207–10, 216,

369; in U.S. West, 365–66. *See also* real
    estate
landfills, 346, 372
Laos, 88, 121
Las Vegas NV, 28, 89, 111, 329, 338–40, 373
Latin America, 7, 41, 65, 90, 96, 104, 153–
    56, 216–21
Latinos, 13, 15, 17, 333, 356
Lázaro Cárdenas, Mexico, 111, 112, 128, 129
Leahy, Terry, 23, 286
Leeds, England, 379–80
legal system, 213, 246, 260, 274, 282, 354,
    368. *See also* U.S. Supreme Court
Leipzig, 108, 120
Lennar (developer), 362, 371–72
Lesotho, 49–50
Levi Strauss, 48, 294
Lexus, 53, 54, 58, 62
LG Display, 265–66
Liberia, 50, 187
Libeskind, Daniel, 322, 338
Libya, 138, 172, 231–32, 263
liquid crystal display (LCD), 74, 75, 265
liquified natural gas (LNG), 76–77, 132, 140,
    146, 148–49, 160–62, 164, 171–72. *See
    also* fuel; gas, natural
Lloyd's, 133, 314
LNG. *See* liquified natural gas (LNG)
loans, 222, 324, 334
locomotives, 52, 68, 81–82, 146, 265. *See
    also* trains
logistics. *See* air freight; airlines; ships;
    trains; trucking
London: airlines in, 72, 73, 90, 95–100,
    104; conditions in, xv; construction
    in, 311–15, 342; historical preservation
    in, 387; power plants in, 227; property
    near, 375, 376; Qatar investments in,
    171, 334; Russian gas industry in, 161;
    shipping in, 125, 126; trains in, 113–14
Long Beach CA, 16, 86, 129, 148
Longhua Science and Technology Park,
    269, 270
L'Oreal, 112, 345, 385
Loreto Bay Homes, 357–58
Los Angeles: airlines in, 93, 97, 98, 100, 101,
    108; commuters in, 357; economy in,

Los Angeles (cont.)

332–37; high-rise building near, 369; immigrants in, 261; mixed-use development in, 363; Northrop Grumman in, 327; population in, 356; shipping in, 123, 124, 129, 130, 131; steel mill near, 188; stores in, 15, 23, 28, 33, 339; train tracks in, 109, 111; trees in, 339

Los Cabos, Baja California, 261, 286

Louisiana, 139, 141, 145, 146, 148

Louis Vuitton, 28, 46, 385

Luanda, Angola, 91, 177

Lufthansa, 72, 90, 92–93, 95–97, 101, 102, 279

Lusaka, Zambia, 105, 122, 200

Luxembourg, 171, 190

Lyon, France, 113–15, 321

Macerich, 31–32, 363

Macquarie, 85, 87

Macy's, 8–9, 11, 28

Madrid, 26, 99, 113, 114, 377

Maersk. *See* A. P. Moller-Maersk

Maine, xii–xiii, 209, 365, 368, 375

Malaga, Spain, 113, 378

Malaysia, 103, 107, 125, 127, 149, 185, 196, 288, 314–15

Mali, 231–32, 233

Malibu CA, 148, 368–69

malls: in China, 293; decline of, 4, 19, 29–30, 292, 390–91; in Dubai, 307; in India, 293–94; in Las Vegas, 338–39; in New York, 345; physical layout of, 27, 30, 32; residential areas near, 32; in San Francisco, 35. *See also* retail stores; shopping centers

Manchester, England, 45, 92, 95, 379–80

Manhattan: automobiles in, 51; buildings in, 340–50; hotels in, 309; housing prices in, 337; Kaaba compared to, 310; Paneras in, 5; parks in, 371; shipping in, 130; stores in, 11, 24, 31, 34–35, 335, 343, 345. *See also* New York City

Manila, Philippines, 106, 293

manufacturers: in Burma, 200; in China, 264–71, 280, 285; in college town, 391; in France, 312; gas use of, 149; in Ger-

many, 62; in India, 275, 280–83; job insecurity with, 276; labor costs of, 81–82; in Mexico, 45, 51; of mining equipment, 201–2; packaging of food, 78; and retailers, 12–13, 84; in Spartanburg SC, 62; supply chains of, 80–81; as "systems integrators," 70–71; in United States, 72, 75, 264, 322, 323, 326; of VWs, 63

Mao Zedong, 237, 271, 272, 274, 383, 386. *See also* communism

Marcellus Shale, 145–46, 148, 325

Marchionne, Sergio, 60, 61

marriage, 245, 271

Marseilles, 114, 125, 127–31, 377

Maryland, 189, 355, 368

Massachusetts, 14–15, 367, 368, 369

Materne Confilux, 222–23

Mato Grosso, Brazil, 218, 219

May Company, 8, 9

McDonald's, 1–7, 39, 283–84

McKinsey study, 227, 243, 254, 302

meat, 205, 226. *See also* chicken; pork

Mecca, 121, 310–11

Medina, Saudi Arabia, 121, 310

Mediterranean Sea, 122, 127, 376

Mediterranean Shipping Company, 124, 125, 127

Melbourne, Australia, 100, 202

Memphis TN, 81, 91, 106, 108, 329

MEND. *See* Movement for the Emancipation of the Niger Delta

Mercedes, 53, 54, 58, 62, 192, 268

metallurgical coal, 180–81

MetLife Building, 349, 350

Metropolitan Transit Authority (New York), 344–45

Mexico: airlines in, 72, 96, 104; auto industry in, 57, 63, 81; banking in, 334; beer in, 42; Coke products, 38; Danone products in, 79; employment in, 261; farming in, 220; food prices in, 206; furniture in, 51; Gecis Global in, 276; LNG terminal near, 148; migration from, 260–62; oil industry in, 135, 151, 153–55, 169; phone company in, 255; processed foods in, 77; production of,

New Mexico, 8, 365
Newmont (gold company), 197–99
New Orleans, 109, 141–42, 218, 361
New Ruralism, 366–67
newspapers, xv–xvi, 18, 389
New Urbanism, 33, 359–63, 369. *See also* urban areas
New York, 16, 326
New York Central, 109, 110
New York City: airlines in, 91, 93, 97, 101, 104; airports of, 344; Cartier stores in, 386; developer from, 336; economy in, 311, 327; European architecture in, 375; glass in, 75; Goldman Sachs in, 327–28; high-rise buildings in, 369; historical preservation in, 383, 387; homelessness in, 333; housing permits in, 354; image of, 293; InBev in, 42; investors from, 337; New Urbanism in, 362; office space in, 316; parks in, 371–72; poultry sales in, 211; roads in, 87; shipping in, 129–31; shopping in outer boroughs, 35; suburbs of, 351, 354–55; trains in, 109; Walmart in, 13, 14. *See also* Manhattan
New York state, 85, 135, 145, 210
New York Stock Exchange building, 348. *See also* stock exchange
New York Times, 197–98, 286, 341, 344, 346–48
Niger, 121, 231–32
Niger Delta, 173–76
Nigeria: airlines in, 91; economy in, 242; farming in, 229, 230, 232; gas-to-liquids fuel in, 172; motorbikes in, 275; Nestlé products in, 79; oil industry in, 138, 173–76; power generation in, 195; railroad in, 121, 122; ships in, 76, 128
Nike, 46, 47, 267, 294
Ningbo, 124–25
Nintendo, 74, 269
Nippon Steel, 186, 189
Nissan, 55, 59, 66–67, 285
Nobel Peace Prize winners, 251, 253
Nokia, 256, 269, 279–81
Nordic Orion (ship), 132–33
Nordstrom, 8, 10–11, 28–30

Norfolk and Western Railway, 109, 110
Norfolk Southern, 108, 109
Norsk Hydro, 162, 194–96
North America: aluminum industry in, 194; auto industry in, 56–58, 63, 64, 66, 67; beer in, 41; gas exports from, 148–49; malls in, 292; oil industry in, 139–54, 167; shipping in, 106, 129–31; steel industry in, 189
North Atlantic, 97, 100
North Carolina, 43–44, 50–51, 70, 224, 352
North Carolina Research Campus, 43–44
North China Plain, 237–38
North Dakota, 135, 150–51, 204, 328
North Sea, 138, 156–57
North Yunfu District, China, 246–47
Norway: airlines in, 91, 96; farm subsidies in, 208; foreign aid of, 250; gas field near, 162; oil industry in, 139, 141, 143, 151, 156–57, 168; Qatar compared with, 171; shipping in, 132; and U.S. fracking, 148
Novorossiysk, 165, 226–27
NTT Docomo, 254, 255
nuclear energy, 147, 170

Oakland CA, xi, 90
office space: in China, 288, 301; in Dubai, 307; in Hong Kong, 295; in India, 304; in Italy, 321; in Japan, 383; in Manila mall, 293; in Moscow, 315–17; near shopping centers, 32–34; in Paris, 319; in United Kingdom, 313, 314, 315; in United States, 329–31, 336–38, 343–46, 348, 350, 351, 356, 361–63. *See also* real estate
Ohio, 52–53, 80, 107–8, 150, 202, 204, 324–25
oil industry: in Africa, 122, 136, 139, 172–77, 242; and air travel, 94; attitudes toward, ix, x, xiv; in Canada, 151–53; carbon dioxide in, 180; in China, 118, 162–66, 266; curse of, 172–73; dominant companies in, 135–39; drilling rights in, 136; and gas fracking, 147; in Iran, 169–70; in Iraq, 168–69; in Kazakhstan, 165–66; in Kuwait, 170–

71; in Mexico, 153–55; in North Sea, 156–57; prices in, 66, 136, 156, 161, 170–72, 174, 207, 317, 330; in Russia, 157–62; in Saudi Arabia, 166–68, 310; and shipping, 76–77, 124, 133; technologies in, 137–39, 143–48, 150–56, 162, 165–67, 171–72; and trains, 116; in United States, 137–44, 147, 327, 330; in Venezuela, 155–56; worldwide production of, 135. *See also* fuel

oil refineries, 154, 155, 175, 176

Oklahoma, viii, 8, 85, 144, 145, 150, 231

Oklahoma City OK, 137, 145

Olympics, 298, 313, 345

Omaha NE, 326, 329

Oman, 127, 138, 279, 294, 393

1 World Trade Center, 34, 75, 344

One Hyde Park, 312, 334

open-air centers, 28–29, 32

Open Skies agreement, 97–99

Orange County CA, 355, 356

orchards, 210, 324. *See also* fruit growers; trees

Oregon, 84–85, 329, 333

ores, 123, 125. *See also* iron ore

Orinoco Belt, 155–56

Oxfam, 39, 233

Pacific Ocean, 88, 118

Pakistan, 44, 45, 88, 103, 120, 163, 169–70, 227, 381–82

palaces, 318, 334–35, 388. *See also* castles

Palestinians, 46, 263

Palm Islands, 306, 309

palm oil, 175, 206, 231

Panama Canal, 112, 130–31, 201

Panama City FL, 359, 366–67

Panera Bread, 5, 390

Pantaloon, 290, 291, 294

Pantene, 79, 386

paper products, 19, 375

Papua, Indonesia, 197–98

Paris: airlines in, 94, 98, 100, 104; conditions in, xv; construction in, 319–21; image of, 293; manufacturing near, 312; office space in, 315; park in, 371; Qatar investments in, 171; trains in, 113, 114

parking areas, 316, 333, 342, 362

parks, 304, 305, 324, 371–75. *See also* environment; public lands

Pasadena CA, 15, 339, 363, 368–69

Peabody (coal company), 180, 182

Pelli, Cesar, 321, 338, 344

Pemex, 153–55

penal systems, 273–75, 288–89. *See also* crime

Pennsylvania: airlines in, 89; coal mining in, 181; farmland easements in, 369; fracking in, 145–46; fuel refinery in, 206–7; Krispy Kreme in, 8; malls in, 28; organic farming in, 215; roads in, 85, 86; suburbs in, 354

Pennsylvania Railroad, 109, 110, 130

Pentagon, 298, 317

peppers, 228, 230. *See also* vegetables

Pepsi, 37, 38, 40

Perlez, Jane, 197–99

Perot, Ross, Jr., 34, 331

Perth, Australia, 194, 202

Peru, 105, 198–99, 212, 220

pesticides, 214, 215, 230. *See also* insects

PetroChina, 152, 162–63

PetroKazakhstan, 164, 165

Petróleos de Mexicanos, 153–55

Petróleos de Venezuela, 135, 155, 156

pharmaceutical companies, 44, 82, 275. *See also* health care

Philadelphia PA, 28, 89, 90, 331, 371

Philippines, 34, 38, 50, 106–7, 185, 252, 277

Phoenix AZ, viii, 89, 102, 331, 354

Piano, Renzo, 315, 341, 344, 361

Piceance Basin, 137–38

pickup trucks, 54, 55, 60, 65, 193. *See also* automobiles; trucks

pineapples, 43, 228

Pingyao, China, 382–83, 387

pipelines: and coal use, 179, 180; for gas, 140, 158, 159, 161, 163, 169, 175, 182; for iron ore, 218; for oil, 137, 144, 151, 153, 157, 164–66, 169, 173, 174, 176

piracy, 133

Pittsburgh PA, 89, 146, 193, 354

Pizza Hut, 4, 283, 284

planned communities. *See* mixed-use development

plastics industry, 146, 326
Pocatello ID, 81, 216
Point Noire, Congo (Brazzaville), 94, 121
Poland, 61, 96, 120, 158, 189, 222, 223, 228, 393
police, 243, 246, 247, 274, 281–82
politics: in California, 332–33; in China, 247, 271–73; in farming, 204, 207–9; and GMOs, 212, 223; and immigration, 261; in India, 234, 243, 278, 281–83, 292; in mining industry, 201; and oil industry, 137, 138, 145, 155–58, 164, 168–69, 177; in suburban planning, 353–54; and U.S. shipping industry, 128. *See also* government enterprises
population: in China, 266, 300–301; in college town, 392; of Dubai, 305–6, 308; in France, 320; in India, 300, 302, 304, 305; in United States, 322, 324–26, 328, 354, 356–58, 368–69
pork, 205, 236. *See also* meat
Porsche, 54, 63
Porta Nuova, 321
ports: Port Arthur TX, 111, 149; Port Authority of New York and New Jersey, 87; Port Elizabeth, 130, 195; Port-Francqui, 121; Port Harcourt, 122, 174; Port Hedland, 185; Port Hueneme, 369; Portland OR, 90, 329; Port of Corpus Christi, 151; Port of Los Angeles, 131; Port of Marseilles, 127–31; Port of New York, 129; Port of Santos, 218; Port of Singapore Authority, 126, 128; Port Sudan, 121
Portugal, 92–93, 114, 176
POSCO, 76, 188–89, 191, 283, 383
Positano, Italy, 378, 379
potatoes, 38, 209, 212, 224, 241. *See also* vegetables
poultry, 221, 232. *See also* chicken; turkey
poverty: in Africa, 233, 241–42, 250–51; and cell-phone use, 259; in China, 245, 263–64; and computer use, 259; in Dallas, 332; in Detroit, 323; and housing, 367; in India, 278; in Los power plants: for aluminum production, 195, 196; in China, 246, 247; in Gabon, 186;

in Germany, 183; in India, 183; in Inner Mongolia, 181–82; in Liberia, 187; in Nigeria, 175; of Reliance Industries, 281, 282; in United Kingdom, 182, 227, 314–15; in United States, 328–29. *See also* electricity; public utilities
Prada, 26, 28, 77
Pradesh, India, 244, 254
Prague, 107, 119
prices: in Africa, 242; of coal, 179, 181, 200; of corn, 204–8; of cotton, 233; of crops online, 260; of fertilizer, 229; of food, 20, 43, 48, 79, 205–6, 211, 239, 287; of gas, 138, 140, 143, 147–49, 157–58, 180; of high-rise construction, 344; of high-speed rail tickets, 114, 117; of housing, 52, 295–96, 298–301, 303, 305, 307, 309, 312, 318, 322–23, 325, 332, 333, 337, 339–44, 346, 347, 351–59, 364–70, 376–80, 383; of industrial power, 195; of Iranian fuel, 170; of iron ore, 185, 186; of land in China, 246, 247; of land in India, 304–5; of land in United States, 346, 349–50, 355, 363, 365–70; of oil, 66, 136, 156, 161, 170–72, 174, 207, 317, 330; of produce in Asia, 233; of production in China, 267, 269; of shipping, 105, 123–24, 266; of soybeans, 219; of steel, 187, 188; in stores, 9, 16, 18, 293, 389; of televisions, 75; of textiles, 43, 46–49; of truck tires, 202. *See also* rent
Prince Rupert BC, 129, 149
private enterprises: in California, 356; in China, 269, 299; in Dallas, 331; European railroads as, 115–16; in Germany, 318, 319; and GMOs, 215; in India, 119, 290; in Kuwait, 170; in Las Vegas, 338; in oil industry, 137, 154–55, 157, 164, 168–69, 175–76; and Russian farming, 226; shipping terminals as, 127; in U.S. West, 365, 366; in Venezuela, 248
Procter & Gamble, 19, 77–80, 385–86
public lands, 139–43, 321, 345, 360, 361, 368–69. *See also* government enterprises; U.S. National Park Service
public utilities, 247, 318. *See also* electricity; water

Pulte homes, 353, 362
Pune, India, 252, 275, 281
Punjab, India, 234, 244, 253
Punta Colonet, Mexico, 112
Putin, Vladimir, 157, 317

Qatar, 158–59, 169, 171–72, 195–96, 315, 334
Qatar Investment Authority, 171, 362
Qingdao, China, 41, 94, 128, 288
Queens NY, 35, 346, 362

railroads. *See* trains
ranchers, 139, 248, 352, 365–66, 374
rapeseed, 213, 227
real estate, 312, 325, 337–38, 340–42, 349–50, 357, 362, 367–69. *See also* commercial space; housing; land; office space
regional planning, 353, 354, 359
Related Companies, 34, 335, 345
Reliance Fresh stores, 291–92
Reliance Industries, 255, 281, 282, 291–92
religion, 167–68, 170
renewable energy, 31, 379. *See also* solar power
rent, 316, 324, 333, 341, 343, 345, 347–50, 383. *See also* prices
restaurants: in author's hometown, vii; in California, 333–34; in China, 284, 297; and fracking boom, 146; in Las Vegas, 339; at malls, 30, 32, 33; in St. Petersburg, 318; in Washington DC, 362. *See also* fast-casual restaurants; fast food; food
retail stores: in Africa, 242; in Brazil, 219; categories of, 27; chain in malls, 27; in China, 293; competition of, 21; deliveries to, 84; in developing countries, 285–94; distribution by, 19–20; growth formulas of, 16–17; in India, 256, 289–92; inventory at, 13–14; in Kansas, 326; in LA Chinatown, 15; in New York, 31, 343, 348; overview of, 8–11; partnerships of, 12–13; physical layout of, 17, 19; showrooming of, 18–19; soft drinks in, 40; in Tijuana, 357; as town centers, 32; Unilever products in, 39. *See also* chain stores; malls; shopping centers

rice, 207, 214, 230–33, 239, 252–53
Rio Grande, 199, 261
Rio Tinto, 185–86, 195, 196, 199, 201, 202
Ritz-Carlton, 335, 361
River Rouge steel plant, 67, 192
Riyadh, Saudi Arabia, 121, 167, 234, 310
roads: in Africa, 121, 122, 229, 242, 311; in Brazil, 218, 220; in California, 357, 368, 372–73; in China, 87–88, 164, 248, 281; in India, 87–88, 243, 275; opposition to tolls on, 85–86; overview of, 84–88; in Saudi Arabia, 311; in South Korea, 384; through Alps, 114–15
Robinsons-May, 8, 334
Rockefeller Center, 345, 350
Rocky Mountains, 110, 181
Rolls-Royces, 54, 106, 172, 296
Rome, 114, 115, 378
Rosneft, 157, 159–60, 162
Rotterdam, 104, 115, 125–27, 131, 132. *See also* Netherlands
Roundup, 212–14
rural areas: in Africa, 241–42, 250–51; in Bangladesh, 259; in China, 238, 245–48, 256–57, 263, 268–69, 301; computers in, 260; consumers in, 39–40; in India, 243, 244, 253, 256, 275, 278, 283, 302; land values in, 351; phones in, 254–60; in Russia, 241; target marketing in, 79; textile employees from, 47–48; in United Kingdom, 375; Walmart in, 18. *See also* migration
Russia: airlines in, 92; auto industry in, 61, 64; bauxite processing in, 194; beef in, 217; beer in, 42; Campbell's products in, 78; coal shipments to, 118; development in, 241, 315–18; farming in, 226–28; iron ore in, 184; oil and gas industry in, 135, 157–62, 164–66, 175; potatoes in, 38; processed foods in, 77; property in, 379; and property in England, 376; roads in, 88; shipping in, 131, 132; steel industry in, 189, 192; trains in, 113, 116, 119, 265; on U.S. fracking, 147. *See also* Soviet Union
Rwanda, 122, 229

shoppertainment, 30–31. *See also* entertainment venues

shopping centers: author's coverage of, xiv; in author's hometown, 390–91; in China, 385; decline of, 29–30; in developing countries, 292–94; in Dubai, 307; on East Coast, 30–31; in Gendale area, 32–33; in Manhattan, 34–35; and New Urbanism, 360, 361, 363; overview of, 27–35; in Paris, 319–20; in Texas, 33–34, 327. *See also* malls; outlet centers; retail stores

Siberia, 132, 164, 194

Sichuan, China, 163, 237

Sicily, 263, 378

Siemens, 256, 265

Simandou iron deposit, 185–87

Simon Property Group, 29, 363

Singapore: airlines in, 69, 71, 72, 93, 100, 103; cameras in, 74; chain stores in, 288; Flextronics in, 281; housing prices in, 299; oil and gas industries in, 172; P&G cosmetics in, 386; property in New York, 349; shipping industry in, 123, 125–28, 279; shipyards of, 76; trains in, 119

Sinopec, 136, 152, 163, 284

ski resort, 364–65

slums, 302, 303–5

smelters, 194, 195, 201

Smith, Adrian, 306–7, 310

Smithfield Foods, 205, 236

snack foods, 38, 77. *See also* food

social problems: and African farming, 231, 232; in Angola, 177; in California and Oregon, 333; in China, 245–48, 270–75; in France, 320; and immigration, 262; in India, 244–45, 278; and mining, 186, 195–200; and oil industry, 155, 172–76; in Russia, 241. *See also* illiteracy; poverty

solar power, 144, 254–56, 367. *See also* renewable energy

sorghum, 41, 242. *See also* grain

South Africa: cell phones in, 258; developer from, 305; e-mail from Jomo Gbomo through, 174; gas company in, 146; and gas-to-liquids fuel, 172; land reform in, 248–49; mining in, 194–97, 199, 200; railroad in, 121; textiles in, 49. *See also* Africa

South African Breweries, 39, 41

South America, 38, 101, 214, 218, 374. *See also specific countries*

South Carolina, 70, 81, 366

South Dakota, 197, 327, 328

Southeast Asia, 39, 292, 293

Southern Company, 179, 180

Southern Pacific railroad, 109, 336

South Korea: airlines in, 100; auto industry in, 67; coffee shops in, 7; construction in, 383; farm subsidies in, 208; food exports in, 239; gas in, 159; shipping industry in, 124; shipyards in, 76; Walmart in, 287

South Sudan, 122, 229. *See also* Sudan

Soviet Union, 135, 226, 316. *See also* Russia

soybeans, 204, 208, 212, 214, 216–20, 232, 239

Spain: airlines in, 90, 92, 96, 99; auto industry in, 57; clothing stores in, 26–27; foreign aid of, 250; LNG to, 148; migrants to, 262–63; phone company in, 255; property in, 377–78, 381; shipping in, 105, 127; toll road companies in, 85, 86; trains in, 113, 114

Spanish language, 17, 276, 340

Sparrow's Point mill, 189, 192

special economic zones (SEZs), 280–81, 283

specialty shops, xiii–xiv, 9, 10, 24

Sri Lanka, 47–48, 163, 279

Stalin, Joseph, 192, 316, 379

Standard Oil Company, 135, 202

Starbucks, 6–7, 25, 35, 39, 76, 284, 285, 323, 332, 390

Staten Island, 87, 372

Statoil, 141, 143, 148, 151, 156, 162, 166, 170

statues. *See* monuments

steam-assisted gravity drainage, 152, 166

steamers (ships), 122–23

steam injection, 143–44

steel: and iron-ore mining, 187, 196; manufacture of, 67, 76, 146, 149, 181, 186–

steel (cont.)
93, 271, 283, 325, 383; mill in Italy, 321; prices of, 187, 188. *See also* mining
Stelco (steel company), 191–92
Stern, Robert A. M., 341, 347
Stewart, Martha, 9, 352
St. Joe's River Camps, 366–67
St. Louis MO, 91, 111, 322, 327, 371
stock exchange, 12, 25, 311. *See also* New York Stock Exchange building
St. Petersburg, Russia, 113, 158, 161, 164, 317–18
Strait of Malacca, 133, 164
Strasbourg, France, 113, 114
strawberries, 216, 222, 223, 236
strip malls. *See* malls; open-air centers
Sual (aluminum company), 194
Subic Bay, 106–7
sub-Saharan Africa, 251, 262. *See also* Africa
suburbs: attitudes toward, xv; in California, 355–58; description of, 285; of Detroit, 323, 324; in Florida, 358–59; in France, 320, 321; industrial areas as, 45; in Italy, 321; and mixed-use developments, 362; in Nebraska, 326; of New York, 354–55, 362; overview of, 351–54; Paneras in, 5; of San Francisco, 337; Target in, 21; Walmart in, 15. *See also* townships
Sudan, 231, 263. *See also* South Sudan
Suez Canal, 131–33
sugar, 205–6, 216–17, 220, 221, 226
sugar beets, 212, 252
sugarcane, 252
suicides, 243, 244, 254, 270
sulfur, 165
Sumitomo, 149, 193
supercenters, 19, 289. *See also* hypermarkets
supermarkets: attitudes toward, xiv, 389; in Boston, 361; Brazilian beef in, 217; Campbell's products in, 78; competition of, 20; in Detroit, 323; Frito-Lay in, 38; GMOs in European, 223; in India, 291; in Los Angeles, 335; in Manhattan, 34, 35; in Qatar, 171; Safaricom tellers

at, 258; Starbucks in, 6; and Walmart, 12, 18, 285. *See also* food; grocery stores
Supervalu, 15, 20
suppliers: of Abercrombie & Fitch, 105; of Carrefour, 288, 290; for Chinese construction, 299; to Chinese shoe factory, 268; and distribution, 39–40; in furniture industry, 50; in global market, 80–81; of Honda in China, 270; in Indian stores, 289–90, 292; in Mexico, 45; of Tesco, 24; use of global, 39, 41, 70; of Walmart, 13–14, 17, 267
SUVs, 55–56, 66, 80. *See also* automobiles
Suzhou, China, 84, 265, 387
Suzuki, 66, 267, 275
Swarovski, 236
Swatch, 77
Swayam Krishi Sangham Finance, 253–54
sweaters, 14, 46
sweatshirts, 45
Sweden, 26, 48, 70, 187, 250, 277
Switzerland: airlines in, 92; business in India, 277; chain stores in, 288; corporations in, 322; farm subsidies in, 208; foreign aid of, 250; Gerber in, 77; GMOs in, 213, 223; mining in, 201; property in, 380; shipping industry in, 125; transport of goods in, 114–15; watches from, 289
Sydney, Australia, 93, 100, 202
Syngenta, 213, 214, 216, 223–24, 252

Taiwan, 75, 107, 269, 287, 288, 306
Taiwan Strait, 87
Taiyuan, China, 117, 236, 270, 383, 385
Tangier, 67, 127
Tanjung Pelapas, 125, 127
tankers (ships), 76–77, 123, 124, 164, 169, 170, 171, 176. *See also* ships
Tanzania, 229, 241–42
Target: in author's hometown, 389; competition of, 16, 17, 19, 21–22, 25; exclusive merchandise at, 9; in Harlem, 24; in malls, 30; in Oklahoma, 391; share of U.S. sales, 12
tariffs, 47–49, 207, 220–21, 222–23. *See also* exports; imports; taxes

tar sands. *See* Athabasca tar sands

Tata, 7, 57, 277, 281–82, 290

Tata Steel, 191, 192

taxes: in Australia, 181; in China, 272, 274; in Dallas, 332; gas, 84–85; and gold mining, 198–99; and Greek shipping, 123; on Hong Kong properties, 296; in India, 280; and iron-ore mining, 186; on McMansions, 367; and online purchases, 18; in Russia, 157, 241; in United States, 81, 323, 324, 326. *See also* tariffs

telephones, 254–60, 302, 364, 366. *See also* cell phones

televisions, 74, 75, 288, 300, 302, 366

Tennessee, 193, 195, 326, 356

Tennessee Valley Authority, 179, 195

Teotihuacán, Mexico, 220, 286

Tesco, 12, 23–24, 217, 267, 286–88, 290

Texaco, 135, 137

Texas: airline routes to, 73, 96; auto industry in, 51, 54, 65, 80; beaches in, 368; cotton from, 50; cropland in, 207; and fracking boom, 150; GMOs in, 214; housing permits in, 354; information technology in, 329; Krispy Kreme in, 8; mixed-use development in, 359; natural gas in, 144, 148, 149, 162; oil industry in, 144, 150, 151, 154, 162, 163, 327; plastics plant in, 146; roads in, 85–86; sheepherders in, 212; shipping in, 124; shopping centers in, 33–34; suburbs in, 351, 352; trains in, 111–12; Walmart in, 12, 13, 17

textiles, 43–50, 200, 203, 266, 280, 304–5. *See also* clothing

Thailand, 57, 88, 93, 233, 288, 382

Thames River, 313–15, 376

theaters, 32, 285, 294, 297, 298, 318. *See also* entertainment venues

ThyssenKrupp mill, 188, 192–93

Tianjin, China, 88, 182, 238, 264, 301

Tibet, 118, 265

Tide, 79, 80

Tiffany, 24, 28, 77

Tijuana, Mexico, 112, 357

Time magazine, 11, 243

Time Warner Center, 34–35, 335, 341

tires, 81, 202

Tishman Speyer, 302, 304, 348–50

tobacco, 77, 157, 217, 249

Tokyo, 90, 92, 98, 383–85

Toll Brothers, 353–55, 362–63

tomatoes, 39, 212. *See also* vegetables

Tommy Hilfiger, 9, 49, 294, 364

Tompkins, Douglas and Kristine, 374–75

Total (oil company), 137, 141, 143, 152, 155–56, 162, 169, 170

tourism. *See* travel and tourism

townships, 305, 353. *See also* suburbs

Toyota, 53, 55, 58, 61, 64–67, 164, 285

tractors, 234, 257, 260

Trader Joe's, 22–23, 24

trains: cost of freight on, 105; in Germany, 318; goods transported via, 83–84, 108–12, 114–22, 130, 151, 164, 182, 229–30, 279, 392–93; high-speed, 102, 112–13, 117, 265, 267, 383; in Hong Kong, 295; for iron-ore, 184–87, 195; in Italy, 321; in Kazakhstan, 165; in Nigeria, 175; overview of, 108–22; in Paris, 319, 320; for passengers, 112–15, 117–18, 121, 122, 265, 302, 311, 363; to Penn Station, 31; tracks for, 109–13, 371; tunnels for, 115; in Washington DC, 361. *See also* locomotives; shipping; transportation

transportation: in Africa, 67, 232, 242, 255; author's coverage of, xiv; in Brazil, 218, 220; in India, 257; in New York, 345; to shopping centers, 31, 32, 320, 360; in South Korea, 383. *See also* air freight; airlines; automobiles; commuting; shipping; ships; trains; trucking

Trans-Texas Corridor, 85–86

travel and tourism: and airlines, 91, 104; in China, 118, 293, 387; at dude ranches, 366; and employment, 261; in England, 379; in Europe, 375, 380–81; in Florida, 367–68; in Grand Canyon, 373–74; to historical sites, 382–83; in Japan, 183; in Kansas, 326; in Mecca, 310–11; in New York, 343, 345; in San Francisco, 337; in St. Lucia, 221; to U.S. national parks, 372–74

trees, 207, 320, 324, 339. *See also* orchards

264, 322, 323, 326; McDonald's in, 1, 7; and Mongolian coal, 118–19; and North Atlantic flights, 97; office space in, 315; oil industry in, 137–44, 147, 150–54, 156, 157, 162, 164, 165; park system in, 372–73; pizza chains in, 4; population in, 300; poverty in, 333; production in, 39, 45; property in Germany, 318, 319; report on Chinese land confiscations, 246–47; report on French housing, 321; retail sales in, 21; and roads, 84–87, 88; sanctions against Iran, 169; in Saudi Arabia, 167–68; shipping industry in, 123, 128, 129, 229–30; shopping centers in, 27; soft drink consumption in, 37, 40; steel industry in, 187, 189–93; suburbs in, 351–59; supermarkets in, 20–23; "supply and command" in, 13; target marketing in, 80; teachers from, 198; textiles in, 43–45, 47, 49–50; theaters in, 297; trains in, 108–13, 116; transport of goods in, 83–84, 106–11; wages in, 266; Walmart in, 12, 287; watches from, 289; water rates in, 238; wine in, 42–43, 225, 226

United States Steel, 186, 191–94, 325

UN Security Council, 164

UPS, 19, 46, 83–84, 106, 107, 392

urban areas: in Africa, 251; author's coverage of, xv; in California, 355; in China, 238, 245–48, 263, 268–69, 298–302, 387; construction in, 295, 298, 346; decline of American, 322–40; in Dubai, 305; families in, 356; in Florida, 370; in India, 290–92, 302; irrigation subsidies in, 209; in Italy, 321; migration to, 261–63; office space in, 351; in Saudi Arabia, 310; in South Korea, 383–84; "suburbs" in, 320, 362; Target in, 21; target marketing in, 79; in United Kingdom, 380; Walmart in, 13, 18, 23, 290. See also downtowns; migration; New Urbanism

Urumqi, China, 236, 288

U.S. agencies: Agency for International Development, 251; Air Force, 107, 327; Border Patrol, 261; Bureau of the Census, 333, 355; Department of Agriculture, 18, 211, 214–16; U.S. Department of Energy, 149; Department of the Interior, 197, 372; Energy Information Agency, 146; Environmental Protection Agency, 199, 207; National Park Service, 372–75; Navy, 146, 362, 371–72; Office of Management and Budget, 372; Postal Service, 19; Supreme Court, 213, 332. See also legal system; public lands

U.S.-EU Wine Trade Agreement, 225

Utah, 202, 328, 364

Vale (iron-ore company), 184–86, 196, 200–201

Valemax bulk carriers, 185, 218. See also ships

Vancouver BC, 110, 129–30, 133

Varanasi, 93, 245

vegetables, 234–35, 236–37, 239, 242. See also specific vegetables

Venezuela, 128, 135, 155–56, 169, 248, 265

Venice, Italy, 91, 114, 337

Victoria's Secret, 35, 47, 233

Vienna, 28, 95, 114

Vietnam, 76, 88, 182, 233, 260, 266, 270

villas, 296, 378–79, 380. See also housing

Viñoly, Rafael, 338, 340, 342

Virgin Group, 97–99, 103, 116

Virginia, 32, 355

Vodafone, 255, 258

Volkswagen, 61–64, 67, 171, 188, 285, 326

Vornado Realty, 31, 338, 345

vw. See Volkswagen

wages: in airline industry, 70, 92, 100; in Australia, 181, 202; in auto industry, 52, 55, 62, 67, 131, 325; at Best Buy, 18; of cell-phone users, 257; in China, 266–70, 285, 299–300; of farmers, 203, 207–8, 230, 233; in furniture industry, 50–51; in gold industry, 198; in India, 276; and labor costs, 81–82; of longshoremen, 131; in Mexico, 206, 261; in Russia, 241; in steel industry, 190; in textile industry, 45, 47–49, 51; in United States, 327; at Walmart, 14–16, 19. See also employees walkable cities, 321, 359, 362, 363, 371, 382

Wall Street, 24, 348

Walmart: in Africa, 249; attitudes toward, x, xiv, 14–16, 389; in China, 267, 287; competition of, 17–23, 25, 289; in Europe and Asia, 286–87; heiress of, 365; in India, 235, 289–90; in malls, 30; in Mexico, 285–86, 357; and New Urbanism, 360; and Norwegian government, 157; organic milk at, 215; overview of, 12–14; and producers, 39, 48–50; shipping of, 130

Walmart Supercenters, 12–16, 17, 19–21

Washington DC, 13, 15–16, 21, 31, 354, 355, 361–62

Washington state, 68–70, 110, 209

watches, 77, 289, 293

water: in Africa, 251; in China, 163, 237–38, 248, 388; at Goldstrike Mine, 197; in India, 243, 304, 305; and iron-ore mining, 187; in Mambilla, 175; management in U.S., 208; in Saudi Arabia, 166, 172, 233–34. *See also* environment; irrigation; public utilities

waterfront property: in China, 297; in Dubai, 306, 307; in France, 376; in India, 302; in Italy, 378, 380; in Japan, 383; in London, 313–15; in St. Petersburg, 318; in United Kingdom, 376; in United States, 336, 346, 354, 368–70, 372–73

weeds. *See* herbicides

Wendy's, 2, 3, 390

Wenzhou, China, 117, 268, 300

West Bengal, 278, 282

Westin hotels, 6, 324

West Virginia, 145, 179, 181, 355

wheat, 203, 212, 217, 226, 227, 234, 236–37, 242, 291

Whirlpool, 12, 312

Whole Foods, 21, 24, 34–35, 324

wholesalers, 13, 289–90, 292

wine, 42–43, 223, 225–26, 236, 288, 339. *See also* alcoholic beverages

Wipro, 277, 278

Wisconsin, 80, 151, 210–11, 328

women, 25, 26, 47–48, 105, 167, 253, 259, 278, 303

Woolworth Corporation, 11, 12, 33

World Bank, 184, 231, 251

World Central International Airport. *See* airports, Al Maktoum International Airport

World Trade Center, 24, 344–46

World Trade Organization, 220–21, 233

World War II, 61, 88, 158, 322, 331, 349, 381

Wuhan, China, 117, 125, 269, 315

Wyoming, 108–10, 180, 212, 364

Xian, China, 302, 387

Xinjiang, China, 182, 236, 237, 288

Yahoo, 174, 329

Yamal Peninsula, 162, 164

Yangtze River, 125, 188, 237–38

Yantian, 84, 124–25, 269

Yellow River, 237–38, 245

yogurt, 79, 216, 222–23

Yokohama, 131, 202

Zambia, 105–6, 199–200

Zara, 26–27, 343

Zhejiang, China, 238, 247, 268

Zimbabwe, 199, 232, 249

Zurich, Switzerland, 92, 115, 380